Microsoft® Windows® XP Power Productivity

Jim Boyce

SYBEX®

San Francisco   London

Publisher: Joel Fugazzotto

Acquisitions and Developmental Editor: Tom Cirtin

Production Editor: Leslie E.H. Light

Technical Editor: Emmett Dulaney

Copyeditor: Tiffany Taylor

Compositor: Craig Woods, Happenstance Type-O-Rama

Graphic Illustrator: Jeff Wilson, Happenstance Type-O-Rama

Proofreaders: Nancy Riddiough, Jennifer Larson, Jim Brook

Indexer: Nancy Guenther

Cover Designer and Illustrator: Richard Miller, Calyx Design

An earlier version of this book was published under the title Windows XP Power Tools © 2002 SYBEX Inc.

Library of Congress Card Number: 2004113403

ISBN: 0-7821-4388-1

Manufactured in the United States of America

10 9 8 7 6 5 4 3 2 1

For Bud, who always fights the good fight.

Acknowledgments

The first edition of this book was my first experience with Sybex, and that experience was a good one. Likewise, this project has been a pleasure to complete, thanks to the good folks at Sybex. I offer my thanks to Tom Cirtin for bringing me the project and helping direct the development, and to Leslie Light and Tiffany Taylor for their invaluable assistance in fine-tuning the content. A special thanks also goes to Emmett Dulaney, who did his usual terrific job of technical editing. Many thanks also to all of the production staff, including the proofreaders, indexer, and the composition folks at Happenstance Type-O-Rama, who put together a great-looking book.

Given that this book builds on a previous edition, I'd also like to mention the key people who contributed to that edition's success: Jordan Gold, Joel Fugazzatto, Ellen Dendy, Pete Gaughan, Pat Coleman, Erica Yee, and Michael Williams. Special thanks also go to Guy Hart-Davis, Kate Chase, and Brian Culp for their contributions to the first edition's content.

Contents

Introduction

Windows XP builds on the many core changes in Windows 2000, adding several very useful features and simplifying (in most cases, anyway) the Windows environment. Features like Remote Desktop extend the functionality of the operating system, and numerous other changes make it easier to use. Other new features add core capabilities such as CD recording, eliminating the need for some third-party applications. Features added in Windows XP Service Pack 2 further improve security and usability.

Windows XP Professional is targeted primarily at business users; Windows XP Home Edition is targeted at home users but can be a useful and less expensive alternative for small offices that don't need some of the more advanced features offered by Professional.

Whichever edition you choose, *Windows XP Power Productivity* will help you make the most of your new Windows operating system. This book focuses on the techniques and tricks that will let you implement advanced features and bend Windows XP to your will, and covers all of Service Pack's 2 features. I also cover many of the excellent third-party applications that extend or enhance Windows XP's features.

Who Is This Book For?

Windows XP Power Productivity is geared toward the intermediate to advanced user who is comfortable using Windows and who wants to know how to make everyday tasks easier to accomplish and how to implement many of Windows XP's advanced features. For example, *Windows XP Power Productivity* explains not only how to host a website under Windows XP Professional, but also how to run CGI applications on the computer, serve up files with FTP, and create a site that submits information using e-mail. Most of the topics in the book are appropriate for both home and business users.

To get the most from this book, you should be well versed in general Windows concepts and have day-to-day familiarity with the standard features of Windows XP. You don't need to have a degree in computer science or even know how your computer works behind the scenes. In every case, I'll tell you how to quickly and easily implement the features discussed in the book.

What Does This Book Cover?

Windows XP Power Productivity is divided into nine parts that cover specific groups of tasks. Part 1, "Installation and Startup," covers a variety of topics related to installation and setup. It starts with an overview of the new features in Windows XP and then covers several methods and options for performing stand-alone and distributed installations. If you're looking for tips on using more than one operating system, you'll find pointers and techniques in Part 1, as well as some very useful third-party applications that make it much easier to support multiple operating systems. Part 1 ends with a look at the many ways you can control Windows XP startup and shutdown.

Part 2, "Customizing and Automating Windows XP," offers advice on ways to improve your day-to-day work experience in XP. It includes chapters that cover customizing the XP interface, shortcuts for working in Windows, tips for printing, useful command-line tools, and how to use and customize the new Windows XP help system.

Part 3, "Managing the System and Applications," will help you with the many setup, configuration, and management tasks you'll face on a regular basis. Chapters in Part 3 cover application installation and tuning, adding and removing Windows XP components, using management consoles, auditing and performance monitoring, and how to manage disk space with quotas.

Part 4, "Hardware," is the place to go for tips and tools that will help you install, configure, and manage hardware. These chapters offer tips on how the Registry works and how to perform some nifty tricks in the Registry, how to install and manage hardware and drivers, and how to choose and manage a file system.

In Part 5, "Communications and Networking," you'll find lots of useful tips and tools for configuring and maximizing Internet and network connections, optimizing TCP/IP, troubleshooting and monitoring network connections, and turning your computer into a server for incoming connections. Part 5 also covers tools that let you use Windows XP remotely, such as Remote Desktop and third-party utilities such as VNC and pcAnywhere.

If you use the Internet or bundled communications applications such as Outlook Express (and I'm sure you do), turn to Part 6, "Internet Applications and Services," for tips on how to optimize the Internet apps included with Windows XP. Part 6 also explains how to make the most of Internet Information Services (IIS) for hosting web and FTP sites, and how to set up a Telnet server. Throughout each chapter, I point out useful third-party tools that extend Windows XP's capabilities.

Part 7, "Managing Users," does much more than just explain how to create and manage user accounts and groups. You'll find extensive discussion of group and local policies, with lots of advice on techniques and policies you can use to apply restrictions and effectively manage users' data for easy recoverability and network roaming.

Part 8, "Backup and Disaster Recovery," is one section I hope you never have to use, but which sooner or later you're bound to need. It covers the methods in Windows XP that you can use to back up and restore a system.

And finally, I round out the book with Part 9, "Security," which covers many of the security-related features in Windows XP. Part 9 explains how to manage certificates, encrypt files for security, and set up a secure connection between computers with IPSec. The final two chapters cover virtual private networking (VPN) solutions and the many security configuration tools included with Windows XP.

Conventions Used in This Book

The following icons indicate helpful tips and warnings. These items are flagged to get your attention because they are worth reading!

TIP   Tips include time-saving information to help you make Windows XP easier to use or more effective.

NOTE   Notes go into more detail on related topics or provide extra resources you can refer to.

WARNING   Warnings flag potential trouble spots (or potential sources of trouble, anyway). Ignore them at your own risk!

New!   The New icon flags material that describes the new features of Service Pack 2.

The book also uses some text conventions to make it more readable. Any code elements—filenames, paths, code lines from configuration files, URLs, and more—are shown `in this font`. And anything that you should actually, literally type is shown **in bold font**.

How to Contact the Author

I always welcome comments, suggestions, and tips from my readers. I invite you to visit my website at `www.boyce.us`, where you'll find lots of additional tips, sample chapters from other books, and, of course, contact information.

Part 1

Installation and Startup

In this section:

- Chapter 1: What's New in Windows XP
- Chapter 2: Standalone Installations
- Chapter 3: Reaping the Rewards of Network, Automated, and Unattended Installations
- Chapter 4: Gaining Control of Windows XP Startup and Shutdown

Chapter 1

What's New in Windows XP?

Windows XP suffers somewhat from a dual personality. In some ways it's a significant release, but in others it's more a maintenance release of Windows 2000. For that reason, Windows 2000 users won't see many major changes other than the interface, although numerous changes under the hood improve Windows' performance and functionality. In addition, new features and accessory applications in Windows XP simplify tasks that were a bit more difficult in Windows 2000.

For Windows 9x, Me, and NT users, Windows XP is a significant change. Not only is the interface considerably different, but the underlying core operating system is completely changed, with several core features either new or improved. The biggest transition is for users migrating from Windows 9x and Me to Windows XP—the additional security features, file system options, and management features in XP make it a distinct shift.

Now, enter Windows XP Service Pack 2. Some consider this a major update to Windows XP, but I see it more as a security overhaul for Windows. Windows Firewall has some significant changes, and Internet Explorer and Outlook Express include more minor changes targeted primarily at Internet security. There are several other changes as well, but users won't see a dramatically different Windows environment or a cornucopia of new accessory applications. Still, SP2 is a major step toward enhancing Windows XP's security and performance overall and well worth installing.

This chapter explores the new and changed features in Windows XP. In addition to an exhaustive feature list, I've included sections that will help users of specific Windows platforms get up to speed quickly on Windows XP's features and functions. The chapter also includes a quick overview of SP2's features. You'll find these features covered throughout the rest of the book where appropriate.

Major Differences between Home Edition and Professional

Windows XP is available in two versions: Home Edition and Professional. Many of the features are the same from one to the other, and both have the same look and feel. Because it's targeted at business users, Professional includes features that aren't really necessary for home users, such as added security, centralized administration, and remote access. The following sections provide a brief overview of the features included in the Professional version that aren't available in Home Edition.

Access Control

When you're sharing a folder under all Windows operating systems, including Windows XP, you can specify *share permissions* that control the level of access that users have to the folder across the network. For example, you might grant users the ability to read the contents of a folder but not to write to it. Both Professional and Home Edition offer the ability to share folders and set share permissions to control access.

Windows XP Professional adds the ability to apply *access control lists* (ACLs) to folders on NTFS volumes. An ACL is a set of specific access permissions for a folder or file granted to specific users or groups. For example, you might grant one group of users the ability to read the contents of a folder and grant another group full control over the contents, including the ability to modify and delete items. Figure 1.1 shows the Security tab of a folder's properties, which you use to configure permissions on the folder.

FIGURE 1.1
Use the Security tab to
specify permissions for
a folder.

TIP   You can apply permissions on a folder or file only on NTFS volumes. FAT volumes support sharing permissions but don't allow you to assign permissions for folders or files.

Permissions you set through ACLs apply for both local and network access. For example, if you don't have permission to read a folder, you'll be unable to read the folder even if you log on locally to that computer.

NOTE   For more information on setting sharing security, see Chapter 18.

Centralized Administration

Windows XP Professional systems can function as stand-alone computers, as members of a workgroup, or in a domain served by Windows NT Server, Windows 2000 Server, or Windows Server 2003 domain controllers. Windows XP Home Edition computers can function as stand-alone computers or as members of a workgroup but don't support domain membership. Domains provide several centralized administrative features, with *centralized security* being one of the most important of those features. Centralized security refers to the ability to control access to resources on multiple systems across the network with a single set of user credentials (account and password).

Domains also provide other important functionality, including the abilities to remotely manage systems and to enforce restrictions and other system properties through group policy.

NOTE   For an explanation of group and local policies, see Chapter 35. Specific uses of group policy are explained in other chapters where applicable.

Encrypting File System

Encrypting File System (EFS) is a core component of Windows XP Professional that isn't available in Home Edition. EFS lets users encrypt folders and files to prevent others from being able to read those files. EFS can be an important tool for protecting data on systems that are susceptible to compromise, such as notebook computers that could be lost or stolen. EFS is also useful for protecting data on removable media.

NOTE   For a detailed discussion of EFS, see Chapter 42.

It's easy to encrypt a folder or file in Windows XP: You simply select a check box in the folder's or file's properties, as shown in Figure 1.2. Windows XP takes care of the encryption and decryption process automatically. However, you should implement an EFS recovery policy, as explained in detail in Chapter 42, to ensure your ability to recover encrypted files if the encryption certificate becomes corrupted or is lost.

FIGURE 1.2
You can easily encrypt
a folder or file through a
single check box in its
properties.

Group and Local Policies

Group policy is another feature supported by Windows XP Professional that isn't supported by Windows XP Home Edition. Group and local policies allow a broad range of properties and restrictions to be applied to Windows XP for a specific computer or user. For example, an administrator can use group policy to redirect a user's `My Documents` folder to a network server, so that the folder is always available regardless of the user's logon location and can be easily backed up.

Group policy has much broader implications than just managing a user's data, however. It provides a means for *change control*, which is the ability to regulate the changes that users can make to their systems and Windows environment. Group policy is also the mechanism through which technologies such as Remote Installation Services (RIS) and IntelliMirror allow administrators to automatically deploy operating systems and applications to computers across the enterprise.

NOTE   Group policies rely on Windows 2000 Server or Windows Server 2003 domain controllers and domain membership. You can apply local policies to Windows XP Professional computers in a domain, workgroup, or stand-alone configuration.

NOTE   For a complete discussion of group and local policies and their implications, see Chapter 35.

Multilingual User Interface Add-On

Windows XP is currently available in numerous localized versions in addition to English. Localization provides menus, dialog boxes, and other elements in a specific language. The Multilingual User Interface Pack is an add-on for Windows XP Professional that allows administrators to switch the user interface elements such as menus, dialog boxes, and Help files into a different language. For more information on this add-on, see www.microsoft.com/technet/prodtechnol/winxppro/evaluate/muiovw.mspx.

Offline Files

Windows XP Professional includes a feature called Offline Files, which allows users to continue to work with network resources even when those resources are unavailable or disconnected from the network. For example, assume a server in your network provides access to a set of common documents that you need to use on a regular basis. Most of the time you're in the office and connected to the network, which means the documents are available from the server. Occasionally, however, you need to use your notebook while out of the office and still work with those documents. With Offline Files, Windows XP creates a local copy of the offline resource on your computer and lets you work with the resource there rather than from its network location. XP makes the transition between online and offline use transparent to the user and provides the mechanism to automatically synchronize changes when the network resource again becomes available.

TIP   You can't use Offline Files on a system that has Fast User Switching enabled. Configure Fast User Switching through the option "Change the way users log on or off" in the User Accounts object in Control Panel.

You enable Offline Files for a particular folder through the Offline Files tab of the folder's properties (see Figure 1.3).

FIGURE 1.3
Enable Offline Files through the Folder Options dialog box.

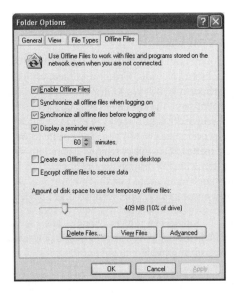

Remote Desktop Connection

Remote Desktop Connection allows you to work with a Windows XP Professional computer from a remote location. For example, you might use Remote Desktop Connection to connect from your home computer to your office computer, in order to access files, printers, or other resources, working with your office PC as if you were physically in the office. You can also use the client portion of Remote Desktop Connection to connect to a Windows 2000 or 2003 Terminal Server.

Windows XP Home Edition includes the client portion of Remote Desktop Connection, enabling you to connect to a Windows XP Professional computer that is configured to allow access to Remote Desktop users (Figure 1.4), or to a Terminal Server. You can't connect to a Windows XP Home Edition computer through Remote Desktop—Home Edition doesn't include the server-side components of Remote Desktop.

FIGURE 1.4
Use Remote Desktop to connect to and use a system remotely.

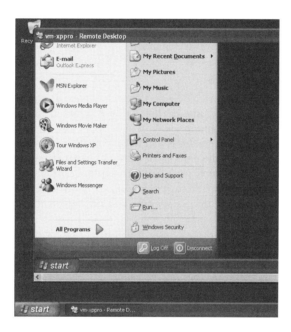

TIP   A handful of third-party applications, such as pcAnywhere, VNC, and Unicenter Remote Control, provide capabilities similar to Remote Desktop for remote access and control. These third-party apps typically provide expanded functionality, such as the ability to let the local user continue working while the remote session is active.

NOTE   For more information on Remote Desktop Connection and its alternatives, see Chapter 23.

Remote Installation Services

Windows XP Professional includes support for Remote Installation Services (RIS), which lets you install Windows 2000, XP, and 2003 on a computer remotely. In a typical RIS deployment, the computer boots from a PXE-compliant network adapter, which allows it to submit a request to a RIS server for service. (PXE stands for Preboot Execution Environment, an open industry standard that allows the system to boot directly from a PXE-compliant network card to initiate an operating system installation or repair.) The RIS server provides the client computer with OS installation options based on the computer's membership in Active Directory. After the user selects the OS options to install, RIS installs the operating system across the network. A system that doesn't include a PXE-compliant network adapter can use a special boot disk created by RIS to allow it to communicate with available RIS servers at boot.

TIP RIS relies on the Active Directory and therefore requires domain membership. Windows XP Home Edition systems don't support RIS.

RIS is primarily a server-side feature requiring either Windows 2000 Server or Windows Server 2003, and it must be configured and managed by a system administrator. For that reason, RIS isn't covered except in passing in this book.

TIP For a detailed discussion of RIS, see *Mastering Windows 2003 Server* by Mark Minasi (Sybex, 2003).

Roaming User Profiles

A *user profile* is a collection of folders and data that make up the majority of a user's working environment. A user's profile includes the My Documents folder, Start menu, Desktop, and other folders. On stand-alone computers and in many network installations, the user profile resides on the local computer. The disadvantage to this is that when you log on from another computer, you don't receive the same desktop settings, documents, or other environment settings as when you log on from your primary workstation. A *roaming* profile overcomes that disadvantage by storing your profile on a network server and copying it to the current logon location. This means that you have the same Desktop, documents, and settings regardless of where you log on—in other words, your working environment follows you around the network.

Scalable Processor Support

Windows XP Home Edition supports a single processor. Windows XP Professional supports up to two processors to provide better performance.

FOLDER REDIRECTION COMPLEMENTS ROAMING PROFILES

As explained in Chapter 37, you can redirect folders from the default profile location to a network server. For example, you might redirect My Documents to a folder on the server. When the user logs on and opens the My Documents folder, he sees the files stored in his folder on the network server, rather than the My Documents folder that would otherwise be stored on his local computer. Redirecting folders in this way helps ensure that the user's documents are always available regardless of logon location. In some ways this might seem to be exactly what roaming profiles achieve. However, folder redirection and roaming profiles are different.

If a user had a roaming profile without folder redirection, the folder would be copied from the server where the profile is stored to the user's local computer at logon. With folder redirection, the folder remains on the server, and the user's computer is redirected to the server when she opens the folder. Folder redirection therefore complements roaming profiles and reduces the amount of data that must be copied across the network during logon.

Software Installation and Maintenance

With Windows 2000, Microsoft introduced a feature called IntelliMirror, which is an umbrella term for a selection of technologies. Windows XP Professional also includes support for IntelliMirror. One of IntelliMirror's major purposes is to let applications be installed, updated, and managed automatically. When a user logs on, group policy and Active Directory membership determine which applications should be installed on the user's computer and which should be made available as an option. Applications that are *assigned* through IntelliMirror appear as if they're already installed on the user's computer. Attempting to start the application causes it to be installed automatically across the network. Applications that are *published* through IntelliMirror are available for installation but aren't installed automatically. Instead, the user can add these applications through the Add Or Remove Programs object in Control Panel.

Most aspects of IntelliMirror are primarily server-side features and are configured and managed at the server level. For that reason, software installation and maintenance are covered only in passing in this book.

TIP   For more information on IntelliMirror and automated application deployment, see *Group Policy, Profiles, and IntelliMirror for Windows 2003, Windows 2000, and Windows XP* by Jeremy Moskowitz (Sybex, 2004) and *Windows 2000 Automated Deployment and Remote Administration* by Christa Anderson (Sybex, 2001).

Windows XP Service Pack 2 Overview

New!

Windows XP Service Pack 2 (at one point called Windows XP Reloaded) incorporates several updates to Windows XP, many targeted at security. XP's features are discussed throughout this book, but this section offers a quick overview to get you up to speed on the new features and changes included in SP2. This section isn't intended to provide a detailed look at each feature but rather to give you a feel for what SP2 contains.

Changes in Networking and Network Security

One of the major changes in SP2 is the introduction of Windows Firewall (Figure 1.5), a replacement for the Internet Connection Firewall (ICF) in Windows XP SP1a and earlier. Windows Firewall incorporates several improvements over ICF, including the following:

Boot-time security   Windows Firewall is enabled during boot with a predefined configuration that prevents connections on all but a limited set of ports. Basic network functions such as DHCP, DNS, and application of group policy are allowed, but other traffic is denied. This protects systems during boot until the user's firewall configuration takes over.

Global configuration   Changes that you make in Windows Firewall apply to all interfaces, simplifying configuration. However, you can still apply unique settings and exceptions to individual interfaces as needed.

Local subnet restriction   You can configure the scope for incoming traffic to restrict it to your own subnet, to all computers, or to a custom list. Local subnet restriction makes it easy to allow connections from your local network while denying those same connections if attempted from the Internet.

Command-line support   The Netsh console command in SP2 now provides command-line configuration and management of Windows Firewall.

On With No Exceptions mode   This mode denies all unsolicited incoming traffic and effectively locks down the computer for everything except solicited outgoing connections without requiring you to reconfigure the firewall's port settings. You can switch back to normal mode with a single mouse click.

FIGURE 1.5
Windows Firewall re-places Internet Connec-tion Firewall and adds several new network security features.

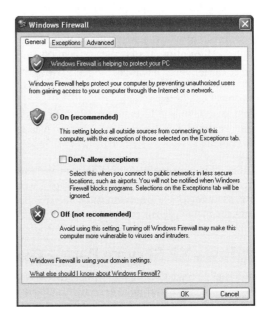

Exception lists   You can use Windows Firewall's exception lists to specify applications that are allowed to listen for incoming traffic on specific ports that are otherwise blocked.

Multiple profiles   Domain users can specify different firewall configurations for different scenarios, easily switching between them. For example, when you're working behind your corporate firewall, you can use a firewall configuration that's different from the one you'd use when connecting from a public location. Workgroup and stand-alone computers have a single firewall profile.

Support for RPC   Windows Firewall allows incoming Remote Procedure Call (RPC) traffic to RPC server applications that run in the Local System, Network Service, or Local Service contexts. You can also add RPC server applications explicitly to the exceptions list to enable those applications to receive RPC traffic.

Group policy   Windows Firewall supports complete configuration through group policy, enabling administrators to easily control personal firewall settings across the enterprise.

Installation and configuration   To simplify configuration, Windows Firewall offers a Restore Defaults feature that quickly restores the firewall to its default settings. You can also configure the default settings for an existing installation and define default settings for unattended installation of Windows XP.

Protocol support   Windows Firewall supports both IPv4 and IPv6 with a single interface, simplifying firewall configuration.

TIP   Windows Firewall is enabled by default when you install SP2. This will concern many administrators because it could cause applications and network connectivity to stop working properly after SP2 is applied. You can mitigate these potential problems during Setup by preconfiguring the firewall settings. For existing Windows XP installations, you can ue group policy to configure the firewall as necessary. Where group policy isn't a viable solution, you can script changes to the firewall settings with Netsh and Windows Script Host. See Chapter 6 for a discussion of Windows Script Host.

In addition to Windows Firewall, SP2 incorporates other network-related changes. For example, the Alerter and Messenger services' startup modes are set to Disabled when SP2 is installed. Prior to SP2, the Alerter service was set by default to Manual, and Messenger was set to Automatic startup. Setting both of these services to Disabled reduces the computer's attack surface for worms, viruses, and other network-borne threats.

NOTE   Don't confuse the Windows XP Messenger service with the Windows Messenger application. The Messenger service transmits simple messages across the local network, whereas Windows Messenger is a desktop conferencing and chat application included with Windows XP. MSN Messenger is a superset of Windows Messenger that offers additional features for MSN users.

Windows Messenger gets an update in SP2. For example, Windows Messenger blocks file transfers if they come from someone not on your contact list or if the file is on the unsafe attachment list defined by Outlook Express. Messenger in SP2 also requires a display name that is different from the contact's e-mail address.

Wireless networking also sees some improvements in SP2 with the addition of a Wireless Network Setup Wizard that greatly simplifies wireless network configuration (Figure 1.6). The wizard creates a set of configuration files that it stores on USB flash drive or floppy disk, which you can use with the wizard on other computers to configure wireless settings. SP2 also adds support for Wireless Provisioning Services, a feature of Windows Server 2003 Service Pack 1 that provides a framework for connecting wireless users to an infrastructure network. Wireless Provisioning Services are targeted at companies that want to offer hotspot wireless access, and inclusion of these capabilities in Windows XP makes it easy for users to connect via wireless hotspots.

Memory Exploit Protection

Windows XP SP2 adds support for Data Execution Prevention (DEP), a feature of newer processors from AMD and Intel that prevents execution of code in memory pages not marked as executable. With DEP enabled, an attempt to run code in unmarked memory causes a processor exception. Preventing the code from executing can help prevent viruses, worms, and other malicious code from running on the computer.

SP2 adds two new startup switches for Windows XP to support DEP:

/NOEXECUTE   Enables DEP. Applications that attempt to run in unmarked pages will fail.

/EXECUTE   Disables DEP. Applications won't generate a processor exception if they attempt to run in unmarked pages. Use this switch to enable known applications to run if they don't function properly with DEP enabled.

TIP   You can use application compatibility settings to disable DEP for specific applications in Windows. See Chapter 7 for a discussion of compatibility options.

FIGURE 1.6
Use the Wireless Network Setup Wizard to quickly and easily set up a small wireless network.

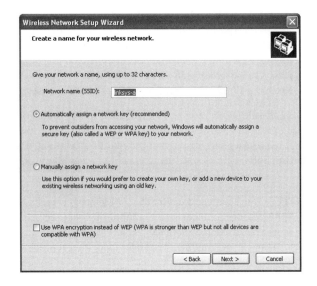

Outlook Express

SP2 adds a handful of features to Outlook Express to improve security. Like Outlook 2003, Outlook Express with SP2 blocks external HTML content. You can configure Outlook Express to allow the content, or you can download it for each message as desired. To help prevent HTML script exploits, you can configure Outlook Express to render downloaded messages in plain text by default. If you need to view the message in HTML, you can click the message and choose View ➢ Message in HTML to render it with HTML.

Internet Explorer

Internet Explorer has several changes in SP2, most of which are targeted at improved security. First, IE incorporates changes for downloading files. You can configure IE to block files from specified publishers and prompt you for others. IE also displays more information about file publishers to help you decide whether to allow add-on downloads. And, it does a better job of detecting and handling add-on crashes, enabling you to block problematic add-ons. Administrators can configure a handful of group policy settings to control these features.

A welcome addition to IE in SP2 is an integrated pop-up blocker. IE blocks all pop-ups by default, but you can configure it to allow pop-ups from specific sites. A new Information Bar (Figure 1.7) displays information about blocking and other security and status information. The Information Bar automatically hides when you navigate away from the page that generated the message.

Along with the pop-up blocker comes a different way to handle windows. IE prevents windows from being opened outside of the viewable area of the Desktop in an effort to prevent sites from hiding content from the user and preventing the user from closing the window. IE with SP2 also enables the status bar for all windows, to let users view information that might otherwise be hidden by a particular site or page.

IE incorporates several changes to help mitigate certain types of exploits. First, binary behaviors—which enable site developers to build functions that can modify HTML tags and their behavior—are blocked in IE's Restricted Sites security zone. In addition, IE applies the ActiveX security model to all instances where URL binding is used to instantiate and initialize an object. This feature is called *Bind-ToObject Mitigation*. IE can also perform *mime sniffing*, which lets IE detect a file type by bit signature rather than file extension and thereby prevent attacks and infections by scripts or other types of masquerading files. In addition, IE incorporates changes to lock down the Local Machine security zone, prevent privilege elevation, and restrict script-initiated pop-up windows.

TIP   You can configure many of IE's new security features with group policy settings.

FIGURE 1.7
The Information Bar displays information about blocked pop-ups and other security messages.

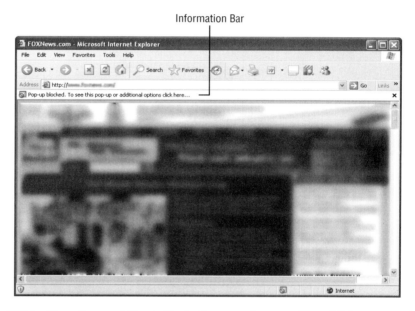

Other changes in SP2 for IE are the capability to block all content from specific publishers, even if the content is signed, and to block all code with invalid signatures. These changes prevent repeated prompts to install otherwise blocked code. IE also prevents a page from accessing objects cached by another site, which can prevent users' personal data from being exposed to potentially malicious sites. In addition, IE now prevents the security context for a given page from being higher than the overall security context for the site's root URL, and it blocks JavaScript navigation if the security context is missing.

NOTE   See Chapter 28 for a complete discussion of SP2 features for Internet Explorer and how to optimize IE's security.

Setup and Configuration

SP2 introduces several changes to Windows XP setup and configuration. First, a trip to the Add Or Remove Programs applet in Control Panel will show you that updates and patches are now hidden from the applet. A check box at the top of the applet lets you turn on or off the display of updates (Figure 1.8). Administrators can control this feature with a group policy setting or Registry modification.

SP2 adds support for new features of Windows Update Services running on Windows Server 2003. Administrators can now deploy updates for drivers, Microsoft Office, SQL Server, and Exchange Server using Windows Update Services. There are several new switches for the Update.exe package installer and a new version 3.0 of the Windows Installer service.

Finally, the Security Center (Figure 1.9) applet in Control Panel provides security-related notifications to users in the areas of virus protection, Windows Firewall, and Windows Updates. You can disable these notifications through the Security Center and through group policy.

FIGURE 1.8

You can turn on or off the display of updates and patches in Add Or Remove Programs.

FIGURE 1.9

Use the Security Center to configure notifications about security-related features.

Where to Go for More Details

This chapter discusses some of the core features in Windows XP that are either new or improved over previous Windows platforms. These are by no means the only changes and improvements, however. There are also significant interface changes, a wealth of new features for remote access and management, improved recoverability, additional system installation and update options, firewalls and other security features, and much more. Rather than cover all these changes in this one chapter, I've opted to describe them throughout the remainder of the book to put them in context. However, several good references are available to help you get an overview of the new features in Windows XP. The following list offers several sources:

◆ *Mastering Windows XP Home Edition*, 3d ed., by Guy Hart-Davis (Sybex, 2004)

◆ *Mastering Windows XP Professional*, 3d ed., by Mark Minasi (Sybex, 2004)

◆ Windows XP Home Edition evaluation web page: www.microsoft.com/windowsxp/home/evaluation/features.mspx

◆ Windows XP Professional evaluation web page: www.microsoft.com/windowsxp/pro/evaluation/features.mspx

◆ Windows XP Service Pack 2 web page: www.microsoft.com/windowsxp/downloads/updates/default.mspx

Chapter 2

Stand-Alone Installations

There isn't much to the installation process for Windows XP—in most cases you pop in the CD, answer a few easy questions, and sit back for half an hour or so while Setup installs and configures the operating system. Usually, the whole process completes without a hitch. This is true for both clean installs and upgrades.

Getting to the point where you insert that CD is the trick, however. You need to consider several issues before you even obtain a copy of Windows XP, much less install it. Do you have enough disk space? What applications will be compatible, and which will cause problems? Should you clone your existing operating system so you can revert to it quickly if Windows XP doesn't live up to your expectations? Not least of all, what is Windows Product Activation, and how is it going to affect you?

This chapter answers these questions and others. I won't cover the installation process except in passing, because there really isn't much to it. Instead, I'll focus on your upgrade options, getting your system ready for Windows XP, and what to expect after it's installed. You'll also find several tips on ways to improve and simplify the installation process as well as update the system.

Understanding Upgrade Options

Upgrading a system gives you a handful of key advantages over installing a clean copy of the operating system. First and perhaps foremost, you don't have to reinstall all your applications. This can save you a lot of time in the installation process. Performing an upgrade also reduces (to some degree) the chance that you might lose data during the process. For example, assume you decide to format your hard disk, install a clean copy of Windows XP, and then reinstall all your applications. You need to back up your documents and other data before the installation and then restore them afterward. Can you be sure you've backed up all the right information? Are you sure you can restore it where it needs to be? How easy will it be to import the data from the backup location?

Although you should certainly back up your crucial documents and other data before performing an upgrade to Windows XP, it isn't likely that a problem will occur during the upgrade that will adversely affect that data. There's a better chance that you'll *introduce* a problem while trying to back up and restore your data. So, performing an upgrade rather than a clean install is not only a lot less work, it's also somewhat safer.

You can upgrade most versions of Windows to Windows XP. Table 2.1 shows the upgrade path for all versions.

As the table indicates, you can't upgrade Windows 3.1, Windows NT 3.51, or Windows 95 systems to Windows XP. Instead, you must perform a clean installation on these systems. Even so, there are some steps you can take on these systems to simplify the migration to Windows XP. See the section "Migrating Applications Manually," later in this chapter, for details.

TABLE 2.1: Windows XP Upgrade Options

EXISTING OS	WINDOWS XP HOME EDITION	WINDOWS XP PROFESSIONAL
Windows 3.1	No	No
Windows 95	No	No
Windows 98	Yes	Yes
Windows 98 SE	Yes	Yes
Windows Me	Yes	Yes
Windows NT 3.51	No	No
Windows NT Workstation 4.0	No	Yes
Windows 2000 Professional	No	Yes
Windows XP Home Edition	N/A	Yes
Windows XP Professional	No	N/A
All server platforms	No	No
All evaluation versions	No	No

Also note from Table 2.1 that you can't upgrade any evaluation or server platform to Windows XP. For example, you can't upgrade Windows NT Server 4.0 to Windows XP Professional. This isn't generally a drawback, however, because it's unlikely you'll want to replace a server operating system with a workstation version. Also, note that you can upgrade from Windows XP Home Edition to Windows XP Professional. So, if you install Home Edition today and later decide you need the features in Professional, you have an easy migration path.

Analyzing and Prepping the System

You should perform several steps before you install Windows XP on a system. This section explains these steps and the tools that are available to help you prepare your system(s) for Windows XP.

TIP This chapter is targeted at single, local Windows XP installations. See Chapter 3 for tips on installing Windows XP across the network and on multiple systems.

Using Upgrade Advisor

Microsoft has developed a tool called Upgrade Advisor that will help you determine if your system is ready for Windows XP. Inexplicably, Microsoft failed to include Upgrade Advisor on the

Windows XP CD. That's too bad, because although you can download the file from Microsoft's website, it's nearly 50 MB in size. Putting it on the CD would have saved a lot of time. If you want to download the tool, point your browser to

`www.microsoft.com/windowsxp/pro/ upgrading/advisor.mspx`

After you download `UpgAdv.exe`, double-click the file to install Upgrade Advisor. The application runs automatically when the installation is complete. Before you move through the advisor to check your system, connect to the Internet; doing so enables Upgrade Advisor to download updates to check for hardware and software compatibility. If you can't connect to the Internet, you can still run Upgrade Advisor, but the data it provides won't be as current as possible.

TIP Running Upgrade Advisor is a good idea even if you decide not to install Windows XP on a system, because Upgrade Advisor can point you to potential problems on your existing OS.

Upgrade Advisor (Figure 2.1) first gives you some background information about application and hardware compatibility. Then, it analyzes your system and provides a report listing any potential problems, as shown in Figure 2.2. You can click each item in the report to obtain more information about the issue and how to resolve it. Using the information provided in Upgrade Advisor's report, start obtaining software patches, device drivers, or other updates that need to be applied to your system prior to installing Windows XP.

TIP Click Save As when Upgrade Advisor displays its report, and save the report to a text file that you can review later.

FIGURE 2.1
Upgrade Advisor offers general information about hardware and software compatibility.

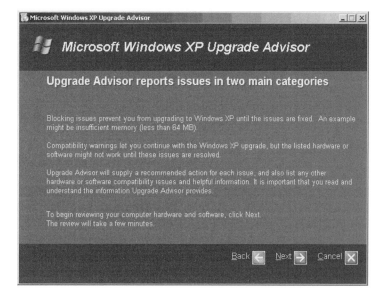

FIGURE 2.2
Upgrade Advisor presents a report of any potential upgrade problems.

Backing Up Your Data

Although it's unlikely that any of your data will be corrupted or lost during an upgrade, you should still back up your critical documents, message store, and any other data you can't afford to lose. In the case of a new installation—such as migrating from an older PC to a newer one—you probably need to perform a backup of your data so you can move it to the new system.

BACKUP OPTIONS

Before you use your current operating system's Backup program to back up your data, make sure you'll be able to read the data in Windows XP. Like Backup in Windows 2000, Windows XP supports backing up to a file, tape, or removable media. The Windows 9x version of Backup can also back up to a file, but not in a format supported by Windows XP. So, backup files that you create in Windows 9x or Me can't be read by the XP version of Backup. This means you won't be able to recover these files from Windows XP if the originals are lost or corrupted.

Restoring tape backup sets created with a different version of Backup is also very iffy. In most cases, you'll be able to restore a backup set if Windows XP supports the tape drive, but only if the tape set was created without software compression. The compression algorithm used in Windows 9x/Me Backup is different from the one in the Windows XP version.

One alternative is to back up your files to a removable disk, second local hard disk, network share, or CD-R/CD-RW. Copy the files rather than backing them up with the Backup utility, and then drag them back to the appropriate locations after you install Windows XP.

Another alternative is to run the original Backup utility under Windows XP. You must set compatibility options on the program to do so. First, copy the Backup program and its support files from the original system to a medium you can read on the Windows XP system after installation. For example, the Windows 9x and Me versions are located in \Program Files\Accessories\Backup. Copy the entire folder to the Windows XP system.

Next, set the path to include the Backup program's support files. In the case of the Windows 9x/Me versions, this is the \Backup\System folder. Right-click My Computer, choose Properties, and click the Advanced tab. Click Environment Variables to open the dialog box shown in Figure 2.3.

FIGURE 2.3
Modify environment variables with the Environment Variables dialog box.

Click Path in the System Variables list and click Edit. In the Edit System Variable dialog box (Figure 2.4), append a semicolon and the additional path string, and then click OK. Close all the dialog boxes.

FIGURE 2.4
Append the additional path string to the existing path variable.

Next, configure the program's compatibility settings. On the Windows XP system, open the folder containing the Backup program, right-click the executable file (such as `Msbackup.exe`), and choose Properties. Click the Compatibility tab, select Run This Program In Compatibility Mode For, and then select the source operating system from the drop-down list. Click OK, then launch the program and perform the restore operation.

TIP At this point, you can see that it would be much simpler to copy the files to a CD, second hard disk, or network share, rather than hassle with getting the older version of Backup to run under Windows XP. Use one of these options, if possible, to save time.

WHAT TO BACK UP

Now that you have some options for backing up your data on the current system, what should you back up?

Documents These include the documents in My Documents as well as any other data files (drawings, databases, checkbook, and so on) that you've created and stored on the system. Make it a habit to keep all your documents under My Documents, if possible, to make it easier for you to back up or move your documents whenever it becomes necessary.

TIP   Use My Documents as the root folder for your documents, and create other subfolders in My Documents to contain specific types of documents. For example, I keep my checkbook in \My Documents\Personal.

Outlook Express folders   The collection of files that hold the data for Outlook Express is called the *store*. You can find the location of the Outlook Express (OE) store this way: Open Outlook Express and choose Tools ➢ Options. Click the Maintenance tab and click Store Folder; the resulting Store Location dialog box shows the path to your OE folders. If others share your computer, make sure to back up their OE folders as well. If your version of Outlook Express doesn't offer the Maintenance tab in the Options, search the system for the folder containing the file Folders.dbx or Inbox.dbx, and back up the entire contents of the folder.

TIP   For more information about moving your Outlook Express message store from one computer to another, see Chapter 29.

Outlook local store(s)   If you use Outlook and have a set of personal folders (these are kept in a PST file), you should back that up as well. If you're using Outlook 2002 or 2003 with multiple accounts, keep in mind that you're probably using multiple PST files, even though you might not be aware of it. Outlook uses PSTs to store Hotmail and certain other accounts separate from your personal folders. Check your Outlook profile for the names and locations of your PST files. Also back up your offline store (OST file) if you're using an Exchange Server account.

Windows Address Book   This address book stores contacts for Outlook Express and other applications that can tap into it (such as your fax program.) Your address book has the name *user*.wab, where *user* is your logon name. Look for this file in the \Application Data\Microsoft\Address Book folder of your current profile folder.

TIP   Your OS system folder (\Windows) *is* your profile folder if individual profiles are turned off in Windows 9x.

Preparing the System

Before you begin installing Windows XP, you should take a few preparatory steps. First, if you're upgrading your existing OS, review your hard disk(s) and delete any old documents or other files you no longer need. Use the Add Or Remove Programs object in Control Panel to uninstall any programs that you no longer use or that you won't use after upgrading to Windows XP. Doing so will make additional space available for Windows XP.

TIP   If you're performing a clean install and either don't need to retain any of your existing files or have backed them up, consider reformatting the disk to start from a truly clean system. Just make sure you can restore your files afterward!

After clearing out the hard disk, consider defragmenting the drive. Doing so ensures the maximum contiguous disk space on the drive and improves performance. All versions of Windows except Windows NT include a disk optimizer, and you can obtain third-party tools such as Diskeeper for Windows NT.

TIP   For more information about Diskeeper, check out the Diskeeper website at www.diskeeper.com/coverpage.asp.

The final step in preparing to install Windows XP is to make sure your hardware is ready for it. Run Upgrade Advisor if you haven't already done so, to check for potential hardware or driver problems. Check the Windows XP Hardware Compatibility List (HCL) to make sure your hardware is compatible with Windows XP; you can find the Windows 2000 HCL at `www.microsoft.com/whdc/hcl/search.mspx`. For Windows XP, Microsoft has supplemented the HCL with the Windows Catalog, available at `www.microsoft.com/windows/catalog`. If you still have questions about driver compatibility for a specific item, check the manufacturer's website for Windows XP compatibility information and upgraded drivers.

Tips for Running Setup

As I mentioned previously, this chapter doesn't cover Setup itself. Rather, I focus on things you can do before and after Setup to simplify the installation process and improve performance. In this section, I offer some tips on using Setup in specific situations.

Installing on a Blank System

The Windows XP CD is bootable, enabling your computer to boot from the CD to run Setup and install Windows XP. This eliminates the need for a boot disk with CD-ROM drivers or for formatting the hard disk beforehand. In order to boot from a CD, your computer must support that feature and have the CD configured as one of the boot options in the BIOS. Boot the system, and enter the BIOS configuration program (the method for doing so varies from one computer to another). Then check your BIOS for a setting that specifies the boot order; be sure to include the CD in the list. The CD need not be the first boot device. If your system boots from a SCSI CD-ROM, you might also need to configure the BIOS to boot from SCSI before IDE. Check with your system's manufacturer or system documentation if you're not sure how to configure these settings.

TIP   If your computer continues to boot from the hard disk even after you've enabled booting from CD in the bios, set the CD before the hard disk in the BIOS boot order.

CREATING BOOT DISKS

If you can't get your system to boot from the CD, you can create a boot disk set that will allow the system to boot, see the CD-ROM drive, and start the installation process. The tool required to create the boot disk set isn't included with Windows XP, but you can download it from Microsoft's website. The download for Windows XP Professional is located at

```
www.microsoft.com/downloads/release.asp?ReleaseID=33291
```
You'll find the files for the Home Edition at

```
www.microsoft.com/downloads/release.asp?ReleaseID=33290
```
Download the appropriate executable file and run it. The utility prompts you to provide six blank, formatted, high-density disks. After the utility finishes copying the files to the disks, insert Disk 1 in the computer on which you want to install Windows XP, and reboot. The system will boot from the floppy, load the necessary CD-ROM driver(s), and start Setup.

Understanding Setup Switches

As I explained earlier, in most cases—whether upgrade or clean install—you insert the CD, boot the system, and let Setup install Windows XP for you with little or no interaction. In some cases, however, you may need to exercise more control over how Setup performs the installation. You can use several switches if you start Setup from a command prompt; these switches control the actions that Setup performs and the way in which it installs Windows XP.

There are two Setup programs, both located in the i386 folder of the Windows XP CD. You can run Winnt.exe on 16-bit operating systems such as DOS, Windows 3.1, or Windows for Workgroups 3.11. You can run Winnt32.exe on 32-bit operating systems such as Windows 9x, Me, NT, and 2000.

Why provide a 16-bit version of Setup if none of those operating systems allow you to upgrade? You might choose to install a clean copy of Windows XP on a system containing an OS version that doesn't support an upgrade, and Winnt.exe gives you the means of starting Setup. It also lets you specify several options to control how Setup runs.

TIP   For the complete syntax of both Winnt.exe and Winnt32.exe, including descriptions of all their optional command switches, see Tables 3.1 and 3.2 in Chapter 3.

Some of the options are the same in both Winnt.exe and Winnt32.exe, but Winnt32.exe offers additional switches not supported by Winnt.exe. In both cases, most of the switches are geared toward distributed or unattended setup. For that reason, all the switches are explained in detail in Chapter 3.

Migrating Applications Manually

When you perform an upgrade, Setup migrates all your applications to Windows XP so you can begin using them as soon as the upgrade is complete. In fact, that's one of the main reasons to perform an upgrade rather than a clean install—it's a real hassle to have to reinstall applications, particularly if you work with as many as I do.

TIP   Before you jump through the hoops to manually migrate an application, make sure it's really necessary. Copy the folder containing the program's executable file to your computer, and double-click the executable. If the program runs without problems, consider yourself lucky; you probably don't need to tweak the Registry or do anything else to continue using the program.

If you have to perform a clean install and you can't copy the application's folder to your new system, you may be able to migrate some of your applications manually and avoid having to reinstall them. The ability to migrate an application manually can be a real time-saver, but it can be a lifesaver, too. What if you've lost the original distribution CD or diskettes for the program, or they've been damaged? With a little luck, you may be able to copy the files from another system, tweak a few settings, and continue using them.

TIP   Migrating an application manually can be time-consuming and is generally useful only when you can't reinstall the application because of lost or damaged distribution media. Reinstall, if possible.

Whether you'll be able to migrate an application without reinstalling depends in large part on three main points, summarized in the following list:

Uses custom DLLs   If the program includes custom DLLs located somewhere other than in the application's folder, you'll need to locate the DLLs and place them in a location where Windows XP can access them.

Installs as a service   If the program installs as a service, you'll have to manually register the service in Windows XP.

Requires Registry settings   Many programs store settings in the Registry. You'll have to copy the Registry key for the application from the original computer or OS to the new one.

TIP   If you're going to reformat the drive when you install Windows XP, make sure to back up the folder containing the application and any subfolders. Also back up your current `Windows` or `Winnt` folder, because some of the application's files might be located in the system root folder.

First, determine if the application uses settings in the Registry. Generally these settings are stored in the `\HKEY_LOCAL_MACHINE\Software` and/or `\HKEY_CURRENT_USER\Software` Registry keys. Before upgrading to Windows XP, click Start ➢ Run, enter **regedit** in the Run dialog box to open the Registry Editor (Figure 2.5), and then look for a key for the application. If you find one, select the key and choose File ➢ Export Registry File to open the Export Registry File dialog box (Figure 2.6).

FIGURE 2.5
Use the Registry Editor to export the application's Registry key.

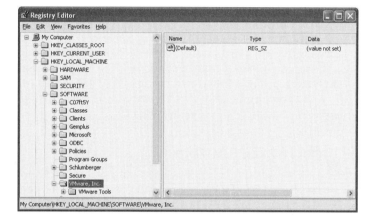

FIGURE 2.6
Save the application's Registry key to a file.

WARNING Make sure you select the application's key rather than a higher-level key. For example, don't select the \HKEY_LOCAL_MACHINE\Software key; instead, select (for example) \HKEY_LOCAL_MACHINE\Software\Adobe\Photoshop. Also, make sure you export *only* the selected branch rather than the entire Registry. Exporting the wrong key or the entire Registry and then importing it into Windows XP could prevent you from booting Windows XP.

Once you've selected the appropriate key in the Export Registry File dialog box, enter a file name for the REG file, select the Selected Branch option, and click Save. Make sure you save the file to a location where you'll be able to read it after installing Windows XP.

Next, locate the folder containing the application, and copy it to your new installation. This may require some planning before you install Windows XP, because you may need to back up the application's folder to a CD, network drive, or other media if you plan to reformat the disk during installation. Place the folder in the same location as on the original installation. For example, if the folder was located in the \Program Files\Adobe\Photoshop folder, place it there again, creating folders as needed.

If you located and exported a Registry key for the application, import that key now. To do so, locate the REG file you previously created, and double-click it to add it to the current Registry.

The next step is to try running the application by double-clicking its executable. If the program runs without any problems, you can stop here. If you receive error messages that the program can't find a DLL, note the name of the DLL and copy it from the original system or your backup copy. Repeat the process for any other missing DLLs.

Updating the System

Microsoft is constantly fixing bugs and adding features to Windows, and the company makes these updates available for download from its website. In previous versions of Windows, you could point your web browser to http://windowsupdate.microsoft.com, and a web-based interface helped you select operating system updates to install. Windows XP uses the same mechanism, but Microsoft has fine-tuned the notification process that Windows XP uses to let you know when updates are available. You can also use an alternative to the Windows Update site if you need to update multiple computers or prefer to download and save the updates so you can apply them when needed (such as after reinstalling your system).

Configuring Windows Update

After you install Windows XP and log in, Windows displays a balloon on one of the tray icons, prompting you to configure Windows Update. You can click the balloon to start the Windows Update Wizard, which lets you configure how Windows Update functions. You can also configure Windows Update through the System object in Control Panel. The only difference is that after configuring settings, the wizard launches your web browser and points it to the Windows Update website. This section explains the Control Panel method.

Open Control Panel and double-click the System icon. Or, right-click My Computer and choose Properties. Then, click the Automatic Updates tab on the System Properties dialog box, as shown in Figure 2.7.

TIP If your Control Panel is configured to show categories, you'll find the System icon under the Performance And Maintenance category.

Use the following four settings on the Automatic Updates tab to configure Windows Update for Windows XP:

Keep my computer up to date   Clear this option if you don't want Windows XP to automatically check for updates.

Notify me before downloading any updates and notify me again before installing them on my computer   Windows XP asks if you want to download updates rather than performing the scan and download automatically. It then prompts you to allow the updates to be installed.

Download the updates automatically and notify me when they are ready to be installed   Windows XP scans for and downloads updates automatically and then prompts you to allow the updates to be installed.

Automatically download the updates, and install them on the schedule that I specify   Windows XP scans for and downloads updates automatically and then installs them at the time you specify with the two associated drop-down lists.

Declined Updates   Click this button to add to the available update list those updates you've previously declined. This option lets you download declined updates.

TIP   You can also check for and apply updates at any time. Access the Windows Update site by pointing your web browser to http://windowsupdate.microsoft.com.

NOTE   If you're using an initial release version of Windows XP without any updates, the Automatic Updates tab will look slightly different from the one in Figure 2.7. The options are essentially the same, however.

New!   If you've installed Windows XP Service Pack 2, the Automatic Updates tab of the System properties will look like the one shown in Figure 2.8. Microsoft didn't change the functionality of the options in the dialog box, but it did reword the options to simplify them. In addition, the Declined Updates button is replaced by a link that reads Offer Updates Again That I've Previously Hidden.

FIGURE 2.7
Use the Automatic Updates tab to configure Windows Update.

FIGURE 2.8

SP2 changes the Automatic Updates tab to simplify the available options.

Downloading Updates for Individual Installation

When you use the Windows Update site, Windows XP downloads and installs the updates without letting you save the download for installation later or on another system. If your job is to manage multiple PCs, or if you like to maintain a library of updates you can apply at any time, you need an alternative to the Windows Update site. Previously, that alternative was the Corporate Windows Update site. Microsoft has revamped the Windows Update site to include the capability to download updates for later installation.

New!

To obtain updates for installation later on your own computer or other computers that you manage, visit the Windows Update website and click the Administrator Options link in the left pane. Click the Windows Update Catalog link in the resulting page.

The Windows Update Catalog, shown in Figure 2.9, lets you search for updates to your version of Windows XP as well as find driver updates. If you click the link Find Microsoft Windows Updates, the site displays a form from which you choose your operating system version and language. You can also click Advanced Search Options to access additional options, such as limiting the search for specific update types.

When you click Search, Windows Update retrieves a list of the updates that match your search criteria. Click the category you want to view (Figure 2.10), scroll through the list, and click Add for each update you want to add to the Download Basket. Then, click Go To Download Basket. In the resulting page (Figure 2.11), you can specify the download location and, if needed, remove updates from the basket before starting the download. When you're ready to download, click Download Now and accept any EULAs that Windows Update displays.

FIGURE 2.9
Use the Windows Update
Catalog to download
updates for distributed
installation.

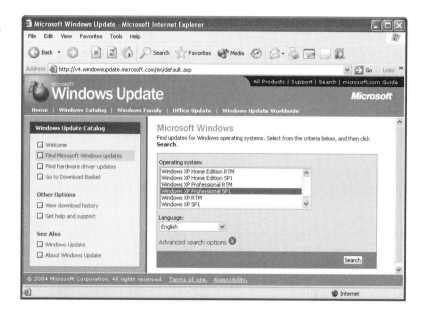

FIGURE 2.9
Use the Windows Update
Catalog to download
updates for distributed
installation.

FIGURE 2.10
Choose the updates you
want to download.

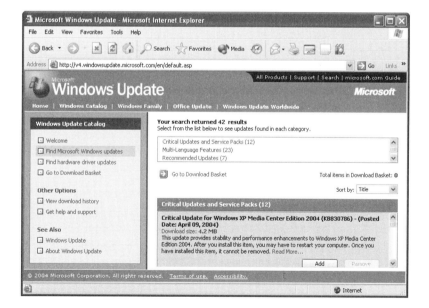

FIGURE 2.11
Review the updates prior
to starting the download.

After the files are downloaded, look in the folder you specified as the drop location. You'll find a `WU` folder that contains several subfolders. Drilling down through the subfolders reveals that each update is stored in its own folder. You can distribute the files as needed on your network or double-click the update's executable to install the update.

Controlling Windows Update with Group Policy

Windows XP offers several group policy settings that enable administrators to control how Windows Update functions. As with other group policies, you can set these policies at the site, domain, organization unit, or local computer level. To explore these policies, run `GPEDIT.MSC` on a Windows XP Professional computer. The policies are located in the `Computer Configuration\Administrative Templates\Windows Components\Windows Update` and `User Configuration\Administrative Templates\ Windows Components\Windows Update` branches.

TIP   Keep in mind that group policies aren't supported on Windows XP Home Edition.

If you want to disable Windows Update, set to Enabled the policy User Configuration\Administrative Templates\Windows Components\Windows Update\Remove Access To Use All Windows Update Features. Users under the scope of the policy will then be unable to access the Windows Update site or receive update notifications from Windows Update.

If you choose to continue to use Windows Update or are installing a Windows Update Services server on your network to host updates, you can use the remaining policies in these two branches to control how updates are identified and deployed. Some of the policies apply to Windows Update globally, some apply specifically to using Microsoft's Windows Update site, and others apply specifically to the use of Windows Update Services. Most of these policies' names make them self-explanatory; if necessary, double-click the policy and then click the Explain tab to learn about the policy's purpose and application.

FIGURE 2.12

Use group policy to disable Windows Update features.

NOTE   See Chapter 35 for a complete discussion of group and local policies. Chapters 36 and 37 discuss specific uses of group policy to apply hardware and software restrictions and manage user data and settings.

Overview of Windows Update Services

Microsoft developed and released a product called Software Update Services (SUS) that enabled a Windows Server to act as an update server for Windows updates and serve as an alternative to the Windows Update website. SUS let administrators control how and when updates were applied. For the second release of SUS, Microsoft has renamed it Windows Update Services (WUS); this new release is slated for release in the first half of 2005.

Why use SUS or WUS to roll out your Windows XP updates? It isn't a good practice to let users download and install their own updates. First, users shouldn't be given the necessary permissions on a system to install updates. Second, updates should be tested for security and compatibility before being deployed across the enterprise, to avoid potential problems. For example, when you install Windows XP SP2, Windows Firewall is enabled by default. This can cause network applications to stop working. For that reason, administrators need to plan for the SP2 deployment to accommodate the firewall.

WUS addresses these potential update problems by giving administrators control over the update process. Users' computers no longer download updates from Microsoft's Windows Update site, but instead download updates from the network's WUS server. Administrators use group policy to control update behavior: disabling users' ability to use the Windows Update site, setting the update behavior for the WUS server, and so on.

TIP   An advantage of moving up to WUS from SUS is that WUS supports upgrades for more than just Windows XP Professional. You can update Windows 2000, Windows Server 2003, Microsoft Office, MSDE 2000, SQL Server, and Exchange Server. Microsoft plans to support updates for other Microsoft applications and operating systems in future stages.

WUS isn't the only solution to rolling out updates to your users. If you need to support other operating systems and applications not supported by WUS, you can turn to Microsoft's Systems Management Server (SMS). Although at the time of the initial WUS release, SMS doesn't use WUS to deploy updates, Microsoft will redesign SMS to use WUS to detect and deploy updates.

Setting up and using WUS is predominantly a server-side issue, so I won't cover it in detail here. For more information about WUS, see

`http://www.microsoft.com/windowsserversystem/sus/default.mspx`
For detailed information about Systems Management Server, see

`http://www.microsoft.com/smserver/default.asp`

Windows Product Activation

In Windows XP, Microsoft introduced a new feature called Windows Product Activation (WPA) as an effort to control piracy and prevent users from installing a single copy of Windows XP on multiple computers. WPA works much like product activation for other products such as Office 2000 and Office XP. After logon, Windows XP determines whether the product has been activated yet. If not, it directs you to either connect to Microsoft over the Internet or call Microsoft to activate Windows XP.

WPA binds each installation of Windows XP to a specific PC. It takes an inventory of a system's hardware and generates a 50-digit string; this string is used to register the product through Microsoft, which provides a 42-digit value for activation. Attempts to activate Windows XP with the same 42-digit value will fail unless the machines are essentially identical.

When you upgrade the system by adding new hardware, Windows XP doesn't perform activation again to change your activation code—you can make all the changes you want to the system after you activate Windows without affecting your system. However, if you have to reinstall Windows XP, there is a good chance that WPA won't recognize the system as being the same if you've made too many hardware changes (a different video adapter, different network adapter, new SCSI host adapter, and so on). The activation will probably fail, but you can call Microsoft to activate the software: Tell the technician you've upgraded the system and are reinstalling Windows XP. You'll receive a new activation code for your new configuration.

WPA is targeted primarily at the retail market. Copies of Windows XP that you purchase through volume licenses such as the Microsoft Open License, Microsoft Select, and Microsoft Enterprise Agreement programs aren't subject to WPA and don't require the same activation steps. If you purchase any retail versions of Windows XP, keep the activation requirements in mind; otherwise, ensure that you purchase Windows XP through a volume-license mechanism, and avoid a mix of open-license and retail copies to eliminate licensing confusion.

TIP   If you've lost your CD case and don't remember your Windows XP CD key, visit www
.magicaljellybean.com to download a copy of Keyfinder. This utility extracts your
Windows XP key from the Registry and can also extract your Office CD key. You can use the latest version of Keyfinder to change the CD key associated with a particular copy of Windows XP.
Or, see `http://support.microsoft.com/default.aspx?scid=kb;en-us;Q328874` to learn
how to use WPA to change the key.

Chapter 3

Reaping the Rewards of Network, Automated, and Unattended Installations

Installing Windows XP on one or just a handful of computers isn't much of a task. You pop in the CD, answer a few questions, and let Setup do its thing. You can be up and running after a donut and a cup of coffee. But if, like me, you frequently need to install Windows XP on 50, 100, or even more computers, installation becomes a headache if your only option is to install on one computer at a time. That many donuts would kill me!

Fortunately, Windows XP gives you several options for installing the operating system in a wide variety of situations. For example, you can install Windows XP from a network share across the network, which eliminates the need for a local CD. You can even integrate service packs and other updates to create a *slipstream installation* share that lets you install Windows XP along with updates and service packs in a single operation—a great timesaver.

You can also create custom Setup files to install Windows XP with custom options in automated or unattended installations. This means you can build an answer file to provide responses to all the questions Setup asks during the installation process. Automated and unattended installation is a handy means for deploying Windows XP across a large number of computers, particularly in situations where the users aren't technically adept.

A third and extremely powerful option is Remote Installation Services (RIS), included with Windows 2000 Server and Windows Server 2003. RIS lets you automatically install Windows 2000, XP, and 2003 to computers across a network, even if the target computer's hard disk is blank. RIS is very useful for deploying an operating system to new hires and for performing disaster recovery. When you combine RIS with the ability to install applications automatically through Microsoft's IntelliMirror technologies, you can essentially automate the entire process of installing the operating system and all applications for a user.

Finally, a handful of options let you create an image of an operating system and deploy Windows XP simply by copying that image to each computer. Each computer receives an exact duplicate of the operating system and applications. This is a great solution for labs and other organizations where you need to install the same set of applications for a large number of users.

I explore all of these installation methods in this chapter, starting with the many switches you can use with the Windows XP Setup programs. You'll use these switches for many of the Setup options discussed in the chapter, so consider them a foundation for the rest of the chapter.

Taming Setup with Switches

As I explained in Chapter 2, there are two versions of Setup: `Winnt.exe` and `Winnt32.exe`. The first is for use on 16-bit operating systems, including DOS, Windows 3.1, and Windows for Workgroups 3.11. `Winnt32.exe` is for all 32-bit operating systems, including Windows 9*x*, Me, NT, 2000, and XP.

The syntax for `Winnt.exe` is

```
winnt [/s[:sourcepath]] [/t[:tempdrive]] [/u[:answer_file]] [/udf:id[,UDF_file]]
[/r:folder] [/r[x]:folder] [/e:command] [/a]
```

The syntax for `Winnt32.exe` is

```
winnt32 [/s:sourcepath] [/tempdrive:drive_letter] [/unattend[num]:[answer_file]]
[/copydir:folder_name] [/copysource:folder_name] [/cmd:command_line]
 [/debug[level]:[filename]] [/udf:id[,UDF_file]]
[/syspart:drive_letter][/checkupgradeonly] [/cmdcons] [/m:folder_name]
[/makelocalsource] [/noreboot]
```

Table 3.1 summarizes the optional command switches for `Winnt.exe`, and Table 3.2 summarizes the optional switches for `Winnt32.exe`.

TABLE 3.1:   *Winnt.exe* Command Switches

OPTION	FUNCTION
`/s[:sourcepath]`	Location of Windows XP source files; must be full local or UNC pathname.
`/t[:tempdrive]`	Location for temporary Setup files and installation partition.
`/u:[answer_file]`	Performs unattended Setup using specified answer file; requires `/s` option.
`/udf:id[,UDF_file]`	Specifies unique ID and uses Unique Database File (UDF) to modify answer file for unattended Setup. ID determines which answers in UDF file are used.
`/r[:folder]`	Creates optional folder that remains after installation; specify folder name as *folder*.
`/rx[:folder]`	Copies folder during Setup but deletes after installation.
`/e`	Specifies command to be executed after GUI-mode Setup completes.
`/a`	Enables accessibility options.

TABLE 3.2:   *Winnt32.exe* Command Switches

OPTION	FUNCTION
/s:*sourcepath*	Location of Windows XP source files; specify multiple sources with multiple /s switches.
/tempdrive:*drive_letter*	Location for temporary Setup files and Windows XP installation partition. You must use the /syspart switch with this switch.
/unattend	Upgrade previous version of Windows XP in unattended Setup mode; implies acceptance of EULA.
/unattend[*num*]:[*answer_file*]	Performs a clean install in unattended mode; *num* is seconds between end of file copy and system restart, and *answer_file* is the file specifying Setup options.
/copydir:*folder_name*	Copies optional folder specified by *folder_name* to the system root folder during Setup; use multiple switches to copy multiple folders. Such a folder isn't removed after completion of Setup.
/copysource:*folder_name*	Copies optional folder specified by *folder_name* to the system root folder during Setup; use multiple switches to copy multiple folders. Such a folder is deleted after completion of Setup.
/cmd:*command_line*	Executes the command specified by *command_line* after Setup but before final system restart.
/debug[*level*]:[*filename*]	Logs information to specified file; 1 = errors, 2 = warnings, 3 = information, 4 = detailed.
/udf:*id*[,*UDF_file*]	Specifies unique ID and uses Unique Database File (UDF) to modify answer file for unattended Setup. *id* determines which answers in UDF file are used.
/syspart:*drive_letter*	Copies Setup startup files to drive and marks the drive active for install in another computer. Setup continues on boot on the other computer. Requires /tempdrive switch. Not available for Windows 9*x* or Me.
/checkupgradeonly	Analyzes the system for upgrade compatibility but doesn't install Windows XP; creates Upgrade.txt (Windows 9*x*) or Winnt32.log (Windows NT) log file in current OS system root folder.
/cmdcons	Installs Recovery Console during Setup.
/m:*folder_name*	Copies files from *folder_name* rather than from the default source location.
/makelocalsource	Copies all installation source files to local hard disk.

TABLE 3.2:   *Winnt32.exe* Command Switches *(CONTINUED)*

OPTION	FUNCTION
/noreboot	Doesn't restart system after final Setup phase.
/dudisable	Prevents Dynamic Update from running during Setup and instead installs only using existing source files. This option prevents Dynamic Update from running even if you specify Dynamic Update options in an answer file.
/duprepare:*pathname*	Prepares distributed installation folder to be used with update files you've downloaded from Windows Update website.
/dushare:*pathname*	Specifies network share in which you have downloaded Dynamic Update files from Windows Update website, and which you've prepared with /duprepare switch. Use this switch during installation to direct Setup to use updated files in specified directory.

As you can see from these two tables, both Winnt.exe and Winnt32.exe support several switches you can use to control the way Setup works and installs Windows XP. I explore all of these switches in the following sections, organized by the function each switch performs.

NOTE   The following sections focus on Winnt32.exe rather than Winnt.exe because you're more likely to be running Setup on a 32-bit operating system.

Specifying the Location of Source Files and Destination

Setup, by default, looks for the Windows XP source files in the same i386 folder where the Setup file (Winnt.exe or Winnt32.exe) is located. In some cases, you may want to specify a different location, such as a network share or a folder on a local hard disk. You may also want to copy all the source files to the local hard disk if the original location (network drive or CD) won't be available after the system restarts to complete Setup.

Use the /s switch to specify the folder where the Windows XP source files are located. The /s switch not only lets you specify a different location for the Windows XP source files, but also lets you speed up the file copy process and distribute the load to more than one installation share on different servers. How? You can specify up to eight /s switches with a single command. Setup copies files from each simultaneously, which speeds up copying and provides load balancing on the installation servers. The following example uses the /s switch to install from three different servers:

```
winnt32.exe /s:\\server1\xpshare /s:\\server2\xp /s:\\server3\xpfiles
```

You can use the /t switch with Winnt.exe to have Setup place temporary installation files and install Windows XP to the specified drive. This is the same as the /tempdrive switch for Winnt32.exe. When you use /tempdrive, you also need the /syspart switch. The following example would install Windows XP from a network share and place the OS on drive D:

```
winnt32.exe /s:\\server1\xpshare /tempdrive:d /syspart:d
```

TIP   Both /tempdrive and /syspart must point to the same primary partition on the target drive.

You can use the /m switch to make Setup copy files from an alternate location rather than the specified or default source folder. For example, assume you've created a folder containing updated driver files, and you want Setup to use those rather than the ones included with Windows XP. If you specify the /m switch, Setup looks in the specified folder for a file and copies it from that location rather than the default. Otherwise, Setup copies the file from the default location. Here's an example:

```
winnt32.exe /s:\\server1\xpshare /m:\\xpupdates
```

Copying Folders During Setup

Another task you might want to perform during installation is to create optional folders and copy existing custom folders to the target system. For example, maybe you have a set of common documents you want everyone to have, or you need to copy a folder for a custom application as part of the installation process. Maybe you need to install custom drivers during Setup.

You can use the /r and /rx switches with Winnt.exe to create folders during installation. With /r, Setup creates the folder and leaves it in place after installation is complete. With /rx, Setup creates the folder during installation but deletes it upon completion. The corresponding switches for Winnt32.exe are /copydir, which copies the folder and leaves it after installation, and /copysource, which copies the folder during installation but deletes it on completion.

There is a key point to understand when you're copying folders with these switches. The folders are always created under the *%systemroot%* folder on the target system—the folder containing Windows (such as \Winnt or \Windows). So, if you want to move the contents of the folder to another location, you need to use the /cmd switch to execute a command to move the files when Setup completes.

Executing Commands After Setup

Let's say you've copied a folder to the *%systemroot%* folder during installation with the /copydir switch, but you want the contents of the folder to be stored in a different final location. Or maybe you want to run a batch file that sets up a certain folder structure on the user's computer or copies certain files from a network server to the user's computer. Both Setup programs give you a switch you can use to execute a command after Setup completes.

The Winnt.exe switch is /e:*command*, and the Winnt32.exe switch is /cmd:*command*. Enclose the command in quotes if it includes embedded spaces, as in the following example:

```
winnt32.exe /cmd:"move c:\windows\CommonDocs c:\CommonDocs"
```

TIP   If a path in the command includes spaces, such as c:\Program Files\CustomApp, you can use the short 8.3 folder name in the command rather than the long name. For example, the \Program Files folder on almost any system has the short name \PROGRA~1 because Windows uses a common naming convention when creating short names.

In addition to or instead of using the /e or /cmd switch, you can use a Cmdlines.txt file to execute commands or include a command in the [SetupParams] section of an answer file.

NOTE   See "Customizing Setup," later in this chapter, to learn how to use alternatives such as Cmdlines.txt and answer files to execute commands and perform other automated Setup tasks.

Prepping a Drive for Another System with */syspart*

You can use the /syspart switch with Winnt32.exe to perform the initial installation steps on a secondary hard disk in preparation for moving that drive to another computer. After you install the drive on the other system and boot that system, Setup continues and completes the installation process. So, /syspart gives you a means of prepping drives for other systems without creating a duplicate image of an existing system. This option is handy if you need to install Windows XP on several new systems that have varying hardware (which makes drive imaging impractical) and can't use RIS or other automated/network-based methods to complete the installation.

The following example would perform an initial installation to drive D: from a network distribution share:

```
winnt32.exe /s:\\server1\xpshare /tempdrive:d /syspart:d /noreboot
```

> **NOTE**   You must use the /tempdrive switch and point it to the target drive when using /syspart.
> You can use an unattended Setup file as well to provide answers to questions that the end user would otherwise see during the final stages of Setup.

Use the /noreboot switch to prevent the computer from rebooting after Setup completes. Also, you should shut down and remove the second drive before rebooting the computer, because Setup marks the drive as active in preparation for booting on the target system.

Managing Dynamic Update

Three switches for Winnt32.exe let you control Dynamic Update during installation. Normally, Setup runs Dynamic Update near the end of the installation process to download and install updates from the Windows Update site. However, you can download updates separately and incorporate them into the installation source files to provide an up-to-date installation in the first pass.

The /duprepare switch modifies an existing Windows XP installation share, adding a dudrvs folder to the share and populating it with update files. You use the /duprepare switch when setting up a distribution share that will later be used by clients to install Windows XP. The syntax for using this switch is

```
winnt32.exe /duprepare:FolderPath
```

Replace the *FolderPath* variable with the local or network path to the folder that contains the Windows XP installation files.

Use the /dushare switch when you run Setup to specify the location of the folder you've prepared with /duprepare. The syntax for using this switch is

```
winnt32.exe /dushare:FolderPath
```

Again, *FolderPath* is the local or, more likely, remote network path to the folder containing the Windows Update files.

One additional switch, /dudisable, lets you prevent Windows Update from running during Setup. This option speeds up the installation process and allows you to control when and if Windows Update executes.

Miscellaneous Switches

You can use a handful of additional switches with `Winnt32.exe`:

/debug   This switch lets you log information to a file during Setup. You can specify one of four logging levels using the numeric variable that goes with the switch:

Level	Logging Performed
1	Logs errors that occur during installation
2	Logs warnings that occur during installation
3	Logs informational messages generated during installation
4	Logs detailed information generated by Setup during installation

/cmdcons   Use this switch to install the Windows XP Recovery Console during installation. You can install the RC along with Windows XP or use this switch to install it at any time after installing XP.

NOTE   For detailed information on installing and using the Recovery Console, see Chapter 40.

/checkupgradeonly   Use this switch to analyze your current OS for compatibility with Windows XP. When you use this switch, Setup doesn't install Windows XP but instead analyzes the system, generates a report, and stores the report as `Upgrade.txt` in the existing operating system's root folder (such as `C:\Windows` or `C:\Winnt`).

NOTE   The following section provides information on how to use the /unattend and /udf switches to perform unattended installations.

Customizing Setup

The switches explained so far let you control how Setup works. Sometimes you'll use these switches as the only method for customizing Setup. In most cases, however, you'll use custom Setup files to control the way Setup runs and the actions it performs. I explain in this section how to create and use custom Setup files.

Overview of Automated and Unattended Setup

Normally, Setup asks several questions during installation to determine how you want it to install Windows XP. If you're installing Windows XP on one or two systems, you'll probably just sit through the installation process and provide the answers yourself. But if you need to install on several systems or need to perform additional tasks during Setup, a custom Setup file is the way to go.

NOTE   Creating and using unattended Setup files is a complex task. You'll find a good overview of the process in this section. For a more detailed look at using unattended Setup files, see *Windows 2000 Automated Deployment and Remote Administration* by Christa Anderson (Sybex, 2001).

SETUP ANSWER FILES

An *answer file* is a text file that contains the answers to questions that Setup normally asks during installation. An answer file contains several sections, each identified by a section name in square brackets. Each section can contain one or more settings. The following listing is a fragment from a typical unattended Setup file:

```
;SetupMgrTag
[Data]
    AutoPartition=1
    MsDosInitiated="0"
    UnattendedInstall="Yes"

[Unattended]
    UnattendMode=FullUnattended
    OemSkipEula=Yes
    OemPreinstall=No
    TargetPath=\WINDOWS

[GuiUnattended]
    AdminPassword="BLINKY"
    EncryptedAdminPassword=NO
    OEMSkipRegional=1
    TimeZone=20
    OemSkipWelcome=1

[UserData]
    ProductID=12345-ABCDE-67890-FGHIJ-12345
    FullName="Jim Boyce"
    OrgName="Jim Boyce, Inc."
    ComputerName=*
```

You can use an unattended Setup file by itself to perform automated or semi-automated installations. All parameters defined by the file will be the same on all systems on which you install Windows XP using the file.

The following example would install Windows XP using the unattended Setup file named `custom.txt` on a network server:

```
winnt32.exe /unattend:\\srv1\install\custom.txt
```

In some situations, you may need to modify the contents of the Setup file during installation to further customize the OS installation. You can use a UDF file for that purpose.

UDF FILES

UDF stands for *Unique Database File*. A UDF file modifies the answers in the custom Setup file. Think of it this way: the Setup file can specify all the answers, but the UDF file replaces some of those answers during installation, overriding selected answers on a per-computer basis. For example, you might use a UDF file to specify computer name, time zone, and a few other properties during installation for each computer.

The UDF file uses the same general format as an answer file. The [UniqueIds] section of the file lists each of the unique sections in the file and typically lists the section where the settings for a particular computer are located. This means you can use a single UDF file to modify any number of individual installations.

Take a look at the following UDF sample:

```
[UniqueIds]
    COMPUTER1=UserData,GuiUnattended
    COMPUTER2=UserData,GuiUnattended
    COMPUTER3=UserData,GuiUnattended
[COMPUTER1:UserData]
    ComputerName=Joe
[COMPUTER1:GuiUnattended]
    AdminPassword="dif984z9"
    TimeZone="  (GMT-05:00) Eastern Time (US & Canada)"
[COMPUTER2:UserData]
    ComputerName=Jane
[COMPUTER2:GuiUnattended]
    AdminPassword="fkuer837x"
    TimeZone="  (GMT-06:00) Central Time (US & Canada)"
[COMPUTER3:UserData]
    ComputerName=Bart
[COMPUTER3:GuiUnattended]
    AdminPassword="8djf7rlcf"
    TimeZone="  (GMT-07:00) Mountain Time (US & Canada)"
```

This example accommodates three different computers, specifying the computer name and an appropriate time zone for the computer during installation, along with the password for the local administrator account. This is a simplistic example, but you can see that it's possible to provide answers for more than one computer in a single UDF file.

To use the UDF file during installation, you need to specify the name of the unattended file, the UDF file, and the unique ID that labels the section you want Setup to use for the current installation. The following code (ignore the fact that this line wraps in print) would install Windows XP on Jane's computer based on the previous UDF example (assuming the file is named custom.udf):

```
winnt32.exe /unattend:\\srv1\install\custom.txt
    /udf:COMPUTER1,\\srv1\udfs\custom.udf
```

Tools for Creating Custom Setup Files

You could create unattended Setup files manually with a text editor. You could also try to stack all the grains of sand on the beach one at a time, but why on Earth would you want to when you could use a bulldozer? That Setup bulldozer is the Setup Manager tool, which Microsoft includes on the Windows XP CD. You'll find Setup Manager in the file \support\tools\deploy.cab. To extract Setup Manager, open a command console and execute the command in the following example. Change the path to the CD drive on your system as needed, and specify the location where you want the file copied for the variable *destination:*

```
expand e:\support\tools\deploy.cab -F:setupmgr.exe destination
```

Next, double-click the extracted `Setupmgr.exe` file to start Setup Manager, which functions as a wizard. As you move through the wizard, you can specify several settings to define the contents of the Setup file.

You can create a new answer file with Setup Manager or modify an existing answer file, and that's the first choice you need to make in the wizard. The second decision you need to make is the type of installation for which the answer file will be used. I'm assuming at this point that you're using Setup Manager to create a file for use in an unattended installation, but you can also create a file for a Sysprep or Remote Installation Services installation. These types of installation are covered later in this chapter.

Within the wizard, you can create a distribution share or direct that the answer file be used to install Windows XP from a CD. After you answer a handful of other questions in the wizard, Setup Manager displays the dialog box shown in Figure 3.1.

FIGURE 3.1
Use Setup Manager to configure the options that Setup will use during installation.

You can click Next to move through the settings pages or use the tree pane at the left to select the settings you want to modify. At the end of the process, Setup Manager prompts you for the name of a Setup file and creates the text file based on the answers you provide.

Setup Manager doesn't create UDF files, but you can use Notepad or any text editor to create the file. Use Setup Manager to create the unattended Setup file you'll use with the UDF file, and then extract to a separate file those sections you need to modify.

Running Commands with *Cmdlines.txt*

A common task you'll probably want to perform during an unattended installation is to execute commands. For example, you may want to copy folders, install drivers, set file or folder permissions, or perform other tasks from a command line. I previously explained the `/e` and `/cmd` switches you can use with `Winnt.exe` and `Winnt32.exe` to execute commands. You can also use the `Cmdlines.txt` file to execute commands during the GUI portion of Windows XP Setup.

Cmdlines.txt is a text file that contains a single section labeled [Commands], followed by each command on its own line, in quotes. Commands you include in Cmdlines.txt need to either run in quiet mode without requiring user interaction or use scripting to accomplish the same results.

Create the folder OEM in the Windows XP distribution folder and place Cmdlines.txt in that folder. Then add the line OEMPreinstall=Yes to the [Unattended] section of your unattended Setup file.

TIP The commands in Cmdlines.txt execute after Setup is finished but before the system reboots. This means that network shares are unavailable, so the commands and any supporting files need to be available locally. If necessary, use the /copydir or /copysource switch or another method to copy the files to the local system.

Running Applications Once after Setup with *[GuiRunOnce]*

Another option for running applications during Setup is the [GuiRunOnce] section of the answer file. Commands you specify in this section execute after Setup completes and the system reboots, but before the user logs on. The [GuiRunOnce] section corresponds to the commands you specify using Setup Manager's Run Once option. They're added to this Registry key:

```
\HKEY_LOCAL_MACHINE\Software\Microsoft\Windows\CurrentVersion\RunOnce
```

TIP Programs and commands that you execute through [GuiRunOnce] need to run in quiet mode without any user input.

Using Sysprep

Sysprep is another tool included with Windows XP that you can use to deploy the operating system. You create an image of an existing Windows XP installation using Sysprep and then replicate the image to other systems using third-party disk cloning software. The target systems' hardware configurations must be identical to that of the source system, making Sysprep useful for deploying Windows XP to multiple computers in a lab situation where you purchase similarly configured PCs in large quantities.

Each Windows XP system needs a unique security identifier (SID). Two computers on the network with the same SID will cause conflicts and lead to problems for both systems. So, Sysprep configures the target image to create a new, unique SID at boot.

Here's the process for duplicating Windows XP using Sysprep:

1. Install Windows XP on the source system. The computer should be a workgroup member (not a domain member), and the administrator password should be blank.

2. Install applications on the source system.

3. Test the source system, and remove any remaining temporary files.

4. Defragment the disk (optional).

5. Use System Manager to create a Sysprep.inf answer file to automate the installation (if desired).

6. Run Sysprep, using switches as needed (described shortly).

7. Duplicate the disk using a third-party utility such as Symantec Ghost.

8. Install the target drive in the target system, and boot it.

When you boot the target system, Setup creates a SID and runs a Setup Wizard that prompts for any remaining information.

TIP You can use the `Sysprep.inf` file to provide those answers, if you prefer, bypassing the Setup Wizard. If you choose to use `Sysprep.inf`, create the file with Setup Manager. Then place the file in the *%systemroot%*\Sysprep folder prior to creating the image.

The syntax for `Sysprep.exe` is

```
Sysprep [-quiet] [nosidgen] [-reboot] [-noreboot] [-pnp]
```

Table 3.3 describes the purpose of each switch.

TABLE 3.3: Optional Switches for *Sysprep*

OPTION	FUNCTION
-quiet	Runs in silent mode without displaying any information dialog boxes
-nosidgen	Doesn't generate a unique SID the next time the system starts
-reboot	Reboots the system when Sysprep is finished
-noreboot	Doesn't reboot the system when Sysprep is finished
-pnp	Forces Plug and Play enumeration on the next reboot

You'll find `Sysprep.exe` on the Windows XP CD in `\Support\Tools\Deploy.cab`. Use the Extract command to extract the file from the archive.

Integrating Service Packs in a Slipstream Installation

As with other Windows operating systems, Microsoft has released service packs for Windows XP to provide a means for easily updating the operating system and deploying new features. Integrating service pack files is an important consideration when you're dealing with Windows XP installations on multiple computers.

Normally, when you install Windows, you first install the operating system and then apply the latest service pack (SP) and any post-SP updates. This is fine for a handful of systems but can be time-consuming if you're installing Windows XP on multiple systems. You could use a combination of Remote Installation Services and IntelliMirror to deploy the operating system and updates automatically, but this method still requires a separate Setup pass to install the SP, as well as a RIS server and Active Directory. To save time, you can create a *slipstream* copy of Windows XP.

A slipstream copy is one in which you've applied a given set of service packs or other modifications to the source files. In other words, it's a copy of the Windows XP source files where the files included in the SP have replaced their original versions. After you create the slipstream copy, you can place it on a network share or burn it to CD for distribution (assuming you've satisfied the necessary licensing requirements).

To create a slipstream Windows XP installation source, first create the folder that will contain the copy (assume `c:\slipstream` for this example). Use the following command to copy the Windows XP source files from the CD in drive D: to the slipstream folder:

```
xcopy d:\i386 c:\slipstream\i386 /e
```

If you have the downloaded version of the service pack, create the folder C:\SP, and then execute the following command from the directory containing the service pack download to expand the SP files. When prompted, specify C:\SP as the location for the extraction. This example assumes you're creating a slipstream with SP2:

```
xpsp2.exe /x
```

Next, switch to C:\SP and execute the following command to copy the service pack files to the slipstream folder:

```
c:\sp\i386\update\update.exe -s:c:\slipstream
```

TIP Replace the path to `Update.exe` if you're using the service pack CD rather than the downloaded version.

Finally, copy the contents of the `c:\slipstream` folder to the network share from which users will install Windows XP, or burn the folder to a CD.

Deploying Windows XP with RIS

Setting up systems can take a huge amount of your time, particularly if you need to install Windows XP on many systems. Installing the OS is also a key task in disaster recovery, not just something you perform for new users or when existing users receive new computers. Although new systems typically come preconfigured with the OS of your choice, you may prefer to provide a custom installation for feature or security reasons.

NOTE *Microsoft Windows XP Power Productivity* focuses primarily on Windows XP rather than Windows 2000 Server or Windows Server 2003. For that reason, this section provides a good overview of Remote Installation Services (RIS) so you'll understand what it is and what it can do, but I don't explain the specific steps to go through to install a RIS server. For detailed information on setting up and using RIS, see *Mastering Windows Server 2003* by Mark Minasi (Sybex, 2003).

When a system goes down because of a drive failure and needs a replacement, you can take a couple of different directions to bring that system back online. One approach is to have spare drives on hand with OS images already ghosted onto them. This requires essentially identical systems throughout the organization and is often impractical. If you're using remote OS installation, however, you can put in a blank drive and let the installation happen almost automatically. The advantage is that the operating system is installed clean on the system and accommodates disparate hardware while requiring little or no interaction with the user or support staff.

TIP The primary benefit of using remote OS installation is reduced IT support time. Whether you're installing systems for new users or existing users, you reduce to almost zero the amount of time required to deploy a new system.

Remote OS installation requires of a handful of key Windows 2000 Server or Windows Server 2003 technologies and features. Remote Installation Services (RIS) is an optional component in Windows Server that works with other Windows components to allow Windows XP to be installed across the enterprise in an automated fashion. This means that you can deploy Windows XP easily to a large number of systems in the enterprise with little administrative interaction, but it also is a means by which you can deploy Windows XP to diskless workstations—those without diskette or CD-ROM drives.

NOTE   Windows Server 2003 also includes RIS, and you can deploy Windows 2000 and XP from Windows Server 2003 RIS platforms. For the purpose of explanation, I'm assuming that you're using Windows 2000 Server as your RIS platform. However, the 2003 implementation is essentially the same.

RIS requires support for the Preboot Execution Environment (PXE), a standard that allows a user to boot directly from a PXE-compliant network card to initiate an OS installation or repair. When a PXE-compliant system boots, it uses DHCP to request an IP address lease from a DHCP server, as well as the address of available RIS servers. It passes its globally unique ID (GUID), which is defined in the system's BIOS. RIS servers listen for that query and respond by providing their IP addresses and the name of the boot image file that the client system can request.

The RIS server then looks up the GUID in Active Directory (AD) to determine if there is a pre-staged account for that GUID/computer. The RIS server downloads the Client Installation Wizard to the computer, which prompts the user to log on. Using the logon information provided, the RIS server looks up the account in AD to determine which installation options it should offer to the user, and then it offers those through the wizard. If no options are configured in AD for the user, RIS starts the installation process without prompting for options, although it does warn the user that the system's hard disk will be reformatted and offers the option of canceling the installation. If no GUID was found in AD that matches the one provided by the client computer, the RIS server creates a computer account in AD with a unique computer name and starts an unattended installation using that name.

What if your systems—or at least some of them—aren't PXE-compliant? You can still take advantage of remote OS installation, because RIS can generate boot diskettes that provide PXE emulation. Rather than boot from a PXE-compliant network adapter, noncompliant systems can boot from the emulator diskette to access the RIS server and its services.

Because you as an administrator can control the options that are offered to users on their logon accounts, you can control which operating system options are installed. Although doing so requires a little planning and configuration beforehand, you still gain the advantage of simplified installation.

RIS relies on AD and group policies to implement the remote OS installation. You don't apply policies at the user level, which means you don't have to prestage installations for every user. Instead, you typically apply the necessary group policy object (GPO) at the organization unit (OU) level, adding or moving users to the OU as needed. If you prefer, you can apply the GPO at the domain or site level depending on the needs of your users and whether those needs are consistent across those levels.

TIP If you decide that RIS sounds like the method you want to use to deploy Windows XP, start by becoming familiar with RIS and how to deploy it. On your Windows 2000 Server or Windows Server 2003 system, use the Add Or Remove Programs object in Control Panel to add the RIS service and its online help. Browse the help to become familiar with the process of installing and configuring the server. Once you've accomplished all the initial planning, the actual process of setting up RIS and creating deployment images isn't difficult. You'll find more information on RIS at www.microsoft.com/WINDOWS2000/en/server/help/sag_RIS_Architecture_Overview.htm.

Other Installation Methods

You can consider a handful of other options to automate and customize the Windows XP installation process, including some useful tools from third-party vendors.

Systems Management Server (SMS)

Systems Management Server (SMS) is an alternative to RIS. You can use SMS, a Microsoft product, to deploy operating systems, updates, and applications. Unlike RIS, which is limited to installing Windows 2000, Windows XP, and Windows Server 2003, SMS can install other operating systems such as Windows 9x and Windows Me.

This ability to install other operating systems is SMS's prime advantage. If you only need to deploy Windows 2000, XP, or 2003, my choice would be RIS because it's (in my opinion) much easier to manage. You can incorporate automatic application deployment through IntelliMirror (group policies) in conjunction with RIS to provide complete system setup for new installations and disaster recovery.

TIP Because of the management overhead involved, you shouldn't try to use both SMS and IntelliMirror to deploy applications. Select the one that best suits your needs, and standardize on it.

You'll find more information about SMS at www.microsoft.com/smserver.

Symantec Ghost

One very popular third-party application for disk imaging is Symantec Ghost. Whereas earlier versions of Ghost functioned primarily to mirror drive images, the latest version is a full-featured tool that lets you deploy Windows XP and other operating systems and applications across the network automatically. Unlike RIS, Ghost doesn't require Windows 2000 Server or Windows Server 2003, so you might find it to be an attractive and less expensive alternative to RIS if you're working in a smaller network or don't currently have a RIS-capable server platform.

Ghost functions essentially in two parts: console and client. The console computer serves as the point of control from which you manage client computers. This computer stores the disk images, configuration settings, and other data that you use to create or deploy OS images to client computers.

Using the Ghost console (Figure 3.2), you can remotely clone existing Windows XP workstations, deploy OS images to client computers, apply Registry changes, migrate user data and settings, and deploy applications and updates. You can easily clone multiple workstations and then make changes as necessary to TCP/IP settings, workgroups, domain membership, and other properties.

For more information on the Symantec Ghost Corporate Edition, visit

http://enterprisesecurity.symantec.com/products/products.cfm?productID=3

FIGURE 3.2
Ghost gives you a single point of control for remotely deploying Windows XP, applications, and settings.

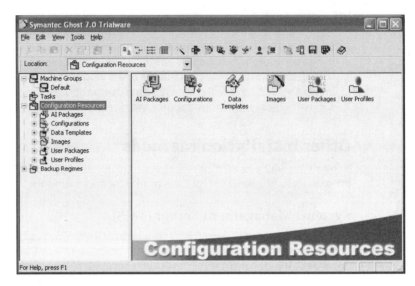

PowerQuest DeployCenter

PowerQuest's DeployCenter is another alternative to RIS for deploying Windows XP and applications across the enterprise. Like Ghost, DeployCenter doesn't require Windows 2000 Server or Windows Server 2003. With DeployCenter, you can create OS images and deploy them to client computers remotely. One very nice feature that DeployCenter offers is a web-based interface that lets you create and deploy operating systems from a remote location via the Internet. So, you can even manage OS installations when you're on the road.

Another benefit you'll find in DeployCenter is support for PXE-compliant systems. DeployCenter can install Windows XP across the network to systems with no operating systems if those systems include PXE-compliant network adapters. Support for PXE significantly simplifies deploying Windows XP to new systems and performing disaster recover. For more information on DeployCenter from PowerQuest, visit `http://sea.symantec.com/content/product.cfm?productid=8`.

NOTE   For more information on PXE, see "Deploying Windows XP with RIS," earlier in this chapter.

Chapter 4

Gaining Control of Windows XP Startup and Shutdown

Windows XP offers several methods for controlling the way the operating system starts and shuts down. For example, the Boot.ini file contains a small number of settings that you can edit, either directly or through the Windows XP graphical user interface (GUI), to specify startup options, such as the length of time the boot menu remains on the screen.

In addition, like other versions of Windows, Windows XP provides a Startup folder that lets you start applications automatically at logon. Although there are no settings to configure for the Startup folder, you can specify a different location for it, if desired. You can also bypass the Startup folder at logon to prevent applications contained in it from starting automatically.

Windows XP also lets you execute scripts at system startup, user logon, user logoff, and system shutdown. In addition to creating scripts to perform a wide variety of actions, you can configure several policies that determine how and when these scripts execute.

This chapter examines these startup and shutdown options, explaining why you might want to change them as well as how to accomplish the change. In most cases, these options are available in both Windows XP versions, but some features that rely on group policy aren't available in Windows XP Home Edition.

TIP Features specific only to Windows XP Professional are identified where applicable in the chapter.

Configuring Boot and Recovery Options in the GUI

Although you can set some boot options by directly editing the Boot.ini file (covered later in this chapter), the Windows XP GUI offers the easiest means of controlling a system's startup options. The boot options include the ability to choose the default OS, the length of time Windows XP displays boot menu options, and what actions, if any, XP should take if the system fails. I examine each of these issues in detail in this section.

Setting System Startup Options

You can set a small number of settings in Windows XP through the GUI; for instance, you can specify which operating system will be treated as the default system on multiboot installations or set the length of time Windows XP displays the boot menu for normal and recovery boot options.

TIP You must be logged on as a member of the Administrators group to configure these settings.

You set system startup options in the Windows XP GUI through the System Properties dialog box, shown in Figure 4.1. You can open this dialog box in one of two ways. The first is to right-click My Computer, choose Properties, and then click the Advanced tab. The second is to open the System object in Control Panel, which takes you directly to the Advanced tab of the System Properties dialog box. (Microsoft's official term for System Properties is a *property sheet*, but for familiarity's sake, I usually refer to it as a dialog box.) Then, click Settings in the Startup And Recovery control group to display the dialog box shown in Figure 4.2.

FIGURE 4.1

Use the Advanced tab of the System Properties dialog box to access startup options.

FIGURE 4.2

Configure startup options for the system through the Startup And Recovery dialog box.

We'll come back to these two dialog boxes several times in this chapter. The following few sections describe specific options available to you here.

SETTING THE DEFAULT OS

Use the Default Operating System drop-down list to select the OS you want Windows XP to boot by default if no other option is selected in the boot menu. This selection corresponds to the value of the `default` entry in the [boot loader] section of `Boot.ini`.

If Windows XP is the only OS installed, there is no need to change the default operating system. However, you might be using Windows XP on a system that also contains Windows 98 or another OS. If that's the case, Windows XP displays a boot menu when you start the system that allows you to select which OS will boot. The default OS is the one that will start if you take no action in the boot menu. You'll probably want to configure the boot options to specify as the default the OS you use most often.

TIP   You can also use the `Msconfig.exe` utility included with Windows XP, as well as any text editor, to modify the `Boot.ini` file.

CONTROLLING BOOT MENU DELAY

Select the Time To Display List Of Operating Systems check box, and specify a value in seconds with the associated spin control, to define the length of time the boot menu will remain on the screen before Windows XP boots the default option. Setting the value to zero or deselecting this option disables the boot menu and causes Windows XP to boot the default OS immediately. This setting corresponds to the `timeout` value in the [boot loader] section of `Boot.ini`.

NOTE   Selecting an option in the boot menu with the arrow keys stops the timer and keeps the boot menu on the screen until you select an option and press Enter.

If you use the default OS most of the time, you can speed up the boot process by reducing the menu display interval from its default setting of 30 seconds to, say, only a few seconds. Doing so makes Windows XP boot almost right away but still gives you the option of selecting a different boot option if you need to. You can set the option to 0 to hide the boot menu altogether.

TIP   If you have only one operating system installed and don't have the Recovery Console installed, Windows XP doesn't display a boot menu. Instead, it begins booting Windows XP immediately.

CONTROLLING RECOVERY MENU DELAY

You may also want to change the length of time that Windows XP displays the boot menu for recovery operations. Use the Time To Display Recovery Options When Needed option to specify how long you want Windows XP to display recovery boot options when the system executes automated recovery.

NOTE   See "Setting Startup Options in Boot.ini Manually," later in this chapter, for details on modifying `Boot.ini` to include additional boot options.

Setting System Failure Options

Although Windows XP is a stable OS, sooner or later an errant program or another problem will cause the system to fail. Although these failures will generally be few and far between, you should consider reviewing and possibly changing the options that determine the actions Windows XP takes in the event of a failure. You configure these settings by opening the System Properties dialog box (shown earlier in Figure 4.1) and then clicking Settings in the Startup And Recovery section to open the Startup And Recovery dialog box (Figure 4.2). The options in this dialog define three possible actions that Windows XP can take in the event of a system failure:

Write An Event To The System Log   Select this option to have Windows XP write an event to the System event log, which you can then view using the Event Viewer console. The event can indicate the source of the failure, although in some cases the system will be unable to write an event, depending on the nature of the failure. This value corresponds to the Registry value

```
\HKEY_LOCAL_MACHINE\SYSTEM\CurrentControlSet\Control\CrashControl\LogEvent
```

Send An Administrative Alert   This option causes the system to generate a network broadcast message to members of the administrative group. This corresponds to the Registry value

```
\HKEY_LOCAL_MACHINE\SYSTEM\CurrentControlSet\Control\CrashControl\SendAlert
```

Automatically Restart   Select this option if you want Windows XP to automatically reboot the system when the failure occurs. Generally, you enable this option for servers and other systems that need to be online as much as possible or that aren't readily accessible to administrative staff who can initiate a reboot. However, you should deselect this option if you're attempting to capture the stop message that is generated when the failure occurs (commonly called the Blue Screen of Death, or BSOD). This setting corresponds to the Registry value

```
\HKEY_LOCAL_MACHINE\SYSTEM\CurrentControlSet\Control\CrashControl\AutoReboot
```

Setting Startup and Failure Options Remotely

As you might have surmised from the Registry information provided in the previous list, you can set these options through Registry modifications as well as through the GUI. If you're setting the options for a single computer, you should generally use the GUI rather than digging into the Registry, because directly editing the Registry is always a somewhat risky proposition; you might make a mistake when changing values and affect the system's operation—or, in the worst case, prevent the system from booting at all.

If you want to configure these settings for multiple computers (and setting them though the GUI isn't practical), you have a couple of options. First, you can use the Registry Editor to connect to another computer's Registry to make the change across the network. To do so, click Start ➢ Run and enter **regedit** in the Run dialog box. In the Registry Editor, choose File ➢ Connect Network Registry to display the Select Computer dialog box (Figure 4.3). Then, type the name of the computer you want to manage, and press Enter or click OK. The Registry Editor adds the remote computer's Registry as a separate key (Figure 4.4). You can then make changes as needed to the remote Registry.

TIP   You can connect to and manage the Registries of Windows 2000, Windows NT, Windows XP, and Windows Server 2003 systems from Windows XP systems, and vice versa.

WARNING   Systems that are configured for Simple File Sharing (SFS) authenticate all network access against the Guest account, so you'll be unable to manage a remote system's Registry if that system is configured for SFS. You could allow Guest access to the Registry, but doing so is an invitation to disaster and should be avoided at all costs. Instead, reconfigure the system for regular file sharing.

FIGURE 4.3
Specify the name of the
computer whose Regis-
try you want to modify.

FIGURE 4.4
Open the key contain-
ing the remote Registry,
and modify settings as
needed.

Another option for modifying the Registry of a remote system is to use Remote Desktop Connection to connect to the remote computer and then open either the Registry Editor or the System Properties dialog box to accomplish the changes. The remote computer must be running Terminal Services (Windows Server computers) or must be running Windows XP Professional with access through Remote Desktop Connection enabled. Managing settings in this way is no different from managing the settings on the local computer, with the exception that you must first establish a Remote Desktop session to the remote computer.

NOTE Currently, no group or local policies define the startup or system failure options. Although you could apply the Registry changes through Windows NT–style policies, I don't recommend mixing NT policies with Windows 2000/XP group policies, for administrative reasons.

NOTE See Chapter 15 for detailed information on how to configure Windows XP systems for remote Registry access. Chapter 23 provides an in-depth discussion of configuring and using the remote-access and management capabilities provided with Windows XP.

Setting Startup Options in *Boot.ini* Manually

As explained previously in this chapter, some of the settings you configure for startup are stored in the system's Boot.ini file. You should make common startup changes through the GUI rather than modify Boot.ini manually; and, due to the potential for disastrous mistakes, you should modify

Boot.ini yourself only when you need to accomplish a change that isn't offered through the GUI. This section explains how to modify Boot.ini, which changes you can make, and why you would make those changes to control startup. For example, you'll need to modify Boot.ini to include the boot entries for another operating system if you clone the existing OS as I explained in Chapter 2.

Modifying *Boot.ini*

Boot.ini is located in the root folder of the boot volume. You can edit the file in Notepad, WordPad, or any other text editor capable of reading and writing text files. You can open Boot.ini directly from Notepad, or you can access it for editing through the System Properties dialog box. On the Advanced tab of System Properties, click Settings in the Startup And Recovery group, and then click Edit in the next dialog box (Figure 4.2). Windows XP opens Boot.ini in Notepad.

WARNING   If you're using a program other than Notepad, make sure you don't save Boot.ini in any format other than as a text file. For example, don't use Word to edit the file and then save it as a Word document. Doing so will prevent your system from booting until the Boot.ini file is restored. Also, make sure the program you use to edit the file does not change the file extension.

NOTE   Windows XP includes a command-line utility called Bootcfg that allows you to make changes to Boot.ini.

The Read-Only and Hidden attributes of Boot.ini are set, and you must change the Read-Only attribute if you edit the file outside of the Startup And Recovery dialog box (such as directly in Notepad). Configure the system's folder options to display hidden files, and then right-click Boot.ini and choose Properties. Deselect the Read-Only option, and click OK. Open the file in Notepad, make the desired changes, and save the file as you would any other text file.

TIP   If you open Boot.ini from the Startup And Recovery dialog box, Windows XP automatically removes the Read-Only attribute from Boot.ini to allow you to make changes. It doesn't restore the attribute when you close Notepad, so consider resetting the Read-Only attribute on the file after you make changes—to prevent unintended changes to it in the future.

Modifying *Boot.ini* Settings

You can modify or add several settings in Boot.ini to change the way the system boots. For example, you might add a second entry in the file, an entry that points to your existing Windows XP installation but boots it with certain troubleshooting options. Maybe, to troubleshoot a problem, you have to boot the system several times in safe mode. You can add one or more entries to Boot.ini that let you select the safe mode boot options from the main boot menu; doing so eliminates the need to press F8 during boot to display such options.

The Boot.ini file contains two sections: [boot loader] and [operating systems].

THE *[BOOT LOADER]* SECTION

This section contains settings that control the way the boot process works. Settings in this section specify the OS that the boot loader boots by default and the length of time the boot menu is displayed. The [boot loader] section can contain two settings:

timeout This value specifies the length of time the boot loader waits for you to make a selection from the boot menu. A value of 0 causes the boot loader to immediately boot the OS using the entry in [operating systems] defined by the value of the default setting. A positive value specifies the number of seconds to display the menu. You can specify a value of –1 to cause the boot loader to wait indefinitely for a menu selection, although you must modify Boot.ini manually to do this (the GUI won't accept a negative value for the setting).

default This value specifies the entry in the [operating systems] section that the boot loader will boot if no other selection is made.

THE *[OPERATING SYSTEMS]* SECTION

This section defines the available operating systems and options for each. By default, this section contains only one entry, which boots Windows XP using all default settings. This section contains other entries if another OS such as Windows 9x, Windows Me, or Recovery Console is present.

The format for an entry in the [operating systems] section depends on the target OS. Windows NT/2000/XP operating systems use the Advanced RISC Computing (ARC) path format for entries. The default entry for Windows XP specifies the physical drive and partition where the OS is located along with the /fastdetect switch (explained shortly). A default entry takes a form similar to the following:

```
multi(0)disk(0)rdisk(0)partition(1)\windows="Microsoft Windows XP Professional"
    /fastdetect
```

The part of the string to the left of the equal sign defines the path to the Windows XP system folder. The data in quotes specifies the description that appears in the boot menu, and the /fastdetect switch disables serial mouse detection on all COM ports (explained in more detail shortly).

BOOT.INI SYNTAXES

You can use three syntaxes in a Boot.ini file to define the ARC (Advanced RISC Computing) path to the system folder. The following sections explain each one in detail.

Multi Syntax

The multi syntax was originally valid only for IDE and ESDI volumes but was expanded to include Small Computer System Interface (SCSI) devices in Windows NT 3.5. When the boot loader boots an installation of Windows XP using the multi syntax, it relies on the system BIOS to load the files necessary to boot the OS. The Ntldr program uses standard INT 13 BIOS calls to locate and load the Windows XP kernel file Ntoskrnl.exe and other files (such as drivers) needed to boot the system. The following is an example of the multi syntax:

```
multi(W)disk(X)rdisk(Y)partition(Z)
```

The following list explains the variables:

Variable	Description
W	The number of the adapter; typically 0
X	The physical disk; always 0
Y	The logical disk number; a value from 0 to 3
Z	The partition number

NOTE For all syntaxes, the first valid value for W, X, and Y is 0, and the first valid value for Z is 1. Primary partitions are numbered first, followed by logical drives.

Typically, the system BIOS identifies only a single adapter for INT 13, which means that the multi syntax can boot Windows XP only from one of two possible disks, on either the primary or secondary IDE chain or on the SCSI bus. The multi syntax supports up to four IDE devices, two each on the primary and secondary chains. The syntax supports the first two drives on the first SCSI adapter, which is the adapter whose BIOS loads first. When the system contains multiple adapters, whether IDE or SCSI, this syntax works only for devices on the first adapter.

SCSI Syntax

This syntax allows the Ntldr program to load a SCSI device driver to access the boot partition rather than rely on INT 13 calls. The following is an example of the SCSI syntax:

```
scsi(W)disk(X)rdisk(Y)partition(Z)
```

The following list explains the variables:

Variable	Description
W	The controller number
X	The physical disk number
Y	The Logical Unit Number (LUN) for the disk; usually 0
Z	The partition number

Signature Syntax

The signature syntax allows Windows XP to support Plug and Play systems in which the SCSI adapter number can potentially vary each time the system is booted. Rather than rely on a static SCSI adapter number, this syntax causes Ntldr to search for and boot from the disk containing the specified signature. The following is an example of the signature syntax:

```
signature(W)disk(X)rdisk(Y)partition(Z)
```

The values for X, Y, and Z are the same as for the SCSI syntax. The value W specifies the disk signature written to the target disk during the text mode portion of Setup, through another installation of Windows XP, or through a previous installation of Windows 2000. The signature—a hexadecimal value—is stored in the disk's Master Boot Record (MBR). Windows XP uses the signature syntax only if the system or boot BIOS doesn't support Extended INT 13, and only if the specified disk is larger than 7.8 GB or the ending cylinder number is higher than 1,024.

BOOT.INI SWITCHES

New!
Boot.ini supports several switches that you can add in order to control the way Windows XP boots. Although you'll most likely use the default value created by Setup to boot the OS, you might add other boot menu selections so you can boot the system differently when needed. For example, you might add an entry that starts a multiprocessor system in single-processor mode, or specify the maximum amount of RAM that Windows XP can use if you suspect a physical memory problem. Table 4.1 lists the available switches and their functions.

TABLE 4.1:   *Boot.ini* Switches and Functions

SWITCH	FUNCTION
/3GB	Moves the 1 GB of kernel and executive components to the 3 GB memory location, allocating 3 GB to user-mode applications (increases user-mode memory from 2 GB to 3 GB).
/BASEVIDEO	Starts Windows XP using the standard VGA driver. Use when a new video driver is preventing Windows XP from starting properly.
/BAUDRATE=*nnnn*	Specifies the baud rate to use for debugging through the system's COM ports. The default rate for a modem is 9,600 and for a null-mode cable is 19,200. This setting causes the /DEBUG switch to activate (see the /DEBUG entry).
/BOOTLOG	Enables boot logging to *%systemroot%*\ntbtlogl.txt.
/BURNMEMORY=*n*	Specifies the amount of RAM (MB) that Windows XP can use. Use this switch to limit physical memory for troubleshooting purposes.
/CRASHDEBUG	Loads the debugger at boot, but the debugger remains inactive unless a kernel error occurs. Use for troubleshooting kernel errors.
/DEBUG	Loads the debugger, and allows it to be activated by any host debugger connected to the system. Use this switch when debugging reproducible errors.
/DEBUGPORT=COM*n*	Specifies the serial port to use for debugging, such as COM1. This switch causes the /DEBUG switch to activate.
/EXECUTE	Starts Windows XP with Data Execution Prevention disabled. DEP, when enabled, prevents applications from running in memory pages not marked as executable.
/FASTDETECT=[COM*n* | COM*x*,*y*,*z*…]	Disables serial mouse detection on the specified port(s). Used by itself, the /FASTDETECT switch disables mouse detection for all ports. Use this switch to speed boot when a device other than a mouse is connected to the specified port(s) at startup.
/MAXMEM:*n*	Specifies the maximum amount of RAM Windows XP can use. This switch is helpful for troubleshooting physical memory problems.
/NOGUIBOOT	Hides the startup progress bitmap during boot.
/NODEBUG	Specifies not to use debugging.
/NOEXECUTE	Starts Windows XP with DEP enabled. Applications can't run in memory pages not marked as executable.
/NUMPROC=*n*	Forces a multiprocessor system to use a specified number of processors. This switch is useful for troubleshooting processor errors and multiprocessor applications.

TABLE 4.1:   *Boot.ini* Switches and Functions *(CONTINUED)*

SWITCH	FUNCTION
/PCILOCK	Prevents Windows XP from dynamically assigning IRQ and I/O resources to PCI devices, instead allowing the BIOS to assign resources.
/SAFEBOOT:switch	Forces Windows XP to boot in safe mode using the specified *switch*, which can be minimal, network, or minimal(alternateshell).
/SOS	Displays device drivers as they're loaded by the boot process. Use this switch to troubleshoot drivers that might be causing a system or boot failure.
/PAE	Allows the system that supports Physical Address Extension (PAE) mode to boot normally. PAE allows software to use more than 4GB of physical memory

NOTE   For more information on PAE and advanced memory issues, consult "Enterprise Memory Architecture" in the *Microsoft Windows Datacenter Server Manual*, included with Datacenter Server and available from TechNet and other Microsoft resources on the Web.

To use any of the switches, edit the Boot.ini file, adding other entries as needed and including the appropriate switches, or modifying existing entries to include the necessary switches.

TIP   The best way to create a new entry for an existing OS installation is to copy and paste from an existing entry. When you add or modify an entry, make sure to change the description so you'll be able to easily identify the function of the entry in the boot menu at startup.

Modifying *Boot.ini* with Bootcfg

Windows XP adds a new utility that you can use to modify the Boot.ini file. This tool—Bootcfg.exe— is a console utility you can run from a command console within Windows XP, from Recovery Console, or in a batch file. You can use this command to modify the local Boot.ini file or the Boot.ini file of a remote computer across the network. That means you can change the way a computer on the other side of the world boots without hopping a plane, train, or slow boat.

NOTE   See Chapter 40 for detailed information on Recovery Console.

Granted, it's so easy to modify a local Boot.ini file on a working system that you'll likely not use Bootcfg to do so very often (instead preferring to use Notepad or the options in the System Properties dialog box). But in some cases, Bootcfg offers the best (or only) solution for modifying Boot.ini files. For example, if you're managing several systems and need to make modifications across the enterprise, Bootcfg allows you to do so through startup scripts, a Telnet session, or other means. You can also use it to make modifications to a local Boot.ini file when you're troubleshooting the system from Recovery Console.

The Bootcfg tool is fully documented in the Windows XP Help documentation. Rather than duplicate that information here, I'll just direct you to the appropriate place. Click Help And Support in the Start menu, and perform a search on **bootcfg**. You'll also find Bootcfg listed in the Windows XP Command-Line Reference.

Working with the Startup Folder

Like earlier Windows platforms since Windows 9*x*, Windows XP provides a `Startup` folder that you can use to start programs automatically when a user logs on. The `Startup` folder is actually two folders, one for the current user and one for all users. Therefore, when you log on, Windows XP starts applications located in both folders—one might start from your personal `Startup` folder, and another might start from the common `Startup` folder. The combined contents of both `Startup` folders are displayed when you click Start ➤ All Programs ➤ Startup.

There is nothing magical about the `Startup` folders, other than the fact that Windows XP searches them at logon and opens any items it finds inside them. These items can be programs, batch files, documents, scripts, or shortcuts—anything you can execute in Windows.

Defining the Location of the Startup Group

The user-specific `Startup` folder is located by default in

```
\Documents and Settings\user\Start Menu\Programs\Startup
```

where *user* is the user's logon name. The common `Startup` folder is located in

```
\Documents and Settings\All Users\Start Menu\Programs\Startup
```

TIP   On systems upgraded from Windows NT, the `Startup` folders are located in *%systemroot%*\ `Profiles`*user*\`Start Menu\Programs\Startup`.

In most cases, you won't need to modify the location of the `Startup` folders, but there is one instance where you might: when you need to redirect several users to the same `Startup` folder(s) across the network. For example, you might want all users to have their own `Startup` folder on their computers but provide a common `Startup` folder—located on a network server—that is shared by all. Doing so would provide all users with the same common startup items and offer an easy way to manage and customize startup items for several users.

RELOCATION BY GROUP POLICY

You have a couple of options for redirecting `Startup` folders. Group policy offers the best solution for computers in a domain, provided you want the whole Start menu redirected to a common location, not just the `Startup` folder. For example, you can use this option to redirect user folders to a common folder on a network server to give them a common set of applications and shortcuts. Or you might redirect each user's Start menu to the user's home folder on a server.

NOTE   Windows XP Home Edition doesn't support group policies. To redirect the `Startup` folder on a Home Edition system, you must edit the Registry, as explained in the following section.

NOTE   This chapter assumes you have some familiarity with group and local policies and how to modify them. For a more detailed discussion of these topics, see Chapter 35.

If you want to redirect the `Startup` folder through policies, open the Active Directory Users And Computers console on a domain controller in the desired domain, right-click the container where you want to apply the redirection policy (domain or organizational unit), and choose Properties. Then click the Group Policy tab, shown in Figure 4.5.

FIGURE 4.5
Use the Group Policy tab
to specify group policy
that redirects folders.

NOTE   You can apply group policies locally if you prefer not to assign policies at a higher level, or if you're working in a workgroup. Run Mmc.exe and add the Group Policy snap-in to the console focused on the local computer. The settings described in the following procedures are available through the Local Computer Policy branch.

TIP   Use the Active Directory Sites And Services console if you want to create a group policy object (GPO) that assigns policies at the site level.

Select an existing policy; or, if you have no policy already defined, click New to create a new one. Then, click Edit to open the Group Policy editor shown in Figure 4.6.

FIGURE 4.6
Edit GPOs through the
Group Policy editor.

In the Group Policy editor, open the branch \User Configuration\Windows Settings\Folder Redirection\Start Menu. Right-click in the right pane and choose Properties to open the Start Menu Properties dialog box. Then, select one of the following options from the Setting drop-down list:

"No administrative policy specified"   Folders won't be redirected unless this policy is defined at an overriding level.

"Basic—redirect everyone's folder to the same location"   This option redirects folders to a common location for all users who are under the policy's scope of management to a single, common folder. You can specify a Universal Naming Convention (UNC) path or specify a local folder. If you specify a local drive and path, group policy will redirect the Start menu to the matching path on the user's local system, so the specified drive and path must exist locally for each user under the scope of the policy. Specify the path in the Target Folder Location field or click Browse to browse for the folder.

"Advanced—specify locations for various user groups"   This option redirects folders to a specified location based on group membership. You add security groups to a list and then specify the redirected folder to be used for each group. Click Add when the Security Group Membership options appear, and select a security group and a path to associate with that group. You can specify multiple security groups and paths in a single GPO.

TIP   You can use the %username% variable in the policy to redirect folders based on username. For example, specifying the path \\server\users\%username%\start would cause the folder to be redirected for a user named jboyce to \\server\users\jboyce\start.

TIP   Group policies are applied in the following order: local policy, site policy, domain policy, OU policy. Therefore, policies applied at the OU level override policies at the site level.

After you specify the path(s) as needed, click the Settings tab of the Start Menu Properties. You can then choose one of the following two options:

"Leave the folder in the new location when policy is removed"   The folder will remain in its redirected location even if the policy is removed.

"Redirect the folder back to the local userprofile location when policy is removed"   This option moves the user's folder back to their local profile location when the policy is removed.

After you finish configuring the policy, close the property sheet and the Group Policy editor. Keep in mind that you can, if needed, link a GPO to other containers in Active Directory. This allows you to use the same GPO for several OUs or domains.

NOTE   For more information on group policies, see Chapter 35. For more information on redirecting folders and other ways to manage user settings and data, see Chapter 37.

RELOCATION BY REGISTRY CHANGES

Group policy offers the best way to redirect folders for multiple users. You can also redirect folders by editing the Registry—a handy method when you need to make the change for only a small number of users or when you aren't using group policies.

The individual user Startup folder is defined by the Registry value *userprofile*\Start Menu \Programs\Startup, where *userprofile* is replaced by the user's current user profile location, describing the Startup folder in the context of the current user profile. For example, this variable points to Documents and Settings*user* for clean installs or systems upgraded from Windows NT. You can change the portion of the string after the variable to relocate the Startup folder to a different location within the user's profile, or replace the whole string to completely relocate the Startup folder.

The Registry entry for the common Startup folder is defined by the value *allusersprofile*\\Start Menu\\Programs\\Startup, where *allusersprofile* points to the Documents and Settings\\All Users folder.

WARNING Improperly editing the Registry can cause various system problems, including the inability to boot the system. Make a backup of your system's Registry before making any changes. See Chapter 15 for detailed information on working with, backing up, and restoring the Registry.

The value for the individual Startup folder is located in the Registry value

```
\HKEY_CURRENT_USER\SOFTWARE\Microsoft\Windows\CurrentVersion\Explorer\User Shell
Folders\Startup
```

The value for the common Startup folders is located in the Registry value

```
\HKEY_LOCAL_MACHINE\SOFTWARE\Microsoft\Windows\CurrentVersion\Explorer\User Shell
Folders\Common Startup
```

Open the Registry Editor and then locate and open the desired key. Make a backup copy of the key, and apply the change. Log off, and then log back on to see the change take effect.

Bypassing the Startup Group

Occasionally you might want to bypass the Startup group and prevent the applications in it from starting automatically when you log on. For example, a startup application might be causing Windows XP to hang. Or perhaps it takes several seconds for the applications to start, and you want to bypass them to speed up logon.

To bypass the Startup folder, hold down the Shift key while logging on. For example, when Windows XP displays the logon dialog box, enter your user name and password. Then, hold down the Shift key and click OK. Continue holding down the Shift key until the Desktop appears and the logon process is complete.

A handful of alternatives to the Startup folder can cause applications to start automatically at logon. These alternatives—and how to bypass them—are covered in the following section.

TIP If you decide you want to permanently prevent a specific application from starting through the Startup folder, open the Startup folder, right-click the item, and choose Delete. Doing so deletes the shortcut from the menu but doesn't uninstall or delete the application itself.

Alternatives to the Startup Folder

In addition to the two Startup folders (one common, one individual), Windows XP provides other ways to start applications automatically at logon. For example, Windows XP also executes applications listed in the following Registry keys:

```
\HKEY_LOCAL_MACHINE\SOFTWARE\Microsoft\Windows\CurrentVersion\Run
\HKEY_LOCAL_MACHINE\SOFTWARE\Microsoft\Windows\CurrentVersion\RunOnce
\HKEY_CURRENT_USER\Software\Microsoft\Windows\CurrentVersion\Run
\HKEY_CURRENT_USER\Software\Microsoft\Windows\CurrentVersion\Runonce
```

If you're trying to bypass the startup applications, and one or more continues to start even though you've either cleared out or bypassed the Startup folders, open the Registry Editor and check the contents of these keys. Make a backup of the Registry key, and then delete the values in this key for those applications you don't want to start automatically. When you're ready to have the applications start automatically again, restore the Registry key, log off, and log back on.

Services can also impact the system at logon. Some applications—including Windows XP components and third-party utilities—are configured to start and run as services. Regardless of the source of the service, you can temporarily configure it to not start automatically, if needed. To do so, open Computer Management Console and then open the Services branch. Locate and double-click the service that you want to temporarily reconfigure. On the General tab, set the startup type to Manual, and then click Stop to stop the service. When you're ready to have the service start automatically again, set its startup type to Automatic and restart the service or log off and then log back on.

NOTE If you've upgraded from Windows 9x, you might also want to check the contents of the WIN.INI file for run= or load= lines that start applications. WIN.INI is located in the system root folder (typically, \WINNT or \WINDOWS).

Startup and Shutdown Scripts

Windows XP supports four types of scripts: startup, shutdown, logon, and logoff. You can use these four types of scripts to automate processes such as mapping drives, starting applications, and so on. You can accomplish a broad range of tasks with scripts, so this chapter doesn't discuss specific script tasks but instead focuses on the mechanics of creating and assigning startup and shutdown scripts.

NOTE See Chapter 37 to learn how to create and manage scripts that run at logon and logoff.

You can assign scripts through group policy. Because group policy isn't supported for Windows XP Home Edition, you can only use policies to execute startup and shutdown scripts under Windows XP Professional.

TIP You can emulate the function of logon scripts in Windows XP Home Edition using the Startup folder: create a batch file and include it in that folder. Use the Registry keys referenced in the preceding section to emulate startup scripts under Home Edition.

When you're ready to create and assign a startup or shutdown script, start by creating the CMD or BAT file that contains the script commands. Then, test and troubleshoot any problems with the script.

When the scripts are working, decide where you'll assign them: at the site, domain, OU, or local level. If you're assigning the policy at the domain or OU level, open the Active Directory Users And Computers console on a domain controller in the domain, and open the GPO where you'll assign the policy. Open the Active Directory Sites And Services console if you're assigning the policies at the site level. Or, to modify the local policy, run Mmc.exe, and load the Group Policy snap-in focused on the local computer (Figure 4.7).

FIGURE 4.7
Use the Group Policy snap-in to modify the local policy.

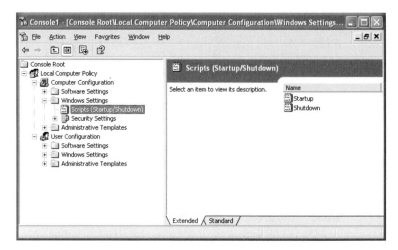

In the policy, open the \Computer Configuration\Windows Settings\Scripts branch. Double-click the Startup policy to open the Startup Properties dialog box. Click Add to open the Add A Script dialog box. In the Script Name field, type the path to the script, or click Browse to browse for it. Add any additional parameters for the script in the Script Parameters field, and click OK. Repeat the process to add other startup scripts as needed, and then close the Startup Properties dialog box.

To specify scripts that run when the system shuts down, double-click the Shutdown policy in the \Computer Configuration\Windows Settings\Scripts branch. Use the same steps described previously to assign shutdown scripts to the computer.

Controlling Script Execution

Policy-defined startup scripts, which execute before other types of scripts, execute synchronously and hidden. The user doesn't see the startup scripts execute, and each script must complete before the next executes. Because the scripts execute synchronously, the logon dialog doesn't appear until all startup scripts have executed.

In most cases, you probably don't need to see the startup scripts execute. However, in cases where you're trying to troubleshoot problems that might be related to the startup scripts, being able to see them execute is critical.

You can control startup script behavior by editing the Registry, but a better solution is to use group policies. Open the MMC, add the Group Policy snap-in focused on the local GPO, and drill down to the \Computer Configuration\Administrative Templates\System\Scripts branch (Figure 4.8). Enable the policy Run Startup Scripts Visible to be able to view the scripts as they execute. Enable the policy Run Startup Scripts Asynchronously if you want startup scripts to be able to run concurrently.

TIP You can use the policy Maximum Wait Time For Group Policy Scripts to specify the maximum amount of time Windows XP will wait for policy-defined scripts to execute. If scripts haven't completed execution by the specified time, Windows XP stops script processing and logs an error to the event log.

FIGURE 4.8
Policies control how
scripts execute.

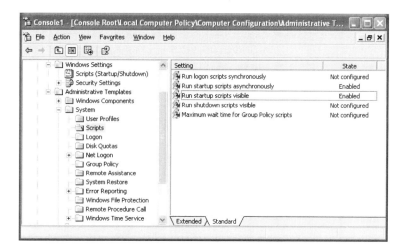

Restricting Shutdown

In most cases, you'll want everyone to be able to shut down a computer. Sometimes, however, it's desirable to prevent certain users from being able to shut down a computer. This is certainly true with servers, but it can also be true for workstations. For example, a particular workstation might be sharing a set of folders that need to be available at all times. Or a computer might be serving as your fax machine and need to be on all the time to receive faxes. You might consider restricting the ability to shut down that particular computer to administrators.

NOTE   You can't control system shutdown for Windows XP Home Edition systems, because they don't support group or local policies.

You restrict the ability to shut down the computer through user rights assignment. Assign these rights through a group policy or local security policy. The right Shut Down The System is located in the \Security Settings\Local Policies\User Rights Assignment branch in the Local Security Policy console or in the \Computer Configuration\Windows Settings\Security Settings\Local Policies \User Rights Assignment branch for group policy.

By default, members of the Administrators, Users, Power Users, and Backup Operators groups can shut down a system. In most situations, you can deny the Users group that right. If users other than those in the Administrators, Power Users, or Backup Operators groups need the ability the shut down the system, create a group specifically for that purpose, and grant that group the right to shut down the system.

To configure the right, open the applicable group or local policy branch as described previously. Locate and double-click the Shut Down The System policy. You can use the resulting dialog box to both remove and add users or groups. Click OK when you're satisfied with the changes, and then close the policy editor.

Part 2

Customizing and Automating Windows XP

In this section:

Chapter 5

Controlling Printing

In this chapter, we'll look at how you can optimize printing, all the way from printer setup to configuration to management. You'll learn to manage how and when printer software communicates with printer hardware, how to set up printer pools and priorities, and how to take advantage of printer spooling. Network printing requires a decent amount of configuration, and in this chapter you'll learn how to make a printer available on the network, how to connect clients to it and set permissions, how to configure a printer to print to the IP address of a network interface print device, and how to redirect print jobs. The chapter ends with a section on Internet printing.

Before you roll up your sleeves, best read the first section, which provides all the background you'll need to get started controlling your printers.

Printing Primer

Much of the discussion about printing in Windows XP is initially a language lesson. It's a necessary evil, however; in order to understand printing, you have to be specific with your terminology. You have to be clear, for example, whether you're talking about a piece of software (the printer) or the piece of hardware that applies ink to a page (the print device), because you'll perform different administrative tasks on both. Following is a quick review of the terms used in a Windows XP print environment.

Printer   A piece of software that provides the necessary translation so that Windows can send information to a print device. The printer is there to provide access to the print device on your desk.

Print device   What is normally referred to (before this section, anyway) as the printer. This is the piece of equipment that turns your electronic files into readable output on a sheet of paper.

TIP   Now, just so you know…it isn't considered proper etiquette to correct people on their use of the terms *printer* and *print device*. The terms are distinguished only for purposes of discussion in computer book chapters that deal with the task of getting ink on a page. So unless you enjoy the role of pariah at social gatherings, keep the distinction between printers and print devices to yourself.

Printer driver   A part of the printer installation that translates document formats into a language that the printer can understand. In other words, because of the work that printer drivers do, all documents look the same to the printer no matter what application they're sent from.

Print server   A computer that has made the printer software resource available on the network by sharing it. Print clients and print servers use the same language to speak to one another—the same one they use to share and request file resources. Therefore, the client and server components between computers must be compatible in order for print clients to submit jobs to a print server. All Windows 9*x* and later computers can be print servers.

Port   A specifically defined pathway that a printer uses to get its translated information to the print device. These pathways of information can be of several varieties, as you'll soon learn.

Print spooler   An area of buffer storage (usually an area on a disk) where documents wait to be serviced. The printer pulls the waiting jobs off the buffer at its own rate. This line-up of print jobs is known as the *print queue*, and the two terms are often used interchangeably. Because the documents are in a buffer where they can be accessed by the printer, you can perform other operations on the computer while the printing takes place in the background. Spooling also lets you place a number of print jobs in a queue instead of waiting for each one to finish before specifying the next one.

Now that we've established that a printer is a piece of software and not a piece of hardware, it shouldn't be too much a leap of faith to imagine that this piece of software, the printer, is just another disk resource that can be shared on a network, as mentioned earlier. You also need to be aware when you configure printing that print devices come in three varieties:

Local   Local printers are devices managed by the software physically installed at your computer. Traditionally, local printers submit their jobs through a parallel port to a device that is sitting right next to your desk, although that isn't always the case (I'll discuss this further in the section on network printing).

Network   These print devices are managed by printers that aren't directly installed on your system. They're accessible over the network, however, as their name implies, and may or may not be located in the same room.

Virtual   These printer types show up as printing options in the Print dialog box of software applications and also are represented as icons in the `Printers And Faxes` folder. These printers don't send jobs to a device that puts ink on paper, but rather they convert a document to a widely readable format. A primary example of a virtual printer is the PDF Writer, which converts documents into the Adobe Acrobat `.pdf` format.

The command-and-control center for printing and faxing is the `Printers And Faxes` folder, which you can open from Control Panel by clicking the Printers And Faxes icon. If you're using Control Panel in Category view, you'll find the Printers And Faxes icon in the Printers And Other Hardware category.

However, you might also want to add a Start menu shortcut to the `Printers And Faxes` folder (this shortcut was present in previous versions of Windows). To do so, follow these steps:

1. Right-click anywhere on the Taskbar or on the Start menu and choose Properties from the shortcut menu to open the Taskbar And Start Menu Properties dialog box.

2. Click the Start Menu tab.

3. Click the Customize button to open the Customize Start Menu dialog box.

4. Click the Advanced tab. Then, in the Start Menu Items section, scroll down the list and ensure that the Printers And Faxes check box is selected.

5. Click OK to close the Customize Start Menu dialog box, and then click OK again to close the Taskbar And Start Menu Properties dialog box.

Now you have an easier way to open the `Printers And Faxes` folder, which is shown in Figure 5.1.

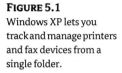

FIGURE 5.1
Windows XP lets you track and manage printers and fax devices from a single folder.

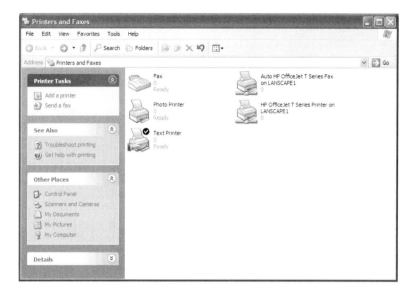

Quick Printing Tips

Usually, the first step in setting up a print environment is to install and configure a local printer, a task that you have likely performed many, many times. To briefly review, you add a printer to the `Printers And Faxes` folder by using the Add Printer Wizard. To start the wizard, open the `Printers And Faxes` folder, and click Add A Printer in the Printer Tasks bar. At the Welcome screen, click Next. The wizard then gives you the choice of adding either a local printer or a network printer, depending on where the printer (software) is located.

The remainder of the screens in the Add Printer Wizard depend on whether you choose to install a local printer or a network printer. If you're setting up a local printer, next you'll select a port that the print device is connected to (usually LPT1) and then find the printer drivers to install. Many of these drivers are included with the XP operating system and are also included on the disk that ships with the print device.

Of course, most printers (whoops, *print devices*) today come with their own setup routine that takes you through this process, even configuring several printing options and settings, without ever having to visit the `Printers And Faxes` folder to launch the Add Printer Wizard. So if you've been able to print successfully for years but have never seen the Add Printer Wizard at work, you aren't alone, and there's no need to worry. The idea is to get the thing to work.

TIP   By the way, if the thing won't work—that is, if your document won't print—it's possible that it has become "stuck" in the print queue (quotes because it's not *physically* stuck, as the word implies, which could be the case were there a paper jam in the physical print device). Try opening the Services MMC snap-in from Control Panel (or Administrative Tools), and then select Stop And Restart the Print Spooler Service. That seems to fix a lot of these types of printing problems. Or simply restart your computer.

Managing Printers

Because the printer is a piece of software, you manage it the same way you manage other pieces of software stored on your XP machine—by configuring options in the software's Properties dialog box.

You can set several attributes in this dialog box, and in this section I've compiled some of the more interesting and/or useful.

Many advanced print configurations rely on your understanding that a printer is a piece of software. Therefore, you can install two or more printers on a system and configure the printers so that both print to the same print device. The configuration options for each printer can be completely different, yet send output to the same machine.

Using two printers to print to the same device can be a great advantage when you quickly want to make several changes to the way a job is printed. Most of today's printers support a wide array of options for paper tray, page size, page orientation, half-toning, print optimization, and so on. For example, one change that I regularly make is to configure a printer to either use or not use photo-quality output. Although the Properties dialog box interface makes it relatively easy to change such printer settings when needed, it can be a little time-consuming when you frequently switch printer settings, particularly if you're trying to change multiple settings at once.

So, to easily switch between separate sets of printer settings, configure multiple printer instances for the same physical print device, each printing to the same print port, and each with its own settings. Give each printer instance a name indicating its function, such as Photo Printer and Text Printer, to make it easy to determine which one you want to use. Then, select the printer instance by name in the application's Print dialog box.

To add and configure a printer instance, follow these steps:

1. Open the `Printers And Faxes` folder, run the Add Printer Wizard, and install the printer a second time.

2. When asked if you want to keep the existing driver files or install new ones, keep the existing files.

3. Right-click the newly installed instance, and choose Properties from the shortcut menu to open the printer's Properties dialog box. Configure the printer's settings as desired, including assigning a descriptive name, and then close the Properties dialog box.

Follow these steps again to add other instances as needed, configuring their settings as required. You'll end up with a Properties dialog box that lists multiple printers for a single port, as shown in Figure 5.2.

FIGURE 5.2
You can configure two or more printers to use the same port and therefore the same print device.

Hours of Availability

You can further manage the use of two or more printers that print to the same device by setting hours of availability for each. Continuing the example from the previous section, I would expect the Photo Printer to print much more slowly than the Text Printer because of its higher resolution. In this example, let's further assume that there is no urgency to the jobs sent to the Photo Printer and that the Text Printer needs to be more readily available. You don't want to wait several minutes for photos to print when you need to print a letter or an invoice and go on to the next task.

In a scenario such as this, it will be useful to configure a schedule for the Photo Printer so that the print device isn't tied up while the Text Printer is trying to have a job serviced. To set printer availability, follow these steps:

1. Right-click the printer you want to configure, and choose Properties from the shortcut menu to open the Properties dialog box for the printer.

2. Click the Advanced tab.

3. The default option for the printer is Always Available. To change this setting, select the Available From radio button, and then set the time when the printer should be available to service jobs.

4. Click OK.

TIP The printer will still be available to receive jobs even when it isn't available. These jobs will wait in the print queue until the printer becomes available. However, keep in mind that the files are queued on the computer's hard disk, so queuing many graphics-intensive or lengthy documents can quickly eat up disk space.

Pooling and Priority

Printer pools and print priorities are typically used in high-volume printing environments, where many printers or many print devices service the printing needs of network users. The two technologies are really two sides of the same coin, as you'll see.

Print pooling associates a single printer with multiple print devices. You typically use a printer pool when many print devices of the same type are located on the network, so that they all understand the instructions of one type of printer driver. The first available print device services the print jobs submitted to a pool. When you configure printer pools, however, you can't specify which print device will receive the job.

TIP For the reason I just mentioned, it's wise to place pooled print devices in close physical proximity to one another, unless you're trying to incorporate your printing scheme with some kind of corporate exercise program.

To configure a printer pool, follow these steps:

1. In the printer's Properties dialog box, click the Ports tab, as shown in Figure 5.3.

FIGURE 5.3
Configuring a print pool
involves just a few clicks.

2. At the bottom of this tab, click the Enable Printer Pooling check box, and then select the check boxes of all the ports from which you want the logical printer to send its ones and zeros. If you don't select the Enable Printer Pooling check box, you'll only be able to configure one port per printer.

3. Click OK.

The flip side of printer pooling is printer priority. Much like configuring a schedule for a printer, you can configure multiple printers to use a single print device. When you set printer priority, you specify how print jobs are sent to the device.

Again, you configure the priority of a printer on the Advanced tab of the printer's Properties dialog box. Using the Priority spin box, you rank the priority of the printer from 1 to 99. The default priority for a printer is 1, the lowest ranking. Any printer that has a higher ranking gets first dibs on the port for which that printer is configured. When the Print Manager on the system polls for print jobs, the printer with the higher priority always print jobs in the queue before jobs in the lower priority printer.

The Print Queue

The print queue is where print jobs go to stand in line before being serviced by the print device. By default, the jobs are deleted from this queue after they have been sent to a print device. This behavior is useful; it keeps the queue from filling up with old documents and consuming unnecessary disk space.

At times, however, it might be better to keep jobs in the print spool even after they have been sent to the print device. For example, if you have a problem with a print job that allows it to complete but not satisfactorily (the printer runs out of toner, for example), you have to open the application and resubmit the job. This might not be a problem for most applications or documents, but for particularly large documents and some applications, reprinting the job from the application could take several extra minutes.

As a safeguard, you can tell XP to keep documents in the queue. Doing so lets you resubmit a document right from the queue rather than having to open the application. If you often print large documents, this could be a real timesaver.

To configure a printer's queue to retain documents, follow these steps:

1. Open the `Printers And Faxes` folder from your location of choice. (I like to keep a shortcut to this on the Start menu.)

2. Open the Properties dialog box for a selected printer, and then click the Advanced tab.

3. Select the Keep Printed Documents check box found near the bottom of the dialog box, and then click OK.

Now documents will be saved in the queue even after printing. Keep in mind that this does require additional disk space and that you'll need to manually remove documents from the queue after they're successfully printed.

Spooling

Like other operating systems, Windows XP supports print spooling. Rather than print directly to the printer, applications send translated, ready-to-print jobs to an area of disk space. The print spool is managed by Windows XP, which in turn takes care of sending the print job to the physical print device. The advantage is that the application doesn't have to wait for the document to finish printing before you can continue using the application. As far as the application is concerned, once the document is in the spool, it's printed. The application can then go about its main function again.

For most people, the default settings for print spooling work fine. In some cases, though, you may need to tweak the settings or turn off spooling. You configure spool settings on a per-printer basis. Follow these steps:

1. Open the `Printers And Faxes` folder, right-click the desired printer, and choose Properties from the shortcut menu to open the Properties dialog box for the printer.

2. Click the Advanced tab.

3. Select the Print Directly To The Printer option.

4. Click OK.

If you choose to use spooling, you can specify that Windows XP start printing as soon as the data starts flowing to the queue, or you can specify that the entire document move to the spool before printing starts. Specifying the latter option can overcome printing problems, particularly with long documents.

TIP There is little reason to change the default spooling options. The time savings gained by sending a job right to the printer is barely measurable; and remember, the spool lets the application get back to business as quickly as possible.

Network Printing

If you're familiar with the concept of sharing folders over a network, you already have the fundamentals of network printing. Just as file sharing is the act of making a file resource available on the network, print sharing makes a print resource available to users who have connectivity.

Making a Printer Available on the Network

You can share a printer when you set up the printer, or you can do it later from the printer's Properties dialog box. To make a printer available for network printing after setup, click the Sharing tab in the printer's Properties dialog box (see Figure 5.4), click the Share This Printer radio button, enter a name for the printer in the Share Name box, and then click OK.

FIGURE 5.4

You specify a share name after you share the printer.

Remember, users will use the share name to make a network connection to the printer. This name doesn't have to match the actual printer name, but use intuitive names when possible. Also keep in mind that any MS-DOS clients of your shared printer won't be able to see names longer than eight characters.

Connecting to a Network Printer

Once you share a printer on the network, print clients can connect to it and send documents to it. If you're setting up a network printer, you're telling the print drivers on your system to send the print job over the network to be managed by a printer that lives elsewhere on a print server. (This is why the language lesson was first.) To add a network printer to a client's `Printers And Faxes` folder, follow these steps:

1. In the `Printers And Faxes` folder, click Add A Printer to start the Add Printer Wizard.

2. At the Welcome screen, click Next to open the Local Or Network Printer screen.

3. Select the A Network Printer, Or A Printer Attached To Another Computer option, and then click Next to open the Specify A Printer screen.

4. You can enter a UNC name for the printer, browse the network for a printer, or connect to a printer on the Internet by entering a URL. You can also search through the Active Directory

(if you're a part of an Active Directory domain) to find a printer after you select Browse For A Printer.

When you confirm your choice, the appropriate print drivers for the network printer need to be installed on your local machine. In a Windows-only environment, this happens automatically: The print server makes the appropriate print drivers available, and the client downloads and installs these drivers automatically.

Now that you've learned how to use the Add Printer Wizard, I want to show you an even quicker way to set up a network printer. To avoid all that clicking, enter the UNC path of the printer (if you know it) in the Open box in the Run dialog box. (Choose Start ➢ Run to open the Run dialog box.) Yep, that's it; the printer will be set up automatically. Upon successful network connection to this shared printer, the contents of the print queue will be displayed, as shown in Figure 5.5.

FIGURE 5.5
You can enter the UNC path to quickly and easily set up a network printer.

You can also connect and install a network printer by browsing for it in Windows Explorer. In the My Network Places folder, double-click the printer you want to set up. After connection is established, you'll see the window shown in Figure 5.5.

Setting Permissions on Network Printers

When a printer is made available from a print server, default printer permissions are assigned that allow the Everyone group (that is, all users) to print and that allow select groups to manage the printer, manage documents sent to it, or all of the above.

Because the printer is available to all users on the network, you may want to limit access for some users by assigning specific printer permissions. For example, you may give all normal users in a department the Print permission and give all managers the Print and Manage Documents permissions. In this way, all users and managers can print documents, but managers can also change the print status of any document sent to the printer. Furthermore, by default the Creator Owner special group has the Manage Documents permission. This means that users can manage all documents that they own. For example, the owner of a document can send a job to the print queue and then cancel its printing if they change their mind.

This behavior is a departure from the behavior of NTFS and Share permissions, in which the Everyone group has the Full Control permission until an administrator tightens security settings. For this reason, you typically won't have to do much configuring of printers' security permissions.

You control which users have access to a shared printer that you make available from your print server through the Security tab of the printer's Properties dialog box, as shown in Figure 5.6.

FIGURE 5.6

You configure the security settings for a printer using the options on the Security tab.

To change the permission settings for a printer, you must have the Manage Printers permission, and then follow these steps:

1. Open the `Printers And Faxes` folder, right-click the printer, and choose Properties from the shortcut menu to open the Properties dialog box for the selected printer.

2. Click the Security tab, and then click Add to open the Select Users Or Groups dialog box.

3. In the Enter The Object Names To Select box, enter the names, separating them with a semicolon. Click OK.

4. In the Permissions section of the Properties dialog box, click the Allow or Deny check box for each permission, as appropriate.

5. Click OK.

TIP If your Windows XP system is part of a domain, the Security tab is automatically displayed in the printer's Properties dialog box. But Windows XP doesn't display a Security tab in the printer's Properties dialog box if you're using Simple File Sharing *and* operating in a Workgroup environment. To see whether you're using Simple File Sharing, look at the list of Advanced settings on the View tab of the Folder Options dialog box. You'll need to make sure that the Simple File Sharing (Recommended) option is cleared in order to display the Security tab.

Network Interface Printing

The printer that is being used doesn't have to be physically connected to your computer or to any other computer in the network. Many companies use the services of a *network interface* print device, which is simply a print device with a network interface card (NIC).

The network interface print device is assigned an IP address, just like any other computer in the network with a NIC. You configure your printer (the software) to print to this address, rather than to a local port such as a parallel or USB port.

Now, here's where it gets a bit tricky—the IP address is also considered a *local* port! Huh? Even though you're sending a print job over the network, technically you aren't printing over the network. The printer is still managed locally, not on a remote print server. (However, a remote print server can certainly print to a TCP/IP port the same as you.) I've beaten it into your head by now (I hope), but it bears repeating: the local and network printing are distinguished by the location of the *software*, not the hardware.

To configure a printer to print to the IP address of a network interface print device, you must set up and configure a standard TCP/IP port. Follow these steps:

1. Start the Add Printer Wizard. At the Welcome screen, click Next to open the Local Or Network Printer screen.

2. Select the Local Printer Attached To This Computer option, clear the Automatically Detect And Install My Plug And Play Printer option, and then click Next to open the Select A Printer Port screen.

3. Select the Create A New Port option. Then, in the Type Of Port drop-down list, select Standard TCP/IP Port. Click Next to start the Add Standard TCP/IP Printer Port Wizard.

4. At the Welcome screen, click Next. On the Add Port screen, enter the IP address of the print device and give the device a name, as shown in Figure 5.7.

FIGURE 5.7
You add and name a
TCP/IP port on the Add
Port screen of the wizard.

5. Click Next, and the wizard's final screen shows you settings information that confirms successful communication with the print device. Click Finish to complete the process.

TIP   Most network interface print devices can self-generate a configuration report, so you can know the IP address of the device. The print device's manual should tell you how to get this report.

Redirecting Print Jobs

The technique of sending print jobs to printer ports that will then send the jobs to network print devices (see why all the terminology was important?) can be a useful troubleshooting workaround.

For example, it can ensure uninterrupted printing when used to redirect the contents of the print queue because a print device is malfunctioning (it's out of toner, there is a paper jam, or various other problems are occurring). You can also use this technique to change the port a printer is configured to use even after the printer is installed. Many network interface print devices also can be connected directly to a computer and may have started life on the network in this way.

Let's say, for example, that the printer connected to your computer has just mysteriously stopped working. Worst of all, you have a big report that needs to be printed. However, your coworker has set up the same type of printer on his computer and shared it. Here's what you can do to solve the problem:

1. Open the Properties dialog box for the printer on your computer, click the Ports tab, and then click the Add Port button to open the Printer Ports dialog box.

2. With the Local Port option selected, click the New Port button to open the Port Name dialog box.

3. In the Enter A Port Name box, enter the name of the port. Use the UNC syntax *servername* *printer*, just as if you were setting up a network printer.

4. Click OK to close the Port Name dialog box, close the Printer Ports dialog box, and then click OK to close the printer's Properties dialog box.

You have now set up the new local port. And remember, even though print jobs will be sent over the network, the port is considered local because the printer software installed locally at your machine manages these print jobs.

Connecting Printers with Scripts

In a networked environment, one common task you'll probably want to perform at login is to connect to remote network printers. You could manually add a printer at each computer, but scripting offers an easier means to connect printers for multiple computers and users.

Connecting a printer from a script is fairly easy; doing so requires that you create a Network script object and then use the AddWindowsPrinterConnection method to connect the printer. Here's a simple VBScript that connects the printer \\server\laserjet to the local computer and names it HP LaserJet:

```
dim oNet
set oNet = CreateObject("WScript.Network")oNet.AddWindowsPrinterConnection
"\\server\laserjet", "HP LaserJet"
set oNet = nothing
```

Typically, you'd incorporate this code snippet into the users' logon scripts.

See Chapter 37 for a complete discussion of how to create logon and logoff scripts. See Chapter 6 for a discussion of Windows Script Host.

Internet Printing

Windows XP supports the Internet Printing Protocol (IPP), which lets documents be sent over the Internet to printers that are available through a TCP/IP connection. So, how are printers available on the Internet? Glad you asked. The ability to print over the Internet is an integral part of the setup of Internet Information Services (IIS). By default, the installation of IIS is supposed to make shared printers accessible through the Internet, and any subsequent printers that are added and shared will be Internet-available as well. However, whether this happens depends on which version of Windows you're installing, as I'll explain in the next subsection. For now, let's assume things are working as advertised.

Once IIS is set up, users who have the appropriate permission levels can view and manage printers from a web browser window. All they have to do to connect to a printer over the Internet is to open a browser window and enter **http://*hostname*/printers** in the Address bar. The ***hostname*** portion of this URL is the name of the print server on which IIS is installed and can be either a name or an IP address, just like when you connect to a website. In this syntax, the **printers** portion of the URL is literal; you type the word **printers**. After you enter this URL and press Enter, your browser displays the page shown in Figure 5.8. From here, the printing options are fairly intuitive; if you can click around on Yahoo to get information, you should have little trouble with the options on this page.

TIP   The process I describe in this section also works on an intranet if you have HTTP connectivity.

FIGURE 5.8

To install and manage a printer, follow the links on the home page of Internet printing on a print server that has IIS installed.

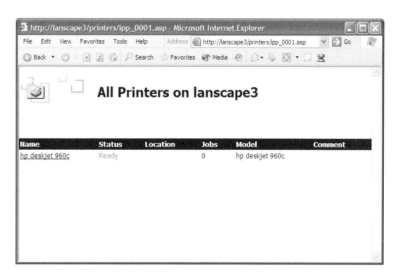

This web page also presents an easy way to set up a network printer on your system. The Printers home page presents you with a hyperlinked list of all shared printers. Follow the link of the printer you want to install, and then choose Connect on the next page (it's at the bottom of the Printer Actions list, as shown in Figure 5.9) to install and set up the printer for your use. You might be prompted to select drivers for the printer you're setting up as part of the installation.

You can also modify the syntax in the Address bar slightly if you want to connect directly to an available printer, bypassing the home page: **http://*servername*/printers/*printername***.

After the Internet printer is installed, you can use the IPP printer exactly the same as you would any other printer installed on your system, either attached locally or available on the network.

FIGURE 5.9

You can install the printer if it isn't already set up.

Setting Up the Printers Virtual Directory

Here's a bug (feature?) that you'll likely encounter when you install IIS under Windows XP Professional. If you notice the setup options for the World Wide Web Publishing Service as you configure IIS from the Windows Components Wizard, you'll see the check box selected that tells you the Printers virtual directory will be created.

This directory is created and configured correctly when you install IIS on a 2000 Server or Windows Server 2003 machine, and Internet printing works exactly as described without further exertion. However, when you try to connect to this print server using a web browser as outlined earlier, you may see a "Page Not Found" error message. In this case, a quick glance at IIS will confirm that the directory hasn't been set up. In Windows XP, as well as in Windows 2000 Professional, you must configure the Printers virtual directory manually, despite what setup tells you, to enable printing from across the Internet.

Fortunately, setting up Internet printing under XP Professional is fairly easy. Follow these steps:

TIP You can follow these same steps to enable Internet printing in Windows 2000 Professional.

1. After you install IIS on the XP system, open the IIS console, right-click the website where you want to add printing capability (normally it's the Default site), and choose New ➤ Virtual Directory to start the Virtual Directory Wizard.

2. Under the site, add a virtual directory with an alias of Printers that points to the *%systemroot%*\Web\printers directory.

NOTE This directory is in a completely different location from the directory set up by the IIS installation, inetpub. Not very intuitive, I know, but I didn't write the software.

3. Set the permissions to include Read and Run Scripts.

4. Open the Properties dialog box for the `Printers` virtual folder, and click the Documents tab.

5. Click Add to open the Add Default Document dialog box.

6. Enter the name **page1.asp**, and click OK.

7. Click the up arrow button to move `page1.asp` to the top of the default documents list. Click OK to apply the change.

8. From a client machine on the LAN or on the Internet, connect to **http://*hostname*/printers**, as discussed earlier. The printers page should be displayed.

TIP   If you can't see the printers from the client browser, stop and restart the website in the IIS console. The client must support IPP to take full advantage of printing across the Internet. Windows XP and 2000 clients natively support IPP. You can find a Windows 9*x* client for IPP on the Windows 2000 Server CD in `\Clients\Win9xipp.cli`. There is currently no IPP client for Windows NT, and at last word Microsoft wasn't planning to release one.

Chapter 6

Scripting Windows XP

Computers are supposed to make our jobs and lives easier, and most of the time, they do. However, sometimes it can seem that computers make more work rather than less. In those situations, it's great to be able to automate tasks so the computer performs most of the work.

For the average user, automating a task generally means creating a macro in an application and running the macro whenever he needs to accomplish the task. For advanced users and administrators, automating tasks often means moving beyond the capabilities of a single application to control the system as a whole or manage multiple systems.

There are several methods for automating Windows XP, including macro recorders and drag-and-drop scripting tools. Although Windows XP doesn't have a built-in macro recorder, it provides a powerful scripting tool called Windows Script Host (WSH). You can use WSH to automate an amazing range of tasks.

WSH scripting isn't for those who have no desire to understand and write programs. If you have some programming background, you'll find it relatively easy to develop scripts for WSH. If you don't have any programming background but are interested in an inexpensive way to get your feet wet, WSH is a great option.

In this chapter, I explore WSH to help you understand what it is and how it works. You'll also learn about the mechanics of writing and running scripts with WSH. I can't teach you to program in this chapter, but you'll gain enough background to understand the capabilities of WSH and learn where to go for more information.

NOTE   The information in this chapter should give you a good start on scripting and illustrates how easy it is to create scripts for local and remote execution. However, scripting is a huge topic, so naturally you need to learn about many other topics and skills, including how to integrate error checking in your scripts. The main scripting URL at Microsoft's website is http://msdn.microsoft.com/scripting.

Understanding Windows Script Host

Windows XP includes a built-in scripting capability called Windows Script Host (WSH) for both the Windows and console environments. WSH is a scripting manager that serves as an interface between scripts and the back-end scripting engines that run each type of script. WSH therefore makes operating system objects and services available to scripts. Following is a list of just a few of the things you can do with WSH:

◆ Display messages in dialog boxes or on the console command line

◆ Map network drives, connect to remote printers, and perform other logon tasks

◆ Read and set environment variables

◆ Read and modify Registry keys

◆ Send mail messages using CDO

◆ Open and manipulate applications, and send keystrokes to applications

◆ Call other scripts

◆ Get information about the current logged-on user

◆ Create shortcuts and work with special folders, such as `My Documents`

◆ Copy files and folders

TIP It's possible that Windows Script Host is disabled on your computer(s). Some administrators and organizations disable Windows Script Host to help prevent virus infections and worm propagation through scripts. WSH can be disabled by renaming the Wscript.exe executable, removing the VBS file extension from association with Wscript.exe, or through a third-party utility such as Symantec's Noscript.exe (`www.sarc.com/avcenter/venc/data/win.script.hosting.html`) or AnalogX Script Defender (`www.analogx.com/contents/download/system/sdefend.htm`).

WSH provides two different mechanisms for running scripts: `Wscript.exe` and `Cscript.exe`. Wscript runs scripts in the Windows environment, and Cscript runs scripts in the console environment. Let's look at a quick example to show you the difference.

Start by creating a text file on the Desktop that contains the following line of code:

```
WScript.Echo("Hello World!");
```

Save the file as `Hello.js`, making sure to remove the `.txt` file extension from the file. Next, let's launch the script using three different methods:

1. Double-click the file. You should see a message box appear on the Desktop.

2. Open a command console, and issue the command that follows. The message box should again appear on the Desktop:

```
C:\Documents and Settings\jim\Desktop>wscript Hello.js
```

3. Use Cscript to execute the file. The text appears in the console rather than in the Windows environment:

```
C:\Documents and Settings\jim\Desktop>cscript Hello.js
```

As you learned in step 1, you can launch scripts from the Windows interface by double-clicking them. Windows uses the file association for the script type to pass the script to WSH for execution. Note that on your system, JScripts might not execute when you double-click. For example, I have Macromedia Ultradev installed, which by default modifies file associations to open JS files in Dreamweaver for editing. If you want to reassociate JS files with WSH, right-click the JS file, and follow these steps:

1. Right-click the JS file you just created, and choose Properties.

2. On the General tab, click Change.

3. Windows Script Host probably won't be listed in the Open With dialog box. Click Browse, browse to *%systemroot%*\System32, select Wscript.exe, and click Open.

4. Click OK to close the property sheet for the file.

Now that you've had an introduction to WSH, it's time to choose your script language. Currently, WSH supports scripts written in Visual Basic Scripting Edition (VBScript) and JScript, which is distantly and indirectly related to Java. The next section explores these two engines to help you decide which is right for you.

Script Engine Options

Visual Basic Scripting Edition (VBScript) is very similar to Visual Basic and Visual Basic for Applications (VBA). If you're familiar with either VB or VBA, you'll have no trouble writing scripts with VBScript. If you don't have any Visual Basic experience, either VBScript or JScript is a good choice for your first script. They offer roughly the same set of capabilities. Either would be an excellent choice for scripting in the Windows environment.

If you're trying to decide which route to choose, consider what you might do later, outside the realm of automating Windows XP. For example, if you want to get into developing ASP web pages or Office macros, VBScript is a logical choice. It's a subset of VB, as is VBA, the scripting language used to automate Microsoft Office applications. VBScript offers a subset of the error handling provided by VB; gives you the ability to easily format dates, numbers, and currency; and provides built-in support for working with COM objects. You'll also be able to easily port your scripts to the Web for ASP. However, keep in mind that earlier versions of Netscape don't support VBScript.

If you're interested in developing web applications for Linux and non-IIS platforms down the road, JScript is a good starting point. JScript borrows from C, C++, and Java, so if you have experience with any of these languages, JScript will feel familiar. JScript is also a good choice if you intend to write a lot of Dynamic HTML (DHTML) code.

Writing Scripts

Now, let's get down to business with scripts. Whole books (many of them) have been written about scripting, and I couldn't possibly cover every use for a script in this chapter. Instead, I'll focus on simple scripts that show how to accomplish specific tasks and illustrate how easy it is to perform some fairly complex tasks with scripts. I'll combine some tasks together out of necessity. At the end of this section you'll find a list of references for more information about WSH, VBScript, and JScript.

Displaying Messages and Working with Variables

I've touched on this topic already in this chapter. Displaying messages is pretty simple and, like many tasks, requires a single statement. However, it's likely that you'll want to output variables as well as static text, so I'll incorporate variables into the samples.

First, let's create a basic script that sets the value of a variable and then displays it in a dialog box along with a static message (Figure 6.1):

```
' Create a text variable
Dim someString
someString = "This is a variable."
' Display a Hello World message, followed by the value of the variable
msgbox "Hello World!" & vbCrLf & someString
```

FIGURE 6.1
This simple message
box was generated from
a script.

The last line uses the & character to concatenate the static message with a carriage return/line feed and the value of the variable value. Here's the same thing using JScript:

```
var someString = "This is a variable.";
WScript.Echo("Hello World!\n" + someString);
```

Notice the use of the \n escape sequence to add a newline character to the message. Table 6.1 lists additional escape sequences.

TABLE 6.1:   Escape Sequences for JScript

ESCAPE SEQUENCE	CHARACTER
\b	Backspace
\f	Form feed
\n	Line feed (newline)
\r	Carriage return
\t	Horizontal tab
\'	Single quotation mark
\"	Double quotation mark
\\	Backslash

Working with Network Shares and Printers

Two common tasks in logon scripts are mapping network-to-network drives and mapping to network printers. In a WSH script, you use the Network object to access network resources. The MapNetworkDrive method supports five properties:

```
MapNetworkDrive LocalDrive, ShareName, Persistence, User, Password
```

The following script uses the MapNetworkDrive method with the Network object to map a remote share \\server1\docs to local drive letter E and makes the mapping persistent (adding it to the user's profile):

```
Dim net
Set net = CreateObject("WScript.Network")
net.MapNetworkDrive "E:","\\server1\docs","True","username","password"
```

Here's the same thing using JScript:

```
var net = WScript.CreateObject("WScript.Network");
net.MapNetworkDrive ("E:","\\server1\docs","True","username","password");
```

Now, let's connect to a remote printer:

```
Dim netPrn
Set netPrn = WScript.CreateObject("WScript.Network")
PrinterPath = "\\server1\HPLaserJet"
netPrn.AddWindowsPrinterConnection PrinterPath
```

Here's the JScript version:

```
var netPrn = WScript.CreateObject("WScript.Network");
var PrinterPath = "\\\\server1\\HPLaserJet";
WshNetwork.AddWindowsPrinterConnection(PrinterPath);
```

The `Network` object supports several other methods, which are described in the following list:

AddWindowsPrinterConnection   This method adds a remote printer connection for Windows applications.

AddPrinterConnection   This method adds a remote printer for DOS, mapping the printer to a local LPT port.

EnumNetworkDrives   This method returns a collection of local drive names and their corresponding remote UNC path mappings. Even-numbered items in the collection are local drive names, and odd-numbered items are UNC path names. The first item is at index zero.

EnumPrinterConnections   This method returns a collection of local printer names and their UNC mappings. Even numbered items in the collection are local printer names, and odd-numbered items are UNC path names. The first item is at index zero.

MapNetworkDrive   This method maps a local drive name to a remote share.

RemoveNetworkDrive   This method disconnects a mapped drive.

RemovePrinterConnection   This method disconnects a remote printer.

SetDefaultPrinter   This method assigns a remote printer as the local default printer.

TIP   See `http://msdn.microsoft.com/library/default.asp?url=/library/en-us/script56/html/wsconaccessingnetworkconnections.asp` to learn more about the `Network` object and how to use these additional methods.

Driving Applications with Scripts

One of the most common uses for the old Windows Recorder was to automate tasks in applications that didn't have their own macro capability. For example, you might have recorded a macro that opened a menu, selected a command, and then processed several other keystrokes or mouse actions.

You can run, activate, manipulate, and terminate applications from a WSH script via the `WshShell` object. I'll focus on the `Run`, `AppActivate`, and `SendKeys` methods, and also touch on the `Sleep` method. `Run` starts the application, `AppActivate` activates it (gives it focus), and `SendKeys` sends keystrokes to the application. `Sleep` causes the script to pause a specified period of time; I'll use the `Sleep` method to help you see the effects of some of the other methods.

Following is the syntax for using the Run method:

```
object.Run(strCommand, [intWindowStyle], [bWaitOnReturn])
```

strCommand is the command to execute, inWindowStyle is the window startup mode, and bWaitOnReturn is a Boolean (a value of true or false) that specifies whether the script waits for the application to finish before the script continues. I'll touch on each of these parameters in the following example.

Here's what the following script will accomplish:

1. Open Notepad, and open Calculator.

2. Activate Notepad again, and send some text to Notepad.

3. Activate Calculator, perform a calculation, and copy the results to the Clipboard.

4. Activate Notepad, insert more text, and then paste from the Clipboard.

Here's the script in VBScript:

```
Set WshShell = WScript.CreateObject("WScript.Shell")
WshShell.Run "%windir%\notepad"
WshShell.Run "%windir%\System32\Calc"
WScript.Sleep 3000
WshShell.AppActivate "Notepad"
WshShell.SendKeys "This is some text in Notepad.{ENTER}"
WScript.Sleep 3000
WshShell.AppActivate "Calculator"
WshShell.SendKeys "2{+}2{ENTER}"
WshShell.SendKeys "%ec"
WScript.Sleep 3000
WshShell.AppActivate "Notepad"
WshShell.SendKeys "Two plus two is "
WshShell.SendKeys "^v"
WScript.Sleep 1000
Msgbox "All Done!"
```

TIP   If you need to specify a long filename path with the Run method, double-quote the command string, such as """C:\Program Files\Windows NT\Accessories\Wordpad.exe""".

In this script, the Sleep method makes the script pause for three seconds at three places in the script and for one second near the end. The last pause gives the script time to paste the results into Notepad before the message box is displayed. Also, note that I used two different methods to access the Copy and Paste commands. For the Copy command, I sent Alt+E+C (for Edit, Copy); for Paste, I sent the shortcut keystroke Ctrl+V.

This sample script also illustrates that SendKeys uses special characters as modifiers. These characters include the following:

( ) { } [ ] + ^ % ~

Table 6.2 explains the purpose of the last four.

TABLE 6.2:   *SendKeys* Modifiers

CHARACTER	PURPOSE
+	Shift
^	Ctrl
%	Alt
~	Enter

For example, the script line that pastes the contents of the Clipboard into Notepad uses ^ as a modifier for Ctrl. The line that enters the calculation 2 + 2 in Calculator, however, sends the plus sign in braces so that it's treated literally rather than as a modifier. So, whenever you need to send the value of a modifier character rather than use it as a modifier, enclose it in braces. You must also enclose the characters

( ) { } [ ]

in braces to have them sent as literals, as in the following example:

```
WshShell.SendKeys "This is a left brace {{} and this is a right brace {}}"
```

See Table 6.3 for a list of special keystrokes and the equivalent SendKeys arguments.

TABLE 6.3:   Special Keys and Their *SendKeys* Arguments

KEY	ARGUMENT
Backspace	{BACKSPACE}, {BS}, or {BKSP}
Break	{BREAK}
Caps Lock	{CAPSLOCK}
Del or Delete	{DELETE} or {DEL}
Down arrow	{DOWN}
End	{END}
Enter	{ENTER} or ~
Esc	{ESC}
Help	{HELP}
Home	{HOME}
Ins or Insert	{INSERT} or {INS}

TABLE 6.3: Special Keys and Their *SendKeys* Arguments *(CONTINUED)*

KEY	ARGUMENT
Left arrow	{LEFT}
Num Lock	{NUMLOCK}
Page Down	{PGDN}
Page Up	{PGUP}
Print Screen	{PRTSC}
Right arrow	{RIGHT}
Scroll Lock	{SCROLLLOCK}
Tab	{TAB}
Up arrow	{UP}
F1	{F1}
F2	{F2}
F3	{F3}
F4	{F4}
F5	{F5}
F6	{F6}
F7	{F7}
F8	{F8}
F9	{F9}
F10	{F10}
F11	{F11}
F12	{F12}
F13	{F13}
F14	{F14}
F15	{F15}
F16	{F16}

In some scripts, you'll need to use Alt, Shift, or Ctrl with other characters. For example, assume you want to simulate holding down the Shift key while the characters S and O are pressed and then releasing the Shift key and pressing the number 2. To do so, you send the Shift and then enclose the combined keys within parentheses, followed by the remaining text. Here's the code:

```
WshShell.SendKeys "+(SO)2"
```

To simulate Shift+S followed by an unshifted O and a 2, you can use the following code:

```
WshShell.SendKeys "+SO2"
```

Here's the same script in JScript:

```
var WshShell = WScript.CreateObject("WScript.Shell");
WshShell.Run ("%windir%\\notepad");
WshShell.Run ("%windir%\\System32\\Calc");
WScript.Sleep (3000);
WshShell.AppActivate ("Notepad");
WshShell.SendKeys ("This is some text in Notepad.{ENTER}");
WScript.Sleep (3000);
WshShell.AppActivate ("Calculator");
WshShell.SendKeys ("2{+}2{ENTER}");
WshShell.SendKeys ("%ec");
WScript.Sleep (3000);
WshShell.AppActivate ("Notepad");
WshShell.SendKeys ("Two plus two is ");
WshShell.SendKeys ("^v");
WScript.Sleep (1000);
WScript.Echo("All Done!");
```

SETTING WINDOW STYLE

Keep in mind that when you launch an application with the Run method, you can specify the window style for the application with the `intWindowStyle` parameter. For example, you might want one application to start in a normal window and another application to start maximized. Table 6.4 lists the integer values that specify the window style; you include the integer with the Run method. The following example starts Calculator minimized:

```
Set WshShell = WScript.CreateObject("WScript.Shell")
WshShell.Run "%windir%\System32\Calc", 3
WshShell.Run "%windir%\notepad", 7
```

You can also specify that the script wait for the application to finish before it continues. To do so, set `bWaitOnReturn` to true. In this example, Notepad won't start until WordPad is closed:

```
Set WshShell = WScript.CreateObject("WScript.Shell")
WshShell.Run """C:\Program Files\Windows NT\Accessories\Wordpad.exe""",3,true
WshShell.Run "notepad",7
```

TABLE 6.4: Integer Values That Define Window State

INTEGER	DESCRIPTION
0	Hide the window, and activate another window.
1	Activate and display the window. If the window is minimized or maximized, the system restores it to its original size and position. Use when displaying a window for the first time.
2	Activate the window, and display it as a minimized window.
3	Activate the window, and display it as a maximized window.
4	Display a window in its most recent size and position. The currently active window remains active.
5	Activate the window, and display it in its current size and position.
6	Minimize the specified window, and activate the next top-level window based on application Z order.
7	Display the window as a minimized window. The active window remains active.
8	Display the window in its current state. The active window remains active.
9	Activate and display the window. If the window is minimized or maximized, the system restores it to its original size and position. Use when restoring a minimized window.
10	Set the show-state based on the state of the program that started the application.

TIP See `http://msdn.microsoft.com/library/default.asp?url=/library/en-us/script56/html/wscondrivingapplications.asp` for more information on automating applications with scripts.

File Management Operations

NOTE See Chapter 18 for more information about managing a file system with scripts.

Copying a file is another common task for a script to perform. You use the `FileSystemObject` object in WSH to manipulate files and folders. `FileSystemObject` supports several methods, but in this chapter I focus on the following:

CopyFile   This method copies a file or folder from one location to another.

CreateFolder   This method creates a folder.

CreateTextFile   This method creates a text file in a specified location.

DeleteFile   This method deletes one or more files.

GetFile   This method returns a `File` object to a specified file.

MoveFile   This method moves one or more files to another location.

TIP It's important to note that you can use multiple methods to copy, move, and delete files. For example, the Copy method will copy files or folders, although only one at a time. Likewise, the Delete method will delete a file or folder.

In addition, the following script also uses the SpecialFolders property of the WshShell object to retrieve the path to the user's My Documents and Desktop folders.

Now, let's create a simple script that performs the following tasks:

1. Create a text file in My Documents, and write some text to the file.

2. Create a folder on the Desktop.

3. Copy the file created in step 1 to the folder created in step 3.

4. Delete the original file from My Documents.

5. Create another text file in My Documents, and write some text to it.

6. Move the file to the second folder, leaving the original in place.

Here's the VBScript version of the script:

```
' Declare the variables
Dim fso, myDocs, myDesktop, file1, file2, folder, fileToCopy, fileToMove, destFile
' Create the file system object
Set fso = CreateObject("Scripting.FileSystemObject")
' Create a shell object
set shell = createobject("wscript.shell")
' Get location of current user's My Documents folder
myDocs = fso.GetFolder(shell.specialfolders("MyDocuments"))
' Get location of current user's Desktop folder
myDesktop = fso.GetFolder(shell.specialfolders("Desktop"))
' Create a text file
Set file1 = fso.CreateTextFile(myDocs&"\File1.txt")
' Write some text to it
file1.Write "This is text file 1."
' Close the file
file1.Close
' Create a folder on the Desktop
set folder = fso.CreateFolder(myDesktop&"\MyTestFolder")
' Get the file to copy
set fileToCopy = fso.GetFile(myDocs&"\File1.txt")
' Set the destination
destFile = folder.Path&"\File1.txt"
' Copy the file
fso.CopyFile fileToCopy, destFile
' Delete the file
fso.DeleteFile fileToCopy
' Create another file
set file2 = fso.CreateTextFile(myDocs&"\File2.txt")
' Write to it
```

```
file2.Write "This is text file 2."
' Close it
file2.Close
' Get the file to be moved
set fileToMove = fso.GetFile(myDocs&"\File2.txt")
' Set the destination
destFile = folder.Path&"\File2.txt"
' Move the file
fso.MoveFile fileToMove, destFile
```

Here is the same script in JScript:

```
var fso, myDocs, myDesktop, file1, file2, folder, fileToCopy,
 fileToMove, destFile;
fso = new ActiveXObject("Scripting.FileSystemObject");
shell = new ActiveXObject("wscript.shell");
myDocs = fso.GetFolder(shell.specialfolders("MyDocuments"));
myDesktop = fso.GetFolder(shell.specialfolders("Desktop"));
file1 = fso.CreateTextFile(myDocs+"\\File1.txt");
file1.Write ("This is text file 1.");
file1.Close();
folder = fso.CreateFolder(myDesktop+"\\MyTestFolder");
fileToCopy = fso.GetFile(myDocs+"\\File1.txt");
destFile = (folder.Path+"\\File1.txt");
fso.CopyFile (fileToCopy, destFile);
fso.DeleteFile (fileToCopy);
file2 = fso.CreateTextFile(myDocs+"\\File2.txt");
file2.Write ("This is text file 2.");
file2.Close();
fileToMove = fso.GetFile(myDocs+"\\File2.txt");
destFile = folder.Path+"\\File2.txt";
fso.MoveFile (fileToMove, destFile);
```

TIP   See http://msdn.microsoft.com/library/default.asp?url=/library/en-us/script56/
html/wsconexecutingfilemanagementoperationsprogrammatically.asp to learn more about
file and folder operations.

Manipulating the Registry

NOTE   There's more on registry scripting in Chapter 15.

Occasionally you might need a script to read from or write to the Registry. WSH provides both
capabilities. Before you blunder through the Registry with WSH, however, keep in mind that incorrect Registry changes can have negative consequences, including preventing a system from booting.

You use the WshShell object to manipulate the Registry. After creating the shell object in the script,
you use the RegRead method to read Registry values and the RegWrite method to write values. You
can use the RegDelete method to delete Registry values or keys.

Let's start with a simple script that reads the system BIOS date and displays it in a message box:

```
' Declare variables
Dim biosDate, sh
' Create the WshShell object
Set sh = WScript.CreateObject("Wscript.Shell")
biosDate = sh.RegRead("HKLM\SYSTEM\CurrentControlSet\Control\Biosinfo\
SystemBiosDate")
msgbox biosDate
```

Here's the same script using JScript:

```
var sh = WScript.CreateObject("Wscript.Shell");
var biosDate = sh.RegRead("HKLM\\SYSTEM\\CurrentControlSet\\Control\\Biosinfo\\
SystemBiosDate");
WScript.Echo(biosDate);
```

WARNING   The previous script is harmless because it simply reads from the Registry. As you begin to write scripts that modify the Registry (such as the ones that follow), keep in mind that an incorrect registry change could affect programs or even prevent the computer from booting. Tread with care!

Next, let's create a short script that creates a Registry key and adds a few values to it. We'll use the RegWrite method for this one:

```
' Create the WshShell object
Set sh = WScript.CreateObject("Wscript.Shell")
' Define the base key name
key = "HKLM\SOFTWARE\MyTestKey\"
sh.RegWrite key & "toast", "wheat", "REG_SZ"
sh.RegWrite key & "eggs", "scrambled", "REG_EXPAND_SZ"
sh.RegWrite key & "intval", 56579, "REG_DWORD"
```

Here's the same script using JScript:

```
var sh = new ActiveXObject("Wscript.Shell");
var key = "HKLM\\SOFTWARE\\MyTestKey\\";
sh.RegWrite (key + "toast", "wheat", "REG_SZ");
sh.RegWrite (key + "eggs", "scrambled", "REG_EXPAND_SZ");
sh.RegWrite (key + "intval", 56579, "REG_DWORD");
```

Now, let's delete those Registry values. The following script removes the Registry values one by one and then removes the key:

```
Set sh = WScript.CreateObject("Wscript.Shell")
key = "HKLM\SOFTWARE\MyTestKey\"
sh.RegDelete key & "toast"
sh.RegDelete key & "eggs"
sh.RegDelete key & "intval"
sh.RegDelete key
```

We can't forget the JScript version:

```
var sh = new ActiveXObject("Wscript.Shell");
var key = "HKLM\\SOFTWARE\\MyTestKey\\";
sh.RegDelete (key + "toast");
sh.RegDelete (key + "eggs");
sh.RegDelete (key + "intval");
sh.RegDelete (key);
```

TIP   See `http://msdn.microsoft.com/library/default.asp?url=/library/en-us/script56/html/wsconmanipulatingsystemregistryprogrammatically.asp` to learn more about managing the Registry with scripts.

Working with Script Arguments

I need to cover one final topic before completing this quick tour of WSH scripting: the use of *arguments*. An argument is a parameter that you pass to the script. For example, assume you want to write a script that will send an e-mail message from the command line. The information you need to provide to the script includes the sender address, recipient address, subject, and message body. So, that's four arguments.

The arguments passed to a script are stored in a zero-based array that you access with the `Arguments` property of the `WScript` object. Extracting the arguments means pulling the information from the array using a zero-based index.

The following e-mail script checks the number of arguments in the array and, if there are four arguments, extracts the arguments, constructs the message, and sends it. Otherwise, the script spits out an error message and terminates:

```
' Declare variables
Dim objArgs, StdOut
' Get the script arguments into the objArgs array
set objArgs = Wscript.Arguments
' Check if there are four arguments
if objArgs.Count = 4 then
    ' Create a new message object
    set objEmail = CreateObject("CDO.Message")
    ' Use the first argument as the sender address
    objEmail.From = objArgs(0)
    ' Use the second argument as the recipient address
    objEmail.To = objArgs(1)
    ' Use the third argument as the subject
    objEmail.Subject = objArgs(2)
    ' Use the fourth argument as the message body
    objEmail.Textbody = objArgs(3)
    ' Send the message
    objEmail.Send
    ' Release the objects
    set objArgs = nothing
    set objEmail = nothing
else
    ' Create an output stream
```

```
   set StdOut = WScript.StdOut
   ' Write an error message to output stream
   StdOut.WriteLine "Incorrect number of parameters - exiting."
End If
```

The following command at a console command prompt executes the script and passes it the required four arguments:

```
C:\myScripts>cscript mail.vbs admin@boyce.us jim@boyce.us "This is
the subject" "This is the body"
```

Here's the JScript version:

```
var objArgs, StdOut, objEmail;
objArgs = WScript.Arguments;
if (objArgs.Length == 4)
  {
    objEmail = new ActiveXObject("CDO.Message");
    objEmail.From = objArgs(0);
    objEmail.To = objArgs(1);
    objEmail.Subject = objArgs(2);
    objEmail.Textbody = objArgs(3);
    objEmail.Send();
  }
else
  {
    StdOut = WScript.StdOut;
    StdOut.WriteLine ("Incorrect number of parameters - exiting.");
  }
```

Running Scripts

If you've followed the examples in the previous sections, you've already had some experience in running scripts. You can execute scripts by double-clicking them, as long as the scripts don't require any arguments. When a script does require arguments, you can take one of two approaches to execute it.

The first approach is to execute the script from a command line using Wscript or Cscript. That's the approach used in the previous section to pass arguments to the mail.vbs script.

You can also create a shortcut to a script and pass arguments to the script through the properties for the shortcut. Using the mail.vbs script as an example, follow these steps:

1. Create a shortcut on the Desktop to your own mail.vbs script.

2. Right-click the shortcut, and choose Properties.

3. Click at the right end of the Target field on the Shortcut tab, and then type the parameters for the script, enclosing text strings in quotes (see Figure 6.2). The following is an example of what the Target field should look like:

   ```
   "C:\Documents and Settings\jim\mail.vbs" admin@boyce.us
   jim@boyce.us "subject" "content"
   ```

FIGURE 6.2
Use the Target field on the
Shortcut tab to specify
script arguments.

TIP You can use the Scheduled Tasks folder, the AT command, or the WinAT tool from the Windows XP Resource Kit to run scripts at scheduled times.

Remote Scripting

WSH version 5.6 adds the capability to run scripts remotely on another computer. To perform remote scripting, you must take a few steps, the first of which is to install WSH 5.6 or later on the remote computer. You can obtain the latest version of WSH from `http://msdn.microsoft.com/scripting`.

The next step is to add your account to the local Administrators group on the remote computer. Then, open the Registry Editor on the remote computer and add the REG_SZ value `HKEY_LOCAL_MACHINE\SOFTWARE\Microsoft\Windows Script Host\Settings\Remote` to the Registry. Set its value to 1 to enable remote scripting, or set its value to 0 to disable remote scripting.

When the remote computer has been configured to enable remote scripting, you can programmatically run scripts on the remote computer. The following example assumes that the scripts are located on the local computer in the folder `C:\Scripts`, that the script to be run is named `SetSecure.vbs`, and that the name of the remote computer is snoopy:

```
Set objCtrl = CreateObject("WSHController")
Set oProc = ojbCtrl. CreateScript("c:\Scripts\SetSecure.vbs", "snoopy")
objProc.Execute
While oProc.Status <> 2
    Wscript.Sleep 100
Wend
WScript.Echo "Remote Script Done"
```

TIP A Status property value of 0 indicates the script hasn't been started. A value of 1 indicates that the script is still running.

Part 3

Managing the System and Applications

In this section:

Chapter 7

Controlling Application Compatibility

You would think that a program written for Windows would work on any Windows operating system, right? Well, that isn't necessarily the case. A program written for Windows 95 might work on Windows XP, but there is a chance that you'll have problems running the application. Forcing all Windows users to upgrade all of their applications each time a new operating system version came out would be a horrible marketing strategy for Microsoft, so it has addressed application compatibility with most Windows releases, and Windows XP is no exception. In fact, Windows XP makes it even easier than previous versions to make applications compatible with the operating system, and this chapter brings you up to speed on how to do that.

You'll also find tips in this chapter about running Linux on your Windows PC. An alternative to running Linux or Unix on your PC is to run an X Window terminal emulator program under Windows that provides access to a Unix- or Linux-based server where the application runs. I'll touch on X Window briefly in this chapter and point you to some X Window solutions for Windows XP.

Using the Program Compatibility Wizard

Windows 2000 introduced a tool called Application Compatibility (`Apcompat.exe`) that let you specify certain compatibility options for a program to allow it to run properly under Windows 2000. Windows XP also includes an application compatibility tool; it's available both as a wizard and directly through the properties for a program's shortcut.

First, let's look at the basic options for setting compatibility options under Windows XP. Then, I'll discuss compatibility issues in more detail.

Basic Compatibility Options

The Program Compatibility Wizard lets you specify the operating system that Windows XP should emulate for the application as well as a handful of other properties such as screen resolution and color depth. The OS options provided by the wizard include the following:

- Microsoft Windows 95

- Microsoft Windows NT 4.0 with Service Pack 5

- Microsoft Windows 98/Me

- Microsoft Windows 2000

To run the Program Compatibility Wizard, click Start ➢ All Programs ➢ Accessories ➢ Program Compatibility Wizard. The wizard prompts you to select the application for which you want to set compatibility options. You can select an installed program, select a program on a CD, or locate the program manually. After you select one of the four operating system choices listed previously, the wizard prompts you for the desired compatibility settings (Figure 7.1). Then, the wizard gives you the opportunity to test the application to make sure it works before finalizing the settings.

If you prefer, you can set program compatibility options manually through the properties for a program's executable or a shortcut to the program. To do so, right-click the program's icon and choose Properties, and then click the Compatibility tab. You can specify the OS as well as the same additional compatibility options provided by the wizard. The only difference is that you don't have the option of testing the settings. However, if necessary you can open the properties again and change them.

TIP You can set properties for an application on a CD, but compatibility settings are saved only for programs installed on a hard disk.

Advanced Compatibility Options

In order to understand advanced compatibility options for Windows XP, you need to recognize the reasons why program compatibility is a potential problem. Some applications expect a specific OS version to be running and balk if the OS returns a different version number. A program might call a Windows API that returns data in a particular format that has changed in a later OS version, or that gives unexpected results because of differences in hardware. For example, early versions of a program might not gracefully handle high-capacity disk drives.

Another potential problem is a change in the location of user data and the Desktop. Windows 2000 and Windows XP both store user data by default in the `\Documents and Settings\`*user* folder, where *user* is the current logon account. Windows 98 uses the `\Profiles\`*user* folder or `\Windows\Personal` folder for user data.

Windows XP addresses compatibility issues during Setup. It uses two database files, `MigDB.inf` and `NTCompat.inf`, to check for hardware and software compatibility problems, and it reports those problems to the user. `MigDB.inf` supports upgrades from Windows $9x$/Me, and `NTCompat.inf` supports upgrades from Windows NT.

ADDING COMPATIBILITY OPTIONS IN WINDOWS 2000

The Windows 2000 Resource Kit includes a tool that you can use to configure certain compatibility options for applications the same way you can in Windows XP. This Resource Kit tool adds a Compatibility tab to the properties sheet for a shortcut to an application, allowing you to set the compatibility mode for the application.

To install the tool, follow these steps:

1. Install the Windows 2000 Resource Kit.

2. Open a command console and execute the following command:

    ```
    regsvr32 c:\winnt\apppatch\slayerui.dll
    ```

3. After the DLL is registered, create a shortcut to the application's executable file.

4. Right-click the shortcut and choose Properties.

5. Click the Compatibility tab, and use the options it provides to select the compatibility mode for the application.

FIGURE 7.1
Use the Program Compatibility Wizard to make a program compatible with Windows XP.

The file *%systemroot%*\AppPatch\SysMain.sdb contains compatibility information and fixes for specific applications. The fixes in SysMain are program-specific and can apply any of several compatibility fixes when the program is loaded, from something as simple as reporting a specific version of the OS the program all the way up to changing the way memory and other system resources are reported to or used by the program.

Windows XP uses Dynamic Update and Windows Update to get the program compatibility information necessary to determine whether a program can run successfully under XP. Dynamic Update works during Setup, downloading updates from the Microsoft Windows Update website. Setup downloads updated drivers, core Windows XP files, and software patches, integrating these updates into the Windows XP installation process. Dynamic Update naturally requires that an Internet connection be available when Setup runs.

Windows XP can also check for compatibility updates when you install an application after Setup is complete. Windows XP checks the Windows Update site for the same types of updates as Dynamic Update. The only difference is that it checks for the updates during program installation rather than Windows XP installation. So, Windows XP uses both the SysMain database and Windows Update to apply compatibility fixes.

APPLICATION BLOCKING

When Windows XP detects a program with a compatibility problem, the OS can take one of two actions: apply a fix to the program and run it, or block the program from running. Windows XP displays a dialog box telling you that the application is incompatible with Windows XP. Depending on the program and its compatibility problems, Windows XP will either let you run the program anyway or will block the program from running. If the program is blocked, you'll have to obtain an update for it.

Compatibility Modes

A *compatibility mode* is a group of fixes that emulate a specific operating system. Compatibility modes are also called *layers*. Each of the OS choices you see in the Program Compatibility Wizard is a compatibility mode. The Windows 95 compatibility mode, for example, applies roughly 50 different fixes to allow programs written for Windows 95 to run on Windows XP. The fixes that each mode applies vary, but common fixes include reporting the selected version of Windows to the application, changing the way Windows manages memory, and specifying the location of data folders. Each mode is naturally tailored to the target operating system to allow the application to run under Windows XP in the context of that target OS.

Windows XP provides three types of compatibility modes:

End-user These are the default modes you'll find on the Compatibility tab and in the Program Compatibility Wizard.

System These include the end-user modes as well as the Limited User Account Security mode, which lets a program run under a limited security context for a user, and the Profiles mode, which controls the way the program works with Windows XP user profiles.

Custom Windows XP provides a CompatAdmin tool you can use to create a custom compatibility mode to apply to a specific program.

It's possible for more than one set of fixes to apply to a program. For example, when Setup installs Windows XP and detects an compatibility problem, it can apply a fix through the SysMain database. You might also apply compatibility options through the Program Compatibility Wizard. Windows XP combines the compatibility settings and applies them all to the program.

Customizing and Extending Compatibility Features

The Program Compatibility Wizard and the Compatibility tab of a program's properties give you the means to set basic compatibility properties. Microsoft offers additional tools you can use to customize and extend compatibility features. You can download these tools as part of the Windows XP Application Compatibility Toolkit from

```
http://msdn.microsoft.com/library/default.asp?url=/downloads/list/appcomp.asp
```

The Application Compatibility Toolkit includes several documents that explain program compatibility issues, offer an overview of the compatibility features in Windows XP, and define test procedures you can implement to determine a program's compatibility with XP. The toolkit also includes a list of other online resources that will help you test and manage program compatibility under Windows XP.

The following sections explain the tools included in the Application Compatibility Toolkit. You can install the tools by downloading the file and double-clicking it.

TIP You can launch the tools from the C:\Program Files\Application Compatibility Toolkit\default.htm page after installation, or click Start ➤ All Programs ➤ Application Compatibility Toolkit.

Compatibility Administrator

New!

The Compatibility Administrator has replaced the Compatibility Administration tool (also called the Application Fix Management Console) in version 3.0 of the Application Compatibility Toolkit. The Compatibility Administrator, shown in Figure 7.2, lets you view and enable or disable existing compatibility database entries. You can also use this tool to create custom fixes for specific applications not already included in the SysMain database. Because you can disable an existing entry, you can create a custom entry for a program already included in the SysMain database.

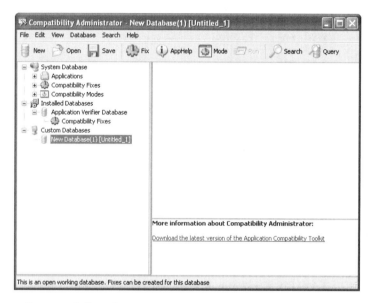

To create a new program fix entry, follow these steps:

1. Open the Compatibility Administrator, and choose Database ➢ Create New ➢ Application Fix to start the Create New Application Fix wizard.

2. Enter the name of the application and vendor name, and then click Browse or enter the path to the program's executable file. Click Next to display the dialog box shown in Figure 7.3.

3. Select an application compatibility mode for the application to configure general settings. You can also select additional compatibility options in the list. Click Next.

4. The wizard prompts you to select additional compatibility fixes. You can select any number of fixes to apply to the application; scroll through the list and select the fixes you want. Click Next.

TIP Click the Show Selected button to view only those fixes that are currently selected in the wizard.

5. The wizard prompts you to add files to the entry for identification. Windows XP uses these files to automatically detect when the application is installed on a system. Adding other files refines the detection process and is particularly useful when you have more than one application that uses the same executable file name. You can add files to the list manually or click Auto-Generate to have the wizard automatically include support files, such as DLLs, from the program's folder. When you're satisfied with the settings, click Next, and then click Finish to create the entry.

When you've finished creating custom program entries in your new database file, choose File ➤ Save to save the database to an SDB file. Next, you need to install the database. You can do so for the local computer through the Compatibility Administrator: Right-click the database and choose Install. You can then distribute the database file to other computers to apply the fixes to those systems. You can use the Sdbinst.exe program included with this tool to install the database on the target systems; the syntax is sdbinst .exe *database_file*.

Sdbinst.exe installs by default in the *%systemroot%*\System32 folder. This method of installing the database is handy when you need to incorporate a database on a target system through a script. If you prefer, you can double-click the database file to add its entries to the Registry. To use this method, place the database file on a network share available to all target users. Then send all users an e-mail message containing a link to the database file on the network share (make sure you create the link as a UNC path rather than an absolute path) with instructions to click the link to install the patch.

The Compatibility Administrator provides a feature you can use to search the local computer and connected network drives for programs that use compatibility fixes. This is handy when you need to know which applications have already been fixed and the fixes that have been applied to them. To search for fixed programs, choose Search ➤ Fixed Programs. The tool displays a dialog box you use to specify the path to search. Click Find Now when you're ready to perform the search. Figure 7.4 shows the results of a search on a typical Windows XP system.

As Figure 7.2 shows, the new Compatibility Administrator includes additional branches in the left pane for viewing and managing application compatibility fixes. For example, the Applications branch lists applications for which fixes are included in the database. You can expand the branch and click an application to view its settings and fixes (Figure 7.5).

The Compatibility Fixes branch lets you view all the installed fixes and a description of what each fix does (Figure 7.6). When you click a fix in the left pane, the description appears in the right pane.

TIP The Compatibility Modes branch lists the standard predefined compatibility modes and lets you view the fixes assigned to each mode.

FIGURE 7.4
You can use the Compatibility Administrator to search local and network drives for fixed applications.

FIGURE 7.5
Use the Applications branch to view information about applications included in the database and the fixes associated with them.

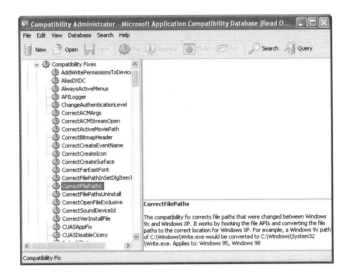

Application Verifier Tool

The latest version of the Application Verifier Tool gives you the means to test programs for compatibility with Windows XP. After you start the tool, click Add (Figure 7.7) to select the program's executable file. Then, in the right pane, select the test settings you want to apply to the program. Click
Run to run the program and allow the Application Verifier Tool to capture any incompatibility problems. Click View Logs to view the log and potential fixes for specific problems the tool encountered
with the selected program.

TIP   See the Help file for the Application Verifier Tool for additional information on testing for program compatibility.

Chapter 8

Adding and Removing OS Components

Unlike most earlier versions of Windows, XP provides no custom Setup option to let you specify which optional components to install and which to omit. Instead, XP's Setup routine installs a one-size-fits-all set of options.

As with almost all clothes, of course, one size never fits all—at least, not comfortably. To get XP working the way you need it to, you're likely to need to add or remove OS components as discussed in this chapter. For example, you might want to add Universal Plug and Play (UPnP) or Print Services for Unix to your installation of XP, or you might want to remove MSN Explorer and all the time-wasting games that the default installation includes.

Even if you're one of the fortunate few whom the standard installation fully satisfies, you'll need to keep your installation of XP up to date to keep it running smoothly and to minimize security and compatibility problems. For this purpose, XP provides the Windows Update feature. You can make Windows Update run automatically, run it manually, or prevent users from running it at all.

Adding and Removing Components

XP includes the Windows Components Wizard, shown in Figure 8.1 (left), for adding and removing components. To run the wizard, log on as an Administrator, display the Add Or Remove Programs window by clicking the Add Or Remove Programs link in Control Panel, and then click the Add/ Remove Windows Components button.

TIP Instead of going through Control Panel and the Add Or Remove Programs window, you can run the Windows Component Wizard by running the program sysocmgr.exe with the /i switch and the location of the *%systemroot%*\inf\sysoc.inf file—for example, **sysocmgr /i:c:\windows\inf\ sysoc.inf**.

Adding Components

The Windows Component Wizard is easy to use. Each selected check box indicates a component that's already installed. Each grayed check box indicates a component that's partially installed. Each cleared check box indicates a component that's not installed.

To add a component, select its check box. If the wizard makes the Details button available, you can click it to display a dialog box in which you can choose subcomponents of the component. For example, Figure 8.1 (right) shows the details dialog for Internet Information Services (IIS), which lets you select the IIS items you want to install. If a subcomponent itself has subcomponents, the wizard makes the Details button available when you select the subcomponent, and you can drill down to the next level to see your choices. (Some components have subcomponents that aren't selected by default, so you'll need to drill down to the Details level to select all the subcomponents if you want to install the full component.)

FIGURE 8.1
The Windows Compo-
nent Wizard is the easiest
way to add and remove
XP components. (left) If
the component has sub-
components, you can
choose those you want to
install. (right).

Once you've chosen the components to add, make sure your XP CD is in the appropriate drive or that your network installation source is available, and click the Next button. The Windows Compo-nent Wizard installs the components, notifies you when it has done so, and returns you to the Add Or Remove Programs window.

Removing Components

The basic way to remove an XP component is, of course, to run the Windows Component Wizard again and clear the check box for the component or subcomponent you want to remove. If another component or service depends on this component or subcomponent, the wizard warns you about the problem and asks if you want to remove the dependent item as well.

NOTE   The Windows Component Wizard removes most components completely when you ask it to. The exception is Internet Explorer, which is too deeply hooked into Windows to be removed. When you choose to remove IE, the wizard deletes its Desktop icon and its entry on the Start menu, but all the program files stay in place. This means "removing" Internet Explorer only gets it out of your interface—you don't save any disk space worth mentioning. (By contrast, removing MSN Explorer nets you a double-handful of megabytes.)

Extending the List of Components in the Windows Component Wizard

As you saw in the previous section, the Windows Component Wizard makes it easy to add and remove components. But it doesn't provide a full list of the components that you can remove. You can remove sev-eral other components, including Automatic Updates, Windows Messenger, and Pinball. (That's right—you can't remove Pinball by removing the other games. Maybe it was a licensing issue.)

WARNING   Before you use this technique to remove components that the Windows Component Wizard hides, run System Restore and create a restore point so that you can easily recover from any side effects XP suffers from the removal of the components.

These are the components you can remove:

Component	Name in `sysoc.inf`
Windows Management Instrumentation	WBEM
Windows Automatic Updates	AutoUpdate
Windows Messenger	msmsgs

Component	Name in `sysoc.inf`
Accessibility Wizard	`AccessOpt`
Multimedia	`MultiM`
Pinball	`Pinball`
WordPad	`MSWordPad`

If you want to remove one of these components, edit the `%systemroot%\inf\sysoc.inf` file in a text editor such as Notepad, and remove the word HIDE from the line that refers to the component you want to remove. For example, the entry for Pinball appears in a line like this:

```
Pinball=ocgen.dll,OcEntry,pinball.inf,HIDE,7
```

Save `sysoc.inf`, and display the Windows Component Wizard again. The previously hidden component or components will appear in the list box.

XP has other components that you can't remove this way, such as COM+ (`com` and `CommApps` in the `sysoc.inf` file), Terminal Server (`TerminalServer`), and Distributed Transaction Coordinator (DTC). Deleting the instance of HIDE in the line that refers to them makes these components appear in the Windows Component Wizard, but you can't deselect their check boxes.

Installing Service Packs and Updates

To keep Windows XP up to date, you need to install any service packs and updates that Microsoft releases to plug security holes, add application compatibility, or add features. XP includes features to check for service packs and updates automatically, but you can check manually if you prefer.

NOTE   Only Administrators can install service packs and run Windows Update.

Using Windows Update

Windows Update is Windows XP's feature that checks automatically for updates and service packs. You can run Windows Update manually or let the Automatic Updates feature check for updates periodically. (You can also prevent the user from running Windows Update. I'll discuss how to do this at the end of the chapter.)

CONFIGURING AND USING THE AUTOMATIC UPDATES FEATURE

Windows XP's Automatic Updates feature is designed to prod you to keep your installation of XP up to date. Depending on the settings you choose, Automatic Updates can automatically check the Windows Update site for critical updates, download them, and present them to you ready for installation.

Automatic Updates initially appears as a nagging icon in the notification area soon after first logon. When you click the icon, Windows XP displays the Automatic Updates Setup Wizard, whose Notification Settings page contains three largely self-explanatory option buttons:

- ◆ "Download the updates automatically and notify me when they are ready to be installed"

- ◆ "Notify me before downloading any updates and notify me again before installing them on my computer"

- ◆ "Turn off automatic updating. I want to update my computer manually"

Once you've dealt with the Automatic Updates Setup Wizard, you can adjust your Automatic Updates settings on the Automatic Updates tab of the System Properties dialog box (right-click My Computer and choose Properties). The Notification Settings group box contains the three option buttons that the Automatic Updates Setup Wizard offers. The Previous Updates group box lets you restore updates you've previously declined.

New!

When you install SP2, the Automatic Updates dialog box changes slightly, but the options are essentially the same as pre-SP2. Only the option names have been changed slightly for SP2.

ACCEPTING OR DECLINING UPDATES

Unless you've turned off automatic updating, Automatic Updates checks the Windows Update Internet site periodically when your Internet connection is open but inactive, to see if new updates are available. When it discovers new updates, Automatic Updates takes the appropriate action depending on the setting you've chosen.

If you chose to download updates automatically, Automatic Update monitors your Internet connection and starts the download when the connection is inactive. If other activity starts on your Internet connection (for example, you start to browse the Web, or your e-mail program checks messages), Automatic Update throttles back its download rate so that it's not hogging all your bandwidth.

When it has downloaded the updates, Automatic Updates displays an Install Reminder icon in the notification area. Double-click the icon to display the Automatic Updates: Ready To Install dialog box.

The three command buttons in the Automatic Updates: Ready to Install dialog box are straightforward:

◆ Clicking the Install button installs all the updates you've downloaded without showing you details of what they are.

◆ Clicking the Details button displays details of the updates and lets you choose which to install. (Again, the default setting is to install all the updates.)

◆ Clicking the Remind Me Later button displays a dialog box that lets you specify a "snooze" time from 30 minutes to 3 days.

If you chose to be notified of available updates without downloading them automatically, you'll see a New Updates Are Ready To Download pop-up from the Windows Update notification area icon. Click the icon to display the Automatic Updates: Updates For Your Computer dialog box (see Figure 8.2), in which you can read brief details of the updates on offer and choose which to download. You can also click the Remind Me Later button to put off downloading the update until a more convenient time.

When you choose to download the updates, Windows Update again uses bandwidth throttling to allow you to use your Internet connection through the download. When the download is finished, Windows Update displays the New Updates Are Ready To Install pop-up in the notification area. Double-click this pop-up or its icon to display the Ready To Install dialog box, and proceed as described earlier in this section.

RESTORING DECLINED UPDATES

If you turn down an update, Windows XP makes available the Restore Declined Updates button on the Automatic Updates tab of the System Properties dialog box. Click this button to make the updates available again.

New!

If you have SP2 installed, the Automatic Updates tab includes a link named Offer Updates Again That I've Previously Hidden. Click this link to display declined updates. This link is dimmed if there are no declined updates.

FIGURE 8.2

In the Automatic Updates: Updates For Your Computer dialog box, choose which updates to download.

PAUSING THE DOWNLOADING OF UPDATES

You can tell when Automatic Updates is downloading updates because the Automatic Updates icon appears in the notification area. If you find your bandwidth has suddenly disappeared, check the notification area for this icon. If necessary, you can pause the downloading of updates by right-clicking the icon and choosing Pause from the shortcut menu. To restart the downloading, right-click the icon and choose Restart.

TURNING OFF THE AUTOMATIC UPDATING SERVICE

Even if you choose the Turn Off Automatic Updating option button, Windows XP continues to run the Automatic Updates service, which is called WUAUSERV. This service supposedly consumes minimal resources, but even so, it won't speed up your computer. Run the Services console, stop the Automatic Updates service, and configure it for Manual startup so that it doesn't run itself the next time you restart XP.

Running Windows Update Manually

To run Windows Update manually, choose Start ➢ All Programs ➢ Windows Update or open Internet Explorer and choose Tools ➢ Windows Update. Internet Explorer displays the Windows Update website (www.windowsupdate.com), from which you scan for updates or perform any of the actions described in the following subsections.

TIP If you're connecting to the Windows Update website through an authenticating proxy that uses NTLM proxy authentication, you may need to select the Use HTTP 1.1 Through Proxy Connection check box on the Advanced page of the Internet Options dialog box in Internet Explorer. (Otherwise, if Internet Explorer uses HTTP 1.0, the Windows Update ActiveX controls don't use the correct keep-alive headers, and NTLM can't authenticate the client.) After you select this check box, close Internet Explorer and restart it for the change to take effect.

REVIEWING YOUR WINDOWS UPDATE HISTORY

To review your Windows Update history, click the View Installation History link on the Windows Update website.

DOWNLOADING UPDATES SO THAT YOU CAN USE THEM ON OTHER COMPUTERS

By default, Windows Update doesn't show you the update files it downloads; instead, it gives you details of their contents and lets you choose whether to install them or pass on them. If you have just one Windows XP computer, this is fine; but if you have two or more, it means that you'll need to download the same updates for each computer. Even if you have enough bandwidth to make minor telecoms' entrails churn with lust, multiple downloads of the same files are a waste of time.

To download the update files in a form in which you can apply them to multiple computers, you need to use the Windows Update Catalog, and you need to use it from a computer running XP (rather than an earlier version of Windows).

To do so, follow these steps:

1. Click the Administrator Options link on the Windows Update website.

2. Click the Windows Update Catalog link on the Administrator Options page.

3. Click the Find Updates For Microsoft Windows Operating Systems link, and use the resulting page to search by operating system. Once you've located the updates, use the Add button to add to your Download Basket the packages you want to download.

4. Click the Go To Download Basket link to display your basket. Specify a download location on your computer, and click Download Now to download the update files.

To install a file you've downloaded, double-click it.

TIP   To install a new device driver on multiple computers with the same configuration, use `unattend.txt` to change the Registry setting of the device driver on the computers.

Preventing Users from Using Windows Update

To prevent users from using Windows Update to update their XP installations, take the following actions under \Local Computer Policy\User Configuration\Administrative Templates in the Group Policy snap-in (Start ➢ Run, enter **gpedit.msc**, and click OK; see the next chapter for details on the MMC):

1. Under \Start Menu And Taskbar, double-click the Remove Links And Access To Window Update item. In the resulting Properties dialog box, select the Enabled option button, and click OK.

2. Under \Windows Components\Windows Update, double-click the Remove Access To Use All Windows Update Features item. In the resulting Properties dialog box, select the Enabled option button, and click OK.

3. Under \Control Panel\Add/Remove Programs, double-click the Hide "Add Programs From Microsoft" Option item. In the resulting Properties dialog box, select the Enabled option button, and click OK.

XP then removes the Windows Update entries from the Start menu and from Internet Explorer's Tools menu, and blocks users from accessing the Windows Update website manually. (The user can go to the Windows Update website, but they receive an Access Denied message that prevents them from accessing any updates.)

Showing or Hiding Components with SP2

New!

Windows XP SP2 simplifies the view in the Add or Remove Programs window by hiding Windows XP updates (such as those installed by Windows Update). If you want to view these updates to review them or remove a particular update, you can un-hide the updates with the Show Updates check box on the Add or Remove Programs window. Select this check box to show updates; clear the check box to hide them.

Chapter 9

Using and Customizing MMC Consoles

The Microsoft Management Console (MMC) is the framework around which most of the tools used to manage Windows XP are built. You use it to create, save, and open collections of administrative tools, called *consoles*. Consoles contain items such as snap-ins, extension snap-ins, monitor controls, tasks, wizards, and documentation required to manage many of the hardware, software, and networking components of your Windows system. You can add items to an existing MMC console, or you can create new consoles and configure them to administer a specific system component.

You need to understand one thing right off the bat: MMC consoles, by themselves, don't perform any administrative functions. Instead, they provide a backdrop that hosts tools that do. The primary type of tool you can add to a console is called a *snap-in*. Other items that you can add include ActiveX controls, links to web pages, folders, taskpad views, and tasks.

The MMC provides a standardized look and feel for all the Windows XP, 2000, and 2003 management tools, which is similar to the look and feel you may be familiar with from working with the file-management utility Windows Explorer. Of course, Windows Explorer, in its current iteration, has been around since Windows 95, so it's assumed that all Windows users are comfortable with this interface. The MMC interface also isn't new to the latest versions of the Windows operating systems. MMC consoles began making their first appearances with some of the BackOffice products installed on the NT 4 platform, such as SQL Server 7, SMS 2, and IIS 4. Thus, the MMC tools should be nothing new to most NT 4 administrators.

One advantage of the MMC interface is that it can run on all Windows 9*x* and Windows NT operating systems, allowing you to manage services running on more advanced Windows operating systems from down-level clients.

Many additional benefits are associated with the MMC management interface, including the following:

◆ It's highly customizable.

◆ You can save and share MMC consoles with other administrators, and you can send snap-ins as e-mail attachments.

◆ You can use most snap-ins for remote computer management.

◆ You can configure permissions so that MMC runs in author mode, which an administrator can manage, or in user mode, which limits what users can access.

In this chapter, we'll look at how you can more effectively use this vital management interface. I'll describe the various MMC components, show you how to create your own MMC tools to better manage your individual networks, and discuss the modes in which you can work with an MMC and the implications of each.

Working with the MMC

Windows XP comes with several preconfigured MMC consoles from which you can do the bulk of administration on any system. One of the first MMC consoles that users new to XP are likely to work with is the Computer Management snap-in. You can open Computer Management, which is shown in Figure 9.1, in a couple of ways:

◆ Choose Start ➢ Control Panel ➢ Performance And Maintenance ➢ Administrative Tools ➢ Computer Management.

◆ Right-click My Computer, and choose Manage from the shortcut menu.

Several snap-ins have been added to this preconfigured console. But before I discuss these snap-ins, let's look at a little terminology regarding the MMC. You're likely to hear the parts of the MMC referred to by various names, so there's nothing definitive about the following:

Console tree   This display shows the organization of the console and allows for easy navigation between the snap-ins.

Details pane   This pane displays information related to the currently selected item in the console tree. You can take care of many administrative tasks using the Details pane.

Action menu   The Action menu provides commands specific to the current snap-in or the currently selected item in the console tree. In other words, the Action menu contains a list of *actions* that can be performed on the selection.

View menu   This menu allows you to choose between several ways of displaying information, like its counterpart in Windows Explorer. The View menu might also include a Customize command, which lets you hide or display the console tree, among other things.

Shortcut menus   Shortcut menus contain only items relevant to the current context. When in doubt, right-click. You'll likely find that the easiest way to carry out an administrative function is to right-click an item and choose a command from the shortcut menu.

FIGURE 9.1

The Computer Management snap-in is preconfigured in Windows XP.

If you're familiar with the NT administrative tools, you're also aware of how different (and much easier to use) the MMC tools are than previous utilities, such as Server Manager and User Manager for Domains. Using the NT administrative tools required that you memorize all the available menus these utilities provided. Conversely, you can use the MMC consoles intuitively by examining the contents of a snap-in's console tree.

Creating a Custom MMC Console

Although creating a specialized snap-in for the MMC requires knowledge of ActiveX programming, creating a custom MMC console requires no programming background whatsoever. All you have to know is how to point and click. To begin to create your own consoles that contain only the administrative tools you commonly need, open a blank MMC and add one or more of the snap-ins available on your system. Remember that by itself, the MMC has no functionality; it's just scaffolding around which the management tools are designed. The management usefulness of the MMC depends on which snap-in is loaded.

On Windows XP computers, you can open a blank MMC console (see Figure 9.2) by choosing Start ➢ Run to open the Run dialog box, typing **mmc** in the Open box, and pressing Enter. When you run this command, you'll experience firsthandthe concept I presented earlier: a blank MMC console is useless until a snap-in provides it with functionality.

FIGURE 9.2
A blank MMC console awaits further instructions.

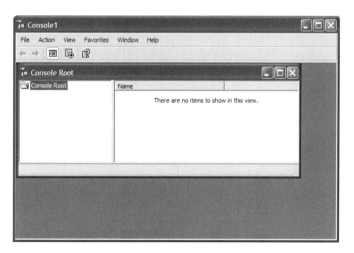

Now it's time to give the console something to work on. To add a snap-in to an MMC, follow these steps:

1. From the MMC console window, choose File ➢ Add/Remove Snap-in to open the Add/Remove Snap-in dialog box.

2. Click the Add button to open the Add Standalone Snap-in dialog box.

3. Select the snap-in you want to add, and click the Add button.

4. At this point, you may be asked which computer you want to manage. In most instances, select the local computer. If necessary, click Finish when you have made your choice.

5. The fun part is that you can keep repeating steps 2, 3, and 4 to add more snap-ins. In this way, you can create a single MMC that gathers all the tools you commonly use into a single location.

6. After you add the snap-ins you want and click Close, you can save the console. Choose File ➢ Save As to open the Save As dialog box. Enter a name for your console, which will be saved with an `.msc` extension by default.

You can save this newly created, customized console anywhere; but one especially useful place to save it is right on the Desktop, where it becomes part of the user profile for the current user. An administrator can then access the custom MMC tool anywhere in a domain environment by implementing a roaming profile. From then on, the administrator need only double-click a single icon on the Desktop to perform all day-to-day administrative tasks.

User Mode versus Author Mode

We've just looked at how to create an MMC console that you can call your own. But you can assign several options to the custom console as you're creating it, and these options define the functionality of the MMC when it's used. There are two general-access options: author mode and user mode. There is one level of author mode, and there are three levels of user mode:

◆ Author mode

◆ User mode, full access

◆ User mode, limited access, multiple window

◆ User mode, limited access, single window

You configure these options in the Options dialog box. When you first open a blank MMC, the default option is set to author mode (if it weren't, you wouldn't be able to add snap-ins). To set the MMC console options for a previously saved MMC, open a blank MMC console and then follow these steps:

1. Choose File ➢ Open, right-click the `.msc` file, and choose Author from the shortcut menu. You can also choose Start ➢ Run to open the Run dialog box, and in the Open box enter `mmc path\filename.msc /a`, if you like to type. Either way, the selected console opens in author mode.

2. Choose File ➢ Options to open the Options dialog box, as shown in Figure 9.3.

3. To change the default mode for which the console is saved, in the Console Mode drop-down list box, select the appropriate mode.

The choices in the Console Mode drop-down list box have the following implications:

Author Mode   You can assign author mode to grant full access to all MMC functionality. Doing so grants users who use this MMC the ability to add other snap-ins, add items to the Favorites menu, and so on.

User Mode - Full Access   All window-management commands and full access to the console tree are provided, but a user is prevented from adding or removing snap-ins or changing the console properties.

User Mode - Limited Access, Multiple Window   Users can create new windows but can't close windows that were visible when the console was saved.

FIGURE 9.3
You can switch between user mode and author mode using the Options dialog box.

User Mode - Limited Access, Single Window This mode prevents users from opening additional console windows, as the name implies. Users see only the window that was visible when the console was saved.

How console changes are saved depends on the mode in which you're working. When you're working with a console in author mode, you're prompted to save your changes when exiting the console. However, when you're working with a console in user mode, changes may be automatically saved. Saving changes is automatic when you close the console if you've cleared the Do Not Save Changes To This Console check box in the Options dialog box.

If the default console mode for the console is one of the user modes, do the following:

◆ To prevent users from editing the console, select the Do Not Save Changes To This Console check box.

◆ To enable users to access the Customize View dialog box, select the Allow The User To Customize Views check box.

However, the MMC console always opens in author mode, ignoring the default opening settings when any of the following apply:

◆ The MMC is already open.

◆ A console has been opened from a shortcut menu.

◆ A console has been opened using the /a switch in the Run dialog box.

TIP If it becomes annoying to see the message "Save console settings to..." every time you close a console that was opened in author mode, you can specify that changes to the console should be saved every time you close the MMC. To do so, set the default mode for the console to one of the user modes, and clear the Do Not Save Changes To This Console check box in the Options dialog box.

Keep in mind that the preconfigured MMC tools are meant to give you easy access to the most commonly performed management tasks without the hassle of adding snap-ins to an MMC each time you want to do something. Probably the best way to use an MMC is to make your own MMC with the snap-ins you commonly use and then always use that tool. Doing so prevents your having to open multiple preconfigured MMC consoles when you have more than one task to manage. Some preconfigured consoles give you access to one snap-in; others, such as Computer Management, give you access to several.

Creating and Using Taskpads

A *taskpad* is a customized page that appears in the Details pane of an MMC snap-in. The big advantage of the taskpad view is that you can create icons that represent several menus, shortcuts, command strings, and/or scripts. Think of taskpads as MMC shortcuts. Just as a Desktop shortcut hides several commands that would be necessary to open a file or run an executable, the icons on the taskpad can hide several steps to achieve a desired administrative goal.

You can create taskpad views as you're setting up your custom MMC consoles, or you can use previously saved consoles. You can't, however, create taskpad views in any of the preconfigured MMC consoles. To create a taskpad view on an existing MMC, open the saved console in author mode using one of the methods discussed earlier, and then follow these steps:

1. In the console tree, select a snap-in item.

2. Choose Action ➢ New Taskpad View (or right-click the snap-in item and choose New Taskpad View from the shortcut menu) to start the New Taskpad View Wizard, shown in Figure 9.4.

3. Follow the on-screen instructions.

This procedure only sets up the taskpad view; it doesn't create any tasks. If you want to create tasks immediately after you create the taskpad view, make sure the Start New Task Wizard check box is checked (it is by default) in the final screen of the wizard.

FIGURE 9.4
The New Taskpad View Wizard helps you create a taskpad view.

Furthermore, you can add or change tasks to the taskpad view at any time. To add a task, follow these steps:

1. In the console tree, right-click the taskpad view, and choose Edit Taskpad View from the short-cut menu to open the Taskpad Properties dialog box.

2. Click the Task tab to display a list of tasks from the selected taskpad view.

3. Click New to start the New Task Wizard, which steps you through the process. Figure 9.5 shows a screen from the New Task Wizard.

NOTE To change an existing task, click the Edit button in the Task tab.

Now, a real-world note about taskpad views: I haven't seen them used often. Because the interface of the MMC is so common for users of the Windows platform, it's easy for most administrators, and even most end users, to learn to use. The prevailing design objective behind the taskpad view is that a taskpad might make it easier for novice users to perform their jobs. For instance, you can add applicable tasks to a taskpad view and then hide the console tree. Users can then begin using tools before they're familiar with the location of particular items in the console tree or operating system.

With that in mind, ask yourself: How often do you delegate administrative tasks to novice users? Probably not often. So even though taskpad views are relatively easy to set up, and adding tasks is simply a matter of stepping through a wizard, you may not find it worth the extra effort to create a taskpad and a task when the MMC by itself is so easy to use.

FIGURE 9.5
Use the New Task Wizard
to add or change tasks.

Chapter 10

It's All About Control: Tools and Techniques for Managing Services

Although the average user doesn't have to deal with services in Windows XP much, if at all, power users often need to manage services. For example, you might need to install an application and configure it as a service so it will start automatically when Windows XP starts. Or perhaps you need to configure the account that a service uses to interact with the system. You might even need to start or stop services running on a computer across the network—or even on the other side of the planet.

Like Windows 2000, Windows XP provides a Services MMC console you can use to manage services for both local and remote computers. In this chapter, I explain how to work with the Services console to start, stop, configure, and perform other management tasks for services. You'll also learn about command-line utilities and techniques you can use to manage services both locally and remotely.

Overview of Services

Many core features in Windows XP are implemented as *services*. A service is a process or set of processes that provides support to other applications. In general terms, a service is an application that performs a specific function in the operating system. Some functions implemented by services include logon, networking, the file system, memory management, scheduling, and print spooling, to name only a few. Most devices in Windows XP are implemented as services through their device drivers.

One of the reasons for implementing operating-system functions and applications as services is to allow the OS to manage them automatically. You can configure services for three different startup modes: automatic, manual, and disabled. The automatic and manual modes let Windows XP or other services start a given service.

TIP   Services can also run without requiring user intervention to start or stop the service, and they can run when no user is logged on.

A second reason for structuring the operating system around services is to provide to the OS a high degree of modularity. Services allow the operating system to be built of relatively small and easily manageable core components that can be replaced, upgraded, or supplemented easily without affecting other OS components. The NTFS file system, for example, is implemented as a service. Other services interact with NTFS to provide other functions. For example, Encrypting File System is a separate service that works in conjunction with NTFS to handle file and folder encryption and decryption.

Another reason for implementing applications as services is to let them interact with the operating system within a given security context. Most services interact with the OS using the System account, but in some situations you might use a different account for a particular service. For example, the components of a server application such as Exchange Server sometimes require security settings different from the System account or other account under which it might run. You can create an account with the necessary rights and privileges and let the application use that account to log on and interact with the system.Why is it important to understand services and how to manage them? If you're a casual user, it probably isn't important. If you need to more closely manage your system or other systems across the network, however, managing services is a core administrative task. You might need to disable a service that is preventing a system from booting properly. You might need to stop a service temporarily while you make system changes. Or maybe you need to install or remove a service. Whatever the case, Windows XP provides a handful of different resources to help you accomplish these tasks. The one you'll use most often is the Services console.

Tips for Working in the Services Console

The Services console is the tool you'll use most often to manage services locally. Services is a snap-in under the Computer Management console. To open the Computer Management console, right-click My Computer on the Start menu and choose Manage. Then, expand the Services And Applications branch to access the Services branch. You can also click Start ➢ All Programs ➢ Administrative Tools ➢ Services to open this console as a stand-alone console, as shown in Figure 10.1.

NOTE This chapter covers most, but not all, of the options and functions in the Services console. For information on creating a custom view in the Services console, see the discussion of taskpads in Chapter 9.

FIGURE 10.1

Use the Services console to manage services.

Managing the View

One change in the Services console from Windows 2000 is the addition of the Extended tab in the right pane. In this view (called a *taskpad*), Windows XP gives you additional information about the selected service, as well as quick links to start and stop the service. The Standard view lists only the five standard columns for each service: Name, Description, Status, Startup Type, and Log On As.

TIP Choose View and then select a different view option to switch among Details (the default view), Large Icons, Small Icons, and List.

By default, the Services console sorts the services by the Name column, which is useful when you want to work with a specific service. However, you can sort the console using the other columns, as well. For example, whenever I reboot a server, I like to check the Services console to verify that all the services configured for Automatic startup are running. The easiest way to do that is to click the Startup Type column to re-sort the service list, as shown in Figure 10.2. I can scan through the list, looking at the Automatic services to make sure they're all started.

NOTE For details on customizing the MMC console, see Chapter 9.

Exporting the List of Services

Occasionally you might find it useful to be able to export a list of the services on a system. For example, maybe you want to create a support database that provides additional information about each service for your support staff and advanced users. Or maybe you need to create a report and include a service list in it.

You can use the Services console to export a list of a system's services to a text file. To do so, open the console and choose Action ➤ Export List to open the Export List dialog box. Select a path and file name for the text file, and then select the desired file format from the Save As Type drop-down list. You can choose either comma-delimited or tab-delimited, in either ASCII or Unicode, depending on the requirements of the application in which you'll be using or importing the list. Click Save to save the file.

FIGURE 10.2
Sort the Services console by Startup Type to quickly determine if all automatic services are started.

TIP   Choose the format for the exported text file according to the application in which you'll use the data. Most database and spreadsheet programs can import both tab- and comma-delimited files.

Configuring Service Startup

Each service has several properties, one of which is its startup type. The startup type determines how (or if) the service can be started. You can configure a service for one of these types:

Automatic   This startup type causes the service to start when the system starts.

Manual   Services with this startup type can be started manually by a user or automatically by a dependent service. They don't start automatically when the system starts.

Disabled   This startup type prevents the service from being started by a user, the system, or a dependent service.

NOTE   The Start button on the General tab of the service's property sheet is dimmed if the startup type is set to Disabled. If you need to start a disabled service, first set its startup type to Manual.

If you want a service to start automatically when the system starts, set its startup type to Automatic. For example, you might want to be able to receive faxes through the Fax service, so you would configure it for Automatic startup. Using this same example, you could set the Fax service to Manual or Disabled if you didn't want the computer to receive faxes.

To configure service startup, open the Services console and double-click the service you want to manage. On the General tab (Figure 10.3 on the left), select the desired type from the Startup Type drop-down list. If you have no other changes to make, click OK to close the dialog box.

TIP   You can set service properties through Recovery Console as well as the Services console, which is handy when you need to disable a service that is preventing a normal boot. See the section "Managing Services from a Console" later in this chapter for more details. See Chapter 40 for details on RC.

FIGURE 10.3
Configure service start-up on the General page. (left) And you can enable or disable a service for a particular hardware profile on the Log On tab. (right)

In addition to configuring startup for a service, you can enable or disable a service for a specific hardware profile. For example, you might want your notebook to receive faxes when it's connected to a docking station at the office but not when you're on the road. So, you could disable the Fax service for the computer's Undocked profile.

To configure service behavior for a hardware profile, open the Services console and then open the properties for the service. Click the Log On tab (Figure 10.3, right), select the hardware profile, and click Enable or Disable, as needed.

Configuring Service Logon

Each service interacts with the system within a specific security context. Most services log on using the SYSTEM account, and generally that's fine. In some situations, however, you might want to change the account that a service uses to authenticate with the operating system.

You configure service logon through the Log On tab of the service's properties, shown in Figure 10.3. The following list explains the options on this page that apply to service logon:

Local System Account   Select this option to have the service log on using the local SYSTEM account.

Allow Service To Interact With Desktop   Select this option if you want to be able to interact with the service when it's running.

This Account   Use this option to specify an account other than SYSTEM for service logon.

Browse   Click this option to display the Select User dialog box (Figure 10.4), which you use to select a local user or built-in security principal for the service.

Password/Confirm Password   Enter and confirm the password associated with the account you specified with the This Account option.

FIGURE 10.4
Use the Select User dialog box to browse for and choose the account you want to use for the service.

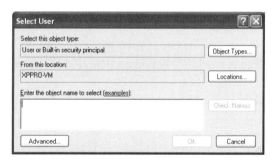

TIP   You don't have to browse for an account if you already know the account name. Just click in the text box beside the This Account option, and enter the account name.

Configuring Recovery Options

You'll find that most services keeping running fine once they're started. Occasionally, however, a service might fail because of problems with the service itself or with an application that relies on the service. In most cases, you don't want the service to just stop and not attempt to recover from the failure; rather, you want it to attempt a restart, generate a notification, or take other appropriate action. You can configure *service recovery* to help Windows XP handle service failures gracefully.

You configure service recovery through the Recovery tab of the service's properties sheet. As Figure 10.5 shows, you can specify the action that Windows XP takes for the first failure instance, for the second failure, and for subsequent failures. Your choices here are described in the following sections.

FIGURE 10.5
Use the Recovery tab to specify how a service should react to a service failure.

Service Failure Options

You can choose an option for each failure situation. These options are as follows:

Take No Action   Windows XP doesn't attempt to recover or restart the service.

Restart The Service   Windows XP attempts to restart the service after a failure.

Run A Program   Windows XP executes the program you specify in the Run Program section of the tab.

Reboot The Computer   Windows XP reboots the computer if the service fails.

Use the Reset Fail Count After option to specify, in days, when Windows XP should reset the fail counter for the service back to zero. If you select Restart The Service for one of the three failure events, use the Restart Service After option to specify the number of minutes you want Windows XP to wait before restarting the service. Increase this value if the system needs time to stabilize after the service fails or if the service has dependent services that stop when it fails, giving the other services time to stop before you restart this one.

The Run A Program Option

The ability to run a program on a service failure can be a valuable tool for handling the service shutdown gracefully. For example, you might use a program to generate an e-mail or pager notification when the service fails, so you'll know about it right away. This is generally more important with servers than with workstations, but the ability is there in Windows XP Professional and Windows XP Home Edition, nonetheless.

To run a program upon service failure, follow these steps:

1. Select the Run A Program option for the desired failure (first, second, or subsequent).

2. Click in the Program text box and enter the path to the program's executable file, or click Browse to browse for it.

3. If the program requires additional command-line parameters (such as an e-mail address or pager number), enter that information in the Command Line Parameters text box.

4. If the program accepts the fail count as a command-line parameter, select the option Append Fail Count To End Of Command Line. Windows XP appends /fail=fc to the command, where fc is replaced by the fail count. This allows the specified program to carry out a particular action based on the fail-count value.

NOTE A program must be written specifically to handle the /fail switch. If not, the script or program will simly ignore the parameter.

The Restart The Computer Option

If you choose the option Restart The Computer for a service, Windows XP will reboot the computer if the service fails. You can configure options that specify how soon the computer reboots and whether it generates a message before it restarts. For example, assume you're using a Windows XP Professional computer as a file server for a small network. You want everyone on the network to receive a notice five minutes before the server reboots, giving them time to save their documents.

To configure these options, follow these steps:

1. Select Restart The Computer from the drop-down list, and then click Restart Computer Options to display the Restart Computer Options dialog box.

2. Specify the number of minutes for the restart delay, and select the Before Restart option.

3. Type in the text box the message you want others to receive when the service fails. Windows XP automatically provides a default message that you can edit as needed.

4. Click OK, and close the service's dialog box.

TIP Other computers must be running the Alerter service to receive notifications. For that reason, you might want to configure the Alerter service on all computers for Automatic startup type.

Managing Services Remotely

You aren't limited to managing only services on the local computer. In many situations, you might need to manage services for other computers across the network. For example, maybe you need to turn on the Alerter service for all the computers in the office, but you don't want to have to go to each one physically to do so. Instead, you can start or configure the service remotely from your own workstation.

Configuring Remote Service with the Services Console

You can use the Services console on the local computer to manage services on a remote computer. You have most of the same options and capabilities managing a remote computer as you do when managing the local computer.

To manage a remote computer's services through the Services console, follow these steps:

1. Open the Computer Management console on your local computer. You can right-click My Computer and choose Manage to open the console.

2. In the console, right-click the Computer Management (Local) branch in the left pane and choose Connect To Another Computer to display the Select Computer dialog box (Figure 10.6).

3. Enter the computer name in the dialog box, or click Browse to browse the network for the computer.

4. After you connect to the remote computer, the branch name changes in the Computer Management console to Computer Management (*computer*), where *computer* is the name of the computer you're managing.

At this point, you can manage services just as you would for the local computer. Double-click the service in question and set its properties as needed through its dialog box.

FIGURE 10.6
Use the Select Computer dialog box to choose a different computer to manage.

Managing Remote Services from a Console

A second method for managing remote services is to use a console session. However, this requires one of two approaches: either the remote computer must be running as a Telnet server, or you need to use a utility included in the Windows XP Resource Kit.

To use the Telnet approach, you first need to configure the remote computer to function as a Telnet server. Once the remote computer is running the Telnet service, you can open a Telnet session on your local computer to the remote computer. The Telnet session is essentially a remote console session. You can then use the `net` command to start, stop, and otherwise manage services. (The `net` command is explained in a later section, "Managing Services from a Console.")

NOTE   Chapter 33 explains the ins and outs of setting up a Telnet server.

A second approach is to use the NETSVC.EXE utility included in the Windows XP Resource Kit. You can use `netsvc` to list installed services, query service status, and start, stop, pause, and continue a service on a remote computer. The syntax for the `netsvc` command is

```
netsvc servicename \\computername /command
```

TIP The Microsoft Windows XP Resource Kit is available directly from Microsoft and from book and software retailers. You can view the Resource Kit documentation online and download Resource Kit tools from the Microsoft site at `http://www.microsoft.com/technet/prodtechnol/winxp-pro/default.mspx`.

For example, you would use the following command to start the Alerter service on a computer named SNOOPY:

```
netsvc alerter \\SNOOPY /start
```

TIP If you're not sure of a particular service's name, use the `/list` parameter to view the list of installed services.

When you use `netsvc`, keep in mind that many services have a display name that is different from their service name. For example, the Internet Connection Sharing service (the display name) has the service name SharedAccess. You can use either the display name or the service name with `netsvc`. Just enclose the display name in quotes if it contains spaces.

TIP For a complete list of `netsvc` commands and its syntax, execute the command **netsvc /?** in a console.

Managing Services with Remote Desktop Connection

A third option for managing services remotely is Remote Desktop Connection, which allows a client running any version of Windows XP to connect to a computer running Windows XP Professional or a server platform, such as Windows 2000 Server, with Terminal Services installed. In the case of Windows XP Professional, the remote computer must have Remote Desktop Connection enabled for incoming connections.

NOTE You enable incoming remote connections through the Remote tab of the properties for My Computer. See Chapter 23 for detailed information on configuring and using Remote Desktop Connection.

When you connect to a Windows 2000 Professional computer with Remote Desktop Connection, the remote computer's current local logon session is terminated. So, using this method works best if no one is using the computer at the time or the user won't be inconvenienced by being kicked off while you manage the services. Use one of the methods described in the preceding two sections if you don't want to force the remote user to log off.

TIP You manage services through Remote Desktop Connection the same way you manage local services. Open the Services console after you establish the remote connection, or open a console and use console commands to manage the services.

Using Remote Assistance to Manage Services

You can use the Remote Assistance feature in Windows XP to manage services remotely. However, this method requires that both the local and remote computers be set up with Microsoft .NET Passports (`www.passport.com`), and the remote user must request assistance from you. This method is useful when you need to configure services across the Internet and don't have a VPN or Telnet connection to the remote computer.

Managing Services from a Console

You can manage services from a command console as well as from the Services GUI console. Using a command console is a good option if you prefer to work in the console rather than the GUI or if you need to manage services through a Telnet session. You can manage services from a console in a regular Windows XP session or from the Recovery Console. Your options are different for each scenario.

Managing Services in a Windows XP Session

You use the `net` command to manage services from a command console, whether that console is running on the local computer or you are connected to a remote computer through a Telnet session. The `net start` command lets you view a list of running services and start a service that is currently stopped. Use `net start` by itself to view the list of running services, or use the following syntax to start a service:

```
net start ServiceName
```

Replace *ServiceName* with the service or display name of the service. If you specify the display name, enclose it in quotes if it contains spaces.

To stop a service, use the `net stop` command:

```
net stop ServiceName
```

Replace *ServiceName* with the service or display name of the service you want to stop.

Managing Services from Recovery Console

Recovery Console (RC) provides a somewhat different set of tools for managing services. The `disable` command, for example, lets you disable a service. This has the same effect as setting its startup type to Disabled in the GUI. Use the following syntax to disable a service or device driver: `disable name`. Replace *name* with the name of the service or device driver you want to disable.

You can use the `enable` command to enable a service that is currently disabled. Unlike the `disable` command, `enable` offers a few options. The syntax for `enable` is

```
enable {ServiceName | DeviceDriverName} [StartupType]
```

Replace *ServiceName* or *DeviceDriverName* with the name of the service or device driver you want to enable. Then, specify one of the following for *StartupType*:

SERVICE_BOOT_START   Use this option to start a device driver when the system boots.

SERVICE_SYSTEM_START   Use this option to start a device driver when Windows XP starts.

SERVICE_AUTO_START   This option corresponds to the Automatic startup type in the GUI.

SERVICE_DEMAND_START   This option corresponds to the Manual startup type in the GUI.

The third RC command you can use to manage services is `listsvc`, which lists the services available on the computer. The `listsvc` command has no options or parameters, but you can pipe it to the `more` command to display one page at a time:

```
listsvc | more
```

NOTE   See Chapter 40 for details on installing and using Recovery Console.

Chapter 11

Monitoring Events

The Windows XP operating system could be considered a busy place, with events of all kinds happening all the time. Some of those events are routine, and some aren't. One key to good system management is to keep a historical record of the routine events and know when nonroutine events occur so you can respond to them. Windows XP provides two main tools for monitoring events: the Event Viewer and Dr. Watson.

The Event Viewer lets you view events related to the system, applications, and security. Some server applications add their own event logs to the system, and you can view these with the Event Viewer, as well. Applications running under Windows XP Professional or Home Edition, however, are unlikely to have their own event logs but instead will log their events to the global Application event log. This chapter will help you become more familiar with the Windows XP logs, the information they contain, and how to manage those logs.

Dr. Watson, on the other hand, is a debugging tool. Unless you're a programmer, it's unlikely that you'll do much with Dr. Watson other than collect some debugging information to send to a technical support engineer. This chapter explains how to do that with Dr. Watson and will help you understand some of the information it gathers.

Tips for Working in the Event Viewer

You can open the Event Viewer as a stand-alone console (Figure 11.1) or as a snap-in in the Computer Management console. Double-click the Event Viewer in the Administrative Tools folder to open the Event Viewer, or right-click My Computer, choose Manage, and click the Event Viewer branch.

TIP The Administrative Tools folder doesn't appear on the Start menu or in the All Programs menu by default. You can turn on the Administrative Tools menu through the properties for the Taskbar. Right-click the Start Menu and choose Properties, click Customize ➢ Advanced, and scroll to the bottom of the Start menu items list to choose an option from the System Administrative Tools group.

As Figure 11.1 shows, there are three standard logs: Application, Security, and System. The Application log is where applications—including many of the accessories and tools included with Windows XP—write status, error, and other information. This is the log you'll use most often when you're trying to troubleshoot a problem with an application.

The Security log maintains security-related events such as logon, logoff, policy change, and a variety of other security/authentication events. You'll use this log to track when other users connect to your computer and monitor other aspects of system security.

NOTE Chapter 13 explains how to configure auditing, which allows you to monitor specific actions such as disk access, logon/logoff, and other important system events and changes.

FIGURE 11.1
Use the Event Viewer to view information about events that occur in Windows XP.

The System log maintains system-wide events that aren't related specifically to security or an application. For example, the System log keeps track of when services start and stop, when the system is rebooted, when Remote Assistance sessions start and stop, and many other system-related events. You'll use the System log when troubleshooting system-wide problems, such as a service failing.

To view an event's properties, double-click the event, or select the event and choose Action ➤ Properties. Figure 11.2 shows a typical event Properties dialog box.

FIGURE 11.2
An event's Properties dialog box shows date, time, event ID, and other information about the event.

The event's dialog box contains several items of information about the event:

Date/Time   These two fields show the date and time the event occurred. The Event Viewer by default sorts the event list by date and time, with the most recent events at the top.

Type   This field shows the type of event being logged. The Event Log uses five different event types:

Error   An error indicates a problem that could cause lost data or lost functionality, such as a service failing to start or a service shutting down.

Warning   A warning indicates an item that could cause problems but isn't as significant as an error. Examples of events that generate a warning are a disk nearing capacity and the time service being unable to synchronize with a time server.

Information   These offer information about successful events for an application, service, or driver. For example, when a service starts successfully, Windows XP logs an Information event to the System log.

Success Audit   These mark successful security events such as logon, logoff, and audited disk access.

Failure Audit   These mark unsuccessful security events. Failure Audit events give you an easy way to monitor for attempted security breaches and troubleshoot authentication and other security-related problems.

User/Computer   The User field indicates the security context in which the event occurred. Most system services run in the context of the System account, and events related to these services list the System account as the user. Application events typically list the application name. The Computer field indicates the computer on which the event occurred. This is almost always the name of the local computer unless you're managing a remote computer's event logs.

Source   This field lists the application or system component that generated the event. For example, when you install a new application from a Windows Installer package, you'll probably see at least a corresponding event with MsInstaller as the source. Service Control Manager is another common source. Almost all service-related events have Service Control Manager as the source.

Category   This field is used most by the Security log, but it can appear in the other logs, as well. This field categorizes the event with labels such as Policy Change, System Event, and Account Logon.

Event ID   This field uniquely identifies a specific event. For example, a successful account logon is event ID 680, and event ID 7036 indicates a successful service startup. The event ID is useful for identifying specific problems and troubleshooting events. For example, you can search the Microsoft Knowledge Base for specific event IDs associated with a particular component, application, or service to help determine the exact cause of the problem.

Description   This field usually offers the most information. For example, the Description field for a successful audit logon/logoff event lists the user, domain, and other authentication properties for the logon event. Think of the Description field as providing details about the event.

Managing the View

The Event Viewer, like most Microsoft Management Console consoles, lets you sort the view using the various columns displayed in the log. For example, you can click the Date or Time field to sort the view by that field. When you're looking for events with a specific ID, you can click the Event column to sort the event list.

TIP   You can choose View ➢ Newest First or Oldest First to specify the chronological order of events in the list.

In addition to sorting the view by column, you can also specify which columns the Event Viewer displays. To do so, select a log and choose View ➢ Add/Remove Columns; use the resulting dialog box to add or remove columns from the view. Select a column and use the Move Up and Move Down buttons to change the column order. For example, you might prefer to have the Date column displayed first rather than the Type column.

Filtering the List

When you're trying to troubleshoot a problem or locate specific events, you can simplify the task by *filtering* the event log. For example, you might want to view only errors and warnings. Or maybe you want to find all events with a specific ID, or all events generated by a specific source. To set a filter, open the log you want to use and choose View ➢ Filter to open a properties sheet similar to the one shown in Figure 11.3.

FIGURE 11.3
Use the Filter tab to specify filter criteria for the view.

The options on the Filter tab are mostly self-explanatory. Select the event type(s) you want to include in the view, and then select source, category, or other criteria to define the filter. Click OK to apply the filter and modify the view. To clear the filter, choose View ➢ All Records.

Using Multiple Views of a Log

In some situations, it's helpful to be able to view the contents of the log in more than one way at a time. For example, maybe you want to view errors in one view and warnings in another. Whatever the case, you can easily open a new view and configure its view settings as needed. To open a new view, select a log and choose Action ➢ New Log View. Or right-click a log and choose New Log View. Select a view and click the Delete button on the toolbar to close the extra view.

NOTE   You can't delete the standard views.

Managing Log Settings

Each log has several settings that determine how large the log can be, what happens when the maximum size is reached, the log's display name and location on disk, and other properties. The default size for each log is 512 KB, and Event Viewer overwrites events when the maximum size is reached. If you're concerned with monitoring system security or keeping a longer historical record of the events that occur on a particular computer, you should modify the log settings.

To change log settings, right-click a log in the left pane and choose Properties, or select the log and choose Action ➢ Properties to open its properties sheet (Figure 11.4). You can change the following options on the General tab:

Display Name   This is the name that appears for the log in the left pane of the Event Viewer.

Log Name   Use this field to specify the path to the log file and the file name. The default location is the *%systemroot%*\system32\config folder.

Maximum Log Size   Use this control to specify the maximum size for the log. There is no direct correlation between maximum log size and any time period. A misbehaving service or application could fill a large log file within minutes (although this isn't common). Set the size according to the amount of space you want to allocate to the log. I typically use a log size of 4 MB on a server and the default 512 KB size for workstations.

Overwrite Events As Needed   Choose this option to allow the Event Viewer to overwrite old events with new ones when the log reaches the maximum capacity.

Overwrite Events Older Than *n* Days   Choose this option to allow the Event Viewer to overwrite events older than the specified number of days when the log reaches the maximum capacity. This option lets you specify a time window for the log.

Do Not Overwrite Events   Choose this option if you don't want the Event Viewer to overwrite any events. You'll have to clear the log manually when it reaches maximum capacity.

Use A Low-Speed Connection   Use this option if you're viewing the log across a slow connection such as a dial-up. The Event Viewer won't automatically download event information when this option is in effect; instead it waits until you open an event.

Restore Defaults   Click to restore the log to its default settings.

Clear Log   Click to clear all events from the log.

TIP   You should save the contents of the log to a file before clearing it, as explained in the next section.

Managing Log Files

As I explained in the previous section, the Windows XP event logs have a specific size limit. When the log reaches that limit, the system takes one of three actions: It overwrites the oldest events with new events, overwrites events older than a specified number of days, or doesn't overwrite events at all. In the last case, Windows XP displays a message that the log is full. It's then up to you to clear the log so Windows can log additional events.

FIGURE 11.4

Use the log's properties sheet to change maximum log size and other properties that determine how the log functions.

Clearing and Saving Logs

You can clear the event logs at any time—you don't have to wait until they fill up. For example, it's sometimes helpful when you're troubleshooting a problem to clear the logs so you have a clean slate and can easily and quickly identify new events. When you clear a log, however, you'll most likely want to save the existing events in case you need to refer back to them later. Saving your logs is particularly important if you later need to track down a security breach.

You can save a log when you clear it, or save the log without clearing it. Right-click a log in the left pane of the Event Viewer, and choose Save Log File As. Select the path and file name for the log (the default extension is .evt), and then click Save.

To save the log when you clear it, right-click the log and choose Clear All Events. Event Viewer asks if you want to save the log. Click Yes, and enter a path and file name for the log.

In addition to saving and clearing logs, you can also open an existing log file. For example, maybe you're trying to track down that security breach I mentioned earlier. To open an existing log, right-click Event Viewer (or any existing log) in the left pane, and choose Open Log File to display the Open dialog box. Locate and select the file, and then select the log type from the Log Type drop-down list. Change the Display Name if you want Event Viewer to use a different name for the log, and then click Open.

Exporting Logs to Other Programs

The Windows XP Event Viewer gives you a reasonable amount of flexibility and capability for viewing and filtering the event logs. In some cases, though, you may want to perform more complex filters or queries on the event logs. You can achieve that by exporting the logs to a database such as Microsoft SQL Server or Microsoft Access. You can also export the events to other programs, as long as those programs can import comma- or tab-delimited text files.

To export an event log, right-click the log in the left pane of the Event Viewer, and choose Export List to open the Export List dialog box. Specify a path and file name, and then select the type of file to create from the Save As Type drop-down list. Click Save to save the file. Then, open the target application, and import the data from the file.

GETTING ADDITIONAL INFORMATION ABOUT SPECIFIC EVENTS

When you're troubleshooting a problem that is dropping event messages in the event logs, and you're looking for more information, the most useful clue is the event ID. The second most useful piece of information is the description. With those items in hand, you can begin searching for answers.

One of the first places to search is the Microsoft website. Open the site, and search on **event id *nnn***, where *nnn* is the ID number of the event. In most cases you'll turn up at least a handful of documents, and in many cases, several dozen documents.

If you have a copy of the Windows XP Resource Kit (or Windows 2000 Resource Kit), open the *Error and Event Messages* document. You'll find standard messages and event IDs for the System, Application, and Security logs. You can also search Microsoft TechNet or MSDN for the specific ID and/or a string from the event's description.

When you're researching events for specific applications, you can check the application's documentation for information about the events. Use the event ID and/or description text to search the application's support website.

Troubleshooting STOP Messages

Windows XP generates a STOP message and halts when the kernel detects an unrecoverable error or the CPU detects an unrecoverable hardware error. STOP messages are referred to fondly by administrators as the Blue Screen of Death (BSOD) because the system prints the messages to the screen in white text on a blue background. The computer is dead at this point; thus the name. Figure 11.5 shows a typical STOP message.

The STOP message contains three parts: bugcheck information, recommended user action, and debug port information. The bugcheck information, located at the top of the message, provides a value called the bugcheck ID. This information can contain up to four developer-defined parameters enclosed in quotes and includes a symbolic name for the error. A common symbolic name for driver-related errors, for example, is IRQ_NOT_LESS_OR_EQUAL.

The first hexadecimal value in the bugcheck string is often the most useful for identifying the cause of the problem or at least finding more information about the potential cause. You can perform a search in Microsoft TechNet, the Knowledge Base on the Microsoft website, or other sources for information about the error. Perform a search on the string **STOP: *error***, where *error* is the hexadecimal value.

The bugcheck section can also contain the hexadecimal memory address associated with the problem and the device or driver experiencing the problem. This information is useful in helping you narrow the list of possible causes.

The recommended user action section describes steps you can take to try to overcome the problem. Some STOP messages display problem-specific resolution steps, but unfortunately, many display the generic information. In most cases, your first step is to restart the computer to determine if the problem reoccurs. If not, consider yourself lucky. If you see the error again after restarting, you'll need to start troubleshooting it. Use the symbolic error name and the hexadecimal value to search the appropriate support site for the STOP message and its potential causes.

TIP The Windows XP Resource Kit document *Error and Event Messages Help* contains STOP error descriptions, including an explanation of each error and the actions you can take to rectify the problem.

FIGURE 11.5
STOP messages offer
information about the
error that caused the
system to halt.

```
*** STOP: 0x0000000A (0x0000015A,0x0000001C,0x00000000,0x80118190)
IRQL_NOT_LESS_OR_EQUAL*** Address 80118190 has base at 80100000 - ntoskrnl.exe


CPUID:GenuineIntel 6.5.2 irql:1f  SYSVER 0xf0000565

Dll Base DateStmp - Name              Dll Base DateStmp - Name
80100000 371cd681 - ntoskrnl.exe      80010000 35e72341 - hal.dll
80001000 35e70768 - atapi.sys         801da000 35e5c313 - SCSIPORT.SYS
80008000 353e319e - Disk.sys          8000c000 36269e3f - CLASS2.SYS
801e3000 36238303 - Ntfs.sys          8001d000 37585465 - Gernuwa.sys
f72f8000 31ec6c8d - Floppy.SYS        f7308000 353e319c - Cdrom.SYS
f750a000 00000000 - Fs_Rec.SYS        f75c9000 00000000 - Null.SYS
f7488000 35eb144b - KSecDD.SYS        f75ca000 00000000 - Beep.SYS
f7348000 353e3184 - i8042prt.sys      f7490000 353e318a - mouclass.sys
f7498000 31ec6c94 - kbdclass.sys      f7360000 35648e19 - VIDEOPRT.SYS
f7040000 35d4a699 - atirage.sys       f74ac000 360ea154 - vga.sys
f73b0000 353e31df - Msfs.SYS          f7050000 353e31d5 - Npfs.SYS
fc4dc000 362043ba - NDIS.SYS          f7290000 375857f0 - AW_HOST.SYS
f751c000 36363522 - Bluesave.SYS      a0000000 3700dc08 - win32k.sys
fc493000 35d4a6b4 - atirage.dll       fb43f000 31ec6e6c - TDI.SYS
fb3f6000 36243c12 - tcpip.sys         f7328000 3a155bf2 - tdimsys.sys
fb3d8000 36129a8d - netbt.sys         f7020000 375dace6 - EL90xBC4.sys
fb3c7000 3610249c - afd.sys           fc4c0000 371e81c6 - TCAITDI.SYS
f7350000 353e35d4 - netbios.sys       f74fc000 31ec6c9b - Parport.SYS
f7474000 353e318f - Parallel.SYS      f755c000 31ec6c9d - ParVdm.SYS
f70a0000 35ef29c4 - Serial.SYS        fb1c4000 35f03aa8 - rdr.sys
fb1b3000 353e362c - mup.sys           fb178000 35b7f615 - srv.sys
fb46b000 346f8058 - spud.sys          fb158000 371e8f5a - tcaicchg.sys
f7000000 353e3626 - Cdfs.SYS

Address  dword dump    Build [1381]                        - Name
f742fd78 80118190 80118190 fb3f77b3 f742fdd8 00000000 805858e8 - ntoskrnl.exe
f742fd7c fb3f77b3 fb3f77b3 f742fdd8 805858e8 fb4122e4 - tcpip.sys
f742fd8c fb4122e4 fb4122e4 f742fec9 fb3f6b92 c03eb660 8012b21b - tcpip.sys
f742fd94 fb3f6b92 fb3f6b92 c03eb660 8012b21b c03eb660 00000202 - tcpip.sys
f742fd9c 8012b21b 8012b21b c03eb660 00000202 8012b406 80670000 - ntoskrnl.exe
f742fda8 8012b406 8012b406 80670000 00000023 00000023 8016d85e - ntoskrnl.exe
f742fdb8 8016d85e 8016d85e 805761a8 00000000 0007ad98 f742ff6c - ntoskrnl.exe
f742fde4 80118190 80118190 00000008 00010246 805761a8 02000000 - ntoskrnl.exe
f742fdfc 80111dc7 80111dc7 805761a8 00000000 00000000 00000002 - ntoskrnl.exe
f742fe2c fb3f6748 fb3f6748 fb412308 80658f08 fb412320 00000000 - tcpip.sys
f742fe30 fb412308 fb412308 80658f08 fb412320 00000000 805761a0 - tcpip.sys
f742fe38 fb412320 fb412320 00000000 805761a0 0242fee8 fb412310 - tcpip.sys
```

In many situations, a STOP error is caused by installing new hardware or device drivers that are either incompatible with Windows XP or buggy. In these situations, and in situations where the problem is caused by a corrupted Registry, you can boot the system using the Last Known Good Configuration. Doing so replaces the current \HKEY_LOCAL_MACHINE\System\CurrentControlSet Registry branch with a backup copy from the last successful boot, thereby replacing any changes that were made when you installed the new device or device driver.

TIP   To boot from the Last Known Good Configuration, press F8 during boot, select Last Known Good Configuration from the boot menu, and press Enter.

Third-Party Event Management Applications

The Event Viewer is a good tool for browsing and monitoring events on the local computer, but it isn't geared toward in-depth analysis or for gathering information from other computers across the enterprise. Several third-party tools extend your ability to monitor and analyze the event logs for both local and remote systems. Most achieve this capability through added services that actively monitor and harvest events from the event logs on multiple systems and then add those events to a database. This gives you the ability not only to view events from a pool of computers, but also to perform much more extensive analysis of events through advanced database queries.

InTrust   This tool collects data from Windows, Novell NDS, and Unix platforms. You can use InTrust to collect, consolidate, archive, and analyze information from event logs and performance counters. It provides hundreds of customizable reports (Quest Software, `http://wm.quest.com/products/intrust/default.asp`).

Argent Guardian   This tool provides a scalable collection and monitoring solution for networks of any size, from small to enterprise. It supports remote and agent-based monitoring of a wide variety of services and applications, not limited to Exchange Server, SQL Server, all Windows event logs, services, SNMP devices, routers and hubs, and NetWare (Argent Software, `www.argent.com`).

LogCaster   This is a suite of network services that perform real-time monitoring and reporting of Windows event logs, TCP/IP devices and servers, Windows system and application services, SysLog devices (Unix/Linux systems, routers, and so on), and other devices and services. LogCaster stores collected data in ODBC-compliant databases that you can access through any database or web connection or through Crystal Reports, which is included with LogCaster. The product includes more than 100 predefined templates, and you can create or modify templates to create custom reports (Ripple Technologies, `www.rippletech.com`).

Using Dr. Watson

Dr. Watson is a debugging tool included with Windows XP. Although you probably won't use Dr. Watson very often, it's a good idea to understand what it is and how it works. You might need to collect debugging information from Dr. Watson to send to support engineers when you're troubleshooting a problem with Windows XP itself or with a specific application. If you know ahead of time how to install debugging symbols, configure Dr. Watson, and collect the resulting data, the support engineer can focus on the problem instead of on helping you set up the system for debugging.

How It Works

Well-designed applications include their own error handlers to detect and perform recovery from specific errors. Here's a simplistic example: If you attempt to open a document file of the wrong type for an application, the error handler prevents the application from opening the file and displays a message to you that the document type can't be used with the application. The difficulty in writing bulletproof programs is anticipating every possible error and incorporating code in the application's error handler(s) to catch and deal with the error so it doesn't crash the program or, worse yet, your system.

An *unhandled error* is one that isn't detected or handled by the application's error handler. When unhandled error occurs, Windows XP looks in the Registry key `\HKEY_LOCAL_MACHINE\Software\Microsoft\Windows NT\CurrentVersion\AeDebug` for a program error debugger. The value Debugger in this key defines the error handler (and points by default to Dr. Watson). The Auto value determines how the debugger functions:

Value	Description
0	The system displays a dialog box indicating that an error has occurred and including two buttons, OK and Cancel. Click OK to terminate the program or Cancel to start the debugger.
1	The system automatically starts the debugger without displaying the informational message. This is the default setting.

Although you can manually modify the Registry to configure these default settings, there's an easier way. Open a command console and type the following command:

```
drwtsn32 -i
```

This means that Dr. Watson starts automatically if an application crash occurs. Dr. Watson creates a text-based log file named `Drwtsn32.log` in the `\Documents and Settings\All Users\Application Data\Microsoft\Dr Watson` folder, and you can view the file with Notepad or any other text editor. Dr. Watson also can optionally create a binary crash dump file that a support engineer can load into a debugger to analyze the cause of the crash. Dr. Watson also writes an event to the Application log, which you can view with the Event Viewer.

TIP You can change the log and crash dump name and path, as explained a little later in this section.

Installing Debugging Symbols

Without any other configuration, Dr. Watson collects and logs useful but somewhat limited information. In order to capture additional and more targeted information, you need to install debug symbols on the system. You can download these symbol files from `www.microsoft.com/whdc/devtools/debugging/symbols.mspx`.

Installing the debugging symbols is a two-step process. First, you need to copy the symbols to a folder on the system. Then, you need to set an environment variable to point Windows XP to them. Proceed as follows:

1. Create the folder `%systemroot%\symbols`.

2. Copy the entire symbol folder/file structure to this folder.

3. Right-click My Computer, and choose Properties to display the System Properties sheet.

4. Click the Advanced tab, and click Environment Variables to display the Environment Variables dialog box shown in Figure 11.6.

FIGURE 11.6
Add the environment variable through the Environment Variables dialog box.

5. Under the System Variables list, click New to open the New System Variable dialog box.

6. Type **_NT_SYMBOL_PATH** in the Variable Name text box, and then enter the path **%systemroot%\symbols** in the Variable Value text box.

In addition to the Windows XP symbols, you can also install debug symbols for specific applications. This is generally most common on a server but is also possible for Windows XP Professional. You install these application debug symbols in much the same way as the system symbols. Copy the symbol files to their own directory, and then add the path to the _NT_SYMBOL_PATH environment variable, separating each path from the next by a semicolon.

Configuring Dr. Watson

You can configure several options that control the way Dr. Watson functions. To do so, click Start ➢ Run, and enter **drwtsn32.exe** to display the dialog box shown in Figure 11.7. The options you can configure are as follows:

Log File Path   This is the path to Dr. Watson's log file. The default path is

```
\Documents and Settings\All Users\Application Data\Microsoft\Dr Watson
```

There is generally no reason to change the path unless you want to store the log in a secure folder. However, you need to make sure the system has the necessary permissions to write to the folder. The log file name is `Drwtsn32.log`.

Crash Dump   If the Create Crash Dump File is enabled, you can specify the path for the binary crash dump file. The default location is the same as for the log file. The crash dump file can be quite large (many megabytes), so make sure you choose a location on a volume with adequate space. The default location is `\Documents and Settings\All Users\Application Data\Microsoft\Dr Watson\user.dmp`.

Wave File   If you enable the Sound Notification option, use the Wave File text box to specify the path to the WAV file that you want Windows XP to play when the error occurs.

Number Of Instructions   This value specifies the number of instructions before and after the current program counter that Dr. Watson disassembles for each thread state dump.

Number Of Errors To Save   This value specifies the maximum number of errors that Dr. Watson records in the log file. This number naturally affects the overall log size.

Crash Dump Type   Use this option to specify the type of crash dump file to capture. Pick the type requested by the support engineer. The default is Mini.

Dump Symbol Table   You can enable this option to have Dr. Watson include the symbol dump table, which includes the address and name for each symbol, in the dump file. Including the symbols considerably increases the size of the file.

Dump All Thread Contexts   Select this option to have Dr. Watson log the state for each thread in the program that generated the error. If you deselect this option, Dr. Watson logs the state of only the thread that caused the error.

Append To Existing Log File   Enable this option to have Dr. Watson append each new crash log to the existing log file. Deselect the option if you want Dr. Watson to overwrite the existing log. Appending to the file can make it very large, so a good practice is to immediately move the log file to a different folder for analysis as soon as the dump occurs. The next crash will then create a new log file.

Visual Notification Select this option to have Dr. Watson display a dialog box when the error occurs. The dialog box closes by itself after five minutes if you don't close it yourself.

Sound Notification Select this option to have Dr. Watson play the WAV file specified in the Wave File text box when the error occurs.

Create Crash Dump File Select this option to have Dr. Watson create the crash dump file when the error occurs. If this option isn't selected, Dr. Watson only creates the log file.

Application Errors This text box displays all the errors for the Event Viewer and Dr. Watson from the system's event logs.

FIGURE 11.7

You can configure several settings in Dr. Watson.

Collecting and Submitting the Data

Unless you're a developer, you probably won't work with the log and crash dump files yourself but will instead send them to a support engineer, who will use a debugger to troubleshoot the error and provide a fix for the problem. I've dealt with Microsoft on several support issues that required me to send debug files to a support engineer. Generally, engineers provide an FTP site you can use to upload the files or sometimes have you e-mail the files, depending on the size. Because the files can be so large, you'll need to compress them using a tool such as WinZip or PKZip. Send the files on their way, and try to wait patiently while the engineer resolves the problem.

Chapter 12

Monitoring Performance

Regardless of the operating system or PC we use, many of us treat optimal system performance like the digital equivalent of the Holy Grail: always pursued yet difficult to obtain. We worry that certain processes slow us down, wonder whether we can eke out just a bit more speed, and debate whether a change in memory or CPU is having the effect we want. This means we need ways to monitor the behavior of various aspects of our system as it performs its work. Tools within Windows XP aid you in doing just that.

If you're primarily familiar with the consumer side of Windows (95/98/Me), you realize that measures of operating performance usually fell to external utilities that you found and installed to allow you to monitor CPU utilization, disk usage, network efficiency, and the like. However, Windows NT 4.0 and later have offered a feature called a *system monitor* and at least a core set of measurement checkers, called *counters*, that allow you to keep an eye on key functions that give you an idea of your system's activity. Those already familiar with NT and 2000's Performance monitoring should be able to transition quickly to the changes here, but may want to review this chapter to refresh their memory.

The Windows XP Performance tool has two primary components: System Monitor, which reports levels of real-time activity for critical features such as CPU, disk, available memory, and network; and Performance Logs And Alerts, used to track user-configured data about system performance and to notify you when potentially important situations arise. Both are available from the Performance option in Administrative Tools in Control Panel.

Windows XP, like add-on utilities that can monitor performance, works by *sampling* data, or taking a discrete time-slice representation of the actual activity of the feature or function being monitored. For some tests, you may want samples taken every 5 seconds, whereas for others, you may want to sample far more rarely. With many options, you can adjust the sampling rate to fit the situation.

In this chapter, you'll learn about using System Monitor and the Performance Logs And Alerts features to help you understand how your system is performing as you work. As you read, don't lose sight of the fact that this data can be useful not just in overall efficiency, but also in monitoring components and services as you troubleshoot problems on a system.

Before You Monitor Performance

Before you begin a systematic analysis of your overall performance and establish a baseline efficiency level from which you can compare earlier and later results, Microsoft recommends you take certain steps spelled out in Help under the Performance section. These include:

- Adjusting the paging file to 1.5 times the amount of physical memory installed on the system
- Turning off any unnecessary services

◆ Turning off screensavers

◆ Using Registry Editor to check and note the nonzero values for the following subkeys:

```
\HKEY_LOCAL_MACHINE\SYSTEM\CurrentControlSet\Control\SessionManager\
   Memory Management
\HKEY_LOCAL_MACHINE\SYSTEM\CurrentControlSet\Services\LanmanServer\Parameters
```

NOTE   As you begin to work, realize, too, that it will be important for you to identify which information to monitor or which log is required to produce the data you most need to analyze. If you're trying to track specific memory utilization, for example, there are many options you won't need to employ, and you may not want to clutter your resources (system and mental) in watching them. You'll learn more about the best counters to use in the next section.

Using System Monitor to Check Real-Time Performance

System Monitor is the part of XP performance monitoring that allows you to get a real-time view of specific aspects of a system's or network's activity. Simply put, System Monitor differs from Performance Logs And Alerts in that you use it to determine what's happening *now*, rather than the more historical view offered by Performance Logs (described in detail in the next section). In this way, they complement each other in helping you perform your analysis.

However, in using either or both tools, you must understand some basic concepts. The work of both is based on items called *performance objects* and *performance counters*.

Performance objects refer to categories of data Windows XP checks through the Windows Registry and collects from monitoring the behavior of select components installed to your system, such as the CPU (processor), memory, disks, and so on. For each performance object, there exists a set of performance counters that can be applied to the object to measure its activity or efficiency.

NOTE   When a system contains multiple items of the same type, such as two network interface cards or two CPUs, each item provides its own counter data.

Here's an example: You want to check the bandwidth and the number of packets received per second on your network interface. The Network Interface would be the performance object you select, and from that, you would choose to monitor the Current Bandwidth counter and the Packets Received/sec counter (from a drop-down list of 17 counters).

NOTE   Performance objects aren't exclusively hardware: processes and services (such as Indexing, Terminal, and RSVP) qualify as well, and both allow you to choose counters under such objects to measure. In addition, the counters available depend on the services installed.

Configuring System Monitor

You open System Monitor by choosing Administrative Tools in Control Panel and clicking Performance. Then select System Monitor from the Console Root.

TIP   To open System Monitor from the command line, type **perfmon.msc**.

System Monitor installs with certain basic information already being monitored, as shown in Figure 12.1. This includes CPU usage (% Processor), the average disk queue length for the physical disk in use, and the number of pages per second moving in and out of memory.

FIGURE 12.1
System Monitor defaults to monitoring several counters.

Familiarize yourself with the System Monitor screen, from the selections available on the Toolbar in the Monitor window itself (major functions are described under Views), to the information display window (in which your view is presented in one of the three formats listed next), to the statistics windows, and the object information panel at the bottom (not available in Report view). Then choose a view that works best for you.

DIFFERENT VIEWS

You can observe your System Monitor information in one of three different views:

Graph (Ctrl+G, or the Graph icon on the Toolbar.) This view records the typical peaks-and-valleys graphical representations of the data being tracked.

Histogram (Ctrl+B, or the Bar Chart icon on the Toolbar.) This view reports the data in classic bar format.

Report (Ctrl+R, or the Report icon on the Toolbar.) This view shows the data in text format.

You can also perform the following key functions using these keys or icons:

Action	Keyboard Shortcut	Button
Clear Display	Ctrl+D	Clear Screen icon
View Current Activity	Ctrl+T	Graph Background icon
View Current Log	Ctrl+L	Round Bar icon
Add Counter	Ctrl+I	Plus sign
Delete Counter	Delete	X sign

ADDING AND REMOVING COUNTERS

To add a counter for an object to be monitored from your current System Monitor screen, follow these steps:

1. Click the Plus sign to add a new counter.

2. From the Add Counters window, choose whether to use the local computer's counter or to choose from a list of recognized systems on the network.

3. Click to open the drop-down list under Performance Object, and select the object you want to track.

4. Click All Counters, or select a specific counter from the drop-down list.

5. Click Add, and then Close or repeat, as needed, until you have all the objects—and their associated counters—you want.

TIP With so many different objects and counters, it can be hard to choose what is most relevant to monitor. Check the "Monitoring for Specific Performance Issues" section, later in this chapter, for recommendations, and then feel free to experiment to find what gives you the best data for your particular situation.

Uncertain what a specific counter will measure? Click the Explain button under the Counters list, and you'll get a pop-up like this one:

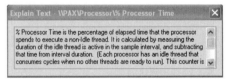

To remove a counter, try one of the following:

◆ From Graph or Histogram view, select the counter to remove in the bottom object information panel, and click the X on the Monitor toolbar.

◆ Also from Graph or Histogram view, select a counter in the bottom object panel, right-click, choose Properties, locate the counter to remove, and click Remove. Click Close.

To change the appearance or properties of a counter in System Monitor, follow these steps:

1. Right-click the counter in the bottom object information panel, and choose Properties.

2. Select among the following tabs and make changes, as needed:

Tab	Functions
General	Basic display options
Source	View, add, or remove data sources (monitor, logging, or database)
Data	Counters being used for that object
Graph	Graph customization options
Appearance	Change background appearance and font

3. Click OK.

Using Performance Logs And Alerts

As with System Monitor, Performance Logs And Alerts uses both performance objects and performance counters as part of its feature set to specify which information must be tracked and logged and, if necessary, to notify you of special problems.

Logs are stored by default in the `[drive letter]`:\PerfLogs folder and store data in a comma- or tab-separated format suitable for importing into applications such as spreadsheets or SQL-capable databases, for long-term tracking and reporting purposes. Also, logs may be started automatically or manually, and they can be viewed both during the collection process and after collection has finished. Through System Monitor, you can view them by clicking the View Log Data icon (Ctrl+L) and choosing the log to review, or by choosing the appropriate log under the Performance Logs And Alerts section of the MMC console:

Counter logs   These logs store information collected by the counters you establish.

Trace logs   These logs collect and store information from system application events tied to one of the following: errors or problems such as page faults, or more normal operations such as disk I/O activity tied to such an event.

Alerts   These logs sends a message via the Messenger service to alert you when conditions being monitored and logged meet conditions, or threshold limits, that you establish.

Setting Up Counter Logs

To establish a counter log (multiple counters can be tracked through each), follow these steps:

1. In the Performance MMC, highlight Performance Logs And Alerts, and then choose and right-click Counter Logs.

2. Select New Log Settings.

3. Provide a name for the log (it must be unique).

4. On the General tab of the next window, note the full log name, and then add objects and counters as desired. At least one counter must be selected before you can proceed. Make changes to sample data intervals and units as needed.

5. On the Log Files tab, make any changes as required for the log file format (binary, binary circular, tab- or comma-delimited text, or SQL database) and for naming automatic logs.

6. On the Schedule tab, set the schedule for this logging procedure. Click OK.

NOTE By default, the following counters are included in basic logging: Memory\Pages/sec, PhysicalDisk(_Total)\Avg. Disk Queue Length, and Processor(_Total)\% Processor Time.

WARNING Although both Windows 2000 and Windows XP name their binary performance log files with the .BLG extension, the two formats differ. You can't directly read XP-created BLG files with Windows 2000. You must either view these files exclusively on XP machines or use the Relog.exe command to convert the XP-created BLG to a Windows 2000–compatible format (*.csv or *.tsv). Here's an example: `relog oldname.blg -f CSV -o newname.csv`.

Setting Up Trace Logs

To configure for a new trace log, perform these steps:

1. Choose and right-click Trace Logs from Performance Logs And Alerts in the Performance MMC.

2. Select New Log Settings.

3. Provide a name for the log (it must be unique).

4. A tabbed window appears with the full current log name displayed. On the General tab, click Provider Status to see what services are available. Then either choose Events Logged

By System Provider (and enable TCP/IP, and so on, as needed) or choose Nonsystem Providers and click Add to include those you want.

5. On the Log Files tab, make any needed changes to the log file type (sequential trace or circular) and the naming convention.

6. Under the Schedule tab, establish the time(s) you want this log to run.

7. On the Advanced tab, you may adjust file buffer sizes. Click Apply, and then click OK.

WARNING Depending on how you have configured your performance tracking, logs may not be immediately available for viewing after you start the tracking process. Most require at least two data samples to be collected to establish the validity of the logging information.

TIP To quickly change parameters for a log, locate it in the list, right-click it, and choose Properties.

Setting Up Alerts

To configure Windows XP to issue an alert to you when conditions match watch criteria you set, do this:

1. Choose and right-click Alerts from Performance Logs And Alerts in the Performance MMC.

2. Select New Alert Settings.

3. Provide a name for the alert (it must be unique).

4. On the General tab, configure the criteria for the alert, based on the counter.

5. On the Action tab, indicate what XP should do when it determines an alert is necessary (just log, send a network message, start a specific log, or run a program, for example).

6. On the Schedule tab, make changes as needed to the schedule for alert scanning. Click Apply, and then OK.

Monitoring for Specific Performance Issues

As mentioned, some counters (and their associated performance objects) are likely to be of more use to you than others; some you may rarely, if ever, try. Table 12.1 offers the top 12 counters you should consider when looking at performance in the typical key areas, such as disk access and memory.

TABLE 12.1:   Top 12 Performance Counters

ISSUE/OBJECT	COUNTER	SIGNIFICANT RESULT
Disk	Physical Disk\% Disk and % Idle	Any major changes
Disk	Physical Disk\Disk Reads/sec and Disk Writes/sec	Below disk manufacturer's specifications
Disk	Physical Disk\Avg. Disk Queue Length	Number of spindles + 2
Memory	Memory\Available Bytes	< 4MB
Memory	Memory\Pages/sec	20 is average; monitor and review paging activity
Network	Network Interface\Bytes Total/sec, Bytes Sent/sec, and Bytes Rec'd/sec	Look for slowdowns
Overall System/Paging	Paging File\% Usage	Above 70%
Printing	Print Queue\Bytes Printed/sec	Any sustained reduction in print capacity
Printing	Print Queue\Job Errors	Sustained or recurring errors may indicate misconfiguration of printer
Processor	Processor\% Processor Time	80 and above—find what is grabbing the CPU's time

TIP   If you want to establish a baseline operating performance review, monitor the system while it's engaged in routine operations. You can monitor again during more extreme periods of activity or for troubleshooting, and compare the results against the baseline. From such a comparison, you may be able to see if your system or some component or service therein simply isn't functioning well under serious workloads and thus, may need replacement or tweaking.

WARNING   Be aware that monitoring many aspects of performance at once can by itself affect overall system efficiency. Reduce your monitoring overhead by using Report view rather than graphical mode, and prioritize the counters you load.

Chapter 13

Auditing the System

Chapter 11 explained the importance of monitoring and responding to events generated by the system, applications, and security processes such as logon and resource access. Chapter 12 explained the importance of monitoring system performance.

When you're concerned with system security, you need to go one step further and *audit* the system. Auditing in Windows XP provides the means by which you can track resource usage, attempted security breaches, and a wide variety of other events that occur on a system that would not otherwise be logged in the system's event logs. For example, perhaps you have a set of folders shared on a computer and want to keep track of unsuccessful attempts to access those folders. Or maybe you want to keep track of unsuccessful logon attempts or other possible security breaches. Auditing lets you do just that.

This chapter first gives you an overview of why auditing is important and how it works. Then you'll learn how to enable auditing for general events as well as audit specific folder resources. If you haven't already done so, you should read Chapters 11 and 12 to get a better understanding of events, performance issues, and the tools provided in Windows XP to monitor both.

NOTE   Windows XP implements auditing through group or local security policy. For that reason, it's available only on Windows XP Professional. Windows XP Home Edition doesn't support auditing because it doesn't implement policies.

Understanding Auditing

In Chapter 11, I defined an *event* as any significant occurrence in the operating system or an application that requires users (usually administrators) to be notified. When a service stops, for example, that's certainly something that needs to be logged to the System event log, at the least. You can keep track of a computer's health by monitoring the event logs and performance counters.

Auditing, however, lets you track the success or failure of specific types of events. For example, maybe you need to monitor logon attempts to determine not only who is logging on successfully, but also when unsuccessful logon attempts occur. Unsuccessful logons might point to attempts to breach a computer's security or perhaps to something far less sinister, such as a user who has forgotten his password and is too embarrassed to admit it or is working after hours and doesn't want to bother an administrator.

Logon and logoff are by no means the only events you can audit in Windows XP. You might also need to audit access to a shared folder to keep track of who uses the folder and the actions they take in it. You can audit many different types of events in Windows XP, in several categories:

Account logon events   Monitor user logon and logoff through a user account.

Account management   Monitor when user accounts or groups are created, modified, or deleted. Monitor when user accounts are renamed, enabled, or disabled. Monitor when a password is set or changed.

Directory service access   Monitor access to Active Directory.

Logon events   Monitor authentication of nonlocal entities, such as network user of a network share or other resource, or a remote service that logs on using a local account (such as the SYSTEM account).

Object access   Monitor access of specific objects such as folders, files, and printers. Auditing in this category also requires configuring auditing properties on the object itself.

Policy change   Monitor when user rights or audit policies are modified.

Privilege use   Monitor the occurrences of a user exercising a right that isn't associated with logon or logoff.

Process tracking   Monitor process execution, such as an application being started.

System events   Monitor global system events such as startup, shutdown, or restart, or events that are related to the system security log or to overall security.

Each of these categories includes several types of events, some of which are general in nature and others that are specific to certain objects. In all cases except object access, auditing is a global action—when you enable auditing for system events, for example, that action results in a range of events being audited. You can't audit one type of system event and not another. The exception is object access: you enable it globally for the system, but you must also turn on auditing for specific objects (more on this later).

Rather than cover every type of event audited for each category, I'll instead explain how to enable and configure global auditing policies in this chapter. You'll also learn how to configure auditing for individual folders, files, and printers.

Enabling Auditing

As I explained previously, you enable auditing by configuring a local or group security policy. For all auditing except object access, setting the policy is all you need to do. The system then begins placing events in the event logs as audited events occur. (Object auditing requires one extra step, as I'll explain in the next section.) First, you need to understand how to configure auditing policies.

If you want to perform auditing on all computers in a given organizational unit, a domain, or an entire site, you should enable auditing through group policy at the appropriate level. For example, assume you want to audit account logon throughout your entire organization. You can enable that auditing policy setting at the site level, or at the domain level if all your computers/users are members of the same domain. To audit account logon only for a specific group of users, you instead place those users in an organizational unit (OU) in the Active Directory and then enable the audit policy for logon in that OU.

Because this book focuses primarily on Windows XP and not Windows 2000 Server or Windows Server 2003, I'll assume that you'll be configuring auditing at the local level rather than through group policies.

TIP   If you need to configure auditing through group policy, open the Active Directory Users And Computers console, open the properties for the container (OU or domain), and create or modify a group policy object (GPO). In that GPO, locate and enable the policy settings for the type(s) of auditing you want to perform.

To configure auditing at the local level, open the Local Security console from the `Administrative Tools` folder. Then, expand the \Security Settings\Local Policies\Audit Policy branch as shown in Figure 13.1.

FIGURE 13.1

Use the Local Security console to enable auditing.

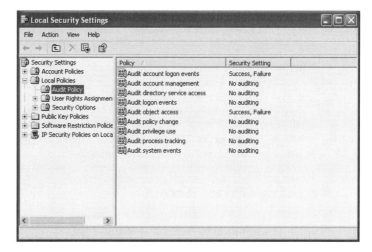

As Figure 13.1 illustrates, there is one policy setting for each of the auditing categories discussed previously. Each of these policies has three possible settings: No Auditing, Success, and Failure. The default value for each policy is No Auditing, so you don't need to take any action if you're not interested in auditing a particular category. Otherwise, double-click the policy for the category in question to open its Properties dialog box, as shown in Figure 13.2.

A key point to understand when you enable auditing is that you can audit two different types of events, success and failure. You don't have to audit both for a given category. For example, you might only audit failure for account logon events to help detect attempts to hack into the system or to identify users who are having difficulty remembering their passwords (or accounts that are being used to attempt a break-in), but not audit successful logons. On the other hand, perhaps you want a record of when each user logs on and from which computer, but you aren't interested in unsuccessful logon attempts. If that's the case, you'll audit success for this category and not audit failure.

As you're rummaging through the audit policies trying to decide which event categories to audit and the type of auditing you want to perform in each one, keep in mind that auditing can generate a huge amount of log activity. For that reason, you should audit only those types of events that have a true relevance to your system, network, or security needs. Otherwise, you may spend quite a bit of your time clearing out the logs or spending a lot of time weeding through the entries to find the ones you need.

FIGURE 13.2

Enable success and/or failure auditing through the policy's properties.

NOTE   Consider whether you're willing to take the time to actively review the logs for the audited events. If all you're doing is filling the logs with events that are never reviewed, reconsider your auditing plans. Decide what's relevant, and then actively monitor and analyze that information.

When you've configured the auditing policies as needed, close the policy console. Windows XP will begin logging events to the event logs according to the policies you've specified.

TIP   One final step you should take is to make sure you've configured the logs' maximum size and overflow behavior so you won't end up with full logs or begin to lose older events as they're over-written by newer ones (unless that's the behavior you want). Open Event Viewer, right-click the Security log, and choose Properties to set log behavior.

Auditing Object Access

When you enable success or failure in the audit policy for object access, you're only making auditing possible. That action alone doesn't cause any object-access events to be logged to the event logs. This is in contrast to the other auditing categories, which begin generating audit events as soon as you con-figure the policy. So, auditing object access is a two-step process. First you enable auditing for object access (success, failure, or both), and then you configure auditing for specific objects. For example, if you want to audit access to a shared folder, you must configure auditing properties for that folder before the system will log access to it.

TIP   If you're concerned that users or administrators are making changes in the Registry, you can turn on auditing in the Registry on a key-by-key basis. The section "Auditing Registry Access," later in this chapter, explains how.

Auditing Folder and File Access

You enable auditing for a file or folder through that object's properties. Open My Computer and browse to the folder or file. Right-click it, and choose Properties to open its properties sheet. Then click the Security tab (Figure 13.3).

FIGURE 13.3
Configure security set-tings for a folder through the Security tab.

NOTE You won't see or be able to access the Security tab unless you configure the computer to use regular file sharing instead of simple file sharing. Configure this option through the folder options. In any folder, choose Tools ➤ Folder Options, click the View tab, scroll to the bottom of the list to locate the setting Use Simple File Sharing, and turn it off. Also keep in mind that you can configure object access only for NTFS volumes; auditing isn't available for FAT volumes.

The Security tab lets you configure access permissions for specific users or groups. Click Advanced to open the Advanced Security Settings dialog box, and then click the Auditing tab (Figure 13.4) to configure auditing for the selected folder or file.

FIGURE 13.4
Enable or disable auditing of a folder or file through the Advanced Security Settings dialog box.

Click Add in the Advanced Security Settings dialog box, and enter the name of the user or group whose access you want to audit. Or, click Advanced in the Select User Or Group dialog box to browse for a user or group. When you click OK, Windows XP opens the Auditing Entry dialog box, shown in Figure 13.5.

FIGURE 13.5
You can audit a broad range of actions for the selected folder or file.

TIP   To audit all users, audit the Everyone built-in group.

In the Auditing Entry dialog box, select Successful for each event for which you want to monitor successful access to the object. Select Failed for each event for which you want to monitor unsuccessful access. The Apply Onto drop-down list lets you specify how the audit settings are applied to the folder, its contents, and subfolders. For example, if you want to audit only the files in the folder and not subfolders, you can select the Files Only option. Select the option This Folder, Subfolders, And Files if you want to audit the current folder, its contents, and the contents of all subfolders. The option "Apply these auditing entries to objects and/or containers within this container only," if selected, restricts auditing to only the selected folder. The contents of subfolders are audited if this option isn't selected.

Back on the Advanced Security Settings dialog box (Figure 13.4) are a couple of options that control how auditing entries are applied throughout the folder structure. You'll probably puzzle over these settings:

Inherit from parent the auditing entries that apply to child objects   When this option is turned on, the selected folder inherits the auditing settings from its parent folder. Clear this check box if you don't want the folder to inherit the auditing settings from its parent.

Replace auditing entries on all child objects with entries shown here that apply to child objects   Turn on this option to clear audit settings in child objects (such as subfolders) and apply the audit settings for the current folder to those child objects.

After you click Apply or OK, Windows XP begins auditing the folder and its contents according to the settings you've specified.

Auditing Printer Access

You can audit printer access in much the same way you audit file or folder access. For example, you might want to monitor attempts to change permissions or take ownership of a printer. To set printer auditing, follow these steps:

1. Open the `Printers and Faxes` folder, right-click the printer, and choose Properties.

2. Click the Security tab, and then click Advanced.

3. Click the Auditing tab, and add a user or group as you would for a folder or file. As Figure 13.6 indicates, the types of events you can audit for a printer are very different from those available for a folder.

As with folders and files, you should be judicious about how you apply printer auditing, particularly in a busy network with lots of printing going on. Monitor only those types of events that will help you track printing problems and potential security issues that are applicable to your network.

Auditing Registry Access

You can use the same basic steps to enable auditing for a Registry key that you use to set up auditing for folders, files, and printers:

1. Open the Registry Editor, right-click a Registry key, and choose Permissions. You can use the resulting dialog box (Figure 13.7, on the left) to restrict access to the selected key.

FIGURE 13.6
You can audit a handful
of events for a printer.

FIGURE 13.7
Use the Permissions dia-
log box to limit access to
a Registry key. (left)
There are a wide range of
events you can audit for a
Registry key. (right)

2. Click Advanced in the Permissions dialog box, and then click the Auditing tab.

3. Add a user or group using the same method described previously for a folder or printer.

The options that Windows XP offers for a Registry key are naturally different from those for other types of objects, as you can tell from the Figure 13.7 (right). As with other types of objects, you can apply the auditing settings to just the selected object or also include child objects, which in this case include subkeys and values.

Tips for Effective Auditing

Just turning on auditing for specific events or objects is pointless unless you follow up with active review and analysis of the events that occur. Windows XP records audited events to the Security log, so you can use the Event Viewer to view these events. Audited events show up with a Type of either Success Audit or Failure Audit, depending on the success or failure of the event. Figure 13.8 shows a handful of audit events in the Security log.

FIGURE 13.8
Audited events appear in the Security log.

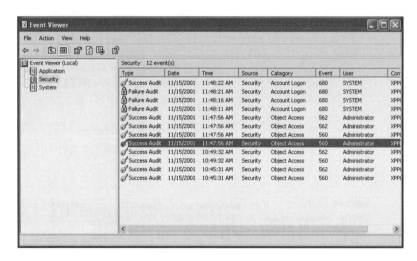

The Event Viewer works fine when you need to review audited events on a small scale or only on a single computer. When you need to expand auditing and analysis to a range of computers or to the entire organization, however, you'll have to turn to other tools. The third-party tools that let you collect data and analyze the event logs give you the same capabilities for analyzing audited events. Check out Chapter 11 for some suggested third-party applications that will let you do just that.

If you choose to enable auditing, you can choose from a handful of approaches:

Audit nothing   You can take the approach that you won't audit any events or objects. This is a valid approach if you're working in a very small network that doesn't have frequent or continuous Internet connections and where none of the users ever have problems or could be considered a potential security risk. If you have such a network, congratulations! You don't need auditing. If your network and users are in the real world, however, it's likely you'll need at least some level of auditing.

Audit everything   In networks that must be completely secure, you can consider auditing all events. Keep in mind that doing so will generate a huge amount of log traffic, so you'll need to adjust your log size accordingly and aggressively archive and analyze your logs. I strongly recommend a third-party solution like those discussed in Chapter 11. You might also consider auditing only failure events and not success events, unless you need a historical record of successful logons or other actions.

Audit specific users   Another approach is to audit only specific users or groups of users. For example, you might audit users who you feel pose an extra security risk or who frequently cause problems by purposely or accidentally attempting to access restricted resources or perform tasks for which they aren't authorized. Keeping records like this will help you guide these users more effectively and, if the need arises, provide a historical record to support termination or other actions.

Audit administrative actions   Except in small networks with only one or two administrators, you should generally monitor actions taken by administrators as well as the attempted unauthorized use of administrative privileges. The latter is important in any size network. In particular, monitor logon for the administrative account or group(s) plus actions taken such as policy changes, account creation or modification, and other administrative tasks that you feel might pose a risk to your network.

Audit folders and files   If you provide access to sensitive documents across the network, you should monitor access and use of those documents. In addition to tracking access, keep a close eye on attempts to change ownership or permissions on a folder or file, both of which can have unwanted security consequences.

What to Audit for Optimum Security

You may be tempted to audit every resource in sight, but doing so is almost never a good idea for a couple of reasons. First, auditing a large number of events may slow the computer because the machine has to perform more actions. Second, for auditing to do you any good, someone has to go through the resulting logs and identify problem events. If that person is you or someone you supervise, you'll want to minimize the amount of time involved in the review.

This section discusses which events to audit for maximum security on your Windows XP Professional systems and suggests remedies to try for various types of hazards. The section is broken down by the types of threats the auditing is intended to counteract or minimize.

Dictionary, Hybrid, or Brute-Force Password Attack

To detect attacks aimed at finding a password by trying a list of words until one works, audit account logon events for failure. (A *dictionary* attack uses known words from one or more languages. A *hybrid* attack mixes numbers, letters, or symbols into known words to search for disguised passwords. A *brute-force* attack tries every possible key combination.)

If you detect failed attacks (or even if you don't), review your password policies carefully to make sure that you require all users to use passwords of at least six characters that include numerals and symbols, that you require them to change passwords frequently, and that you prevent them from reusing passwords they've used before. If you need truly strong security, consider replacing your passwords with biometric authentication devices.

Entry Using a Stolen Password

To learn when someone has entered the system using a stolen password, audit account logon events for success. Because auditing account logon events for success will show you all successful logons by authorized users as well, you'll need to do some sleuth work to sort the authorized logons from the unauthorized.

If you detect an unauthorized entry, assess the damage and determine effective countermeasures. At the very least, you'll need to force a password change for the user account involved. If you're in doubt about unauthorized entries, force all users to change their passwords immediately.

Unauthorized Use of Computers

To check for users using computers they aren't authorized to use (for example, workstations in the wrong section of the network), audit account logon events for success. If you discover unauthorized use of computers, close the loophole by changing the appropriate policy.

Misuse of User Privileges

To check for users misusing their privileges, audit the appropriate privilege uses for success. Curtail or remove the appropriate privileges from offending users.

WARNING   Don't audit privilege use continuously. Doing so will produce massive amounts of data, and you'll need to trawl through large numbers of legitimate events to uncover any instances of abuse.

Misuse of Administrator Privileges

To check for administrators misusing their privileges or unintentionally making changes they shouldn't, audit account-management events and policy changes, both for success. Boost your communication channels or rein in your administrators as necessary.

File Security Breaches

To check for breaches to your file security, audit the appropriate files and folders for success and failure of access and change. For example, to find out who has been viewing the files in a particular folder, audit the folder and its files for List Folder/Read Data access for success; to find out who's been trying to view the files, audit List Folder/Read Data access for failure.

To prevent access to the files and folders in question, remove permissions for their folders from everyone but those users and groups allowed to access them. For greater security, locate the files or folders on another drive or server to which the offending users don't have access.

Printer Efficiency and Insecurity

To find out whether users are having problems with certain printers, audit printer failure events. If you detect problems, fix the printers or the users' access to them.

In most cases, you won't want to audit printer success events, because if your printers are used moderately or heavily, the auditing will log a large number of events. However, you may want to audit printer success events for a short period—especially for printers that use expensive media—to determine whether users are using printers they aren't supposed to print to. If they are, remove their permissions to do so.

Unauthorized Actions or Use of Programs

To detect users running unauthorized programs, or to monitor a user for unauthorized actions, audit process tracking for success. If the program is installed on the user's computer, remove it and use policies to prevent her from reinstalling it or installing other programs. If the program is installed elsewhere, remove the user's access to it.

Virus Threat

To detect unauthorized processes being run by a virus, script, or other malware, audit write access for program files and system files (EXE and DLL files) for success and failure and process tracking for success and failure. Monitor the System log actively while doing so.

Chapter 14

Using Disk Quotas

In a small network with one user per computer, controlling disk space isn't generally a big issue. If someone fills up a disk, you or that user can clear out old documents or unused applications as needed. As the network begins to grow and as multiple users begin to use the same computer, controlling disk space becomes increasingly important.

Limiting disk usage is also important on a server. You don't want one user filling up the server with MP3 or AVI files. Disk usage is just one reason; that kind of activity also indicates (to be diplomatic) a lack of sufficient focus on the job. By limiting disk activity, you can not only prevent users from carelessly filling up a disk, but also limit their ability to purposely load up the server with junk.

You can impose *disk quotas* to control the amount of space a user can use on a local computer as well as on a server. You can control disk quotas in a few different ways depending on where the volumes are located and which users should be affected. In this chapter, I explain three different quota methods: setting them directly, using mounted volumes, and applying them through group policy.

Understanding how to set disk quotas is an important issue even if you have a relatively small network with no dedicated server. You might have in place now, or put in place down the road, a Windows XP Professional computer to act as a file server. If that's the case, you should consider applying disk quotas to the computer to avoid potential problems later. A disk filling up isn't just an inconvenience to the user—it can cause services to fail and in some situations render the computer effectively useless. That makes disk quotas doubly important.

Applying Quotas to a Disk

A *disk quota* is just what its name implies: It's a limit—or quota—on the amount of disk space a given user can fill on a volume. You apply disk quotas on a per-volume, per-user basis. This means that the quota defines the total amount of space the user can have on the volume. It isn't limited to a specific folder, but rather to the volume. You can set two different quota levels. The first acts as a warning level; when this quota level is reached, Windows XP issues a warning message to the user. This gives the user the opportunity to do their own housecleaning and weed out old documents or other files.

TIP The term *volume* refers to a physical or logical drive, such as C:, D:, and so on.

The second limit acts as a stop on the user's ability to store files on the computer. Windows XP issues a message to the user that the maximum amount of space has been used and prevents any further additions to the volume by that user. This forces the user to clean up their act. Although quotas won't eliminate an Administrator's need to monitor disk usage, they do put the impetus on the users to manage their own folders more effectively.

TIP   Quotas work equally well on Windows XP Professional and Home Edition. If you have children who share a computer, it's a good idea to set quotas to prevent one or two from using up the entire volume with games, downloads, or other files. It also helps teach them good work habits and computer management skills.

Quotas function through junction points in the file system, which allow specific file-system features to be implemented by drivers other than the primary file-system drivers. Quotas are one example of the use of junction points; encryption is another. Because quotas rely on junction points, which rely on the NTFS file system, you can apply quotas only to NTFS volumes. You can't apply quotas on a FAT volume.

Setting Global Quota Settings

Perhaps the easiest way to set disk quotas is directly through the properties for the volume. To do so, open My Computer, right-click the volume, and choose Properties. Then click the Quota tab (Figure 14.1).

FIGURE 14.1

Use a volume's Quota tab to set quotas.

Setting up disk quotas for a volume is a two-step process. You first configure the general settings that apply for all users. Then, you add users to the quota entry list and specify the amount of space they can use. If a user doesn't have an explicit quota entry for a volume, you can configure the volume's global quota properties to include default values for quota and warning limits and have those settings apply to new users. Windows XP checks the quota entries and, if it doesn't find one for the user, creates one based on the default settings. This gives you the means to automatically apply the same quotas to all users without having to create individual quota entries.

TIP   As you'll learn in the next section, you can modify the quota entry for any user. A good plan of attack is to set reasonable quota defaults and then modify individual user quota entries as needed to increase or decrease the quota settings for users who need more or less than the default amount of disk space.

To enable quotas, select the Enable Quota Management option on the Quota tab. This makes available the remaining options on the tab:

Enable quota management   Use this option to enable or disable quotas for the volume. When this option is enabled, Windows XP applies the quota settings for the volume. Clear this option if you don't want any disk-usage limits applied to the volume.

Deny disk space to users exceeding quota limit   Enable this option if you want Windows XP to prevent users from using any more space on the volume if they exceed their quota limit. Clear this option if you only want to warn users but not impose a physical limit. In a way, not denying space defeats the purpose of disk quotas, so I generally recommend that you enable this option unless you have a compelling reason to warn rather than enforce.

Do not limit disk usage   Select this option if you don't want to apply a disk quota to new users who have no disk quota yet on the volume. In general, I don't recommend using this option, but instead suggest you apply a default quota using the following setting.

Limit disk space to   Select this option to set a default quota for any user who doesn't have an existing quota entry for the volume. This value specifies the maximum amount of space the user can fill. If you select the Deny Disk Space option described previously, the user is denied the ability to use more space when this limit is reached.

Set warning level to   Use this option to set the amount of space used that will generate a warning message. As with the preceding setting, this sets the default value for new users who have no existing quota entry on the volume. Windows XP creates a new quota entry for the user with this setting and the Limit Disk Space To setting on first access.

Log event when a user exceeds their quota limit   This option adds an event to the System log when a user exceeds the quota limit specified in their quota entry for the volume. This option gives you a means of notification and analysis to help plan and manage disk usage, particularly if you use a third-party event-log analyzer like those discussed in Chapter 11.

Log event when a user exceeds their warning level   This setting adds an event to the System log when a user exceeds the warning limit specified in the quota entry for the volume. Use this option in conjunction with the preceding one to plan and analyze disk usage.

Setting Quota Limits for a User

As I explained in the previous section, you can set default quota values for a volume and let Windows XP apply those quotas to everyone. You don't have to set individual users' quota settings unless they need custom values. A second approach is to manually create quota entries for specific users and not apply default settings to other users. This, in effect, applies quotas to a selected group of users but lets all others use as much space as they want on the volume. Think about how you want to restrict disk usage and choose a method accordingly. Just remember that even if you decide to use default settings and apply quotas to all users, you can modify the settings for any user as needed.

To modify quotas for a user, or to create an explicit quota entry, open My Computer, right-click the volume in question, and choose Properties. Click the Quota tab, and then click Quota Entries to display the dialog box shown in Figure 14.2.

FIGURE 14.2

You can view, add, and modify quota entries for users as needed.

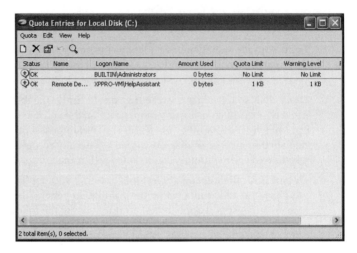

The Quota Entries dialog box shows all existing quota entries for the volume. It also displays useful information, such as the settings for the user, amount currently used, percent used, and status, which indicates whether the user is within quotas or has exceeded the warning or limit levels.

To create a new quota entry for a user, choose Quota ➢ New Quota Entry. Windows XP opens the Select Users dialog box, which you use to enter or browse for the user account. After you select the user, Windows XP displays a dialog box similar to the one in Figure 14.3. Set the warning and limit values and click OK.

Double-click any quota entry to open the Quota Settings dialog box (Figure 14.3) for the user, to enable/disable quotas or to set the warning and limit levels for the selected user.

TIP   You can't apply quotas to groups. So, the Select Users dialog box limits the search to user accounts and excludes groups.

FIGURE 14.3

Change a user's settings through the Quota Settings dialog box.

Copying Quotas from Volume to Volume

Let's say that over time you have fine-tuned the quota settings on a particular volume, but even with quotas in place, you still need to add more disk space. So, you decide to add a new volume to the computer. You don't want to have to set up all the quotas again; instead, you want to impose the same quotas for the new volume as for the old one. Windows XP makes it easy to do just that.

You can export the quota entries from a volume to a file and then import those settings in the other volume. To export the settings, open the properties for the source volume and click the Quota tab. Click Quota Entries to open the Quota Entries dialog box, and choose Quota ➢ Export to open the Export Quota Settings dialog box.

Once you have exported, open the Quota Entries dialog box on the target volume and choose Quota ➢ Import. Select the file you exported and click Open to add the quota entries.

Setting Quotas on Remote Volumes

You can apply quotas to a remote volume in much the same way you apply quotas to a local volume. The remote volume must be shared at the root of the volume and you must be a member of the Administrators group for the remote computer.

To set quotas on volumes that fit those criteria, first open My Computer and map a local drive letter to the remote share. Then right-click the mapped volume in My Computer and choose Properties. Use the Quota tab of the remote volume's properties to set quotas just as you would for a local volume.

How Compression Affects Quotas

Disk compression is a feature of NTFS volumes that allows a file to use less space on the disk than it would if uncompressed. When Windows XP tracks disk usage for quotas, it considers the uncompressed size of the file, not the compressed size. A 100 MB file that compresses down to 60 MB would still count as 100 MB against the user's quota, so you (or the user) can't use compression to get around the quota limit for files.

However, Windows XP does consider the compressed size of *folders* rather than the uncompressed size. A folder that takes up 400 MB compressed but would have an uncompressed total usage of 700 MB counts as only 400 MB against the quota.

NOTE   See Chapter 18 for a more detailed discussion of compression.

How Conversion Affects Quotas

You can convert FAT volumes to NTFS without a loss of data. FAT volumes don't track file ownership, but NTFS volumes do. So, when Windows XP converts a FAT volume to NTFS, it needs to assign ownership to each file on the volume. It automatically makes the Administrator the owner for all files. If you enable quotas on the converted volume, this means that all the existing files count against the Administrator account's quota limit. This typically isn't a problem, because in most cases you won't apply a quota limit for Administrators. If you need to apply a limit, however, check the total disk usage right after converting the volume. Then add that amount to whatever quota limit you plan to give Administrators.

How Ownership Affects Quotas

As the previous section hints, quotas are directly tied to ownership. So, ownership is an issue you consider when setting quotas. Conversely, you need to consider quotas when changing ownership of a folder or file. If you change ownership, that folder or file is counted against the new owner's quota limit. If that's not a problem, you don't have to worry about it. Otherwise, you might need to either increase the new user's quota or not make the ownership change.

Applying Folder-Specific Quotas with Mounted Volumes

As I explained previously, quotas are volume-specific: You can't set one quota on a folder and set a different quota on a different folder. For example, you can't have a 20 MB limit in `C:\Program Files` and a 200 MB limit in `C:\users\you`. At least, that's the case if both folders reside on the same physical disk. But how can you have two folders in the same directory structure (both appearing under C:, for example) that reside on different physical disks? You use one or more mounted volumes, another feature made possible by NTFS 5 junction points.

A *mounted volume* is a volume that you mount into an empty NTFS folder. For example, assume a computer's physical drive C: is running low on disk space. You need to add several additional applications. You can install a new disk, move the contents of the existing `C:\Program Files` folder to the new disk, and then mount the new disk in the now empty `C:\Program Files` folder. To the user, it appears that drive C: suddenly has a lot more free space. In reality, it's a different disk.

One side benefit of mounted volumes is that the mounted volume can have different quota settings from the host volume. So, you might mount a volume as `C:\Users` with a completely different set of quotas than the settings applied to the physical C: volume. For example, users might have a 5 MB limit on the host volume but a 200 MB limit on the mounted volume, which appears as `C:\Users`.

There isn't anything magical about setting up different quota settings for mounted volumes. However, you might need to change the way you get to the quota settings. You can mount a volume to an empty NTFS folder and that mounted volume doesn't have to have a drive letter. So, you can't just right-click the volume in My Computer to access the Quota tab in its properties; instead, you need to use the Disk Management console. Right-click My Computer, select Manage, and click the Disk Management branch in the Computer Management console. Right-click the mounted volume and choose Properties. You'll then have access to the volume's Quota tab, where you can set quotas as you would for a nonmounted volume.

NOTE   For a detailed discussion of how to configure and use mounted volumes, see Chapter 18.

Applying Quotas with Policies

Although you can apply quotas manually, as explained earlier in this chapter, there are many situations where you might prefer to apply quotas through group or local policy. For example, let's say that you have 50 workstations shared by several hundred users (a computer lab in a school would fit that scenario). You want to impose a disk quota so that each user can have only 5 MB of data. You could go to each computer and manually configure the quota default settings, but there is a much easier way, provided those computers are domain members. You can apply the quota settings through group policy, which allows you to configure the settings once from a central location and have them applied to all the computers.

You can apply quotas through group policy or local policy. The former requires the Active Directory Users And Computers console and the latter requires the Group Policy console focused on the local computer. Setting quotas through local policy rather than group policy is your only policy-based method of imposing quotas if the computers belong to a workgroup rather than a domain. It takes just as long—if not longer—to set local quotas through local policy as it does to set them through the volume's properties. The benefit is that any new volumes you add to the computer will have the same quotas automatically, without the need to set them. This isn't a major advantage but it's helpful, nonetheless.

Setting Quotas with Group Policy

You can set group policy at the site, domain, or organizational unit (OU) level. This section assumes you're setting the policy at the OU or domain level. If you're setting quotas at the site level, use the Active Directory Sites And Services console rather than the Active Directory Users And Computers console.

To set policies, follow these steps:

1. Open the Active Directory Users And Computers console on a domain controller. Right-click the domain or OU and choose Properties.

2. Click the Group Policy tab (Figure 14.4), and open an existing group policy object (GPO) or create a new one.

TIP   You can't apply a GPO to the built-in Users container. If you need to apply quotas or other policies to a group of users, create an OU and move their accounts to that OU.

FIGURE 14.4
Use the Group Policy tab to access and edit group policy objects.

3. In the Group Policy editor (Figure 14.5), expand the \Computer Configuration\Administrative Templates\System\Disk Quotas node. You'll see several policies that correspond to settings on a disk's quota tab. These group policy settings are self-explanatory.

4. Double-click a policy, and set its value as needed. The last policy, Apply Policy To Removable Media, if enabled, causes the quotas to be applied to removable media in addition to fixed media.

FIGURE 14.5
Use the Group Policy editor to modify policies.

Setting Quotas with Local Policy

To set quotas with local policy, follow these steps:

1. Click Start ➢ Run and enter **MMC** in the Run dialog box.

2. When the MMC opens, choose File ➢ Add/Remove Snap-In. Click Add.

3. Choose Group Policy in the Add Standalone Snap-In dialog box (Figure 14.6) and then click Add.

FIGURE 14.6
Select Group Policy in the Add Standalone Snap-In dialog box.

4. The console automatically focuses the snap-in on the local computer, as shown in Figure 14.7. Click Finish to add the console, then click Close, and finally click OK to return to the console.

FIGURE 14.7
Group policy is automatically focused on the local computer.

5. Expand the \Local Computer Policy\Computer Configuration\Administrative Templates\ System\Disk Quotas node and set the policies in that node as needed. See the previous section if you need an explanation of the individual policies.

6. Close the Local Computer Policy console.

Applying Quotas from a Command Console

In some situations, you might find it helpful to be able to manage quotas from a command line. For example, perhaps you need to incorporate quota tasks in a batch file or you want to manage quotas on a remote computer from a Telnet session. The `fsutil` command lets you do just that.

TIP You can use `fsutil` as part of an administrative script to create quota reports or set disk quotas as part of the setup process when you add a new user.

The `fsutil` command has several uses. The following list shows its syntaxes:

```
fsutil quota disable VolumeName
```

Use this syntax to disable quota tracking and enforcement on the volume specified by *VolumeName*.

```
fsutil quota enforce VolumeName
```

Use this syntax to enforce quota tracking and limits on the volume specified by *VolumeName*.

```
fsutil quota modify VolumeName Threshold Limit [UserName]
```

Use this syntax to modify an existing quota entry or create a new one on the volume specified by *VolumeName*. The *Threshold* value specifies the value at which Windows XP issues a quota warning. The *Limit* value specifies the hard-quota limit for the entry. *UserName* specifies the domain or user name for which to apply the settings.

TIP   Specify the values for *Threshold* and *Limit* in bytes.

```
fsutil quota query VolumeName
```

Use this syntax to list quota entries on the volume specified by *VolumeName*.

```
fsutil quota track VolumeName
```

Use this syntax to track quotas on the volume specified by *VolumeName*.

```
fsutil quota violations
```

Use this syntax to search the application and event system logs for quota violations for threshold limits being reached.

Part 4

Hardware

In this section:

Chapter 15

Understanding and Managing the Registry

In the good old days of Windows 3.*x*, Windows stored the majority of its settings in text-based INI files. Some Windows applications still use INI files to store application settings. However, the majority have moved their settings to the Windows Registry. As this chapter explains, the Registry serves as the main data repository for the Windows XP operating system and for application settings.

Most tasks that you'll need to perform don't require you to know much at all about the Registry. Although it's where most settings are stored, various elements in the GUI give you the means of modifying these settings. When you make changes in a Control Panel applet, for example, you're actually indirectly modifying settings in the Registry.

In some situations, however, modifying the Registry is the only way—or the quickest way—to make system or application changes. You need an understanding of how to work in the Registry for that reason alone. In addition, you need to know how to back up and restore the Registry. This chapter explains the Registry and how to work with local and remote registries. For detailed information on backing up and restoring the Registry, see Chapter 38.

Understanding the Windows XP Registry

The Windows XP Registry stores information about the operating system configuration, system hardware, security settings, rights, working environment settings (Desktop properties, for example), and many other types of information. Setup creates the Registry when you install Windows XP, and the operating system modifies the Registry when you add or remove hardware or modify hardware or operating system settings. Most applications also modify the Registry to store their settings.

The Windows XP Registry is a single logical entity divided into subtrees. Each subtree contains *keys*, which can contain subkeys and values. A *subkey* is just a branch of a subtree. *Values* are the actual items in the Registry that store data.

The Registry includes two physical subtrees, HKEY_LOCAL_MACHINE and HKEY_ USERS. These are often abbreviated as HKLM and HKU. The HKLM subtree stores hardware- and system-related data; HKU stores user-related data.

These two physical subtrees are divided into five logical subtrees, called *hives*. Microsoft defines a hive as a body of keys, subkeys, and values rooted at the top of the Registry hierarchy. The five logical hives are as follows:

HKEY_LOCAL_MACHINE   This hive stores information about the local hardware and operating system configuration. These settings aren't user-specific but are instead the same regardless of the current user.

HKEY_CLASSES_ROOT This hive, abbreviated HKCR, contains the settings that define file association data. This hive is created from \HKLM\Software\Classes and \HKCU\Software\Classes. The values in the HKCU key take precedence over the HKLM key, making the values user-specific. So, Windows XP can store different file-association data for each user.

HKEY_CURRENT_USER This hive stores the current user's profile, which includes the desktop settings, Start menu, application settings, and so on. This hive is an alias of the \HKU*SID* key, where *SID* is the current user's security ID.

HKEY_USERS This hive stores the user profiles for users who log onto the computer locally. This includes the default user profile. There are individual keys for each user SID.

HKEY_CURRENT_CONFIG This hive stores hardware information such as installed devices, device drivers, device settings, and so on. This hive is an alias of the key

```
\HKLM\System\CurrentControlSet\Hardware Profiles\Current
```

Each hive comprises two files: the Registry file and the log file, both of which are stored in the *%systemroot%*\System32\Config folder. The Registry file contains the Registry structure and values for the hive, and the log file functions as a transaction log for hive modifications. Table 15.1 lists hives and their corresponding files.

TABLE 15.1: Registry Hive Files

HIVE	FILES
\HKEY_LOCAL_MACHINE\SAM	Sam and Sam.log
\HKEY_LOCAL_MACHINE\SECURITY	Security and Security.log
\HKEY_LOCAL_MACHINE\SOFTWARE	Software and Software.log
\HKEY_LOCAL_MACHINE\SYSTEM	System and System.log
\HKEY_CURRENT_CONFIG	System and System.log
\HKEY_CURRENT_USER	Ntuser.dat and Ntuser.dat.log
\HKEY_USERS\DEFAULT	Default and Default.log

TIP You'll also find .sav files in the Config folder. These are backup files created after the text portion of Setup and are used only if the GUI portion of Setup fails.

The majority of these files reside in the *%systemroot%*\System32\Config folder. The exceptions are the Ntuser.dat and Ntuser.dat.log files, which reside in each user's profile folder. On a system with a clean install of Windows XP, the profile folder is \Documents and Settings*user*, where *user* is the user's logon name. On a system upgraded from Windows NT to Windows XP (or from NT to 2000 and then to XP), the user profiles are stored in *%systemroot%*\Profiles*user*.

Figure 15.1 shows the Registry Editor (covered later in this chapter) to illustrate the Registry's logical structure.

FIGURE 15.1
The Registry comprises
five logical hives.

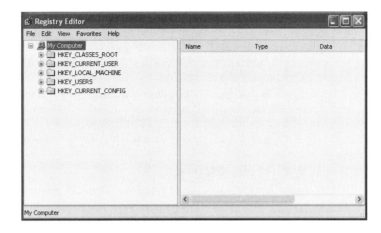

HKEY_LOCAL_MACHINE

The HKLM hive stores hardware and operating system settings that are system-wide. The HKLM hive contains a handful of subkeys:

HARDWARE This subkey stores hardware configuration information. Windows XP creates the contents of this key when the system boots.

SAM This subkey contains security data for local user accounts and groups.

SECURITY This subkey defines the local security policy.

SOFTWARE This subkey contains data about installed applications.

SYSTEM This subkey contains values for device drivers, startup, services, and other system-wide values.

The settings in HKLM are used if there are no corresponding settings in the HKCU key. Otherwise, the settings in HKCU take precedence. However, some items—such as device drivers—always come from the HKLM key and not the HKCU key.

HKEY_USERS

This hive stores information about users who log on to the computer locally. The first key in this hive is .DEFAULT, which stores the default user profile that Windows XP uses to create the profile for a user the first time that user logs on. The rest of the keys in this hive define the profile for specific users. Each user's settings are stored in a separate key, which has the user's unique SID as its key name.

TIP In most cases, you won't be able to identify a user from a SID, which makes it difficult to make changes in the HKU key. However, you shouldn't make Registry changes directly in most cases, anyway. If you need to change values for a user, log on as that user and make the changes through the Control Panel or other GUI methods. Or, log on as the user and make the changes in the HKCU hive, which points to the current user's key in HKU.

HKEY_CURRENT_USER

This key is an alias for the \HKU*SID* key for the current user. When you log on, the HKCU hive points to your Registry key in the HKU hive. If you make a change to keys or values in HKCU, the changes are actually made to \HKU*SID*, where *SID* is your security ID.

HKCU contains several subkeys. The AppEvents subkey, for example, contains application event settings such as WAV files that are associated with specific operating system events (that annoying startup sound, for example). This key also contains several other subkeys that define the command console, Control Panel, working environment, identities (such as for Outlook Express), network settings, remote access settings, and much more. In essence, all user-specific settings are visible through HKCU.

HKEY_CLASSES_ROOT

This hive stores file associations. Windows XP builds this hive from \HKLM\Software\Classes and \HKCU\Software\Classes. Values in HKCU take precedence over HKLM, giving each user custom file associations. This means that one user can have a particular file type associated with one program, whereas another on the same computer can have a different application associated with that same file type.

HKEY_CURRENT_CONFIG

This hive stores hardware configuration data such as device drivers, device settings, and so on. HKCC is an alias of \HKLM\System\CurrentControlSet\Hardware Profiles\Current. HKCC contains two main keys, Software and System. The Software key contains settings for system fonts and a few applications. The System key stores a partial copy of \HKLM\System\CurrentControlSet.

Working with Keys and Values

A Registry key is really just a container for other keys and for values. Keys provide the structure for the Registry, and values store the data. You can create several types of values in the Registry:

REG_BINARY This type stores a single item of data in binary format. The Registry Editor displays these values as hexadecimal numbers.

REG_DWORD This type stores a single data item as a four-byte number. The Registry Editor can display these values using binary, hexadecimal, or decimal formats.

REG_EXPAND_SZ This is a variable-length string that stores information with expandable variables (thus the name). The variables are enclosed in percent signs and expanded at the time of use by the system or an application. For example, the *%systemroot%* variable expands to the actual path to the Windows XP system folder.

REG_MULTI_SZ This type stores multiple string values as a single Registry value. The strings are separated by commas, spaces, or other character delimiters.

REG_SZ This type stores fixed-length strings, one string per value. It's the most common type of Registry value.

REG_FULL_RESOURCE_DESCRIPTION This type stores nested arrays. This value type is commonly used to store the resource list for a device driver or hardware component.

NOTE You'll learn in the next section how to create and modify keys and values in the Registry.

Using the Registry Editor

Previous versions of Windows, including Windows 2000 and Windows NT, provided two different programs for editing the Registry. Windows XP combines (finally!) the features of both these Registry editors into a single program. You can use the Registry Editor (Figure 15.2) to browse the Registry to check settings; create, modify, or delete keys and values; and set permissions on keys. You can also use the Registry Editor to manage a remote Registry.

FIGURE 15.2
Use the Registry Editor to view and make changes to the Registry.

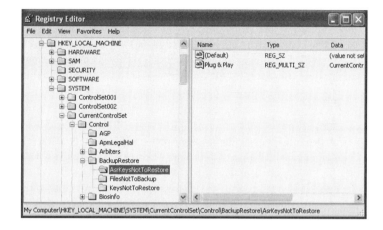

NOTE   See the section "Managing a Remote Computer's Registry," later in this chapter, for information on how to access and manage a remote Registry.

As Figure 15.2 illustrates, the Registry Editor shows the five Registry hives as expandable branches in the left pane. You can navigate the Registry structure in the left pane and view subkeys and values in the right pane.

The Registry Editor is easy to use, so I won't cover it in detail in this chapter. Instead, I'll give you a few tips on using it more effectively.

Copying Key Names

When you're working with the Registry, it's sometimes useful to be able to extract the key name. For example, maybe you need to document a particular change, and you want to reference the Registry key in the document. You can open the Registry Editor and the document and manually type the key in the document, character by character. Or, you can use the Clipboard.

Just select the desired Registry key, and choose Edit ➢ Copy Key Name to copy the key name to the Clipboard. Then switch to the document where you want to use the key name, and paste the text into the document.

Favorite Registry Keys

The Registry Editor in Windows XP lets you maintain a list of "favorite" Registry keys. I realize that Registry keys are probably your least favorite thing, but the ability to save a key to a Favorites list helps you navigate quickly to frequently used keys. Some of the keys you'll use more often than others are buried deep in the Registry structure, and you can click your fingers raw getting to them.

To add a key name to the Favorites list, follow these steps:

1. Browse to the key and choose Favorites ➤ Add To Favorites.

2. Specify the name you want to appear in the list, and click OK.

3. Choose Favorites ➤ Remove Favorite to open a dialog box you can use to remove an entry from the Favorites menu.

Note that adding a Registry key to the Favorites menu adds it to the Favorites menu in the Registry Editor, not to your Favorites folder where URLs are stored.

TIP If you want to copy your Registry favorites from one computer to another, or back them up so you can easily restore them on your computer if they get deleted, export the Registry key \HKEY_CURRENT_ USER\Software\Microsoft\Windows\CurrentVersion\Applets\Regedit\Favorites and import it on the other system. Just double-click a REG file to import it.

Last-Used Key

Another feature that the Registry Editor implements by default is to automatically open the key that you had open when you last closed the Registry Editor. This can be handy, particularly if you're experimenting with a setting and need to make frequent changes to it. However, it can also be a security risk—you might not want someone else to open the Registry Editor and see where you were last working.

You can prevent the Registry Editor from keeping track of the previous key from session to session:

1. Open the Registry Editor and locate the key

   \HKEY_CURRENT_USER\Software\Microsoft\Windows\CurrentVersion\Applets\Regedit

2. Double-click the value LastKey, clear the value, and click OK.

3. You need to set permissions on the Regedit key to prevent it from displaying the last-used key. In other words, if a particular user doesn't have Full Control in this key, the Registry Editor can't read the LastKey value and therefore can't display it. Right-click the key

   HKEY_CURRENT_USER\Software\Microsoft\Windows\CurrentVersion\Applets\Regedit

   and choose Permissions.

4. Remove the Full Control permission for any user you don't want to be able to see the previous session's last-used key.

TIP As an alternative, you can collapse all branches and select My Computer in the left pane prior to closing the Registry Editor.

Exporting and Importing Registry Keys

There are lots of situations in which you'll want to export or import a portion of the Registry. For example, you can move application settings from one computer to another by exporting the appropriate portion of the Registry. It's even possible to avoid reinstalling certain applications by copying their files and Registry key to the other computer.

When you export a portion of the Registry, the result is a text file with an .REG extension. Here's a sample of a portion of a typical REG file:

```
Windows Registry Editor Version 5.00

[HKEY_CURRENT_USER\Software\Microsoft\Windows\CurrentVersion\Internet Settings]
"User Agent"="Mozilla/4.0 (compatible; MSIE 6.0; Win32)"
"IE5_UA_Backup_Flag"="5.0"
"NoNetAutodial"=dword:00000000
"MigrateProxy"=dword:00000001
"EnableNegotiate"=dword:00000001
"ProxyEnable"=dword:00000000
"EmailName"="IEUser@"
"AutoConfigProxy"="wininet.dll"
"MimeExclusionListForCache"="multipart/mixed multipart/
x-mixed-replace multipart/x-byteranges "
"WarnOnPost"=hex:01,00,00,00
"UseSchannelDirectly"=hex:01,00,00,00
"EnableHttp1_1"=dword:00000001
"PrivacyAdvanced"=dword:00000000

[HKEY_CURRENT_USER\Software\Microsoft\Windows\CurrentVersion\
Internet Settings\5.0]

[HKEY_CURRENT_USER\Software\Microsoft\Windows\CurrentVersion\
Internet Settings\5.0\Cache]
"Signature"="Client UrlCache MMF Ver 5.2"
...
```

The lines contained in square brackets [] define a Registry subkey. The lines that follow the key name are the settings included in the specified branch.

When you export from the Registry, you can export the entire Registry or just the selected branch. I can't think of a situation in which you would want to export the entire Registry; you'd end up with a huge REG file. You could export the Registry as a backup, but you're better off using the Backup applet to back up the system state data.

To export a portion of the Registry, open the Registry Editor and select the key you want to export. Choose File ➢ Export to open the Export Registry File dialog box. Enter a name for the REG file, verify that the Selected Branch option is selected, and click Save.

When it comes time to import a REG file, you have two options. You can open the Registry Editor, choose File ➢ Import, and then select the file. The easier method, however, is to double-click a REG file. Windows XP then imports the contents of the file (after prompting you to verify the import).

In some situations, you might want to distribute a REG file to multiple users. For example, let's say you're creating a custom category list in Microsoft Outlook, and you want everyone in the company to use the same categories. There are a couple of ways to distribute the categories. You can either create an e-mail with the categories assigned or export the part of the Registry where the categories are stored.

To distribute a REG file, you can attach it to an e-mail and send it to everyone who needs it. If your mail server blocks REG attachments (which I strongly recommend), you can instead place the REG file on a network share and e-mail a link to the UNC path of the REG file. Recipients can then click the link to download and import the Registry file.

Setting Permissions on Registry Keys

Just as you can with many other objects in Windows XP, you can apply permissions to Registry keys to specify the actions that specific users or groups can take in the selected key. For example, you can prevent others from accessing your Registry remotely by changing the permissions on the winreg key (explained later in this chapter).

Setting permissions can have implications for you as well as for other users. For example, in the section "Last-Used Key," earlier in this chapter, I explained that you can prevent the Registry Editor from automatically opening the last-used key in the next session by setting permissions on the key where that information is stored. So, if the Registry Editor can't read that key, it can't open the last used key and instead opens at the root of the Registry.

WARNING Be judicious in your application of permissions in the Registry. Incorrectly applying permissions could prevent you from accessing important keys in the Registry or even stop your system from functioning.

You can use the same method in either Professional or Home Edition to set permissions on a Registry key. Open the Registry Editor, select the key on which you want to set permissions, and choose Edit ➢ Permissions to display the dialog box shown in Figure 15.3.

You can use this dialog box to add or remove users and groups and to modify the permissions that each of those users or groups has in the selected key. The Permissions dialog box gives you access to only a few permissions. To set advanced permissions, click Advanced to open the Advanced Security Settings dialog box. The Advanced Security Settings dialog box includes two options that determine how permissions are applied:

Inherit from parent the permission entries that apply to child objects When this option is enabled, the selected key inherits permissions from the parent key.

Replace permission entries on all child objects with entries shown here that apply to child objects Select this option to apply the selected Registry permissions to all subkeys of the currently selected key.

FIGURE 15.3

Use the Permissions dialog box to restrict access to a Registry key.

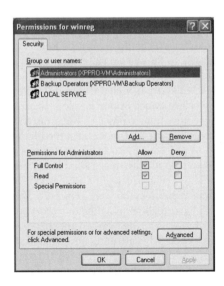

You can also apply special permissions when you need to fine-tune access to a particular key. In the Advanced Security Settings dialog box, select a user or group and click Edit to display the Permission Entry dialog box shown in Figure 15.4. Table 15.2 lists the advanced permissions and their effect.

TABLE 15.2:   Registry Permissions

PERMISSION	EFFECT
Query Value	View the key.
Set Value	Set Registry values.
Create Subkey	Create keys.
Enumerate Subkeys	List/view subkeys.
Notify	Open the key with Notify access.
Create Link	Create links to a key.
Delete	Delete a key.
Write DAC	Determine who has access to a key.
Writer Owner	Determine key ownership.
Read Control	Remotely access Registry objects.

FIGURE 15.4
You can set several advanced permissions on a Registry key.

Working with Hive Files

The Registry Editor also gives you the ability to open, modify, and save a hive separate from your computer's own current Registry hives. Although you might puzzle over why you would want to do this, there are a handful of good reasons. For example, let's assume you have a system that won't let anyone log on because of an improper Registry change. The problem computer boots and can be seen on the network, however. The solution is to load the appropriate Registry hive file, make the modifications, and close the file.

TIP If one of your computers won't boot because of a Registry problem, you can use the Recovery Console to copy the hive file from the problem computer to a working computer, make the necessary changes, and then replace the damaged copy. Because the hive file is probably larger than the capacity of the computer's floppy drive, you'll have to copy it to a removable media such as a Zip disk. Or, if the system uses FAT instead of NTFS, you can boot the system to a Windows 9x boot disk and install a minimal network client on the computer so you can access the files across the network.

You can also use the Registry Editor to open a user's portion of the Registry to make changes for a particular user. The user portion of the Registry is contained in `Ntuser.dat`, which Windows XP stores in the user's profile folder, such as `\Documents and Settings\user`.

To load a hive and modify it, follow these steps:

1. Open the Registry Editor on a working system.

2. Click either HKEY_LOCAL_MACHINE if you're opening a system hive or HKEY_USERS if you're opening a user hive.

3. Choose File ➢ Load Hive to display the Load Hive dialog box. Browse for and select the hive file, and click Open.

4. The Registry Editor prompts you for the hive name. Enter the name under which you want the hive to appear in the editor. For example, if you're opening Joe's user hive, you might use the name **Joe's Hive**.

TIP You can open a hive only if it isn't in use. If you're opening a user hive from a remote computer, that user can't be logged on at the time.

5. The added hive appears under the selected key, as shown in Figure 15.5. You can expand the hive to access keys and values just as you would for a local hive. As with a local hive, Windows XP immediately applies changes to the added hive's file when you make those changes in the Registry Editor.

6. When you're finished working with the hive, select it in the left pane and choose File ➢ Unload Hive.

Managing a Remote Computer's Registry

You can use the Registry Editor to view and modify a remote computer's Registry in much the same way you modify a local Registry. For example, you might want to apply a Registry change to several computers across the network and find that the easiest method is to make the change through the Registry Editor. Or, using the example in the previous section of a computer that won't allow local logon but can still boot, you could connect to the remote computer's Registry to change the setting that is preventing logon.

FIGURE 15.5
You can load and modify an external hive in the Registry Editor.

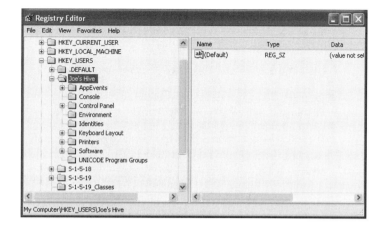

Accessing a Remote Registry

Modifying a remote Registry through the Registry Editor is easy:

1. Open Registry Editor on your local computer, and choose File ≻ Connect Network Registry to display the Select Computer dialog box.

2. Enter the remote computer's name or browse for the computer, and then click OK.

3. Registry Editor adds a new branch to the left pane that includes two subkeys: HKEY_LOCAL_ MACHINE and HKEY_USERS. You can use the same methods in these subkeys to modify keys and values in the remote Registry as you would for the local Registry. Figure 15.6 shows Registry Editor with two remote Registries opened.

4. When you've finished viewing or making changes to the remote Registry, choose File ≻ Disconnect Network Registry. Select the Registry you want to disconnect, and click OK.

FIGURE 15.6
Each remote Registry appears under its own branch in the Registry Editor.

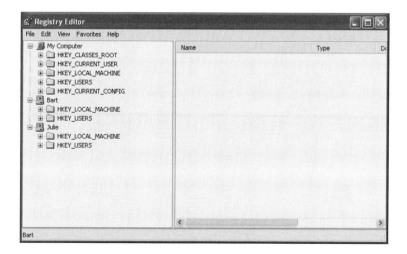

Restricting Remote Registry Access

Your ability to access a Registry remotely depends on the permissions you have in the remote Registry. The permissions on the key

```
\HKEY_LOCAL_MACHINE\System\CurrentControlSet\Control\SecurePipeServers\winreg
```

control which users can access a Registry remotely. By default, the Administrators group has Full Control and can therefore access the Registry remotely. The Backup Operators group has Read permission, as does the LOCAL SERVICE group.

To restrict access or to grant a specific user or group the ability to access the Registry remotely, you must modify the permissions on the key. To do so, open the Registry Editor, select the key

```
\HKEY_LOCAL_MACHINE\System\CurrentControlSet\Control\SecurePipeServers\winreg
```

and then choose Edit ➤ Permissions. Use the Permissions dialog box to add users or groups and assign the desired permissions.

In many situations, you'll probably want to allow limited remote Registry access. For example, the Directory Replicator service needs remote access to perform replication, and the Spooler service on a remote computer needs remote access to your Registry to be able to print to your shared printer(s).

You can take two approaches to allowing selected remote Registry access. The first approach is to grant the remote account the necessary permissions to your Registry. This generally isn't very practical. Instead, you can use the AllowedPaths key to specify specific Registry keys for which remote users and services can bypass the security set on the winreg key. To do so, follow these steps:

1. Open the Registry Editor and open the key

    ```
    \HKEY_LOCAL_MACHINE\System\CurrentControlSet\Control\
    SecurePipeServers\winreg\AllowedPaths
    ```

2. Double-click the Machine value to open the Edit Multi-String dialog box shown in Figure 15.7

3. Add to or modify the list of Registry keys that can be accessed remotely, and then click OK.

4. Restart your computer to make the change take effect.

FIGURE 15.7

The list of accessible keys is stored as a REG_MULTI_SZ data type that you can edit with the Edit Multi-String dialog box.

The Remote Registry Service

Windows XP uses the Remote Registry service to enable remote computers to access the local Registry. The Remote Registry service starts automatically. If you stop this service, remote users and services won't be able to access your local Registry. Doing so can add an additional layer of security for your system as long as your local computer provides no services to other computers on the network (such as printing, replication, and so on). If that's the case, you can configure the Remote Registry for manual startup to prevent it from starting when the system boots.

NOTE   Windows XP Home Edition doesn't include the Remote Registry service, so you can't remotely manage the Registry of a Home Edition computer.

Scripting Registry Changes

It's a simple matter to make changes to the Registry on a single computer with the Registry Editor, and it's almost as easy to make changes on a remote computer. Sometimes, however, you may need to make a change to the Registry on many computers, perhaps as part of a custom application installation or a security change. One of the easiest ways to make these types of global changes is to script them with Windows Script Host (WSH).

TIP   For detailed information on the Windows Script Host, see Chapter 6.

The `WshShell` scripting object enables you to modify the Registry. There are three common tasks you may want to accomplish with the Registry through a script: reading values, writing values, and deleting values. Three methods of the `WshShell` object—`RegRead`, `RegWrite`, and `RegDelete`—enable you to perform these tasks programmatically.

Let's look at a sample script that incorporates all three tasks. The scenario is that you have a custom application you're installing on several computers, and you want to script the Registry changes for it. In this example, the script displays a value from the Registry in a dialog box, creates a key, writes a couple of values to the key, deletes the values, and then deletes the key:

```
' Declare variables
Dim compName, sh, val1, val2
' Create the shell object
Set sh = WScript.CreateObject("Wscript.Shell")
compName = sh.RegRead("HKLM\SYSTEM\CurrentControlSet\Control\ComputerName\
ActiveComputerName\ComputerName")
msgbox "You are running this script from " + compName
' Create the key
sh.RegWrite "HKLM\Software\MyCustomApp\", "", "REG_SZ"
' Write two values to the key
sh.RegWrite "HKLM\Software\MyCustomApp\Installed", 1, "REG_DWORD"
sh.RegWrite "HKLM\Software\MyCustomApp\DefaultAppPath",
"C:\Program Files\MyCustomApp\bin", "REG_SZ"
'Display a dialog showing the values
val1 = sh.RegRead("HKLM\Software\MyCustomApp\Installed")
val2 = sh.RegRead("HKLM\Software\MyCustomApp\DefaultAppPath")
msgbox "Computer: " + compName + vbCrLf + "Installed: " + cstr(val1)
 + vbCrLf + "Path: " + val2
```

```
' Delete the two values
sh.RegDelete "HKLM\Software\MyCustomApp\Installed"
sh.RegDelete "HKLM\Software\MyCustomApp\DefaultAppPath"
' Delete the key
sh.RegDelete "HKLM\Software\MyCustomApp\"
```

Note that when you're working with a key rather than a value, you must include the trailing \ character. If you're specifying a value, you omit the trailing \ character.

The following sites offer information about the RegWrite, RegRead, and RegDelete methods, respectively:

http://msdn.microsoft.com/library/default.asp?url=/library/en-us/script56/html/
wsmthregwrite.asp

http://msdn.microsoft.com/library/default.asp?url=/library/en-us/script56/html/
wsmthregread.asp

http://msdn.microsoft.com/library/default.asp?url=/library/en-us/script56/html/
wsmthregdelete.asp

Chapter 16

Working with Device Manager

Managing hardware in Windows hasn't always been an easy task. Prior to Windows 9*x* and the introduction of Device Manager, managing devices was primarily a matter of kicking real-mode drivers in Autoexec.bat or System.ini when the devices needed configuration changes. Device Manager made that task much easier by putting a graphical interface on the process.

Windows XP has its roots in Windows NT, and whereas device management in NT isn't all it's cracked up to be, Windows 2000 made a big leap with its own Device Manager console. You'll find the same console in Windows XP, making device management in Windows XP relatively easy.

As a power user, you won't have any problem working in Device Manager to manage hardware settings, so I don't cover the nuts and bolts of it in this chapter. Instead, I focus on ways to make it easier to use Device Manager, such as changing the way it displays information to help you identify and manage resources. This chapter also explains how and why to create device logs with Device Manager to provide a historical record of changes you make to systems.

In larger organizations, the ability to remotely manage systems can be a real boon to power users and system administrators. So, this chapter also covers some of the remote-management options.

Tips for Running Device Manager

Windows XP includes Device Manager as a snap-in for the Computer Management console, as shown in Figure 16.1. To open Device Manager, right-click My Computer, choose Manage, and then click the Device Manager node in the left pane.

FIGURE 16.1
You'll find the Device Manager in the Computer Management console.

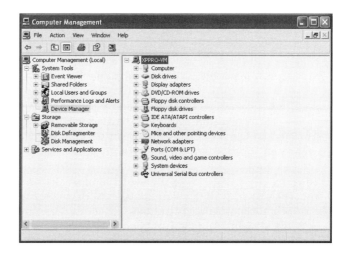

The Computer Management console is a catch-all, containing management tools you might not use very often. For example, I never use the Indexing Service, WMI Control, and Removable Storage consoles on a Windows XP system. Although they certainly apply to XP systems—and you might need them—there are probably just as many people who don't use them. So, when you're working with devices, you might want to either work solely with Device Manager or incorporate it into your own custom console.

Using Device Manager by Itself

Device Manager is a standard MMC console contained in the file Devmgmt.msc, located in the %systemroot%\Sytem32 folder. You can open this console file to work with Device Manager by itself. One way to do that is to create a shortcut to Devmgmt.msc on your Desktop or in the Start menu. Or, you can double-click the MSC file to open the console. Figure 16.2 shows Device Manager running by itself.

FIGURE 16.2

You can use Device Manager by itself.

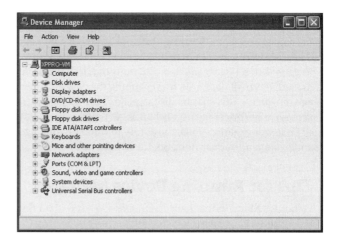

TIP   You can also add the Device Manager snap-in to a new console. In most cases, you'll also add other snap-ins to the console, as discussed in the next section.

Creating a Custom Management Console

Device Manager lets you view and set properties for a device, such as IRQ usage, DMA, and other resources, as well as install or update drivers. When you're managing devices, however, it's sometimes helpful to have other consoles at hand. For example, you might need to stop and start services when you modify hardware settings, so having the Services console and Device Manager together can come in handy. I prefer Device Manager, Services, and Event Viewer in one console when managing devices. This mix gives me access to all the information I need to troubleshoot a device, locate an available resource, and otherwise manage the system's devices (Figure 16.3).

You can easily create your own custom console with these snap-ins or any combination you choose. To do so, click Start ➢ Run and enter **MMC** in the Run dialog box. Choose File ➢ Add/Remove Snap-In and then click Add and add the desired snap-ins. For each, Windows XP asks for the focus for the snap-in; select the Local Computer option.

FIGURE 16.3
Create a custom console to include the snap-ins you use most frequently.

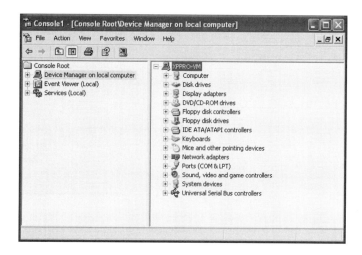

TIP   If you need to compare the settings on a remote computer with those on the local computer, add two instances of Device Manager: one focused on the remote computer and one focused on the local computer.

Running Device Manager in Administrator Context

When you log on using an account that is a member of the Administrators group, you increase the security risk to your system because applications that run when you're logged on can run in an Administrator context. This means the applications have the potential to make changes you might not like. For example, you might connect to a malicious website that downloads and executes an application on your computer that deletes files or compromises your system security in other ways. You also give Trojan horse applications and worms greater access to the system and therefore greater potential to do damage when you run in the Administrator context. For that reason, you should use an account that is a member of the Users or Power Users group for regular work and use an Administrator account only when you need to make system changes.

When you do need to make a change, however, it can be a real hassle to have to close all your programs, log off, and then log on again. Fortunately, you can take a different approach—just run Device Manager or other administrative application in the Administrator context. You use the runas command to do that.

TIP   You can use runas to run any application in a different user context. This chapter focuses on Device Manager.

You can use one of two methods to launch Device Manager in an Administrator context. If you have the Administrative Tools folder on the Start menu, click Start ➤ All Programs ➤ Administrative Tools. Then hold down the Ctrl key and right-click Computer Management, and choose Runas from the context menu. In the Run As dialog box (Figure 16.4), select The Following User and then select the Administrator account from the drop-down list.

FIGURE 16.4
Use the Run As dialog
box to select an account
with administrative
privileges.

You can also use the `runas` command in a command console to launch the Device Manager console. Open a command console, change to the *%systemroot%*\System32 folder, and issue the following command:

```
runas /user:administrator "mmc.exe devmgmt.msc"
```

Windows XP will prompt you for the password for the Administrator account. After you enter the password, you see a message that Windows XP is trying to start the program as the specified user, then Device Manager will open, and you can manage the system as if you were logged on as an Administrator.

NOTE On a Windows XP Home Edition system, the first account created during Setup serves as an Administrator account. Replace `administrator` in the command line with the appropriate account name on a Home Edition system.

Controlling Device View

Device Manager, by default, lists the system devices sorted by device type, such as computer, disk drives, display adapters, and so on. This view is useful when you need to locate a specific device. But this isn't the only view Device Manager offers; its other views can come in handy when you need to manage devices in other ways.

For example, maybe you're trying to resolve an IRQ or a DMA conflict between devices. Rather than search through each device to find its resource settings, you can change the view to show resources by type and view a list of IRQ assignments and the devices that use them. This is a much better view for identifying resource conflicts.

Device Manager provides four views:

Devices By Type This default view, shown in Figure 16.2, lists devices by their type, such as monitor, display adapter, disk drive, CD-ROM drive, keyboard, and so on.

Devices By Connection This view shows devices according to their connection to the computer. All devices connected to a SCSI adapter, for example, appear together under that adapter. All devices connected to the IDE controller on the motherboard show up under the IDE controller. Other devices appear under their respective connections. Figure 16.5 shows Device Manager in Device By Connection view.

FIGURE 16.5

Use the Device By Connection view to show devices according to the way they're connected to the computer.

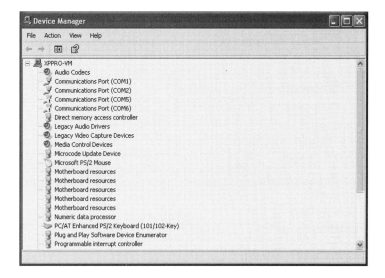

Resources By Type This view shows resource usage sorted by device. The resource categories include Direct Memory Access (DMA), Input/Output (I/O), Interrupt Request (IRQ), and Memory. Each category shows the resources used and the device that is using each one. Figure 16.6 shows the Resources By Type view. You might use this view when you're trying to identify an available resource.

NOTE This view doesn't show unallocated resources. Unused IRQs, for example, don't show up in the IRQ list.

FIGURE 16.6

Use the Resources By Type view to determine which resources are assigned to which devices.

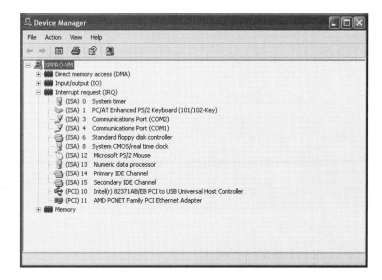

Resources By Connection   This view (Figure 16.7) shows resource use sorted by device connection. It's similar to the Resources By Type view, except that the resource list is organized by device connection rather than device type. You might use this view when you're trying to determine the resources being used by all devices on a given connection (such as all devices on a SCSI or IDE host adapter).

Showing Hidden Devices

By default, Device Manager hides certain types of devices, such as all non–Plug and Play drivers. This includes the IPSec driver, NDIS system driver, TCP/IP protocol driver, and several others. Device Manager also hides a handful of other devices.

In most situations, you won't need to view or work with the hidden devices. If you do, however, you can easily configure Device Manager to show them. To do so, choose View ➤ Show Hidden Devices. The hidden devices will then show up in your view.

FIGURE 16.7
Use Resources By Connection to view resource assignments according to device connection.

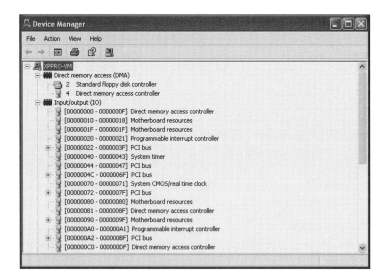

Creating Device and Configuration Logs

Windows XP can create system restore points that enable you to easily restore the system to a specific condition. For example, assume you're about to install some software or a new device. To be safe, you create a system restore point prior to making the change. Then, you install the software or device. If the system is unstable after the change, you can restore the system to the previous state, which is defined by the restore point. Chapter 39 covers System Restore in detail.

In addition to using System Restore, you should also create device configuration logs that will help you troubleshoot problems that might occur with your system's hardware. For example, assume you change a device's DMA or memory settings and a few days later notice a problem with a device. The problem could be a resource conflict. Having a record of the change you made can help you locate and troubleshoot the problem.

TIP   It's a good idea to print a system summary before taking your computer to be serviced. The summary serves as a record of what's in your computer. Most repair shops are reputable, but it doesn't hurt to have a hard copy on hand just in case.

You can use Device Manager to print or save a system summary. The system summary includes information about your OS version and service packs, registration information, BIOS, processors, physical RAM, and other system properties. The summary also lists information about your disk drives, CD-ROM drive, and device resource usage.

You can also print a detailed listing for a specific device or for an entire device class (such as all disk drives, for example). In most cases, I don't recommend printing a device or class report, because you'll end up with lots of pages. This is particularly true if you print a complete system report, which includes a system summary and details for every device.

Device Manager gives you the means to print a report but not save it to disk, the latter being a much better option when you need to generate a full system report (because of the quantity of data). However, you can get around that limitation by printing the report to a generic text printer. If you haven't already done so, run the Add Printer Wizard and create an instance of the Generic/Text Only printer pointed to FILE as the port. Then, print the report to a file.

To print a report, open Device Manager, click the computer in the right pane, and choose Action ➢ Print to open the Print dialog box (Figure 16.8). Choose a report in the Report Type group, choose the printer, and click Print. With each report type you get a system summary; your selection determines whether you also get detailed information as well.

FIGURE 16.8

You can print three types of reports in Device Manager.

Managing Devices on a Remote Computer

Device Manager lets you connect to a remote computer and view devices and their settings on that remote computer. However, Device Manager operates in read-only mode when connected to a remote computer. In effect, you can look but not touch—you can make changes through Device Manager only on the local computer, not on a remote computer. That isn't very convenient when you need to troubleshoot a computer located in another part of the building and it's really a drag if that computer is on another continent (unless you're shooting for a company-paid vacation).

You have a few options for managing devices remotely, most of which require some means of remote access other than a plane ticket. The first (and easiest) option is to use Remote Desktop Connection to connect to the remote computer. You can then open Device Manager on the remote computer and make whatever changes are needed, just as if you were sitting at the remote computer. You can use other remote-access tools instead of Remote Desktop Connection to connect to and manage a remote computer; third-party tools such as pcAnywhere and VNC are good examples.

NOTE   See Chapter 23 for detailed information on setting up and using Remote Desktop Connection.

You have a couple of options for managing remote systems from a console, although this is limited primarily to stopping and starting services. You can connect to the remote computer using a Telnet session (if the remote computer is acting as a Telnet server) or use the netsvc command to manage the remote services.

NOTE   See Chapter 10 for details on remote service management tools, including netsvc.

Chapter 17

Configuring Hardware

Some people love to tinker with computer hardware; others hate it. The rest of us think about our computer's hardware only when one of two things happens: we need to add a new gadget, or one that is already installed fails and needs to be replaced. Windows 2000's incorporation of Device Manager and Plug and Play (PnP) support went a long way toward simplifying device installation and management. Windows XP builds on those capabilities to make device management just as easy.

In order to effectively manage computer hardware under Windows XP, you need to understand some basic concepts. In the first few sections in this chapter, I take you through device drivers and PnP to give you the background you'll need to add, remove, and configure devices under Windows XP. You'll also learn how to update and replace device drivers.

Installing devices is an easy task in Windows XP, so you shouldn't have any trouble with the mechanics of adding or removing devices. Rather than focus on device installation, this chapter explains how to disable and enable them. The ability to disable devices lets you prevent XP from using a device without having to remove it. This is handy when a device would otherwise conflict with another in the system, and you don't want Windows to keep trying to install it for you at each boot. You can disable one of the devices to avoid the conflict, enabling it and disabling the other when you need to use it. It's also handy when you're experiencing problems with the system, and you want to temporarily shut down a device for troubleshooting.

Resource usage is another important hardware topic you need to understand to effectively manage hardware. In this chapter, I explain how devices often use DMA, I/O, IRQ, and memory resources and how to configure them. For example, you might need to change the DMA channel a device uses to prevent a conflict with another device. This chapter explains how.

Working with Drivers

You don't need to know the ins and outs of Windows XP device drivers and how they work to manage devices. It is important, however, to have a basic understanding of the function that device drivers play and how to work with them.

Understanding Drivers

A *device driver* is a program, usually small, that serves as a means of communication between a device and the operating system. Typically vendors implement device drivers as `.sys` files, sometimes supplementing them with Dynamic Link Libraries (DLL files). With a few exceptions, the device driver loads at system startup, enabling Windows XP to communicate with the associated device.

Windows XP includes a large library of drivers for generic equipment types as well as specific third-party devices. These drivers are stored in the *%systemroot%*`\Driver Cache\i386\driver.cab` file. When Windows XP detects a new device, the operating system looks in the `driver.cab` file for an appropriate driver and, if it finds one, installs that driver and any associated files for the device. If Windows XP can't find a driver, it prompts you to specify the location of the driver files. Some devices provide a Setup program that takes care of installing the driver and any other support software. You've no doubt been through these processes before, so it won't be new to you.

In Windows XP, as in Windows 2000, drivers are either *signed* or *unsigned*. Microsoft implemented driver signing to provide additional security for the operating system, but mainly to improve system stability.

Signed drivers have a digital signature attached to them. The signature signifies that the driver has passed certain compatibility and performance requirements from Microsoft's Windows Hardware Quality Labs. The signature also ensures that the driver hasn't been modified by a virus or Trojan horse application or subjected to other unwanted changes. Digital signing doesn't guarantee that a driver is completely free of bugs, but it reduces the likelihood. Later, in the section "Signed vs. Unsigned Drivers," I explain the mechanism that Windows XP provides to prevent unsigned drivers from being installed and the issues to consider when installing drivers.

Viewing Device Driver Properties

Before you go through the trouble of searching for an updated device driver, take the time to determine what version you have now. You don't want to go through the hassle of updating a driver only to find that you already have the latest version.

To view the driver's properties, open Device Manager and locate the device. Double-click the device to open its properties sheet, and then click the Driver tab (Figure 17.1).

FIGURE 17.1
You can manage a
device's driver through
the Driver tab.

As Figure 17.1 shows, the Driver tab lists general information about the provider, driver date, version, and whether the driver is signed. You can click Driver Details to display a dialog box that shows the path to each of the files. Click a file to view its version, provider, and other information.

NOTE   Some drivers consist of a single file. Others use two, three, or more, depending on the device.

With the version information in hand, you can check the vendor's website or other sources to determine whether a newer version of the driver exists.

Getting Device Information with *driverquery*

Windows XP Professional includes a command-line tool you can use to get information about the drivers on a system. You'll find the program `driverquery.com` in the *%systemroot%*\System32 folder. The syntax for the command is

```
driverquery [/S system [/U username [/P [password]]] [/FO format]  [/NH] [/SI] [/V]
```

Table 17.1 lists the parameters and variables.

TABLE 17.1:   *driverquery* Parameters

PARAMETER	DESCRIPTION
/S *system*	Specify the system from which to display driver information. Omit to use the local system. Specify *system* in the form *computer* or *domain\computer*.
/U *username*	Specify the user context in which the program will run.
/P *password*	Specify the password for the user name specified with the /U switch. Omit to be prompted for the password.
/FO *format*	Specify the format for the driver information output. Replace *format* with TABLE, LIST, or CSV.
/NH	Suppress the column header for the TABLE or CSV format.
/SI	Display information about signed drivers.
/V	Verbose mode; display detailed information.

When used without any parameters, `driverquery` lists information about drivers on the local system as shown in the following sample output using the default TABLE output mode.

```
Module Name  Display Name           Driver Type   Link Date
============ ====================== ============= ======================
ACPI         Microsoft ACPI Driver  Kernel        8/4/2004 1:07:35 AM
ACPIEC       ACPIEC                 Kernel        8/17/2001 3:57:55 PM
aec          Microsoft Kernel Acous Kernel        2/13/2004 9:20:15 AM
AFD          AFD Networking Support Kernel        8/4/2004 1:14:13 AM
agp440       Intel AGP Bus Filter   Kernel        8/4/2004 1:07:40 AM
Arp1394      1394 ARP Client Protoc Kernel        8/4/2004 12:58:28 AM
AsyncMac     RAS Asynchronous Media Kernel        8/4/2004 1:05:02 AM
atapi        Standard IDE/ESDI Hard Kernel        8/4/2004 12:59:41 AM
ati2mtag     ati2mtag               Kernel        1/27/2004 8:56:55 PM
```

```
ATIBTCAP      ATI TV Wonder Video Ca Kernel      11/5/2002 6:14:42 PM
ATIBTXBAR     ATI TV Wonder Video Cr Kernel      11/5/2002 6:13:59 PM
ATIVTUTW      ATI TV Wonder TV Tuner Kernel      11/5/2002 6:13:56 PM
ATIVXSTW      ATI TV Wonder Audio Cr Kernel      11/5/2002 6:13:57 PM
ATIXBAR       ATI TV Wonder WDM Audi Kernel      11/5/2002 6:13:57 PM
Atmarpc       ATM ARP Client Protoco Kernel      8/4/2004 12:58:29 AM
audstub       Audio Stub Driver      Kernel      8/17/2001 3:59:40 PM
Beep          Beep                   Kernel      8/17/2001 3:47:33 PM
Bridge        MAC Bridge             Kernel      8/4/2004 12:59:56 AM
BridgeMP      MAC Bridge Miniport    Kernel      8/4/2004 12:59:56 AM
BT848         ATI TV Wonder BtCap, W Kernel      4/24/2001 12:53:58 PM
BTTUNER       ATI TV Wonder TVTuner, Kernel      11/5/2002 6:13:56 PM
```

Verbose mode displays considerably more information, such as start mode, state, status, the amount of memory used by the driver, and more. Verbose mode generates a wide listing that you'll have difficulty viewing in a console, but you can redirect the output to a file and view it in Notepad. The following example redirects to a file:

driverquery /V > DriverInfo.txt

Use the LIST output mode when you want to display the driver information in a vertical list, with each driver separated from the next by a blank line:

```
Module Name:      ACPI
Display Name:     Microsoft ACPI Driver
Driver Type:      Kernel
Link Date:        8/4/2004 1:07:35 AM

Module Name:      ACPIEC
Display Name:     ACPIEC
Driver Type:      Kernel
Link Date:        8/17/2001 3:57:55 PM

Module Name:      aec
Display Name:     Microsoft Kernel Acoustic Echo Canceller
Driver Type:      Kernel
Link Date:        2/13/2004 9:20:15 AM

Module Name:      AFD
Display Name:     AFD Networking Support Environment
Driver Type:      Kernel
Link Date:        8/4/2004 1:14:13 AM

Module Name:      agp440
Display Name:     Intel AGP Bus Filter
Driver Type:      Kernel
Link Date:        8/4/2004 1:07:40 AM
```

Use the CSV format when you want to output the information in comma-delimited format for import into a spreadsheet or database. Generally, you'll redirect the output to a file rather than the display when using the CSV mode. The following is a sample output using CSV mode:

```
"Module Name","Display Name","Driver Type","Link Date"
"AFD","AFD Networking Support Environment","Kernel ","8/17/2001 8:30:36 PM"
"AsyncMac","RAS Asynchronous Media Driver","Kernel ","8/17/2001 3:55:29 PM"
"atapi","Standard IDE/ESDI Hard Disk Controller","Kernel ","8/17/2001 3:51:49 PM
"Atmarpc","ATM ARP Client Protocol","Kernel ","8/17/2001 3:46:40 PM"
"audstub","Audio Stub Driver","Kernel ","8/17/2001 3:59:40 PM"
"Beep","Beep","Kernel ","8/17/2001 3:47:33 PM"
"cbidf2k","cbidf2k","Kernel ","8/17/2001 3:52:06 PM"
"Cdaudio","Cdaudio","Kernel ","8/17/2001 3:52:26 PM"
"Cdfs","Cdfs","File System ","8/17/2001 10:33:34 PM"
"Cdrom","CD-ROM Driver","Kernel ","8/17/2001 3:52:25 PM"
"Disk","Disk Driver","Kernel ","8/17/2001 3:52:31 PM"
"dmboot","dmboot","Kernel ","8/17/2001 3:58:34 PM"
"dmio","Logical Disk Manager Driver","Kernel ","8/17/2001 3:58:27 PM"
"dmload","dmload","Kernel ","8/17/2001 3:58:15 PM"
"Fastfat","Fastfat","File System ","8/17/2001 10:39:54 PM"
"Fdc","Floppy Disk Controller Driver","Kernel ","8/17/2001 3:51:22 PM"
```

TIP Use the /NH parameter if the program in which you'll be importing the information doesn't need the first line of the file to include the column or field names. For example, exclude the column headings if you're importing the data into an existing database that already has the fields defined.

The driverquery tool can be truly useful for displaying information about drivers on a local or remote computer, but it's most useful for gathering information for analysis in a database, spreadsheet, or other data analysis tool.

TIP You can use the driverquery command from a local console to retrieve information about drivers on a remote system that is located on your network. For systems not on the local network, connect with a Telnet session and use driverquery in the Telnet session to retrieve information from those remote systems. Keep in mind that you need to make a connection only to a Telnet server on the remote LAN, and you can use the driverquery tool to retrieve driver information from any computer on that remote LAN—you don't need a Telnet session to each remote computer.

Driver Compatibility

In general, Windows XP is particular about the drivers you install, and whenever possible you should use a driver written specifically for Windows XP. In a pinch when no XP driver is available, however, you should be able to use a Windows 2000 version of a driver without any problems. Although there is the possibility of an exception, most drivers written for Windows 9x and NT won't work well, if at all, under Windows XP. If you have a device you need to use under Windows XP, and the vendor doesn't offer a 2000 driver or an XP driver, you can try installing the available driver. However, back up your critical files and/or create a system restore point before installing the driver. Then, test the system fully after installation to make sure everything is working properly.

NOTE   See Chapter 39 for detailed information on creating system restore points and restoring a system using this method.

Updating/Replacing Device Drivers

Most hardware vendors continue to improve on their drivers after the initial release, incorporating bug fixes and in some cases adding support for new features. So, it's a good idea to check periodically for updated drivers and replace them if you're looking for additional features. This is particularly true if you're experiencing a problem with a device. Check the vendor's website for driver updates, and also check your computer manufacturer's site for updated drivers. You'll need the device name and model, which you can generally find in Device Manager. Just expand the device branch to view the device name and model of devices under the selected branch.

WARNING   I subscribe to the old adage, "If it ain't broke, don't fix it." Not the most grammatically correct bit of wisdom, but still good advice. If you're satisfied with the way a device is working, don't go looking for updates. You might find that a new driver introduces problems you didn't have before.

When you're ready to upgrade the driver, you can use one of two methods, depending on the way the vendor has packaged the driver. In some cases, the vendor includes a Setup program that you can run to update the driver. If so, run the Setup program and follow its prompts to install the update. Otherwise, you can update the driver through Device Manager.

TIP   Installing or removing devices requires administrator privileges. You must either log on as a member of the Administrators group or supply the administrator password when prompted by Windows XP.

Follow these steps:

1. Open Device Manager and locate the device whose driver you want to update.
2. Double-click the device to open its properties sheet, and click the Driver tab.
3. Click Update Driver to start the Hardware Update Wizard.
4. Follow the prompts provided by the wizard, pointing it to the location where your new driver files are located. If you have a CD or floppy, browse the disk for a `Windows XP` folder or, lacking that, a `Windows 2000` folder (or a folder obviously intended for those platforms, such as `W2K` or `WXP`). If you downloaded the files to your hard disk, select the download location, instead.

Rolling Back after an Upgrade

Windows XP keeps track of changes that you make when you update a driver or add a new device. So, if you update a driver and find that it doesn't give you the performance or features you were looking for, or it introduces new bugs or problems you didn't have before, you can easily roll back the system to use the previously installed driver. This is similar in a way to restoring the system from a restore point, but rolling back a driver affects only the selected driver. It has no other impact on the system state.

To roll back a driver, open Device Manager and then open the properties for the device. Click the Driver tab, and then click Roll Back Driver. Windows XP prompts you to confirm that you want to perform the rollback and then accomplishes the task for you.

TIP   If you haven't updated the driver for a device, and therefore no backup driver exists, Windows XP displays a dialog box that gives you the option of launching the Troubleshooter to troubleshoot the device. Click No to cancel or Yes to start the Troubleshooter.

Uninstalling a Driver

There are a handful of circumstances in which you might want to uninstall a driver. You might want to remove it to reinstall the driver from scratch. You might not be using the device and want to prevent the device driver from loading or consuming any system resources. Or perhaps you've determined that the current driver is buggy, and you want to remove it until you can obtain an updated driver. Uninstalling the driver prevents it from loading but doesn't remove the device. When it's time to get the device going again, you only need to reinstall the driver, not the device. This can save you a bit of time.

To uninstall a driver, open Device Manager and open the properties sheet for the device. Click the Driver tab, and then click Uninstall. Windows XP prompts you to confirm the deletion and then removes the device driver's files and corresponding Registry entries.

If you're removing the driver for a PnP device, the device must be plugged in. So, for removable devices such as PC Card network adapters, modems, and so on, make sure the device is plugged in, and then remove the driver. You can unplug the device after removing the driver.

TIP   You can reinstall drivers for a PnP removable device without removing and then reinserting the device. To do so, open Device Manager, and choose Action ➢ Scan For Hardware Changes. Windows XP will redetect the device and install its driver. Windows also detects the device— whether you want it to or not—each time the system boots.

Signed vs. Unsigned Drivers

As I explained previously in this chapter, driver signing helps ensure that drivers are fully compatible with Windows XP and have been tested for performance and reliability. It's therefore always preferable to use signed drivers rather than unsigned ones.

In some situations, however, you find that you can't get a signed driver for a device. Maybe the device manufacturer chose not to go through the added effort and expense to have the driver certified and signed (not a good indication of quality, unfortunately). Or perhaps the device is relatively old and the manufacturer chose not to write a driver for Windows XP, or the company is out of business. Whatever the situation, you can use unsigned drivers. You can also control the way Windows XP handles unsigned drivers.

CONTROLLING DRIVER SIGNING LOCALLY

If you attempt to install an unsigned driver, Windows XP displays a warning dialog box that gives you the option of either continuing with the installation or canceling it. You can configure other behavior for unsigned drivers, as well. To do so, open the System properties sheet from Control Panel and click the Hardware tab. Click Driver Signing to open the dialog box shown in Figure 17.2.

You can choose one of three options: have Windows XP ignore driver signing and always install drivers, have it prompt you (the default), or always prevent unsigned drivers from being installed. If you're logged on as an administrator, you can choose the option Make This Action The System Default to apply the setting to all users of the local computer.

FIGURE 17.2
Configure how Windows XP handles unsigned drivers through the Driver Signing Options dialog box.

CONTROLLING DRIVER SIGNING WITH GROUP POLICY

In a large network, it usually isn't practical to configure Windows XP's driver-signing behavior through the method I described previously. In these situations, it's much easier and more effective to apply the behavior through a group policy.

NOTE You can apply the behavior locally by modifying the local policy. Open the MMC, and add the Group Policy snap-in focused on the local computer. Then modify the policy as explained in this section for group policies.

To configure group policies for driver signing, follow these steps:

1. Open the Active Directory Users And Computers console on a Windows 2000 or Windows .NET domain controller for the applicable domain.

2. Right-click the domain or organizational unit, and choose Properties.

3. Click the Group Policy tab, and then edit an existing group policy object or create a new one.

4. Expand the \Computer Configuration\Windows Settings\Security Settings\Local Policies\ Security Options branch. Open the Unsigned Driver Installation Behavior policy, and select Define This Policy Setting.

5. Choose one of the following from the drop-down list:

    Silently Succeed This option allows unsigned drivers to be installed without prompting or warning.

    Warn But Allow Installation This option prompts the user to allow or prevent the driver to be installed.

    Do Not Allow Installation This option blocks unsigned driver installation.

TIP You can define the policy at the site level to apply to all domains, if desired. To do so, use the Active Directory Sites And Services console to set the policy rather than the Active Directory Users And Computers console.

Stopping and Starting Device Drivers

Although you'll most often disable a device to prevent Windows XP from using it, you may occasionally want to stop or restart a device driver. You can determine which device drivers can accept a stop or start command by listing the services with `driverquery` (explained in detail in the previous section, "Getting Device Information with *driverquery*"). Use the /V switch to create a verbose listing, and then check the value for the service in the Accept Stop column. If this value is TRUE, you can stop and start the service.

You can stop and start certain services through Device Manager. To do so, choose View ➤ Show Hidden Devices to display the non-PnP devices. Open the properties for the device whose driver you want to stop, and then click the Driver tab. Click Stop or Start as appropriate.

TIP If you want to test your ability to stop and start a service, try stopping and starting the Beep driver. It's a relatively low-priority service that won't be missed.

You can also stop and start drivers using the `net` command. Open a console, type **net stop** *driver*, where *driver* is the device driver's name. Use **net start** *driver* to start the driver again.

TIP For more information on working with services and the `net` command (as well as its remote cousin, `netsvc`), see Chapter 10.

Managing Plug and Play

In its earliest incarnation, Plug and Play (PnP) worked sporadically at best. Over time, however, manufacturers and Microsoft have worked together to improve PnP's performance from the system, device, and operating system perspectives.

PnP has several requirements in order to work properly and allow automatic installation and configuration of hardware. First, the system's BIOS must support PnP. All new systems support PnP, as do many older systems. A quick scan through an older system's BIOS setup program for PnP-related settings will tell you whether the system supports PnP.

The second requirement to support PnP device management is a PnP-compliant operating system. Windows 95 was the first of Microsoft's OSes to support PnP, and support has only improved in later versions, including Windows XP.

Third, the device itself must support PnP. This means the device must be able to provide an identification string to the operating system so the OS can identify the device manufacturer, type, model, and so on. The OS needs this information to automatically install support for the device (more on this shortly). Also, the device must be able to provide the OS with a list of its required resources, including such system resources as DMA channel and IRQ, as well as the drivers it requires.

Finally, the device must be designed to detect and respond to PnP events such as directives to power down the device (where applicable) or other hardware control events. With a true PnP-compatible device, Windows XP can dynamically load and unload drivers as needed. Unplug a PC Card network adapter, for example, and Windows XP can shut down the driver until the device is reinserted, at which time it restarts the driver.

ISA-bus devices (8-bit or 16-bit ISA adapters) generally don't support PnP. Most PCI-bus devices do support PnP. PC Card (formerly PCMCIA) and USB devices are by definition PnP devices. So, with rare exceptions, all the devices sold today that connect to the system through PCI, PC Card, USB, or FireWire (IEEE 1394) interfaces support PnP. Devices that connect through a standard serial or parallel port can support PnP, but the likelihood is less than for the other interface types.

PnP Device Installation

The beauty of PnP is that it automates the device installation process. So, there isn't a lot for me to tell you about installing PnP devices, except briefly how it works.

When you install a PnP device and boot Windows XP (or connect the device to a PnP-compatible bus such as USB), the operating system reads the ID string stored in the device's firmware or BIOS. XP then looks in its driver index—which it builds from the files in the *%systemroot%*\Inf folder—for a match. If it finds one, it installs the appropriate driver file(s) and makes any other needed system modifications to support the device. When the process is finished, Windows XP displays a message informing you that the installation is complete.

TIP   Many PnP devices require that you install the software that comes with the device before installing the device itself. This adds the driver files to Windows XP's driver index and allows the OS to install the drivers automatically.

If Windows XP can't find a driver for the PnP device, it starts the Found New Hardware Wizard, which prompts you for the location of the drivers for the device. This is the same method XP uses for non-PnP devices that it's able to detect.

NOTE   Windows XP detects non-PnP devices in much the same way it detects PnP devices, by querying the devices for ID strings. The main difference is that the PnP devices let Windows XP automatically configure the device. Non-PnP devices don't support configuration by the OS. However, Windows XP is at least able to identify and install the appropriate driver for most non-PnP devices and enable you to specify any required settings such as IRQ or other resources.

Managing Devices

As I explained in the chapter introduction, I don't cover adding and removing hardware per se in this chapter, because you shouldn't have any problems accomplishing that. Instead, this section focuses on how to manage devices that are already installed in the system.

Enabling and Disabling Devices

Occasionally you might have two devices that need the same resources, or a device might seem to be preventing an application or another device from working properly. Although you could remove the device, you might prefer to disable it. Doing so shuts down the device but makes it an easy matter to get it going again when you need it—you can just enable it again.

TIP   If two devices conflict with one another and you don't need to use them at the same time, you can create two hardware profiles and disable one device in each profile. Then, boot with the appropriate profile when you need to use a specific device.

To temporarily disable a device, open Device Manager, and open the properties for the device to be disabled. On the General tab, select Do Not Use This Device (Disable) from the Device Usage drop-down list, and click OK. To reenable the device, open the General tab again, and select Use This Device (Enable) from the drop-down list; then click OK.

Device Resource Use

Most devices use some type of system resource. These resources include Interrupt Request Line (IRQ), Direct Memory Access (DMA) channel, I/O base address, and memory address. The system has a limited amount of each resource type, and as you add more devices, the potential for resource conflicts increases. You may occasionally need to modify the resources used by a device to overcome a resource conflict.

Fortunately, resource conflicts in Windows XP are rare unless your system contains multiple legacy devices (non-PnP adapters). Most devices don't require DMA, so the system can usually accommodate all DMA-needy devices with the available DMA channels. The same is generally true for devices that require an I/O base address or a memory range.

The exception to this plethora of resources is the IRQ resources available on the system. With earlier systems, IRQ allocation was a real problem, and finding an available IRQ for a device in an already heavily populated system was difficult. Thankfully, Windows XP takes advantage of the fact that most of today's devices that require an IRQ are PCI devices; in addition, most of today's motherboards provide Advanced Configuration and Power Interface (ACPI) compliance, which enables them to share IRQs among multiple devices. So, it isn't uncommon to see two or three devices in a Windows XP system using the same IRQ.

TIP   Although some devices support sharing IRQs, they also refuse to work correctly if they're sharing an IRQ. Everything might look good with the device's drivers and resources, but it still might not work. Sharing IRQs can be a hit-or-miss proposition.

CONFIGURING RESOURCE SETTINGS

The combination of PnP and ACPI means that you seldom have to make any resource configuration changes for devices in Windows XP. In fact, you often can't change resource settings directly in Device Manager but instead must force changes by removing a specific IRQ from PnP availability in the system's BIOS. However, changing resource settings is necessary when you have one or more non-PnP devices in the system. This section explains how to view and change resource settings.

TIP   If you open the Resources tab of a device's properties sheet and the Use Automatic Settings check box is selected and dimmed, you can't modify the resource settings for the device.

To change resources for those devices that support it, follow these steps:

1. Open Device Manager, open the properties sheet for the device, and then click the Resources tab (Figure 17.3).

TIP   If the device isn't using any resources, the Resources tab contains a single button: Set Configuration Manually. Click this button to make the tab change so it looks like the one in Figure 17.3.

2. If the option Use Automatic Settings is selected, clear it.

3. Select the resource (I/O range, IRQ, and so on) from the Resource Settings list, and click Change Setting. If you receive the error "You cannot modify the resources in this configuration," you must select a different configuration from the Settings Based On drop-down list.

4. In the resulting dialog box—which differs slightly according to the resource type—choose the resource setting you want to use, and click OK.

NOTE   If the resource value you select is already in use by another device, Device Manager shows the conflicting device in the Conflict Information list. You can then either select a different value or change the resource usage on the other device.

Managing Hidden Devices

I've already discussed, to some degree, the existence of hidden devices in Windows XP and the fact that you can view and manage them in Device Manager. Hidden devices are primarily non-PnP drivers, but there are a handful of others.

To view the hidden devices, open Device Manager and choose View ➤ Show Hidden Devices. Device Manager then refreshes the display to show additional branches and devices.

You can manage hidden devices in much the same way you manage other devices in Device Manager. The General tab for a hidden device's properties sheet, for example, lets you enable or disable it.

The Driver tab, though, is somewhat different from the Driver tab for other types of devices. For most hidden devices, you can use the Driver tab to stop and start the driver as well as configure its startup method. In general, you probably won't have to stop or start these devices except in the situations I suggested earlier in this chapter. Unless you're directed to do so by a support engineer, I don't recommend changing the startup type for a service unless you understand the implications of the change and how it will affect not only the device but also other devices and system services.

Chapter 18

Managing the File System

Several advanced features in Windows XP can baffle even the most experienced users. IPSec, encryption, and some other features can seem like a foreign language.

There are also a couple of *basic* features that can confuse users, and the file system is one of them. In order to choose between FAT and NTFS file systems, for example, you need to know the advantages and disadvantages of each. In order to set up a fault-tolerant volume, you need to understand not only what RAID is all about, but also the difference between basic and dynamic disks.

This chapter explains several key features associated with the file system options in Windows XP. I also cover how to configure disks and volumes, including how to use compression and how to optimize volumes in other ways.

Another feature you'll find handy for NTFS volumes is the ability to mount a volume to an empty NTFS folder. You could, for example, increase the apparent size of drive C: when it nears capacity by installing a new drive and mounting it into a folder in drive C:. This would let you go from, say, a nearly full 4 GB disk to a 40 GB disk without replacing the existing drive or moving any files.

Windows XP also supports Redundant Array of Independent Disks (RAID), which lets you extend and protect volumes. Windows XP Professional supports RAID level 0, which offers improved performance but no fault tolerance. I discuss RAID levels in detail later in the chapter.

Windows XP adds some new wrinkles for sharing folders and files, and I try to iron out those wrinkles for you in this chapter, as well. The new Simple File Sharing (SFS) can be difficult to understand (paradoxically), particularly if you're experienced with the file-sharing mechanisms in Windows 2000 and other platforms. I'll even show you a trick to get around SFS in Windows XP Home Edition when you need better sharing security.

Configuring Disks and Volumes

The Disk Management console is the main tool you'll use to manage disks and volumes. It's included in the Computer Management console, or you can add it to your own custom console. Figure 18.1 shows the Disk Management console with the Disk List view in the top pane and Graphical View in the bottom pane.

Disk Management offers four views:

Disk List   This option organizes the view as a list by physical disk.

Volume List   This option organizes the view as a list by logical volumes.

Graphical View   This option shows physical disks and logical volumes using a graphical view rather than a list.

Hidden   This option hides the bottom pane.

FIGURE 18.1
Use the Disk Management console to partition, format, and perform other disk operations.

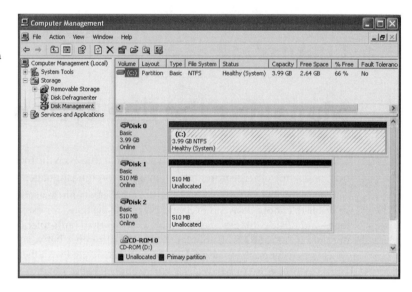

TIP You must be logged on with an account that has administrator privileges in order to run Disk Management. You can use the `runas` command to launch the console in an administrative context if your current logon account doesn't have it. See the section "Running Disk Defragmenter in Administrator Context," later in this chapter, to learn more about `runas`.

Some disk operations, such as setting the volume label, aren't covered in this chapter because they're relatively basic and easy to accomplish. You should have no problems with those tasks. Instead, the remainder of the chapter focuses on more advanced disk topics and those that aren't self-evident from the Disk Management console.

WARNING If you're coming to Windows XP from Windows NT, understand that Windows XP commits all disk changes as soon as you make the changes in the Disk Management console. This is different from Windows NT, which requires that you manually commit disk changes (such as deleting a partition) to make them take effect.

Understanding Basic and Dynamic Disks

The disks supported by DOS and all versions of Windows prior to Windows 2000 are now called *basic disks*. Non-Itanium, 32-bit systems (your average PCs) support a maximum of four partitions per basic disk. These partitions can be either *primary partitions* or *extended partitions*. A primary partition functions as a single logical drive. Extended partitions can contain multiple logical volumes. A disk can include up to four primary partitions, or up to three primary partitions and one extended partition.

Systems with a 64-bit Itanium processor support both basic and dynamic disks. These systems also support a new type of disk-partitioning schemed called GUID Partition Table (GPT), which supports a theoretically unlimited number of unique partitions per disk. GPT also supports volumes up to 8,192 EB (exabytes) in size and primary and backup partition tables for redundancy. Windows XP 64-Bit Edition runs on Itanium processor–based systems. It can read/write but can't boot from a basic disk.

TIP   GUID stands for globally unique ID.

Windows 2000 introduced a new type of disk called *dynamic disks,* and Windows XP Professional carries forward support for dynamic disks. Professional supports features on dynamic disks that it doesn't support on basic disks. This includes the ability to create the following types of volumes:

Simple   This volume type comprises space from a single dynamic disk. It can use a single region on a disk or multiple regions on the disk that are linked together. You can extend a simple disk to include additional space, and extending a simple volume onto other physical disks makes it a spanned volume.

Spanned   These volumes comprise space on more than one physical disk, enabling you to create a larger volume than what's available on a single disk. You can extend an existing spanned volume to further increase its capacity.

Striped   This type of volume provides better performance by striping the data for a single logical volume across two or more disks. The performance increase comes from distributing the read/write load across multiple disks. Striped volumes don't offer any fault tolerance. If one disk in a striped set fails, the entire volume is lost.

RAID   There are several levels of RAID, but Windows XP Professional supports only RAID level 0, or striped volumes (see the previous item). RAID 0 doesn't provide any fault tolerance. To gain that, you need to move up to RAID 1, disk mirroring, or RAID 5, stripe sets with parity. These RAID levels are supported by Microsoft's Server platforms, such as Windows 2000 Server and Windows Server 2003.

NOTE   Windows XP Home Edition doesn't support dynamic disks and therefore doesn't support the features made possible by dynamic disks such as spanned and striped volumes. Throughout the remainder of this chapter, any discussion of spanned and striped volumes or of dynamic disks applies only to Windows XP Professional.

NOTE   See "Creating and Managing Advanced Volumes," later in this chapter, for more details on RAID levels and their benefits.

Compatibility is the main advantage offered by basic disks. Systems with operating systems prior to Windows 2000 don't support dynamic disks. This is an issue only on systems that dual-boot between Windows XP (or Windows 2000) and Windows NT, Me, or 9x. If you're only running Windows XP on the computer, you don't have to worry about compatibility, except in one situation: disaster recovery. If you're using basic disks with a FAT file system and something happens to a system that prevents it from booting, you can boot with a Windows 9x or DOS boot disk and still gain access to the files. On systems with NTFS, you can use Recovery Console to attempt to recover the system.

NOTE   Windows NT supports simple, spanned, striped, and RAID volumes, but not through dynamic disks. Windows 2000 and Windows XP support existing volumes of these types on basic disks but require a dynamic disk to create new ones.

When you're deciding which disk type to use, consider whether you want to create spanned or striped volumes. If you do, you'll need to convert your disks to dynamic disks.

Converting between Basic and Dynamic Disks

You can convert a basic disk to a dynamic disk without losing any data on the disk:

1. Open the Disk Management console, and change the view to show either Disk List or Graphical View. Both of these views show the disk type for each physical disk (Figure 18.2).

2. Right-click the disk, and choose Convert To Dynamic Disk. Disk Management to display a dialog box with all drives listed.

3. Place a check beside each disk to convert, and click OK.

FIGURE 18.2

The Disk Management console identifies a disk's type.

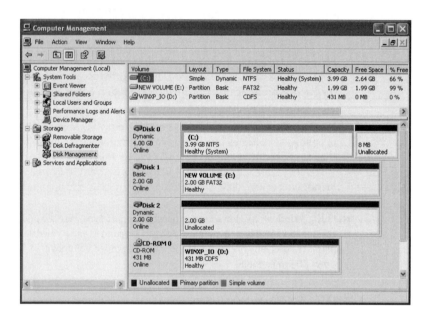

TIP When Disk Management converts the disk from basic to dynamic, it must dismount the disk, making it unavailable. If you're sharing folders on the disk, first disconnect all users. You can use the Shared Folders branch of the Computer Management console to close files and disconnect users.

You can revert a dynamic disk to a basic disk, although the volumes on the disk must be empty. To revert a disk, first back up all the volumes on the disk and remove the volumes and partitions. Then, right-click the disk and choose Convert To Basic Disk. Disk Management reverts the disk without any additional prompts or input.

Creating and Activating Partitions

It's a simple matter to create a partition. Just right-click the disk and choose New Partition to start the New Partition Wizard. The wizard prompts you for the partition type, size, driver letter or path (explained in the next section), format, and compression attribute. You should have no trouble creating partitions with the wizard.

You do need to keep one thing in mind, however. If you're going to boot from a partition, that partition must be active. I can't tell you how many times I've cloned a disk to replace an existing smaller drive and forgotten to activate the boot partition on the new disk!

It's easy to activate a partition: Open Disk Management, right-click the partition, and choose Mark Partition As Active. When you reboot, the system will boot from the active partition.

TIP   You can also use the FDISK console utility to activate a partition.

Changing a Drive Letter or Path

Each volume can have a drive letter associated with it, be mounted in an empty NTFS folder, or both (or neither). You can also create a volume that has no drive letter or path association, although there isn't any way to use it, so that's an unlikely scenario.

To assign a different drive letter to a volume, regardless of the drive's type (hard disk, CD, and so on), follow these steps:

1. Open Disk Management, and right-click the disk. Choose Change Drive Letter And Paths to open a dialog box.

2. Click Change if you want to modify the existing drive or path assignment, or click Add to add one.

3. The resulting dialog box is essentially the same except for its title (Figure 18.3). Both options are available only if you currently have no letter or path assigned to the volume. Otherwise, the one you currently *don't* have is available. Choose a drive letter from the drop-down list, or enter the path to an empty NTFS folder, and then click OK.

FIGURE 18.3
Use the Add Drive Letter Or Path dialog box to add or change drive letter assignments.

TIP   To remove a drive letter or path assignment, open the Drive Letter And Paths dialog box, select the item to remove, and click Remove.

Formatting Volumes

Earlier in this chapter, I discussed the pros and cons of FAT and NTFS. You can format a volume as FAT, FAT32, or NTFS, using one of three methods.

FORMATTING WITH THE DISK MANAGEMENT CONSOLE

The first is to use the Disk Management console. To do so, right-click a volume, and choose Format. Click Yes when asked if you're sure you want to format the partition. You'll see the Format dialog box shown in Figure 18.4.

FIGURE 18.4

Use the Format dialog box to specify a file system and other properties for the volume.

The dialog box contains two options worth singling out here:

Perform A Quick Format   Select this option if you want to clear out the file-allocation data and not check the disk for errors. This speeds up formatting on a drive that has previously been formatted.

Enable File And Folder Compression   Select this option to enable the compression attribute for the volume. All folders and files created on the volume will be compressed by default.

CLUSTER SIZE

In most cases, you can accept the default allocation unit (cluster) size suggested by Windows XP, but you can manually select a value if you want a specific cluster size. The smaller the cluster size, the more efficiently (in most cases, and up to a point) the disk can store data. Larger cluster sizes lead to wasted space due to *cluster slack*. Here's why: when you create a new file, Windows XP allocates space on the disk in clusters. Let's say the disk's cluster size is 32K. If you create a file that is 2K in size, the remaining 30K is wasted—Windows XP can't allocate the remaining space to another file, although it can use the space if the file grows in size.

Having a small cluster size can lead to highly fragmented files, reducing performance. That's why I recommend that you let Windows XP choose the cluster size. Storage efficiency usually isn't a big deal unless you're cramped for disk space. With today's inexpensive high-capacity disks, cluster size won't have enough impact to make it worth worrying about. You'd be better off using the time you spend worrying about cluster size cleaning out all the unused files and other junk littering your hard disk.

FORMATTING FROM MY COMPUTER

The second option you have for formatting a disk is to right-click the disk in My Computer and choose Format to open the Format New Volume dialog box shown in Figure 18.5.

You have essentially the same options as with the Disk Management console, with a few exceptions that have to do with disks. You can only choose FAT as the file system for a disk. In addition, you have an option, Create An MS-DOS Startup Disk. Choose this option to format a disk and make it a bootable DOS disk. You can use the disk to boot the system to a command prompt for trouble-shooting or recovery purposes.

FORMATTING WITH THE *FORMAT* COMMAND

The third option for formatting a disk is to use the format command from a console. There is no real advantage to using format rather than the GUI methods unless you're using the command from a script or want to format a diskette with a nondefault number of tracks per disk side or sectors per track. To view the syntax and options for format, open a console and enter **format /?** at the console prompt.

FIGURE 18.5

Use the Format New Volume dialog box from My Computer to format disks.

Converting Between FAT and NTFS

If you format a disk as FAT or FAT32 and later want to convert it to NTFS, you can do so without losing any data on the disk. You can even do it without rebooting the computer, unless you're converting the system partition.

You use the `convert` console command to convert a volume from FAT to NTFS. The syntax for `convert` is

```
convert volume /FS:NTFS [/V] [/CvtArea:filename] [/NoSecurity] [/X]
```

In most cases, you can use a simple form of the command to convert a disk. The following example would convert drive E: to NTFS:

```
convert E: /FS:NTFS
```

TIP You can use the command to convert the system volume to NTFS, but Windows XP will ask if you want to schedule the conversion for the next reboot. If you agree, the conversion takes place during the next startup.

Table 18.1 explains the parameters for the `convert` command.

TABLE 18.1:   Options for the *convert* Command

SWITCH	DESCRIPTION
volume	Specify the drive letter followed by a colon, volume mount point, or volume name.
/FS:NTFS	Convert the volume to NTFS.
/V	Run in verbose mode, providing additional status information.

TABLE 18.1: Options for the *convert* Command *(CONTINUED)*

SWITCH	DESCRIPTION
/CvtArea:*filename*	Specify a contiguous file in the root directory to be the placeholder for NTFS system files.
/NoSecurity	Converted files and directories have permissions giving everyone access.
/X	Force the volume to dismount first if necessary, causing all opened handles to the volume to be invalid.

The /CvtArea, /NoSecurity, and /X parameters are new for Windows XP. The /CvtArea parameter lets you specify the location in the disk's root directory of the NTFS master file table (MFT), which NTFS uses to store file allocation data. Using this parameter prevents fragmentation of the MFT, which improves NTFS performance.

Use the /NoSecurity parameter when you want to convert a disk to NTFS but not apply the default NTFS permissions that Windows XP would otherwise apply to it. FAT volumes don't have any permissions, so convert normally assigns Full Control for all users and groups. When you use the /NoSecurity parameter, convert assigns the following permissions to folders and files on the volume instead:

User or Group	Permissions
Administrators	Full Control
Local Administrator	Full Control
System	Full Control
Creator Owner	Full Control
Users	Traverse Folder/Execute File, List Folder/Read Data, Read Attributes, Read Extended Attributes, Read Permissions, Create Files/Write Data, Create Folders/Append Data (correspond to the Read & Execute, List Folder Contents, and Read global permissions)

Use this option when you want to ensure high security for the volume. You can apply whatever permissions are necessary after convert finishes its job.

By default, convert prompts you to specify whether it should dismount a volume before converting it. Dismounting the volume makes it unavailable and is a good idea to help ensure a problem-free conversion. You can use the /X parameter to direct convert to dismount the volume without prompting you.

NOTE The time required to convert a volume depends almost entirely on the amount of data on the disk. If you're converting a volume that others need to access, and it contains lots of data, consider converting the data after hours when it won't be missed.

Unfortunately, convert won't convert a volume from NTFS to FAT. In Windows XP itself, there is no way to convert an NTFS partition to FAT or FAT32. Without a third-party utility, you must back up the volume, reformat it, and restore the files. You can, however, use a utility such as Norton PartitionMagic (`www.powerquest.com/partitionmagic/`) to convert the file system, with a few caveats. The NTFS partition can't contain compressed files, sparse files, reparse points, or encrypted files. The NTFS partition also must be error-free, so you might need to perform a check and repair on the volume with chkntfs before performing the conversion.

TIP NTFS *reparse points* are the mechanism by which Windows XP implements several file-system features. These include mounted volumes, compression, encryption, sparse files, and offline storage. In effect, reparse points are like flags in the file system that direct Windows XP to pass processing of the data that follows to a different file-system driver. When the NTFS driver comes to a reparse point indicating an encrypted file, for example, it passes the operation to the EFS subsystem for processing.

Another advantage that partitioning tools like PartitionMagic provide is the ability to merge NTFS partitions. You could merge two 4 GB partitions on the same disk into a single 8 GB partition.

WARNING When you convert an NTFS partition to FAT or FAT32, extended NTFS data such as permissions, alternate data streams, and quotas is lost.

Optimizing Disk Performance

Even with the relatively low cost of high-capacity disks, it's still important to optimize disk capacity and performance. In this section, I examine two methods for improving disk capacity and performance: defragmentation and compression.

Disk Capacity and Fragmentation

In order to understand why fragmentation occurs and what impact it has on the system, as well as how allocation size affects capacity, you first need to understand a little about disk structure.

A *sector* is the smallest unit of storage space on a disk. The sectors are arranged in circular *tracks* around the disk. The tracks from one platter to another form a *cylinder*. When Windows XP allocates space on disk, it does so using *clusters*. A cluster is a group of sectors. The number of sectors in a cluster is defined when you format the disk. Remember the allocation unit size I described earlier in the section on formatting? That's the cluster size.

The cluster size has a lot to do with disk capacity. Let's say you format a disk with a large cluster size—64K in this example. The smallest amount of space that Windows XP can allocate is 64K.

You create a new file that is 20K in size. When Windows XP stores the file, it allocates one cluster, or 64K, for the file, and the 20K of data goes into the 64K cluster. The end result is that the OS has wasted 44K of space, since Windows XP won't store any other data in the unused space in the cluster. It's like putting a small present in a large box—you're wasting the additional space inside the box.

TIP This disk capacity waste is often called *sector slack*.

Many people have the misconception that NTFS is more efficient than FAT because of its difference in file-system structure. In fact, NTFS is just as susceptible to sector slack as FAT. NTFS is more efficient because it uses a smaller default cluster size that ranges from 512 bytes to 4 KB. Using a smaller cluster size means less sector slack and more efficient storage.

NOTE FAT can't address as many clusters as NTFS and is therefore forced to use larger cluster size as the disk size increases. The result is increased sector slack and less efficient storage.

On the other side of the efficiency coin is *fragmentation.* Windows XP tries to allocate contiguous clusters for a file, or clusters that reside side by side in a track on the disk. This makes for faster reading and writing, because the disk heads don't have to move as much to write or read the file. As files change or more files are added to an already fragmented drive, a file can become fragmented—that is, stored in noncontiguous clusters. This reduces performance because the OS has to skip around the disk to pull together all the pieces of the file. The more file changes that occur, the more fragmentation becomes a potential problem.

Cluster size is the common thread between disk capacity and fragmentation. A small cluster size leads to less sector slack and higher capacity, whereas a larger cluster size leads to less fragmentation. This might seem like a Catch-22 if it weren't for the availability of a defragmentation tool for Windows XP. You can use a small cluster size to improve disk capacity and efficiency and still avoid excess fragmentation, as long as you periodically defragment the disk.

TIP When you format an NTFS volume, let Windows XP use the default cluster size or manually specify a cluster size of 4K or less for best performance.

Another disadvantage to using a cluster size larger than 4K on an NTFS partition is that you can't use compression on the volume. So, I recommend you stick with the default cluster size for NTFS partitions.

Tips for Defragmenting Disks

Windows XP includes a tool to analyze fragmentation on FAT and NTFS disks and to defragment them, if necessary. The Disk Defragmenter is a console snap-in that resides in the Computer Management console by default. However, you can create your own MMC console and add the Disk Management snap-in to it, if you wish. Figure 18.6 shows the Disk Defragmenter console.

FIGURE 18.6
Use the Disk Defragmenter to defragment FAT and NTFS volumes.

It isn't difficult to figure out the Disk Defragmenter—right-click a volume and choose Analyze to create a fragmentation report, or choose Defragment to start the defragmentation process. Disk Defragmenter handles the task without any further intervention from you. For that reason, I'll just offer some tips on defragmenting drives rather than explain in detail how to use this tool.

RUNNING DISK DEFRAGMENTER IN ADMINISTRATOR CONTEXT

First, you must be logged in as administrator (or Owner for Home Edition systems) in order to defragment a disk. This doesn't necessarily mean that you must log off and log on again with an account with administrator privileges. Instead, you can use `runas` to launch the Disk Defragmenter console in an administrator context.

Open My Computer, and browse to *%systemroot%*\System32, right-click `Dfrg.msc`, and choose Run As to open the Run As dialog box. Select the option The Following User, select Administrator from the drop-down list, and type the appropriate password. Then click OK to launch Disk Defragmenter.

AUTOMATIC DEFRAGMENTATION

Unfortunately, there isn't any mechanism in Windows XP to schedule the Disk Defragmenter to run automatically. Although the Disk Defragmenter console uses two other programs, `Dfrgfat.exe` and `Dfrgntfs.exe`, neither of these support command-line operation, which would make it possible to schedule the defragmentation with the AT command, Scheduled Tasks folder, or other mechanisms. So, defragmenting a disk is purely a manual process with the Disk Defragmenter console.

In order to gain the ability to defragment automatically, such as at a scheduled time, you need to move to a third-party tool such as Executive Software's Diskeeper. Diskeeper was the first defragmentation tool for NTFS and continues to be a leader in defragmentation technology for Windows platforms. You'll find more information about Diskeeper at `www.diskeeper.com`.

Using Disk Compression on NTFS Volumes

Windows XP supports on-the-fly compression that lets you increase a disk's apparent capacity. Unlike compression methods for Windows 9*x* and Me, compression in Windows XP doesn't require that you compress an entire volume. Instead, you can compress specific folders or even individual files.

There is one limitation for disk compression in Windows XP (and in all other Windows operating systems)—you can't compress FAT volumes. You can only compress folders and files on NTFS volumes. This isn't much of a drawback, because NTFS is a better choice than FAT in almost all cases, anyway.

Compressing a volume, folder, or file is easy. To compress an entire volume, follow these steps:

1. Open My Computer, right-click the volume, and choose Properties.

2. On the General tab (Figure 18.7 on the left), select the option Compress Drive To Save Space, and click OK.

3. Windows XP displays the Confirm Attribute Change dialog box. You can apply compression either to only the root of the volume or to the entire volume. If you select the latter, all existing folders and files on the volume are compressed, and any new folders or files you create will also be compressed.

FIGURE 18.7

Use the volume's General tab to enable the compression attribute. (left) Use the Advanced Attributes dialog box to set the compression attribute for a folder or file. (right)

TIP You can set a volume's compression attribute when you format the volume. Look for the Enable File And Folder Compression or Enable Compression check box in the Format dialog box (it depends on whether you're formatting from My Computer or Disk Management).

You use a similar method to compress a folder or file:

1. Right-click the item, and choose Properties.

2. On the item's General tab, click Advanced to display the Advanced Attributes dialog box (Figure 18.7 on the right).

3. Select the option Compress Contents To Save Disk Space, and click OK. As when you compress a volume, Windows XP prompts you to choose whether to compress subfolders and their contents.

I've used the term *set the compression attribute* rather than *compress the folder* because unless you direct Windows XP to compress the subfolders and their contents, the only thing that happens is that Windows XP sets the value of the folder's compression attribute—it doesn't compress anything. When you create new files in the folder, however, they're compressed because Windows XP checks the compression attribute and acts accordingly.

TIP Compression and encryption are mutually exclusive. You can compress a file but not encrypt it, and vice versa.

MOVING AND COPYING WITH COMPRESSION

You need to consider compression when you move or copy files between folders and volumes. When you move or copy files, those files take on the compression attribute of the target folder, with a couple of exceptions (explained shortly). For example, if you copy a file from an uncompressed volume to a compressed volume, the new copy of the file will be compressed. Likewise, if you copy a compressed file to an uncompressed volume, the file is uncompressed.

There are two exceptions to this behavior:

◆ The object retains its original compression attribute if the target folder is on the same volume as the source folder.

◆ The object is uncompressed if it's copied or moved to a FAT volume, because FAT doesn't support compression under Windows XP.

IDENTIFYING COMPRESSED FOLDERS AND FILES

By default, compressed folders and files look just like their noncompressed counterparts. You can configure Windows Explorer to display the title under compressed folders and files in blue to identify them as compressed. To do so, with any folder open, choose Tools ➢ Folder Options, and then select the option Show Encrypted Or Compressed NTFS Files In Color from the View tab.

Working with Zipped Folders and Files

Windows XP supports a second kind of compression that you can use on both FAT and NTFS volumes and that doesn't function at the operating system like NTFS compression.

You're probably familiar with ZIP files, which are compressed archives that can contain files and folders. The ZIP format is a standard compression format supported by several software vendors, and it has become the most popular choice for compressing files for distribution. One of the most popular tools for zipping and unzipping files is WinZip (`www.winzip.com`).

Windows XP adds support for zipped archives, treating them like compressed folders. You can view a ZIP file's contents as if it were a folder: double-click the folder, and Windows XP opens a window to display its contents, just as it does for a regular folder. A zipped file appears as an icon with a zipper, as shown in Figure 18.8.

In most cases, you can work with a ZIP file and its contents just like a regular folder. To extract a single file, for example, open the ZIP file and drag the file to the Desktop. You can also right-click a ZIP file and choose Extract All to extract the ZIP file's entire contents to a folder. The Extraction Wizard prompts you for the destination and lets you specify a password for password-protected ZIP files.

FIGURE 18.8
Windows XP lets you work with ZIP files without any add-on software.

To add a new ZIP file, right-click in a folder and choose New ➤ Compressed (Zipped) Folder. Specify a name for the file and, after it's created, drag files to it to add them to the archive.

The main advantage of using Windows XP's ZIP capabilities is that you don't need to install an application such as PKZIP or WinZip to handle archives. However, Windows XP's ZIP capabilities are limited. If you want the full complement of features—such as ability to span disks, perform encoding, or apply a password—you need a third-party tool.

TIP If you decide to install a third-party ZIP application like WinZip, keep in mind that the direct access you have in Windows XP will no longer be available. Instead, the ZIP application takes over all ZIP file actions. However, some of the third-party applications offer the same capability to treat ZIP files as folders.

Managing Volumes from a Console

Windows XP includes a couple of tools you can use to manage volumes from a command console. You'll probably do most of your disk management from the GUI, but you might occasionally need to perform tasks from a console or to incorporate functions into a batch file. The two tools are fsutil and diskpart. Both offer gut-level access into the file system.

The *fsutil* Command

fsutil lets you manage both FAT and NTFS file systems. This utility gives you quite a bit of power over the file system, so you should use it with care.

TIP You must be logged on as an administrator to use fsutil.

fsutil is actually a set of commands rather than a single command. The following sections briefly explain each of the subcommands you can use with it. The fsutil command is fully documented in the Windows XP Help system, so I won't cover these options in detail here. For information on specific options or usage, open Help And Support Center in Windows XP and search for the keyword **fsutil**.

The syntax for using fsutil is

```
fsutil subcommand options
```

•

BEHAVIOR

Use this subcommand when you want to query or set certain properties or behavior of the file system. For example, you can control how Windows XP uses short 8.3-format file names, enable or disable update of the Last Access Time (LAT) attribute for a folder or file, set the reserved size for the MFT zone, and specify how often quota violations are logged to the system log (the default is one hour).

TIP You can view short filenames with the dir command. Open a command console and execute the command **dir /X**. The fifth column in the resulting output shows the 8.3 short filename.

DIRTY

The dirty subcommand lets you query or set the value of a volume's *dirty bit*. When the dirty bit is set, it indicates that the file system could be in an inconsistent state. For example, there might be corrupt directory entries, or data might be waiting in the write buffer that hasn't been committed to disk.

When the system boots, the Windows XP kernel calls `Autochk.exe` to check volume status. If the dirty bit is set, `Autochk` initiates a check of the disk with `chkdsk /f`.

You can query the status of a volume's dirty bit with the `dirty` subcommand. You can also use it to set the bit to force a check of the volume when the system reboots. The following two examples check the bit and set it, respectively:

```
fsutil dirty query c:
fsutil dirty set c:
```

TIP   You can specify the drive letter followed by a colon, as in these examples, or specify a mount point or volume name.

FILE

You can use the `file` subcommand to perform a range of file operations. The following list explains the options you can use with the `file` subcommand:

createnew   Use this option to create a file of a specified length that contains all zeros for its data. For example, you might use `createnew` to create a large file to test file-system performance.

findbysid   Use this option to find files by the security ID (SID) of the user who owns the files. This is useful for listing all files on a volume that are owned by a given user.

queryallocranges   Use this option to query the allocated ranges for a file, which is useful if you're trying to determine whether a file contains *sparse regions* (regions with all zeros for data).

setshortname   Use this option to set the short 8.3-format filename for a file.

setvaliddata   Use this option to specify the valid data length (VDL) of a file on an NTFS volume.

setzerodata   Use this option to replace a range of data in a file with zeros. If the file is a sparse file, setting a range to zeros has the effect of releasing the clusters used by the range back to the OS, making them available for other files.

FSINFO

The `fsinfo` subcommand of the `fsutil` command lets you query information about drives, volumes, and file-system statistics. This subcommand offers several options:

drives   This option lists all the drives on the system.

drivetype   This option displays the drive type of a specified drive—for example, showing Fixed Drive for a hard disk, Removable Drive for a floppy drive, or CD-ROM Drive for a CD drive.

ntfsinfo   Use this option to list detailed information about an NTFS volume, such as number of sectors, total number of clusters, free clusters, and location of the MFT zone.

statistics   This option lists file-system statistics, such as log file, metadata, and MFT reads and writes.

volumeinfo   This option displays information about the volume, such as the name, serial number, and file-system type.

HARDLINK

Use the hardlink subcommand to create *hard links* to a file. A hard link is a directory entry for a file. On NTFS volumes, each file has at least one hard link but can have multiple hard links, enabling it to appear as if it resides in multiple directories. However, there is only one copy of the file. Users can use a file through any of its hard links—they're handled at the file-system level and are transparent to the user, who sees a file in the directory where the hard link exists. Windows XP deletes a file only after all hard links to it are deleted.

OBJECTID

Object identifiers (OIDs) are used by the Distributed Link Tracking Client service and File Replication Service to track objects such as files, directories, and links. You can use the objectid subcommand to create, delete, query, and set OIDs, but it's unlikely that you'll ever need to do so. In fact, you can wreak havoc on the file system by incorrectly modifying OIDs, so stay away from this subcommand!

QUOTA

The quota subcommand offers several options to help you manage quotas on NTFS volumes. You can use quota to disable, enforce, modify, query, or track quotas on a specified volume. You can also use it to search a volume for quota violations.

REPARSEPOINT

Reparse points are objects in the NTFS file system that act as flags to the operating system; such a flag indicates that the file or directory associated with the reparse point needs to be handled by a different driver or subsystem. For example, encryption is implemented using reparse points. The NTFS driver begins to read an encrypted file and comes to the reparse point that contains data indicating the file is encrypted. NTFS then passes the operation on to the EFS subsystem, which takes care of decrypting the file on the fly. Other features such as mounted volumes and the Distributed File System (Dfs) rely on reparse points. You can use the reparsepoint option to query or delete reparse points on an NTFS volume.

SPARSE

A *sparse* file contains one or more regions of unallocated space. The unallocated space would otherwise be filled with zeros or no data. Sparse files enable Windows XP to more efficiently manage disk space, because the space that would otherwise be used by the file for the empty data isn't allocated to the file. Instead, only the space required for the nonzero data is allocated, along with a relatively small amount for the reparse points that enable the OS to recognize the sparse data areas. You can use the sparse subcommand to query for and set sparse ranges in a file.

USN

This subcommand lets you manage the update sequence number (USN) change journal, which maintains a complete log of all changes to files on a given volume. Several services use the USN change journal, including the Indexing Service, File Replication Service, Remote Installation Service, and Remote Storage. Although you can use the usn subcommand to create, delete, and query in the USN change journal, you'll probably never have to do so.

VOLUME

Use the `volume` subcommand to dismount a volume or query the amount of free space on the volume. Dismounting a volume makes it unavailable but is necessary for certain actions such as converting a volume from FAT to NTFS.

The *diskpart* Command

The `diskpart` command isn't new to Windows XP—it was previously included in the Windows 2000 Recovery Console. What's new is its presence in Windows XP outside of Recovery Console.

`diskpart` lets you perform a wide range of disk-management tasks, which you can accomplish dynamically from a command console or through a script or batch file. You can create `diskpart` scripts as text files and run them through `diskpart` to automate disk-management tasks. `diskpart` returns an error code when it encounters an error, enabling you to troubleshoot problems with the script.

TIP In addition to using the syntax `diskpart` *subcommand,* you can also use this command by typing **diskpart** at the command line and pressing Enter. The prompt will change to DISKPART>. You can then type subcommands directly or type **?** for a list of available commands.

The following list summarizes the subcommands supported by `diskpart` and the functions they perform. For a detailed discussion of each subcommand, open the Help and Support Center in Windows XP and search for the keyword **diskpart**:

`active`   Use this subcommand to mark a partition as active. A partition must be active to enable the computer to boot from the partition.

`add disk`   Use this subcommand to add a disk to a mirror set. You can only mirror simple volumes on dynamic disks. Neither Windows XP Professional nor Home Edition supports mirrored volumes; this subcommand applies only to Windows 2000 Server and .NET Server platforms. You can, however, manage mirrored volumes on a server from a Windows XP workstation.

`assign`   You can assign a drive letter or volume mount point to a volume with this subcommand. You can't assign a different drive letter to the system or boot volumes, to the volume that contains the paging file, or to any OEM partition or GPT partition other than a basic MSDATA partition.

`break disk`   Use this subcommand to break a mirrored volume. This subcommand applies only to Windows 2000 Server and .NET Server platforms (see the `add disk` subcommand).

`clean`   You can remove all partitions and formatting from a volume with the `clean` subcommand. On MBR-based disks, the MBR and hidden sector data are overwritten. On GPT disks, the GPT partition data (including the Protective MBR) is overwritten. You can use the `all` parameter with the `clean` subcommand to replace all data on the disk with zeros, effectively wiping the disk's contents.

`convert basic`   Use this subcommand to convert a dynamic disk to a basic disk. The dynamic disk must be empty.

`convert dynamic`   Use this subcommand to convert a basic disk to a dynamic disk. `diskpart` retains any existing data on the basic disk during the conversion.

`convert gpt`   This subcommand lets you convert an empty, basic MBR-based disk on an Itanium-based computer to a basic disk with GPT partition style.

`convert mbr`   Use this subcommand to convert an empty, basic disk containing a GPT partition to a basic disk with an MBR partition.

`create partition efi`   This subcommand creates an Extensible Firmware Interface (EFI) system partition on a GPT disk. This subcommand only applies to Itanium-based systems.

`create partition extended`   Use this subcommand to create an extended partition. A disk can contain only one extended partition, although the extended partition can contain multiple logical drives.

`create partition logical`   Use this subcommand to create logical drives in an extended partition.

`create partition msr`   This subcommand creates a Microsoft Reserved (MSR) partition on a GPT disk. The subcommand applies only to Itanium-based systems.

`create partition primary`   Use this subcommand to create a primary partition on a basic disk. A disk can contain up to four primary partitions.

`create volume raid`   This subcommand creates a RAID 5, or striped set with parity, volume on a Windows 2000 Server or Windows Server 2003 platform. Windows XP doesn't support RAID 5 volumes.

`create volume simple`   Use this subcommand to create a simple volume on a dynamic disk. Simple volumes can comprise a single region on a disk or multiple regions on the same disk.

`create volume stripe`   This subcommand lets you create a striped volume using two or more dynamic disks. Striped volumes represent RAID 0, which offers performance improvements but no fault tolerance.

`delete disk`   Use this subcommand to delete a missing dynamic disk from the disk list. You can use the `override` parameter to delete all simple volumes from the disk.

`delete partition`   You can delete a partition on a basic or dynamic disk using this subcommand. You can't delete the system partition, boot partition, or partition containing the paging file.

`delete volume`   Use this subcommand to delete a volume. You can't delete a system or boot partition, or the partition containing the paging file.

`detail disk`   This subcommand displays detailed information about the selected disk and its volumes.

`detail volume`   Use this subcommand to list the disk on which the current volume resides. For example, you would use this command to view the disks used by a spanned volume.

`exit`   This subcommand exits the `diskpart` command.

`extend`   Use this subcommand to extend the current volume. You can extend a volume on a basic disk only to unallocated space on the same disk, but volumes on dynamic disk can be extended to any dynamic disk.

`help`   Use this subcommand (or /?) to display a list of `diskpart` commands.

`import`   Use this subcommand to import a foreign disk group into the local computer's disk group.

`list disk`   This subcommand displays a list of the disk on the system and information about them, such as size, free space, and partition style.

`list partition`   Use this subcommand to list the partitions in the current disk.

`list volume`   This subcommand lists the volumes on all basic and dynamic disks.

`online`   Use this subcommand to bring an offline disk or volume online.

`rem`   Use this subcommand to add comments to a `diskpart` script, just as you would add comments to a batch file.

`remove`   You can use this subcommand to remove a drive letter or mount point from the current volume. Use the `all` parameter to remove all drive letters and mount points.

`rescan`   Use this subcommand to scan the computer for new disks that have been added.

`retain`   This subcommand prepares a simple volume on a dynamic disk to be used as a boot or system volume. For *x*86-based computers, `retain` creates a partition entry in the MBR. On Itanium-based computers, this subcommand creates a partition entry in the GPT.

`select disk`   Use this subcommand to select a specific disk and shift the focus of `diskpart` to it. Most of `diskpart`'s subcommands operate on the disk with the current focus.

`select partition`   This subcommand lets you select a partition and shift focus to it.

`select volume`   Use this subcommand to select a volume and shift focus to it.

Using Mounted Volumes

Mounted volumes are a handy feature introduced in Windows 2000 and carried over into Windows XP. Essentially, mounted volumes enable you to mount any volume into an empty NTFS folder. The volume then appears as a part of the directory structure of the hosting volume. For example, let's assume the one hard disk in your computer is running low on space. You have all the programs you need, but you're running out of room for documents. So, you add a new hard drive to the computer, move the contents of the `Documents and Settings` folder to it, and mount the new drive into the now-empty `Documents and Settings` folder. The result is that you now have lots of space for documents and other data.

Mounted volumes offer another useful capability. Quotas apply at the volume level, so there is no way to apply quotas to a folder that are different from those that apply to the volume hosting the folder. You can get around that limitation by applying the different set of quotas to another volume and then mounting the volume into an empty NTFS folder on the host volume. The result is that the mounted volume has different quota settings from the host volume, even though the mounted volume appears as a folder on the host volume.

Setting up mounted volumes is easy. You can mount any type of volume; it doesn't have to be NTFS. However, the host volume must be formatted with NTFS, because mounted volumes rely on reparse points, a feature supported only by NTFS. Also, the directory in which you mount the volume must be empty.

Follow these steps:

1. Create the target folder on the NTFS host volume, or empty an existing folder.

2. Open the Disk Management console, right-click the volume to be mounted, and choose Change Drive Letter And Paths. Click Add to open the Add Drive Letter Or Path dialog box (shown earlier in Figure 18.3).

3. Type the path to the empty NTFS target folder, or click Browse to browse for it. Click OK, and then close the Change Drive Letter Or Path dialog box.

The mounted volume is represented by a drive icon rather than a folder icon (Figure 18.9) in the host directory structure when you view the folder locally as well as across the network.

FIGURE 18.9
The mounted volume
is represented by a
drive icon rather than
a folder icon.

Creating and Managing Advanced Volumes

As I mentioned previously, in the section "Understanding Basic and Dynamic Disks," Windows XP Professional supports two advanced volume types: spanned volumes and striped volumes. This section explains how to manage these types of volumes.

NOTE   Unlike Windows 2000 Server and Windows Server 2003 platforms, Windows XP doesn't support mirrored volumes (RAID 1) or stripe sets with parity (RAID 5). The highest (and only) level of RAID supported in software by Windows XP is RAID 0—striped sets. Windows XP Home Edition doesn't support dynamic disks, spanned volumes, or striped volumes. Windows XP Professional lets you create advanced volumes on dynamic disks but not on basic disks.

Managing Spanned Volumes

A spanned volume uses space from two or more disks to create a single logical volume. Why would you do such a thing? Let's say you're running out of space on drive E: (your main data drive), and you need more space. You could install a new hard drive and mount it into an empty NTFS folder on drive E: to increase the apparent size of the volume. This approach has the potential disadvantage that most of your free space is now available only in the mounted volume. A better solution would be to add a new drive and create a spanned volume, giving you a logical drive E: that encompasses the space on both drives. You can add up to 32 disks to a spanned volume to create a potentially huge volume (although a couple is probably all you'll ever use).

WARNING   If you dual-boot the computer with an operating system such as Windows 98 that doesn't support dynamic volumes, don't convert the drive to a dynamic disk. If you do, the other OS will no longer work.

If you decide to create a spanned volume, keep in mind that it doesn't offer any fault tolerance. If one disk in the spanned set dies, you'll lose all the data in the spanned volume, including the data stored on the disk that is still functioning.

TIP   You can manage spanned volumes created on basic disks with Windows NT, but you can't create or expand spanned volumes on basic disks with Windows XP. Instead, you must create or expand them on dynamic disks.

CREATING A SPANNED VOLUME

You use the Disk Management console to create a spanned volume. Follow these steps:

1. In the console, right-click the unallocated area on the disk that will serve as the first part of the spanned volume, and click New Volume to start the New Volume Wizard.

2. Click Next, choose Spanned, and then click Next.

3. In the Select Disks screen (Figure 18.10), select the other disk to add to the volume set, and click Add. If you don't want to add the entire disk to the set, change the space allocation using the control labeled Select The Amount of Space In MB. Click Next.

4. Specify the drive letter or mount point, and then follow the remaining prompts to complete the process.

FIGURE 18.10
You can use only a portion of a disk for a spanned volume by changing the amount allocated.

TIP   If you have only one drive with available disk space, you need to extend an existing volume rather than create a new one.

The new volume appears in My Computer as a single volume. In Disk Management's graphical view, the volume is labeled as a single volume, but you can view and work with the individual disks (Figure 18.11).

EXTENDING A SIMPLE OR SPANNED VOLUME

You can increase the size of a simple or spanned volume, adding additional unallocated space to it, by *extending* the volume. For example, assume you added a new disk to a computer. Now, you want to add the new disk to your existing simple volume to create a spanned volume. You do that by extending the existing volume to include the additional space.

NOTE   If you extend a simple volume, it becomes a spanned volume. You use the same process to extend both simple and spanned volumes.

FIGURE 18.11
A spanned volume in
Disk Management

The process for extending a volume is a lot like that for creating the spanned volume:

1. Open Disk Management, right-click the existing volume, and choose Extend Volume to start the Extend Volume Wizard.

2. Click Next, select the disk containing the unallocated space that you want to add to the volume, and click Add.

3. Adjust the amount of space to be allocated, if desired, and then click Next. Click Finish to complete the task.

Following are a few notes that apply to extending volumes:

◆ A volume must contain no file system (unformatted) or must be formatted as NTFS to be extended. You must convert FAT/FAT32 volumes to NTFS before you can extend them.

◆ You can't extend a simple volume on a disk that was upgraded from a basic disk to a dynamic disk. You can extend only volumes created on a dynamic disk.

◆ You can't extend system or boot volumes.

◆ You can't extend striped volumes.

◆ If you extend a simple volume onto multiple disks, it becomes a spanned volume and can't be striped.

◆ You can't delete any portion of a spanned volume. Instead, you must delete the entire volume.

Managing Striped Volumes

A *striped volume* is one in which the data is written across multiple disks that appear as a single logical volume. Unlike a spanned volume, in which a file would probably reside on only one disk, files in a striped volume are typically spread across all drives in the set because Windows XP distributes the write operations to multiple disks.

Striped volumes, which represent RAID 0, provide increased performance, particularly on systems with SCSI drives. These disks can read and write independently of the other disks in the system. With the file system distributed across multiple disks, read/write times decrease and performance increases because the workload is divided among the disks in the set. However, striping offers diminishing returns as more drives are added to the set, so a set of two or three drives is optimal.

Striped volumes offer no fault tolerance, however. If a single disk in the set fails, the volume is broken and all data is lost. Before you rush off and stripe your disks, understand that you'll gain performance but will still need to rely on backups or other methods to ensure survivability of your files in the event of a disk failure.

TIP To gain fault tolerance, you need to move up to RAID 1 (mirroring) or RAID 5 (stripe sets with parity). Neither of these is supported by Windows XP, although you can install RAID hardware in a computer to implement them. There are other levels of RAID, as well, but they pertain mainly to server environments and therefore fall outside the scope of this book.

You use much the same method to create a striped volume as you do to create a spanned volume. The only difference is that you select Striped in the New Volume Wizard. See the earlier section "Creating a Spanned Volume" if you need more information.

Understanding and Implementing Sharing

It isn't difficult to share a folder with other users on the network, but there are some security issues to consider, particularly if you aren't familiar with NTFS permissions. Windows XP also adds a new twist on sharing by introducing Simple File Sharing. This section of the chapter focuses mainly on Simple File Sharing and security but also explains briefly the process for sharing folders in Windows XP.

Understanding File-Sharing Options

Before you begin sharing files, you need to choose between the two sharing methods: classic or Simple File Sharing.

SHARE PERMISSIONS VS. NTFS PERMISSIONS

The classic sharing mechanism in Windows XP is the same as that in Windows 2000 and Windows NT; it functions as a combination of *share permissions* and *NTFS permissions*. When you share a folder, you can set limited permissions for the share itself. These permissions include Full Control, Read, and Change. The share permissions control access to the share from the network. For example, if a user is assigned Read permission in the share, he can read the data but not modify it.

NTFS volumes offer an additional layer of security that provides much more granular—that is, detailed—control over folder and file access. In addition to setting share permissions on a folder, you can also set NTFS permissions on the folder and/or its contents. For example, assume you're sharing the folder C:\Docs on your computer. The folder contains several other folders. Some users need access to some of the folders, and other users need access to different folders. You also want to restrict users to only the folders they specifically need. The answer is to use NTFS permissions.

To enable all the users to access the shared folder across the network, you grant Full Control to the built-in Everyone group when you share the folder. Then, you remove the Everyone group from the NTFS permissions for each folder and add the users who need access to each item, giving them whatever level of access is appropriate. The end result is that the share permissions allow everyone to get into the share, but NTFS permissions control what they can do once they're in.

TIP   NTFS permissions apply to local as well as network access of a folder or file and are the mechanism by which you can secure folders or files against local access from others who log on to your computer. NTFS permissions are available only on NTFS volumes. FAT volumes support only share permissions and therefore provide no local security.

It's important to understand the interaction between share permissions and NTFS permissions. The most restrictive permission applies, so you might grant Everyone Full Control through share permissions but grant only Read permission through NTFS permissions. The result is that unless a user is a member of another group that explicitly has less restrictive permissions, she will have only Read ability in the folder.

NOTE   Also take into account group membership when you're setting up sharing. Group membership is cumulative, and a user receives the permission granted to his account as well as the permissions granted to each group of which he is a member.

Simple File Sharing

Now, enter Simple File Sharing (SFS). I believe that Microsoft introduced SFS mainly to insulate Windows XP Home Edition users from the intricacies of NTFS permissions. Sharing a folder with SFS enabled is easy and requires only a few clicks of the mouse. The disadvantage is that you have much less control over access. SFS controls access to folders using the system's Guest account, so all users have the same level of access in the folder—either Full Control or Read, depending on how you share the folder.

You can easily share your own documents with other users on the network with SFS. You can also make your My Documents folder private, which prevents other users from accessing it locally. I cover each of these tasks later, in the section "Sharing and Securing Folders and Files."

CHOOSING A FILE-SHARING METHOD

Windows XP Professional includes in the GUI the ability to switch between classic sharing and SFS. To switch, open the Folder Options dialog box (choose View ➤ Folder Options from any folder, or use the Folder Options icon in Control Panel) and click the View tab (Figure 18.12). Scroll to the bottom of the Advanced Settings list, and use the Use Simple File Sharing check box to enable or disable SFS.

FIGURE 18.12
Use the View tab to configure SFS.

Windows XP Home Edition users normally don't have the ability to disable SFS, which would make it seem that SFS is the only way share files. Although SFS is the default mechanism in Home Edition, you can still use classic sharing. The secret is safe mode.

When you boot a Home Edition computer in safe mode, the sharing mechanism reverts from SFS to classic. If you right-click a folder and choose Sharing And Security, you'll see the same Sharing tab that Windows XP Professional users see when SFS is turned off. You can assign share permissions, selectively apply access, and configure NTFS permissions for the folder. When you reboot the computer in normal mode, SFS once again becomes the default sharing mechanism.

What happens to folders you share in safe mode and reboot in normal mode? The changes you made still apply. If you open the sharing properties for the folder, you'll see the usual SFS interface with the folder shared. Whatever NTFS permissions you applied are still valid.

As an advanced user, I prefer classic sharing because I'm used to it, but also because I prefer greater control over what I share. Nevertheless, SFS is a good option for inexperienced users who only occasionally need to share a folder on their systems and don't need the added security offered by NTFS permissions.

TIP Certain features are difficult or impossible to implement if SFS is enabled. For example, you can't configure NTFS permissions if SFS is enabled. All access to the computer from the network is authenticated with the Guest account when SFS is enabled, which affects the ability to access a Registry remotely and other network features. If you enable SFS and then down the line can't get a feature to work as you might expect, try turning off SFS to see if the problem goes away.

Sharing and Securing Folders and Files

There isn't much to sharing folders. The process varies slightly depending on whether you're using SFS. If you use classic sharing, keep in mind that Windows XP controls access based on the permissions assigned to accounts or to groups. If your computer belongs to a domain, Windows XP uses the domain accounts and groups to authenticate access by network users to your shared folders. If you're a member of a workgroup, you need to use local accounts and groups to control access to shared folders. If the latter is the case, create accounts or groups as needed before diving into sharing.

WARNING Take the threat of viruses and worms into account when you configure sharing and permissions. Viruses such as Nimda use a new method of attack: They search for improperly secured network shares and infect files they find there. You can avoid a lot of aggravation and potential downtime by removing the Everyone group from sharing and NTFS permissions on a shared folder.

CLASSIC SHARING

You can use classic sharing whether or not you're sharing from an NTFS volume. However, if you're sharing from a FAT volume, you won't have any more options using classic sharing than you would using SFS. Keep that in mind when you decide which sharing method to use.

To share a folder, follow these steps:

1. Set the necessary NTFS permissions on the folder and its contents to control access (assuming you're sharing a folder on an NTFS volume). To do so, locate and right-click the folder, and choose Properties. Click the Security tab (Figure 18.13), add or remove users or groups as necessary, and then assign them the desired permissions. Click Apply when you're happy with the permissions.

FIGURE 18.13
Use the Security tab
to configure NTFS
permissions.

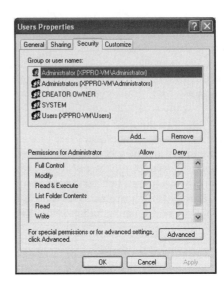

WARNING   I always set NTFS permissions first because I'm securing the folder and files before making them available on the network. It's like closing each horse's stall before opening the barn door—they won't get out unless you let them out. If you share the folder first, you might forget to apply NTFS permissions and thereby expose your data to unwanted access.

2. Click the Sharing tab (Figure 18.14), and select Share This Folder. Windows XP uses the folder name as the default share name, but you can change it if you wish. This is the name by which users on the network see the folder when they browse the network.

FIGURE 18.14
Use the Sharing tab to
share a folder.

3. If you wish, you can limit the number of concurrent connections to the folder. Windows XP supports up to 10 concurrent connections, so choosing Maximum Allowed will allow up to 10 connections. In most cases, this won't put much of a burden on your computer or the network, but you can select Allow This Number Of Users and specify a lower number, if you wish.

TIP You'll need to move up to Windows 2000 Server or Windows Server 2003 if you need more than 10 concurrent connections.

4. Click Permissions if you want to change share permissions. In the Permissions For Users dialog box (Figure 18.15), add and remove users or groups and assign permissions as desired. Click OK, and then click OK to close the folder properties and begin sharing the folder.

FIGURE 18.15
Use the Permissions For Users dialog box to set share permissions.

SHARING WITH SFS

The process is a bit simpler with SFS:

1. Right-click the folder, and choose Sharing And Security to open the Sharing tab shown in Figure 18.16.

2. Select Share This Folder On The Network, and then change the share name, if desired.

3. Choose the option Allow Network Users To Change My Files if you want to grant Change permission in the folder. Click OK to start sharing the folder.

What's the effect in terms of classic sharing? When you share a folder with SFS enabled, Windows XP shares the folder and grants the built-in Everyone group Full Control if you selected Allow Network Users To Change My Files. If you don't select this option, XP grants the Everyone group Read permission.

FIGURE 18.16
Use the Sharing tab to
share a folder with SFS
enabled.

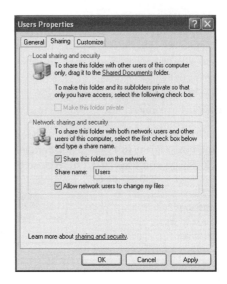

If the folder resides on an NTFS volume, Windows XP sets the access control lists (ACLs) on the folder to give Everyone Modify permission if you selected Allow Network Users To Change My Files. If not, Windows XP sets the ACLs to grant Read & Execute permission.

SHARING YOUR DOCUMENTS OR MAKING THEM PRIVATE

Regardless of which sharing method you use, you'll find your documents are available directly through My Computer. You can share your documents folder or make it private. To share it, right-click the folder and choose Sharing And Security. Use the same method to share the folder as you would for any other.

TIP   To quickly share your documents, drag the folder to the Shared Documents folder. Doing so creates a shortcut in Shared Documents to your documents folder.

To make your documents folder private, choose the option Make This Folder Private. Then, click OK.

NOTE   This option is available only if the folder you're attempting to change is located in the \Documents and Settings*username* folder for the username you're currently logged in as. This option also requires NTFS. In addition, keep in mind that even Administrators can't gain access to the contents when they're made private. It's the equivalent of granting NTFS Full Control permissions to *System* and *Username* and granting no one else any rights at all.

Hiding Shares

When you share a folder, it's visible to other users who browse your computer on the network. This is fine if the folder contains information you want to share with everyone, or if you don't mind that those people who don't have access can still see the folder on the network. In some cases, however, you might want to hide the folder so that it doesn't appear when users browse the network. Anyone who knows that the folder is there, however, can still connect to it if they have the necessary permissions.

Hiding a share is easy—just add a $ character as the last character of the share name. For example, you might share the folder Docs on a computer named Bart as Docs$. When someone needs connect to the share, they can map a drive or browse to \\bart\docs$ and work with the folder.

The ability of the $ to hide the share exists because, although remote Windows computers *do* see your share, they don't display it. Unix/Linux computers running a Samba client can see all Microsoft shares, even those with a $ on the end. Be sure you don't relax your security just because you think a share is hidden from everyone.

> **TIP** Windows XP creates administrative shares for each disk in the system. Drive C:, for example, is shared as C$. XP shares the *%systemroot%* folder as ADMIN$. Windows XP also creates a handful of other hidden shares depending on the services that are running. You can connect to these shares on a remote computer as long as you're a member of the Administrators group on the remote computer.

Command-Line Tools for Sharing

You may occasionally find it useful to share folders or map a drive letter to a remote share from a command console. You can use the net command to do just that. To share a folder, use the following net syntax:

```
net share sharename=drive:path
```

Replace *drive:path* with the path to the folder you want to share. You can use some additional parameters to control the number of connections, add a description for the share, set offline caching options, and so on. Execute the command **net help share** at the command console to view the syntax for these parameters.

To map a local drive letter to a remote network share, use the following syntax:

```
net use drive: \\server\share\subshare\...
```

Replace *drive:* with the local drive letter to map to the remote share. Replace *server* with the name of the computer sharing the folder. Replace *share* with the name of the share on the remote folder, and replace *subshare* with the name of a folder inside the remote share. You can specify multiple *subshares* to drill deeper into the remote share's directory structure.

> **TIP** For a list of available net subcommands, type **net** with no other parameters. Then, type **net help subcommand** to get more information about the syntax and use for specific subcommands.

Managing the File System with Scripts

If you have the responsibility of managing several systems, at some point you may want to automate certain file-system tasks. For example, perhaps you need to create a set of folders on 20 workstations and copy files from a server to those workstations. You could accomplish the task manually, but a script would make the process much easier.

> **TIP** Chapter 6 explains Windows Script Host (WSH) in more detail. This chapter focuses specifically on methods you can use to manage the file system with scripts.

You use `FileSystemObject` in WSH to manipulate the file system. `FileSystemObject` supports many methods and properties, but I'll focus specifically on the following methods and properties in this section:

`CopyFile`   This method copies a file or folder from one location to another.

`DeleteFile`   This method deletes one or more files.

`MoveFile`   This method moves one or more files to another location.

`CreateFolder`   This method creates a folder.

`CreateTextFile`   This method creates a text file in a specified location.

`GetFile`   This method returns a `File` object for a specified file.

`GetFolder`   This method returns a `Folder` object for a specified folder.

`SpecialFolders`   This property of the `WshShell` object lets you retrieve the path to the user's My Documents and Desktop folders.

TIP   You can create scripts for WSH using either Visual Basic Scripting Edition (VBScript) or JScript. This section focuses on VBScript. For more information on JScript and WSH in general, see `www.microsoft.com/scripting`, which redirects you to MSDN content about scripting technologies for Windows.

Managing Files and Folders

In this example, assume that you're moving a file from a specific folder of the user's My Documents folder to a user-specific folder on a network share. Then, you'll delete the file from the user's computer.

Let's start with some basics (no pun intended). The scripts should define the variables to be used and then create a file system object with which you can use the methods I've described previously. Here's the first part of the script:

```
' Declare variables
Dim fso, myDocs, myFolder, serverFolder, user, fileToCopy, fileToMove, fileToDelete
' Create the file system object
Set fso = CreateObject("Scripting.FileSystemObject")
' Create a shell object
set shell = createobject("wscript.shell")
```

Now you need to get the path to the user's My Documents folder:

```
' Get location of current user's My Documents folder
myDocs = fso.GetFolder(shell.specialfolders("MyDocuments"))
```

Next, get the username by reading an environment variable, and then set the destination directory on the server and create the folder:

```
' Get the user's logon account name
user = sh.ExpandEnvironmentStrings("%username%")
serverFolder = "\\docserver\" & user & "\"
sh.CreateFolder serverFolder
```

You now copy the file from a subfolder of My Documents to the server:

```
' Get the file to copy
set fileToCopy = fso.GetFile(myDocs&"\My Templates\Proposal.dot")
' Set the destination
destFile = serverFolder & "Proposal.dot"
' Copy the file
fso.CopyFile fileToCopy, destFile
fso.DeleteFile fileToCopy
```

The final two lines of this sample script copy the file from the source to the destination on the server and then delete the original. If you wanted to move the file instead, you could replace these two lines with the following one:

```
Fso.MoveFile fileToCopy, destFile
```

Keep in mind that this sample is intended only to show you how to create and manipulate file system objects. It doesn't include any error handling, which should be included in any production script. For example, you should verify that the file has been copied prior to deleting the original. Also, bear in mind that you must run the script under a user context that has sufficient privileges in the source and destination directories.

Creating and Writing to a Text File

Another common file-related task you might want to perform from within a script is creating and writing to a text file. For example, you might want to log script-related events to a file.

Creating a text file and writing to it file is relatively easy:

```
' Set up the variables
Dim myLogFile
' Create a text file
myDocs = fso.GetFolder(shell.specialfolders("MyDocuments"))
Set myLogFile = fso.CreateTextFile(myDocs&"\ScriptLog.txt")
' Write some text to the file
file1.Write "The backup script has started."
' Other script statements would go here…
' Close the file
file1.Close
```

Part 5

Communications and Networking

In this section:

Chapter 19

Modem and Dial-Up Networking Configuration

There usually isn't much to setting up a modem and making dial-up connections work. In most cases, Windows XP will automatically recognize the modem and install the appropriate driver for it. Setting up a dial-up connection is then just a matter of specifying the phone number, server type, and other general properties.

For those reasons, I won't cover modem or dial-up connection configuration in detail in this chapter but will instead focus mainly on related topics. For example, I explain why dial-up connections sometimes don't work even if your modem is dialing and attempting to connect to the remote server. The chapter also covers scripting, dialing rules, and other more advanced topics.

If you have more than one modem or are willing to invest a little money in another modem to improve your dial-up connection's performance, you'll be interested in the section on multilink. This feature in Windows XP lets you aggregate two or more dial-up connections to increase overall throughput. For example, you might aggregate two 56K dial-up connections to achieve a theoretical connection speed of 112K. That's still not as good as a broadband connection such as DSL, but any improvement is usually worthwhile.

Modem Configuration Tips

Modem installation and configuration in Windows XP is generally easy, but there are a few issues to consider and a few potential problems. This section offers tips for these situations.

TIP The Phone And Modem Options object in Control Panel gives you access to the majority of modem configuration tools and properties.

The Standard Modem

As I mentioned in the introduction, there isn't much to setting up a modem in Windows XP. In most cases, Windows XP automatically recognizes the modem and installs support for it. Sometimes, however, Windows XP doesn't properly recognize a modem and installs it as a Standard modem using a generic driver. I used to own and operate an ISP with about 1,000 customers (I'm glad that's over!), and it's my experience that the Standard modem often causes connection problems. Whenever a customer called Support with a connection problem, the first thing we checked was the modem type. Installing the right driver invariably fixed the problem and allowed the customer to connect without further problems.

Check your system to make sure it's using the right modem driver. If Windows XP didn't correctly detect your modem and instead installed one of the Standard modem drivers, update the driver. If you can't get a new driver from the modem manufacturer, consider replacing the modem with a new one.

NOTE   To update the driver, open the properties for the driver in Device Manager or in the Phone And Modem Options object in Control Panel. Click the Driver tab, click Update Driver, and follow the wizard's prompts to install the new driver.

Performing Diagnostics and Logging

On those rare occasions when you need to troubleshoot a modem connection, you can use a couple of Windows XP features that simplify the process.

QUERY THE MODEM

First, you can query the modem to make sure Windows XP is communicating with it. To do so, follow these steps:

1. Open the Phone And Modem Options object in Control Panel, and click the Modems tab.

2. Select the modem in the list, click Properties, and then click the Diagnostics tab (Figure 19.1).

3. Click Query Modem. Windows XP queries several registers in the modem and displays information about the modem and its configuration in the dialog box.

FIGURE 19.1

Use the Diagnostics page to query the modem.

NOTE   If Windows XP indicates a status of "Not Present" for the modem, you can't choose Properties to query the modem. This status can indicate a defective modem, or in the case of an external modem, a modem that is not turned on or connect to the computer.

If Windows XP is unable to query the modem, your modem either isn't working or isn't properly connected to the computer (external). If you're setting up the modem and it hasn't worked successfully, there is also the chance that you've configured it incorrectly. Check the COM port assignment to make sure you're using the right port. Also check in Device Manager for a COM port conflict.

TIP   If you install an internal modem on a COM port that your computer also has enabled on the motherboard or an add-on card, you should disable that system COM port to avoid potential port conflicts.

SEND COMMANDS TO THE MODEM

Another troubleshooting technique is to communicate directly with the modem, sending it configuration and test commands to determine whether the computer can communicate with the modem and the modem can dial out.

You can use HyperTerminal, which is included with Windows XP, to communicate with the modem. To establish a connection using HyperTerminal, follow these steps:

1. Click Start ➤ All Programs ➤ Accessories ➤ Communications ➤ HyperTerminal. The first time you run HyperTerminal, Windows XP recommends it to be the default Telnet program. I prefer the command-line version, but HyperTerminal works well as a Telnet client—the choice is up to you.

2. After you respond to the prompt, HyperTerminal displays the Connection Description dialog box. Enter a name for the connection, such as Modem Direct, choose an icon for the connection, and click OK.

3. In the Connect To dialog box's Connect Using drop-down list, choose the COM port assigned to the modem (Figure 19.2). Click OK.

4. In the Port Settings dialog box, select a port speed from the Bits Per Second drop-down list. I recommend 9600 for testing purposes. Use the default settings (8, none, 1, hardware) for the other settings, and click OK.

FIGURE 19.2
Select the modem's COM port from the Connect Using drop-down list.

When you click OK, HyperTerminal starts a connection to the modem. Type **AT** and press Enter. You should receive the response OK. If you don't see the AT as you type it, you need to turn on local echo:

1. Choose File ➤ Properties, and then click the Settings tab.

2. Click ASCII Setup to display the ASCII Setup dialog box (Figure 19.3).

3. Select Echo Typed Characters Locally, and click OK. Click OK to close the properties sheet, and try the AT command again.

FIGURE 19.3
Use the ASCII Setup dia-
log box to enable local
echo of typed characters.

If you receive OK in response to the AT command, try dialing. Issue the command **ATD*number***, replacing *number* with the phone number you want to dial. If the modem starts dialing, you can type **ATH** to hang up the connection. If the modem successfully dialed, the problem likely lies in your communications program. There's an outside chance that the modem driver is wrong, but I'd look at the connection settings before looking for problems with the driver.

TIP   You can use lots of other commands to initialize or configure a modem. Check your modem manual for a complete list of commands.

If you receive an error message in response to AT, you likely have a problem with the modem itself, with the driver, or with the connection between the computer and modem. Check these and try again. If the modem responds to AT but gives you an error, such as no dial tone, check the connection between the modem and phone line.

TIP   You can shut down the computer and then start it again to reset an internal modem. For an external modem, cycle power on the modem and then use Device Manager to scan for device changes to redetect the modem. Check the connection again after the reset.

CHECK THE MODEM LOGS

Another modem-troubleshooting technique you can use in Windows XP is to check the modem logs. Windows XP creates a log when it detects a modem, and you can use this log to identify potential problems with detection. Check the file *%systemroot%*\ModemDet.txt for the port on which a modem was detected and other status messages. Windows does not always create this file, so it may not exist on your computer.

Windows XP also creates a modem log for each modem as you use it. The modem logs are located in the *%systemroot%* folder and are named ModemLog_*ModemName*, where *ModemName* is the model name of the modem. For example, the log file for the ancient but functional Intel 400e I use for incoming faxes is named ModemLog_SatisFAXtion Modem 400e.txt.

NOTE   I'm hanging onto my Intel 2400 baud external modem just in case Intel wants it for their corporate museum some day. I would entertain bids, however. The worst thing is that I fondly remember the days when 2400 baud was fast enough for anything you cared to do online.

Each log file contains the initialization commands that Windows XP sends to the modem, as well as modem responses and other information. The log can be particularly useful in tracking down initialization or communication problems.

Using Additional Configuration Strings

In some cases, you may need to use additional configuration strings for a modem. To put it simply, these are other modem commands that you direct Windows XP to send to the modem when it initializes the modem to start the dial-up session. For example, you might need to enable error-correction methods or change other settings that aren't available through the GUI.

Check the modem documentation to determine the commands you need to send to the modem. Then, open the properties for the modem and click the Advanced tab. In the Extra Initialization Commands text box, type the initialization string you need to send to the modem. You can also click Change Default Preferences to change properties such as initial port speed, data protocol, and flow control method.

Configuring Dial-Up Connections

Setting up a standard Internet connection is relatively easy to accomplish; in most cases, you can run the New Connection Wizard and let Windows XP create the connection based on the information you provide, such as phone number, account name, and password. This section of the chapter focuses on the additional issues you might face for certain connections or when using a connection from a different location.

TIP   To run the New Connection Wizard, click Start, right-click My Network Places, and choose Properties to open the Network Connections folder. Click Create A New Connection in the left pane to start the wizard.

Setting Dialing Rules

Dialing rules let you specify the way Windows XP dials a connection—for example, using a credit card to dial, dialing the area code, dialing a prefix to access an outside line, disabling call waiting when it initiates the call, and other dialing tasks. Dialing rules are based on calling location, so if you're calling from a particular area code, a hotel, or a location that requires other special dialing steps, you can specify a set of rules accordingly.

BASIC RULES

To configure dialing rules, follow these steps:

1. Open the Network Connections folder, right-click the connection, and choose Properties. Or, in the Connect dialog box prior to dialing, click Properties.

2. On the General tab of the connection's properties, click Use Dialing Rules.

3. Click Dialing Rules to open the Phone And Modem Options dialog box. Select an existing location and click Edit, or click New to create a new dialing location. Figure 19.4 shows the resulting Edit Location dialog box.

TIP   You can also access the Phone And Modem Options dialog box from Control Panel.

4. Use the General tab to specify the dialing location name, area code, prefixes to dial for local and long-distance calls, and a handful of other settings. The settings on the General tab are self explanatory.

FIGURE 19.4
Use the Edit Location
dialog box to specify dialing rules.

AREA CODE RULES

Use the Area Code Rules tab to create rules that govern the way Windows XP treats specific area codes for the selected dialing location. For example, if you're dialing from area code 218 and need to dial other numbers in the 218 area code, you might need to specify which ones should be dialed as long distance and which ones should be dialed as local calls without the area code.

Click New to open the New Area Code Rule dialog box (Figure 19.5) to enter the area code and specify which prefixes should be dialed as long-distance numbers. To dial only certain prefixes as long-distance numbers, choose Include Only The Prefixes In The List Below, click Add, and add the prefixes.

FIGURE 19.5
Use the New Area Code
Rule dialog box to specify
prefix rules.

CALLING CARDS

Setting up Windows XP to use a calling card to dial a number is perhaps the most difficult rules task. Windows XP includes several predefined card types to make it easier to set up your own card. Open the Dialing Rules tab on the Phone and Modem Options dialog box, select a location, and click Edit. Then click the Calling Card tab (Figure 19.6 on the left).

FIGURE 19.6

Windows XP includes several calling card types. (left) Plus you can edit an existing card to suit your specific needs. (right)

Look through the list of predefined cards to see if yours is included. If so, select the card from the list and then enter the account number and PIN (if any) in the text boxes on the Calling Card tab. If you need to fine-tune the card's settings, select the card and click Edit to open the Edit Calling Card dialog box (Figure 19.6 on the right).

TIP   The process for creating a new card is much the same as editing an existing card. Just click Add instead of Edit, and then fill in the desired settings.

The General tab lists the card name, account number, and PIN. Click the Long Distance tab to change the access number Windows XP should dial to use the card and/or the other information to be dialed when using the card, such as the sequence in which it dials specific items.

The Long Distance, International, and Local Calls tabs list the sequence in which items are dialed when using the card. You can use the Move Up and Move Down buttons to change the sequence as needed. Click an item's button if you need to add that item to the dialing sequence; in some instances, this brings up a dialog box to choose details for that item. For example, click Wait For Prompt if you need Windows XP to wait for a response or for a message to end before sending the next dialing string. When you click Wait For Prompt, Windows XP displays the dialog box shown in Figure 19.7.

If you need to dial a string of numbers or the * or # character, click Specify Digits to enter the digits to be dialed. Windows XP dials those digits at the specified point in the dialing sequence.

The settings on the International and Local Calls tabs are the same as on the Long Distance tab. However, these settings apply when Windows XP detects that you're dialing an international or a local call, respectively.

FIGURE 19.7
Use the Wait For dialog
box to include a pause in
the dialing string.

The best way to check the number sequence without actually dialing it is to open the connection after you set the dialing rules and then check the numbers shown in the Dial drop-down list (Figure 19.8). You can also click Dialing Rules to view the dialing string.

TIP   Calls that come in when you're online can disrupt the connection if call waiting is enabled. You can disable call waiting for the duration of the call through the General tab of the Edit Location dialog box. Select To Disable Call Waiting Dial, and then enter the dialing string for your phone system that disables call waiting. Common strings include *70, 70#, and 1170. Check with your phone company to determine the appropriate string.

MANUAL OR OPERATOR-ASSISTED DIALING

In some cases, you might find it easier to dial the connection yourself or have an operator do it rather than let Windows XP do it. This is particularly true if you only need to use the calling card a couple of times—in many cases, you can dial the connection yourself and be finished with the dial-up session in the amount of time it would take to finish setting up the card.

FIGURE 19.8
The Dial drop-down list
shows the number to be
dialed.

Setting up manual/operated-assisted dialing isn't exactly intuitive, because Windows XP doesn't offer those settings through the dial-up connection's properties. Follow these steps:

1. Open the `Network Connections` folder, and choose Advanced ➢ Operator-Assisted Dialing.

2. Double-click the connection you want to dial.

3. Pick up the handset. Dial the number, calling card, and any other dialing strings, and then click Dial.

4. Hang up the handset after the modem takes over the line (immediately, in almost every case).

To disable operator-assisted or manual dialing, open the `Network Connections` folder and choose Advanced ➢ Operator-Assisted Dialing to remove the check from the menu.

Choosing Authentication Settings

Windows XP supports several authentication methods for dial-up connections, and you can assign multiple authentication methods for a dial-up connection. Windows XP attempts the connection using the authentication methods in decreasing order of security provided. You configure the method(s) for a connection through the Security tab for the connection (Figure 19.9).

FIGURE 19.9

Use the Security tab to configure authentication methods for a connection.

The Security Options group gives you access to three authentication options:

Allow Unsecured Password   This option allows the use of Password Authentication Protocol (PAP), which transmits passwords in plain text. This option provides the least security because passwords can be easily sniffed from the PPP packets. Windows XP will also attempt a connection using CHAP, SPAP, MS-CHAP, and MS-CHAP v2 with this option selected.

Require Secured Password   With this option, Windows XP attempts a connection using CHAP, MS-CHAP, and MS-CHAP v2 (all explained later in this section). The password is encrypted, providing much better security and considerably reducing the possibility that the password will be compromised. PAP and SPAP aren't attempted.

Use Smart Card This option offers excellent security for systems that contain a smart-card reader. Windows XP uses the credentials stored in the smart card to authenticate the connection to the remote server. Windows XP uses EAP for authentication (more on this later).

You can also set advanced authentication methods—for example, restricting the connection to a specific authentication method, or using a method such as EAP that provides better security. Click Advanced on the Security tab, and then click Settings to display the dialog box shown in Figure 19.10.

FIGURE 19.10

Set authentication options through the Advanced Security Settings dialog box.

The Data Encryption drop-down list lets you specify whether Windows XP uses encryption for the connection. You can choose between the following:

No Encryption Allowed Windows XP drops the connection if the server requires encryption.

Optional Encryption Windows XP attempts encryption but allows the connection even if the server declines encryption.

Required Encryption Windows XP disconnects the connection if the server doesn't offer encryption.

Maximum Strength Encryption This option requires 128-bit encryption.

Whether you choose to use encryption depends on whether the server supports it and whether you require maximum security for data.

If you're setting authentication from the Advanced Security Settings dialog box, you also need to choose the protocol(s) to use for the connection:

PAP Password Authentication Protocol uses plain text to transmit the password to the dial-up server. This makes the password susceptible to compromise, so you should use PAP only in situations where it's unlikely that someone can intercept your password or where the remote server only supports PAP.

SPAP Shiva Password Authentication Protocol was developed by Shiva Corporation, a remote-access technology company that has since been acquired by Intel. SPAP allows connections to Shiva products such as the Shiva LAN Rover. Like PAP, SPAP provides less security than the other authentication methods offered by Windows XP, so you should use it only when connecting to a Shiva access device that doesn't offer stronger security.

CHAP Challenge Handshake Authentication Protocol, also known as MD-5 CHAP or simply CHAP, uses a standard mechanism for encrypting the authentication process. CHAP is supported by various remote access servers, including non-Microsoft servers. It offers better security than PAP or SPAP because of its encryption, but it doesn't provide the same level of encryption—and thereby increased security—offered by either MS-CHAP version or by EAP.

TIP If you're configuring a Windows 2000 Server or Windows Server 2003 computer to support CHAP, keep in mind that passwords must be stored on the server using reversible encryption. You can enable reversible encryption for each account through the Store Password Using Reversible Encryption option on the Account tab of the user's properties (Active Directory Users And Computers console). You can also configure reversible encryption on a global basis through group policy in \Security Settings\Account Policies\Password Policy.

MS-CHAP Microsoft Challenge Handshake Authentication Protocol is a version of CHAP developed by Microsoft and supported by the company's remote-access platforms (such as Windows 2000 Server and Windows Server 2003 RRAS). With this protocol, the authentication server sends the client a challenge containing the session ID and an arbitrary challenge string. The client responds with the user name assigned to the dial-up connection and an encryption of the session ID, challenge string, and password. The server validates the credentials and authenticates the session if they match the credentials stored on the server. This protocol provides better security than CHAP.

MS-CHAP v2 Version 2 of the Microsoft Challenge Handshake Authentication Protocol improves on MS-CHAP's security. With this protocol, the remote server sends the client a challenge containing the session ID and an arbitrary challenge string. The client responds with the user name, an arbitrary peer challenge string, and a one-way encryption of the server's challenge string, peer challenge string, session ID, and password. The server validates the response and returns a success/failure and an authenticated response based on both challenge strings, the encrypted client response, and the password. The client validates that authentication data and accepts the connection if it's valid. The client terminates the connection if it can't validate the authentication data provided by the server. So, MS-CHAP v2 offers two-way authentication and, therefore, excellent security.

EAP Extensible Authentication Protocol allows the client and server to negotiate an authentication method from the methods supported by the server. The client and server must both support the same EAP types in order for authentication to succeed.

Windows XP supports two EAP types: EAP-MD5 CHAP and EAP-TLS. EAP-MD5 CHAP works much like CHAP but sends challenges and responses as EAP messages. It authenticates clients using user names and passwords.

EAP-TLS uses certificates to authenticate remote clients, using a secured private key exchange between the client and the server. EAP-TLS is the most secure method of authentication offered by Windows XP because it uses certificates for authentication. Windows 2000 Server and Microsoft .NET Server platforms support EAP-TLS only in domain environments—the Routing and Remote Access Service (RRAS) doesn't support EAP-TLS on a stand-alone RRAS server.

CONFIGURING AUTHENTICATION

Choosing and setting up authentication methods for a dial-up connection is usually easy. If your dial-up server doesn't have advanced authentication requirements (you're dialing an ISP, for example), you can generally leave the settings at their default values. In those cases where stronger security is needed and is supported by the dial-up server, you can use the Advanced Security Settings dialog box previously shown in Figure 19.10.

Select the desired encryption option from the Data Encryption drop-down list. If you aren't using EAP, select the protocol(s) you want the connection to be able to use in the Allow These Protocols list. If the user credentials on the dial-up server are the same as your local user credentials, select the option "For MS-CHAP based protocols, automatically use my Windows logon name and password." Doing so causes Windows XP to use your local user name and password for authentication.

For dial-up scenarios requiring EAP, select the Use Extensible Authentication Protocol option, and then choose the EAP method from the drop-down list. If you choose the Smart Card Or Other Certificate option, click Properties to display the dialog box (Figure 19.11).

FIGURE 19.11
Configure the EAP certificate and other options in the Smart Card Or Other Certificate Properties dialog box.

The following list summarizes the options in this dialog box:

Use My Smart Card   Select this option if you have a smart-card reader on the local computer and want to authenticate on the remote server using the credentials stored in your smart card.

User A Certificate On This Computer   Select this option to use a certificate installed on the local computer to provide authentication.

Validate Server Certificate   Select this option to check that the certificate on the server has not expired.

Connect Only If Server Name Ends With   Use this option to specify a domain name for the remote dial-up server and prevent a connection if the server doesn't reside in the specified domain. If you were connecting to a server in the sybex.com domain, for example, you would enter **sybex.com** in this text box.

Trusted Root Certificate Authority   Select the root certification authority (CA) in the certification hierarchy for the server's certificate. This requires that the server's certificate be verified for authenticity against the specified root CA.

Use A Different User Name For The Connection   Select this option if the user name stored in the smart card or associated with the certificate isn't the same as the user name on the remote server.

NOTE   See Chapter 41 for detailed information on obtaining and installing certificates on your computer.

Scripting

Most dial-up servers don't require connection scripts, but a few holdouts and older servers still require scripts. For example, you need a script to connect to CompuServe's network.

Windows XP includes four predefined scripts that you can use for connecting to specific types of servers. These scripts are stored in *%systemroot%*\System32\ras:

Cis.scp   Use this script to connect to CompuServe.

Pppmenu.scp   Use this script to establish a PPP connection to a remote-access server that uses a menu to offer connection options.

Slip.scp   Use this script to connect to a server that uses Serial Line Interface Protocol (SLIP) to establish the connection.

Slipmenu.scp   Use this script to establish a SLIP connection to a remote-access server that uses a menu to offer connection options.

In most cases, you can use the scripts as-is or make only minor modifications to the scripts to apply them to your situation. To select a script, open the Security tab of the connection's properties and click Run Script. Click the drop-down list to select the desired script, or click Browse to browse the computer for it. After you select the script, you can click Edit to open the script in Notepad for editing.

TIP   You can view the script in action to troubleshoot it or watch its operation. Select the Show Terminal Window option on the Security tab to monitor the script's progress.

It's unlikely that you'll need to do anything other than make minor changes to existing scripts, and you probably won't need to create your own from scratch. For that reason, I'll just point you in the right direction for more information rather than offer pages and pages of content on scripting here. In Windows XP, open the Help And Support Center, and search on the key phrase **connection script**. The document "Basic Structure of a Script" under the Suggested Topics category offers a good introduction to scripting. You'll also uncover several additional documents that explain scripting commands and syntax.

TIP   Although I haven't run across this problem yet with Windows XP, it's my experience that Windows 2000 sometimes has difficulty getting the password to authenticate for a CompuServe connection. You could try re-creating the connection, but my preferred solution has always been to modify the Cis.scp file to explicitly send the password rather than use the $PASSWORD variable to pull it from Windows XP. If you choose this route, edit Cis.scp and replace $PASSWORD with your actual password in quotes. Note that this exposes your password to anyone who has access to the script file. To avoid that, store the password in an NTFS folder with permissions set to prevent access by unauthorized users.

Using Callback for Security and Cost

Windows XP provides callback features to enable a remote-access server to call back your computer to initiate a connection. There are two reasons to use callback: cost and security.

Having the server call you back reverses any long-distance charges that might otherwise apply. Naturally, for this to work, the remote server must be configured for callback and must be able to dial a long-distance call. Commercial remote-access services are very unlikely to support callback at all, much less callback to a long-distance number. Instead, reversing long-distance charges through callback is applicable only to remote-access services provided by your company. Unfortunately, Windows XP doesn't support callback as a dial-up server, so you'll need to use Windows 2000 Server or Windows Server 2003 platforms (or third-party RAS servers) as your remote-access servers to enable callback.

Security is another reason to use callback. You can configure remote-access policies on a Windows 2000 or Windows Server 2003 RRAS server to call a user back at a specific number. Doing so ensures that the user can connect only from a specific location and considerably lessens the possibility that someone else can obtain the user's credentials and use them to gain unauthorized access.

NOTE You configure callback for a specific user through the Dial-In tab of the user's account in Active Directory on the server.

To configure a dial-up client to use callback from Windows XP, right-click My Network Connections, and choose Properties to open the Network Connections dialog box. Choose Advanced ➢ Dial-Up Preferences, and click the Callback tab. You can choose from three options:

No Callback You connection won't use callback even if it's offered by the server.

Ask Me During Dialing When The Server Offers Windows XP displays a prompt asking if you want the server to call you back. The prompt appears only if the server offers callback.

Always Call Me Back At The Number(s) Below Use this option if you want the server to call your computer back at a specific number. If your computer has more than one modem and the server supports multilink, you can specify the number for each modem and have the server call back each one to create a multilink connection.

A Windows 2000 or 2003 RRAS server supports three callback options:

No Callback This option prevents the user from being called back by the server.

Set By Caller This option allows the server to call the user back at the number from which the user called (requires caller ID) or at the number requested by the caller (which could be different from the dialing number).

Always Callback To This option lets the RRAS server administrator specify a number for the user that the server always uses to call back the remote user, even if his computer requests a different number.

Improving Performance with Multilink

In the previous section, I touched briefly on multilink, which lets you aggregate two or more connections to create a single logical connection with a bandwidth equal to the added bandwidth of all connections. For example, you might aggregate two 56K connections for a theoretical connection speed of 112K.

There are two requirements for using multilink on a dial-up connection:

♦ Your computer must have two or more modems, each connected to a different phone line.

♦ The remote server must support multilink connections.

The actual throughput you get depends on a variety of factors. As you experiment with multilink, you may find that it doesn't offer a noticeable improvement in throughput, particularly if you're aggregating two 33.6 K or 56 K modems. Still, it's worth a try if you're trying to get the most possible bandwidth out of your existing dial-up connections.

Also keep in mind the requirements of the dial-up server and the way the service bills you for the multilink connection. You can't use two or more different accounts to establish a multilink connection. Instead, each call uses the same user credentials to authenticate. This means you can't use your and your neighbor's dial-up accounts to make multilink work. It also means that the dial-up provider needs to deal with the fact that you're using one account to dial into more than one modem at a time. ISPs that offer unlimited access are very unlikely to support multilink because it reduces their customer-to-modem ratio without increasing revenue. Some support multilink but charge you for two accounts. Those ISPs that offer metered (time-limited) access are much more likely to support multilink. In this situation, your account is debited time according to the number of connections you're using. Use two connections for an hour, and you're docked two hours on your account.

Setting Up a Multilink Connection

To set up multilink, follow these steps:

1. Install all the dial-up devices you want to use for the connection.

2. Open the properties for the connection. On the General tab (Figure 19.12), place a check beside each of the devices you want to include in the connection.

3. Select the option All Devices Call The Same Numbers if you use a single dial-up number to connect to the RRAS server. Otherwise, clear this option, click a modem in the list, and enter the phone number it should dial in the Phone Number field; then click the next modem and enter its dial-up number. Click OK.

TIP You don't have to use multilink every time you use a connection that is configured for multilink. Just deselect one of the modems, and then dial the connection.

FIGURE 19.12
Use the General tab to configure multilink.

Dynamic Multilink Connections with BAP/BACP

Windows XP supports Bandwidth Allocation Protocol (BAP) and Bandwidth Allocation Control Protocol (BACP). BAP lets multilink be adaptive to bandwidth requirements. If bandwidth utilization drops below a certain point, BAP enables multilink connections to be dropped to reduce cost. BAP also allows multilink connections to be added as bandwidth utilization grows.

BACP performs a single function. If both peers of a multilink/BAP connection send a request to add or drop a link at the same time, BACP elects one as a favored peer and responds to its request, rejecting the request for others. This prevents both connections from being dropped or more than one additional link being created at a time.

A computer running Windows XP can use multilink and BAP to aggregate outgoing connections, subject to whether the called remote access server supports multilink and BAP. In addition, a Windows 2000 or Windows Server 2003 running RRAS and serving as a remote-access server for incoming connections can support multilink and BAP to calling clients.

To configure BAP on a Windows XP client, follow these steps:

1. Click the Options tab of the connection's properties.

2. In the Multiple Devices group, select from the drop-down list the method you want to use to initiate the multilink connection. To use BAP, choose Dial Devices Only As Needed.

3. Click Configure to display the Automatic Dialing And Hanging Up dialog box (Figure 19.13), where you set the parameters the client will use to determine when to request new links or drop existing links. The options in this dialog box are self-explanatory.

FIGURE 19.13
Configure BAP through the Automatic Dialing And Hanging Up dialog box.

Chapter 20

Configuring LAN Connections

As is true for most other hardware configuration tasks, Windows XP makes it relatively easy to install and configure network hardware. Even so, getting your network up and running the way you want requires that you understand the settings you can configure for your network card and clients, and which protocol(s) to choose. You can also modify a handful of advanced network settings to fine-tune a system's performance.

In this chapter, I explain how to work in and customize the Network Connections folder. For example, you might not realize that you can rename your network connections or why you'd want to do such a thing.

This chapter also covers network configuration, starting with network adapters. The settings vary from one adapter to another, but there are common settings you can change. You also need to decide which protocols and services to use on your network and how services should be bound to protocols for each connection. For example, you shouldn't bind the File and Printer Sharing service to TCP/IP for external connections, to avoid someone being able to access your system from the Internet. There are some mitigating factors, however, which I discuss later in the chapter.

This chapter also explains how to configure network clients and change logon options. I round out the chapter with a look at the advanced settings you can configure for your network connections through the Network Connections folder.

Managing the Network Connections Folder

Like its predecessor, Windows 2000, Windows XP integrates your network and dial-up connections into one location. Windows 2000 users are probably familiar with the Network and Dial-Up Connections folder. Microsoft has opted to rename the folder Network Connections in Windows XP, eliminating the distinction between LAN and dial-up connections. Figure 20.1 shows the Network Connections folder on a typical system.

To open the Network Connections folder, click Start, right-click My Network Places, and choose Properties. You can also open it through the Network Connections icon in Control Panel.

Changing the View

Windows XP uses the Tile view as the default for the Network Connections folder. This view shows the connection name, status, and device associated with the connection. If you have several connections or want more information, you may prefer a different view. For example, the Details view includes the same information plus the device type, owner name, and phone number or network address of the connection. Figure 20.2 shows the Details view.

FIGURE 20.1

Use the Network Connections folder to manage network settings.

FIGURE 20.2

The Details view offers additional information about connections.

To switch views, choose View and select the type of view you want. If you choose the Details view and want to customize it, choose View ➤ Choose Details to open the dialog box shown in Figure 20.3. You can select which columns to display and change the order of the columns using the Move Up and Move Down buttons. You can also change the column order and columns displayed directly in the view. To do so, click and drag a column to change its location. Right-click any column to display a menu you can use to turn on or off the various columns.

FIGURE 20.3
Use the Choose Details
dialog box to change the
columns displayed and
their location.

Simplifying the Folder for Multiple Adapters

Although most Windows XP computers typically have only one network adapter (and possibly several dial-up connections), you may run across a computer now and then that contains two adapters. A good example is a computer that functions as an Internet gateway, sharing its broadband Internet connection with other computers on the network. One NIC connects to the DSL modem or cable modem (or router), and the other connects the computer to the LAN.

Windows XP names the first connection Local Area Connection and names subsequent connections Local Area Connection 2, Local Area Connection 3, and so on. This doesn't make it easy to differentiate between the adapters. The simple solution is to rename the connections. For example, rename the adapter for the Internet connection to WAN, Internet, or something similar. You can also shorten the LAN connection's name to LAN or Local, for example. This lets you identify the cards at a glance, which is particularly helpful if you have two identical adapters in the computer.

To do this, right-click the connection's icon, and choose Rename. Type the name you want, and click OK.

TIP   I include the IP address in the connection's name if the computer has an assigned address. If the computer has two NICs that both take their addresses dynamically, I include the first three octets of the address. This helps me recall the NIC addresses at a glance.

Configuring Adapters

Most network adapters offer at least a few settings you can configure to change the way the card handles the connection and certain protocols. These settings vary from one card to another; some are common to all, and others are implemented only on some cards.

WARNING   If you don't understand a particular setting and don't have a specific reason to change it, leave it alone. You might find yourself juggling the settings to try to get the connection to work again.

It's difficult to explain all the possible settings, because they're device-dependent. One setting you might want to change is the speed and duplex mode of the card. Cards that support both 10 Mbps and 100 Mbps speeds set the speed automatically by default. The cards sense the connection speed and mode at startup and configure the speed accordingly. If you're connecting to a switch with defined speeds and modes for each port (or at least for your port), you can explicitly set the speed and mode for your adapter.

TIP Check your network card's documentation for information on the other settings offered by your card.

Open the properties for the connection and, on the General tab, click Configure to open the properties sheet for the card. Then click the Advanced tab. Find the setting that offers the following options, and select according to your desired configuration:

10 Mbps Full Duplex   The card operates at 10 Mbps and can send and receive at the same time.

10 Mbps Half Duplex   The card operates at 10 Mbps and doesn't send and receive at the same time.

100 Mbps Full Duplex   The card operates at 100 Mbps and can send and receive at the same time.

100 Mbps Half Duplex   The card operates at 100 Mbps and doesn't send and receive at the same time.

100 Mbps full duplex offers the best performance, but it requires that the other devices with which you communicate support the same speed and mode.

TIP In a few cases, I've seen network problems crop up when I've set a card to explicitly use 100 Mbps Full Duplex, and I've resolved the problem by moving to either AutoDetect or 100 Mbps Half Duplex. I've also seen cases where the card autodetected the correct settings but had to have the setting explicitly set to function properly.

The only other settings you'll probably need to change for a network adapter are the resource settings it uses. However, even this isn't likely, because most of today's network adapters fully support Plug and Play; thus Windows XP can dynamically assign the I/O range, memory range, and IRQ used by the card. If you're working with a legacy card or need to change the properties for another reason, you can do so through the Resources tab of the network card's properties.

Choosing Protocols

Network protocols are the language by which networked devices communicate. In the earlier versions of Windows, the most common protocol was NetBEUI for Microsoft networks and IPX/SPX for Novell NetWare networks. Over the years and in the past few iterations of the Windows platform, TCP/IP has become the protocol of choice for performance and compatibility reasons.

NOTE See Chapter 21 for a complete discussion of TCP/IP and its configuration.

Which protocol is right for your situation? Let's look at the three most common protocols.

NetBEUI

Although it isn't considered the protocol of choice these days, NetBEUI is still a good option for small networks because it requires no configuration. However, Windows XP doesn't install NetBEUI by default, so you have to add it manually, which dilutes that ease-of-use a bit. Also, NetBEUI isn't routable, which is both a good thing and a bad thing, depending on what you're trying to accomplish.

Not being able to route NetBEUI is a problem if your network sits on multiple segments and traffic needs to pass through one or more routers. TCP/IP is generally the best bet in these situations.

NetBEUI can be handy in networks that are directly connected to the Internet and in which you want to provide an added measure of security against attacks from the Internet or unauthorized access to files on the LAN. In this scenario, you need two protocols, NetBEUI and TCP/IP. You bind NetBEUI to the File and Printer Sharing service, which means it's used for file and printer sharing on the LAN. You unbind TCP/IP from the File and Printer Sharing service, which prevents remote users on the Internet from browsing files on your LAN. You could also substitute IPX for NetBEUI and achieve the same results.

NOTE You might think that this is an unlikely scenario to be able to browse other computers over an Internet connection, but I have seen it happen myself over more than one type of broadband connection (such as a home DSL connection). It's also possible over a dial-up connection.

However, I don't recommend this type of poor-man's firewall. Windows XP now sports its own firewall, which you can use to protect a small network from various types of attacks. An even better solution is a hardware-based firewall that can provide not only protection from attacks but also content-filtering to prevent users from browsing to undesirable sites.

New! **TIP** Internet Connection Firewall in Windows XP SP1 and earlier has been replaced by Windows Firewall in Service Pack 2. See Chapter 24 for a discussion of Windows Firewall.

Is NetBEUI still a good choice? If you're setting up a small network that isn't connected to the Internet, and you don't want to hassle with any configuration, NetBEUI is a good solution. In almost all other situations, TCP/IP is the way to go.

TCP/IP

TCP/IP is actually a suite of protocols, of which the two primary ones are Transmission Control Protocol (TCP) and Internet Protocol (IP). TCP/IP is the protocol suite used by the Internet and has become almost universal, even for small networks. Windows 2000 used TCP/IP as its default protocol, and Windows XP follows suit.

With TCP/IP, each network device must have a unique IP address, which can be statically assigned or dynamically assigned. There are two means for dynamic assignment:

DHCP A DHCP server manages a pool of IP addresses and assigns an address to a computer (or other device) when it starts up. A device can also release and renew its address. You'll find that most hardware firewalls can act as DHCP servers. A computer that shares its Internet connection through Internet Connection Sharing (ICS) functions as a DHCP server. You might also have one or more computers running one of Microsoft server platforms (such as Windows 2000 Server or Windows Server 2003) on the network and functioning as a DHCP server.

APIPA Automatic Private IP Addressing (APIPA) used by Windows XP provides a means for allocating IP addresses automatically without a DHCP server. When the computer boots, it looks for a DHCP server and, finding none, assigns itself an IP address from a common nonroutable (private) address range. The end result is that all the computers on a network can assign their own addresses through APIPA, which means no configuration is required.

Windows XP uses TCP/IP as its default protocol, installing TCP/IP automatically during XP installation. If you do nothing to modify the network installation during installation, Setup installs TCP/IP and configure it for dynamic addressing.

Although TCP/IP requires some configuration and more thought than NetBEUI, I still recommend it in almost all situations. Configuring TCP/IP isn't rocket science, and even novice users can have success with it if they understand what's needed.

IPX/SPX

This protocol is used primarily in older Novell NetWare networks. If your LAN includes one or more NetWare servers, IPX/SPX is a possible protocol. However, NetWare also supports TCP/IP, and TCP/IP is a better choice if only to improve network administration and eliminate the need for multiple protocols for computers that need access to both NetWare servers and the Internet.

What's the bottom line? I recommend TCP/IP in all situations unless you have a compelling reason to use a different protocol. That's why this book focuses primarily on TCP/IP.

Working with Network Clients

In addition to a network protocol, you also need a network *client*. The client provides the mechanism for access to shared network resources. If you're going to do file or printer sharing on the network, you'll need a client.

Windows XP provides two network clients: Client for Microsoft Networks and Client Service for NetWare. The former lets you access shared resources on a Microsoft-based network, such as one with Windows NT, Windows 2000, or Windows 2003 servers. You also use this client to access shared resources on a peer-to-peer network of Windows computers (all versions) with no dedicated servers. You'll use the Client Service for NetWare in a NetWare environment—one with one or more NetWare servers.

The next two sections cover both clients. To add a client, open the properties for the network connection, and click Install. Select Client, click Add, and follow the prompts to select and install the client.

Client for Microsoft Networks

You set the properties for the Client for Microsoft Networks through the properties for the connection where it's installed. Open the connection's properties, and double-click Client For Microsoft Networks in the General tab. Figure 20.4 shows the resulting dialog box.

The dialog box contains two settings:

Name Service Provider This option specifies the method Windows XP uses to locate other computers on the network. Choose between Windows Locator and DCE Cell Directory Service. Windows Locator is the default selection and is applicable to most situations. The other option, DCE Cell Directory Service, enables the computer to communicate with a DCE computer running the Name Service Interface Daemon (NSID), which provides name services for the network.

Network Address If you selected the DCE Cell Directory Service option from the Name Service Provider drop-down list, you must specify the address of the DCE name server.

FIGURE 20.4
Client for Microsoft Networks configuration

TIP   Client for Microsoft Networks corresponds to the Workstation service in Windows NT.

Client Service for NetWare

Unlike the Microsoft client, the NetWare client doesn't offer the ability for configuration through the `Network Connections` folder. Instead, you need to use the CSNW icon in Control Panel to configure the NetWare client. Figure 20.5 shows the resulting dialog box.

FIGURE 20.5
Use Client Service for NetWare dialog box to configure the NetWare client.

NOTE The NetWare client does appear in the properties for the connection in the Network Connections folder, but you can't configure the client from there.

The Client Service for NetWare dialog box contains the following settings:

Preferred Server This is the server that your computer connects to by default when you log on and which displays information about the resources available on the NetWare network. Use this option if your NetWare network isn't running Novell Directory Services (NDS).

Default Tree And Context If your network uses NDS, use this option to specify the NDS directory tree and context for your user account.

Print Options Set various print parameters through these options.

Login Script Options Select this option if you want your logon script to run each time you log onto a NetWare server or NDS tree.

Setting Advanced Network Properties

There are a handful of advanced settings you can configure for network connections. With the Network Connections folder open, choose Advanced ➢ Advanced Settings to open the Advanced Settings dialog box (Figure 20.6).

FIGURE 20.6
Use the Advanced Settings dialog box to change provider order and other advanced settings.

Controlling Bindings

The Connections group on the Adapters and Bindings tab lists the network connections in the order in which they're accessed by network services. In most cases, you'll want to keep LAN connections at the top followed by dial-up connections. In a few rare cases—such as when you work primarily through a dial-up connection rather than your LAN connection—you may want to change the order. If that's the case, click a connection, and click the up or down arrow to change its order in the list.

When you click a connection, Windows XP displays the *bindings* for the connection in the Bindings group. If a particular client or service is bound to a connection, Windows XP allows that item to function through the connection. For example, if the File and Printer Sharing service is bound to a particular connection, remote users can access your shared files and printers through that connection. However, you generally don't want File and Printer Sharing bound to a public connection such as a dial-up connection or WAN link (the network adapter connected to your cable or DSL modem, for example). The answer is to unbind the service from the connection. That's as simple as clearing the check box beside the File and Printer Sharing service in the Advanced Settings dialog box.

TIP You can unbind a client or service from a network connection through the connection's properties—you don't necessarily need to use the Advanced Settings dialog box to do it. Just open the properties for the connection from the Network Connections folder, and then clear the check box beside the item on the General tab.

Each service or client in the Bindings group of the Advanced Settings dialog box lists the protocols that are bound to it. This is different from the properties for the connection, which only show whether a protocol is enabled for the connection. They don't show whether a given protocol is bound to a specific client or service the way the Advanced Settings dialog box does.

You can bind or unbind one or more protocols for a specific client or service through the Adapters And Bindings tab of the Advanced Settings dialog box. To do so, select the connection, locate the client or service in the Bindings list, and clear the check box to unbind it, or place a check beside it to bind it. For example, assume you're using NetBEUI as your local protocol and TCP/IP for Internet connectivity. You would bind NetBEUI to the File and Printer Service but not to TCP/IP. Removing the binding for TCP/IP would remove the possibility that remote Internet users could browse your shared resources.

TIP Using NetBEUI as a local protocol is one way to reduce unauthorized access to a computer's shared resources, but it's no substitute for a firewall.

Setting Provider Order

The Provider Order tab of the Advanced Settings dialog box (Figure 20.7) lets you specify the order in which Windows XP uses network providers when multiple providers are present. For example, if you have both a NetWare client and a Windows client, but you use the Windows client most often, you can move it to the top of the list, giving it higher priority and therefore making Windows XP access it first by default. This can improve network performance and streamline browsing for resources.

You can also change the order of print providers through the Provider Order tab. Changing the order determines which print method Windows XP uses when multiple providers are available. For example, if you use Internet Printing Protocol (IPP) to print to printers on the network with HTTP rather than use the LanMan print service, you can change the order of the services so HTTP Print Services comes first in the list.

To change the provider order, open the Network Connections folder and choose Advanced ➢ Advanced Settings. Click the Provider Order tab, select the item whose order you want to change, and then click the up or down arrow to move the item to the desired location in the list.

FIGURE 20.7
Use the Provider Order
tab to control the order
in which Windows XP
uses network providers.

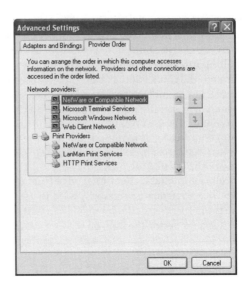

Bridging Connections

In a typical small network, all computers reside on the same media. For example, all the computers in your office may be connected by twisted-pair cable through a small hub or switch, and all the computers reside on the same network. Having all computers on the same network in this way is usually best because it simplifies network setup and management.

The same holds true in a small home network. If all your computers use the same media and are on the same network, it's much easier to share resources and connect them to the Internet. In some cases, however, it isn't possible or practical to have all computers on the same network. For example, let's assume you have a handful of computers connected in your office through twisted-pair cable on one or two switches. All the computers have a single network adapter, reside on the same logical network, and can share resources. They can all also access the Internet through a DSL router connected to the network.

However, now you need to add several computers in the manufacturing area, but it's located 100 feet away in a different building and you don't want to run cable to it. Instead, you decide to use wireless access points to connect the two networks. So, one computer in your office network (computer X) will have two network adapters: one for the wired LAN and one for the wireless LAN. One of the computers in the manufacturing area (computer Y) will also have two adapters: one for its local LAN and one to connect to the office network. The result is three networks: the office network, the network between computers X and Y (the wireless network), and the manufacturing network.

Without bridging connections, X can see Y and vice versa because they're on the same wireless network, but the computers on either LAN are unable to see across the wireless network to the other LAN. Plus, computers on the manufacturing network won't be able to get out on the Internet through the office LAN.

The solution is to *bridge* the connections. In this scenario, you create two bridges: You bridge the connections on X to allow the office LAN to see the wireless network, and you create a second bridge on Y's two connections to allow the manufacturing LAN to see the wireless network. The end result is that each LAN can now see across the wireless network to the other LAN. Then, all the computers can communicate and access the Internet.

To bridge connections, you must log on to the target computer using the Administrator account. You can bridge any Ethernet, IEEE 1394, or Ethernet-compatible wireless network adapters, but you can't bridge dial-up, VPN, or direct cable connections. You also can't bridge a connection that has Internet Connection Sharing or Internet Connection Firewall enabled.

TIP Although you can bridge an adapter that has a public IP address to an adapter that has a private address—in effect creating an Internet gateway—you should not do so. Instead, use Internet Connection Sharing to create the gateway. Better still, install a hardware-based firewall/router on the network and use that as the Internet gateway.

When you're ready to create a bridge, open the `Network Connections` folder and select one of the two adapters to include in the bridge. Hold down the Ctrl key, and click the other adapter. Then right-click one, and choose Bridge Connections. Windows XP creates the bridge and then creates a new section in the folder named Network Bridge. It moves the two bridged connections to this section and creates a new icon to represent the bridge.

You can't make changes to a network adapter's settings directly when it's part of a bridged connection. Instead, you must make changes through the Network Bridge icon. Right-click the icon and choose Properties to display the dialog box shown in Figure 20.8.

FIGURE 20.8
Use the Network Bridge dialog box to modify the bridge or settings for adapters in the bridged connection.

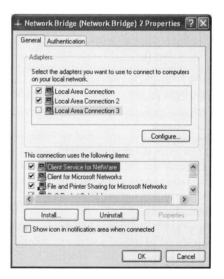

As the figure illustrates, the General tab shows the adapters included in the bridge and the services, clients, and protocols used by it. As with an unbridged connection, you can enable or disable specific items by checking or clearing the check box beside the item. To add another adapter to the connection, place a check beside it.

The Authentication tab configures Windows XP's use of 802.1x authentication. This draft standard was developed by several wireless vendors, Microsoft, and PC vendors in conjunction with the IEEE and addresses the potential security issues that arise from otherwise unprotected wireless LANs. For example, if a wireless LAN in your apartment connects to your DSL connection, it's possible for your neighbors to tie into your wireless LAN and gain access to the Internet through your connection (not to mention possibly access your files).

The Authentication tab lets you specify the types of authentication that the computer uses when connecting to the network. Although the 802.1x security standard is designed for wired LANs, it applies primarily to wireless LANs. For that reason, I cover the options on the Authentication tab in the following section.

Securing a Wireless Network

As I briefly mentioned in the previous section, security for wireless networks is a potential problem and should be a major concern for you if you implement wireless solutions at the office or at home. If you don't have proper security mechanisms in place, it's possible for someone to gain unauthorized access to your network and potentially to your Internet connection, essentially stealing services from you and from your Internet service provider.

A wireless access point—the device through which you connect to the network—broadcasts its service set identifier (SSID) to potential wireless clients. This makes the wireless network visible to clients looking for a network. There are a few steps you can take to reduce the possibility that an unauthorized user can identify your wireless network, much less connect to it.

The first change to make is to modify the SSID of your access point(s) to a nondefault value that isn't easy to guess. For example, set it to an arbitrary string of letters and numbers. Don't use your phone number, address, or other information that an unauthorized user might easily guess. If possible, turn off SSID broadcast. The downside to turning it off is that the wireless network won't appear when you browse for a network in Windows XP when adding a new computer, but the upside is that doing so decreases the likelihood that an unauthorized user will find your network.

WARNING   Windows XP provides the ability to browse for wireless networks and discover SSIDs. There are third-party and freeware applications that can discover wireless networks for other operating systems, so you should do everything you can to inhibit the ability of these platforms to identify your network.

Next, check out the access point to determine whether it allows you to configure the network as either open or closed. In an open network, wireless clients that specify Any as the station name or that specify no station name at all can still connect. In a closed network, the station name must be specified. Select the closed option, if available.

You should also change the default password or community string for the access point. Many default to using the common SNMP community string `public`, making it easy for savvy users to get into the access point if they succeed in determining the SSID.

Another security step you can take is to switch from dynamic addressing to static addressing. If your network includes a firewall or router that assigns addresses dynamically through DHCP, turn off DHCP and assign addresses in an arbitrary private subnet. Don't use the common 192.168.0.n subnet, for example, but go with something like 192.168.52.n. At the very least, this increases the number of addresses a potential unauthorized user has to go through to find your subnet.

Windows XP supports Wired Equivalent Privacy (WEP), a set of services that provides additional security for wired networks. WEP allows a certificate to be used to authenticate network clients and also supports encryption to secure data from sniffing. To configure the wireless connection, open the `Network Connections` folder, open the properties for the wireless adapter, and then click the Wireless Networks tab (Figure 20.9 on the left).

FIGURE 20.9

Use the Wireless Network tab to configure security for wireless LANs. (left) Enable WEP and configure security through the Wireless Network Properties dialog box. (right)

Figure 20.9 (left) shows a typical configuration, with an Orinoco PC Card connection to an Orinoco RG1000 Residential Wireless Gateway with an SSID of 089c41. To configure security, select a wireless network from the Available Networks list (multiple networks may be listed) and click Configure to display the Wireless Network Properties dialog box shown in Figure 20.9 on the right.

Select Data Encryption (WEP Enabled) to enable WEP. The option Network Authentication (Shared Mode) determines whether a network key is used to authenticate to the wireless network. If your access point requires a network key, select this option. The key itself may be provided on the wireless adapter; if so, you can use the default option The Key Is Provided For Me Automatically to make Windows XP use that key automatically. Otherwise, clear this option and then specify the network key string, format, length, and index using the options provided.

NOTE   The key is defined by the access point and is often by default the same as the network name. To increase security, consider changing the key from the default value to something difficult to guess, such as an arbitrary string of digits.

The last option in the dialog box specifies whether the connection is to another wireless computer or to an access point. Select this option if you're connecting directly to another computer and not through an access point.

If your access point is configured to not broadcast its SSID, you'll need to connect to the wireless network manually. To do so, click Add on the Wireless Networks tab. In the Wireless Network Properties dialog box, enter the SSID of the access point and the authentication information as I described previously. Then click OK.

Setting Up a Wireless Network with SP2

New!   Windows XP Service Pack 2 introduces a new feature called the Wireless Network Setup Wizard. This wizard makes it much easier to configure wireless network settings on multiple computers on the network. In a nutshell, the wizard helps you create the settings needed for a wireless client to connect to the wireless network and then copies those settings onto a USB flash drive or disk, which you can use with the wizard on other computers to configure the client.

TIP The Wireless Network Setup Wizard isn't geared toward configuring wireless settings for a large number of computers at once, but it can be useful for helping you set up a small wireless network. It can also be handy in a situation where you need to routinely configure wireless connections for new users. You can create the data on the flash drive or diskette and keep it handy for times when you need to set up a notebook for a new user.

To use the Wireless Network Setup Wizard, follow these steps:

1. Log on to a computer with a wireless adapter, and double-click the wireless connection icon in the tray.

2. Choose View Wireless Networks on the General tab of the wireless connection properties, and then click the link "Set up a wireless network for a home or small office" (Figure 20.10).

TIP You can also start the wizard from the Network Connections folder. To do so, click the link in the Network Tasks pane.

FIGURE 20.10
Click the link on the General tab of the wireless connections properties to start the wizard.

3. The wizard prompts you for the settings for the wireless network and saves them to a USB flash drive or a disk (Figure 20.11). Note that you can save the settings to any hard disk on the computer, as well. However, you won't be able to easily transport those settings to other computers!

TIP If you delete the information from the USB flash drive or diskette and want to easily re-create it, run the wizard again on the source computer and choose Add New Computers Or Devices in the wizard. The wizard will then write the settings to the device you specify.

FIGURE 20.11
The wizard saves the settings to a USB flash drive by default.

When you need to set up a device, plug the flash drive into the new computer's USB port. The data includes an `Autorun.inf` file that launches the Setup program to configure the computer. If you're working from a floppy diskette, run the `SetupSNK.exe` file on the diskette. After you run the wizard, insert the device back in the source computer and click Next. The wizard lists the devices that have been added to the network (Figure 20.12). The last page of the wizard also gives you the opportunity to print the settings and clear them from the flash drive, if desired.

FIGURE 20.12
The wizard lists the devices that have been added to the network.

Chapter 21

Configuring and Optimizing TCP/IP

Transmission Control Protocol/Internet Protocol (TCP/IP) is an group of network protocols (sometimes called a protocol suite) essential to Internet and other network communications through the operating system.

Whether you realize it or not, you use it every day in going online. Yet what is more important for you to understand is that TCP/IP's proper configuration and optimization can be key to achieving the best results (read: the fewest hassles) in your communication.

In this chapter, you'll get a fuller understanding of what TCP/IP is and the job it does, how to configure it, and ways to optimize it for best results. Then, in the following chapter, I'll take you through both the monitoring and troubleshooting of TCP/IP connections.

NOTE This chapter focuses specifically on IPv4. See `http://www.microsoft.com/technet/prodtechnol/winxppro/plan/faqipv6.mspx` for details on IPv6 and Windows XP.

TCP/IP Overview

If you're looking for a de facto standard for network communication, TCP/IP is it.

As I mentioned, TCP/IP isn't a single network communication protocol. Instead, it's an aggregate of different protocols, which work together to provide a host of both simple and advanced communication services and are supported by virtually all current-issue network operating systems and packages. You'll find TCP/IP built into Unix, for example. These different protocols come together under the umbrella of TCP/IP to serve as the protocol "bridge" linking different and divergent systems and networks for communication. The need to interconnect different networks—what eventually became the global Internet—is the reason TCP/IP was developed. Because of this versatility, TCP/IP has grown to become the dominant technique used in a variety of networking environments, for home users connecting to the Internet as well as small and large organizations.

TCP/IP supports functions and processes such as virtual private networking (VPN), internal IP routing, and network-based printing; and it permits multiple addresses to be tied to one or more network interface cards (adapters), a capability commonly known as *multihoming*. Also, tools built into TCP/IP provide a host of diagnostic and service functions for monitoring and troubleshooting connections and configuration (covered in detail in Chapter 22).

Here are just a few of the protocols bound together under the name TCP/IP:

- Address Resolution Protocol (ARP)
- Internet Control Message Protocol (ICMP)
- Internet Group Management Protocol (IGMP)
- Internet Protocol (IP)
- Transmission Control Protocol (TCP)

Configuring TCP/IP

Since TCP/IP is installed by default with Windows XP, your job becomes configuring it for proper communications.

In this section, you'll learn more about the terminology—and the technology behind the terms—of TCP/IP communications, including IP addresses and their assignment, and the IPConfig tool used to verify the communications. I'll also tell you how to obtain and supply the necessary parameters such as an IP address or whether to obtain one automatically if you're logging onto the Internet from a dial-up Internet provider.

Before we launch into the terms and details, follow these steps to access your current TCP/IP properties:

1. Open My Network Places, and right-click the Local Area Connection option. (If you have more than one connection/connection type, you may have more than one TCP/IP configuration in place for each particular circumstance.)

2. Click Internet Protocol (TCP/IP), and Choose Properties.

3. Check the General tab, and note the configuration information.

4. Click the Advanced button to open the Advanced TCP/IP Settings. You'll see these four tabs:

IP Settings	Used for establishing communications parameters; discussed in the next section
DNS	Domain Name System; discussed later under "Using DNS"
WINS	Windows Internet Naming Service; discussed later under "Using WINS"
Options	Discussed later under "Configuring Other TCP Properties and Tools"

We'll talk about checking and properly configuring these settings as we go.

Internet Protocol Addressing

IP addresses act as unique identifiers for every computer system connected either to a network or to that bigger network known as the Internet. They have to be unique, of course, because communication would get confusing otherwise.

Here's a simple example of how IP addressing works. I use a popular network-messaging program to send notes back and forth in real time to colleagues and friends. When I send the message, TCP/IP is involved in the process of communicating with my provider and helping to send my message out to the messaging service's server. That message gets stamped with my system's IP address, because the IP inserts both the source and destination IP address into a packet when data is sent. So when the other party sees my message and replies, that response arrives back at my location rather than being sent to some user logged in from Tibet, because it gets routed through the Internet to my unique IP address. This is why the uniqueness is so key to proper communications and why mistakenly duplicating an existing IP address can create a mess.

The IP address gets bound to the interface, such as the installed network interface card (or the NIC integrated into the motherboard itself) or other network adapter. An IPv4 address is a 32-bit address, usually organized into four *octets* (four sequences of eight bits each) and taking a form something like 192.168.63.1 or 169.254.0.2.

You can configure TCP/IP in Windows XP (and elsewhere) and assign these unique IP addresses either automatically through options in XP or manually (see "Manual IP Addressing," later in this chapter).

Every IP address is made up of two components: a network portion and a host portion. How you determine which sets of numbers are network portions and which are host portions depends on the type, since there are different classes of IP addresses. A Class A IP address uses only the first set of numbers as the network portion, with the rest identifying the host portion; a Class B network portion is defined by the first two octets, whereas a Class C IP address uses the first three sets of numbers to identify the network.

IP Address Types

There are two major types of IP addresses:

Public IP addresses   These are used for devices connecting to the Internet.

Private IP addresses   These take the same format as public IP addresses, but they're specifically used for systems on a network that don't connect directly to the Internet and can't be accessed from the outside world. For example, if you're on a workstation on a 10-node network, that network requires only one public IP address to connect to the Internet, whereas each individual workstation (including yours) needs its own authorized private IP address.

You should know a bit more about these IP address types since you may ultimately have reason to use more than just a public IP address, particularly if you're involved in a networked environment. After all, even a small home network can employ more than a few IP addresses: Each node on the network needs (at least) one, and one is assigned by your Internet provider for connecting online.

TIP   Ever wonder exactly who establishes and keeps track of the untold number of unique IP addresses? This is the job of the Internet Assigned Numbers Authority (IANA), which (along with other organizations it delegates to) provides access companies and others with lists of available public IP numbers for assignment. Permitted address ranges for private IP addresses were established some years ago, and their usage is governed by RFC 1918; these are used and reused over and over, without any need to go through a formal assignment (again) by the IANA.

PUBLIC IP ADDRESSES

This type of IP address is required for access to the Internet. It's typically assigned by an Internet service provider (ISP) or access company through a list of available IP addresses supplied to them by the IANA.

Public IP addresses can be either *static* (the same IP address is always used, usually because of a fixed connection to the Internet, as occurs through many types of broadband Internet access) or *dynamic* (randomly assigned during each Internet connection, as is more typical with dial-up Internet access).

PRIVATE IP ADDRESSES

Private IP addresses are just that—drawn from a list of available, valid IP addresses identified by IANA. These are typically employed on a network where individual nodes don't have direct Internet connectivity (because they would then need a public ID address).

Does this mean you can't connect to the Internet if you use the private IP address route? Absolutely not, because you can configure these nodes to share an Internet connection that has been established on a system (or server) that *does* have a public IP address, using either a hardware-based router, Windows XP's Internet Connection Sharing, or a third-party communications proxy program such as WinProxy. Table 21.1 lists private IP address ranges for each address class.

TABLE 21.1:   Private IP Address Ranges

CLASS	FROM	TO	CIDR MASK	DECIMAL MASK
Class "A" or 24 Bit	10.0.0.0	10.255.255.255	/8	255.0.0.0
Class "B" or 20 Bit	172.16.0.0	72.31.255.255	/12 or /16	255.240.0.0 or 255.255.0.0
Class "C" or 16 Bit	192.168.0.0	192.168.255.255	/16 or /24	255.255.0.0 or 255.255.255.0

IP Address Assignment Methods

Windows XP directly supports four different methods for performing IP address assignment within TCP/IP:

Dynamic Host Configuration Protocol (DHCP)   This is the default method for IP address assignment under Windows XP. It's used to automatically configure both IP addresses and other necessary options for all clients in a network based on a DHCP server.

Static IP addressing   This method involves the manual assignment of a fixed IP address, which is usually used in special circumstances and/or where DHCP and APIPA are unavailable or undesired.

Automatic Private IP Addressing (APIPA)   This is another automatic configuration method, used when a DHCP server is unavailable or unwarranted.

Alternate IP configuration   This new method in Windows XP is used to configure one primary and one secondary IP assignment. Alternate configuration can be helpful when you have multiple connection options, such as when you use your laptop at work to establish one type of connection and then at home or on the road to connect via another method. The primary configuration is tried first, and if it's not available, the secondary configuration is tried.

Each of these methods is covered in later sections of this chapter.

Manual IP Addressing

As a rule, wherever possible, you should choose automatic IP address assignment over manual configuration.

When you learn more about DHCP-style IP address assignment in the next section, you'll see that Windows XP is configured by default to make services available for the automatic assignment of IP addresses. Also, be aware that by choosing to manually assign these IP addresses, you become responsible for their validity (uniqueness, following a valid number range, and so on) and their administration and that you're effectively bypassing the normal safeguarding measures built into TCP/IP.

Thus, if you develop a problem when manually assigning the addresses, you may want to work through or around it by removing the self-enforced assignments and going the automatic route instead, to facilitate the establishment of basic network communications. Once you have your setup functioning correctly, you can always go back and tinker.

Also, be aware that you can use a mix of both manual and automatic IP address assignment—this is a common practice in almost every major network environment.

DISABLING AUTOMATIC TCP/IP CONFIGURATION

In some circumstances, such as certain situations in which you may have to later use static addressing for IP address configuration, you may find it necessary to disable automatic TCP/IP configuration. Now, why would you need to do that, since (as you'll read later under the APIPA section) automatic configuration is ignored when static addressing is used? You may have an IP assignment situation in which you've set up the static IP address correctly, yet the configuration behaves as if it's still using (you suspect) its automatic assignment. The Registry tweak outlined here forces the disabling of automatic configuration in such a case, ruling out this issue in troubleshooting a connectivity issue.

The best way to do this is by editing the Registry; you should follow the usual precautions in protecting the integrity of your Registry. Once you've done that, follow these steps to permanently disable automatic configuration:

1. Load the Registry Editor.

2. Locate this Registry key:

   ```
   HKEY_LOCAL_MACHINE\SYSTEM\CurrentControlSet\Services\Tcpip\Parameters
   ```

3. Add the following entry to the key:

   ```
   IPAutoconfigurationEnabled: REG_DWORD
   ```

4. Assign this entry a value of 0.

5. Save your changes, and exit the Registry Editor.

MANUALLY CONFIGURING YOUR TCP/IP PROPERTIES

If you choose to manually configure your system for special reasons or because you don't have a situation in which you can use DHCP or APIPA, follow these steps:

1. From Network Connections, right-click the Local Area Connection entry (or the desired one, if more than one exists for your setup), and choose Properties.

2. On the General tab, click to select Internet Protocol (TCP/IP), and click the Properties button.

3. On the new General tab, select Use The Following IP Address, and then type in the appropriate information, including a value for IP address, subnet mask, and default gateway. Click OK twice to save your changes and exit.

NOTE See "Other TCP/IP Properties and Tools," later in this chapter, for information on configuring the default gateway and other properties.

STATIC ADDRESSING

One example where you may need to set up static addressing occurs when you have a computer connecting to an ISP or access company that requires you to use a specific, static address to access their servers. They will usually provide this address to you in the documentation or e-mail accompanying the opening of your account with them.

To manually configure a static IP address under TCP/IP, follow the steps in the preceding section, and enter the address you need.

Automatic IP Addressing

The chief means of automatically assigning IP addresses are Dynamic Host Configuration Protocol (DHCP) and Automatic Private IP Addressing (APIPA).

DYNAMIC HOST CONFIGURATION PROTOCOL (DHCP)

One of the protocols wrapped under the umbrella of TCP/IP, DHCP was first conceived as a common, easily implemented way to allow for automatic configuration of IP addresses and other parameters. DHCP is enabled by default in Windows XP.

This method works under a distributed process called *leasing,* where a DHCP server keeps and manages a list of valid IP addresses available for a network. When a client system logs into the server, the server configures and leases a dynamic IP address to the client; this means IP address assignment occurs on the fly, and the IP for a particular node on the network can change frequently but automatically without user configuration.

Also, the DHCP leases these IP addresses for a specific chunk of time, referred to as the *lease duration*. When a client obtains a lease and begins using it, the meter begins running. Halfway through the lease duration, the client automatically sends a request to extend the lease to the DHCP server, to make sure a session doesn't time out or otherwise fail because of an expired lease. The DHCP, on its end, grants that request again and again until the client stops requesting an extension (for example, because the client has been shut down or otherwise removed from the need for an IP address assignment). This helps ensure that leased IP addresses will return to the DHCP queue for reassignment.

By design, DHCP effectively avoids pesky address conflicts and other issues that typically crop up with manual IP address assignment and configuration.

You also don't need an intricate network to use the services of DHCP, since Windows XP's Internet Connection Sharing employs it, for example, in distributing Internet access to other systems, even on a small home network. ISPs also may use DHCP and require you to adjust your configuration for this process (for example, Obtain An IP Address Automatically) under your TCP/IP properties.

DHCP does more than assign IP addresses. It manages addresses for features such as print and news servers, and it configures other TCP/IP parameters including the default gateway and the subnet mask.

Since DHCP is installed and enabled for you when you set up Windows XP, it's already there, waiting for use. See the next section for instructions for setting up TCP/IP to use this automatic configuration and for the rules of how Windows XP handles the issue of whether to use DHCP, APIPA, or alternate configuration to assign IP addresses.

AUTOMATIC PRIVATE IP ADDRESSING (APIPA)

Using APIPA, you can automatically allow Windows XP to configure the system to assign private IP addresses to each node on the network—no DHCP server or manual IP address assignment is required.

However, some special conditions are placed on APIPA's use. Unlike some of the other methods mentioned here, APIPA configures the IP address and subnet mask *only*. Any other settings (such as default gateway and IP addresses for either DNS or WINS servers) are left unconfigured. Thus, it should only be used on a network with just one subnet and where no routers are connected.

Also, because we're talking about the assignment of private IP addresses and without the added configuration setup, it's not wise to use this for either a home area network (HAN) or a small office's LAN where a direct connection to either an intranet or the Internet is used.

I said earlier that Windows XP uses that protocol by default to configure IP addresses automatically. However, what happens when a DHCP server is unavailable? Windows XP then looks at the Alternate Configuration tab and makes a judgment call whether to use APIPA or these alternate parameters to configure the IP address.

If APIPA is chosen (and under normal conditions, it wll be), then an IP address is assigned using a very specific range (169.254.0.1 to 169.254.255.254). These addresses are reserved for APIPA use only and won't be found anywhere on the Internet. APIPA also sets the subnet mask to a default setting of 255.255.0.0.

Because Windows XP looks to DHCP first and then falls back to either APIPA or alternate configuration, how you enable these to work is roughly the same for all three (at least, as long as you have an alternate configuration established). If you choose to force a manual configuration through the use of static addressing, however, all automatic configuration is ignored.

Follow these steps to assign your IP addresses automatically:

1. From Network Connections, right-click the Local Area Connection you want to adjust, and choose Properties.

2. In the Internet Protocol (TCP/IP) Properties window, select Obtain IP Address Automatically.

Configuring for a Default Gateway

A *gateway,* by definition, is any device used for common access to an external source. With Internet Connection Sharing, for example, the single system directly accessing the Internet serves as a gateway to the other systems on the network sharing the service. But particularly as it relates to TCP/IP, the gateway is the address of a specific, reachable IP router.

Understand that, to add a default gateway, you have to manually configure your TCP/IP properties, including the IP address and the subnet mask, as well as add the default gateway information. To do this, follow these steps:

1. From Network Connections, select the connection you want to configure, and then click Change Settings Of This Connection.

2. On the General tab, click to select Internet Protocol (TCP/IP Properties), and then click Properties.

3. Choose User Configured, click Use The Following IP Address, and then supply the IP address, subnet mask, and default gateway. If necessary, fill in the primary and alternate information for either or both DNS and WINS servers. Click OK.

WHAT IS A SUBNET MASK?

A *subnet* is a subdivision of an IP network—often used for better performance control and security—where all devices share one or more IP address prefixes. For example, nodes on a subnet may all have IP addresses of the form 192.168.0.*xxx*; here, *xxx* is the unique identifier for each device.

A *subnet mask* is the method of identifying the various devices within a subnet, providing a 32-bit number (usually taking the form of 255.*xxx.xxx.xxx*) needed to allow a device sending an IP packet to identify both the network ID and host ID sections of a particularly IP address for accurate handling and routing. When a device prepares to send an IP packet, it compares the destination IP to its own, trying to first determine whether both are on the same subnet. If they are on the same subnet, the device resolves the destination's MAC address using ARP (see the preceding chapter) and sends it directly. If they aren't on the same subnet, the IP packet is sent instead to the default gateway's IP address.

TCP/IP-Based Name Resolution

Ever try to recall—accurately—more than a few IP addresses? Since everything covered here needs an IP address *and* each IP address must be unique, you end up with a lot to remember. For most people, they're much tougher to use on a regular basis than a normal name identity.

Thus, it becomes the job of a process called TCP/IP *name resolution* to convert those unique IP addresses into unique name identities. This gives you the option of looking for a computer called Pax rather than trying to remember 192.168.0.5 (the Pax system's IP address on the network). Although virtually all of the methods discussed here can resolve both from name to IP and from IP to name, these methods are chiefly used for resolving names to IP addresses; that's why the process is called name resolution.

Windows XP directly supports several types of TCP/IP name resolution, including

◆ Domain Name System (DNS)

◆ Windows Internet Naming Service (WINS)

◆ HOSTS

◆ LMHOSTS

◆ Broadcast

I'll discuss the first two in some detail, and then tell you how the next two are used. The last type (broadcast) is briefly described under LMHOSTS.

Using DNS

Domain Name System (DNS) is a directory service that translates domain names into IP addresses. When DNS is used on a network for name resolution (meaning, whenever you use a domain name), the network looks to a hierarchical, distributed database (called the *domain namespace*) stored either within the network or on the Internet. That database stores specific mappings of DNS domain names to related data, which includes IP addresses and user-friendly names, for easy lookup. When the network queries the DNS server, it's searching on the data stored in that database to try to come up with an IP address linked to that particular domain so that it can convert that domain into an IP address. As soon as an appropriate match is made, the process is finished. If it can't make a match based on the listings contained in the local database, it jumps to other available DNS servers trying to find a match. If it can't find a match anywhere, a DNS error is reported back.

DNS is the default name resolution system used with Windows XP clients, and a DNS host name is automatically collected from the client's computer name when XP is installed. To see your DNS host name, double-click the System icon in Control Panel, and choose the Computer Name tab.

A primary DNS suffix is used to identify the DNS domain to which a specific host belongs. Under normal conditions, when you're working with a small network, a workgroup, a stand-alone system, or even a Windows NT domain, a DNS suffix may not be needed and won't be established *unless* you manually specify one.

You can either establish your first DNS suffix or modify your existing one by following these steps:

1. Open the System applet in Control Panel, and choose the Computer Name tab.

2. Click Change.

3. Click More.

4. In the DNS Suffix And NetBIOS Computer Name window, type the new DNS suffix required, and click OK until you exit.

TIP   To change this setting automatically each time a system changes its domain affiliation (membership), be sure to click to check this option in the DNS Suffix window.

NOTE   A secondary DNS suffix is the alternate one to use if the first isn't available.

Using WINS

When you read about DNS in the preceding section, you learned that the distributed database stores results of mapping a *domain* name or host name to other information, including (importantly) the IP address. Now let's look at Windows Internet Naming Service (WINS), which maps *computer* (NetBIOS) names to their respective IP addresses.

WINS is a server-based process that uses a distributed database to track and update these NetBIOS/computer name-to-IP address listings. The updating part is critical, because if DHCP servers are configured to assign IP addresses dynamically, these IP addresses (and the names they associate with) can change from session to session. One strong benefit here is that WINS facilitates the way you can locate computers, even on remote networks. Another is that WINS is compatible for use with clients and servers running earlier versions of Windows.

Two different elements form what we refer to as WINS:

WINS server   This is the administrative part. It handles the distributed database and is responsible for both name queries and name registrations.

NetBIOS over TCP/IP (NetBT, as client)   This network component is used for backward compatibility with non–Windows 2000 and XP systems that are still using the basic network input/output operating system (NetBIOS) included with earlier versions of Windows. It's also used to perform computer name–to-IP address mapping and name resolution.

If DHCP is used for autoconfiguration of the IP address, WINS information (server parameters) should be automatically set. However, let's go through the steps of configuring Windows XP to use WINS, while also being sure that you have enabled DHCP:

1. From Network Connections, right-click Local Area Connection (or the appropriate connection if you use more than one), and choose Properties.

2. From the list of protocols, select Internet Protocol (TCP/IP), and then click the Properties button.

NOTE   If you don't use autoconfiguration through the DHCP assignment method, you *must* configure your WINS connection manually.

What you do next depends on whether you have a DHCP server already established to work with WINS. If you do, choose Obtain An IP Address Automatically, and click OK. If you don't, then follow these steps:

1. On the General tab under TCP/IP Properties, click the Advanced button.

2. Select the WINS tab.

3. Click Add, which opens the TCP/IP WINS Server dialog box.

4. Provide the name of the WINS server you want to use, and click Add again.

TIP   If you have more than one WINS server you can use, you can add additional ones here. To change the preference order in which Windows XP checks these servers, select the desired server from the list, and then click the up arrow to move it higher in the list or the down arrow to move it lower.

Using a HOSTS File

What if you don't have access to a DNS server for domain/host name-to-IP address resolution?

This is the role of the HOSTS file, a static table of local host computers that provides host-name resolution whenever DNS isn't available (or when it's available but not all hosts may be registered). You can use it to store a list of static entries for the systems to which you regularly connect.

A sample HOSTS file is located in the *%systemroot%*\System32\Drivers\Etc\ folder. This is a simple text file, which you can edit to add the names of remote hosts plus IP addresses to which you connect; or, you can use its format to create your own (remember to save it in text-only format). The syntax for an entry for a host named Pax1 at boyce.us might look like this:

```
192.168.68.10          pax1.boyce.us
```

Using an LMHOSTS File

Windows XP sees any system that is neither configured as a WINS server nor a WINS client as being a *broadcast* or *b-mode* computer, because of the way such a system uses IP broadcasts for NetBIOS name resolution rather than the WINS name resolution type. What's different here is that the system's cache is called on to store registered address/name mappings gathered from an LMHOSTS file (*LM* stands for local machine, referring to that system's hosts listing).

The LMHOSTS file is a straight text file containing the NetBIOS or Microsoft NT domain name as well as the IP address of remote computers or (backup) domains to which you connect. Such computers can be any system inside or outside your local subnet. The contents of this file are read into the cache, and when Windows XP wants to try to identify a remote computer, it looks first in the cache. If it can't identify the remote computer through stored mappings, it then moves to IP broadcasts to try to resolve the name. If that fails, it goes back and parses the entire LMHOSTS file.

A sample LMHOSTS file (lmhosts.sam) is provided for you in the *%systemroot%*\System32\ Drivers\Etc folder. You can edit this version to add necessary computers, but you must save it to lmhosts, rather than lmhosts.sam, to have the file recognized for use.

TIP   For the LMHOSTS file to be most effective, you need to add the NetBIOS name and IP address of every remote system you regularly connect with.

Other TCP/IP Properties and Tools

In the following sections, I discuss a variety of further TCP/IP options:

- Setting up multiple gateways
- Configuring TCP/IP filtering
- Using class IDs
- Taking advantage of IPConfig

Using Multiple Gateways

As was the case in early versions of Windows (including NT 4), you can set up multiple gateways for a single workstation, if necessary. This situation may occur if you have multiple network adapters installed, all pointed at different other systems or devices acting as gateways. This has the added benefit of allowing data to switch to the second gateway, for example, if the first one is unavailable.

Follow these steps to add one or more additional gateways:

1. From Control Panel, click Network Connections.

2. Select and right-click the desired connection, and choose Properties.

3. Select TCP/IP, and click Properties.

4. On the General tab, click Advanced.

5. On the IP Settings tab (opened by default), go to Default Gateways, and click Add.

6. In the TCP/IP Gateway window, type in the desired gateway address, and click Add. Click OK.

Using TCP/IP Filtering

Filtering here means a way to try to better control the data traffic reaching the Windows-based machine being configured for TCP/IP.

TCP/IP in Windows XP includes a set of input filters specifically designed to work with local host traffic only; these filters are typically used when you're not configuring for more advanced data traffic management, such as you might have through an external application, Routing and Remote Access, or even IPSec.

By default, TCP/IP filtering is turned off in Windows XP. To turn it on and configure it for use, follow these steps:

1. From Network Connections, select the local area connection you want to modify, right-click, and choose Properties.

2. On the General tab, select Internet Protocol (TCP/IP), and then click Properties.

3. Click Advanced.

4. On the Options tab, select TCP/IP Filtering, and then click Properties.

5. In the TCP/IP Filtering window, click to select Enable TCP/IP Filtering.

6. Under their respective sections, provide the port numbers for all TCP and UDP ports, plus the IP protocols you want to enable filtering to check. You must click Permit Only before you're allowed to add these ports. Click OK until you exit.

NOTE   Concerned about security, or have questions about establishing IP security under Windows XP? You'll find this covered in Chapter 43.

Using Class IDs

Starting with Windows 2000, Windows operating systems support the use of class IDs, used by DHCP to distinguish which class of PCs a particular workstation or client belongs to. Classes can help identify particular groups of devices, such as those residing in a particular department, and customize those locations to which they have access, the priority with which requests are handled, and the length of DHCP lease periods used.

For example, based on class ID, you can give a much longer lease period to people who log on directly through the network than to workers dialing in from home or a remote location.

By design, a DHCP server handles requests based on the available class IDs presented to it.

Class IDs are set using the IPConfig tool, discussed in the next section. You must log in on an administrator account in order to set class IDs, and use one of the following syntaxes:

```
ipconfig /setclassid [classIDname]
ipconfig /setclassid [adaptername] [classIDname]
```

WARNING   Failure to specify the new class ID when using the /setclassid option purges any current class ID established.

Using IPConfig

IPConfig is a command-line tool available in Windows XP to help verify the proper setup of TCP/IP and its communication with other systems and networks. Specifically, IPConfig confirms the configuration parameters available on the host, with the host here defined as any device on the network that isn't responsible for forwarding data packets between subnets.

NOTE   If you recall the WINIPCFG tool available in earlier versions of Windows, you're probably already aware that it isn't included with Windows XP. IPConfig replaces it.

NOTE   Another such tool, the Ping utility, is discussed in the next chapter.

By default, IPConfig displays the following information for each adapter to which TCP/IP has been bound after it has completed its verification (as shown in Figure 21.1):

◆   Assigned IP address

◆   Subnet mask

◆   Default gateway

However, switch options available for use with IPConfig allow you to customize (to some degree) the result output depending on your specific needs. These options are detailed in Table 21.2.

FIGURE 21.1
IPConfig gives this screen output.

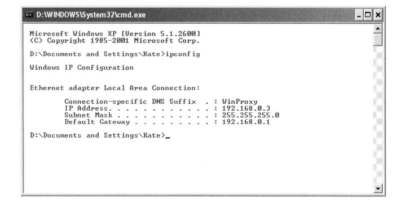

TABLE 21.2: IPConfig Switch Options

OPTION	PURPOSE
/all	Displays all available TCP/IP configuration information.
/displaydns	Displays info from the DNS resolver cache.
/flushdns	Clears the DNS resolver cache.
/registerdns	Reregisters DNS names after it refreshes all DHCP leases.
/release *adapter*	Releases the IP address (specified adapter only).
/renew *adapter*	Renews the IP address (specified adapter only).
/setclassid	Resets the DHCP class ID to a specific setting.
/showclassid	Displays the DHCP class ID(s) available for the specified adapter.
/?	Displays online help; use the |more option to break the text into different screens.

The syntax used in conjunction with IPConfig follows conventions such as these (typed from the command line):

```
ipconfig /all
ipconfig /displaydns
ipconfig /renew adapter
ipconfig /setclassid adapter class_ID
```

The results of `ipconfig /all` are shown in Figure 21.2. When you're using the `/renew` switch, replace the variable with the name of a specified adapter (wildcards are supported).

FIGURE 21.2
ipconfig /all reports
all available TCP/IP data.

TIP   If you fail to provide the name of the specified adapter for either /release or /renew, then these will be applied to all adapters bound to TCP/IP.

WARNING   If you force a static IP address assignment, you won't be able to release it with the ipconfig /release command; you must reconfigure the TCP/IP properties instead.

TIP   Need to see if APIPA is currently enabled on the system? Go to the Command Prompt, and type **ipconfig /all**. Make sure the entry marked Autoconfiguration Enabled reads Yes and that it provides a valid IP address in the range of 169.254.0.1 to 169.254.255.254.

Switching between Network Settings

In some situations, you might want to use two different sets of network settings on a notebook. For example, assume you connect to your office LAN with a PC Card NIC and use the same NIC for your home connection (or for connection in a different office). But the settings at the office are different from those at home. You have to switch settings each time you move your computer from one network to the other. That can be a real pain.

Windows XP maintains information about the installed PC Cards based on their slot. Using the slot location as an indicator is the best means for managing settings, because you might have two identical adapters in the notebook's PC Card slots. The slot number is a unique piece of information and therefore a good means for tagging the settings.

This bit of behavior means that you can move a PC Card from one slot to another and have Windows XP maintain different settings for it in the new location. As you might have guessed, this makes it easy to switch networks. Just switch the card to the appropriate slot and boot the computer. You don't even need to use hardware profiles to accomplish the change.

Alternate IP configuration is an option under a TCP/IP setup's properties that lets you provide an alternate (secondary) IP address. The PC I'm using right now has one IP address for its primary work and communication, and another (the alternate IP) for sharing broadband Internet services through the main network via WinProxy.

To configure this option, follow these steps:

1. Under Network Connections, right-click the connection to which you want to add an Alternate Configuration, and choose Properties.

2. Click Internet Protocol (TCP/IP), and then click Properties.

3. Select the Alternate Configuration tab.

4. Either choose Automatic Private IP Address or select User-Configured, and then provide the desired IP address and other information. Click OK twice.

We're done here, but you may be wondering how you can monitor TCP/IP performance and activity, as well as how you can work through difficulties you may encounter both in configuration and use. Jump to Chapter 22, where I'll take you through all that and more.

Chapter 22

Troubleshooting and Monitoring TCP/IP Connections

Sometimes, it can be difficult enough resolving an issue with what should be a simple communication between two computers directly connected together. After all, it could be a problem with configuration, the cable, or many other aspects.

Imagine how much more complicated troubleshooting becomes when a lot more hardware, software, and distance intervenes between two systems trying unsuccessfully to communicate with one another. If you've ever tried to get the IP address for another user on the Internet, you've seen that your attempts go through any number of *hops*—different locations your data message bounces to en route to its ultimate destination. A problem at any one of those hops could mean that data gets rerouted, slowing everything down; or it could be that data dies out in the ether, and you have to determine where the problem lies.

Even before we get into a situation where we need to troubleshoot, we tend to want to monitor our data transmissions to make certain they're efficient and that all channels along the route are open and ready to both forward and receive data. This obsession strikes everyone from casual home users who have just installed their first network to seasoned network administrators who always keep their eyes on the data traffic, trying to anticipate a possible bottleneck or connectivity failure before it occurs by watching how swiftly and efficiently data moves.

Such watching—and fixing—is the focus of this chapter. You'll learn about the structure underlying TCP/IP monitoring and troubleshooting, as well as when and how to use the most common relevant commands. At the end, you'll get a quick look at several third-party utilities available to cover some of the work done by these commands; sometimes multiple tasks are rolled into one graphical interface.

Internet Control Message Protocol (ICMP)

A major part of how you both monitor and troubleshoot TCP/IP configurations and the overall health of the network (of whatever type) your data moves across is tied to a part of the TCP/IP suite, Internet Control Message Protocol (ICMP). This isn't exclusive to Windows XP, since ICMP is a TCP/IP standard and, as such, crosses platforms, operating systems, and network environments.

ICMP's role is to provide a sort of behind-the-scenes communications system by which both hosts and routers can exchange information related to data control and status, as well as report errors that are encountered.

NOTE An IP *datagram* is a packet of information containing two distinctive parts: an *IP header* containing source and target addresses and other key administrative information, and what is often referred to as the *IP payload*, or the meat and potatoes of the data being transmitted. ICMP messages, by design, are contained within IP datagrams.

Automatically, without your intervention, ICMP issues messages in the event that certain conditions are seen and/or reported. These include:

◆ An IP datagram can't reach its target address.

◆ A router or gateway can't forward datagrams at an appropriate transmission speed.

◆ An IP router, seeing the packets, redirects the host (sender) to use a different (usually more efficient) route to its destination.

Different types of ICMP messages are used in this process. The ones discussed most often in this realm are these:

Echo Request messages   These messages are used to determine whether an IP node, host, router, or gateway is available for contact/data transmission.

Echo Reply messages   These reply messages are sent in response to Echo Request messages, reversing the path followed by the Echo Requests.

In addition to the situations that cause an automatic ICMP message to be issued, the commands discussed in the next section detail ways you can initiate ICMP messages to troubleshoot, because these commands send those messages as part of their run-time process. Before we move on, I strongly encourage you to try these commands as you go, so you get a feeling for the wealth of information about your connections that can be gleaned from the results—once you train your eye to look through the mass of numbers to see the real data.

TCP/IP Commands

If you've been using the Internet for a while, you may have run a few of the commands that evaluate your connection(s) and data transmission performance, such as `ping` or `tracert`, to check either the status of your Internet service provider's access server or that of a specific website. Some commonalities about working with these commands are worth noting in one place, rather than under each separate command reference.

First, all of these commands are accessible only from the command line (*not* from Start ➤ Run). You execute them by following these short steps:

1. Open the Command Prompt.

2. Type the command you want to use, along with switches and the IP address you wish to check. Press Enter.

3. Check the screen, where the results will be reported.

As with other types of commands, you can stop the actions of many of these commands at the command prompt by pressing Ctrl+C or pause them by pressing Pause.

NOTE   Typing a command alone (without any parameters at the end) displays information and available options for that command.

You may find it useful to open the Command Prompt console window to its full capacity, since the results from some of these commands can be extensive. You can also use the pipe symbol (|) with the keyword `more` to break the output into distinct screens, pausing between each. For example, to pause between screens using `tracert`, you could type at the command line **tracert www.boyce.us |more**.

TIP   You can redirect the results of some commands from the screen to a text file (or printer), if desired. For example, to send the results of a `ping` command against IP address 192.168.0.1 to a text file called `pinglog.txt` in your `Logs` folder, type **ping 192.168.0.1>c:\logs\pinglog.txt**.

To make your job easier when you issue certain commands routinely every time you run a check, you may want to roll them into a batch.

Finally, be aware that testing network connectivity often involves testing more than one connection at once. This means you're likely to use a mix of commands as you work, and you may execute them differently (using varying parameters, for example) against each major point along a connection route to try to pinpoint a failure or slowdown. If that last process sounds painstaking, it should; that's what is sometimes required of you in tracking and resolving a TCP/IP communications issue.

Let's look at the commands you're most apt to use in normal TCP/IP monitoring and trouble-shooting, along with when and why you might use them.

WARNING   Many of the switch options available for these commands *are* case sensitive. Beware.

ping

The `ping` command is overwhelmingly the most common of the TCP/IP commands for troubleshooting IP-level connectivity. It works—as many commands do—by sending ICMP Echo Request messages to a destination IP address you want to test and then reporting vital facts about what hops the process took and how responsive these were in passing your data (in this case, the ICMP request) along to its intended addressee.

An example of how this command is used happens when you can't open a particular website through a browser (even though you can open other sites) or can't connect to a mail server. You can use the `ping` command to send a test packet to the problematic server or other destination IP address to see whether you get any response or whether the operation times out along the way. If it does, other commands discussed here can help you narrow down whether the destination isn't responding or whether a point along the way isn't available for routing your test packet.

The syntax for the `ping` command is

```
ping [-switch switch_value] target_IP_address
```

For example, this command

```
ping -l 30 208.149.106.51
```

means to ping the IP address 208.149.106.51 (the target) using 30 bytes of data. The results of this command can be seen in Figure 22.1. Table 22.1 is a list of available switch options for the `ping` command.

FIGURE 22.1

Use ping to test connectivity and response.

```
D:\>ping -l 30 208.149.106.51

Pinging 208.149.106.51 with 30 bytes of data:

Reply from 208.149.106.51: bytes=30 time=695ms TTL=115
Reply from 208.149.106.51: bytes=30 time=739ms TTL=115
Reply from 208.149.106.51: bytes=30 time=743ms TTL=115
Request timed out.

Ping statistics for 208.149.106.51:
    Packets: Sent = 4, Received = 3, Lost = 1 (25% loss),
Approximate round trip times in milli-seconds:
    Minimum = 695ms, Maximum = 743ms, Average = 725ms

D:\>
```

WARNING Use the ping command with care, since repeated, frequent pinging affects overall traffic on its own and may interrupt the session of a user logged in at the system being pinged.

TABLE 22.1: *ping* Switch Options

SWITCH	FUNCTION
-a	Resolves an address to its hostname.
-f	Sets the "Don't fragment" flag within the packet to prevent routers along the path from fragmenting it; used for monitoring possible Path Maximum Transmission Unit (PMTU) issues.
-i *value*	Sets the value of the Time To Live (TTL) field.
-j *hostlist*	Specifies that the packet should take a "loose" source route along the *hostlist* (see Chapter 26).
-k *hostlist*	Specifies that the packet should take a "strict" source route along the *hostlist*.
-l *size_value*	Pings using the specified (by *size_value*) number of bytes for the packet's data field.
-n *count*	Specifies a number (*count*) of Echo Request messages to send; by default, the *count* value is 4.
-r *count*	Enables the Record Route option within the IP header to chronicle the route taken by the ICMP Echo Request (each hop gets its own entry in the route table); valid *count* values are 1–9.
-s *count*	Enables the Internet Timestamp option within the IP header to chronicle the time both the Echo Request and the Echo Reply Request reach each hop along the route; valid *count* values are 1–4.

TABLE 22.1:   *ping* Switch Options *(CONTINUED)*

SWITCH	FUNCTION
-t	Specifies to keep sending Echo Request messages until interrupted (by Ctrl+Break, Pause, or Ctrl+C).
-v *TOS_value*	Enables and specifies a value for the Type Of Service (TOS) field in the ICMP Echo Request message's IP header; by default, this is set to 0 with a valid range of 0–255.
-w *timeout_value*	Forces a maximum amount of time (in milliseconds) to wait for an Echo Reply message answering an Echo Request message before a timeout is declared; by default, this is set to 4,000 (4 seconds).

tracert

The tracert command is used to check the path that data takes in trying to reach its destination. It works like the ping command in that it sends multiple ICMP Echo Request as well as Echo Reply packets out and then reports on the results as the data moves through each different router on its journey.

If you're looking for specific packet-to-router information, you'll probably do better using the pathping command (see the preceding section).

The syntax to use with the tracert command follows either of the following two conventions:

```
tracert [IP_address]
tracert -d [hostname]
```

For example,

```
tracert -d www.example.com
```

There is only one switch for tracert, and it's described in Table 22.2.

TABLE 22.2:   *tracert* Switch Option

SWITCH	FUNCTION
-d	Restricts the display output from the tracert command for easier readability.

pathping

The command pathping is typically used to detect packet loss and monitor network latency (that is, transit time, especially the lag time lost due to bottlenecks or errors). As its name implies, pathping is like the ping command but performs its work by looking at intermediate hops along the route a packet takes. The purpose of pathping isn't so much to determine whether there is a data logjam but rather to identify where things are getting hung up by looking at the path step by step.

When you see the results, note that the information is largely broken into two parts: The hops path is listed first, followed by specific statistics per hop, the number of packets lost versus sent, and the IP address.

The syntax for this command follows this convention:

```
pathping [-switch switch_options] IP_address_or_name
```

For example, by using this command

```
pathping -n -p 500 www.example.com
```

I'm checking (by pinging) all routers along the path. The -n switch tells it not to try to resolve the IP address of intermediate routers, and -p 500 forces pathping to wait 500 milliseconds (½ second) between consecutive pings. Table 22.3 lists the switches available to modify the pathping command.

TABLE 22.3: *pathping* Switch Options

SWITCH	FUNCTION
-g *hostlist*	Tells pathping to send ICMP messages using the loose source route option contained in the *hostlist* file.
-h *value*	Specifies the maximum number of hops to use, where *value* equals the number of hops; by default, this is set to 30.
-n	Tells pathping not to resolve the IP addresses of intermediate routers, to save time.
-p *value*	Sets the amount of time (in milliseconds) to wait before each new ping is issued; by default, this is set to 250 ms (¼ second).
-q *value*	Sets a specific number of ICMP Echo Request messages to transmit to each router along the data path, where *value* equals the number of messages; by default, this is 100.
-r	Forces pathping to check to see if every network device along the data path supports the Resource Reservation Protocol (RSVP), which is used to reserve a chunk of bandwidth as a dedicated data stream. If you receive a "Destination Unreachable" error, it's usually because RSVP isn't supported by one or more hops.
-t	Attaches a tag to the Echo Request message to check each network device along the path to be sure it supports layer-2 priority (used to assign a level of priority to a message) functionality. If one or more devices don't, this could be a point of concern.
-w *value*	Establishes a set amount of time (in milliseconds) to await an Echo Reply message after pinging, where *value* is the number of milliseconds; by default, this is 3,000 ms (3 seconds).

NOTE Only the -p switch option forces pathping to ping each intermediate hop individually.

arp

The arp command is used to both reveal as well as to change entries contained in the Address Resolution Protocol (ARP) cache. This cache is used to store tables (one for each installed Ethernet or Token Ring network adapter) containing IP addresses and their respective resolved addresses.

The syntax used for this command follows either of these conventions:

```
arp [-switch option]
arp [-switch option [InetAddr] -switch option [IfaceAddr]]
```

where *InetAddr* stands for an IP Internet address and *IfaceAddr* represents a network adapter interface address, which are both shown in decimal notation. You can also use an Ethernet address (*EtherAddr*) presented in hexadecimal notation, taking the form (for example) 00-50-DA-C3-00-24.

NOTE Under normal conditions, the contents of the ARP cache scroll out over time as new entries replace them, with one exception: The -s switch option allows you to make entries to the ARP cache that are static and don't scroll out with time (except when TCP/IP itself is stopped and then started, as might occur with a shutdown/restart). If you have ARP entries that should be added each time TCP/IP restarts, Microsoft recommends that you place them in a batch file and add this batch file to your Scheduled Task entries so that it can be reexecuted regularly.

Table 22.4 lists arp command switches.

TABLE 22.4: *arp* Switch Options

SWITCH	FUNCTION
-a *InetAddr*	Reveals the most recent ARP cache tables for each installed adapter. This is often used with the –N switch, as in arp -a 208.169.62.15 -N 10.0.0.99.
-d *InetAddr* [*IfaceAddr*]	Used with *InetAddr*, deletes the entry for the Internet address specified. To remove all entries for a specific adapter, use -d with *IfaceAddr*.
-g *InetAddr*	Identical to the -a switch.
-N *IfaceAddr*	(Note uppercase.) Specifies the IP address of the network adapter; typically used secondary to the -a switch.
-s *InetAddr EtherAddr*	Writes a static entry to the ARP cache that resolves the IP address of the Internet address to the physical address of the adapter address specified in *EtherAddr*. For example: arp -s 10.0.0.99 00-50-DA-C3-00-24.

netstat

The netstat command is used to display information about all active current TCP connections as well as all ports that are engaged in listening for transmissions. It also goes well beyond this to show all vital Ethernet statistics (including both total bytes and packets sent/received) and the IP routing table, plus IP protocol version–specific statistics for the connection, including IPv4 and IPv6.

Of specific interest to you in monitoring and troubleshooting may be the information compiled by the command, including these categories:

Proto   The command shows the type of protocol in use (TCP or UDP).

Local Address   This category lists both the local system's IP address and the port number in use for the operation. If the port isn't established or available, `netstat` displays an asterisk (*).

Foreign Address   The command reports both the IP address and the port number for a specific remote system.

State   This category gives the state of the connection. Ten states are recognized:

CLOSE_WAIT	FIN_WAIT_1	LISTEN	TIMED_WAIT
CLOSED	FIN_WAIT_2	SYN_RECEIVED	
ESTABLISHED	LAST_ACK	SYN_SEND	

The syntax for `netstat` follows this convention:

```
netstat [-switch switch_option] [interval]
```

For example, the command

```
netstat -e -s 30
```

displays the Ethernet statistics by protocol for all protocols available and then redisplays them every 30 seconds. Running `netstat` without any switches or parameters displays statistics for the active connections (as shown in Figure 22.2).

FIGURE 22.2
Use `netstat` to see Ethernet statistics by protocol.

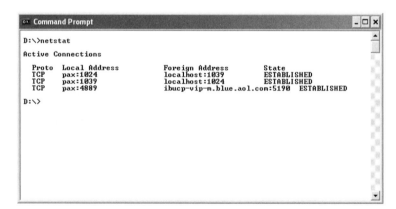

Table 22.5 lists the `netstat` switches.

hostname

The `hostname` command is used to display the name of a computer (the host). It's useful if you're doing other command-line procedures and need to verify the name of the system for troubleshooting or monitoring.

The syntax of this command is simply `hostname`. No switches are available for it.

TABLE 22.5:   *netstat* Switch Options

SWITCH	FUNCTION
-a	Results in a list of all current and active TCP connections along with the listening TCP and UDP ports.
-e	Displays Ethernet statistics, including how much data (in bytes) has transmitted. This switch is often combined with the -s switch option.
-n	Gives a report of all active connections but without resolved names, and with both addresses and port numbers expressed numerically only.
-o	Reports active TCP connections but specifically includes the process ID (PID) for each of these connections. You can then match the PID to corresponding processes contained in the Processes tab in Windows Task Manager.
-p *protocol*	Shows active connections only for those using the protocol specified by the *protocol* switch (such as TCP, UDP, TCPV6, and UDPV6). When used with the -s switch option, it can display the connections by various types of protocols (the ones previously stated plus ICMP, IP, ICMPV6, and IPV6).
-r	Works like the route print command to display the entire contents of the IP routing table.
-s	Shows statistics by protocol (by default, for TCP, UDP, ICMP, and IP, plus IPv6 if that protocol has been installed under Windows XP).
interval	Tells the command to redisplay chosen data every *interval* number of seconds.

route

The route command, as you might expect, is highly focused on the route a packet of data takes in reaching its destination and then answering with a reply, as you see with Echo Request and Echo Reply messages. Specifically, you can use this command to both show and edit entries contained in the IP routing table; each route identified and taken by your data transmissions gets its own entry in this master routing index.

This command is a little different than others in this chapter because you can issue certain commands in conjunction it, each performing a specific function (add [entry], change, delete, and print) against entries in the IP routing table. You can also use other nonswitch parameters with this command, as indicated in Table 25.6.

The syntax to use for this command is as follows:

```
route [-switch switch_option] [command_and/or_parameter]
```

For example, issuing this command as configured

```
route print
```

prints the entire contents of the IP routing table, whereas this command

```
route delete 10.0
```

deletes all IP routing table entries that start with the IP address 10.* (obviously, wildcards are supported).

TABLE 22.6:   *route* Switch and Parameter Options

SWITCH	FUNCTION
-f	Removes entries from the IP routing table, except the following: nonhost route (defined as a route with a netmask of 255.255.255.255), loopback network route (where the destination is 127.0.0.0 and the netmask is 255.0.0.0), and multicast route (destination 224.0.0.0 and netmask 240.0.0.0). When run with a route-supported command, the entries are cleared before the command is executed.
-p	Used only with two commands: add (adds a new route and uses it to initialize the IP routing table anytime TCP/IP is stopped and restarted) and print (produces a list of persistent routes, found in the \HKEY_LOCAL_MACHINE\System\CurrentControlSet\Services\ Tcpip\Parameters\PersistentRoutes key in the Windows XP Registry).
Command	Simlar to the -p switch with four commands supported: add to add an entry to the IP routing table, change, delete, and print.
Destination	Specifies the final destination of the route. It can be an IP address for a host route, an IP network address, or a default route destination of 0.0.0.0.
Gateway	Specifies the gateway address (which can be a directly reachable router's IP address, the IP address of a interface attached to the subnet, and so on).
if *Interface*	Specifies the interface index for a connection-reachable interface. Use the route print command to display a list of interfaces and their corresponding interface indexes to use with this parameter. (Case isn't significant for this or the next two options.)
mask *Netmask*	Specifies the netmask or subnet mask used for a particular network destination. It can be the (sub)netmask of an IP network address, a host route (255.255.255.255), or a default route (0.0.0.0).
metric *Metric*	Designates the levels of efficacy in routes to a particular destination appearing in the IP routing table, using a number (integer from 1–9,999). The lower the metric value, the better (and faster) the route.

nbtstat

nbtstat stands for (TCP/IP) *NetBT statistics* and is used to show (in table format) both protocol statistics and current connections for any NetBT communications. This command is useful for troubleshooting as well as general information. It can also be used to refresh the NetBIOS name cache and registered entries in WINS (see the previous chapter for details)—it's especially helpful when you want to dump current entries in favor of a fresh list. It also works with the NetBIOS name table, which is a listing of the various NetBIOS names representing installed and running NetBIOS applications.

Be aware that with nbtstat you need to respect case sensitivity when adding switch parameters, because the case used here can alter the results you get from executing the command. The switches for this command are described in Table 22.7.

TABLE 22.7:   *nbtstat* Switch Options

SWITCH	FUNCTION
-a *RemoteName*	Shows the NetBIOS name table of the remote computer, where *RemoteName* must be the NetBIOS name of this remote system.
-A *IPAddr*	(Note uppercase.) A variation of the -a switch. You provide the IP address of the remote system and then get the NetBIOS name table for it.
-c	Shows the entire contents of the NetBIOS name cache (local system) along with both the NetBIOS name table and resolved IP address.
-n	Shows the NetBIOS name table (local system). Check the Registered column to see if the NetBIOS name for the system is registered as either broadcast or with a WINS server for name resolution.
-r	Displays relevant statistics for NetBIOS name resolution. Where WINS is used, it provides the total number of names that have been resolved and registered (for either broadcast or WINS).
-R	(Note uppercase.) Dumps the contents of the NetBIOS name cache (local system), and then looks in the lmhosts file to reload entries marked with the #PRE tags (see the preceding chapter).
-RR	(Note uppercase.) First releases and then reloads NetBIOS names (local system) for a system registered with a WINS server.
-s	Shows information about both NetBIOS client and server sessions, and then tries to resolve the destination IP address to a name.
-S	(Note uppercase.) Same as -s, but lists remote systems by the destination IP address (no name resolution).
interval	Forces nbtstat to refresh the listing for selected statistics every *interval* seconds.

The syntax to follow for this command is

```
nbtstat [-switch switch_parameter] [interval]
```

This example,

```
nbtstat -a PAX
```

displays the remote computer's (whose NetBIOS designation is PAX) NetBIOS name table (see Figure 22.3). This example

```
nbtstat -R
```

releases all the NetBIOS names currently registered with the designated WINS server and then reregisters them all.

FIGURE 22.3

Use nbtstat to check IP statistics.

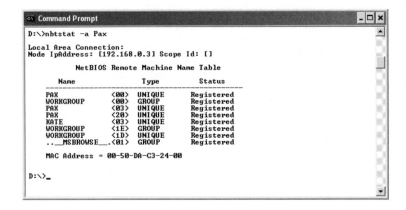

```
Command Prompt                                                    _ □ ×
D:\>nbtstat -a Pax

Local Area Connection:
Node IpAddress: [192.168.0.3] Scope Id: []

            NetBIOS Remote Machine Name Table

      Name               Type         Status
   ---------------------------------------------
   PAX          <00>  UNIQUE      Registered
   WORKGROUP    <00>  GROUP       Registered
   PAX          <03>  UNIQUE      Registered
   PAX          <20>  UNIQUE      Registered
   KATE         <03>  UNIQUE      Registered
   WORKGROUP    <1E>  GROUP       Registered
   WORKGROUP    <1D>  UNIQUE      Registered
   .._MSBROWSE__.<01>  GROUP       Registered

   MAC Address = 00-50-DA-C3-24-00

D:\>_
```

netsh

netsh is a command-line scripting tool that establishes its own console within the command console, so to speak, from which you can see or change the network configuration of the system from which you're working (you can be working locally—at the keyboard—or remotely). By console within a console, I mean that you execute netsh first (or netsh diag for diagnostics), and the command prompt turns into a Netsh (or Netsh diag>) prompt from which you then run specific netsh commands. Different commands are available depending on the type of network service you're checking, including DHCP, Interface IP, routing, general diagnostics, and more.

Because of the volume and breadth of commands covered under netsh, you may want to refer to them directly by using Windows XP Help And Support to search on **netsh**. There, you'll find all these commands, their conditions, and their switches laid out for you depending on the troubleshooting or modifications you need to perform.

TIP   Type netsh -? to view a list of switches and command syntax for the netsh command.

Chapter 23

Remote Access: Using, Monitoring, and Managing

Remote access services under Windows aren't completely new, although they've gone through some changes in Windows XP. Formerly, however, they were known strictly as Terminal Services—aptly named as a way to remotely log on via terminal (remote console) to a server or a system acting in that capacity. Seasoned professionals have used something like these remote services for many years to resolve issues remotely for clients and employers, through external applications like VNC, pcAnywhere, and Carbon Copy.

In Windows XP, the Remote Desktop Connection option noted in this chapter is what was formerly called the Terminal Services client, and Remote Desktop basically uses the same infrastructure.

Terminal Services, however, had a (perhaps undeserved) reputation for being difficult to configure and troubleshoot; it was typically used only in commercial or heavy-duty use environments or by technicians who often had to log on from remote locations to fix problems that others on-site could not.

Remote access services under Windows XP make this process much more friendly for average users looking to increase their control over one or more other systems while sitting at a single PC. For instance, one method allows you to do this from a web browser. Configuring remote access requires almost no time, and the remotely controlled systems can be non-networked systems within your home or office, or can be located across the state, the country, or the world. The most common use is to provide someone working from home a way to connect with their host system at the office—and not just to exchange files, but to work very much as though you were sitting at the keyboard in the office.

In this chapter, you'll learn about Remote Desktop services, their requirements, how to manage them, and how they're configured and used, as well as some troubleshooting techniques to get around common problems related to their use. Then I'll finish by discussing two major third-party applications that largely duplicate the kind of functionality available in Windows XP.

Remote Access Overview

Remote Desktop comprises two components—Remote Desktop Connection (RDC) and Remote Desktop Web Connection (RDWC)—and serves as the client front-end for Terminal Services.

There are many situations in which remote access to a Windows XP system might be desirable, including these general categories:

- Working on an office system from home

- Working on a home system from the office

- Evaluating, working on, or repairing someone else's system

- Performing system administration when you're on the road

TIP Here's a different use. The other night, the monitor connected to my XP system flaked out. I couldn't get it to stay on consistently, and it's tougher to troubleshoot with no display. I logged on through Remote Desktop over my network and was able to proceed with my work—exactly where I left off.

This is achieved by setting up a Terminal Services server on the XP system and then configuring it to accept incoming connections as well as determining which users should have access in this manner.

Remotely, someone with either Remote Desktop or the older Terminal Services client installed can—with a valid user name and password and access through either the Internet or a network—log on to the remote XP system and work from the same Desktop, with the same applications and files available, as someone sitting at the keyboard of that remote system. In fact, if you come in during the middle of a session being conducted by a user at the console, you receive their working Desktop—populated by its open applications, running processes, and on-screen messages.

But this situation also raises questions, such as "How will I keep the wrong people out?", "How vulnerable does this leave my system?", and "How do I control the situation remotely?"

Read on to find the answers.

Managing and Securing Remote Access

Clearly, working remotely presents a unique set of problems related to access and security. Authorized users need a way into the system, yet you need to keep everyone else out, including anyone who may try to hijack your transmitted data, your passwords, and even your hardware (some Trojans and computer viruses can act against printers, for example).

Remote Desktop and its associated services for remote access can employ one or more security schemes to try to maintain adequate protection. These include the following:

- Requiring password authentication at logon (rather than automatic connections)
- Establishing suitable encryption levels for local-to-remote connections and transfers
- Turning off printer and file redirection
- Disabling Clipboard sharing

You can force any of these options—and others—by configuring the Terminal Services group policy to enable or disable them. Specific settings for each option are included in the next section. You'll learn how to work with Terminal Services group policy in the next section.

NOTE As you read, you'll see that I discuss two aspects of Remote Desktop: Remote Desktop Connection and Remote Desktop Web Connection. The end result of both is the same: the ability to log onto your XP machine remotely. The chief difference is that you access RDC like any normally installed program, whereas you can use RDWC from any supporting web browser, without extra software installed on other systems.

TIP Be sure to read "Adding and Removing Remote Desktop Connection Users" later in this chapter, because you must add users for access to RDC and RDWC before they can successfully login remotely. If you set this up and still find that you or another user can't connect, look at your user assignments first.

Adding the Terminal Services Snap-In

You can effectively manage and control many aspects of Remote Desktop (including basic configuration) through the Terminal Services group policy (Figure 23.1), available as a snap-in under Microsoft Management Console (MMC). These aspects are *not* configured by default.

FIGURE 23.1

Load the group policy snap-in to configure remote access.

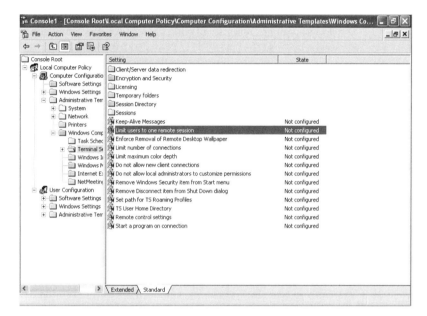

The features and functions you can set and manage here include the following:

◆ Setting time and requirement limits based on situations and types of users

◆ Establishing a remote user's range of services (view or full control)

◆ Permitting or preventing Windows Messenger

◆ Forcing a program to run each time a remote connection is successfully made

◆ Specifying how the remote Desktop will appear

Let's go through the steps for loading this group policy:

1. From a command prompt (or click Start ➤ Run), type **mmc** to launch the management console.

2. From MMC, choose File ➤ Add/Remove Snap-In, and then click Add.

3. In the Add Standalone Snap-In window, click Group Policy, and then click Add. Click Finish in the Select Group Policy Object window.

4. Back in the Add Standalone Snap-In window, click Close. Click OK to exit the Add/Remove Snap-In window.

5. At the console, click \Local Computer Policy\Computer Configuration\Administrative Templates\Windows Components\Terminal Services.

Later in this chapter, you'll learn about command-line options for managing and controlling your connections as well.

Requiring Password Authentication

A password is required at all times for any user trying to connect remotely. However, RDC allows users to set up a password that can be automatically used as part of the login process rather than typing it in each time. Doing so, of course, means that anyone with access to the system could log on remotely, because the password is provided for them.

To prevent users from bypassing the password screen (and thus defeating one level of security), use the Terminal Services group policy to require Always Prompt Client For Password, located in the Encryption And Security branch.

Choosing Encryption

Remote Desktop by itself is equipped to use the highest form of encryption available (the 128-bit standard for financial and other secured transactions). However, you need to enable and enforce it (which you can do using the same process you'll read about in a moment).

However, as you'll soon learn in this chapter, you may need to use the actual (older) Terminal Services client (which Remote Desktop replaces in Windows XP) when connecting remotely to an XP system from a Windows 2000, Windows NT, or even a Windows for Workgroups system. The older client does not by default support 128-bit encryption.

In situations when you're working with the older access client, you can choose to reduce your level of encryption to Client Compatible, in which case Remote Desktop uses the highest level of encryption possible that doesn't interfere with communications between itself and the client (connecting) system. You do so by opening \Terminal Services\Encryption And Security and enabling the option Set Client Connection Encryption Level Properties, as shown in Figure 23.2.

FIGURE 23.2
Use group policy to determine the encryption level.

Disabling Redirection

To disable file redirection, select Do Not Allow Drive Redirection in the Client/Server Data Redirection branch from the Terminal Services group policy. To turn off printer redirection, choose Do Not Allow Printer Redirection.

Use the Do Not Allow Clipboard Redirection option in the Client/Server Data Redirection branch to remove a user's ability to perform this function.

About Firewalls and Remote Access

One of the chief jobs of a firewall (such as the one included with Windows XP or the many others like BlackIce and Zone Alarm that are also available) is to protect your system or network from unwanted access, including port snooping (which occurs when someone scans your ports, trying to find one open so they may enter and/or attack).

Naturally, however, your communication depends on the ability to use necessary ports to exchange data. Thus, a delicate balance must be struck between "open for what you need" and "closed for everyone else." One of the ways you can achieve that balance is by understanding what programs and utilities require exactly which ports to be open. In this way, a firewall can map acceptable use to the necessary ports so it doesn't block your desired communications, while monitoring any activity involving the other ports.

As I walk you through remote access services, including some third-party ones, note that I usually mention the ports typically used by the operation(s). Combine that information with what you'll learn about Windows XP's Windows Firewall in Chapter 24, and you can better configure your firewall to keep data flowing unobstructed.

Remote Desktop Connection

Remote Desktop Connection is the client software for remote access. When you choose to work from something as ubiquitous as a web browser (meaning remote access is available from devices that are more mobile than a desktop PC), you can also use Remote Desktop Web Connection, discussed later in this chapter.

NOTE   RDC and its associated Terminal Services initially connect using port 80 and then settle into communications using port 3389. Note these numbers for your firewall configuration.

Remote Desktop Connection Requirements

When I talk about configuring RDC, I mean a two-step process. Both the primary system you're configuring *and* the remote system must be set up to work together, and that requires the remote system to have software installed that allows this functionality and connection to occur.

The Windows XP system acting as the host for remote connections needs to have RDC (Terminal Services) installed and set up for use. It must also have a means—network, dial-up phone line, or broadband continuous connection—for letting remote systems contact it.

The remote system needs one of two client software packages:

Remote Desktop Connection   This package is already available, but might not be configured under Windows XP. You can install it to Windows 95/98 and Windows NT 4 systems using the Windows XP install CD, following the steps provided next, in "Installing Remote Desktop Connection Manually."

Terminal Services Client This package is available with Windows 2000 Server and Windows Server 2003; see "Installing and Using Terminal Services Client" later in this section.

You also need a connection method, as well as a client interface. It can take the form of any of these:

♦ Virtual private network (VPN)

♦ Local area network (LAN)

♦ Dial-up modem connection or broadband access (see "Working with a Dynamic IP Address," later in this chapter)

TIP Before you install and configure RDC functionality, be sure your connection method works properly. By doing so, you'll avoid reaching the point that you're trying to connect remotely, can't, and have to wonder whether it's the connection itself or your configuration of Remote Desktop that's at fault.

Installing Remote Desktop Connection Manually

In two situations, you may need to perform a manual installation of RDC:

♦ You can't find Remote Desktop Connection installed to your Start ➢ All Programs ➢ Accessories ➢ Communications menu.

♦ You need to install it on a non-XP system (95/98 or Windows NT 4) in order to connect with an XP-based Remote Desktop–connected system.

To perform this manual installation, follow these steps:

1. On the non-XP system you want to connect to using Remote Desktop Connection, run Setup from your Windows XP installation CD, and choose Perform Additional Tasks.

2. On the Additional Tasks screen, select Set Up Remote Desktop Connection.

3. When the InstallShield Wizard opens, click I Accept under the License Agreement, and then click Next.

4. When prompted, provide your information under Customer Information, and then select to install this program either for all users on this system or just for you. Click Next.

5. Click Install.

Configuring Remote Desktop Connection

Follow these steps to configure your client RDC for connection with the Windows XP–based server:

1. From Windows Start ➢ All Programs ➢ Accessories ➢ Communications, select Remote Desktop Connection.

2. In the Remote Desktop Connection window, click Options. The lower section of the window opens and displays five tabs.

3. On the General tab, select the computer you want to connect to, and then provide your user name, password, and domain (if applicable). If desired, click Save My Password.

4. On the Display tab, you can adjust your normal viewing settings. Doing so is useful if the system you're connecting to has a monitor with much different quality or a different display adapter, and you need to make adjustments for optimal display.

TIP   Those connecting via slower, dial-up connection rates should use only 256 colors. The more colors used, the more bandwidth is required to keep the display fresh in a timely manner.

5. On the Local Resources tab, you can set these options:

Remote Computer Sound   This option determines whether to play sound invoked on the remote computer via your local system or at all.

Keyboard   This option lets you modify Windows key combinations.

Local Devices   You can check or uncheck access to local devices such as disk drives, printers, and serial ports.

6. On the Programs tab, you can set up a specific program to run every time you connect to a remote system. Doing so is helpful if you always need to execute the same application or utility each time.

7. On the Experience tab, you can configure how the two systems connect (dial-up modem, broadband, LAN) and whether to allow certain features such as the Desktop background, themes, and bitmap caching during your remote session.

TIP   You can also use the General tab to save your current connection settings, which are then stored to a file ending with .rdp. Use the General tab again, and choose Open to reopen these saved settings.

WARNING   If you hit serious performance problems, turn off extra features under the Experience tab such as Desktop background and themes.

NOTE   If you find you can't add an available computer to your connect list, check to be sure the computer you want to connect to has the Terminal Services client or Remote Desktop Connection installed and/or is configured to allow this access.

WORKING WITH A DYNAMIC IP ADDRESS

The best way to use remote access in Windows XP is with existing network or high-speed broadband Internet access, but it's also best if the XP system hosting the remote connection has a static (fixed) IP address or a recognized Internet name.

The problem with a dial-up access situation for the XP host is that you must know the current IP address of the host (which can change with each connection) in order to connect. You can find this address by using the ipconfig /all command at the command console, but you need to do so each time a new connection is established if you don't have a static IP address or recognized name for the host system. Otherwise, remote users—including you logging on from another location—won't be able to find the host to connect.

PRIORITY OF ACCESS

Since only one user can be logged on (at the console or remotely) to Windows XP at any one time, RDC and RDWC (and Terminal Services) prioritize access by type of user. That way, if two people try to log on at the same time, the person with administrator access always wins. Exact logon behavior, however, depends on whether Fast User Switching is enabled.

When one administrator is already logged on and a second administrator tries to log on, the second administrator has the ability to bump the currently connected user. However, when two users of normal stature conflict, the first person to connect can continue his session while the one who attempts to log on later receives a message that a user (identified) is currently logged on.

Enabling Fast User Switching affects how a user's session is terminated in the event of an administrator override. If Fast User Switching is turned on, the user currently on the system is disconnected but not logged off; they can continue their session once the administrator has logged off. If Fast User Switching is off, the user is logged off and disconnected.

Also, when Fast User Switching is enabled and a second user tries to log on while another user is already logged in, the current user receives a message like this:

```
<Domain or Computer Name>\<username> is trying to connect to this computer. If you
allow, you will be disconnected, but you can resume later. Do you want to allow
this connection?
```

WARNING   Reserve administrator status for a very select few. If others need to log on, they can be given normal user or Remote Desktop user status.

Loading Remote Desktop Connection

First, be certain you have a valid connection in place (dial-up modem, broadband, or network). Then, follow these steps to launch RDC:

1. Choose Start ➤ All Programs ➤ Accessories ➤ Communications ➤ Remote Desktop Connection.

2. In the Remote Desktop Connection window, select the name of the computer you want to connect to, and click Connect.

If your connection is good, you're using a valid account (see the following section), and no one else is logged on to the system (see the preceding section), you should be logged on properly and able to begin work as the remote Desktop opens before you.

Adding and Removing Remote Desktop Connection Users

As I tipped you to earlier, a user can't connect remotely unless she's been added as a user for this service.

When RDC is installed and configured for use, a new type of user becomes available: Remote Users. Administrators automatically have access to remote connection features, but it's neither good security nor good practice to make everyone who may connect remotely to the hosting XP system an administrator.

By following these steps, you can add new people to your remote access services:

1. From Control Panel, double-click the System icon, and choose the Remote tab.

2. Be sure the Allow Users To Connect check box is checked, and then click Select Remote Users.

3. In the Remote Desktop Users window, you may already see a list of user accounts currently configured to use Remote Desktop access (by default, this initial listing only displays administrators). To add more users, go to step 4. If you don't need to add any additional users to this list, click Cancel until you fully exit.

4. Click Add.

5. In the Select Users window, Users should be listed under Select This Object Type. Click Locations if you need to change the location to look for these users.

6. In the Enter The Object Names To Select text box, type the name of a user you want to add. Click Check Names.

7. If a match is found, click OK in the Select Users dialog box. The name is then added to your list. Highlight the name, click Add, and then click OK until you exit. If a match isn't found, you get the Select User window again with a message telling you to verify the user name.

NOTE You can use the same basic process to remove users from your active Remote Users list by clicking Remove rather than Add in step 7.

Changing the Remote Desktop Connection Port

RDC by default uses port 3389. In most cases you won't need to change this port, but in some situations it can be useful to configure RDC for a different port. For example, I like to have remote access to my main workstation and my server, both of which sit behind a firewall. However, my firewall doesn't offer one-to-one network address translation (NAT). Instead, I have to use port forwarding to send port 3389 to the private IP address of one of the two computers so I can access it through RDC. I could change the port-forwarding rule every time I need to access the other computer, but doing so would require me to enable remote management for the firewall—something I don't like to do, for security reasons.

The solution to this scenario is to change the port on which one of the computers is listening for RDC. It only takes a quick Registry change and a reboot to make that happen:

1. Open Registry Editor, and navigate to the `HKEY_LOCAL_MACHINE\SYSTEM\CurrentControlSet\ Control\Terminal Server\WinStations\RDP-Tcp` key.

2. Double-click the PortNumber value.

3. In the Edit DWORD Value dialog box, click Decimal.

4. In the Value Data field, highlight the existing port and type the new port. Choose a port not in use by any other service on the computer.

5. Click OK, close the Registry Editor, and then reboot the computer. To test that it's now listening on the new port, open a command console and execute the command NETSTAT -AN. Look for the port in the Local Address column and Listening in the Status column.

After you reboot the computer, it will be ready to accept RDC connections on the new port. Configure your firewall to port-forward traffic for the specified port to the private IP address of the target computer. Then, on the client computer, open RDC and enter the public IP address of the firewall, followed by a colon and the port number of the target computer. For example, 216.239.31.4:13200 would attempt a connection to 216.239.31.4 on port 13200.

Managing Remote Systems Using Terminal Services

With older Windows NT/2000 systems, which didn't include the new RDC, you'll need to install and configure the Terminal Services client to connect to the XP system.

You'll learn about that in this section, but I'll also tell you about some special commands related to Terminal Services that are available for use from the command console only when you're logged in remotely. These commands can help you exercise control over your remote connections and monitor the connections made to the computer.

INSTALLING AND USING TERMINAL SERVICES CLIENT

If you want to connect from a system running Windows 2000 Server, you can install Terminal Services and configure it for use by performing these steps:

1. Open Windows Explorer, and locate the folder named
   %systemroot%\System32\Clients\Tsclient.

2. Right-click this folder, select Properties, and then select the Sharing tab.

3. Select Share This Folder. Click OK.

TIP   If you can't access the option to share this folder, be sure you're logged on with an administrator, server operator, or power user logon account.

MANAGING TERMINAL SERVICES FROM THE COMMAND LINE

Certain commands are supported under Terminal Services—and by extension, Remote Desktop—and allow you to monitor, change, and otherwise control the Terminal Services server-client environment and its connections from the command line. You can use these commands to look up session information by session ID, session name, or even user name. They can also be used to copy profiles from one user to another; to kill, shut down, or shut down and reset connections; and to send messages to other users, among your many options.

How you use these commands is often poorly documented, because some requirements are imposed to be sure that not just anyone logged on can execute them.

Before you can use the Terminal Services commands, you must make sure you're set in three different areas:

1. Enable the use of remote commands under Terminal Services group policy.

2. Be logged on to the remote Windows XP system using the Remote Desktop/Desktop Web/ Terminal Services client with an account that allows their use (such as administrator). This is the only time these commands may be used. If you try to use them outside of this session, you'll receive a message that they aren't recognized.

3. Run them from the command console, either directly or through a batch file.

To enable the use of remote commands (this is disabled by default), follow these steps:

1. Load the Terminal Services MMC snap-in, as described earlier in this chapter.

2. Under \Local Computer Policy\User Configuration\Administrative Templates\Windows Components\Terminal Services, double-click Remote Control Settings in the right pane.

3. On the Setting tab, select Enabled. Under the Options drop-down list, you can choose how these settings are enabled, ranging from View Session Without User's Permission to Full Control With User's Permission. Click OK. You may then close the console.

WARNING It may be necessary to shut down and restart Terminal Services—or even to restart the system acting as the server—to apply configuration changes so that remote commands are available to those logging in from the client.

Table 23.1 lists key commands for managing remote sessions from the command console.

TABLE 23.1: Key Commands for Terminal Services

COMMAND	PARAMETERS	FUNCTION
change logon	/enable	Allow logons from other users from client sessions (rather than the console).
	/disable	Disallow other users logging on in this same session.
	/query	Determine status (enabled/disabled).

TABLE 23.1:   Key Commands for Terminal Services *(CONTINUED)*

COMMAND	PARAMETERS	FUNCTION
change port	*PortA=PortB*	Change (map) the serial port specified by *PortA* with the serial port specified by *PortB* (with COM ports 1–4 usually supported).
	/d:*porta*	Delete the mapping applied to the COM port specified by *portA*.
	/query	Display mapping information for the port.
change user	/execute	Turn on *.ini file mapping to the home directory (by default).
	/install	Turn off *.ini file mapping to the home directory (this is necessary when you're installing applications to the terminal server itself).
logoff	*SessionID*	Log off the session specified.
	SessionName	Log off the session specified.
	/server:*ServerName*	Specify the terminal server from which the session you want to log off is running. The current server is used when none is specified.
msg	*UserName*	Specify the name of the user to whom you want to send a message.
	SessionID	Specify the ID of a session to contact.
	SessionName	Specify the name of a session to contact.
query process	*	Display all processes running for all current sessions.
	/id:*nn*	Specify the ID of a session whose processes you want to query.
	ProcessID	Identify the ID of the process you want to check.
	ProgramName	Identify a particular program (use full name including .exe file extension) whose processes you need to check.
	/server:*ServerName*	Specify another server (besides the current one) in the query.
	SessionName	Identify all the processes running in a particular session.

TABLE 23.1: Key Commands for Terminal Services *(CONTINUED)*

COMMAND	PARAMETERS	FUNCTION
	/system	Include all system processes in the query results.
	UserName	Check all the processes running for a specific user.
query session	/connect	Query a terminal server about currently active connection settings.
	/counter	Display information gleaned from current counters, including a total count of sessions (created, disconnected, and reconnected).
	/flow	Check current flow-control settings.
	/mode	Show line settings currently in effect.
	SessionID	Specify a particular session ID to check in the query.
	SessionName	Specify a particular session name to check.
	UserName	Query about a session by a specific username.
query termserver	/address	Reveal both network and node addresses for all terminal servers.
	/continue	Turn off a pause between screens when displaying query results.
	/domain:*Domain*	Specify a particular domain on which to query terminal servers (useful only if it's not the current domain).
query user	/server:*ServerName*	Specify a different terminal server in running a user query.
	SessionID	Specify a particular session ID to query for user data.
	SessionName	Specify a particular session name to query for user data.
	UserName	Check by a specific username.
register	*FileName*	Register the specific file named by this parameter.
	/system	Register the file, and also register it as system global resource file.
	/user	Register the specified file as a user global resource.

TABLE 23.1:   Key Commands for Terminal Services *(CONTINUED)*

COMMAND	PARAMETERS	FUNCTION
	/v	Turn on verbose mode for more detailed information.
reset session	SessionID	Reset the session specified.
	SessionName	Reset the session specified.
	/server:ServerName	Specify the server hosting the session you want to reset.
shadow	SessionID	Control the session specified.
	SessionName	Control the session specified.
	/server:ServerName	Identify the terminal server running the session you want to control.
tscon	SessionID	Connect to the session specified.
	SessionName	Connect to the session specified.
	/dest:SessionName	Specify the name of the destination connection you want to use.
	/password:pw	Connect using the password specified by *pw*.
tsdiscon	SessionID	Terminate the connection specified.
	SessionName	Terminate the connection specified.
	/server:ServerName	Identify the terminal server where the connection is occurring *if* it isn't the current session (and server) in use.
tskill	/a	Kill the process for all sessions running it.
	/id:SessionID	Terminate the process running in the identified session.
	ProcessID	Terminate the process specified.
	ProcessName	Terminate the process specified.
	/server:ServerName	Specify a terminal server where the process you want to kill is running (used when this isn't the currently used terminal server).
	/v	Turn on verbose mode for more details.

TABLE 23.1: Key Commands for Terminal Services *(CONTINUED)*

COMMAND	PARAMETERS	FUNCTION
tsprof	/copy	Copy the user configuration information for the person identified as *SourceUser* to that of the person identified as the *DestinationUser*.
	DestinationUser	Identify the user account to which you're copying a source user's information.
	/domain:*Domain*	Specify the domain (when it's not the present one).
	/local	Apply profile operations only to local accounts.
	/profile:*ProfilePath*	Specify the Terminal Services profile path.
	/q	Reveal the current profile path of a user.
	SourceUser	Specify the existing user account upon whose profile you want to perform an operation.
	/update	Specify that the profile path information for a specific user name should be updated.
	UserName	Identify a particular user account for updating or query.
tsshutdn	/delay:*LogOffDelay*	Whereas tsshutdn allows an administrator to shut down (and reboot, if desired) a terminal server, this switch allows you to specify how much time to wait between logging off users and shutting down.
tsshutdn	/powerdown	Shut down the terminal server completely (where available, because of hardware/software support).
	/reboot	Reboot the terminal server post-shutdown.
	/server:*ServerName*	Specify the terminal server to shut down if not the current one in use.
	/v	Turn on verbose mode for more details.
	WaitTime	Specify a set amount of time between notifying users that a shutdown is about to occur and forcing their logoff so the shutdown can happen.

TIP For more information about these and other Terminal Services commands, use Help And Support under Windows XP and search on the phrase in question.

Remote Desktop Web Connection

Remote Desktop Web Connection (RDWC) is not just a cool capability but a useful enhancement to standard remote connections, because you can work remotely through a supporting web browser (such as Internet Explorer 6). If your Windows XP system, for example, has a supporting web server with RDWC installed, you can log on and use your XP system from another computer—say, one at work or at home—using the browser.

The difference, as you might guess, between Remote Desktop and RDWC (because the latter can use a browser as its access medium), is that the web connection requires that the service be installed to a supporting web server, such as you find with Internet Information Services (IIS).

TIP A common misconception about RDWC is that it enables a Remote Desktop Connection over port 80. However, RDWC only uses port 80 to allow the remote client to connect to the server and download the ActiveX control. The connection still occurs by default over port 3389, but it's displayed in the browser rather than the RDC client software. See the section "Changing the RDWC Port," later in this chapter, for more details.

Unlike RDC, this web component is optional and not included in your installation. You must add it through Windows.

In addition, the requirements change slightly. For example, RDWC must be installed to a valid web server on one system, where files are copied automatically to the *%systemroot%*\Web\ Tsweb folder to support the process. If you can't install RDWC to a web server, you won't have this functionality.

For clients to work with RDWC, they need the following available:

◆ A TCP/IP connection either to the Internet or to a network

◆ A compatible web browser (Microsoft IE 4.0 or later)

NOTE You must be logged on as an administrator in order to install and configure this option.

WARNING You may also need to have Windows Internet Naming Service (WINS) or another name-resolution method such as DNS configured, in order for RDWC to work. See Chapter 21.

Installing Remote Desktop Web Connection

Follow these steps to install RDWC:

1. From Control Panel, click Add Or Remove Programs, and then click Add/Remove Windows Components to launch the Windows Components Wizard.

2. Select Internet Information Services from the list, and click Details.

3. In the resulting Subcomponents window, select World Wide Web Service, and then click Details.

4. In the next Subcomponents window, select Remote Desktop Web Connection. Click OK, and then click Next.

NOTE When Remote Desktop Web Connection is installed, it brings with it two default web pages: `default.htm`, which can be used as a home page to replace the default RWDC page in the browser, and `connect.asp`, a connection-specific page. These files can be customized for your use.

Configuring Remote Desktop Web Connection

Once RDWC is installed, you need to adjust the settings under Directory Security for your web server/site to allow for anonymous logons. To do this, follow these steps:

1. Launch Internet Information Services, which is available from the All Programs list under Administrative Tools.

2. Expand the folders until you locate and select *computername*\Web Sites\Default Web Site\tsweb (the Terminal Services web folder), where *computername* is the name of the system on which you're setting up RDWC.

3. Right-click the folder, and choose Properties.

4. Select the Directory Security tab.

5. In the Anonymous Access And Authentication Control section, click Edit.

6. In the Authentication Methods window, select the Anonymous Access check box. Click OK twice to apply and exit.

Using Remote Desktop Web Connection

Once you have RDWC installed and configured for use on your system, you should double-check (if possible) that the remote system you want to contact is available online.

When you have done this, make certain you have a valid connection in place (dial-up modem, broadband, or network), and follow these steps to connect to web server where Remote Desktop Web is installed:

1. From the remote or client system, launch Internet Explorer.

2. Type the address for the hosting web server into the browser's Address line, following this format: **http://name/tsweb/**, where *name* is the name of the web server and *tsweb* is the default web for this purpose.

3. When you connect to the Remote Desktop Web Connection default page, provide the name of the computer to which you want to connect in the Server box.

4. Click Connect.

5. You'll be prompted to log on to the other system using a valid username and password (preferably, one with permissions to allow your work).

NOTE   You can adjust the screen size by clicking the Size drop-down box and selecting the size you want to use.

NOTE   You may be prompted during this process to accept the download of a Terminal Services Control (RC2) file. Click Yes to accept it.

Once you've done this, you'll see the Desktop—including open files and applications, if any— available on the other system from your browser, as shown in Figure 23.3. Begin working as you normally would, with this caveat: If someone is on the remote system when you log on, they'll find they are locked out of their work (and will be notified of this situation) until someone with administrator access logs on from the console.

FIGURE 23.3
Use Remote Desktop Web Connection to work from the browser just as you work from the Desktop.

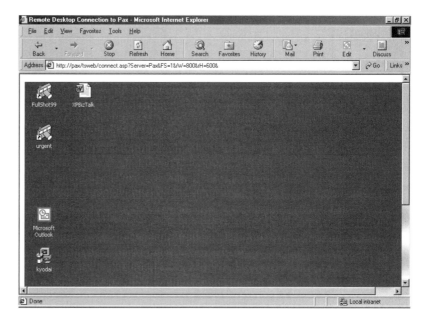

NOTE   Be aware that since RDWC is working from a website, port 80 must be available, along with port 3389 (or whatever you change it to per the following section).

Changing the Remote Desktop Web Connection Port

RDWC, like RDC, uses port 3389 for RDC traffic. Port 80 is used to enable the browser to connect to the RDWC server and download the ActiveX control. The ActiveX control then makes the connection to the RDC server on port 3389 and displays the session in the browser. This means port 3389 must be opened in the firewall, and—assuming your firewall is performing NAT—port 3389 must be port-forwarded to the target computer.

Earlier in this chapter, in the section "Changing the Remote Desktop Connection Port," I explained that it's useful in certain situations to change the port used by RDC. You may also want to change the port that RDWC uses. For example, assume you've configured your workstation to use port 3390 rather than 3389 for RDC. Now, you want to be able to connect using your browser and RDWC. There are a couple of steps to take to make RDWC work with a nonstandard port:

◆ Change the RDC port in the Registry.

◆ Modify the `Default.htm` file in the target computer's `TSWEB` virtual directory to include the port specification.

◆ Configure the firewall to port-forward the specified port to the target computer.

The first step is to change the RDC port in the Registry. Keep in mind that you can't use separate ports for RDC and RDWC. Instead, they both use the same port, because the same Terminal Services service handles connections for both. The only difference is the application used by the connecting client to display the session. So, if you've already configured your computer to listen on, say, port 3390 for incoming RDC traffic, you don't need to make a separate change for RDWC.

TIP   If you haven't configured the custom RDC port yet, see the section "Changing the Remote Desktop Connection Port," earlier in this chapter to learn how.

With the Registry changed to reflect the new custom port number, let's modify the `Default.htm` document:

1. On the target computer where RDWC is already installed, open `\%systemroot%\web\tsweb\Default.htm` in Notepad or an HTML editor.

2. Search in the file for `MsRdpClient.AdvancedSettings2`; you should find four statements in the Device Redirection Options section of the file that begin with this string.

3. Add a fifth line to the section:

```
MsRdpClient.AdvancedSettings2.RDPPort = 3390
```

   Replace the specified port with your custom port number, if it's different from 3390, and then save the file.

To connect to the remote computer with RDWC, you must be able to hit its TSWEB virtual directory. If there is already a computer on the network to which port 80 traffic is being forwarded, you must use a different port for the target computer. Here's an example using port 8080:

1. Open the IIS console from the Administrative Tools folder on the target computer.

2. Open the `Web Sites\Default Web Site` branch in the IIS console.

3. Right-click Default Web Site, and choose Properties.

4. On the Web Site tab, click Advanced.

5. In the Advanced Multiple Web Site Configuration dialog box, click Add.

6. In the TCP Port field, type **8080**. Leave the Host Header field blank for now, and click OK. Click OK to close the Advanced Multiple Web Site Configuration dialog box, and then click OK to close the properties for the website. Then, close the IIS console.

7. Change your firewall's configuration to forward ports 8080 and 3390 to the target computer. Add other port-forwarding pairs for other computers to which you want to direct RDWC traffic. Keep in mind that the pairs must be unique.

At this point, the firewall and target computer are configured and ready to accept connections for RDWC on the nonstandard port. Now, how to you make the connection? Follow these steps:

1. Connect to the target computer's TSWEB virtual directory.

2. Assuming your network's single public IP address is 216.239.31.4 and you've configured the target computer for port 8080 in IIS, open Internet Explorer and connect to `http://`

`216.239.31.4:8080/tsweb`. When your browser hits the page, the nonstandard port setting will be set by the configuration script contained on the page.

3. In the Server field on the page, enter the public IP address by itself with no port information. Specify other options such as screen size, and then click Connect. The client will attempt a connection on the specified IP address using the port contained in the configuration script.

Troubleshooting Remote Desktop

In this section, you'll learn how to troubleshoot some of the more common issues encountered when using RDC. Some of the problems you may encounter are to be expected. If you're using a slow dial-up connection through an analog modem, for example, you may find your remote connection intolerably slow. For very slow dial-ups, you're either going to sit waiting at times or learn to be moderate in what you run remotely. Where possible, use broadband access for remote work. When my satellite connection is running at its best speed, I notice relatively little difference compared to working directly at the console.

You also have to use common sense in working with a remote system. If the remote system tends to run slowly, it won't seem any faster through a remote connection. If the remote system is laboring under a borderline amount of installed RAM, you have to respect that and not demand too much. Finally, if a remote system has problems—for example, it's behaving in a flaky manner before you connect—you're going to feel them remotely through your system in the form of errors, slowness, and so on. Likewise, if the system you're connecting with is running low on virtual memory or is overburdened with open applications or problems, you may want to at least restart the system before you attempt the remote connection.

Can't Log On

Always be sure that you're trying to connect to the right system and that you're using a valid user name and password for access. Policy settings and permissions may also limit your access to a remote site, so verify them. If necessary, try logging on with an administrator account to see if it's available to someone with advanced privileges; if it is, then the problem may be with policies and permissions limiting the other account you were using.

If you're using RDWC, be sure you're not trying to log on as a remote to the same system on which you're currently working. You can't. Also make certain you're using the right URL to connect, following the convention `\\computername\tsweb`.

Remote Desktop Can't Find the XP System

Before you do anything else, try to test the computer name or IP address on a system where you know connections work. If the other system can't find the Windows XP system, then the XP system may be unavailable (it's crashed, for example, or shut down, or something else is preventing Terminal Services from allowing connections). Check the XP system's functionality and remote configuration as soon as possible.

If you can log on in one way or another from a different system, your current system may not be configured for name resolution (see Chapter 21), you may not be using the same address, or there may be a problem with your connection. Test it by trying to reach other sites, through your web browser or other means. If you can't reach anything, restart your system (just to be sure) and then check your communications hardware (modem) for physical connections, as well as review your TCP/IP settings.

Can't Run Programs Remotely

Check the account you're using and its privilege level. Also be sure that you haven't configured anything in group policy that may restrict this functionality.

Try more than one program. If necessary, you can use the `reset session` command in Terminal Services to try to reset the Windows XP–based server. In some of my sessions, I've experienced a short-term lockup, probably due to Internet traffic congestion, and found that one or more programs had a tendency to stall afterward. Resetting the server and reconnecting usually gets me back to the point where I can work normally.

Chapter 24

Configuring and Sharing Internet Connections

Although there aren't as many people with computers connected to the Internet today as you might think, the odds are still good that you want to either connect or improve the connection you already have. For example, maybe you're thinking about installing DSL or cable broadband service and are looking for tips on connecting your home network. Or, perhaps you're looking for ways to connect your office network to the Internet.

This chapter explains how to configure, optimize, and share an Internet connection. Whether you use a dial-up connection or broadband, you can share that connection with users on your local network. So, everyone on the network can check their e-mail, browse the Internet, and perform other Internet-related tasks even if you have only one modem, one phone line, and one dial-up account.

If you're experienced with networking, you probably won't need any help connecting your network to the Internet. You'll still find lots of useful information in this chapter, such as how to protect your network with a firewall, how to optimize TCP/IP settings for clients on the network, and even how to enable routing on a multihomed computer (one with multiple network adapters).

If you're not up to speed with networking or don't have a network in place now, this chapter will help you connect your network quickly and safely to the Internet. I don't cover general networking topics in this chapter, but you can refer to Chapters 20, 21, and 22 to get the local network operational and ready for the Internet connection.

NOTE See Chapters 19 through 21 for help configuring modem and network connections. Chapter 21 explains how to configure TCP/IP connections.

Options for Sharing Internet Connections

How you share an Internet connection with other users depends on the type of connection, how your network is structured, and a few other issues. In this chapter, I explain the possibilities and how to configure each one.

NOTE See the section "Sharing through a Router" if you want an alternative to Internet Connection Sharing.

Internet Connection Sharing

One of the easiest ways to share an Internet connection is through Windows XP's Internet Connection Sharing (ICS) feature. ICS is designed for situations where one computer is connected directly to the Internet and you want to allow the other computers on the network to access the Internet through that computer. The Internet connection can be a dial-up connection or a broadband connection. Figure 24.1 shows a typical dial-up scenario, and Figure 24.2 shows one broadband possibility.

FIGURE 24.1
You can share a dial-up connection with ICS.

FIGURE 24.2
You can also share a broadband connection with ICS.

With the broadband scenario, the DSL/cable modem connects directly to the computer through its network card. A crossover cable eliminates the need for a hub or switch between the two devices. In some situations, the DSL or cable modem installs directly in the PC and takes the place of a network card. Some broadband modem devices provide the IP address for the connection. Those that don't provide the IP address require a router or network adapter to provide the address.

If your system uses a cable or DSL modem that connects directly to your computer's network interface or installs internally in your computer, you'll need to add another network adapter to that computer and connect it to the rest of the local network. Then, share the Internet connection with ICS. The other computers on the network will connect to the Internet through the second adapter.

ENABLING ICS

When you dial into an Internet service provider (ISP), the dial-up connection receives a dynamically assigned IP address that resides on the ISP's subnet. If you have a broadband connection, the DSL or cable modem is assigned an address in the ISP's subnet, either dynamically or statically. In most cases, that's the only IP address you'll get from the ISP. It would be impossible to share one IP address with multiple computers without some means of address translation or routing. ICS uses a combination of routing and network address translation (NAT).

You enable ICS on the network interface that connects to the Internet. This interface receives an IP address that resides in the ISP's subnet, placing your computer on the ISP's network. When you enable ICS, Windows XP assigns the static IP address 192.168.0.1 to the local network interface. Figure 24.3 illustrates the scenario.

FIGURE 24.3
ICS assigns a static IP address to the computer.

Static addresses in 192.168.0.*x*
subnet or addresses assigned
through DHCP by gateway

192.168.0.1
statically assigned address

Second network card
with ICS enabled

Internet

DSL/cable modem/router

Any other computers on the local network must have an address in the same 192.168.0.*x* subnet (with subnet mask 255.255.255.0), and they must have the ICS computer set as their default gateway. Packets from these other computers go to the ICS computer, which routes them out through the Internet connection. The ICS computer not only acts as a router but also performs NAT, replacing the source computer's IP address with its own. When the packets come back, the ICS computer removes its IP address from the packet, restores the original source address, and forwards the packet on to the client.

To share an Internet connection through ICS, follow these steps:

1. Open the `Network Connections` folder on the computer that will share its connection.

2. Right-click the connection to the Internet—whether dial-up or broadband—and choose Properties.

3. Click the Advanced tab. Figure 24.4 shows the Advanced tab for a dial-up connection.

4. Select the option "Allow other network users to connect through this computer's Internet connection" if you want to share this Internet connection with other computers on the network.

FIGURE 24.4
Use the Advanced tab to
enable ICS.

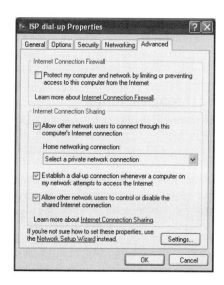

TIP The Advanced tab is similar for a broadband connection, except the option "Establish a dial-up connection whenever a computer on my network attempts to access the Internet" isn't present.

CONTROLLING AUTOMATIC CONNECTION

If you're sharing a dial-up connection, the option "Establish a dial-up connection whenever a computer on my network attempts to access the Internet" determines whether your computer automatically dials the connection. When a client attempts to connect to the Internet through an application such as Internet Explorer, the packets get routed to the ICS computer, which then determines whether there is a current connection to the Internet. If not, and this option is enabled, the ICS computer dials the connection. The dial-up remains connected until you manually disconnect it at the ICS computer or it reaches its specified inactivity period and disconnects automatically. If this option is disabled, the client's connection attempt times out and fails.

TIP See the later section "Configuring Client Timeout" to prevent a client from timing out before the connection is established.

The "Establish a dial-up…" option also applies to a broadband dial-on-demand connection such as a VPN connection to your office LAN. Windows XP makes the connection automatically if this option is enabled and a client attempts to connect to the Internet through the shared connection.

LETTING THE CLIENT CONTROL THE CONNECTION

The option "Allow other users to control or disable the shared Internet connection" determines whether the client can control the connection state of the Internet connection. For example, assume you share a dial-up connection with an inactivity timeout of 20 minutes. Someone else on the network opens Outlook Express to check their e-mail. The session takes less than a minute. They walk away, and the dial-up remains connected for another 19 minutes before finally timing out and disconnecting.

Another potential problem is that the user's session might time out and fail before the dial-up finishes connecting. For example, say it takes 45 seconds for the dialer to connect, authenticate, and establish the Internet connection. But the user's program waits only 30 seconds before it assumes there is no connection and fails.

If you enable the option "Allow other users to control or disable the shared Internet connection," other users on the network can force the connection to dial first before they open the e-mail program, browser, or other application. They can also disconnect the connection when they're finished, rather than wait for the connection to time out. They connect and disconnect the connection using the Internet Gateway icon in their `Network Connections` folder.

Sharing through a Router

Broadband Internet connections typically offer other possibilities for sharing. If your system uses a DSL or cable modem that connects directly to your computer's network interface, or which installs internally in place of a network card, then ICS is your means for sharing the connection with others. If a router sits between your computer and the broadband connection, however, you share the connection differently. You also have more options.

Figure 24.5 illustrates a typical broadband connection with a hardware router. You can also install a software-based router such as WinRoute (described later in this chapter) to let one connection work as a router and share its Internet connection. Let's look at the hardware solution first.

As Figure 24.5 shows, the router sits on both the ISP's subnet and your local network subnet. The router might be incorporated into the cable/DSL modem, or it could be a separate piece of equipment.

FIGURE 24.5
Multiple computers can
share a router-based DSL
connection.

Public IP address

Internet

DSL router

192.168.0.1

Hub or switch

Static address in 192.168.0.*x* subnet or
addresses assigned dynamically by router

Sharing an Internet connection in this situation isn't much of a chore: Just configure the router's LAN interface with the desired private IP address for your network. Configure its wide area network (WAN) interface with the IP address assigned to you by your ISP. This might be a private or public address, depending on how the ISP has structured its network. It's also possible that the WAN address is assigned dynamically by the ISP rather than statically. In either case, configure the WAN address according to the ISP's requirements.

The next step is to configure your workstations so they reside in the router's LAN IP subnet. For example, assume you assigned the address 192.168.0.1 to the router with a subnet mask of 255.255.255.0. Assign addresses in that same range and with the same subnet mask to the other computers on the network. Then, specify the router's LAN port address (in this case, 192.168.0.1) as the default gateway for all computers.

The main advantage offered by a router is the flexibility to use different addressing schemes on your local network. ICS forces you to use the range 192.168.0.*x*. With a router, you can use any private address range. For example, perhaps you want to use the 10.10.10.*x* subnet. The router doesn't care— it will translate the traffic regardless of its source address. You just need to make sure the router's LAN interface resides in the same subnet as the local network.

I'm assuming that you'll be connecting a limited number of computers through the shared connection. That makes static IP addressing a workable solution for assigning client addresses. As the number of computers increases, dynamic addressing makes more sense from an administrative standpoint. Without ICS, Windows XP doesn't work as a DHCP server. So, you'll need to install a DHCP server of some kind on the network. Virtually all DLS/cable routers also function as DHCP servers. If you have Windows NT Server, 2000 Server, or Windows Server 2003 on the network, you can use its DHCP service to assign client addresses. If not, you can use a third-party DHCP server application to provide dynamic addressing.

NOTE   For a complete description of how DHCP works, see Chapter 21.

A search for DHCP on your favorite download site will no doubt turn up at least a handful of third-party DHCP server applications or integrated server suites that provide DHCP and that run under Windows XP. I cover one of the more popular solutions in the next section.

TIP   Check out www.jhsoft.com for Simple DNS Plus, a commercial server suite that provides DHCP services.

USING A SOFTWARE-BASED ROUTER

If you want the flexibility of a router without putting in another piece of hardware, consider using a software-based router solution such as Kerio's WinRoute Lite or WinRoute Pro. Both versions provide DHCP, network address translation, routing, and several other features. The Pro version adds an integrated firewall, URL filtering, a proxy server, and several other excellent features.

You'll need two network adapters in the routing computer if you decide to go this route (no pun intended). One interface will connect to the Internet, and the other will connect to the local network.

Configuring Clients to Access the Shared Connection

Getting to the Internet through a shared connection requires that the client computers be configured properly. I've already touched on addressing in the previous sections. The following section explains how to configure the address at the client.

Assigning Addresses

You can assign the other computers on the network the appropriate address range and default gateway manually or let the ICS computer or your DHCP server assign the addresses. If you prefer to configure the client systems manually and are using ICS, give them a static IP address in the range 192.168.0.*x* with subnet mask 255.255.255.0 and the default gateway 192.168.0.1. You can use a different address range if you have a hardware or software router in place.

The easiest solution, however, is to let the ICS computer assign the IP configuration. ICS lets the connection-sharing computer act as a mini-DHCP server. You configure the client computers to take their IP address dynamically, and the ICS computer assigns the IP address, default gateway, and DNS servers to the clients when they boot or refresh their address lease.

To configure the client settings, follow these steps:

1. Open the Network Connections folder, and open the properties for the client's network connection.

2. Locate the TCP/IP protocol in the list of installed components, select it, and click Properties.

TIP   For platforms other than Windows XP, right-click the Network Neighborhood folder (or My Network Places) on the Desktop, and choose Properties to set the connection properties.

3. To assign a static IP address, click Use The Following IP Address. Enter the private IP address for the computer in the IP Address field, and specify the appropriate subnet mask.

4. Enter the IP address of the router or ICS computer in the Default Gateway field.

5. Enter the DNS servers your ISP has provided to you in the DNS Server fields.

TIP Dynamically assigning addresses is much easier. Just select the option Obtain An IP Address Automatically. This also takes care of assigning the DNS servers, assuming the device functioning as the DHCP server has been configured with DNS server settings.

Configuring Client Timeout

After using ICS for a while with a dial-up connection, you've probably run across the problem that your client computer times out waiting for ICS to establish the connection. For example, your web browser might report your home site as unreachable because TCP times out before the server can establish the connection.

TCP sets an initial retransmission timer of three seconds when it attempts the first data transmission for a connection. TCP doubles the retransmission timeout value for each subsequent connection attempt, and by default attempts retransmission two times. So, the first attempt is made at 3 seconds, the second at 3 + 6 seconds, and the third at 3 + 6 + 12 seconds, for a maximum timeout of 21 seconds. Increasing the initial retransmission timer to 5 seconds results in a total maximum timeout of 5 + 10 + 20, or 35 seconds.

To increase the initial TCP retransmission timeout value for a Windows XP computer, use the Registry value

```
\HKEY_LOCAL_MACHINE\System\CurrentControlSet\Services\Tcpip\Parameters\InitialRtt
```

The InitialRtt value is a REG_DWORD with a valid range from 0–65,535 and specifies the timeout in milliseconds.

The number of connection attempts is defined by the Registry setting

```
\HKEY_LOCAL_MACHINE\System\CurrentControlSet\Services\Tcpip\Parameters\
    TcpMaxDataRetransmissions
```

The TcpMaxDataRetransmissions value is also a REG_DWORD with a valid range of 0–65,535.

TIP Neither of these Registry settings exists by default—you'll have to create them.

Firewalls, NAT, and Security Planning

Whether you use a dial-up connection or a dedicated Internet connection, you need a firewall to protect your systems from being compromised and your network from denial-of-service and other attacks. Other methods such as NAT can help secure your network from intrusion, but these methods can't offer the same protection as a firewall. Let's look at your options.

Windows XP's Internet Connection Firewall

Windows XP includes its own firewall, called Internet Connection Firewall (ICF), which you can use to protect your systems. In most cases, you need to run it only on the computer that is sharing its Internet connection—you don't have to run it on every computer. In fact, running it on every computer can affect your ability to share files and printers on the network.

NOTE The firewall in Windows XP SP2 is called simply Windows Firewall. See the section "SP2's Windows Firewall," later in this chapter, for details.

Enabling and configuring ICF is relatively easy. To enable ICF, open the `Network Connections` folder, right-click the Internet connection, and choose Properties. Click the Advanced tab, and select the option that begins Protect My Computer And Network.

ALLOWING ACCESS TO INTERNAL SERVICES

Next, click Settings to open the Advanced Settings dialog box (Figure 24.6). The Services tab lets you specify port-to-address mapping that allows Internet users the ability to access servers inside your firewall. For example, if you host a web server on your network, you'll open port 80 for HTTP traffic to reach the server.

FIGURE 24.6
Use the Advanced Settings dialog box to configure services and security.

ICF lets you map different services to computers inside the firewall. These services can be running on a single computer or on multiple computers. However, you can only direct traffic for a particular service to a single computer.

Select the service that you want Internet users to be able to access. When you click the check box, Windows XP displays a Service Settings dialog box similar to the one shown in Figure 24.7. As the figure illustrates, you can enter the IP address or host name for the target computer, but you can't change the port assignments.

FIGURE 24.7
Specify the host name or IP address of the server in the Service Settings dialog box.

TIP If you specify a host name, the ICF computer must be able to resolve that name to a local IP address inside your network.

The Services tab contains nine predefined options that cover the most commonly used services. However, you can add other services to suit your needs. For example, you might need to add a service option to allow pcAnywhere or VNC connections to an internal server. Or, perhaps you want to redirect all incoming traffic on port 80 to a different port on an internal server. You can accomplish both tasks by creating a custom service:

1. Click Add to open an empty Service Settings dialog box.

2. Enter a name for the service as you want it to appear in the Services tab, and include the IP address or host name of the internal computer providing the service.

3. In the External Port field, enter the port that external computers use to access the service. For HTTP traffic for example, enter 80.

4. In the Internal Port field, enter the port on the internal computer that is listening for the traffic.

NOTE Why would you have a web server functioning on a port other than 80? Perhaps you've installed a third-party web server on a computer that's also running IIS, which is providing access to the computer's printers. So, you configure the third-party server to use port 8080 (for example) and continue to use port 80 for IIS.

CONFIGURE SECURITY LOGGING

Use the Security Logging tab (Figure 24.8) to specify how you want ICF to handle access through the firewall. The settings on the Security Logging tab include the following:

Log Dropped Packets Record in the log file all packets that the firewall drops (doesn't allow to pass through the firewall). Use this option to maintain a record of potential attempted attacks on your network or to troubleshoot attempts to access services from the LAN that aren't allowed by the firewall.

Log Successful Connections Record all successful connections from both inside and outside the firewall. This can result in lots of data being logged but is useful for troubleshooting.

Name Specify the path and name of the log file.

Size Limit Set the maximum size for the log file. Windows XP drops older log entries when this size is reached.

CONFIGURING ICMP

ICMP stands for Internet Control Message Protocol. The `ping` command is the most common use for ICMP. As Chapter 22 explained, `ping` lets you troubleshoot connections by sending ICMP echo requests. If the packets come back, you've verified connectivity between the two devices. If you receive a Request Timed Out error instead, there could be a problem with the connection. Another possibility is that a firewall is dropping ICMP packets, because `ping` is one tool that hackers and other miscreants use to launch a denial-of-service attack on a computer.

The ICMP tab (Figure 24.9) of the Advanced Settings dialog box lets you specify how ICF should handle ICMP packets. Each check box identifies a particular ICMP request, and selecting the option directs ICF to allow the computer to respond to the request. For example, select Allow Incoming Echo Request if you want to be able to use `ping` from other devices to check connectivity to the local computer.

FIGURE 24.8
Configure logging on the
Security Logging tab.

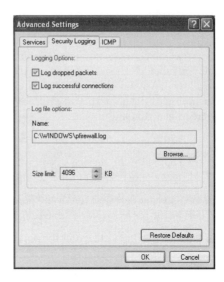

FIGURE 24.9
Use the ICMP tab to con-
figure how ICF handles
ICMP packets.

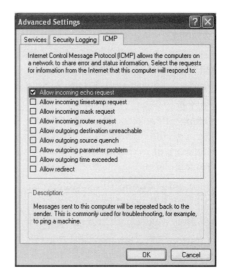

SP2's Windows Firewall

New!

Windows XP Service Pack 2 replaces ICF with a new firewall called Windows Firewall. This firewall is in many ways similar to ICF, but it's also very different. For example, when you install SP2, Windows Firewall will be enabled by default. This section explains how to configure and use Windows Firewall, how it's different from ICF, and how to control it with group policy.

ENABLING OR DISABLING WINDOWS FIREWALL

Windows Firewall initially applies the same settings to all interfaces, so you don't have to configure each interface separately if your computer contains more than one. You can, however, modify settings individually for each interface as needed.

To configure Windows Firewall, open the Windows Firewall applet from Control Panel. Figure 24.10 shows the Windows Firewall property sheet, which you use to configure the firewall globally.

FIGURE 24.10
Use the Windows Firewall applet to configure Windows Firewall.

The General tab lets you enable or disable the firewall. The Don't Allow Exceptions option, when enabled, directs Windows Firewall to ignore the settings you've configured on the Exceptions tab.

ABOUT SCOPE

Before I go any further in this Windows Firewall discussion, you should understand a little about *scope*. Firewalls, including Windows Firewall, use rules to determine whether to allow packets through the firewall. In addition to other properties, rules have a scope that determines how the rule is applied.

Windows Firewall offers three scopes:

◆ *Any computer*—The rule applies to any computer, regardless of its address. This scope applies the rule to the local network and the Internet.

◆ *My network (subnet) only*—The rule applies only to computer on the same subnet as your own, which means computers on your local network only.

◆ *Custom list*—You can build a custom list of addresses for which a rule should apply. For example, you might want to allow Remote Desktop Connection traffic from a handful of other computers on your local network as well as from a couple of computers on the Internet.

CONFIGURING EXCEPTIONS

Windows Firewall automatically adds a few exceptions to the Exceptions tab, shown in Figure 24.11. These exceptions allow specific applications to work through the firewall. The preconfigured exceptions include the following:

File and Printer Sharing This rule enables computers on your own subnet (your local network) to access file and printer sharing on your computer.

Remote Assistance This rule allows incoming Remote Assistance traffic to your computer from any source, including the Internet.

Remote Desktop This rule allows incoming traffic on port 3389, which is used by Remote Desktop Connection and Remote Desktop Web Connection (see Chapter 23).

UPnP Framework This rule supports devices that use Universal Plug and Play for network device discovery and configuration. The rule uses subnet scope, limiting UPnP traffic only from the local network.

Windows Messenger This rule allows other computers, including those on the Internet, to communicate with Windows Messenger on your computer.

FIGURE 24.11
Use the Exceptions tab to allow applications to work through the firewall.

You can use the Exceptions tab to add two types of exceptions to Windows Firewall: applications and ports. When you add an application, you're telling Windows Firewall that addresses under the scope of the rule can communicate with the application. You specify the application by path and executable. To add an application, follow these steps:

1. Open the Exceptions tab, and click Add Program to display the Add A Program dialog box (Figure 24.12, left).

2. The Programs list contains a selection of programs. You can click Browse to locate other programs not included in the list. Select a program, and then click Change Scope to display the Change Scope dialog box (Figure 24.12, right).

3. Select one of the three scopes described earlier in this chapter. If you choose the Custom List option, click in the text box and type the list of addresses to be allowed through the firewall; separate addresses with commas.

FIGURE 24.12

Use the Add A Program dialog box to configure Windows Firewall to allow traffic to a specific application. (left) Set the scope for the selected application. (right)

You can also add a port to the Exceptions list. Adding a port directs Windows Firewall to allow traffic through the specified port. For example, if you're using VNC for remote access, you'll likely open port 5900, which VNC uses for incoming connections.

To open a port in Windows Firewall, follow these steps:

1. Open the Exceptions tab, and click Add Port to display the Add A Port dialog box (Figure 24.13).

2. In the Name box, type the name of the application that will be using the port, or enter a description that will help you identify why the port is open.

3. In the Port Number box, enter the port number you want to open.

4. Choose either TCP or UDP, depending on the type of traffic that must move through the port.

5. As when you're adding an exception for an application, you can click Change Scope to specify which addresses are allowed in through the specified port.

FIGURE 24.13

Use the Add Port dialog box to add a firewall port.

CONFIGURING INTERFACES DIFFERENTLY

The changes that you make through the Windows Firewall applet in Control Panel apply to all network interfaces. In some situations, you'll want to make changes only to a specific interface. For example, you might want your local network interface to be relatively open, with your Internet connection locked down tight. The approach is to configure Windows Firewall globally to be locked down and then modify the settings for the local interface to open it as needed.

To configure settings for a specific interface, do the following:

1. Open the Windows Firewall applet from Control Panel, and then click the Advanced tab.

2. The Network Connection Settings group (Figure 24.14, left) lists the interfaces. A check beside an interface indicates that the interface is protected by Windows Firewall. Absence of a check indicates that Windows Firewall is turned off for that interface. To disable Windows Firewall on a specific interface, clear the check box beside the interface, and click OK.

3. To configure firewall settings for a particular interface differently from the others, click the interface in the list, and then click Settings. Windows Firewall displays the Advanced Settings dialog box shown on the right in Figure 24.14.

4. The Services tab shown on the right in Figure 24.14 lets you specify a computer on the network that acts as a server for the specified protocol. When you place a check beside a service, Windows Firewall displays the Service Settings dialog box shown on the left in Figure 24.15. Here you specify the host name or IP address of the target computer that is hosting the service.

5. If the service you need to configure isn't displayed, click the Add button on the Services tab. Windows Firewall opens the Service Settings dialog box, this time with all the options enabled. Enter the name of the service and the host name or IP address of the computer that hosts the service. In the External Port box, enter the port on which remote computers will attempt to connect to the service. In the Internal Port box, enter the port on which the local server is listening for the incoming traffic.

6. The ICMP tab of the Advanced Settings dialog box (Figure 24.15 on the right) lets you specify how Internet Message Control Protocol (ICMP) traffic is handled by the interface. If you're not sure what a particular option means, click it, and read the description in the Description field. Place a check beside an option to allow that type of ICMP traffic.

MANAGING ADVANCED SETTINGS

In addition to interface-specific settings, the Advanced tab of the Windows Firewall dialog box includes other advanced options you can set. For example, click Settings in the Security Logging area to open the Log Settings dialog box (Figure 24.16), which lets you specify if and how Windows Firewall logs information about connections. You can specify the location of the log, the maximum log size, and the type of events to be logged.

FIGURE 24.14

Use the Advanced tab to configure advanced settings. (left) Use the Advanced Settings dialog box to configure individual interfaces. (right)

FIGURE 24.15

Specify a server on the Service Settings dialog box. (left) Use the ICMP tab to specify how Windows Firewall handles ICMP traffic. (right)

FIGURE 24.16
Configure the log with
the Log Settings dialog
box.

If you click Settings in the ICMP area, Windows Firewall opens the ICMP Settings dialog box, which is similar to the ICMP tab shown previously in Figure 24.15 on the right. Use this dialog box to configure global ICMP options for Windows Firewall.

Finally, if you want to restore Windows Firewall to its out-of-the-box default settings, click the Restore Defaults button.

IMPORTANT SERVICE PACK 2 FIREWALL CHANGES

As I write this, SP2 has just been released and there is considerable harping in the computer media about SP2, most often directed at Windows Firewall. Although Windows Firewall will introduce problems for some companies and individuals, it won't break the Internet as some overzealous critics might contend. You simply need to understand the implications of Windows Firewall before deploying SP2. This section summarizes the key features of Windows Firewall in SP2:

On by default   It's true that SP2 enables Windows Firewall by default when you install SP2. However, the first dialog box you see when you log on is one that gives you the option of turning off Windows Firewall. That is a simple fix for any applications that might otherwise have problems working with Windows Firewall.

Boot-time security   A boot-time component of Windows Firewall is enabled at boot, protecting the computer during the boot process while the network interfaces are enabled and before Windows Firewall is fully enabled. The boot firewall blocks all traffic except common protocols required to boot the system, such as DHCP, DNS, and application of group policy. You can't configure the boot-time firewall. If you disable Windows Firewall, the boot-time firewall is disabled, as well.

Global configuration   As I've already explained, Windows Firewall gives you the capability to configure firewall settings globally for all interfaces. You can then make changes to customize the firewall's rules for individual interfaces.

Scopes   In Windows Firewall, you can specify the scope for a rule. The scope determines the source addresses to which the rule is applied. You can use global scope, subnet scope, or a custom address/subnet list.

On with no exceptions   This mode directs Windows Firewall to ignore any exceptions you've configured for the firewall globally or for a particular interface. Typically, you'll use this mode when you're connecting to the Internet from a nonsecure location such as a public hotspot.

Full group policy support Windows Firewall supports a broad range of group policies, enabling system administrators to control users' firewall settings across the enterprise. Many problems that might otherwise be introduced into a network by the installation of SP2 and Windows Firewall can be avoided through appropriate application of group policy to configure the firewall as needed. See the section "Controlling Windows Firewall with Group Policy," later in this chapter, for details.

Support for RPC Windows Firewall in SP2 handles Remote Procedure Call (RPC) traffic differently from ICF. Any RPC server application that is running in the Local System, Network Service, or Local Service security context can request that Windows Firewall open the necessary ports to enable the service to handle incoming requests. You can also add an RPC application to the exceptions list to enable the application to accept incoming traffic on dynamically assigned ports.

Multicast responses Windows Firewall allows a unicast response for three seconds on the same port from which a multicast or broadcast packet arrived, enabling applications and services to alter firewall policy for multicast and broadcast client/server situations.

IPv4 and IPv6 support Windows Firewall supports both the IPv4 and IPv6 protocols with a single firewall and interface, eliminating the need to configure two firewalls on systems that use IPv6.

CONTROLLING WINDOWS FIREWALL WITH GROUP POLICY

As I mentioned in the previous section, Windows Firewall supports a broad range of group policy settings to enable administrators to control users' firewall settings across the network.

NOTE Group policy requires a Windows 2000 Server or Windows Server 2003 Active Directory domain and membership in the domain. Local policies can be configured on workgroup members but can't be managed or applied remotely.

To configure firewall settings, open the Computer Configuration\Administrative Templates\Network\Network Connections\Windows Firewall policy branch (Figure 24.17). Here you'll find two sub-branches: Domain Profile and Standard Profile. The Domain Profile policies control Windows Firewall when the computer is connected to the Active Directory network. The Standard Profile policies control Windows Firewall when it isn't connected to the domain, such as when the user takes a notebook computer on the road and connects to a public network. The policies in each branch are the same; the only difference is in when they're applied.

The best way to get a handle on Windows Firewall policies is to view explanation text for each policy. To do so, switch to Extended view in the Group Policy console, click a policy, and read the explanation of its purpose. Or, double-click a policy, and then click its Explain tab.

Third-Party Software-Based Firewalls

ICF is a useful firewall, combining a reasonable level of security with easy configuration. However, it trades features for ease of use. If you need better control over what the firewall does and doesn't allow, or if you need to perform more advanced NAT, you need a different firewall.

One of the most popular third-party software-based firewalls is ZoneAlarm from Zone Labs (www.zonelabs.com). ZoneAlarm is free for personal and nonprofit use and provides good protection from intrusion and various attacks. ZoneAlarm Pro adds lots of other features, including expanded e-mail protection, the ability to track the source of an attack, restricted zones, custom security levels, and much more.

FIGURE 24.17
Use group policy to configure Windows Firewall.

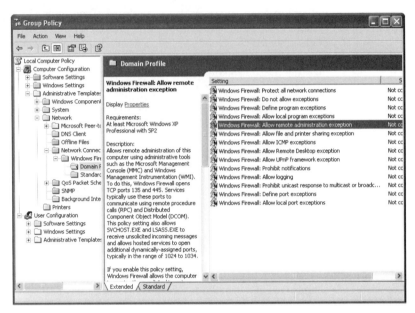

Another product worth considering is Tiny Firewall from Tiny Software at www.tinysoftware.com. This inexpensive firewall offers several advanced features including the ability to verify the authenticity of applications. This prevents an application from impersonating an authorized application to infect your system or cause other havoc.

Also check out Kerio Personal Firewall, at www.kerio.com. Like TPF, this firewall is easy to configure; but it offers some advanced features, including application verification.

Hardware-Based Firewalls

In many cases, a typical software-based firewall isn't practical or doesn't offer the necessary level of protection. For example, if you're hooking up a DSL or cable broadband connection, you need a DSL/cable router. Why not put in a router that also functions as a firewall, and kill two proverbial birds?

One of the features that a hardware-based router offers—that many workstation-class, software-based firewalls don't offer—is content filtering. This option enables the router to restrict access to specific websites that fall into certain categories, such as those that contain pornography. The firewall maintains a list of prohibited sites and their categories and blocks access to them if you've configured the router to do so.

Another important difference in many hardware-based firewalls is support for one-to-one NAT, which enables you to direct traffic for a specific public address to a private address. Although software-based firewalls and most inexpensive hardware-based firewalls support limited one-to-one NAT, more expensive firewalls support configuration of multiple NAT pairs. This is an important consideration if your network is supported by multiple public IP addresses that need to be routed to various private addresses on your network.

Check out www.sonicwall.com, www.linksys.com, www.netgear.com, www.dlink.com, and many other companies for hardware-based firewalls.

Enabling Routing on a Multihomed System

Windows XP does not, by default, providing routing services between two network interfaces. For example, assume you have a computer with one network card at 192.168.0.1 and a second card at 10.10.10.1, connecting two networks. Windows XP won't route packets between the two networks. You can, however, turn on IP forwarding to enable XP to route the packets.

Open the Registry Editor, and then open the branch

```
\HKEY_LOCAL_MACHINE\SYSTEM\CurrentControlSet\Services\Tcpip\Parameters
```

Look for the setting IPEnableRouter. Set the value to 1 to enable IP routing on all of the computer's interfaces.

Chapter 25

Supporting Wired or Dial-Up Incoming Connections

All of Microsoft's Windows operating systems have supported incoming connections, either through built-in support or through add-ons. Support for incoming connections lets you set up a Windows XP computer to act as a dial-up server. For example, you might connect a modem to a computer in the office to allow a small number of customers or business associates to access files on that computer. This lets you grant access to the system without putting it on the Internet or going through the bother of setting up an FTP site or website.

In addition, you can set up Windows XP to support other types of incoming connections. For example, you can use a null-modem cable between two computers to create a small network. So, if you have a notebook without a network adapter, you can connect your notebook to your desktop computer through the serial or parallel port to create a mini-network for sharing files.

An easier solution, if both computers include infrared ports, is to set up infrared connections for sharing. This solution offers the beauty of no cables and very little installation hassle.

This chapter explains how to set up each of these types of incoming connections.

Configuring Incoming Dial-Up Connections

As I mentioned in the introduction, Windows XP can support incoming connections from dial-up lines. For example, you can configure Windows XP to allow remote users to dial into a modem connected to the computer to access its files or even print to its printer. You can use this option when it isn't possible or practical to set up the computer to accept incoming connections through a hardwired connection such as the Internet. For example, you might not have a broadband Internet connection to the computer, or your ISP's firewall might prevent users from connecting to your computer.

TIP   You can use Internet Information Services (IIS) to share files with users on the Internet.

Windows XP can support one incoming dial-up connection. However, it can also support one each of the other types of incoming connections (infrared and direct cable), for a total of three. If you need to support multiple remote users over the same type of connection (such as several concurrent dial-up connections), install Windows 2000 Server or Windows Server 2003, which support an unlimited number of remote-access users.

It's important to understand that in addition to gaining access to shared resources on the computer that is acting as the dial-up server, the remote client can also optionally access the network on which the dial-up server is located. So, a remote client can dial into a Windows XP computer and then use the resources of the LAN as if the remote computer were connected directly to the network. The client could access shared network volumes, shared printers, and other network resources (such as an e-mail server). You control whether the remote client has access to the network when you configure the incoming connection (explained shortly).

If you're hoping to provide 56 Kbps dial-up speeds for a remote client, I have to dash your hopes. Providing 56 Kbps dial-up connections requires a digital link from the phone company to the modem pool, which is typically provided by a T1, fractional T1, or other digital broadband connection. You can't dial into an analog 56 Kbps modem with another 56 Kbps modem and get 56 Kbps performance. If the two modems are compatible, the fastest connection possible is 33.6 Kbps. In many cases, the best connection you'll get is 28.8 Kbps because of compatibility issues between the two modems.

Even at these slower speeds, a dial-up connection can still offer advantages you can't otherwise enjoy. For example, you might configure your home computer as a dial-up server so you can access your home files, printers, or even shared Internet connection when you're on the road. Or maybe you need to grab a file from the office when you're working at home, and a dial-up connection to your office computer could be the solution.

Understanding the Security Risks

When you configure a Windows XP computer as a dial-up server, by default the computer allows the remote caller to access the local network to which the dial-up server is connected. For example, assume you set up your office computer as a dial-up server. When you connect from home, you can access not only your own computer but also any resources shared on the office network.

The ability to access network resources is an important and powerful tool, but it's also a potential security risk. In order to dial in and connect, the remote caller must have or know an account on the dial-up computer. If one of the accounts is compromised, and that account has been granted dial-in permissions, an unauthorized user can potentially gain access to network resources. Securing all network resources with NTFS and share permissions is one step in securing the network, but you should still consider dial-up servers in a network to be a security risk for shared resources.

Dial-up access also poses other potential risks. Allowing dial-in connections bypasses the firewall if one is in place on your network, providing a potential back door into your network for viruses, Trojan-horse programs, and hackers. For that reason, you should install a Windows XP dial-up server only if you fully understand and accept the security risks involved.

Setting Up the Connection and Using Callback

Your first step in setting up a dial-up server is to install the modem and verify that it's working. You don't necessarily need to dial out with it—just open the modem's properties and use the Diagnostics tab to verify that you can query the device. When the modem is working, you can start setting up the connection.

You configure a Windows XP computer to act as a dial-up server through the Incoming Connections icon in the `Network Connections` folder. By default there is no such icon, so you need to create a new connection to create it.

Log on as administrator, open the `Network Connections` folder, and click the Create A New Connection link in the left pane. Select Set Up An Advanced Connection, and click Next. Select Accept Incoming Connections, and click Next. The wizard displays the available connection devices, as shown in Figure 25.1. Select the modem, and click Next.

FIGURE 25.1
Select the device(s) that
will accept incoming
connections.

You can specify whether the dial-up server will support incoming VPN connections. You don't
need to support VPN to allow the remote caller to access the local computer or the LAN, so choose Do
Not Allow Virtual Private Connections and click Next. The wizard then prompts you to specify the
local users who can dial in (Figure 25.2).

FIGURE 25.2
Select the users who can
dial in.

You can select multiple users to grant those users the ability to dial in. You can also change the
user's full name or password through the wizard; double-click the account to open its properties.

You can use the Callback tab to specify whether the server will call back the remote user. This
allows you to essentially reverse the connection charges. For example, if you're working from home
and need to dial into your office computer to work, and the call is long distance, you can use the Callback properties to configure your office computer to dial you back at home. The company then picks
up the tab for the call.

TIP To view the Callback tab, click a user in the User Permissions page of the wizard and click Properties,
then click the Callback tab.

The other reason to use callback is to increase security. You can configure each account to use a specific callback number. This helps prevent unauthorized access to the dial-up computer and LAN, because not only must the remote caller have the necessary logon credentials, but he must also be calling from a specific number. Select one of the following options to use callback:

Do Not Allow Callback   The server won't call back the remote user, even if the remote user requests it. Ultimately, this means the user will incur long-distance toll charges for the call.

Allow The Caller To Set The Callback Number   The remote user can specify the number for callback when the initial connection is made.

Always Use The Following Callback Number   The server will call back the remote user at the specified number, even if the user requests a different number.

You don't need to configure any special settings at the client to use callback. Windows dial-up clients automatically attempt to negotiate a callback session. From the remote computer, dial the server; the client and server negotiate a callback protocol, as well as other protocols (such as authentication). After the server authenticates the client, the client, recognizing that the server accepts callback, initiates the callback. A dialog box appears on the client's computer requesting the callback number; Figure 25.3 shows a Windows 98 client in a callback session. If the account requires callback to a specific number, you can't change the number from the client. Otherwise, enter the callback number complete with area code and dialing prefix, if needed. When you click OK, the computers disconnect, and the client waits for a call back. The server then dials the specified number to reestablish the connection. You can also click Cancel if you want to continue the existing connection without a callback.

FIGURE 25.3

Specify the callback number when you first establish the connection.

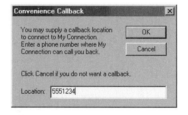

After setting callback options, click OK, and then click Next in the wizard. Review the network components that are enabled for the connection in the Networking Software list. Clear the check box beside any item you don't want used for the connection. For example, if you have more than one network protocol installed and only want to use one, clear the other(s). When you're satisfied with the settings, click Next, and then click Finish.

TIP   If your modem doesn't answer, it could be that the modem initialization string isn't set to enable auto-answer. On a Windows 98 computer, open the connection's properties and click Configure on the General tab. Click the Connection tab, and click Advanced. In the Extra Settings field, type **ATS0=1**, and then close the dialog boxes (ATS0=1 sets the modem to auto-answer on the first ring). For Windows XP and 2000 computers, open the modem's properties in Control Panel, and set the initialization string through the Advanced tab.

Controlling Access to the Network

As I mentioned earlier in this chapter, you can configure the dial-up server to allow the remote caller to access the network as well as the server. This ability is set on a per-protocol basis. If the client is negotiating two different protocols, one can deny network access and the other can allow it. Follow these steps:

1. Right-click the Incoming Connections icon in the `Network Connections` folder, and choose Properties.

2. On the Networking tab, double-click the network protocol that you want to configure.

3. In the resulting protocol property dialog box, select the option Allow Callers To Access My Local Area Network if you want the remote caller to be able to access network resources. Clear this check box to restrict the remote caller to accessing only those resources available on the dial-up server. Figure 25.4 shows the dialog box for the TCP/IP protocol as an example.

FIGURE 25.4
Use the properties for the protocol to allow or deny network access.

TIP　If the dial-up server allows multiple protocols, make sure you configure the settings for each protocol to allow or deny access as appropriate for your situation.

Configuring Incoming Hardwired Connections

Although a dial-up connection can be a handy way to connect to a remote computer or network, it doesn't give you stellar data speeds. In some situations, you may want to use a hardwired connection between two computers. For example, perhaps you have a desktop computer at home and a notebook that you use at work and at home. You don't have a network in place at home, but you want to connect your notebook and desktop systems at home to share some files or a printer.

You have a couple of different options for connecting the computers. This section explains two options: using network cards and a crossover cable, or using a null-modem cable attached to the computers' serial or parallel ports.

NOTE　See the section "Using Infrared Devices and Connections," later in this chapter, if both computers provide infrared support or if you're looking for a solution to allow your notebook or other infrared-capable devices to connect to a computer that currently has no infrared support.

Network Adapters and Crossover Cables

The first option for connecting two computers doesn't require Windows XP's remote access features—you only need a network adapter in each computer and a network *crossover cable*. In a crossover cable (unlike a standard network cable), the send and receive lines are crossed. This enables the two computers to communicate without going through a hub or switch. Think of it as holding two phone handsets together, microphone to speaker.

The advantage of this method is that you get high data throughput speeds (up to 100 Mbps if the adapters support 100 Mbps speeds). It's also easy to set up. Just install the network adapter, connect the two computers with the crossover cable, and your network is up and running. You avoid the expense of a hub or switch.

TIP   You don't need to disconnect the cable from the desktop computer when you aren't using the mini-network. Leave the cable connected and accessible so you can easily plug it into the notebook or other computer when needed.

USB-to-USB Connections

Another option to consider if both computers have USB ports is to connect them through USB. Parallel Technologies (www.lpt.com) offers a USB-to-USB cable that lets you connect two computers through their USB ports. The cable, in effect, acts like a pair of USB network adapters. For that reason, this method uses the built-in network features of the two computers' operating systems rather than Windows XP's remote-access features. This USB cable option supports transfer speeds of up to 6 Mbps. The price of the cable is comparable to the price of two network adapters and a crossover cable, making it an attractive alternative to the option I discussed in the previous section.

Serial or Parallel Port Connections

You can also use a serial (COM) or parallel (LPT) port to connect two computers. This option does require Windows XP's remote-access features, as well as an appropriate cable to connect the two computers. Parallel port connections offer faster data throughput than serial connections, so you should choose a parallel connection for best performance.

Your first step in setting up a direct cable connection between the two computers is to make sure you have the right cable. You can purchase a cable or make your own. I suggest you buy one and avoid the hassles inherent in making the cable. Parallel Technologies (www.lpt.com), which I mentioned in the previous section, sells serial and parallel port cables that work for direct cable connections with Windows XP.

You can also find cables for direct cable connections at most computer retailers. If you're not sure which one to get, either ask the salesperson or check the cable to see that it matches the pin-outs shown in Tables 25.1 and 25.2. You can also point your web browser to

```
http://support.microsoft.com/default.aspx?scid=kb;EN-US;Q310576
```

or search the Microsoft Knowledge Base for article Q310576, which shows the pin-outs.

When you have the right cable in hand, you're ready to hook up the computers. Connect the cable to an available port on each computer.

TABLE 25.1: Serial Cable Pin-Outs

9-PIN	25-PIN		25-PIN	9-PIN	DESCRIPTION
Pin 5	Pin 7	connects to	Pin 7	Pin 5	Ground–Ground
Pin 3	Pin 2	connects to	Pin 3	Pin 2	Xmit–Rcv
Pin 7	Pin 4	connects to	Pin 5	Pin 8	RTS–CTS
Pin 1 and 6	Pin 6	connects to	Pin 20	Pin 4	DSR–DTR
Pin 2	Pin 3	connects to	Pin 2	Pin 3	Xmit–Rcv
Pin 8	Pin 5	connects to	Pin 4	Pin 7	CTS–RTS
Pin 4	Pin 20	connects to	Pin 6	Pin 1 and 6	DTR–DSR

TABLE 25.2: Parallel Cable Pin-Outs

25-PIN		25-PIN	DESCRIPTION
Pin 2	connects to	Pin 15	N/A
Pin 3	connects to	Pin 13	N/A
Pin 4	connects to	Pin 12	N/A
Pin 5	connects to	Pin 10	N/A
Pin 6	connects to	Pin 11	N/A
Pin 15	connects to	Pin 2	N/A
Pin 13	connects to	Pin 3	N/A
Pin 12	connects to	Pin 4	N/A
Pin 10	connects to	Pin 5	N/A
Pin 11	connects to	Pin 6	N/A
Pin 25	connects to	Pin 25	Ground–Ground

SETTING UP THE HOST

On the computer that will act as the server (host), open the Network Connections folder. If Incoming Connections doesn't already exist, run the Create A New Connection wizard as explained in the earlier section "Configuring Incoming Dial-Up Connections." When the wizard prompts you to select the connection device or port, select the port to which you've connected the cable. Complete the wizard as you would for a dial-up connection (although you naturally can't configure callback options).

TIP You actually have two ways to set up the host. When you run the wizard, you can choose the option Connect Directly To Another Computer instead of Accept Incoming Connections. If you choose this route, select Host when prompted to specify whether you're setting up the host or client. When you complete the wizard, you'll have an Incoming Connections icon in the Network Connections folder.

Setting Up the Client

The process for setting up the client is very similar. On a Windows XP computer, open the Network Connections folder, and run the Create A New Connection wizard. Select the option Connect Directly To Another Computer, and then select Guest. When you're prompted for the name of the computer to which you're connected, you can specify any name—this is the name for the connection, not the host's computer name (although they can be the same). Select the appropriate port to finish the wizard.

To set up a client on a Windows 98 or Me computer, first make sure the Direct Cable Connection software is installed. Click Start ➤ Programs ➤ Accessories ➤ Communications ➤ Direct Cable Connection. If this item doesn't exist, open Control Panel and use the Add/Remove Programs applet to add the software. Click the Windows Setup tab, and select Direct Cable Connection under the Communications group. After the software is installed, click Direct Cable Connection in the menu to start the connection wizard. Select the Guest option, and follow the wizard's prompts to specify the other properties, such as connection port.

Using the Connection

The guest connection works much like a dial-up connection. On a Windows XP client, open the Network Connections folder, and double-click the connection's icon. Windows XP displays a connection dialog box (Figure 25.5), in which you enter the user name and password for the account on the host computer. Click Connect to initiate the session.

FIGURE 25.5
Specify the user name and password for the connection.

The process is a little different on a Windows 98 or Me computer. Click Start ➢ Programs ➢ Accessories ➢ Communications ➢ Direct Cable Connection.Windows displays a dialog box similar to the one shown in Figure 25.6. Click Connect to initiate the session.

FIGURE 25.6

Use Direct Cable Connection to connect in Windows 98.

After you connect the two computers, the host appears essentially like a node on the network, as if it were connected by a standard network connection. You can browse resources on the host through the My Network Places folder and even map local drives to shared resources on the host.

Chapter 26

Optional Networking and Management Components

Windows XP includes several optional networking services. Many of these are general TCP/IP tools. For example, the RIP Listener is a service that lets a Windows XP computer listen for route updates from routers that use the Routing Information Protocol (RIP) version 1. Although you wouldn't need to listen for RIP updates in most scenarios, the service is useful for improving routing and network performance in certain dial-up situations.

The Simple TCP/IP Services included with Windows XP allow an XP computer to respond to requests from other computers for certain optional TCP/IP functions. For example, the Quote of the Day service allows the computer to return quotations taken from a text file. The Simple TCP/IP Services also include Character Generator, Daytime, Discard, and Echo tools, all of which are explained in this chapter. In most cases, these tools are useful only in environments where Unix-based systems are also present.

Simple Network Management Protocol (SNMP) allows remote monitoring and management of devices including routers, switches, computers, and other types of devices. The SNMP service included with Windows XP lets clients access SNMP data across the network.

Print Services for Unix, another optional networking service included with Windows XP, allows Unix clients on your network to access printers connected to an XP computer. This lets you share your printer with those Unix systems. The service also enables a Windows XP computer to print to printers hosted by Unix-based hosts.

TIP Microsoft offers a free add-on for Windows Server called Services for Unix, which provides extensive Unix/Windows integration.

The Universal Plug and Play service included with Windows XP makes it possible for an XP computer to discover and control Universal Plug and Play devices on the network.

New! Peer-to-Peer enables peer-to-peer network services to communicate between computers without intermediary servers. The optional Peer-to-Peer networking component installs support for Microsoft's new peer-to-peer functionality and also configures Windows Firewall to support the ports used by this technology.

This chapter explains how to find and install each of these services—and configure them where appropriate.

RIP Listener

Routers use one of two methods to route network traffic: static routing or dynamic routing. A *static* route is one that the router administrator manually enters in the router's firmware. *Dynamic* routing lets a router build its routing table from information it gathers from adjacent routers. This allows routers to respond on the fly to network events such as a new router coming on line or a router going down. Each time a router boots, it rebuilds its routing table. The routing table initially contains only the routing table entries for physically connected networks, but the router can add other routes dynamically as it learns them.

RIP, which stands for Routing Information Protocol, is a common routing protocol. A router using RIP periodically broadcasts announcements regarding routes. This enables adjacent routers to modify their routing tables accordingly. Therefore, a router begins using RIP announcements to build its routing table after it boots.

TIP Each router is sometimes referred to as a *hop*, and a packet's hop count is increased by one each time it passes through another router. RIP is relatively easy to configure but is limited to a maximum of 15 hops, making it suitable mainly for small to mid-sized networks. RIP considers any destination more than 15 hops away to be unreachable.

RIP also provides for *triggered updates* in addition to broadcast updates. These updates are triggered when a router detects a network change, such as an interface going down. The router then broadcasts the change to adjacent routers, which modify their routing tables accordingly. When the interface comes back up, the router that recognizes the change broadcasts a triggered update to adjacent routers, which again modify their routing tables to accommodate the change.

RIP v2 provides additional features not supported by RIP v1, such as authentication for security, support for Variable Length Subnet Masks (VLSM), and route filtering. RIP v2 also supports multicast broadcast of RIP announcements and several other features. RIP v1 routers are forward compatible with RIP v2 routers, enabling them to coexist.

The RIP Listener service included with Windows XP allows an XP computer to listen for RIP v1 announcements and adjust its routing table accordingly. In the vast majority of situations, RIP Listener isn't needed on a workstation. However, if a multihomed Windows XP computer is serving as a router or connects to a remote network through a dial-up or direct connection, the RIP Listener service can improve network performance by reducing the number of hops required for outgoing packets to reach their destination. Rather than be routed through a less efficient route and require a remote router to reroute the packets, the Windows XP computer can route them according to the new routes defined through the RIP announcements. Using the RIP Listener lets the computer update its routing table itself, without the need for you to manually add or modify the routing table.

TIP RIP Listener can also listen for RIP v2 announcements that are sent as subnet-level broadcasts, but it doesn't receive RIP v2 multicast announcements.

One of the most common uses for RIP Listener is to simplify workstation configuration when more than one gateway is available. As Figure 26.1 illustrates, a computer with multiple gateways to other LANs or to the Internet can use RIP Listener to update its routing table based on RIP announcements from its adjacent routers. This helps the computer determine the most efficient route for a given packet.

Therefore, the main advantage of RIP Listener is that traffic gets routed more efficiently, providing faster network response. It also reduces the number of hops for a given packet, which reduces the workload on the routers involved.

FIGURE 26.1
RIP Listener lets a computer build its routing table dynamically from adjacent routers.

Using RIP Listener on a Windows XP computer is easy because you don't need to configure the service. Follow these steps:

1. Open the Add Or Remove Programs object in Control Panel, and click Add/Remove Windows Components.

2. Open the Network Services item, place a check beside RIP Listener, click OK, and then click Next.

3. Windows XP prompts you for the Windows XP CD or location of the Windows XP source files, copies the files, and then starts the service. You don't need to perform any additional configuration.

TIP   The RIP Listener service appears in the Services console. You can stop and start RIP Listener there, if needed.

Simple TCP/IP Services

Windows XP includes a set of services that support features offered by most Unix platforms. These services include the following:

Character Generator   This component sends data from the 95 printable ASCII characters and is useful for troubleshooting printer problems.

Daytime   This component returns messages containing the day of the week, month, day, year, current time, and time zone. It's most often used programmatically to monitor differences in this information compared to that from other computers.

Discard   This component discards all messages received on the port without responding to or acknowledging them. It can also be used programmatically to discard unneeded messages.

Echo   This component echoes messages that it receives, which is useful for testing and debugging.

Quote of the Day   This component returns one or more lines of text from *%systemroot%* System32\Drivers\Etc\Quotes. Windows XP creates a sample file that you can use as is or modify to add other quotes.

If your computer resides in a Unix environment and you want to use these components, you can add them through the Add Or Remove Programs object in Control Panel. To do so, click Add/Remove Windows Components, and then open the Network Services item. Select Simple TCP/IP Services, click OK, click Next, and insert the Windows XP CD when prompted.

SNMP Service

As I mentioned in the introduction, SNMP stands for Simple Network Management Protocol; it's an Internet standard for gathering information about network devices and managing those devices. For example, many routers, switches, and other devices use SNMP as the primary mechanism for remote monitoring and management. An administrator doesn't have to be physically present at a router to configure it but instead can rely on an SNMP-based management tool to interface with and configure the router.

SNMP is also often used to monitor and manage computers. SNMP management applications let network administrators gather information about the computers on their networks for inventory and management purposes; often, the application scans the network for SNMP devices automatically. Windows XP doesn't include an SNMP management application, but you can use one of several third-party management tools as well as Microsoft's own Systems Management Server (SMS). Some network management tools you might want to consider are as follows:

◆   Tivoli NetView

    http://www-306.ibm.com/software/tivoli/

◆   Hewlett-Packard OpenView

    http://www.managementsoftware.hp.com/

◆   Computer Associates UniCenter

    www.ca.com

◆   Microsoft Systems Management Server

    www.microsoft.com/smsmgmt/default.asp

Windows XP includes the SNMP agent that lets a management application collect information from the Windows XP computer. This chapter explains how to install and configure the SNMP service on a Windows XP workstation.

Installing the SNMP Services

There are two SNMP services for Windows XP. The first is the SNMP agent, which allows SNMP information to be collected and provided to management applications. The second is an SNMP provider, which allows that information to be provided to management applications through the Windows Management Interface (WMI). You need the latter only if you plan to use management applications that use WMI.

You add the SNMP service to a computer in the same way you add other optional components:

1. Open the Add Or Remove Programs item in Control Panel, and click Add/Remove Windows Components.

2. Open the Management And Monitoring Tools item, and select Simple Network Management Protocol. Also select WMI SNMP Provider if your management applications are WMI-based.

3. Click OK, click Next, and provide the Windows XP CD or path to the XP installation files when prompted.

Configuring SNMP

After you install the SNMP service, you need to configure each computer for SNMP. This is one of the few Windows XP components that you configure through the Services console. Open the Services console and double-click the SNMP Service to display the properties sheet for the service, and then click the Agent tab (Figure 26.2).

FIGURE 26.2

Use the Agent tab to configure general SNMP settings and services used by SNMP.

The Agent tab contains the following options:

Contact   Specify the person who is the contact for this computer. You can enter a name, an e-mail address, or other identifying information.

Location   Specify the physical location of the computer.

Physical   Select this option if you want SNMP to report information about physical devices such as hard disks.

Applications   This option specifies that the computer uses applications that send data using TCP/IP.

Datalink And Subnetworks   This option specifies that the computer manages a bridged network connection.

Internet   This option specifies that the computer functions as an IP gateway for other clients.

End-To-End   This option specifies that the computer is an IP host.

In addition to configuring general information for SNMP, you also need to configure community names and traps. The community name essentially serves as a password. All SNMP devices that need to communicate do so using the community name. Many devices use the community name `public` by default, although configuring your SNMP devices to use this default community name is a security risk. Instead, you should use an SNMP community name that isn't easy to guess.

You configure community names and trap destinations on the Traps tab of the SNMP service properties (Figure 26.3, on the left). To do so, follow these steps:

1. Type a community name in the Community Name combo box, and click Add To List.

TIP   You can configure a computer for more than one SNMP community. Doing so enables the computer to communicate in multiple groups of computers and provides a means for administrators to logically group computers for management purposes.

2. Click Add to open the SNMP Service Configuration dialog box.

3. Enter the host name, IP address, or IPX address of the computer that needs to receive SNMP notification messages from the computer. You can add multiple trap destinations to send notifications to multiple computers.

FIGURE 26.3

Use the Traps tab to configure SNMP community names and traps. (left) Use the Security tab to configure properties for incoming SNMP messages. (right)

The community names specified on the Traps tab are used to authenticate outgoing SNMP messages only. You configure security for incoming SNMP messages through the Security tab (Figure 26.3, on the right).

The options on the Security tab include the following:

Send Authentication Trap   Select this option to have the computer send an SNMP authentication trap message to all hosts in the trap list if the computer receives an SNMP request from a host that isn't in the communities listed on the Security tab.

Accepted Community Names   Click Add to add a new community name and specify the community rights, or select an existing community and click Edit to edit the current rights. These rights include the following:

None   This setting prevents the host from processing any SNMP requests.

Notify   This setting lets the host send trap notifications only to the communities configured in its trap list.

Read Only   Select this option if you don't want the host to process SNMP SET requests. In effect, this allows management applications in the specified community to read SNMP information but doesn't let them cause the computer to modify its configuration.

Read Write   Select this option to allow the host to respond to SET requests, enabling management applications to cause the computer to change its configuration through SNMP.

Read Create   Select this option to let the host create new entries in the SNMP tables.

NOTE   The communities specified on the Security tab apply to incoming SNMP requests only. Use the Traps tab to configure communities for outgoing SNMP messages.

Accept SNMP Packets From Any Host   Use this option to let the computer process SNMP requests from all hosts specified in the Accepted Community Names list.

Accept SNMP Packets From These Hosts   Use this option to apply a higher level of security for SNMP. With this option selected, the computer process SNMP messages only from selected hosts. You specify the host name, IP address, or IPX address of the allowed host(s). Click Add to add a host to the list of allowed hosts.

Setting SNMP Properties with Group Policy

Although you can configure SNMP properties through the properties for the SNMP service, you'll find it more efficient to set SNMP properties through group policy if you have a relatively large number of computers in a domain environment. Group policy lets you apply the SNMP properties across the site, domain, or organization unit (OU) automatically, without requiring that you modify settings at each individual computer.

To configure SNMP policies, edit the group policy object at the desired level (site, domain, OU, or local computer). Open the \Computer Configuration\Administrative Templates\Network\SNMP branch (Figure 26.4). Open the Communities policy, and add the communities in which the computer should belong. This setting corresponds to the Accepted Community Names property in the SNMP service.

Use the Permitted Managers policy to define the SNMP management hosts to which the client will respond. This policy corresponds to the list associated with the option Accept SNMP Packets From These Hosts in the SNMP service properties.

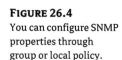

FIGURE 26.4
You can configure SNMP properties through group or local policy.

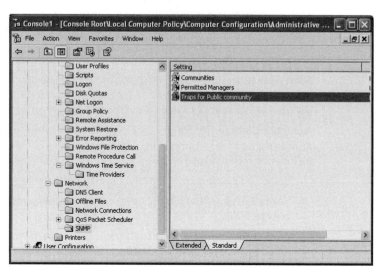

Use the Traps For Public Community policy to specify the hosts that should receive SNMP traps from the computer. This policy corresponds to the list of hosts in the Traps tab of the SNMP service.

TIP SNMP properties set through group policy override SNMP settings configured locally on the computer through the SNMP service properties.

Print Services for Unix

Print Services for Unix allows Unix (or Linux) hosts on the network to print to a printer hosted by a Windows XP computer and, vice versa, allows a Windows XP computer to print to a printer hosted by a Unix-based computer that uses the line printer daemon (LPD). Print Services for Unix adds support for LPR ports to Windows XP

TIP Check out Microsoft's web site at www.microsoft.com/windows/sfu/default.asp for details on Services for Unix, Microsoft's free add-on that provides more extensive Unix/Windows integration.

To connect to a printer on a Unix host, you must install Print Services for Unix and then add the printer driver for the remote printer and configure its LPR port. Follow these steps:

1. Open the Add Or Remove Programs object in Control Panel, click Add/Remove Windows Components, and add Print Services for Unix, which is located under the Other Network File And Print Services item.

2. Run the Add Printer Wizard, click Next, and choose Local Printer Attached To This Computer.

3. Clear the option to automatically detect and install the printer, and then click Next.

4. Select Create A New Port, choose LPR Port from the drop-down list, and then click Next.

5. In the Add LPR Compatible Printer dialog box (Figure 26.5), enter the fully qualified host name or IP address of the Unix host that manages the remote printer. Also enter the name of the printer or the print queue on the remote computer, and click OK.

Windows XP checks communication with the remote print server and displays a warning if it can't locate the remote server. You have the option to continue anyway.

FIGURE 26.5
Specify the remote Unix host name and printer or queue name.

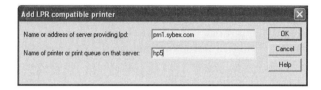

TIP If Windows XP displays a warning that it can't communicate with the remote Unix host, and you discover after installing the printer that the host name or printer/queue name is incorrect, just change those properties. Open the properties for the printer, click the Ports tab, and click Configure Port to change the port settings.

Universal Plug and Play

The Universal Plug and Play service in Windows XP allows a Windows XP computer to detect and control Universal Plug and Play (UPnP) devices on the network. These devices include printers, network storage devices, and other devices that provide resources on the network. When Windows XP detects a new UPnP device, Windows displays notification in the tray. UPnP devices also appear in My Network Places, giving you quick access to these devices and the resources they provide.

UPnP User Interface, which supports UPnP devices in the Windows XP interface, doesn't install by default when you install Windows XP. This is fortunate, because the UPnP service included with the initial release of Windows XP suffers from an unchecked buffer bug that, if exploited by a hacker, can enable the hacker to gain complete control over the computer. This UPnP service can also be exploited to accomplish a denial-of-service attack against the computer and the network in which it resides.

If you choose to use the UPnP service, you should apply the latest patches to ensure that you prevent the attacks I've described. To install the UPnP service, open the Add Or Remove Programs item in Control Panel, and click Add/Remove Windows Components. You'll find UPnP User Interface in the Networking Services item.

After you install UPnP, there are no additional configuration steps you need to take. However, you do need to install the patch. You'll find a detailed description of the problem and the patch in Microsoft Knowledge Base article Q315000:

```
http://support.microsoft.com/default.aspx?scid=kb;en-us;Q315000
```

This article includes links to the patch files. You can also access the updates through the Windows Update site.

Peer-to-Peer

New!

In the Advanced Networking Pack for Windows XP, Microsoft introduced a new feature called Peer-to-Peer Networking Infrastructure. This new component is a developer platform to facilitate creation of peer-to-peer (P2P) applications for information sharing, personal communication, real-time application collaboration, and other functions. The component is integrated into Windows XP with SP2 and can be added or removed through the Add Or Remove Programs applet in Control Panel.

When you add the Peer-to-Peer component in Windows XP, Setup adds the components to Windows XP that are necessary to support P2P applications designed for the Peer-to-Peer Networking Infrastructure. In addition, installing the component configures Windows Firewall to allow connections on port 3540 for Peer Name Resolution Protocol (PNRP) and port 3587 for Windows Peer-to-Peer Grouping. Both of these are added with scope for any computer, enabling connections from the Internet.

TIP I focus in this section on how to add the P2P component to Windows XP. For details on Microsoft's Peer-to-Peer Infrastructure and related technologies, see www.microsoft.com/windowsxp/p2p/default.mspx.

You'll find the Peer-to-Peer component in the Networking Services item in the Add Or Remove Programs applet. Simply add the component to add P2P support; there are no additional configuration requirements.

Chapter 27

Creating and Managing Database Connections

Windows XP, like other Windows platforms, can host databases and support connections from local applications and remote clients to those databases. For example, if you host a website on Windows XP to publish information on your intranet, you might connect a database to your website to allow users to browse or update the database through a web browser. You might also create a database connection on your computer to allow a local application to hook into the database. For example, perhaps you want Microsoft Excel to be able to easily reference information in a database.

Database connections are supported by Open DataBase Connectivity (ODBC). This chapter explores ODBC and explains how to configure and use ODBC connections. I'll include some code examples you can incorporate in your website to view and modify databases hosted by ODBC connections.

Because this book focuses on Windows XP, not Microsoft Office, this chapter focuses on creating ODBC connections to use with Internet Information Services (IIS) to enable remote clients to view and modify databases across the Web. For details on configuring and using ODBC with a local application, search the application's Help content for details.

Overview of ODBC

ODBC in effect serves as a transaction coordinator between a client and a database hosted on, in this case, a Windows XP computer. The client makes standard database calls to the ODBC driver on the server computer. The ODBC driver translates those calls into the format required by the hosted database and also massages the information coming from the database so it can be returned to the client. So, ODBC acts as a middleman between the client and the database.

An ODBC connection is defined by a Data Source Name (DSN). Windows XP offers three types of DSNs:

User DSN   A user DSN is visible only to the logon account that was active when the DSN was set up. Use this type of DSN when you want only your own logon account (or some other specific account) to be able to use the DSN and the underlying database.

System DSN   A system DSN is visible to local services and all users who log on to the system where the DSN is hosted. Use this type of DSN when you want to provide database connectivity to multiple local users and through IIS for web-based access.

File DSN   A file DSN can be used by any user who has the same ODBC driver installed. Generally, you use a file DSN when you want to create the same ODBC connection on multiple computers. The settings for a file DSN are stored in a file on the local computer.

NOTE   In this chapter I focus specifically on creating system DSNs because that's what you need to enable IIS to host a database for web access.

Perhaps the best way to understand ODBC is to set up a connection and put it to work. The next section explains how to set up DSNs.

Configuring ODBC Drivers and DSNs

You use the Data Sources applet in the Administrative Tools folder to create and manage DSNs and configure other ODBC properties. Figure 27.1 shows the ODBC Data Source Administrator.

FIGURE 27.1

Manage ODBC with the ODBC Data Source Administrator.

The first three tabs, User DSN, System DSN, and File DSN, let you create and manage each of the three types of DSNs. Each of these three tabs works much the same as the next, because there is no difference in how you configure the same type of ODBC driver for each DSN type. In other words, you create a user DSN or a system DSN for a Microsoft Access database the same way. The tab you use to create the DSN determines who has access to it.

You can configure most ODBC drivers through two dialog boxes. The main exception is the SQL Server driver, which uses a wizard for configuration. Many of the properties for an ODBC connection are common among the different ODBC driver types. Therefore, configuring one ODBC driver is much like configuring another. For that reason, I'll focus specifically in this chapter on two drivers: Microsoft Access and Microsoft SQL Server.

TIP   See Table 27.1 for an explanation of the options for each of the ODBC driver types.

Configuring a Microsoft Access ODBC Connection

Before you begin configuring an ODBC connection for a Microsoft Access database, first create the database, and then add fields to it as needed. The database need not contain any records. You can add records from a web interface that you develop later or add them in Access—it's your choice.

When the database is designed and saved to disk on the computer where the ODBC connection will be hosted, follow these steps:

1. Open the ODBC Data Source Administrator.

2. Click the System DSN tab, and click Add to open the Create New Data Source dialog box.

3. Click Microsoft Access Driver (*.mdb) in the list, and click Finish. The console then displays the ODBC Microsoft Access Setup dialog box shown in Figure 27.2.

4. In the Data Source Name box, type a name to describe the ODBC driver. Although you can use spaces in the name, don't do so—you'll avoid potential connection problems later.

5. Enter a description in the Description box; feel free to use spaces and any other characters you wish here.

6. Now it's time to select the database to be used for the driver. Click the Select button, browse to the location where you've saved the database, select it, and click OK.

7. In most cases, you'll want to protect the connection with a username and password, so click Advanced to open the Set Advanced Options dialog box (Figure 27.3). Enter a login name and password, and click OK.

FIGURE 27.2

Use the ODBC Microsoft Access Setup dialog box to add an Access DSN.

FIGURE 27.3

Set a username and password to protect the database.

That's all you need to set for most situations. See Table 27.1 for all the options for each ODBC driver. Table 27.2 lists advanced options.

TABLE 27.1: Common ODBC Driver Options

OPTION	DATABASE	USE / TIPS
Advanced	Access	Sets advanced options; see Table 27.2.
Approximate Row Count	dBase	Determines whether table sizes are approximated.
Buffer Size	Access, MS Oracle	Access: Specifies the buffer size for disk I/O; a larger size increases memory use but improves performance. Oracle: Specifies the size (bytes) of buffer that holds fetched data. The Oracle driver requires you to specify rows to fetch; the Microsoft driver returns enough rows to fill the buffer.
Collating Sequence	dBase, Paradox, FoxPro	Selected language affects sorting.
Compact	Access	Removes empty spaces in records to conserve space. Doesn't compact password-protected databases due to possible data loss or the inability to access the database.
Connect to Database in Read-Only Mode	Oracle	Enable the option to open the database in read-only mode, preventing changes.
Create	Access	Creates a new Access database compatible with Microsoft Access version 7.x or later.
Data Source Name	Access, dBase, Excel, MS Oracle, Oracle, Paradox, Text, FoxPro	Name for the data source.
Database Type	FoxPro	Either a Visual FoxPro database or Free Table directory, according to the type of data in the source.
Default	Text	Lists all files in the data-source folder.
Define Format	Text	Displays the Defined Text Format dialog box and specifies a file format for the data source.
Deleted	FoxPro	Includes deleted records in the data source.
Description	Access, dBase, Excel, MS Oracle, Oracle, Paradox, Text, FoxPro	Optional description for the driver instance.
Enforce ODBC DayOfWeek Standard	MS Oracle	Sets the result set to ODBC day-of-the-week format; Sunday=1 and Saturday=7. Deselect for Sunday=7 and Monday=1.

TABLE 27.1: Common ODBC Driver Options *(CONTINUED)*

OPTION	DATABASE	USE / TIPS
Exclusive	Access, dBase, Paradox, FoxPro	Specifies exclusive access to the database; locks the file for use by a single user. Deselect for shared mode.
Extension/Extensions List	Text	Shows file extensions displayed for the data source. Type an extension in the Extension ield, and click Add.
Fetch Data in Background	FoxPro	Improves performance by having data fetched in the background.
Include REMARKS in Catalog Functions	MS Oracle	Has the driver return Remarks columns for the SQLColumns() result set. Deselect to improve performance if not needed.
Include SYNONYMS in SQLColumns	MS Oracle	Has the driver return column information for Tables, Views, and Synonyms with a SQLColumns()API call. Deselect to improve response time.
Library	Oracle	Specifies the name of the translation library. Not supported on all versions.
Net Style	Paradox	Network style for this data source.
Null	FoxPro	Enables the driver to include null fields.
Option	Oracle	Specifies a numeric value passed to the translation library when the library is called by Oracle ODBC driver. Not supported on all versions.
Options	Access, dBase, Excel, Paradox, FoxPro	Displays the Driver section of the dialog box to show additional options.
Page Timeout	Access, dBase, Paradox	Specifies the amount of time an unused page remains in the buffer.
Path	FoxPro	Enter a FoxPro database path, or click Browse.
Prefetch Count	Oracle	Number of rows that the application can fetch at one time. Increasing this number increases the memory required to hold rows. Specify a value that matches the number of rows you want to see.
Read Only	Access, Excel	Prevents the database from being changed.
Repair	Access	Click to select and repair an Access database.
Rows to Scan	Excel	Integer from 1–32767 that defines the number of rows the driver will scan in the data when setting columns and column data types.

TABLE 27.1: Common ODBC Driver Options *(CONTINUED)*

OPTION	DATABASE	USE / TIPS
Select	Access	Browse for and select an Access database.
Select Directory	dBase, Excel, Paradox, Text	Path to the folder containing the database.
Select Indexes	dBase	Index file(s) to use with the data source.
Select Network Directory	Paradox	Specifies the network directory after you enter a username.
Select Workbook	Excel	Select the Excel file used as a data source.
Server/Service Name	MS Oracle	Oracle database from which the driver will retrieve data.
Show Deleted Rows	dBase	Select to show rows marked as deleted; deselect to hide deleted rows.
System Database	Access	Select a shared system database.
Translation	MS Oracle	Select an ODBC translator for connection. No translation is performed by default.
Use Current Directory	dBase, Excel, Paradox, Text	Select to make the application's current directory the directory from which the data source is opened.
User Name/User ID	MS Oracle, Oracle, Paradox	Specifies the account to be used to access the data source.
Version	dBase, Excel, Paradox	Select a client version for the connection.

TABLE 27.2: Advanced ODBC Driver Options

OPTION	DESCRIPTION
Login Name	Username for the data source if the connection requires authentication (recommended). The default password for Access is Admin.
Password	Password associated with the Login Name field. The default password for Access is an empty string.
DefaultDir	Default directory for the driver to use.
Driver	Enter a custom name for the driver, if desired.

TABLE 27.2: Advanced ODBC Driver Options *(CONTINUED)*

OPTION	DESCRIPTION
FIL	Specifies the file type of the data source. The default is MS Access for Microsoft Access.
ImplicitCommitSync	Specifies how changes that occur outside transaction are written to the database. With the default (Yes), the Access driver waits for commits in an internal/implicit transaction to be completed. This ensures that changes are written correctly to the database. This option impacts performance.
MaxBufferSize	Sets the same option for the data-transfer buffer as the Buffer Size option in the Setup dialog box.
MaxScanRows	Number of rows to be scanned when setting a column's data type based on existing data. Valid values are 1–16, with a default of 8. Use 0 to cause all rows to be scanned.
PageTimeout	Length of time (in tenths of a second) that an unused page remains in the buffer. The default is 0.5; the value must be greater than 0.
ReadOnly	Value of 1 makes the database read-only. A value of 0 allows database changes.
SafeTransactions	If 0, all transactions are committed immediately. When set to 1, all transactions are saved to disk only on a commit operation.
Threads	Number of background threads for the engine to use. Increase beyond the default value to improve performance for large or active database.
UserCommitSync	When Yes, the driver waits for commits in user-defined transactions to be completed. When set to No, one transaction can override another. Should be set to Yes in a multiuser environment; can be set to No to improve performance in a single-user environment.

Configuring a SQL Server ODBC Connection

If you have SQL Server running on the network, you can create an ODBC connection to a SQL database. The ODBC connection need not be hosted by the SQL Server. Instead, you can reference a database across the network. For example, you might configure a Windows XP Professional computer as a web server for the intranet. The web server would host the access pages and ODBC drivers for the database, which is located on a different server.

The ODBC Data Source Administrator provides a wizard for configuring a SQL Server data source. Follow these steps to configure a SQL Server data source:

1. Open the ODBC Data Source Administrator, and click the System DSN tab.

2. Click Add to open the Create New Data Source dialog box, select SQL Server, and click Finish.

3. In the first wizard page (Figure 27.4), enter a name for the data source in the Name field. This name appears in the Data Sources list in the DSN tab.

FIGURE 27.4
Enter a DSN name and
select the SQL Server.

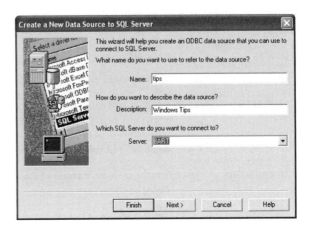

4. Specify an optional description in the Description field.

5. In the Server field, specify the IP address or name of the SQL Server computer or click the drop-down arrow and choose a server. Click Next.

6. In the second page (Figure 27.5), choose options using the following list as a guide:

FIGURE 27.5
Specify authentication
and connection options.

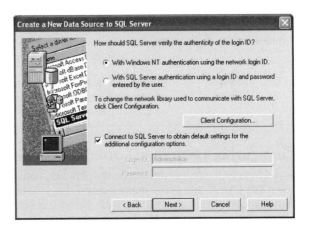

With Windows NT authentication using the network login ID   Select this option to have the ODBC driver request a trusted connection to the server. The driver uses the current client logon username and password to authenticate the request on the server. The specified username must have an association on the SQL Server to a SQL Server login ID.

With SQL Server authentication using a login ID and password entered by the user   Select this option to have the driver require the user to specify a SQL Server login ID and password for all connection requests.

Connect to SQL Server to obtain default settings for the additional configuration options
Select this option to have the driver connect to the SQL Server to obtain settings for the options in the remaining wizard pages. When you click Next, the driver connects to the specified SQL Server and presets many of the remaining options. Deselect this option to prevent the driver from connecting to the server to obtain settings.

Login ID/Password Specify the username you want the driver to use to connect to the specified SQL Server to retrieve settings for the remaining wizard pages. This login ID and the associated password aren't used for the client connections after the data source is created.

Client Configuration Click to open the Add Network Library Configuration dialog box shown in Figure 27.6. Use these options to specify the network configuration for the data connection. In most cases, you shouldn't have to use settings other than the defaults.

7. Click Next to show the third wizard page (Figure 27.7). Choose options using the following list as a guide:

FIGURE 27.6
Choose a protocol and set other network configuration options.

FIGURE 27.7
Specify the database and other options.

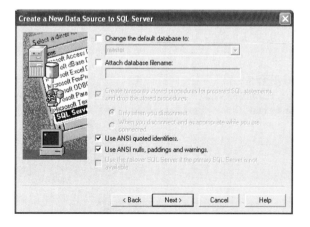

Change the default database to   Choose from this list to specify the database for the data source, overriding the default database for the specified login ID. Deselect this option to use the default database defined for the specified login ID.

Attach database filename   Specify the name of a primary file for an attachable database, which is used as the default database for the data source. Specify a full path and filename.

Create temporary stored procedures for prepared SQL statements and drop the stored procedures   Select this option to cause the driver to create temporary stored procedures to support the SQLPrepare ODBC function. Deselect the option if you don't want the driver to store these procedures.

Only when you disconnect   Select this option to have the stored procedures for the SQLPrepare function dropped only when the SQLDisconnect function is called. This reduces overhead but can lead to a build-up of temporary stored procedures. In situations where SQLPrepare calls are used extensively without disconnecting from the database, you shouldn't use this option.

When you disconnect and as appropriate while you are connected   Select this option to have stored procedures dropped when SQLDisconnect is called, SQLFreeHandle is called for the statement handle, SQLPrepare or SQLExecDirect is called to process a new SQL statement on the same handle, or a catalog function is called. Using this option adds more overhead but helps prevent a build-up of temporary stored procedures.

Use ANSI quoted identifiers   Enforce ANSI rules for quotation marks so that they can be used only for identifiers, including table and column names. Character strings must be enclosed in single quotes.

Use ANSI nulls, paddings, and warnings   Specify that the ANSI_NULLS, ANSI_WARNINGS, and ANSI_PADDINGS options are set on when the driver connects to the data source.

Use the failover SQL Server if the primary SQL Server is not available   Have the driver attempt connection to the failover server if supported by the primary SQL Server specified for the connection. If a connection is lost, the driver cleans up any current transaction and then attempts to reconnect to the primary server. Failing that, the driver attempts to connect to the failover server.

8. Click Next to open the final wizard page (Figure 27.8). Use the following list as a guide to choose options:

FIGURE 27.8
Specify the database and other options.

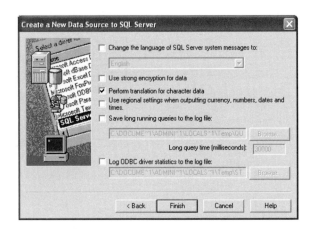

Change the language of SQL Server system messages to   If the SQL Server is configured to use multiple languages, choose from this list the language for system messages. The option is available only if more than one language is installed on the SQL Server.

Use strong encryption for data   Use this option to require SSL encryption between the client and server.

Perform translation for character data   If this option is selected, the driver converts ANSI strings sent between the client and server using Unicode. With this option enabled, the client computer must have the code page used by the SQL Server for translation to happen correctly. If this option is deselected, the driver performs no ANSI translation. If the client is using a different code page than the SQL Server, extended characters in ANSI strings could be interpreted incorrectly. However, if the client uses the same code page as the SQL Server, the extended characters will be interpreted correctly.

Use regional settings when outputting currency, numbers, dates, and times   Choose this option to have the driver use the client's regional settings to display currency, numbers, dates, and times. Use this setting only for client applications that display data, not for applications that process data.

Save long running queries to the log file   If this option is selected and a log file is specified, the driver logs any queries that exceed the value of the Long Query Time value.

Long query time (milliseconds)   Specify a value in milliseconds to define the threshold value for long queries. See the previous option.

Log ODBC driver statistics to the log file   Enable this option to have ODBC driver statistics logged. Specify the path to the log file.

Hooking Into ODBC from the Web

At this point, the ODBC driver is ready to begin handling connections through the DSN you just created. As I explained earlier in this chapter, I'll focus on web-based network access rather than on individual client applications. So, the next step is to build a set of web pages to hook into the database through the ODBC driver.

The great thing about ODBC is that it hides the database from the client. Without ODBC, you'd have to build database-specific web applications for each database type. With ODBC, you can use the same general structure to connect to, display, and modify a database.

Two of the most popular web development applications are Microsoft FrontPage and Macromedia Dreamweaver. Both of these applications provide an interface for defining database connections and building pages that display data. Before I explain how to build data access pages with them, I'll give you an example you can put to use right away. This sample will help you begin to understand what is involved in connecting to a database from a web page.

The following script is a hit counter for Active Server Pages (ASP) that you can use to record page hits on a website hosted by IIS, whether on Windows XP or on Windows Server:

```
' Hit counter by Jim Boyce, www.boyce.us
' Define the connection string for the database
connStr = "dsn=counter;uid=mycounter;pwd=mypassword;"
' Declare some variables to hold data
Dim clientIPAddress
```

```
Dim clientBrowser
Dim clientReferrer
Dim pageURL
' Get the client's IP address
clientIPAddress = Request.ServerVariables ("REMOTE_ADDR")
' Get the client's browser type
clientBrowser = Request.ServerVariables ("HTTP_USER_AGENT")
' Get the referring page from which the current page is accessed
clientReferrer = Request.ServerVariables ("HTTP_REFERER")
' Get the page being requested (the current page)
pageUrl = Request.ServerVariables ("HTTP_URL")
' Create a database connection object
set cn = Server.CreateObject("ADODB.Command")
' Open the connection using the connection string
cn.ActiveConnection = connStr
' Define a SQL command to insert data into the database
cn.CommandText = "INSERT INTO Hits (page, clientIPAddress, clientBrowser,
    clientReferrer) VALUES ("&"'"&pageURL&"'"&","&"'"&clientIPAddress&"'"&","&"
    '"&clientBrowser&"'"&","&"'"&clientReferrer&"'"&")"
' Execute the SQL command
cn.Execute
' Close the database connection
cn.ActiveConnection.Close
' Release the cn object to reclaim memory
set cn = nothing
```

TIP   For more information about the hit counter and to download an empty copy of the database, see www.boyce.us/articles/freecounter.asp.

The bits of this script that manipulate the database are few:

```
connStr = "dsn=counter;uid=mycounter;pwd=mypassword;"
set cn = Server.CreateObject("ADODB.Command")
cn.ActiveConnection = connStr
cn.CommandText = "INSERT INTO Hits (page, clientIPAddress, clientBrowser,
    clientReferrer) VALUES ("&"'"&pageURL&"'"&","&"'"&clientIPAddress&"'"&","&"'"
    &clientBrowser&"'"&","&"'"&clientReferrer&"'"&")"
cn.Execute
cn.ActiveConnection.Close
```

In a nutshell, you must specify the connection string, which includes the DSN name and the user account and password associated with the DSN (if any). Then, you create a connection object, open it, specify a SQL command string, execute the string, and close the connection. Depending on the purpose of your web application and database, you might perform several SQL commands before closing the connection.

TIP   You can take many other actions programmatically to access a database from an ODBC connection. For example, you can query the server for a list of DSNs, query the server for the list of tables in a database, and perform many other tasks that fall outside the scope of this chapter. If you're a beginner to ODBC and web development, you'll find a good start to database integration in the remaining sections of this chapter.

Now, let's look at how to add database connections in FrontPage and Dreamweaver.

Creating a Data-Access Page in Dreamweaver

Dreamweaver makes it relatively easy to add a data-access page, although its greater range of options makes the task a bit more difficult to accomplish than in, for example, FrontPage. However, Dreamweaver gives you lots of flexibility in setting up connections and includes several features that help you build relatively complex data-access pages with little effort.

In this example, I'll use an ASP page; but as you'll see in the steps, you can choose a different server platform, if needed. Follow these steps if you're using Dreamweaver MX 2004:

1. Open the site, and start a new ASP page.

2. Choose Window ➢ Databases to display the Databases window (Figure 27.9).

3. If you haven't already done so, set up the server model for the site: Click the site link to open the Site Definition dialog box, and then click Testing Server in the Category list (Figure 27.10). If the testing server is already specified, skip to step 7.

FIGURE 27.9
Use the Databases window to set up a connection.

FIGURE 27.10
Specify the testing server.

FIGURE 27.11
Specify settings to connect to the server.

4. From the Server Model drop-down list, choose the type of server on which the page will be hosted.

5. Select the type of access you have to the server, whether FTP or local/network. The dialog box changes to display additional options that vary according to the option you selected. Enter the data necessary to connect to the server (Figure 27.11). Click OK when you're finished.

6. Click the Document Type link in the Databases window, and choose the scripting language you're using.

7. Click the + icon button at upper left in the Databases window, and choose Data Source Name to open the Data Source Name dialog box (Figure 27.12).

FIGURE 27.12

Use the Data Source Name dialog box to set up a connection.

NOTE At this point, you can choose a DSN on the testing server or one on the local computer. I prefer to place the DSN on the server, get it running, and allow Dreamweaver to pull queries from the server. However, you may not be able to configure the ODBC connection right away; so, a workable alternative is to create the DSN on the local computer for development purposes, copy the database to the server, and create a DSN there when you're ready to publish the page.

8. In the Connection Name field, enter a descriptive name for the connection.

9. If you're using a server-based DSN, choose the option Using DSN On Testing Server, click the DSN button, select the existing DSN from the list in the resulting Select ODBC DSN dialog box, and click OK. If you're using a local DSN, choose the option Using Local DSN, and then choose the DSN from the Data Source Name drop-down list.

10. Enter the username and password for the DSN in the User Name and Password fields, and then click Test. If your settings are correct, you should receive a message that the connection was made successfully. If you don't, check your settings and try again.

11. Click OK to close the Data Source Name dialog box. The database will now appear in the Databases window, as shown in Figure 27.13.

TIP The following steps explain how to add a recordset to a page. If you're connecting to a DSN hosted by a Windows XP computer with SP2 installed and using the original release of Dreamweaver MX 2004, Dreamweaver won't be able to read the tables from the server. You can obtain a patched MMHTTPDB.JS script file from Macromedia to fix this problem and enable Dreamweaver to work with a DSN hosted on an SP2 machine. See www.macromedia.com/support to obtain the fix.

FIGURE 27.13
The database appears in
the Databases window.

FIGURE 27.13
The database appears in
the Databases window.

Next, you need to add a recordset (query) to the page. To do so, follow these steps:

1. Choose Window ➤ Bindings to display the Bindings window.

2. Click the + icon button, and choose Recordset to open the Recordset dialog box (Figure 27.14).

FIGURE 27.14
Use the Recordset dialog
box to create a recordset.

3. Change the default name in the Name field to something more descriptive to help you identify the contents of the recordset (optional).

4. Select the connection to the DSN from the Connection drop-down list.

5. Choose a table from the Table drop-down list.

6. To include all fields from the table, choose the All option in the Columns group. Or, choose Selected and then hold down Ctrl and click the fields you want included in the recordset.

7. Click Test to test the recordset. Dreamweaver displays a Test SQL Statement window with the results of the query (Figure 27.15). Click OK to close the window.

FIGURE 27.15

You can test the results of your query.

8. Click OK to close the Recordset dialog box.

At this point, the recordset appears in the Bindings window. Although you can drag a field from the recordset to a page, doing so will cause the page to display that field only for the first row in the recordset. It's more likely that you'll want to create a results page that displays the complete contents of the recordset. One method is to create a repeated region. To do so, drag a field to the page, and then click the field to select it. Choose Insert ➢ Application Objects ➢ Repeated Region to display the Repeat Region dialog box (Figure 27.16). Specify the number of records to display, or choose All records, and then click OK.

FIGURE 27.16

Use the Repeat Region dialog box to repeat a field on a page.

If you're trying to build a page that lists records in the database and provides links to a results page that displays the records, Dreamweaver makes it easy for you with a wizard. Start a new page, and then choose Insert ➢ Application Objects ➢ Master Detail Page Set to open the dialog box shown in Figure 27.17.

FIGURE 27.17
Add a master page with
the Insert Master-Detail
Page Set dialog box.

In the top half of the dialog box, specify the items you want included on the master page. From the Link To Detail From drop-down list, choose which item you want Dreamweaver to create a link to the record detail page. Then, in the bottom half of the dialog box, enter the name of a new results page in the Detail Page Name field. Dreamweaver will create the page for you when you click OK.

This concludes the primer on database connectivity with Dreamweaver. At this point, you've created a database connection, a recordset, and even a master-detail page set. You can build additional database connectivity into your site through the other options in the Insert ➤ Application Objects menu. Keep in mind that you can modify the pages that Dreamweaver creates automatically for you to suit your needs.

TIP   See the Dreamweaver documentation to learn more about building data-connected pages and sites.

Creating a Data-Access Page in FrontPage

FrontPage, like Dreamweaver, makes it relatively easy to create data-enabled pages for a website. You can use a DSN hosted on the local computer or on a remote computer. In this section, I'll explain how to connect to a DSN and build a data-enabled page with FrontPage.

The first point to understand is that FrontPage looks for a server for DSNs depending on the type of web you've opened. If you open a disk-based web, FrontPage looks to the local computer for DSNs. To work with a DSN on a remote server, you must open the web from that server—in other words, open it as a server-based web.

If you don't have a remote server set up yet but still want to develop the site or experiment with database integration, you can configure a DSN on the local computer and use it within a disk-based web for development. Then, when the site is ready to go live, copy the database to the target server, set up a system DSN on the server using the same properties as the local DSN (username, password, and so on), and publish the site to the server. The site should function properly, working from the DSN on the server.

TIP   When you work with a server-based web in FrontPage, all changes you make to a page or to the web as a whole are made live on the site. This is one reason why in many situations it's best to work from a local DSN and disk-based web and then move the database and DSN to the server just prior to publishing the web.

As with Dreamweaver, FrontPage offers several ways to add database integration to a page, including coding the page manually. Since this is an introduction, I'll focus here on using a wizard to build a database query results page:

1.   Create the DSN on the remote server (for a server-based web) or on the local computer (for a disk-based web).

2.   Open the web, and Choose Tools ➢ Web Settings to open the Web Settings dialog box. Click the Database tab.

3.   Click Add to open the New Database Connection dialog box (Figure 27.18).

FIGURE 27.18
Use the New Database Connection dialog box to create a connection to a DSN.

4.   Choose System Data Source On Web Server, and click Browse. In the System Data Sources On Web Server dialog box, click the DSN you want to use, and click OK.

5.   Click Advanced, and enter the username and password values for the DSN in the Advanced Connection Properties dialog box. Click OK.

6.   Click OK to close the New Database Connection dialog box, and then click OK to close the Web Settings dialog box.

7.   Open an existing page or add a new page to the web, and give the page an `.asp` file extension.

8.   Choose Insert ➢ Database ➢ Results to start the Database Results Wizard.

9.   Choose the option Use An Existing Database Connection. From the drop-down list, select the connection you created in steps 2 through 6. Click Next.

10.   From the Record Source drop-down list, choose an existing table if you want to pull from a table, or choose an existing query if you want to use a query in the database as the source for the data. Or, you can specify a custom SQL query against the database. To do so, choose Custom Query,

and click Edit to display the Custom Query dialog box (Figure 27.19). Click in the SQL Statement box, modify the SQL statement as desired, and then click OK.

FIGURE 27.19
Build your own query in the Custom Query dialog box.

11. The next wizard page lets you choose which fields from the database to include on the page. Click Edit List to add or remove fields. Click More Options to display the More Options dialog box (Figure 27.20), where you can create a filter for the query, set record ordering, limit the number of records returned (or disable the limit), and specify the message that is displayed if no records are found that match. Click OK when you're finished, and then click Next.

12. The Step 4 of 5 wizard page lets you choose how the data will appear on the page (Figure 27.21). The data can be displayed in a table, as a list, or in a drop-down list. Use the latter when you want to include items from a database in a form.

FIGURE 27.20
Set additional options in the More Options dialog box.

FIGURE 27.21
Choose how the data will be displayed.

13. The final page of the wizard gives you the option of either showing all records together or grouping them (you specify the number of records per group). This option isn't available if you're displaying the data in a drop-down list. Click Finish to complete the wizard.

You now have enough background in FrontPage database operations to create connections to DSNs and build simple query-results pages. With some experimentation and the FrontPage Help documentation, you should be able to broaden your skills to include using database fields in forms and working with data in other ways.

Overview of Advanced ODBC Options

To round out this chapter on ODBC, let's take a brief look at some of the additional options you can configure. To configure these settings, open the ODBC Data Source Administrator. You'll find the following tabs in addition to those already discussed:

TIP   I don't cover the advanced options in detail in this chapter because you should seldom need to use them. I mention them here mainly so you know they exist if you ever need them.

Drivers   This tab lets you view the ODBC drivers that are installed on your system. You can't add or remove drivers here; the tab serves only to let you view information about installed drivers.

Tracing   This tab lets you configure logging for ODBC. You can specify the location of the log file, specify additional tracing options, and start or stop tracing.

Connection Pooling   This tab lets you specify whether ODBC drivers can reuse open connection handles to the database server. Pooling can improve performance by reducing the overhead involved in establishing new connections. By default, Oracle and SQL Server connections are pooled but all others aren't.

Part 6

Internet Applications and Services

In this section:

Chapter 28

Optimizing Internet Explorer

Microsoft Internet Explorer 6.0 is ready to use the minute you finish installing it, which occurs by default. But like so much else in Windows, computing, and even life, Internet Explorer may work a great deal better for you and your specific needs if you explore options for optimization and advanced configuration.

In this chapter, I'll take you through some of the options available to you for advanced configuration, focusing on features such as AutoComplete and Content Advisor as well as security functions. Then we'll finish with a close look at how Windows XP Service Pack 2 changes and improves Internet Explorer.

TIP Throughout this chapter, you'll make most adjustments by opening the Internet Options properties sheet (Tools ➤ Internet Options).

Optimizing IE Advanced Settings

When web browsers first arrived on the scene after the general birth of the World Wide Web in 1993, we were happy to just have them load a web page. Now, especially in the Windows environment, the browser has become the window not just to the rest of the world, but to the Desktop. With this comes a need for more functionality and more options.

Many of the options you can configure in Internet Explorer 6 are self-explanatory. This section will focus on some less-covered but highly useful tools you can enable and configure, such as AutoComplete for assisting with website addresses and web form field entry, and certain advanced options you can set to improve the overall performance, security, or efficiency of the browser.

Working with AutoComplete

The AutoComplete feature has been around for a few IE versions now. Its name tells you the function it performs: it tries to automatically complete an entry for you. This entry can be a URL for a website or for a drive and folder on your system, or anything you might type into a field on a form on a website, such as your home or work address, phone number, e-mail address, or username.

AutoComplete works—when enabled—by recording entries you have typed before and storing them in encrypted format as part of your browser history. When you return to a site or folder and begin typing the word, phrase, or address again, AutoComplete performs an ultra-fast search of like entries and expands the field to reveal located possible matches. You can either continue typing or click one of the choices AutoComplete presents to you, as shown in Figure 28.1.

FIGURE 28.1
AutoComplete presents a list of possible matches.

The vast majority of the time, enabling AutoComplete can be a real time-saver, since it will try to complete not just web addresses but frequently used usernames and passwords, too, such as you might use to log on to a secured and/or subscription website.

However, just as with other such convenience options, you run into obvious security problems. If you're logging onto your company's secured website to work from home, enabling AutoComplete means that anyone else who sits down at your system—or connects to your XP system remotely— could access the same site just as easily. For an online vendor site, the username and password may be tied to a credit card, Social Security number, or other information, which could make it very easy for someone else at your keyboard to access and "borrow" it.

Also, if you're concerned with privacy but don't happen to clear your AutoComplete entries or IE history before someone else uses your system, they'll be presented with your AutoComplete match list, which might give them a clue where you've visited, along with any phone numbers, addresses, and so on that have been recorded in the course of your work.

NOTE Website designers who use IIS and who want to suppress a user's ability to use AutoComplete for usernames and passwords when visiting their sites should check out Article Q290641 in the Microsoft Knowledge Base at http://search.support.microsoft.com.

ENABLING OR DISABLING AUTOCOMPLETE

In IE6, AutoComplete is enabled by default, while a subcomponent of it called Inline AutoComplete (used to try to finish a line based on best matches if the user has previously typed a similar line) is not.

To disable AutoComplete for most of what you do (websites), From Internet Explorer, choose Tools ➢ Internet Options. On the Content tab, click AutoComplete, and uncheck all the boxes.

To enable the use of the Inline AutoComplete feature, choose Tools ➢ Internet Options and, from the Browsing group on the Advanced tab, click to check Use Inline AutoComplete. Click OK until you exit.

MODIFYING AUTOCOMPLETE SETTINGS

You have some options, although limited, for when and how AutoComplete works. For example, as shown in the previous section, turning it off for web addresses turns off its match feature for those items, so it won't try to complete them for you. You can do the same for forms, as well as usernames and passwords, by following the instructions for disabling in the preceding section and choosing which options you want to keep.

DELETING AUTOCOMPLETE ENTRIES

Entries within the IE history are kept in a single store, so there is no clean, neat way to remove individual entries expeditiously. You basically have two options: clear all of AutoComplete's recorded entries, or remove them one at a time from the match list as it appears.

To empty all of the entries, choose Tools ➢ Internet Options; then, from the History group on the General tab, click Clear History. Click OK.

You can remove individual entries from the AutoComplete list, with one caveat. This can be done only while you're in the process of typing information on a web-based form or username-password field on a website. As you work, and AutoComplete presents you with a match list, locate and select the entry you want to delete and then press the Delete key.

Configuring Advanced Settings

The Advanced Settings tab under Tools ➢ Internet Options (Figure 28.2) lets you specifically configure your browser to use (or to prevent the use of) various supported options, including these major categories:

Accessibility   These are special options for those who don't download images, who use alternative input methods, or who have a physical limitation.

Browsing   Various options are included here, including whether to notify the user when a download is complete, whether to underline links, and so on.

HTTP 1.1 Settings   Options here are for compatibility with an earlier standard.

FIGURE 28.2
When a website doesn't act as expected, this tab is the best place to check for potential problems.

TIP   IE previously included a Java virtual machine (VM) from Microsoft that enabled IE to run Java applets. On computers where the old Microsoft VM is installed, you'll see a Microsoft VM section in the Advanced settings. However, on most later systems, the Microsoft VM section is absent. If you need to run Java applets in IE (many sites use Java), browse to `http://java.com/en/index.jsp` to download Sun's Java VM.

Multimedia   Check here for entries regarding audio and graphics related to websites and how IE handles them.

Printing   Click to check if you want to print background images from websites.

Search From The Address Bar   Indicate how to handle web searches conducted from here (whether to try to make the closest match to what you typed).

Security   These options are discussed in the next section.

Optimizing Internet Explorer Security

Considering the breadth of the Internet along with the vast number of different types of files that can be run or opened through the browser, it makes sense that security in Internet Explorer takes a categorized approach to how secured options should be handled, based on the type of website or file.

IE does this by dividing its range into distinct zones, each of which can be configured differently depending on the level of restriction desired. You can add sites to these zones so that they can be covered by the specific rules configured for that zone.

In this section, we'll tackle zones, talk about cookie management as administered by IE6, and step through the enabling and configuration of Content Advisor, which can prevent the browser from accessing specific sites or types of sites.

Content Zones and Security Settings

Internet Explorer 6 supports four different zones, each of which has its own security settings that you can configure for individual preferences and needs:

Internet   This zone offers settings for generalized Internet use. It applies to all sites that you haven't assigned to another zone.

Local Intranet   This zone includes specific websites and pages that are part of an intranet (internal web network).

Trusted Sites   These sites are designated as ones that should be safe (containing no offensive or damaging content).

Restricted Sites   Sites in this zone may contain either offensive or damaging content.

All of these security zones can be user-configured to adjust the security level from virtually none to high. Each zone can be configured differently, if desired (and it frequently is).

ADJUSTING IE SECURITY ZONE SETTINGS

You can adjust your IE security zones on the Internet Options Security tab (Figure 28.3), following these instructions:

1. From Internet Explorer, select Tools ➢ Internet Options.

FIGURE 28.3

Customize your IE security zones.

2. Select the Security tab.

3. Click a zone, and then click Custom Level.

4. In the Security Settings window, you can click to select individual options (Disable, Enable, Prompt before doing) under each listing, such as ActiveX downloads, file downloads, and more.

5. Click OK until you exit, or return to step 3 to repeat this operation for another zone.

NOTE   From step 3, you can also choose Default Level, which restores the zone to its default security status. Likewise, at the bottom of the window described in step 4, in the Reset Custom Settings section, you can click the drop-down list box to choose your desired security level, and then click Reset. Doing so clears your previously configured security back to default levels.

ADDING SITES TO (AND REMOVING SITES FROM) A SECURITY ZONE

You can't add sites under the Internet zone, but you can add sites to the other zones. Adding a site to a zone causes that site to be treated with the settings associated with the specified zone.

To add a site to a zone, or to remove one you've added, follow these steps:

1. Open the Security tab of the Internet Options dialog box.

2. Click the desired web content zone, and click Sites.

3. In the resulting dialog box, to add a site, type the desired web address under Add This Web Site To The Zone, and click Add. The URL you typed now appears in the list of sites for the zone.

   Or, to remove a site, select the URL you want to remove from the Web Sites list, and click Remove.

4. Click OK.

NOTE   One zone differs from these instructions: the Local Intranet zone has an intervening screen of options specific to sites that may be available on your network or intranet. To add sites to (or remove sites from) this zone, click Sites, and on the Local Intranet screen, click Advanced to reach the add/remove screen.

Working with Advanced Security Settings

When we looked at the Advanced tab under Internet Options earlier in this chapter (Figure 28.2), you saw that some security settings are available for configuration. Now let's examine the terminology provided here, to make sure you understand the implications of these settings.

For example, when options refer to *certificates*, it's important to realize that many (usually commercial) websites like Microsoft and others use security certificates to help identify them as a trusted source. These certificates are issued by an Internet certification authority, such as VeriSign, to attest that a site or a file you download from such a site is from the right source (and not a destructive entity trying to masquerade as a vendor you'd trust). This system isn't foolproof, since someone a few years ago managed to get a certificate issued to him in the name of a company with which he had no association.

The option identified as Signatures On Downloaded Programs refers to a unique digital signature attached to many types of files that try to verify the author/creator of a file. Visual Basic for Applications, for example, allows you to digitally sign code you develop for Office XP and other applications. IE lets a user establish a trust relationship based on that digital signature, always permitting such a signed file to be downloaded even if others are blocked.

SSL refers to Secure Sockets Layer, a special protocol used with online vendors, financial organizations, and subscription-only sites to try to prevent online snoopers from attempting to steal unsecured personal or financial information you may send through the browser. An SSL-enabled website transaction is considered secure and is subject to 128-bit encryption.

Managing Cookies

Cookies are text files containing a (usually) small store of information related to who you are and the areas you may have visited on a particular website. This information is passed to your browser from the web server hosting a website you visit and stored on your system for later retrieval.

For example, if you visited the *New York Times* website to read articles, cookies there might store information about which articles you've already read, so that when you revisit, you can tell (by a change in color) whether you've read a particular article. Other cookies are used to pass administrative access to a particular person to work on a secured website.

Cookies are a controversial topic, because many people choose not to have anything on their systems that could track and identify their Internet usage. They feel cookies are an intrusion forced onto their systems, and they block them at all costs.

Usually, cookies are fairly innocuous in nature (letting a site identify you so it can greet you by name or offer selected preferences), although the information data store about you that's possibly being kept by vendors who employ cookies on their sites may not be so harmless. However, the vendors' accumulation of data about you is more frequently tied to your particular viewing or spending habits and other information they can glean from how you use their site.

Let's go through the cookie-management features of Internet Explorer 6.

WARNING   Some sites will block you from accessing parts of the website or the entire website if you choose to block all cookies.

Adjusting Cookie Security

By default, Windows XP is configured to handle the acceptance or rejection of a cookie based on the level of security you've set. This runs the range from having cookie management turned off (Accept All Cookies), from Low through High, to Block All Cookies.

To adjust your overall cookie security level, open the Privacy tab of the Internet Options (Figure 28.4). Move the slider bar up to increase the security level or down to decrease it (text to the right tells you the significance of each level).

TIP   Click Import to import a set of cookies from another source.

Overriding Windows XP Cookie Management

You have the option of overriding Windows XP's designed (by security level) method of handling cookies. To do so, click Advanced on the Privacy tab. In the next screen, click to check Override Automatic Cookie Handling.

You then have the option to choose from the following settings, for both first-party (special to you) and third-party cookies (a third-party cookie is offered to you from a website you're visiting but is actually sent by a third party, such as another vendor or company):

Accept Automatically receive the cookie.

Block Automatically refuse the cookie.

Prompt Ask before accepting.

If desired, click to check Always Allow Session Cookies to let IE cache session cookies. Click OK to return to Internet Options.

But what if you frequently visit websites that need a different cookie security level than you configure for most of the sites you browse? Internet Explorer allows you to bypass the regular security level on a site-by-site basis. You can do this as follows:

1. From Internet Explorer, select Tools ➢ Internet Options.

2. Select the Privacy tab. In the Web Sites section, click Edit.

3. Under Per Site Privacy Actions, type the name of the website, and then click either Allow (if you normally have cookie security set to a high level but want to change it for this site) or Block (if you normally set security very low but you specifically want to reject cookies from a particular site). Click OK.

NOTE From this same window, you can remove one site on your existing list or remove all sites.

Working with Content Advisor

Content Advisor has also been with us in Internet Explorer for some time, devised as an effort (mostly) to try to keep younger or sensitive eyes from getting access to unwanted content.

Like most content watchdog programs, such as CYBERSitter and Net Nanny, the idea is to develop guidelines for what types of content are deemed acceptable, and then to allow the user to visit only those sites that meet or exceed the configured guidelines (sort of like the movie rating system here in the U.S.). Also like most programs, Content Advisor works only as well as it is configured and managed. This means that if you're a parent using Content Advisor to try to keep your kids out of sexually oriented sites (or an employer trying to do the same for people working in the office), you need to supplement the use of this tool with real monitoring, so that you can catch sites your children manage to access around your guidelines and then change your rules to fit.

When you configure Content Advisor for use, you must provide a supervisor's password, and you must use that password whenever you make changes to the configuration.

Enabling and Configuring Content Advisor

Let's go through the process of enabling Content Advisor and then configuring it for the job you want it to do. One word of warning before we start: be prepared to go back and adjust your ratings later, as needed. You may have to tweak it a bit before you find the right level of access balanced with restriction.

To set up Content Advisor for use, follow these steps:

1. In IE, choose Tools ≻ Internet Options.

2. From the Content tab, under Content Advisor, click Enable. (If you already have Content Advisor enabled, click Settings, and then type the supervisor password.)

3. In the Content Advisor window, select the Ratings tab.

4. Click to select a category (Language, Nudity, Sex, or Violence), and then move the slider bar to the right to reduce the exclusion level for that category (as you move the slider, the screen informs you what each level covers) or to the left to increase the level.

NOTE   Click More Info from the Ratings tab to see additional detailed information about each rating level and how these ratings are determined.

5. Move to the Approved Sites tab, and provide the URL of any websites to allow and the conditions for each (Always Allow or Never Allow) or click Remove to remove a website already on the list.

6. Move to the General tab, where you can set user options (such as allowing users to view all nonrated websites), create a supervisor's password, or find more information or configure options under Ratings Systems.

7. Move to the Advanced tab, and select, if desired, a ratings bureau (an organization that creates and manages rating system lists) to use in helping you secure your browser from unwanted sites. You can also import Platform for Internet Content Selection (PICS) rules here.

8. Click OK to close the Content Advisor properties.

TIP If the Settings button under Content Advisor is grayed out, this indicates Content Advisor hasn't been enabled.

Resetting a Lost Content Advisor Password

What happens when you forget your Content Advisor password? It's probably no overstatement that thousands of people uninstall or reinstall IE, trying vainly to disable the Content Advisor feature and allow them to work without limitations.

The by-the-book process, from Microsoft, is to call the company: they'll walk you through the fix. You can't scream at them for this, since Content Advisor was created to help keep children (among others) from visiting sites that might contain inappropriate material. Telling everyone how to reset the password would defeat the whole purpose of having it.

But let's cut to the chase, so to speak, by following these steps to reset your Content Advisor password when needed:

1. Load RegEdit.

2. Locate and double-click the key identified as

   `HKEY_LOCAL_MACHINE\Software\Microsoft\Windows\CurrentVersion\Policies\Ratings`

3. Delete the key value.

4. Exit RegEdit.

5. Use Windows Explorer or another method to look in your *%systemroot%*`\system` folder, and right-click the `ratings.pol` file. Select Rename, and rename this file to **`ratings.old`**.

6. Shut down and restart the system.

7. When the system is back up, launch Internet Explorer.

8. Choose Tools ➢ Internet Options.

9. Select the Content tab, and click Enable (or Disable) Ratings.

10. When prompted, type in a new password, and click OK.

Changes in Internet Explorer for Service Pack 2

New! Service Pack 2 for Windows XP makes several changes and enhancements to IE to improve usability and security. This section provides an overview of these changes and enhancements.

Pop-Up Blocking

SP2 adds a pop-up blocker to IE. When a page is blocked, the Information Bar (a new element that appears between the toolbars and the page area) displays an informational message about the blocked page. You can click the Information Bar to view pop-up blocker settings for IE. You can also choose Tools ➢ Pop-Up Blocker ➢ Pop-Up Blocker Settings to display the Pop-Up Blocker Settings dialog box (Figure 28.5).

FIGURE 28.5

Use the Pop-Up Blocker Settings dialog box to configure pop-up blocking.

In the upper half of the dialog box, you can enter the URL for a website from which you don't want the pop-up blocker to block pop-up windows. For example, if you visit a site that uses pop-up windows to display information you want to see, you need to add the site's URL here.

Although the FAQ associated with the link on the Pop-Up Blocker Settings dialog box indicates that you can view a blocked pop-up by clicking the Information Bar and choosing Show Blocked Pop-Up, the command doesn't appear to exist. However, you can click the Information Bar and choose Temporarily Allow Pop-Ups, and then refresh the page to view any pop-ups. Or, choose Always Allow Pop-Ups From This Site after clicking the Information Bar to add the site to the Allowed sites list.

You can also configure the blocking level from the Pop-Up Blocker Settings dialog box. From the Filter Level drop-down list, choose the level of blocking you want. Use the Notifications And Filter Level group to optionally have IE play a sound when a pop-up is blocked, and to enable or disable the Information Bar for pop-ups. If you deselect the option Show Information Bar When A Pop-Up Is Blocked, IE won't display the Information Bar for blocked pop-ups.

Internet Explorer Information Bar

The IE Information Bar is new in SP2. As I explained in the previous section, the Information Bar appears when IE blocks a pop-up and gives you access to the pop-blocker settings. The Information Bar also appears at other times, including when a site

◆ Tries to open a pop-up window

◆ Attempts to install an ActiveX control

◆ Attempts to download a file to your computer

◆ Attempts to run active content on your computer

◆ Tries to run an ActiveX control in an unsafe manner

When the Information Bar does appear, you can click it to get more information about the action that IE blocked. For example, when a site tries to install an ActiveX control, you can click the Information Bar and direct IE to allow the ActiveX control to be installed.

To configure the Information Bar, open IE and choose Tools ➢ Internet Options, click the Security tab, and then click Custom Level. Then, choose an option for each of the Information Bar actions based on the list in Table 28.1.

TABLE 28.1:   Options for the Information Bar

INFORMATION BAR ACTION	SETTING
Pop-up blocker	Show Information Bar When A Pop-Up Is Blocked
Downloads	Automatic Prompting For File Downloads
ActiveX controls	Automatic Prompting For ActiveX Controls

Add-On Management and Crash Detection

Add-ons for IE extend IE by adding features not found in the core browser, such as the capability to view other types of files, run Java applets, play media, and perform additional tasks. SP2 adds a new feature to IE to make it easier to view the add-ons installed for IE and to manage those add-ons. To manage add-ons, open IE, and choose Tools ➢ Manage Add-ons to display the Manage Add-ons dialog box (Figure 28.6).

By default, the Manage Add-ons dialog box shows only those add-ons that are currently loaded in IE. To view all add-ons, choose the option Add-ons That Have Been Used By Internet Explorer from the Show drop-down list.

You can also enable or disable add-ons using this dialog box. To do so, click an add-on, and then click Disable or Enable in the Settings area. Some add-ons can also be updated; if the add-on supports updating, the Update ActiveX button becomes available when you click the add-on. Click this button to start an update check for the item, and if available, download the update.

FIGURE 28.6
Manage IE add-ons with the Manage Add-ons dialog box.

In addition to the new management interface, IE also provides better crash protection for add-ons. When possible, IE will detect a problem with an add-on and give you the option of disabling it.

Additional Security Enhancements

SP2 incorporates several security enhancements in addition to those I've already mentioned. These changes and enhancements include the following:

Local machine zone lockdown SP2 locks down the local machine zone with additional security restrictions to help prevent exploits that attempt to elevate privileges and gain access to the local file system and other local resources.

MIME handling To mitigate exploits from downloaded files, SP2 enables IE to perform MIME sniffing to attempt to determine file type based on bit signature rather than file extension. IE can then block execution of a file, potentially avoiding a virus infection or other attack. In addition, IE with SP2 won't elevate the privileges of a file if the file's application (as defined by its MIME type) is unable to load the file.

Download protection SP2 adds several group policy settings that administrators can use to control how and when IE allows file downloads. These policies are located in the Administrative Templates\Windows Components\Internet Explorer\Security Features\Restrict File Download branch. The policies here let you specify which processes can download files and whether IE prompts on download. SP2 also provides a more consistent user interface for prompting about file downloads.

Binary behaviors and *BindToObject* mitigation   Binary behaviors allow site developers to dynamically modify HTML tags and resulting behavior, without exposing the underlying code on the page as a script. Binary behaviors can be used to exploit systems through malicious web code. By default, IE blocks binary behaviors in the Restricted Sites zone. SP2 also applies the ActiveX security model to all situations where URL binding is used to create an instance of and initialize an object, which mitigates several IE exploits.

Object caching   IE with SP2 no longer allow a web page to access objects that were cached from another site, which can help prevent exposure of user data.

Window restrictions   In addition to controlling pop-up windows, IE with SP2 also imposes certain other window restrictions to help improve security. For example, IE won't let a window open outside of the viewable area of the desktop; this change prevents a malicious site from hiding content from the user. In addition, IE with SP2 always enables the status bar for all windows.

Zone-elevation blocks   IE with SP2 prevents the security context for any link on a page from being higher than the overall security context of the root URL. In addition, JavaScript navigation is blocked where the security context is absent.

Untrusted publishers   IE with SP2 now offers users the capability to block all signed content from specific publishers. This feature blocks the content without repeated prompts and also blocks installation of code without valid signatures.

Group Policy Additions

As I briefly mentioned in the previous section, SP2 adds several new group policy settings to let administrators control security aspects of IE. You can set these policies either through machine (Computer Configuration) or user (User Configuration) policies. The policies are located in the Administrative Templates\Windows Components\Internet Explorer\Security Features branch.

In large part, these new group policies enable administrators to define restrictions for specific processes to control the actions in IE that those processes can perform. For example, the settings in the Restrict File Download branch determine whether automatic prompting is enabled for file downloads that aren't initiated by the user.

Each of the new security policy branches contains three policies:

Process List   Use this policy to specify a list of processes (based on the process executable name) to which the policy applies.

Internet Explorer Processes   This policy controls the security behavior for processes started by IE.

All Processes   This policy applies the security settings to all processes.

Chapter 29

Outlook Express

Outlook Express is the component of Internet Explorer that allows you to send and receive both e-mail and Usenet newsgroup messages.

When you set up your e-mail account here, a wizard guides you through the steps. You supply the necessary information, such as username and password, as well as mail server names, which you usually determine from previous account settings or obtain from your e-mail provider.

With this kind of ease, we'll turn our attention to slightly more advanced Outlook Express configuration issues, such as creating and managing more than one identity, migrating messages from different mailer software, and setting up special other types of e-mail accounts—such as the free, web-based Hotmail or online service accounts—to send and receive messages through Outlook Express instead.

Account Management in Outlook Express

In this section, I'll take you through transferring data (addresses, messages, settings) from a different e-mail program, such as Eudora, into your new base of operations in Outlook Express (OE). Then you'll learn about establishing and using additional identities under OE to help you manage situations in which more than one user will be using it for e-mail.

Importing Accounts and Messages

All too often, changing PCs—or even installing a new hard disk in one PC—means you have to either start fresh with your e-mail or go through a moderately complicated process to restore your old settings and messages for use under the newly configured e-mail program.

OE automates this process in many ways through its Import function, allowing you to bring mail account settings, address book entries, and messages (both e-mail and newsgroup-based) into it using a few simple steps. You can import from all the major mailer programs, including Microsoft Outlook and Microsoft Exchange, as well as Netscape Communicator and Eudora (and export to these formats, as well).

TIP   What if you have an address book or other entries stored in text format or available only in a incompatible mailer program? Comma-delimited (.csv) text files can be imported using the same processes described in the next few sections. For other incompatible mailers, export your address book and other data in text or .csv format, and then try to import it into OE.

IMPORTING ACCOUNT SETTINGS

Account settings specify how Outlook Express communicates with your mail servers (both the outgoing e-mail's Simple Mail Transfer Protocol [SMTP] and the incoming e-mail's Post Office Protocol [POP]).

Information provided within these settings includes the following:

- Username and password

- E-mail identity (usually, *username@provider*.com)

- Names of the SMTP and POP servers

- Any special accommodations (such as requiring logon authentication)

To import account settings from your currently installed and configured mailer software, do this:

1. In Outlook Express, choose File ➢ Import ➢ Mail Account Settings.

2. When prompted, select the appropriate mailer program to use as the source of the mail account settings you wish to import. Click Next.

3. The mail settings for the other mailer's account are displayed. You can then do either of the following:

   - Click Change Settings and follow the wizard to make any necessary changes to the existing account settings.

   - Click Accept Changes to accept them as displayed.

4. Click Next, and then click Finish.

The account you imported should now be displayed under Tools ➢ Accounts ➢ Mail.

If your prior mail account is stored elsewhere (for example, on another system) using Outlook Express, follow these steps:

1. On the old system, load Outlook Express.

2. Go to Tools ➢ Accounts, and select the Mail tab.

3. Choose the desired mail account (if more than one exists), and click Export. Click OK to finish.

4. Locate the file OE exported the accounts to (a file ending in .iaf), and copy it to the system with the new OE installation.

5. From OE on this machine, go to Tools ➢ Accounts, and select the Mail tab.

6. Click Import, and specify the location of the .iaf file you just exported. Click OK.

IMPORTING ADDRESS BOOK ENTRIES

These steps permit you to import your Address Book from another mailer into OE:

1. In OE, click the address book icon.

2. From Address Book, choose File ➤ Import ➤ Other Address Book. (If you're importing the contents of another Windows Address Book (`.wab`) file, choose Address Book (WAB) instead.)

3. Locate and select the other address book you want to bring into Outlook Express, and click Open.

4. You are prompted to select the type of address book. Once you've done so, click Import.

IMPORTING MAIL MESSAGES

If you're anything like me, your mail software becomes something of an historical vault for communications. I frequently back up the message base, and I always transfer messages from one mailer to another when I either switch computers or add a new mailer to one of the systems in my office.

But before you get down to the basics of message migration, here's a recommendation to consider: If your current mail software has a Compact or Condense feature to clean up spaces in the message store index, run it before you import the message store into Outlook Express.

TIP   Where possible, perform manual housekeeping on your current message base (and address book) to remove advertising and other material you don't want to follow you.

Now, to import messages from your previous mailer into OE, follow these steps:

1. Choose File ➤ Import ➤ Messages.

2. In the Select Program window, choose the program from which you want to import messages, and click Next. Verify your selection, and click Next again.

3. Select either Import All Folders (to import every folder available in the other mailer) or Select Folders (to choose from specific folders). Click Next, and then click Finish.

Using and Managing Identities in Outlook Express

When you launch OE for the first time, part of the configuration process involves creating an identity for you. An identity in OE is much like a user profile, storing information specific to the person identified by the label.

With OE, more than one identity can be established to allow more than one user (or even one user who wants to maintain different accounts and settings under more than one identity) to use the mailer. It can be used by two or more people sharing a single copy of OE on a PC at home or at work. This saves time and foul-ups, because without multiple-identity support, you'd have the pesky issues of manually changing names and mail accounts each time you sent mail on an e-mail account other than your default (primary) account.

The primary identity in OE—the one loaded by default when OE launches and used by default when an application doesn't ask which identity to use for sending mail—is called the *main identity*. Each subsequent identity is labeled by whatever name you provide for it when you add the new identity.

Unlike user profiles, you don't have to log off the Desktop to let another person log in to send e-mail. You can switch identities right from OE, do your mail, and switch back to the first person with just a few pop-up windows prompting you to choose.

Each identity gets its own

◆ Set of folders, such as Inbox

◆ Subfolders (if you create them)

◆ List of contacts

◆ User settings (under Tools ➢ Options)

The following steps allow you to establish another identity under OE. If you need more than one, repeat the steps:

1. Choose File ➢ Identities ➢ Add New Identity.

2. In the New Identity window, type in the name you want to use for the new identity. If desired, click to check Require A Password.

Once the identity has been created (instantly), you'll be asked if you want to switch to it.

To switch to an identity that has already been created, choose File ➢ Switch Identity. In the Switch Identities window, select the identity to which you would like to switch, and click OK.

NOTE   If you respond Yes to the prompt asking "Do you want to switch identities?" immediately after you create one, you'll be asked for information about this new identity's mail account and Internet connection.

Outlook Express Changes in Service Pack 2

New!

Service Pack 2 adds a set of features to OE to improve security and do a better job of blocking spam. For example, like Microsoft Outlook 2002 and later, OE blocks external HTML content until you explicitly download it. This external content is sometimes referred to as *web beacons*, and spammers occasionally use external content to validate e-mail addresses. Blocking the content helps prevent the spammer from determining a valid address. In addition, OE won't attempt to connect to the Internet if external content is blocked when you view a message.

To configure content blocking, choose Tools ➤ Options, and click the Security tab (Figure 29.1). The option Block Images And Other External Content In HTML E-mail, when enabled, causes OE to block external content. When content has been blocked, the InfoBar, located just above the message in the preview pane, displays a warning that content has been blocked. Click the Infobar to download the external content if you want to view it.

FIGURE 29.1

Use the Security tab to configure external content blocking.

This latest version of OE, as with previous versions, enables you to configure the program to read HTML messages in plain text to help prevent HTML-scripted exploits. SP2 improves usability for this feature by making it easier to read messages in HTML when you aren't concerned about the message content. To have OE render a message using HTML, choose View ➤ Message In HTML.

One final change that SP2 applies to OE is targeted at developers rather than end users. OE includes an Attachment Execution Service (AES) Application Programming Interface (API) that supports attachment checking for OE and for external applications. An application developer who needs to check an attachment in your OE mail store can call the AES API rather than develop his own code within the application to accomplish the same task.

Chapter 30

Hosting Websites

Windows XP Professional includes Internet Information Services (IIS), a collection of components and services that lets you host a website on a Professional computer. Although Windows XP Professional is limited to a maximum of 10 concurrent connections, IIS nevertheless provides a means for you to share resources with other users through mechanisms different from those you might otherwise use. For example, you can use IIS to share documents with users across the Internet.

IIS also makes it possible to share printers through TCP/IP, including allowing remote Internet users to connect to and print to your printer. You might use this as an alternative to a fax machine or to provide easy access to printers from the LAN for inexperienced users.

NOTE   See Chapter 5 for details on setting up IPP (Internet-based) printing.

This chapter explains installing and configuring IIS as well as setting up specific web services. You'll find detailed information in this chapter on how to set up a web server, share files with others through FTP, and use FrontPage Server Extensions to support publishing from FrontPage. I'll also explain how you can run CGI and Perl scripts on your computer, which enables you to run counters, submit forms through e-mail, and perform a host of other tasks not possible or practical without a knowledge of programming. If you're looking to secure your website, you'll find information on using certificates and Secure Sockets Layer (SSL).

This chapter also looks at a small number of web-development tools you might want to consider if you're looking for an easy way to develop your website. You'll find that it's easy to create websites that support Dynamic HTML (DHTML) for special visual effects, serve dynamic content from databases, use feedback forms, and create other high-end content for your website.

Overview of Internet Services in Windows XP

In Windows XP Professional, Internet Information Services (IIS) comprises components and features that let a computer function as a web server, FTP server, or SMTP relay agent (relaying e-mail). IIS also includes additional components that support these core services. For example, FrontPage Server Extensions allow a computer running Microsoft FrontPage to publish to the web server. The following sections offer an overview of each component.

NOTE   Windows XP Home Edition doesn't include IIS or a version of Personal Web Server (PWS). Check out www.tucows.com or other software download sites for freeware and shareware webhosting solutions for Home Edition.

The World Wide Web Service

The World Wide Web Service allows a Windows XP Professional computer to serve a single website. Windows XP Professional is limited to a maximum of 10 concurrent connections, so a maximum of 10 users can access the website at any one time. This is a problem if you're hosting a public Internet site (unless your site is incredibly unpopular), but it's a great solution for hosting a site for internal use by other users on your LAN. For example, you might use a Windows XP Professional computer running IIS to provide links to documents, support information, policies, printers, or other information or resources.

TIP Consider Windows 2000 Server or Windows Server 2003 if you need to host more than one website on a single computer, or if you need to provide more than 10 concurrent connections to your web server.

Windows XP Professional can also be useful as a *staging server*. You use a staging server to publish and test a website before publishing it to its final server. Since you're only testing the site, it doesn't matter that you're limited to one site and a maximum of 10 users—unless you're stress-testing the site. If that's the case, you're better off staging to a server that matches closely, in hardware and OS, the final target server.

File Transfer Protocol Service

The FTP Service lets a Windows XP Professional computer host an FTP site, which lets users share files. If the computer is connected to the Internet, remote Internet users can access the files.

FTP provides an excellent means for sharing documents, drivers, or any other type of file that needs to be available to multiple users, but which you don't want to share through conventional means (such as a network share). Users can access the FTP site through a web browser, with a third-party FTP application such as FTP Explorer, or from a command console. As with websites, IIS under Windows XP Professional can serve one FTP site, and the site is limited to a maximum of 10 concurrent connections.

NOTE See Chapter 32 for details on setting up and managing an FTP site.

SMTP Service

Simple Mail Transfer Protocol (SMTP) is an Internet standard that defines e-mail transfer. SMTP is the most widely used mechanism for transferring mail across the Internet.

The SMTP Service in Windows XP doesn't give you the means to turn a Windows XP Professional computer into a full-blown e-mail server. It does, however, let you set up the computer for *mail relay*. For example, you might create a form on your website that collects information and forwards it through e-mail. The SMTP Service can receive the message and forward it to its destination or route it to another SMTP server that will process the message.

The SMTP Service also accepts incoming messages. It doesn't provide a mailbox structure like Exchange Server or other e-mail servers but instead places incoming messages into a drop folder. You can develop applications that monitor the folder and direct e-mail to specific users, or you can use third-party applications for the same purpose.

NOTE See Chapter 31 for details on setting up and managing an SMTP virtual server.

Hosting a Website

I've been in the Internet service business for several years, and one of my main experiences in that time has been setting up and managing web servers. So, I can offer you some useful insight into hosting websites with IIS. This section explains not only how to set up and configure a single site in IIS, but also some ways to work around the one-site-only limitation imposed by IIS under Windows XP Professional.

Installing IIS

IIS installs through Control Panel just like most other Windows XP components. However, you have some control over which components Setup installs.

To install IIS, follow these steps:

1. Open Control Panel, and then open the Add Or Remove Programs item.

2. Click Add/Remove Windows Components.

3. If you only select Internet Information Services from the components list, Setup installs the World Wide Web service and support files (such as documentation) but doesn't install the FTP or SMTP service.

4. To add or remove components, select Internet Information Services, and click Details (Figure 30.1). Select the components to install, click OK, and then click Next to complete the installation.

5. Windows XP prompts you for the Windows XP CD or the location of the installation files.

FIGURE 30.1
You can add or remove components from IIS.

TIP   Make sure you install the IIS snap-in so you'll be able to configure and manage your sites.

If you don't plan on publishing to your website using FrontPage, you can omit the FrontPage Server Extensions. If you select FrontPage Server Extensions for installation, Setup automatically sets up the Default Web Site for publishing though FrontPage. You don't have to add the extensions separately.

TIP   Setup doesn't by default install the Scripts virtual directory for the World Wide Web service. Double-click the service in the components list to open the details for the service, and then select the Scripts item. Doing so causes Setup to create the Scripts virtual folder. However, Setup doesn't place any scripts in the folder. This saves you the trouble of creating the folder if you plan to use it to store scripts for your website.

Setting Up the Site

With IIS installed, you're ready to set up your website. Windows XP automatically creates a site called Default Web Site when you install IIS (Figure 30.2). In the initial release of Windows XP, you could modify this site as needed to define your own site or delete the site and create a new one. The advantage to keeping the original site and modifying it as needed is that you save yourself the trouble of configuring the basic settings, specifying the site folder, adding FrontPage Server Extensions (if needed) to the site, and other setup tasks. IIS has been changed in Windows XP since the original release to restrict you to a single site—the Default Web Site. You can't delete the site or create another new site, but you can still modify the Default Web Site to suit your needs.

To configure the site, open the Internet Information Services console from the `Administrative Tools` folder. Expand the server and Web Sites nodes, right-click Default Web Site, and choose Properties to display the properties sheet for the site.

NOTE The following sections explain how to configure common website properties. Other configuration issues, such as setting up security for the site, are covered later in this chapter.

IP ADDRESS, PORT, AND HOST HEADER

Each website has three properties that determine how it responds to client browser requests: the IP address, port number, and host header. You set these on the Web Site tab of the site's properties (Figure 30.3). By default, IIS sets up the site to respond to all unassigned IP addresses. This is an issue only on a computer with more than one IP address. In this default configuration, IIS monitors incoming traffic for all IP addresses not assigned to other sites (not applicable on a Windows XP computer anyway) and responds to requests on those addresses.

You don't need to worry about changing the IP Address setting under Windows XP, because the default setting enables IIS to respond to all requests to the site even if the computer has multiple IP addresses. However, you do need to change the IP address if the computer has multiple IP addresses and you want IIS only to respond to a specific address. Select the IP address from the drop-down list if you want to assign a specific address to the site.

FIGURE 30.2

Use the IIS console to manage the Default Web Site and Default FTP Site.

FIGURE 30.3
Use the site's properties
sheet to configure the site.

The default TCP port for HTTP—the protocol used for web traffic—is port 80. In most cases, you should leave your site configured for the default port. This allows a client to connect to your website through a browser without having to specify the port number in the URL. For example, you can get to my website by entering the URL www.boyce.us. If I changed the port to, say, 8080, you would have to type the URL www.boyce.us:8080 to get to the site.

You should generally change the port number only for one of three reasons: to hide the site from casual browsing, to enable the site to run on the same computer as another site with the same IP address and host header, or to enable the site to run on a computer that includes other hosting software—in addition to IIS—that is using port 80. In most cases, you can leave the port at the default of 80.

TIP   If you decide to change the port, you need to tell clients what port to use or place a link to the URL (with port) on a page served by another server, enabling the client to link to your site.

The host header also serves to identify the website in conjunction with the IP address and port. When a browser connects to a site, it passes the web server the host header, such as www.boyce.us. The web server then checks the host header to determine which site to provide.

The host header isn't needed if you're hosting only one site. Clients can get to your site either through the IP address or through a URL. The URL can take the form http://*computer*, where *computer* is the network computer name of the Windows XP computer hosting the site. Or, you can create a DNS host record in the DNS zone in which the computer resides and let clients use the host name in a URL. If the host name were www, the URL would be http://www.boyce.us. The host name jim would enable the client to use the URL http://jim.boyce.us to reach the site. If you're relying on DNS records to allow clients to reach your site, click Advanced on the Web Site tab of the site's properties, and then click Add. Specify the IP address, port, and host header, and click OK.

TIP   Windows 2000 and Windows XP computers can register their host names with a Windows 2000 Server or Windows Server 2003 DNS server automatically. This allows hosts that use DHCP to obtain an address dynamically to still have a valid and current host record in their domain zone records. So, if your IP address changes because of an address lease change, remote clients can still connect to your website using your host name or network name, because the record is updated on the DNS server.

HOME DIRECTORY AND PERMISSIONS

The Home Directory tab (Figure 30.4) lets you specify the folder in which the website's files are located, as well as general permissions for the folder. You can specify a folder on your local computer as the home directory, use a shared folder on another computer on the LAN, or redirect the site to a different URL.

FIGURE 30.4

Use the Home Directory tab to specify where the site's files are located.

In addition, you can specify the permissions that clients have on the directory. In most cases, you should grant only Read permission and deny Write, Script Source Access, and Directory Browsing. Restricting the site to Read permission helps protect the site against hacking and other potential security threats.

NOTE   You can configure an application for the site, but in general you don't need to do so for a typical site. It's unlikely that you'll run server applications on a Windows XP Professional computer, so application configuration isn't covered in this book.

If you configure a site for directory browsing, clients can connect to the site and browse the underlying folder structure. This is generally a bad idea unless you're using the site to provide access to documents, because it exposes all the files in the site to the client.

TIP   If you want to allow directory browsing to simplify file access, create a virtual directory at the root of the folder you want to make available, and then enable directory browsing in the properties for the virtual directory.

DEFAULT DOCUMENTS

One additional property you need to set initially for the site is the default document, which lets a user view your default page without having to include it in the URL. For example, assuming the default page for www.boyce.us is index.htm, a client can point a web browser to www.boyce.us, and IIS displays the index.htm page automatically. This is the same as entering www.boyce.us/index.htm but eliminates the need for the client to know your main document name.

IIS automatically assigns four default documents to the website: `default.htm`, `default.asp`, `index.htm`, and `iisstart.asp`. `default.htm` and `index.htm` are the most commonly used, but you can use any document for the site. To use a different document, open the Documents tab of the site's properties (Figure 30.5), click Add, and add the document to the list. Use the up and down arrow buttons to change the order of the documents in the list. IIS searches the folder for a matching document in the order listed, and the first one found is served to the client.

FIGURE 30.5
Use the Documents tab to specify the site's default document.

OTHER SITE PROPERTIES

You can configure many other properties for the site that determine how IIS handles the site and how clients access it. The remaining properties that apply to the types of sites typically hosted on a Windows XP Professional computer are explained later in this chapter as they apply to specific issues, such as providing site security.

Providing Site Security

Web server security is an important issue, particularly as the threat of viruses, worms, and hackers continues to grow. It's therefore important that you have an understanding of the security issues involved in hosting a website and how to configure IIS to afford the protection your site requires. This section covers the most common security issues.

General Site Security

First and foremost, I recommend that you host your site files on an NTFS partition to give you control over them. Without the protection that NTFS provides, it's much easier for someone with access to your computer to modify the files and present site content that could be embarrassing or damaging to you or your company. It's also easier for hackers to exploit potential security holes to access your system and your site's content.

You should also consider how you'll make the site available for publishing content. You generally have three options: publish the files locally or through the LAN, use FTP to publish to the computer, or (in the case of FrontPage) use FrontPage Server Extensions to publish to the server. Given that the target server is running Windows XP Professional, it's a good bet that you'll be doing your website development on the same computer. So, publishing the files locally is the most likely scenario and one that involves the least security risk. As long as you use NTFS for the target partition and make sure you don't grant the Everyone group anything other than Read permissions, you should be in good shape. However, you'll also need to grant the IUSR account Read access, as I explain in the next section. You should also review the permissions on the folder to make sure that any other users or groups who should not have Write or Change permission on the folder have the appropriate permissions. This advice also holds true for any situation in which you need to publish to a computer across the LAN. Make sure you apply the appropriate permissions to the folder and its subfolders, and connect to the share using credentials that have the necessary permissions in the folder.

If you need to use FTP to publish to the server from a different computer, make sure you configure the computer's FTP site to provide the appropriate security, restricting access as needed to the folder containing the website.

TIP   See Chapter 32 for complete details on hosting and FTP site under Windows XP Professional.

The last option for publishing is to use FrontPage Server Extensions and develop/publish the site from FrontPage. FrontPage Server Extensions provide a means for controlling authoring permissions to prevent unauthorized access.

Perhaps one of the most important things you can do is to ensure that you keep your operating system up to date with the latest security patches. You can obtain the patches by pointing a web browser to `windowsupdate.microsoft.com`. You should also consider implementing a firewall in front of the server to help prevent denial-of-service (DoS) and other attacks aimed at your server.

In addition, consider implementing auditing for the site in an effort to detect unauthorized access or attempted access. See Chapter 13 for a discussion of how to audit security for Windows XP.

Anonymous versus Authenticated Access

IIS supports two types of access to a site, anonymous and authenticated, although the former isn't a technically accurate description. *Anonymous access* allows anyone with a web browser to connect to the site without providing any user credentials. IIS doesn't actually allow unauthenticated access, however. When you install IIS, Setup creates a user account named IUSR_*computer*, where *computer* is the computer's name. On a computer named Snoopy, for example, the account would be IUSR_SNOOPY. IIS then uses this account to authenticate all anonymous requests for access to the site.

For *authenticated access*, the site or page is protected by NTFS permissions and is only accessible to users who specify an appropriate username and password. This gives you a means of restricting access to a site or page, preventing anonymous users from browsing it. You can protect the site or page with a single set of user credentials or create a separate account for each user.

To configure authentication for a website, open the IIS console, right-click the site, and choose Properties. Then click the Directory Security tab. Click Edit in the Anonymous Access and Authentication Control group to display the dialog box shown in Figure 30.6.

FIGURE 30.6

Use the Authentication Methods dialog box to configure anonymous and authenticated access.

If you don't want to allow anonymous access to the site, clear the Anonymous Access checkbox. You can use the Basic Authentication and Integrated Windows Authentication options if you want to authenticate users against local accounts. With Integrated Windows Authentication (IWA), the client's browser first attempts to authenticate using the current logon credentials. If that fails, the server prompts the client for a username and password. With Basic Authentication, the server prompts for the credentials without attempting to authenticate using the existing logon credentials.

Basic Authentication is less secure because the password isn't encrypted. However, Basic Authentication allows for authentication through a proxy server, but IWA doesn't. If you need to authenticate through a proxy server, use Basic Authentication. Otherwise, use IWA for the additional level of security it provides.

WARNING   Although you can change the account that IIS uses for anonymous logon, I don't recommend doing so because it can lead to unforeseen authentication problems.

Restricting Access to Specific Pages or Folders

In some cases, you might want to offer anonymous access to a site but restrict access to certain parts of the site, whether a single page or an entire folder and its contents. If that's the case, configure the site to allow authenticated access, set the NTFS permissions on the file or folder to remove the IUSR account from the list, and then add any accounts that need access, granting them the appropriate level of permissions (Read, Change, and so on) depending on the function of the particular item.

You can also apply security at the folder level, whether that folder is a physical folder or a virtual folder. To do so, open the IIS console, open the site, right-click the folder, and choose Properties. Use the same procedure to configure security that you use to configure site-level security (see the previous section.)

Restricting Access by Address or Domain

Windows NT Server, Windows 2000 Server, and Windows Server 2003 give you the ability to restrict access to a site by the IP address, subnet, or domain of the client. Windows XP Professional, however, doesn't provide this feature. Although the controls for accessing it are located on the Directory Security tab, the controls are disabled. If you need to restrict access based on address, subnet, or domain, you'll need to move the site to a server platform or configure rules in your firewall to control access (which is outside the scope of this book).

Using SSL to Secure a Site

You can use Secure Sockets Layer (SSL) to provide additional security for clients. SSL uses a certificate to encrypt data between the client and server, making that data secure from interception and hijack. For example, you might use SSL to secure the site for authoring, enabling a remote client to publish to the site with greater security.

OBTAINING THE CERTIFICATE

In order to use SSL, you must obtain and install a certificate on the Windows XP Professional computer that is acting as the web server. You can obtain the certificate from a public certification authority (CA) such as VeriSign (www.verisign.com) or Thawte (www.thawte.com). Or, if your network contains a stand-alone or enterprise CA, you can obtain the certificate from the local CA.

TIP Windows 2000 Server and Windows Server 2003 platforms include Certificate Services, which allows the server to function as a stand-alone or enterprise CA. A Windows XP computer can't function as a CA.

The method you use to obtain the certificate varies slightly depending on the CA. The easiest method is to use the IIS console, as follows:

1. Open the IIS console, and open the properties for the website.

2. Click the Directory Security tab, and then click Server Certificate to start the Web Server Certificate Wizard.

3. In the wizard, specify that you want to create a new certificate and that you want to prepare the certificate request now but send it later.

4. On the next page of the wizard (Figure 30.7), enter a descriptive name such as **Web Server Certificate** in the Name field. It's unlikely that you'll need to change any of the other options on this page for a site hosted on a Windows XP Professional computer, so I won't cover those (they would lead to a lengthy discussion of topics outside the scope of this book).

5. The remaining items of information required by the wizard are for the most part self-explanatory or adequately explained by the wizard. When you're prompted for the Common Name, however, what you enter depends on how the site is accessed. For a site publicly available on the Internet, enter the host header (such as www.boyce.us) as the common name. For an intranet-accessed site, specify the computer's DNS or NetBIOS name. The wizard automatically uses this name unless you enter a different name.

TIP If users will connect to the secure site through its IP address rather than a host name, use the IP address as the common name.

FIGURE 30.7
Use the IIS console to
create a certificate
request.

FIGURE 30.7
Use the IIS console to
create a certificate
request.

6. Open a web browser on the computer that will function as a server, and connect to `http://server/certsrv`, where `server` is the CA's computer name. The CA presents a web-based wizard that steps you through the process of requesting the certificate (Figure 30.8).

7. Click Next, choose Advanced Request in the wizard, and click Next.

FIGURE 30.8
The CA uses a web-based
wizard to process your
certificate request.

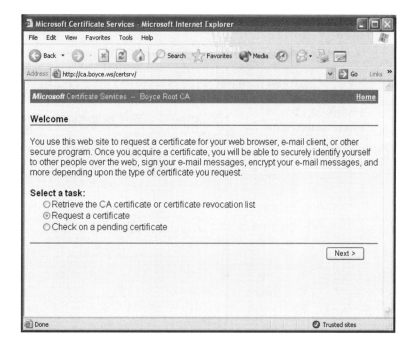

8. In the following wizard page (Figure 30.9), choose the option to submit a request using a Base64-encoded file. Click Next.

FIGURE 30.9
Request the certificate using a Base64-encoded file.

9. On the next page (Figure 30.10), click Browse to browse for and select the certificate request file you created through the IIS console. Then, click Read to enter the data into the form. You can also open the file in Notepad to cut and paste the data.

FIGURE 30.10
Import the request file.

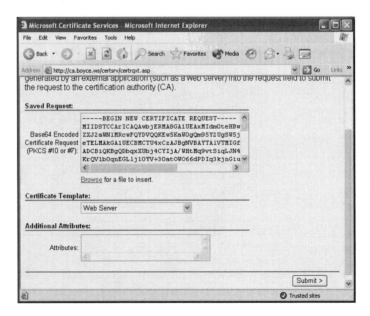

10. Select Web Server from the Certificate Template drop-down list, and click Next.

TIP You won't be able to browse to the file on your local computer unless you add the CA's URL to your list of trusted sites. You do this through the Security tab in Internet Explorer's options. If the CA doesn't use SSL for certificate requests, you need to clear the option Require Server Verification For All Sites In This Zone.

11. Depending on how the CA is configured, the CA will either provide you with the certificate immediately or will prompt you to return to the CA later to retrieve the certificate after it has been issued by an administrator. If the CA issues the certificate immediately, select the option to download it.

If you use a commercial CA such as VeriSign, you'll have to pay for the certificate. These services also use a web-based wizard to prompt you for the information needed to create the certificate. When the certificate is ready, the wizard downloads it to your computer.

12. After the certificate is downloaded to the server, reopen the IIS console, and open the properties for the website.

13. On the Directory Security tab, click Server Certificate.

14. Choose Process The Pending Request And Install The Certificate, and click Next.

15. Browse to the location of the certificate file you obtained from the CA. Click Next, and follow the remaining prompts to complete the installation.

CONFIGURING THE SITE FOR SSL

After you install the certificate, you'll probably want to modify some of the SSL-related settings for the site. Open the properties for the site in the IIS console, and click the Directory Security tab. Click Edit under the Secure Communications tab to open the dialog box shown in Figure 30.11.

FIGURE 30.11
Use the Secure Communications dialog box to configure SSL settings.

The following list summarizes the options on the Secure Communications dialog box:

Require Secure Channel   Select this option to require the clients to use SSL to connect to the website. Clearing this option allows unsecured and unencrypted access to the site.

Require 128-Bit Encryption   Choose this option to require stronger 128-bit encryption.

Client Certificates   Use Accept Client Certificates to enable clients to use client-side certificates to authenticate on the website. Require Client Certificates forces the clients to authenticate using a client-side certificate. Use Ignore Client Certificates for a publicly available website.

Enable Client Certificate Mapping   This option maps client-side certificates to local computer accounts on the server, enabling the client to use a certificate to authenticate on the server.

Enable Certificate Trust List   You can enable this option to specify a list of CAs that are trusted by this website. Only certificates issued by a trusted CA will be granted access.

TESTING IT

At this point, you should be ready to test SSL connections to the website. Point your browser to `https://SiteURL`, where `SiteURL` is the URL for your web server. Make sure you use `https` rather than `http` in the URL.

If you're unable to successfully connect to the site or you receive a warning such as the one shown in Figure 30.12, check the certificate to make sure you specified the appropriate host header in the Common Name field for a public site or the computer's machine name for an intranet site. Note that in Figure 30.12, the only problem with the server's certificate is that it was issued by a CA not explicitly trusted by the client computer. If you obtain a certificate from a public CA instead of issuing your own, public clients generally won't see this warning, because their computers are probably configured to trust the public CA. For internal clients, make sure to add your local CA to the trusted authorities on each client.

FIGURE 30.12
This warning can indicate an incorrectly configured certificate.

Using Custom Error Pages

IIS provides common error pages for specific errors such as the requested page not existing (the 404 error). Most of these error messages are pretty boring, and you might want to either spice up the error messages a bit or include additional information. For example, you can provide a link to your home page or to a corporate page when a 404 error occurs.

The default error pages are stored in *%systemroot%*\help\iisHelp\common as HTML documents. You can either modify these pages or create your own from scratch. If you choose the latter option, follow these steps:

1. Create the file, and place it in the common folder just mentioned. I recommend you give the file a new name rather than overwrite the default document for the error in question.

2. Open the IIS console, and open the properties for the site.

3. Click the Custom Errors tab (Figure 30.13). Select the error for which you want to change documents, and click Edit Properties to display the Error Mapping Properties dialog box.

4. Enter the path to the custom file, and click OK.

5. Repeat the process for any other custom errors, and then close the properties for the site.

FIGURE 30.13
Use the Custom Errors tab to define custom error documents.

Using Counters

Although your website will be limited to a maximum of 10 concurrent users, you may want to keep track of how many hits the site gets or (perhaps more important) who is visiting your site. You have several options for including a counter on the site.

FrontPage, for example, includes a visible counter that you can easily add to a page. To add an invisible counter, you'll either need to code one yourself or subscribe to a service such as thecounter.com that offers site tracking. Many of these, including thecounter.com, offer free visible counters and paid hidden counters. Adding the counter to your site is as easy as copying the script code provided by the counter site to your web page. The counter site will explain the process when you obtain the counter script.

NOTE In most cases, you don't need to add Perl/CGI support to the web server to support a counter. The exception is when the script is written as a Perl script.

If you don't want the trouble or expense of obtaining a counter from a counter service, I have another solution for you—an ASP-based counter that records page hits to a Microsoft Access database. Here are the contents of `counter.asp`:

```
' Hit counter by Jim Boyce, www.boyce.us
MM_counter_STRING = "dsn=counter;uid=mycounter;pwd=mypassword;"
Dim clientIPAddress
Dim clientBrowser
Dim clientReferrer
Dim pageURL
clientIPAddress = Request.ServerVariables ("REMOTE_ADDR")
' Exclude hits from your own network, change IP addresses to suit your network
If clientIPAddress <> "216.239.31.4" and left(clientIPAddress,7) <> "192.168" then
        clientBrowser = Request.ServerVariables ("HTTP_USER_AGENT")
        clientReferrer = Request.ServerVariables ("HTTP_REFERER")
        pageUrl = Request.ServerVariables ("HTTP_URL")
        set cn = Server.CreateObject("ADODB.Command")
        cn.ActiveConnection = MM_counter_STRING
        cn.CommandText = "INSERT INTO Hits (page, clientIPAddress, clientBrowser,
        clientReferrer) VALUES ("&"'"&pageURL&"'"&","&"'"&clientIPAddress&"'"&",
        "&"'"&clientBrowser&"'"&","&"'"&clientReferrer&"'"&")"
        cn.Execute
        cn.ActiveConnection.Close
End If
set cn = nothing
```

This script assumes the following:

◆ You created a Data Source Name (DSN) on the server that points to the Microsoft Access database where the hit data will be stored. The DSN is named *counter* and uses *mycounter* as the username and *mypassword* as the password. See Chapter 27 to learn how to set up and manage DSNs.

◆ The database includes the fields specified in the code.

Note that the `If` statement in the script checks the value of the `clientIPAddress` variable and executes the nested statements only if the `clientIPAddress` value isn't 216.239.31.4 and not in the 192.168.n.n private subnet. The former happens to be the public IP address of my server at www.boyce.us, and the latter is the private subnet I use on the local network. Including this statement prevents hits from my own internal LAN (such as from my workstation) from being included in the hit counter. If you want to record all hits, remove the `If` and `End If` statements or place an apostrophe (`'`) character at the beginning of them to turn them into comments. Otherwise, change the `If` statement to reflect your own server's public address and private IP subnet.

TIP   You probably don't want to type all this code yourself or go through the trouble of creating the database. Point your browser to www.boyce.us/articles/freecounter.asp to copy the code and download an empty counter.mdb database.

What do you do with `Counter.asp`? Place it in a folder named `counter` under the root of your website, and then include the following lines at the beginning of each page whose hits you want to count:

```
<%@LANGUAGE="VBSCRIPT"%>
<!--#include file="counter/counter.asp" -->
```

Make sure each page you're counting has an `.asp` extension.

Using Perl and Other Server-Side Applications

In some situations, you may want to add the ability for your server to process CGI or Perl scripts. For example, maybe you'd like to host a bulletin board such as the one offered at `www.ikonboard.com`. Or perhaps you want to have clients enter information in a form and have that form e-mailed to you. There are lots of great scripts out there that you can use on your web server, but you need to add script support to your server.

One of the best options is to use ActivePerl, available from `www.activestate.com`. ActivePerl is free for both commercial and noncommercial use.

When you install ActivePerl, Setup creates the necessary application association to handle scripts with a PL extension. To handle scripts with a CGI extension, you need to modify the site's configuration as follows:

1. Open the IIS console, and open the properties for the site.

2. Click the Home Directory tab, and click Configuration to open the Application Configuration dialog box.

3. Click Add to open the Add/Edit Application Extension Mapping dialog box (Figure 30.14).

4. Enter

   ```
   C:\Perl\bin\Perl.exe "%s" %s
   ```

   in the Executable field, and then enter **.cgi** in the Extension field. Enter **GET,HEAD,POST** in the Limit To field, and click OK.

NOTE   Change the path to `Perl.exe` if you installed ActivePerl in a different folder.

FIGURE 30.14
Use the Add/Edit Application Extension Mapping dialog box to add a mapping for CGI scripts.

After you install Perl and configure the site, create a folder—either physical or virtual—named `cgi-bin`. You can use a different name if you prefer, but this is the most commonly used name. Place your custom scripts in this folder. Many commercial scripts use their own folder structure, so you can create their folders either under the root of your website or as a subfolder under the `cgi-bin` folder.

Generally, you also need to modify the scripts to specify the path to the script root as well as specify the path to the Perl interpreter. If you installed ActivePerl in the default location, the path to Perl is `c:/perl/perl.exe`. Change this path in your scripts as needed. The path is specified most often in the first line of the script.

E-Mailing Form Results

One function you might want to perform is to e-mail the contents of a form either to yourself or someone else. For example, you might use a form to allow clients to request information about a service, get support, or provide feedback on the site. How you accomplish this bit of magic depends on your development platform.

E-Mail Forms from FrontPage

If you create the site in FrontPage, it's relatively easy to set up a form for e-mail submission:

1. Create the form, and then right-click it and choose Form Properties (Figure 30.15).

2. Choose the Send To option, and enter the target e-mail address in the E-Mail Address field. You can also have the form sent to a file specified by the URL in the File Name field. Clear this field if you only want the form submitted by e-mail.

TIP   You must publish the form to the server through FrontPage through the URL in order for special scripts such as e-mail forms to work. You can't publish the site with FTP.

3. Click Options to open the Saving Results dialog box, and then click the E-Mail Results tab (Figure 30.16).

FIGURE 30.15
Use the Form Properties
dialog box to configure
the target e-mail address.

FIGURE 30.16
Configure form e-mail
properties through the
E-Mail Results tab.

4. Choose the format for the message from the E-Mail Format drop-down list. Select the option Include Field Names if you want FrontPage to include the field name for each field in the message along with the form content.

5. Specify the subject for the message in the Subject Line field and the reply address in the Reply-To-Line field. Click OK to close the dialog box.

TIP   To include as the reply address the e-mail address of the person filling out the form, include a field on the form in which the user enters his address. Then, select the option Form Field Name beside the Reply-To-Line field, and enter the name of the field on the form that contains the user's e-mail address.

You can perform additional functions through FrontPage with the form. For example, you can redirect the user to a confirmation page after they submit the form. You can also retain values from the form to use elsewhere (such as in the confirmation page). Check the FrontPage documentation, or *Mastering Microsoft FrontPage 2002 Premium Edition* (by Peter Weverka and Molly E. Holzschlag; Sybex, 2001), for more information on using forms in FrontPage.

E-Mail from Non-FrontPage Sites

One of the most popular tools for e-mailing forms on non-FrontPage servers is FormMail, developed by Matt Wright (`www.scriptarchive.com`). You can use the `formmail.pl` script without charge, provided you retain the copyright information and attribution in the script.

On Unix systems, `formmail.pl` relies on the Unix sendmail program to send the message. Windows XP systems don't have sendmail, so you need to take a little different route. A handful of different solutions are available to you. You can create your own script to send the message through the SMTP service on the server or on a different server. For a sample script and additional information to help you create such a script, see the Microsoft Knowledge Base article Q221495:

```
http://support.microsoft.com/default.aspx?scid=kb;en-us;Q221495
```

Another option is to use a third-party e-mail utility on the computer and use a modified version of `formmail.pl`. There are a few different e-mail utilities, but the one I've found useful in the past is Blat, which is free. You'll find Blat at www.blat.net.

To install Blat, copy the `Blat.exe` program executable to the `%systemroot%` folder on the Windows XP Professional computer that is acting as the web server. Then, open a command console on the server, and execute the following command to install and configure Blat:

Blat -install *server sender*

Replace *server* with the IP address or fully qualified domain name of the SMTP server to be used for sending the e-mail. Replace *sender* with the e-mail address you want Blat to use by default as the sender for the e-mail. To view other options, type **Blat** without any other options or parameters.

Next, you need to obtain and install a copy of `formmail.pl` that has been customized to use Blat. You'll find such a copy of `formmail.pl` at www.scriptarchive.com/formmail.html. Copy the script to your web server's script folder (typically `cgi-bin`). Then, create the form and include the following hidden form fields:

`recipient` Specify the e-mail address to which you want the form to be mailed. The following is sample HTML code for the tag:

```
<input type="hidden" name="recipient" value="jim@boyce.ws">
```

`required` Specify the names of fields on the form that must be filled in by the user. Typically this value includes the user's e-mail address and name, but it can include other fields, as well. Separate the fields by commas, as in the following example:

```
<input type="hidden" name="required" value="realname,email">
```

`subject` This field specifies the subject for the e-mail. The following is an example:

```
<input type="hidden" name="subject" value="Book Request">
```

`title` This is the title for the confirmation page that the script displays when the message has been sent. The following is an example:

```
<input type="hidden" name="title" value="Thanks for your request!">
```

Add any other fields to the form (as visible fields) that you want included in the message. Then specify `POST` as the method for the form, and specify the path to `formmail.pl` as the action. For example, you'll specify `cgi-bin/formmail.pl` if the `formmail.pl` script is located in the site's `cgi-bin` folder. When the user clicks the Submit button, FormMail processes the form contents.

Chapter 31

Using the SMTP Service

Windows XP Professional includes an SMTP service as part of Internet Information Services (IIS) that enables a Windows XP Professional computer to act as a mail relay server. Although the SMTP service doesn't enable Windows XP to function as a full-spectrum mail server complete with mailboxes for incoming mail, it can serve to deliver outgoing mail or placing incoming messages in a drop folder where another program or service can process them.

The SMTP service can be particularly useful when you need to relay messages for a website or for other applications. This chapter explains what SMTP is and how it works, as well as how to install and configure the SMTP service for Windows XP Professional.

Overview of SMTP and the SMTP Service

Simple Mail Transfer Protocol (SMTP) is the primary standard for delivering e-mail messages across the Internet. By contrast, Post Office Protocol 3 (POP3) is one of the most common protocols used by e-mail programs for retrieving mail from a mail server. So, SMTP and POP3 (or other protocol such as Internet Access Message Protocol [IMAP]) work together to provide both delivery and receipt of e-mail.

Here's a typical scenario when you send an e-mail message from a typical e-mail client like Outlook Express:

1. When you click Send in your mail program, the program contacts the SMTP server specified in the account properties.

2. When a connection has been established, the client uses SMTP to transfer the message to your mail server.

3. Your mail server initiates an SMTP connection to the SMTP server for the destination domain for the e-mail message (based on the domain specified in the recipient address) and delivers the message to the destination server.

4. The recipient's e-mail client uses POP3 or another protocol (not SMTP) to pull the message down to the recipient's computer.

There are certainly other scenarios, as well. For example, your mail server might actually be a mail relay agent, passing its messages to another SMTP server up the line, which takes care of delivering the messages to their target domains. Or, perhaps the receiving SMTP server for a particular domain is acting as a front-end server for several other servers, and after accepting the message, it forwards the message on to another server for delivery or further processing.

Where does the Windows XP SMTP service fit into the picture? It can't serve as a full-blown mail server, but it can certainly act as a forwarding agent. For example, assume you have set up a Windows XP computer to act as a Web server for your intranet. You want to incorporate some e-mail forms for submission of trouble reports, purchase orders, or other items on your intranet site. Windows XP's SMTP service can act as the mail relay, accepting mail from the forms and submitting it to your company's mail server.

NOTE The SMTP service can also deliver incoming messages to a drop folder on the computer, but some other process needs to monitor the folder for new messages and then process those messages. Windows XP has no feature for doing that, so I don't cover using the SMTP service in that way in this book.

Installing and Configuring the SMTP Service

It's a simple matter to install the SMTP service for Windows XP. The service is included as a subcomponent of IIS. Follow these steps:

1. Open the Add Or Remove Programs applet in Control Panel, and click Add/Remove Windows Components.

2. Click Internet Information Services, and then click Details.

3. Select SMTP Service, click OK, and click Next.

4. Insert the Windows XP CD when prompted, and click OK to complete the installation process.

TIP If you've installed the SMTP service and it doesn't appear in the IIS management console, remove IIS altogether and reinstall it from the Add Or Remove Programs applet. Be sure to back up your website, if any, before doing so.

Now that the SMTP service is installed, you're ready to start configuring it. The following section explains how.

Configuring the Default SMTP Virtual Server

When you add the SMTP service, IIS creates a Default SMTP Virtual Server. This virtual server appears in the IIS console (Figure 31.1), where you manage its settings and control the service.

TIP IIS configures the SMTP service to start automatically when the computer starts. You can control service startup through the Services console in the Administrative Tools folder.

IIS supports only one SMTP Virtual Server on Windows XP, but one should serve your needs. If not, you can use the SMTP service on Windows 2000 Server or Windows Server 2003 to create multiple SMTP servers.

To configure the SMTP server, right-click Default SMTP Virtual Server, and choose Properties. The following sections explain the settings you can configure for the server.

CONFIGURING GENERAL PROPERTIES

The General tab of the SMTP virtual server's properties (Figure 31.2) lets you set the address on which the server will respond, specify connection options, and enable logging.

FIGURE 31.1

Use the IIS console to manage the SMTP Virtual Server.

FIGURE 31.2

Configure address, connection, and logging settings on the General tab.

By default, the virtual server is configured to respond on all IP addresses for SMTP traffic. In almost all cases, you can leave the IP address property set to All Unassigned, which causes the service to listen for SMTP traffic on all IP addresses. This is only an issue if the Windows XP computer has more than one network interface. If you want the computer to respond to SMTP traffic only on a specific interface, choose the interface's IP address from the drop-down list.

The service also defaults to using port 25 for SMTP. The only reason to change the port is to in effect hide the SMTP server from users on your network. If they don't know the port, they can't configure their e-mail programs to use the computer to send out mail. If you want to change the port, click Advanced, click Edit, and enter the desired port in the resulting Identification dialog box.

NOTE   Even if you change the port, there is nothing to prevent someone from using a port scanner on the network to locate the service. However, if you have users who are sharp enough to use a port scanner, you have other problems!

The two connection options on the General tab of the SMTP Virtual Server's properties let you control the number of connections and timeout limit for each connection. The SMTP service in Windows XP is limited to 10 concurrent connections, and although you can enter a larger number in the Limit Number Of Connections To field, the value reverts back to 10 the next time you open the dialog box.

If you're having problems with the SMTP service or want to keep track of the traffic it's handling, you can select the Enable Logging option to turn on logging. Choose a log file format from the Active Log Format drop-down list, and then click Properties to set additional logging properties (Figure 31.3)

FIGURE 31.3

Set the log frequency and location on the General Properties tab.

TIP In most cases, the Microsoft IIS Log File Format option should provide the information you need to track the SMTP service. If you want to log additional information, or you need the logs in a specific format for review by a third-party application, choose one of the other two formats as required by the application.

The General Properties tab for the log, shown in Figure 31.3, lets you configure how frequently IIS creates a new log and the log file location. The Extended Properties tab becomes available if you choose either of the two non-IIS log file formats; here, you can choose the items you want to include in the log (Figure 31.4).

FIGURE 31.4

Choose which items to log from the Extended Properties tab.

CONTROLLING ACCESS TO THE SERVER

The Access tab of the SMTP virtual server's properties (Figure 31.5) is the place to go to control who can use the SMTP server, to set up a certificate to enable SSL for the server, and to apply relay restrictions.

FIGURE 31.5

Use the Access tab to control who can use the server.

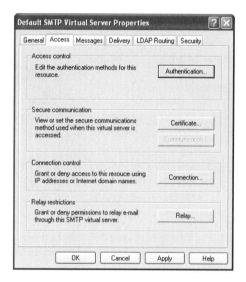

Authentication

To set the authentication methods the server will support, click Authentication to open the Authentication dialog box. The SMTP service supports three types of authentication:

Anonymous   This option allows connections to the SMTP server without any authentication. You should disable anonymous access unless you aren't concerned about people using the SMTP server to send messages without specific authorization. However, you'll have to configure your website or other service(s) using the SMTP server to specify a username and password when sending messages. An alternative to disabling anonymous access is to apply IP address restrictions to deny access to all computers other than those that should have access to the SMTP service. I explain later in this section how to configure connection restrictions based on address or subnet.

Basic authentication   Use basic authentication when you need authentication but the remote client or application won't support Integrated Windows authentication (explained next).

Integrated Windows authentication   With this option, the client's Windows account credentials are used to authenticate on the SMTP server. You must create a matching account on the Windows XP computer hosting the SMTP service.

SSL

You can install a certificate on the Windows XP computer hosting the SMTP service to enable the use of SSL to secure traffic between the client and server. If you need SSL, it's likely that you really need Windows Server as your SMTP platform. For that reason, I don't cover SSL in detail in this chapter. See Chapter 30 to learn about certificates and configuring SSL properties. The process for an SMTP virtual server is much the same as for a website.

Connection Control

A great way to prevent unauthorized users from sending mail through the SMTP server is to create a list of IP addresses that are allowed to connect to the server. To configure this list, click Connection on the Access tab to open the Connection dialog box (Figure 31.6).

FIGURE 31.6
Restrict access to the server by specifying a list of addresses that are allowed to connect.

Here, you have two choices: specify a list of addresses that will be denied access, or specify a list of addresses that will be allowed access. In most cases, the latter makes the most sense because you're explicitly stating the computers that can connect to the server. Choose the option Only The List Below, and then click Add to open the Computer dialog box. You can enter individual IP addresses, specify a group of computers by subnet, or specify a domain. If you choose the latter, the client computers must have host records in the DNS zone for the specified domain.

Controlling Relay

Next, consider how you'll restrict the ability to *relay* through the SMTP Virtual Server. Message relay enables a client or other server to send a message through the SMTP server to another destination server. In other words, the SMTP service relays the message to its destination.

Open relays, or servers that indiscriminately allow message relay, are a spammer's dream. So, you should configure relay restrictions on your SMTP server to prevent unauthorized people—including those in your own company—from relaying through the server.

To configure relay settings, open the properties for the virtual server, click the Access tab, and click Relay to open the Relay Restrictions dialog box (Figure 31.7). As when you restrict connections, you can specify a list of individual addresses, subnets, and domains that are either allowed to relay or not allowed to relay. In general, I recommend that you use the option Only The List Below to explicitly define the list of computers that can relay. Click Add, and specify an individual address, subnet, or domain name.

You can also use the option at the bottom of the dialog box to allow anyone who can authenticate on the server to use it to relay messages. If you enable this setting, configure the e-mail clients for any users who need to relay to use a valid set of account credentials on the Windows XP computer. In Outlook Express, for example, you set this option on the Servers tab of the account properties. Select the option My Server Requires Authentication, click Settings, and specify the username and password.

FIGURE 31.7
Restrict relay to prevent
spamming through your
server.

CONFIGURING MESSAGE LIMITS

The Messages tab of the SMTP virtual server's properties (Figure 31.8) contains several settings that limit message size, number of recipients, and other items.

FIGURE 31.8
You can impose restrictions on message size and other items.

The Messages tab contains the following settings:

Limit Message Size To (KB) The server rejects messages larger than the specified size. The default is 2 MB (2048 KB). Sending servers that support Extended SMTP and send an EHLO command to initiate the connection to the server will detect the maximum message size advertised by the server and not attempt to send messages larger than the specified size. Those servers that send HELO to initiate a connection won't detect the limit, will attempt to send the message, and will receive an error.

Limit Session Size To (KB) This is the total size, in KB, that the server will accept for all messages (body only) during a single session with a remote server. The value should be greater than the individual message limit.

Limit Number Of Messages Per Connection To This value specifies the maximum number of messages that are transmitted in a single connection session. Keep this number relatively low (such as the default) to maintain performance.

Limit Number Of Recipients Per Message To Set the maximum number of recipients per single message with this option. Some servers generate a nondelivery report (NDR) if this maximum is exceeded. Servers running the Microsoft SMTP service send the maximum and then open another connection to send to the remaining recipients.

Send Copy Of Non-delivery Report To Enter the e-mail address to which you want to send a copy of all NDRs generated by the SMTP service. Receiving the NDRs can help you identify problems with the server or your network.

Badmail Directory Specify the location where the SMTP service should place undeliverable messages. You should review this folder periodically and clear out its contents to conserve disk space.

SETTING DELIVERY OPTIONS

The Delivery tab (Figure 31.9) lets you set how the SMTP service attempts message delivery and what actions it takes if delivery fails.

The Outbound group of controls determines how many times the service attempts to deliver a message and the time it waits between attempts. The Delay Notification value determines when the service sends a notification to the sender indicating that the message has been delayed in delivery. The Expiration Timeout value specifies the point at which the service considers the message undeliverable and generates a nondelivery receipt to the sender. The values in the Local control group specify these same values but for local delivery of messages.

FIGURE 31.9
Configure message delivery options on the Delivery tab.

If you need to specify how your SMTP server makes connections to remote mail servers for outbound delivery, click the Outbound Security button to open the Outbound Security dialog box. Here you specify the type of authentication required by the remote server(s). If you're sending messages out to the Internet and not routing through a local mail server, you'll likely need to keep the Anonymous access default. Otherwise, choose the type of authentication required by the remote server(s).

To control connection limits and the port used for outgoing connections, click Outbound Connections on the Delivery tab to open the Outbound Connections dialog box. Here you specify the maximum number of concurrent outbound connections, which defaults to 1,000. You can also specify the connection timeout, the number of concurrent connections allowed per domain, and the port to be used for making the connections. The default port is 25; change the port value only if you're connecting to a server specifically configured to respond on the specified port.

Finally, you can click Advanced on the Delivery tab to open the Advanced Delivery dialog box (Figure 31.10), which contains the following options:

Maximum Hop Count   Specify the maximum number of servers through which an outgoing message can be relayed. If the hop count is exceeded, the service generates a NDR.

Masquerade Domain   Specify in this field the local domain name you want listed in the Mail From field in the message header for outgoing messages.

Fully-Qualified Domain Name   Specify the fully qualified name of the SMTP server to identify the sending server to remote servers.

Smart Host   Specify the name of another mail server through which you want to route all outgoing messages. Use this option when you don't want your Windows XP SMTP server to try to deliver messages itself to their destination, but instead you want it to relay the messages to your primary mail server or other SMTP relay server.

Attempt Direct Delivery Before Sending To Smart Host   Choose this option to have the SMTP service attempt to deliver messages itself before sending them to the smart host for delivery. The service will send the messages to the smart host only if it can't deliver them itself.

Perform Reverse DNS Lookup On Incoming Messages   If this option is enabled, the SMTP service attempts to validate that the IP address of the sending server resides in the DNS records for the sending server's reported domain. The SMTP service doesn't reject the message if reverse lookup fails. Instead, the service places the word *unverified* beside the sending server in the message header.

FIGURE 31.10
Use the Advanced Delivery dialog box to set additional delivery options.

LDAP Routing

The LDAP Routing tab (Figure 31.11) of the SMTP virtual server's properties lets you use Lightweight Directory Access Protocol (LDAP) to perform address resolution and message routing. With LDAP routing enabled, the SMTP service attempts to resolve addresses using LDAP queries to the specified LDAP server. For example, assume you have a Windows 2000 Server or Windows Server 2003 domain. You can specify a domain controller in the domain as the LDAP server, and the SMTP service will look up sender and recipient addresses in the domain.

FIGURE 31.11
Configure LDAP address resolution on the LDAP Routing tab.

It's unlikely that you'll be using a Windows XP mail relay agent in such a network, so I don't cover LDAP routing in detail in this chapter. For more information about how to configure LDAP, click Help on the LDAP Routing tab.

Specifying Server Operators

The Security tab of the SMTP service's properties lets you specify which users can manage the SMTP service. By default, members of the local Administrators group can manage the service. If you need other users to be able to configure the SMTP server, click Add, and add their user account or group to the Operators list.

Implementing a Full-Blown E-Mail Server

As I mentioned at the beginning of this chapter, the SMTP service included with Windows XP won't enable the computer to function as a full-blown e-mail server complete with user mailboxes or support for pickup protocols like POP3 or IMAP. The SMTP service is intended solely as a mail relay tool.

If you're looking for a complete mail solution and want to run it on Windows XP rather than Windows Server, several options are available. A search on your favorite shareware site should turn up several e-mail server applications that will run on Windows XP. Following is a list of several with links to more information about them:

IMail Server   This is one of the more popular, full-featured mail server products and is used by a number of Internet service providers (ISPs) and small- to medium-sized companies. Available in three versions, the product supports a wide range of features including broad protocol support, anti-spam and antivirus integration, customizable web access, and much more: www.ipswitch.ca/products/imail.htm.

ArGoSoft Mail Server Pro   The freeware version supports SMTP and POP3 and includes web-mail capability, enabling you to check your mail with a web browser. The Plus and Pro versions add several other features including IMAP, customizable web output, support for multiple domains, and much more: www.argosoft.com/mailserver.

Merak Mail Server   This product is available in several versions to support various feature requirements. The Lite version supports a maximum of 12 users, with other versions offering an unlimited number of users. Options include integrated webmail and support for access by WAP devices: www.merakmailserver.com.

Winmail Mail Server   This product supports SMTP, POP3, IMAP, and webmail access, as well as IMAP public folders. It also supports several options for secure messaging, such as SSL and TLS: www.magicwinmail.net.

WorkgroupMail Mail Server   This mail server is available in three versions: Home, Professional, and Enterprise. The Home version is limited to 5 users, and the other two versions are unlimited. The product offers several features for message filtering, autoresponse, virus scanning, and content filtering: www.workgroupmail.com/.

Chapter 32

Hosting FTP Sites

Internet Information Services (IIS) in Windows XP Professional includes an FTP service that you can use to exchange files with other users. File Transfer Protocol (FTP) is an Internet standard. Not long ago, FTP was the primary means for making files available to other users across the Internet. Today, HTTP is rapidly replacing FTP as the method of choice for publishing files on the Internet. When you link to a file on a web page, far more often than not it's an HTTP link to the file rather than an FTP link.

Even though HTTP is now more common for file sharing, FTP is still an important service and an attractive alternative to HTTP, particularly when you need to share a relatively large number of files (particularly binary files). When you set up an FTP site, you only need to create the folder structure under the service and place files in the folders—you don't have to create individual links on a page to each file. With HTTP, you need to either create individual links or enable directory browsing for a folder.

FTP is also a primary means for publishing websites for non-FrontPage servers. All web-development platforms—including FrontPage—support FTP as a publishing method. So, if you're using any develop-ment tool other than FrontPage, it's a good bet that you'll need to set up the FTP service on the server, if for no other reason than to publish your website.

This chapter explains how to install and configure the FTP service under Windows XP Profes-sional, set up an FTP site, and provide security for the site. I also offer a few tips for handling a few potential problems you might run across, as well as how to access the FTP site from the client side.

Hosting an FTP Site

Setup doesn't install the FTP service by default when you install Internet Information Services (IIS), unless you explicitly select the FTP service during installation. To add the FTP service, open the Add Or Remove Programs item in Control Panel, and click Add/Remove Windows Components. Expand IIS in the component list, select FTP, and then follow the remaining prompts to install the service. With the service installed, you can begin setting up your FTP site.

Configuring the Default FTP Site

When you install the FTP service, Setup automatically creates a default FTP site. Although you can't create new FTP sites in IIS under Windows XP, you can modify the default FTP site to suit your needs.

TIP If you need to host multiple FTP sites, switch to Windows 2000 Server, Windows Server 2003, or a third-party FTP hosting application.

To configure the site, open the IIS console (Figure 32.1), right-click the default FTP site, and choose Properties.

FIGURE 32.1
Use the IIS console to
manage your FTP site.

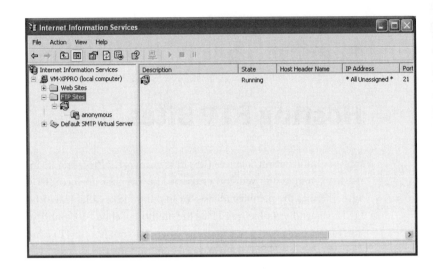

CONFIGURING GENERAL PROPERTIES

Use the FTP Site tab (Figure 32.2) to configure the site's general properties. The Identification group of controls lets you specify the name for the site as it appears in the IIS console, the IP address it will use, and the TCP port. The default port is 21; you should use a nonstandard port only if clients know the port beforehand or if you create a link on a web page to the FTP site's URL that includes the port. An example of an FTP URL that includes the port number is `ftp://ftp.boyce.us:10000`.

TIP Generally, the only reason to use a nonstandard port is if you have another service running on the computer that uses the standard port. This would be the case only if you're running another FTP server on the computer in addition to IIS.

FIGURE 32.2
The FTP Site tab
controls the general
settings for the site.

The Connection group lets you specify the maximum number of connections and the Connection Timeout value. As with a website, Windows XP Professional is limited to 10 concurrent FTP connections, so the only reason to change the number of connections is to limit access to fewer users. The Connection Timeout value controls how long a connection can be inactive before IIS disconnects it, requiring the client to connect again. The default is 900 seconds, but you might decrease the value if you have one or more clients who tend to time out frequently because of network problems. With only 10 available connections, you probably don't want connections tied up because of timeout issues. However, if you set the timeout too low, IIS will drop connections unnecessarily. If you feel you're having problems with connections being unavailable due to timeout, consider decreasing the timeout value to 180 seconds (three minutes).

The Enable Logging option lets you turn on logging of FTP sessions. I recommend that you turn on logging unless you don't provide public access to the FTP site, the site is available only to a limited number of people, and you aren't concerned about security for the files and/or server. In all other cases, I recommend that you turn on logging, if for no other reason than to provide an evidence trail that will allow you to prosecute someone who hacks into or abuses your system. You can choose between the IIS log file format and the extended W3C format, which offers additional formatting options. Select the desired format from the list, and then click Properties to display the log properties shown in Figure 32.3.

FIGURE 32.3

The General Properties tab configures the log frequency and path.

As Figure 32.3 illustrates, you can specify how frequently IIS creates a new log, choosing between log frequency and log file size. If you want to continue with a single log file indefinitely, select the Unlimited File Size option. However, you should periodically check the size of the log to make sure it isn't growing out of control. IIS can log a lot of data in a file without making it overly large, but you should monitor the log file anyway. When the log grows uncomfortably large (takes a long time to load in WordPad, for example), write it to a CD-R or other removable media.

If you choose the W3C log format, IIS displays an additional Extended Properties tab for the log (Figure 32.4). IIS by default logs only certain information about each session. You can choose the Extended Properties option and select additional items to include in the log. I recommend that you at least include the username in the log if you're providing nonanonymous FTP services, giving you the ability to track who is using the FTP server and when.

FIGURE 32.4
Use the Extended Properties tab to specify the log's contents.

VIEWING CURRENT CONNECTIONS

IIS gives you the ability to view the current connections to the FTP server as well as to disconnect specific users. To view current connections, open the properties for the FTP site in the IIS console, and, on the FTP Site tab, click Current Sessions to display a dialog box similar to the one shown in Figure 32.5. If you enable authenticated access to the FTP server, the user's logon name identifies the user. Otherwise, the password that the user enters for the anonymous account identifies the user.

To disconnect a user, click the user in the list and click Disconnect. Or, click Disconnect All to close all sessions. Keep in mind that file transfers that are active will be terminated (and incomplete) when you close the connections.

CONFIGURING AUTHENTICATED AND ANONYMOUS ACCESS

Like the World Wide Web service in IIS, the FTP service supports both anonymous and authenticated access. Also like the World Wide Web service, anonymous FTP access isn't truly anonymous in the sense that IIS uses the IUSR account I discussed in Chapter 30 to authenticate all anonymous users. So, although you might not know who an anonymous FTP user is—since they can provide a bogus e-mail address for the password when they log in—at least IIS is authenticating the access against an existing account.

FIGURE 32.5
Use the FTP User Sessions dialog box to view current user sessions.

You should configure the FTP service for anonymous access if you don't care who accesses the site and its files. If you want to maintain control over who has access and who doesn't, you should turn off anonymous access and rely on user accounts to protect your site.

NOTE   One reason to allow *only* anonymous access is to prevent users from logging onto the FTP server with an account that has administrative privileges. Administrative access could present a security risk to the computer and the files hosted on your FTP server, because an account with administrative privileges is likely to have full control over the folders and files—something you might not want.

To configure access methods for FTP, open the IIS console, right-click the default FTP site, and choose Properties. Click the Security Accounts tab (Figure 32.6). Select the option Allow Anonymous Connections if you want to allow anonymous users to access the FTP site. This option doesn't prevent users from logging on with a different, valid user account, however. If you want to prevent users from logging on with anything other than the computer's IUSR account (anonymous access), also select the option Allow Only Anonymous Connections. IIS will then reject any attempts to connect using any username other than anonymous.

If you want to prevent anonymous access to the site, clear the option Allow Anonymous Connections. Users must then provide a valid local account with the necessary rights to log onto the FTP site (explained shortly).

TIP   Although you could change the account that the FTP service uses for anonymous logon, I don't recommend it. Leave the default IUSR account in place, and allow IIS to control the password (through the option of the same name).

For remote users to connect to the FTP service, the account they provide must have the right to log on locally. Setup grants the IUSR account this right when you install IIS. You need to grant this right to any other accounts that are authorized to use the FTP service. You could assign the right on a per-user basis, but I recommend you create a local group named ftp-users (or something similar), grant this group the right to log on locally, and then add accounts to the group as needed.

FIGURE 32.6

Configure access with the
Security Accounts tab.

To create the FTP group, follow these steps:

1. Open the Computer Management console, and expand the Local Users And Groups branch.

2. Right-click the Groups node, and choose New Group to open the New Group dialog box.

3. Specify the group name, and then click Add to add local accounts to the group.

4. After populating the group, click Create, and then close the dialog box.

After you create and populate the group, you need to grant it the right to log on locally as I mentioned earlier:

1. Open the Local Security Policy from the Administrative Tools folder.

2. Expand the branch \Security Settings\Local Policies\User Rights Assignment, and then double-click the Log On Locally right to display the Log On Locally Properties dialog box.

3. Click Add User Or Group, enter the name of the group you just created, and click OK.

   If you want to browse for the group, click Object Types, click to check Groups, and click OK. Click Advanced, search for the recently created FTP users group, and then close the dialog box and the policy editor.

Now it's time to test the FTP service. You don't need to log on from another computer. Just open a command console, and type **ftp localhost**. Or, enter **ftp** and, at the ftp> prompt, type **open localhost**. Enter the necessary account credentials when prompted. If the logon fails, verify the account credentials, and check that the account is included in the local ftp-users group. Also check the methods you've allowed for authentication on the FTP server, and then try again.

NOTE You can use the ftp command from a console to perform all FTP client tasks. You can also use a web browser or one of several third-party FTP utilities. See the later sections of this chapter for information on using Internet Explorer and third-party applications.

Although the Security Accounts tab contains an FTP Site Operators control group, you can't modify the list of operators for the site. Operators can make certain changes to a site but not to IIS general settings or settings that apply to the server as a whole. By default, IIS adds the Administrators group to the list. You must use Windows 2000 Server or Windows Server 2003 platforms if you need to control operators on a more granular level.

TIP Controlling operator access on a Windows XP Professional computer isn't really necessary, because you can host only one site. Nevertheless, it would be nice to be able to designate a different user as an operator to offload some of the administrative tasks for FTP. Perhaps Microsoft will add this capability in the future.

CONFIGURING WELCOME, EXIT, AND MAXIMUM CONNECTIONS MESSAGES

You can customize your FTP server to present custom messages to clients when they log on and off the FTP server, or when they attempt to log on but no more connections are available. For example, you might want to add a legal disclaimer to your welcome banner that informs the user that the site is monitored for unlawful use, violators will be prosecuted, and so on. Or maybe you just want to offer a friendly greeting to anyone connecting to the site. To do this, follow these steps:

1. Open the properties for the FTP site, and click the Messages tab (Figure 32.7).

2. In the Banner text box, type the text that you want the user to see prior to logging on.

3. Enter in the Welcome text box the message you want displayed following successful authentication.

4. In the Exit box, type the text that users should see when they log off.

5. Enter in the Maximum Connections box the text the FTP server should display when there are no more available connections.

FIGURE 32.7

Configure FTP service messages through the Messages tab.

CONFIGURING THE HOME DIRECTORY

The last tab in the FTP site's properties—Home Directory (Figure 32.8)—lets you specify the location of the FTP site's root folder. This is the folder in which anonymous users are placed and the folder in which authenticated users are placed if they have no home directory (see the next section).

As Figure 32.8 illustrates, you can specify a local folder or a network share on a remote computer as the root for the FTP site. Specifying a network share lets your computer function as the entry point to the site but allows the files to actually be hosted on a different server. For example, you might place the root folder on a server that gets backed up regularly to ensure availability of your FTP files in the event your computer suffers a catastrophic failure.

The Home Directory tab also controls the general permissions for the site. You can allow Read or Write access, or a combination of the two. Enable Read access to allow users to download files; enable Write access to allow them to upload files. Then, use NTFS permissions on individual folders to control read/write ability on a more granular basis.

FIGURE 32.8

Use the Home Directory tab to specify the location of the site's root folder.

The Directory Listing Style group controls how directory listings appear to remote users when they use the dir command from an ftp console or when they browse a directory using a web browser or graphical FTP client. Select the Unix option to display permissions and other directory information in Unix format, similar to what you would see when listing a directory on a Unix computer with the ls -1 command. Select the MS-DOS option if you want the directory to look similar to the results of a dir command in a command console on a Windows-based system.

PLACING USERS IN A SPECIFIC DIRECTORY AT LOGON

One handy feature provided by IIS for FTP is that it checks for a folder name that matches the user's credentials during logon and, if it finds a match, places the user in that folder after authentication. For example, if I log onto the account with the username jboyce, and the FTP server contains a folder, either physical or virtual, named jboyce, that folder becomes my initial folder after I log in.

You can use this feature in a couple of ways as it suits your needs. First, you can use it to quickly direct remote users to their own folders. Create a virtual directory for each FTP client, and configure the permissions as necessary on each folder to provide the desired security. Make sure to set the alias for the directory to match the user's logon name. When the user logs on, she is automatically placed in her "home" directory.

TIP This little trick works for the anonymous account, as well. Create a virtual directory with the alias anonymous, and when anonymous users log on, they're placed in that folder initially. This is a good way to direct anonymous users to specific content.

You can also use virtual directories to provide specific types of content. For example, you might create virtual directories with the aliases drivers, documents, tools, and so on. Users could then log on with a generic username (assuming you've created a matching account) and immediately be directed to the associated content.

Adding Virtual Directories

The directory specified in the Home Directory tab of the FTP site's properties is the root directory for the FTP site's overall folder structure. If you create physical subfolders under the specified root, the remote users also see these folders as subfolders under the root. Your site isn't limited to physical folders, however. You can also create *virtual directories*.

A virtual directory is assigned an alias that serves as the client-side folder name—the folder name the user sees when connecting to the folder. When users connect to a virtual directory, IIS redirects them to the actual folder, whether it's located on the same computer or on a network share. The user, however, doesn't see the virtual directories when browsing the FTP site. For example, assume your FTP site has its root folder at c:\inetpub\ftproot. This folder has no physical subfolders. Also assume that the user connects with the anonymous account, and there is no virtual directory named anonymous. So, IIS places the user in the site's root folder. But the user sees only the contents of the root folder—no other folders are visible, because the virtual folders aren't enumerated.

There are a handful of ways for the user to wind up in a virtual folder:

Alias-to-account mapping The user logs on with a username that matches the virtual directory's alias.

Specifying the alias with the *cd* command The user is working from an FTP console and uses the cd *alias* command to switch directories, where *alias* is the virtual directory alias.

Specifying the alias in the URL The user includes the virtual directory alias in the connection URL, such as ftp://ftp.boyce.us/doorknobs. In this case, doorknobs is the virtual directory alias.

Specifying the alias as the initial folder in an FTP client Most third-party FTP clients let you specify the initial folder for the connection and automatically place you in the folder after authentication.

To create a virtual directory, open the IIS console, right-click the FTP site, and choose New ≻ Virtual Directory to start the Virtual Directory Creation Wizard. The wizard prompts you for the alias, the actual path to the folder (which can be a local drive or UNC path), and the desired permissions for the folder. If you specify a UNC path, IIS prompts you for the user credentials it must use to connect to the remote share.

TIP You can create multiple levels of virtual directories. When you're creating the directory, right-click the folder that will serve as the root of the virtual directory.

Providing Site Security

I've already touched on site security in my discussion of authentication. Given the 10-connection limit of Windows XP Professional, I assume that you're using Windows XP to host an FTP site on an internal network rather than the public Internet. However, if you're using it to provide FTP services to the public, I then have to assume that you're providing files to friends and family rather than the public at large. Otherwise, you should be using a server platform without a connection limit.

I don't recommend that you allow anonymous access on an FTP server connected to the Internet unless you're prepared to have every nut from here to the next solar system putting files on your computer (more on this in the next section). Instead, grant access to people on an individual basis, either creating an account for each one or giving out the username and password for a common account, but only after obtaining identifying information from each person.

Your other alternative is to give anonymous users Read access but to give Write access only to users with a specific account. To accomplish this, first set up the FTP site's folders on an NTFS volume. Configure the site to allow anonymous and authenticated access, as I explained earlier in this chapter. Then, configure NTFS permissions so that the IUSR account has only Read permission and the other accounts have Write permission. You can assign Write permission on an as-needed basis or grant your FTP users group Write permission if everyone except anonymous users should have the ability to upload to the site.

TIP You can configure NTFS permissions on a per-folder basis, giving you lots of flexibility in the type of access each user will have.

Another important consideration is the location of your FTP root folder for the site. Make sure you place the root folder on an NTFS volume if at all possible, and don't use a folder that contains any sensitive system files. For example, *never* use the root of a system drive as the root of your FTP site. Also avoid using the \Inetpub folder as the root; instead, use the default \Inetpub\ftproot.

If you use FTP to publish your website to the server, you'll also need to set up a secure FTP virtual directory that points to the website's root folder. Make sure the site resides on an NTFS volume, and then configure the permissions on the folder and all subfolders so the publishing account has change permission in the folders.

TIP The IUSR account doesn't, by default, have explicit permissions in the \Inetpub folder or any of its subfolders. Instead, Windows XP grants the built-in Users group Read & Execute, List Folder Contents, and Read permissions. The IUSR account is implicitly a member of the Authenticated Users group, which is an explicit member of the Users group. This is why the IUSR account (and therefore anonymous users) can read files from the website.

One final bit of advice I offer is that you make sure to turn on logging through the FTP Site tab and select the W3C Extended Log File Format I described earlier in this chapter. Configure extended logging to include the source IP address, date and time, and username. The date and time are as important as the IP address, because they give you a means to identify the remote user. The user's IP address could vary if he connects to the Internet through a dial-up connection, but the user's ISP can identify the user based on its connection logs. The IP address tells the ISP which port was used to log on to its service, and the date and time help the ISP determine which user was on that port at the specified time.

Tips for Dealing with Miscreants

If you open your FTP site to anonymous upload, I guarantee it won't be more than a few weeks at best before some joker (if not several) starts using your server to host pornography or other unwanted content. I forgot to turn off anonymous access when I set up one of my home servers, and I was the recipient of some questionable content within a matter of days. What's worse, the scum-sucking, bottom-feeding person who did it set up a corrupt folder structure that took me a few days to delete. Once I figured out the method they used, however, the solution was easy.

It's possible under certain circumstances to create folders that use reserved system names as folder names. For example, you can create a folder called COM2 and place in it all the files you like. When you try to delete the folder, however, Windows XP will politely tell you that you can't delete the folder. That's one method hackers and crackers use to put content on a system and prevent the average user from removing it without reformatting the volume (one reason to place your FTP site on its own disk drive or logical drive).

You can delete folders with reserved names using one of two methods. If the folder resides on an NTFS volume, open a command console, and issue the command `del` with the folder name identified with at least one wildcard. To delete the folder LPT2, for example, use the command **del LPT?**.

If the folder or file resides on an NTFS partition, you need to take another approach. The Windows 2000 and Windows XP Resource Kits include a tool called `RM.EXE`. This is a POSIX application that allows you to remove folders and files, including those with reserved names. The following example would remove a file named `COM1` from the `c:\inetpub\ftproot` folder:

```
rm -d "//C/inetpub/ftproot/COM1"
```

As the sample illustrates, POSIX uses a path structure different from DOS/Windows. POSIX commands are case sensitive, so you must enter the path using its actual case. In addition, the example assumes you have placed the `RM.EXE` executable in a folder that is on the current path.

If you need to recursively remove an entire folder tree, use a command similar to the following, replacing the path with the appropriate path to the folder you want to delete:

```
rm -r "//C/Program Files/App"
```

Another method hackers use is to create a folder with an empty long filename. This makes it nearly impossible to delete the folder even with the `rm` command, because you can't use the `cd` command to change to a folder with an empty name. In most cases, you can use the `rm` command to remove the entire folder tree, but sometimes you may want to preserve the tree and delete only the folder with the blank name. The trick is to use the folder's short name, not the long name, to delete the folder:

1. Open a command console, and use the `cd` command to move to the folder that contains the blank-named subfolder.

2. Type **dir /X** to view the short names for the items in the folder. Note the short name for the folder that has the blank long name.

3. Use the `rm` command with this short name to delete the folder.

Finally, and perhaps most important, take to heart my suggestions about security in the previous section, and make sure you actively monitor the FTP service's logs. If you find that someone has been abusing your FTP site, take whatever legal remedies you can against them. If nothing else, make sure to notify the remote user's ISP, if possible.

Third-Party FTP Applications

If you want to simplify FTP, particularly for uploading and downloading multiple files and folders, consider using one of the many third-party FTP clients available on the Internet. These tools offer features such as easy file and folder handling, the ability to save connections settings and connect to a server with a single click, the ability to restart an interrupted transfer, and much more.

A search of your favorite software download site (mine is www.tucows.com) will likely turn up at least 100 FTP utilities of one kind or another, and probably more than that.

I've tried several FTP apps over the years, and although I can't say that these are necessarily the best, I've had good luck with them:

BulletProof FTP Server This FTP server offers full support for the FTP standard and adds other advanced features like transfer restart, group management, real-time statistics and monitoring, quotas, and lots more. Best of all, the server supports multiple IP addresses, enabling you to host multiple FTP sites: www.bpftpserver.com.

BulletProof FTP   The client version provides the typical graphical interface and adds a multiple-file download queue and the ability to restart interrupted downloads: `www.bpftp.com`.

VShell   This server application functions as an alternative to Telnet and FTP for secure remote access and file transfer. This SSH2 server provides strong encryption and several other features to offer secure network access, remote administration, and file transfer: `www.vandyke.com/products/vshell/index.html`.

Crystal FTP Pro   This FTP client includes all the usual features you'd expect from an FTP client, and it also lets you download up to eight files at a time while you continue to browse the FTP site. It includes a built-in Tetris game, but I could do without that: `www.casdk.com`.

Internet Neighborhood Pro   This FTP tool functions as a Windows shell addition rather than a stand-alone program. So, you can browse FTP sites through the standard Windows Explorer interface. The program supports transfer restart and lots of other handy features, such as the ability to save a file directly to an FTP site from an application: `www.knoware.com/index.php?pg=./products/inpro/index`.

Chapter 33

Setting Up a Telnet Server

Have you ever wished you could connect to a computer and manage it remotely, but you didn't want to go through the expense of a third-party remote-control application like pcAnywhere? Even though Windows XP now includes the ability to manage a remote computer through Remote Desktop Connection, and even though free remote-control applications are available (notably VNC, covered in Chapter 23), you might desire a different method of remote access and control. Telnet can give you that ability.

Telnet is an Internet standard that lets you connect to a remote computer and run a console session on that computer. Windows XP includes the software necessary to turn the computer into a Telnet server, enabling remote users to connect to the computer and work from a console session.

In this chapter, I explain how to set up the Telnet service in Windows XP and configure the computer for remote Telnet access. The chapter not only covers basic configuration but also examines security, how to run startup scripts, and third-party Telnet programs you might find useful.

TIP   Windows XP Professional includes the Telnet service, but Windows XP Home Edition doesn't. However, you can use a third-party Telnet server under Home Edition.

Setting Up a Telnet Server

Setup installs the Telnet service under Windows XP Professional during installation but doesn't configure the service for automatic startup. So, getting your computer up and running as a Telnet server is a simple matter of starting the service. You can then fine-tune the configuration to control security, change the logon banner, and specify other settings.

TIP   Users must be members of the TelnetClients group (which does not exist by default) or the Administrators group to connect to the computer through Telnet. Simply having the right to log on locally doesn't provide that ability. See the section "Configuring System Security," later in this chapter, for more information.

Starting the Service

To configure the service, open the Services console (Figure 33.1) from the Administrative Tools folder or the Services branch of the Computer Management console. Locate the Telnet service in the service list, and click the Start button on the toolbar or the Start link if you're using the Extended tab.

FIGURE 33.1
Start and stop the Telnet service through the Services console.

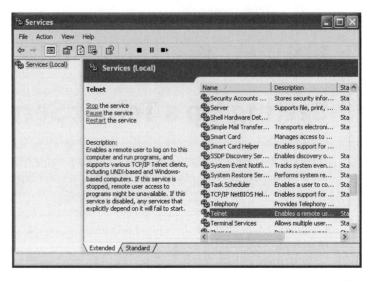

If you want to be able to connect to the computer through Telnet at any time, consider configuring the Telnet service for automatic startup. Double-click the Telnet service in the Services console, and select Automatic from the Startup Type drop-down list (Figure 33.2). Before you do so, however, you should read the section "Configuring System Security," later in this chapter, to make sure you aren't exposing your system to a security risk.

FIGURE 33.2
Configure the service for automatic startup if you want access to it all the time.

Setting the Logon Banner

When a user logs onto a Windows XP Telnet server, the Telnet service opens a command console for the user and executes a default logon script. This script is located in *%systemroot%*\System32\Login.cmd. The script by default displays the simple welcome message specified by the echo commands in the file. You can use the message as is, but I recommend that you modify it to at least warn remote users that the system is restricted to authorized users only and that access is audited. This should give you some legal recourse if someone hacks into your system through the Telnet service (assuming you catch them).

To modify the logon banner, change the contents of the Login.cmd file. The following is a sample:

```
echo *==============================================================
echo Welcome to host.boyce.us. Access to this computer is restricted
echo to authorized personnel only! Access to this computer is audited
echo and monitored regularly. Legal action will be taken against any
echo unauthorized users. Have a nice day!
echo *==============================================================
```

Changing the Home Directory

Another function that the Login.cmd script performs is to change to the user's home directory. The last line of the script accomplishes this change:

```
cd /d %HOMEDRIVE%\%HOMEPATH%
```

The cd command is the same one you use in any command console. The /d switch allows a change of drive as well as directory, in case the user's home directory is located on a different volume from the system volume. The script replaces the *%HOMEDRIVE%* and *%HOMEPATH%* variables with the path to the user's home directory. When I log on as jboyce, for example, the script puts me in C:\Documents and Settings\jboyce.

Using these variables allows the Telnet service to open the console session for the user in his own directory, and that's the behavior you'll want in most cases. In some situations, however, you may want to place the remote users in a specific folder. You can accomplish this by replacing the variables with the appropriate path. For example, if you want all remote Telnet users to have their consoles open rooted in F:\telnet, then you can change the last line of the script to the following:

```
cd /d f:\telnet
```

NOTE   You need to create the specified folder on the specified volume first. Also keep in mind that the logon script applies to all users, so if you change the location, it will apply to all Telnet users.

Running User-Specific Startup Scripts

In Windows XP, as in other Windows platforms, each user can have a script that runs when the user logs on. The logon script is defined in the user's profile and can be either a batch (BAT) or command (CMD) file. Typical uses for the logon script include mapping network drives, executing programs, and connecting printers.

To assign a logon script, open the Computer Management console, and open the \Local Users And Computers\Users branch. Double-click a user account to open its properties, and click the Profile tab (Figure 33.3).

NOTE I cover other profile properties in Chapter 37. This chapter focuses specifically on logon scripts for Telnet access.

FIGURE 33.3
Specify the logon script in the Logon Script field.

Here's where it gets a bit tricky. The Windows logon service and the Telnet service look in different places for the user's logon script. The Windows logon service looks in the NETLOGON share on the computer for the scripts, and the Telnet service looks in `%systemroot%\system32\repl\imports\scripts`. On a Windows NT Server platform, the NETLOGON share points to this same folder. On a Windows 2000 Server or Windows Server 2003 platform, however, the NETLOGON share typically points to a subfolder of the SYSVOL folder on the domain controller.

Here's the catch: the folder doesn't exist on a Windows XP Professional computer, even though the Telnet service passes it to the client as part of the path! So, if you want a Telnet client to run a custom logon script, you need to create the folder `%systemroot%\system32\repl\import\scripts`. Then, create a folder for the user who matches the user's logon name and place the script in that folder. Open the user's profile and enter **%username%*scriptname*** in the Logon Script field, where *scriptname* is the filename of the script.

When you're setting up the Telnet script, keep in mind that Windows logon also looks to the profile for the user's logon script, even though that script might be located in a different folder. Although you could share the `%systemroot%\system32\repl\import\scripts` folder as NETLOGON, you don't have to—you can share a different folder by that name if you like. The end result of doing so is that you'll have one script for Windows logon and a different script for Telnet logon. However, you need to maintain the same folder structure for both folder locations. In other words, if you specify `%username%` as the path for the logon script in the profile, then both locations—NETLOGON and the `import\scripts` folder—must have a folder that matches the username, and both of those folders must contain the appropriate script.

I see this behavior—two different services looking for the logon script in a different location—as a bug. There is the possibility that Microsoft will change this behavior in a future patch. Most administrators would probably prefer a consistent treatment of logon scripts to avoid having to manage two sets of scripts.

Configuring System Security

Telnet offers yet another way for remote users to access your computer. Each method of access offers certain security risks. This section examines the risks and also explains how to configure user accounts to allow Telnet access.

NOTE   See the later section "Using the Telnet Administrator" to learn how to specify the authentication methods supported by the Telnet service.

Protecting Your System

Providing Telnet access to your computer is, in general, more of a security risk than sharing a folder on the network. When you share a folder, the user is restricted to that folder. However, gaining Telnet access is just like sitting in front of the computer locally. You can change drives and folders using cd and other commands. This means that unless you use NTFS and protect all folders with appropriate NTFS permissions, a remote Telnet user can gain access to all folders and files.

Before you go to the trouble of setting up accounts for Telnet access, consider the security implications of allowing Telnet access. Convert your volume(s) to NTFS, and then make sure you review the permissions on *all* folders and restrict access as needed. I strongly recommend that you perform these tasks before allowing any access through Telnet.

Setting Up Accounts

In order for a remote user to connect to a Windows XP computer running the Telnet service, the user must be a member of a local group named TelnetClients. Windows XP doesn't create this group by default; you must create it to grant Telnet access to users.

To create the account, follow these steps:

1. Open the Computer Management console, and expand the Local Users And Computers branch.

2. Right-click the Groups node, and choose New Group.

3. In the following dialog box (Figure 33.4), enter **TelnetClients** in the Group Name field. You can also add a description of your choice in the Description field.

4. Click Add, and then enter the username or browse for a user to grant Telnet access. Add any other users as needed, and click OK.

5. Close the New Group dialog box and the Computer Management console.

A Telnet user must have the right to log on locally to the computer. You don't need to grant the TelnetClients group the right to log on locally, because the members already have this right through membership in the built-in Users group. However, if you *deny* the TelnetClients group the right to log on locally, no one other than administrators will be able to connect through Telnet. This would defeat the whole purpose for the TelnetClients group. The bottom line is this: any user you allow Telnet access also has the ability to log on locally. In most cases, this won't be a problem, particularly if you protect your system with NTFS permissions.

FIGURE 33.4
Create a group named
TelnetClients to allow
Telnet access.

TIP Members of the Administrators group are an exception to the requirement for membership in the TelnetClients group. These users can access the computer through Telnet without being members of the TelnetClients group.

Using the Telnet Administrator

If you have worked with the Telnet service in Windows 2000 or Windows Server 2003, you're probably at least somewhat familiar with the `tlntadmn` program that lets you configure and manage the Telnet service. This program has been changed considerably in Windows XP. The Windows 2000 version provided a management menu, whereas the Windows XP version functions as a command-line tool. This makes it handy for scripting but makes it more difficult to manage Telnet service settings. I hope that Microsoft will at some point provide a GUI interface for configuring the Telnet service. In the meantime, we'll have to make do with `tlntadmn`.

Managing Sessions

You can use `tlntadmn` to manage Telnet client connections to your computer. You can view information about sessions, kill (disconnect) a session, and send a message to a remote user.

To work with a session, you first need to know its session ID. Open a command console, and type the following to see output like the lines presented here:

```
C:\>tlntadmn -s all
2

2 telnet session(s)

ID    Domain    UserName        Client         LogonDate   LogonTime    IdleTime
-----------------------------------------------------------------------------
372   VM-XPPRO  jboyce          192.168.0.11   1/25/2005   9:48:37 AM   0:04:52
920   VM-XPPRO  administrator   192.168.0.15   1/25/2005   10:22:13 AM  0:06:31
```

The session ID appears in the first column. You can then use a couple of other options with tlntadmn to kill the session or send a message. To kill a session, use the following syntax, replacing *ID* with the session ID:

```
tlntadmn -k ID
```

In some cases, you may want to send a message to a remote user. For example, perhaps you need to reboot or shut down your computer. Sending a message allows the remote user to exit the session first. Use the following syntax to send a message, replacing *ID* with the session ID:

```
tlntadmn -m ID Type your message here, no quotes needed
```

Configuring the Server

You can also configure the Telnet service with the tlntadmn program using the config parameter and a corresponding option. The syntax for this format of the command is

```
tnltadmn config [config_option]
```

Following is a list of the actions you can perform and the associated option:

Set the default domain for usernames   Set the domain against which user accounts are authenticated if it's different from the local computer. Here's an example:

```
tlntadmn config dom = mydomain
```

Set the mapping of the Alt key   Map the Alt key to Ctrl+A so the Telnet server will interpret Ctrl+A as pressing the Alt key. Here's an example:

```
tlntadmn config ctrlakeymap = yes
```

Set the idle session timeout   Specify the amount of time a session can be idle before it's disconnected. This example sets the timeout to 1 hour, 30 minutes, 20 seconds:

```
tlntadmn config timeout = 1:30:20
```

Enable idle session timeout   Specify whether the Telnet server should disconnect idle users when the session timeout is reached. Here's an example:

```
tlntadmn config timeoutactive = yes
```

Set the maximum number of login failure attempts before disconnecting   Specify the number of failed logins allowed before the server disconnects the session. The default is three. For example:

```
tlntadmn config maxfail = 2
```

Set the maximum number of connections   Specify the maximum number of concurrent connections allowed with this option. For example:

```
tlntadmn config maxconn = 20
```

Set the Telnet port   Specify the port used by the Telnet service. The default is port 23. Here's an example:

```
tlntadmn config port = 5200
```

Set the authentication mechanism   The server can use NTLM or unencrypted authentication. If you enable both methods, the server attempts NTLM and then, failing that, attempts unencrypted authentication based on the credentials provided by the client. The following example would turn off NTLM and turn on password authentication:

```
tlntadmn config sec = -NTLM +passwd
```

Specify the name of the audit file   Set the name of the log file used by the Telnet server if it's other than or in addition to the event log. For example:

```
tlntadmn config fname = c:\logs\telnet.log
```

Specify the maximum size of the audit file   Set the maximum size (in MB) of the log file if you're using a log file in addition to or in place of the event log. This example sets the size to 4 MB:

```
tlntadmn config fsize = 4
```

Specify the mode of operation   Set the mode of operation for the Telnet server, choosing between `console` and `stream`. Console mode is most often used for screen-oriented programs; stream mode is more for dumb terminal operations (it's more efficient for command-line tasks). Here's an example:

```
tlntadmn config mode = stream
```

Specify where to log   You can configure Telnet to log to the event log, a log file, or both. For example:

```
tlntadmn config auditlocation = eventlog
```

Specify events to audit   Specify the types of events to log. Choose among administrative logon, user logon, and failed logon. The following example would log successful logons but not failures:

```
tlntadmn config audit = +admin +user -fail
```

TIP   Issue the `tlntadmn` command without any options to view the status of current settings.

Managing a Remote Server

You can use the `tlntadmn` command to manage the Telnet service on the local computer or use it to manage the service on a computer elsewhere on the network. However, `tlntadmn` works only for Windows XP and Windows Server 2003 computers. You must use the Windows 2000 version of the program if you need to manage a Windows 2000 Telnet server.

To connect to and manage a remote Telnet server on the LAN, include the computer name in the `tlntadmn` command. The following example would set the maximum number of connections on the Telnet server named snoopy:

```
tlntadmn \\snoopy config maxconn = 20
```

You can also use `tlntadmn` from within a Telnet session to a remote Windows XP computer. Open the Telnet session, and, in the console, issue the appropriate `tlntadmn` command.

Third-Party Telnet Applications

Like FTP, Telnet is a service that developers seem to have pursued with a passion, and the result is a wide selection of Telnet applications. The vast majority are client applications that add support for additional terminal emulation and other features. A handful of Telnet servers are available as well. The following two programs are worth consideration:

Absolute Telnet SSH This Telnet client provides all the standard Telnet features and adds support for Secure Shell 1 (SSH1) and Secure Shell 2 (SSH2), which provide several compression methods, X11 forwarding, port forwarding, and other features. The program supports file transfer through xmodem, ymodem, and zmodem protocols, as well as secure file transfer: `www.celestialsoftware.net`.

SecureCRT In addition to support for the Telnet protocol and standard features, this program also provides support for SSH, smart card–based authentication, file transfer protocols, port forwarding, font scaling, and much more. The program can work from the notification area to reduce Desktop and Taskbar clutter: `www.vandyke.com/products/securecrt/index.html`.

Part 7

Managing Users

In this section:

Chapter 34

Managing Users and Groups

If you're moving to Windows XP from Windows 9*x* or Windows Me, two topics are probably new to you: user accounts and groups. Although these other operating systems use accounts of a sort, they aren't at all like the user accounts used in Windows NT, 2000, and XP.

It's important that you understand users and groups to use Windows XP, and it's even more important that you use them effectively and securely. They are the mechanism by which you secure your computer and its shared resources. They are also the means by which you access shared resources on other computers.

Although you can assign rights and permissions on a user-by-user basis, in most cases you should do that only when you have a very small number of accounts. Even then, using groups to assign those rights and permissions often provides a more logical method for security organization. This chapter explains the role that user accounts and groups play in Windows XP security, both locally and across the network. I explain how to create users and groups and configure group membership.

New in Windows XP is a feature called *fast user switching*, which allows you to log on to a computer and use it without logging off the current user or closing his programs. For example, your spouse might be using the computer, but you need to check your e-mail before going out. You can log on, use the computer, and log off without making your spouse close any programs.

The final topic I cover in this chapter is user profiles. A user profile consists of the information that makes up a user's working environment; it includes `My Documents`, the Start menu, and other items, such as logon and logoff scripts. Managing user profiles might include, for example, locating a home directory on a server rather than on the local computer.

NOTE Chapter 37 goes into more aspects of user accounts, especially user profiles and logon/ logoff scripts.

Understanding Groups

Groups in Windows XP provide a way for you to assign rights and permissions to multiple users without having to assign those rights and permissions separately to each user. As such, groups are a tool you can use to simplify security administration.

For example, assume that you work in a company with a relatively small network of 50 users. You have certain files on your computer that 10 of those people need to be able to read, 10 others need to be able to modify, and the rest should have no access to at all. If you assigned the permissions without groups, you would need to assign the rights to each account. With groups, however, you can create two groups—one for read access and the other for change access—and make the appropriate user accounts members of the required group.

If you think a bit about this example, you'll probably realize the drawback of using a workgroup in this situation rather than a domain. In order for users to have individually recognized access to the shared folder, each user must have a local account on your computer. This means creating (in this example) 20 user accounts on your computer for those 20 users.

In a domain, each user would already have an account in the domain and these accounts would be managed by the network administrator. You would then grant access to your local share using these domain accounts; but again, the best option is to create a group and place in the group those accounts that need access. Otherwise, you need to add each account to the access control list (ACL) for the shared folder.

There is an alternative that you might consider for this situation and others like it that would otherwise require you to create multiple accounts on your computer. You could create two generic accounts, one called Read and the other called Change. Assign permissions accordingly to the shared folder using these two accounts. Then, give the account and password to the people who need access. They can connect to the share using the supplied user credentials to gain access.

The downside to this approach is the relative lack of auditing capability it offers. Although you could audit access by these two accounts, you would have no idea who was using the accounts. By creating and using individual accounts and groups, you can accurately audit which users are connecting to the shared resource.

Local and Domain Groups

You don't need to understand domains to really understand groups and how to use them, but an understanding of domains can be very useful when your computer resides in a workgroup and must interact with a domain. An understanding of domains is also naturally helpful where your Windows XP systems are domain members.

Domains act as a security boundary that serves to simplify security administration. The domain contains accounts for all users in the domain and users can authenticate against their domain account to access resources located anywhere in the domain. This means you don't need to create an account on every computer containing a resource that a given user needs to use. Instead, you grant access to each resource using that single domain account. If you're sharing a folder on your local computer, this means that when a remote user tries to connect to the share, Windows XP communicates with the domain controller to authenticate the user based on her domain account.

Multiple domains form a *domain forest* and domains in the forest can be grouped together hierarchically to form *domain trees*. The first domain in a domain tree is the *root domain*. Other domains in the tree are called *child domains*. The domain directly above a particular domain is that domain's *parent domain* and the domain directly below it is called its *child domain*. Figure 34.1 illustrates a domain hierarchy.

TIP You can't create domains on a Windows XP computer. Domains require the Windows NT Server, 2000 Server, or Windows Server 2003 platform. In addition, logical domain relationships are different from NT to the other two platforms. My discussion of domains in this chapter assumes Windows 2000 Server or later.

In Windows XP, there is only one kind of group: local. This means that the group resides on the local computer. Likewise, local user accounts also reside on the local computer.

FIGURE 34.1
A domain hierarchy begins with a forest and ends with individual members.

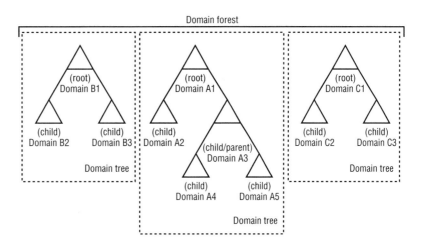

Note: Each root domain is a parent domain of those domains directly under the root.

A domain uses three group types, each with a different scope: domain local, global, or universal. Groups with universal scope—called *universal groups*—can contain groups and accounts from any domain in the domain tree or forest. They can be granted permissions in any domain in the entire domain forest.

Groups with global scope—called *global groups*—can contain groups and accounts only from the domain in which the group is defined, but they can be granted permissions in any domain in the forest.

Groups with local domain scope—called *domain local groups*—can contain accounts and groups only from their own domain and can be granted permissions only in the local domain.

A local group can naturally contain local user accounts. If the Windows XP computer resides in a domain, however, a local group can also include user accounts from the domain. Because this book focuses on Windows XP, I'll assume that you're creating local groups and want to add both local and domain accounts to the groups.

Creating and Managing Local Users and Groups

Windows XP provides two tools for creating user accounts and one for creating groups. In this section, I explain how to use these tools to create groups and accounts.

Creating and Managing Groups

You use the Local Users And Groups branch of the Computer Management console to create and manage groups in Windows XP. Right-click My Computer and choose Manage to open the console, then expand the Local Users And Groups branch (Figure 34.2).

TIP   You can add the Local Users And Groups snap-in to a stand-alone MMC console or to a custom console and then use that console instead of the Computer Management console to manage users and groups.

FIGURE 34.2

Use the Local Users And Groups snap-in to create groups.

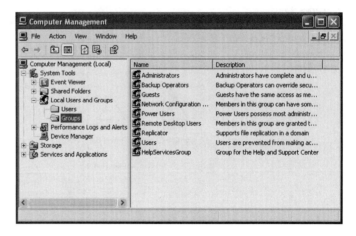

The Groups branch shows all the existing groups on the local computer. There are several built-in groups:

Administrators   Members of this group have complete control over the computer and can perform all functions, including adding hardware, modifying the configuration, and managing users and groups.

Backup Operators   This group allows members to bypass certain security restrictions to perform backups. However, members of this group can't view files for which they don't have the necessary permissions. Instead, they can only back up these files.

Guests   Members of this account, by default, have the same permissions as members of the Users group. The exception is the Guest account, which has additional restrictions.

Network Configuration Operators   This group allows members to modify certain network configuration items.

Power Users   These users have most of the same rights and permissions as administrators but lack certain rights, such as the ability to take ownership of a folder or file.

Remote Desktop Users   This group exists to support the Remote Desktop feature in Windows XP. Members of this group have the right to log on locally, giving them the ability to connect to the local computer using Remote Desktop.

Replicator   This group is used to replicate data within a domain. In most cases, you won't need to add accounts to or remove accounts from this group.

Users   Members of this group have the right to log on locally and this group is intended to support local users of the computer. Users can't make configuration changes to the computer (with minor exceptions) and they can run certified applications but not legacy applications.

HelpServicesGroup   This group is used by the Help and Support Center and supports the Remote Assistance feature in Windows XP.

You can add users to these groups as needed rather than create new groups. For example, when you need to give another person access to a computer, create an account for them in the built-in Users group.

The main reason to create a new group is to assign permissions and rights to a group of users that are different from the permissions and rights assigned to an existing group. For example, perhaps you want to create a group to support remote FTP access to your computer. You would grant this group the right to log on locally but deny them access to any folders other than the FTP folders.

To create a group, right-click the Groups node in the Local Users And Groups console and click New Group to open a dialog box where you specify the name of the group and an optional description. Then click Add to open the Select Users dialog box.

You can enter the names of the accounts directly in the text box or click Advanced to expand the dialog box (Figure 34.3) to search for accounts. If you choose the latter, click Find Now in the Select Users dialog box to search the default location (typically, the local computer). You can also click Locations to open a dialog box to search the domain if the computer is a domain member.

FIGURE 34.3

Search for and select users with the Select Users dialog box.

To simplify the search for accounts in a domain or on a local computer with lots of groups and accounts, click Object Types to open another dialog box. Clear the check box beside Built-In Security Principals, and click OK. Windows XP will then only search for user accounts.

Repeat the process to add other users or groups to the group. When you've added all the desired accounts and/or groups, close the New Group dialog box.

You can easily add members to a group after it's created. To do so, open the Local Users And Groups console, and then open the Groups branch. Double-click the group to open its properties and click Add to add other users or groups.

Creating and Managing User Accounts

Creating a user account is almost as easy as creating a group. In the Local Users And Groups console, right-click Users, and choose New User to display the New User dialog box (Figure 34.4). Enter the desired account name in the User Name field, the user's real name in the Full Name field, and an optional description for the account in the Description field. Enter the password for the account, and verify the password.

FIGURE 34.4
Add a user account with
the New User dialog box.

> **TIP** You can also use the User Accounts object in Control Panel to create and modify user accounts. See the later section "Other User Management Tasks" for more information.

Next, specify the following options, click Create to create the new account, and click Close to close the dialog box:

User Must Change Password At Next Logon   Choose this option to require the user to specify a new password the next time he logs on.

User Cannot Change Password   Select this option to prevent the user from changing passwords. This option is useful for accounts used by services to prevent someone from changing the password, which would prevent the service from starting.

Password Never Expires   Select this option if you don't want the account to be subject to password aging.

Account Is Disabled   Select this option to disable the account, which prevents it from being used.

MODIFYING GROUP MEMBERSHIP

When you create an account, Windows XP makes it a member of the Users group. You can modify group membership afterward to add other groups or change the default membership. To change membership, open the Local Users And Groups console and double-click the user account to open its properties; then click the Member Of tab.

To remove an existing group, select the group and click Remove. Click Add to add one or more groups with the Select Groups dialog box (Figure 34.5). You use the Select Groups dialog box in much the same way you use the Select Users dialog box.

> **TIP** Any user can be a member of more than one group. Membership in multiple groups is a common means for achieving custom security settings.

FIGURE 34.5

Add groups to a user's properties through the Select Groups dialog box.

RESETTING AN ACCOUNT PASSWORD

In Windows NT, the password for an account is available within the account's properties. Windows 2000 and XP are a bit different, however. To change the password, follow these steps:

1. Right-click the account and choose Set Password.

2. Windows XP displays a warning that changing the password could prevent the user from logging on. Click Proceed to display the Set Password dialog box (Figure 34.6).

3. Enter and confirm the password, and click OK.

FIGURE 34.6

Change the password with the Set Password dialog box.

NOTE   See "Recovering from Lost Passwords," later in this chapter, for information on changing a password with a password reset disk.

You can use the User Accounts object in Control Panel to change the password hint that Windows XP uses to prompt you for a password when you enter the password incorrectly. The following section explains how to configure the password hint.

Other User-Management Tasks

Although I prefer the Local Users And Groups console for user and group management, you can also use the User Accounts object in Control Panel to perform certain account-management tasks. These include changing the password, changing the picture associated with the account, and adding a .NET password to an account.

TIP   The picture for an account appears beside the account name in the Welcome screen.

SETTING A PASSWORD AND PASSWORD HINT

You can change a password as well as the password hint that Windows XP displays to help remind you of your password. Follow these steps:

1. Open Control Panel and open the User Accounts link.

2. Select an account. Click Change My Password to display the window shown in Figure 34.7.

NOTE   Change My Password becomes Change <user's> Password if you choose a password other than your own.

3. Enter the current password and the new password in the fields provided.

4. Enter the desired password hint in the last field and click Change Password.

FIGURE 34.7

You can specify a word or phrase that Windows XP will display as a password hint.

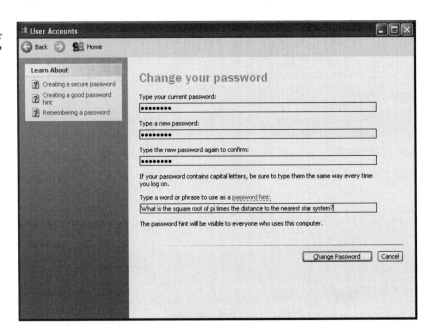

TIP   The password hint can help you guess a forgotten password, but it also can help someone else hack into your system locally if you use a hint that is too easy to guess

CHANGING YOUR ACCOUNT PICTURE

The Welcome screen displays a small picture beside each user account. Windows XP chooses a picture at random from a small selection of images. However, you can specify the picture that you want Windows XP to use for a particular account. The image need not be a specific size—Windows XP will resize it as needed. You can specify an image in GIF, BMP, JPG, or PNG format.

TIP XP resizes the image so the largest side is 48 pixels, with a maximum image size of 48×48 pixels

To change the picture, click the Change My Picture link in the User Accounts window. Select one of the sample images or click Browse For More Pictures to select from a different location.

SETTING UP A .NET PASSPORT

Microsoft has created an authentication mechanism called the .NET Passport that you can use to authenticate your identity on several websites, including Microsoft's sites. Windows Messenger also uses your .NET Passport as the means by which you log on to the Messenger service and other users can contact you. Assigning a .NET Passport to your user account enables you to use the passport to authenticate on these sites and services while logged on to Windows XP.

To assign a .NET Passport to an account, open the User Accounts link in Control Panel and click Set Up My Account To Use A .NET Passport. Windows XP starts a wizard to help you through the process of assigning your existing .NET Passport or creating a new one. All you need is an e-mail account to set up a passport.

MODIFYING YOUR NETWORK PASSWORD CACHE

Windows XP can maintain the user credentials that you use to access network resources such as shared folders, secured websites, printers, and other resources. For example, if you have a membership to a particular site, you can have Windows XP save your password so you don't have to enter it each time you visit the site.

To manage your password cache, follow these steps:

1. Open the User Accounts link in Control Panel and click your user account.

2. In the left pane, click Manage My Network Passwords to open the Stored User Names And Passwords dialog box (Figure 34.8).

FIGURE 34.8
Modify your password cache with the Stored User Names And Passwords dialog box.

3. To modify an existing password entry, click the item in the list and click Properties. In the dialog box for the item, specify the user name and password, and, if desired, change the name of the network resource.

   Or, to create a new password entry, click Add in the Stored User Names and Passwords dialog box. Specify the URL to the server or the UNC path for LAN resources, along with the user credentials to use to authenticate for the resource.

RECOVERING LOST PASSWORDS

Forgetting a password for a user account isn't a big deal as long as you know the administrator account password—just log on as an administrator and change the user's password as needed. When you lose the administrator password, however, the situation is more serious. You can't make any changes to the system without the administrator account. Fortunately, there are a couple of ways to recover the administrator password, as well as a way for users to recover their own passwords without help from an administrator.

Using a Password Reset Disk

Windows XP adds a new feature called a *password reset disk* that enables you to recover an account if you forget the password. The reset disk works for the administrator account as well as other user accounts. However, it can't recover a password unless it resets the password. You must create the recovery disk with the existing password, which means you must create the disk before you forget the password!

To create a password recovery disk, do the following:

1. Open the User Accounts link in Control Panel and click the account for which you want to create the disk.

2. In the left pane, click Prevent A Forgotten Password. Windows XP starts a wizard that steps you through the process of creating the recovery disk.

3. When prompted, insert a formatted disk and provide the current password for the account.

Here are the steps to recover the account with the password reset disk:

1. Boot the computer and select the account at the Welcome screen.

2. Enter any password and press Enter. Windows XP displays a warning message about your password.

3. Insert the reset disk in the floppy drive and click Use Your Password Reset Disk.

4. Follow the prompts provided by Windows XP to create a new password.

Using a Third-Party Recovery Tool

Without a password reset disk, one of the best options for recovering a forgotten password is to use a third-party password recovery tool. Several are available, but two are worth mentioning here.

The first is Winternals ERD Commander. In addition to enabling you to reset the administrator password, this tool boots otherwise unbootable systems from a CD and can recover lost files, recover Windows XP restore points, and accomplish several other recovery tasks. Look for more information at www.winternals.com.

If you're looking for a free password-recovery solution, check out Offline NT Password and Registry Editor. You can use this tool to boot the computer from a CD image and reset the administrator password for the local computer. You'll find more information at http://home.eunet.no/~pnordahl/ntpasswd.

Deleting the SAM File

Another, more drastic solution is to delete the file that holds the security database, contained in the Security Account Manager (SAM) file, which is part of the computer's registry. I recommend using this method only if you can't get another method to work, or you don't care that you'll lose the accounts on the computer and need to re-create them.

To use this approach, follow these steps:

1. Boot the system using Recovery Console.

2. Change to the *%systemroot%*\system32\config folder.

3. Rename the file sam to sam.old.

4. Reboot the computer. Your administrator account will now have a blank password, but all other accounts will be deleted.

5. Log on using the administrator account, change the account's password, and re-create any accounts and groups as needed.

Managing Users and Groups from a Console

The net command included with Windows XP provides a console-based tool for managing users and groups. The net user command manages user accounts on the local computer and net group manages groups.

The net command, when used without any other parameters, lists the user accounts on the computer. You can use the command to add and remove accounts, change an account's active status, change passwords, and accomplish other tasks. You can also set several other properties, including the account expiration, home directory, and profile location.

Type **net help user** at a command prompt to view the syntax and options for this command.

TIP   The net   group command only works on a domain controller and can't be used on a Windows XP computer to manage groups.

Fast User Switching

Windows XP offers a feature called *fast user switching* that allows another person to log on and use the computer without requiring that an existing user shut down all programs and log off. For example, let's say you're using the computer and your significant other wants to check e-mail, but you have several programs running. Fast user switching lets the other user log on, use the computer, and log off without affecting your running applications. When you log back on, your applications and Desktop are just the way you left them.

To enable fast user switching, open Control Panel and open the User Accounts link. Click Change The Way Users Log On Or Off to display the logon and logoff options shown in Figure 34.9. Select Use Fast User Switching and then click Apply Options.

FIGURE 34.9

Enable or disable fast
user switching through
the User Accounts dia-
log box.

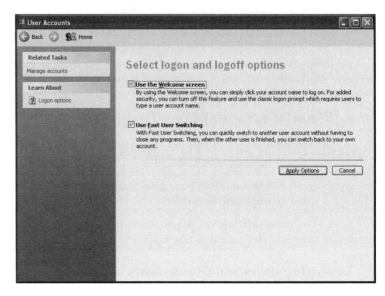

To switch users, click Start ➤ Log Off and then click Switch User. Windows XP prompts you to log
on. When you're ready to switch back, use the same procedure to change to the previous account.

NOTE A handful of features are not available when Fast User Switching is turned on. If you turn on
Fast User Switching and then realize that something isn't working as before, that's the likely reason.

Chapter 35

Understanding Group and Local Policies

In Windows 2000, Microsoft introduced a new feature to take the place of the system policies in Windows NT and Windows 9*x*. This new feature—called *group policies*—makes possible a wide range of capabilities to simplify data management, system administration, and security. For example, you can use group policies to automatically install operating systems and applications to client computers, which offers an excellent method for deploying new systems and accomplishing disaster recovery.

Group policies allow for more effective user data management. You can redirect user folders from the local computer to a network server to simplify disaster recovery and to provide easier data backup and recovery.

Group policies also provide a means to apply restrictions and impose *change control* on users' working environment. Change control refers to an administrator's ability to prevent certain user-initiated changes such as changing workstation configuration, adding or removing hardware, and so on.

Windows XP, like Windows 2000, also supports local policies, which are a local implementation of group policies defined and applied at the local computer level. Group policies require a Windows 2000 Server or Windows Server 2003 domain, but local policies are also available in a workgroup environment. In this chapter, I explain how to use and configure group and local policies.

Overview of Group and Local Policies

Group and local policies, introduced in Windows 2000 and expanded upon in the Windows XP and Microsoft Server 2003 platforms, provide a means of applying settings to the operating system and related environment during logon. These policies take the place of the system policies found in Windows 9*x* and Windows NT.

TIP   For a searchable database of group policy settings, check out www.boyce.us/gp, then click the List All Policies link.

There are literally hundreds of policy settings that you or a network administrator can apply through group and local policies. For example, group policies can be used to automatically define aspects of the user's working environment such as Desktop settings and the location of the user's profile. Policies also control the elements that the user sees in the Windows environment, such as the volumes listed in My Computer, items that appear in Control Panel, and icons that appear on the Desktop.

Group and local policies are a component of Microsoft's Directory Enabled Client Management (DECM) group of technologies. Policies work in concert with other features and services such as Remote

Installation Services (RIS) to provide a means for deploying operating systems and applications, managing user data, and controlling the actions that a user can perform within Windows. In effect, policies let you dynamically configure the operating system and working environment.

Policies can be applied at four different levels: site, domain, organizational unit (OU), and local. Policies are also separated into two categories: group and local. To use group policies, a computer must reside in a Windows 2000– or Windows Server 2003–based domain. The system administrator defines the policies in Active Directory (AD) at the appropriate level (site, domain, or OU); the same policy can have different settings at different levels. For example, the administrator might deny a particular user right at the site level but grant that right to an OU. The effective policy setting would then give the members of the OU that right, because the policies are applied in a layered fashion. Local policies apply first, then site, then domain, and then OU. The last policy applied takes precedence when the same policy is defined at multiple levels.

Because this book focuses on Windows XP and not Microsoft's server platforms, I'll focus this chapter on local policies. You can configure essentially the same policies at the local level that you can apply through AD. When the computer resides in a domain, the local group policies can be overridden by policies at higher levels. So, you can configure local policy, but there is no guarantee that the policies you define won't be replaced by group policy. When the computer resides in a workgroup, however, the local policies are the only ones that apply. So, local policies are a great way to automatically configure computers in a workgroup.

Many of the features made possible by group policy aren't available through local policy, however. The ability to automatically install operating systems and applications is a primary example. These capabilities require a Windows 2000 Server– or Windows Server 2003–based domain, a RIS server, and other resources. Even so, you can still use local policies to configure Desktop and working environment settings, apply disk quotas, and configure other Windows XP operating system settings. Local policies are particularly useful for applying restrictions and change control on computers that are shared by multiple users.

Why bother with local policies? The main reason to use local policies in a workgroup environment is to specify settings that you want applied to multiple users of the same computer. For example, you might want to configure properties for Internet Explorer that are different from the default settings and have these settings applied to all users of the computer. Or, perhaps you want to remove certain items from the Start menu, turn off personalized menus, hide the system tray (now called the *notification area*), or apply other changes for the computer, either for multiple users or just for yourself. Local policies provide a one-stop shop for changing almost all of the properties that define how your computer looks and functions.

TIP   Most of the policy settings correspond to values in the Registry. Although you can change the settings in the Registry manually, policies provide a more logical organization and a safer method for settings management.

You use two very different methods to manage group policies versus local policies. You create and edit group policies through the Active Directory Users And Computers console or the Active Directory Sites And Services console, both on the server. Neither of these tools is included with Windows XP. However, you can use the Group Policy console, which is included with XP, to manage local policies.

TIP   This chapter provides an overview of local and group policies and explains how to manage them. Chapters 36 and 37 focus on specific applications of local policy, such as applying user restrictions and redirecting user data.

Working with the Group Policy Console

The Group Policy console offers the same general structure for managing local polices that the Active Directory tools offer on a server for managing group policies. The only difference is that those policies that can't be set at the local level don't appear in the Group Policy console.

Follow these steps:

1. To open the console, choose Start ➢ Run and enter **MMC** in the Run dialog box.

2. Choose File ➢ Add/Remove Snap-In to display the Add/Remove Snap-In dialog box.

3. Click Add, select Group Policy from the snap-in list (Figure 35.1), and click Add. Then, click Close and click OK.

FIGURE 35.1

Select the Group Policy snap-in from the list.

4. In the Select Group Policy Object dialog box, specify Local Computer in the Group Policy Object field (Figure 35.2). Click Finish.

FIGURE 35.2

Select Local Computer as the group policy object to edit.

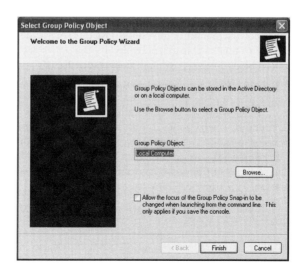

TIP You can use the Local Security Policy Editor in the `Administrative Tools` folder to modify various security policies, which form a subset of the local policies.

As Figure 35.3 illustrates, the Group Policy console includes two main branches: Computer Configuration and User Configuration. The Computer Configuration branch contains policies that apply to the computer and User Configuration contains policies that apply to the user.

FIGURE 35.3

Use the Group Policy console to manage local policies.

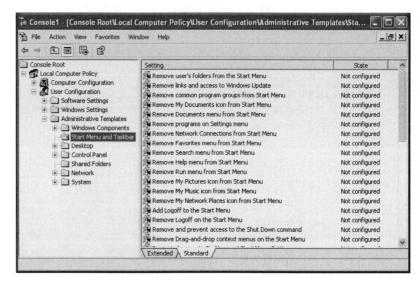

The Group Policy console works just like most other MMC consoles. To configure settings for a particular branch, select the branch. The policies that reside in the branch appear in the right pane, as Figure 35.3 shows. To change a policy, double-click it in the right pane to open a dialog box similar to the one shown in Figure 35.4. Use the Setting tab to configure the policy, choosing Not Configured, Enabled, or Disabled:

Not Configured This option indicates that the policy isn't configured, so no change is made to the Registry to modify the policy. Use this setting when you want Windows XP to use the default behavior for the feature controlled by the policy setting. However, understand that the policy could be defined at a different level (site, domain, or OU), overriding the local policy.

Enabled This option applies the policy to the user or computer.

Disabled This option specifies that the policy won't be applied to the user or computer.

Depending on the policy, the Setting tab might offer additional controls to set specific policy properties. For example, the Hide These Specified Drives In My Computer policy includes a drop-down list that you can use to select which drives to omit from My Computer.

Most of the settings also have an Explain tab (Figure 35.5) that provides a detailed explanation of the policy's function, how to use it, and other policies that work in conjunction with the selected policy.

FIGURE 35.4
Use the Setting tab to
configure the policy.

FIGURE 35.5
Find detailed informa-
tion about a policy on the
Explain tab.

Using the Group Policy console isn't difficult and the Explain tab generally does a good job of explaining the purpose of a given policy. For those reasons, and because there are hundreds of policies, I don't cover each policy in detail in this chapter. Instead, I offer some tips in the following sections that will help you identify the different policy branches and accomplish specific tasks.

My advice is that you spend several hours poring through the Group Policy editor, analyzing each policy to figure out what it does and how it will help you configure your computer the way you want or impose restrictions for users as needed. Start by reading the following sections to get an idea of the things you can control through policies.

Computer Configuration

The Computer Configuration branch, as I mentioned previously, contains policy settings that apply to the computer. The following sections explain what types of settings you'll find in each branch.

Software Settings

This branch is used by group policy to install applications automatically through DECM. There are no settings you can control locally. Instead, these policies must be set through group policy at a higher level.

Windows Settings

The Windows Settings branch contains several branches that control security, user rights, password policies, and related security settings.

SCRIPTS

The Scripts branch specifies the startup and shutdown scripts for the computer. These scripts, as their names imply, execute when the system starts and when it shuts down.

NOTE   For information on using startup and shutdown scripts, see Chapter 4.

SECURITY SETTINGS

The Security Settings branch gives you access to policies that control the way Windows XP handles logon, auditing, user rights, software restrictions, and other security-related features:

Account Policies   The Password Policy branch contains policies that control how Windows XP treats passwords. You can require that XP retain a password history to help ensure that users don't continue to reuse the same password. You can also configure other password-related settings such as password aging, minimum password length, and password complexity requirements.

The Account Lockout Policy branch specifies what actions Windows XP should take when a logon failure occurs (such as a user entering the wrong password). For example, you can configure XP to lock the account after a specified number of failed logon attempts and you can also specify how and when the account is subsequently unlocked.

Local Policies   The Local Policies branch contains three sub-branches that control auditing, user rights assignment, and various security-related settings. For example, you can rename the Administrator and Guest accounts, control users' ability to make device changes and install device drivers, and specify what the user sees during logon.

Public Key Policies   This branch contains one setting, Enroll User And Computer Certificates Automatically, which determines whether Windows XP automatically installs certificates on the computer. It also determines whether Windows XP automatically renews expired certificates and performs other certificate-related tasks.

The Encrypting File System branch lets you configure data recovery agents for EFS. The recovery agents allow encrypted data to be recovered if the certificate that was used to encrypt the data is lost or removed.

NOTE   See Chapter 42 to learn how to develop and implement an EFS recovery strategy.

Software Restriction Policies   Use this branch and its policies to control which applications a user can run and the paths that a user can access. For example, you might configure policies in this branch to prevent users from executing specific types of files, such as batch files or scripts. You can also specify which software publishers are trusted to determine whether applications from those publishers can be installed.

IP Security Policies   IP Security (IPSec) provides a means to encrypt and secure IP traffic between computers. The IP Security Policies branch contains the policies that determine how the local computer handles IPSec connections to other computers.

NOTE   See Chapter 43 for a detailed discussion of IPSec and how to use it.

Administrative Templates

This branch contains a wealth of application and operating system settings:

Windows Components   This branch contains policies that control NetMeeting, Internet Explorer, Terminal Services, the Task Scheduler, Windows Installer, and Windows Messenger. The primary reason to modify these policies is to control how these applications run or to prevent users from running specific applications, even if they are installed. For example, you can prevent the user from running Windows Installer, which effectively prevents the installation of most applications.

System   This branch controls system-wide settings such as the way scripts execute, how Windows XP manages user profiles, application of disk quotas, and logon. The branch contains several other branches that control properties including Remote Assistance, the Windows Time Service, and other features.

Network   This branch provides settings that control network properties and behavior for the computer. You can configure settings and behavior for DNS and offline files, prevent the use of ICS and ICF, prevent connection bridging, enable and configure QoS, and configure SNMP.

NOTE   See Chapter 26 for a discussion of SNMP.

Printers   This branch controls several properties for printing. For example, you can specify whether new printers added to the computer are published in Active Directory, enable or disable Internet-based printing to a printer on the computer, and specify a custom web page that appears in the left pane of the Printers folder to help users with printing problems.

User Configuration

The User Configuration branch contains policies that apply to users rather than to the computer.

TIP   As with the Computer Configuration branch, the Software Settings branch contains no policies that you can define at the local level.

Windows Settings

The Windows Settings branch lets you define logon and logoff scripts for users on the computer. The Public Key Policies branch contains a single policy, Autoenrollment Settings, that determines whether Windows XP automatically installs, updates, and renews user certificates.

The Internet Explorer Maintenance branch is the place to go to control the way IE looks and functions. You can change such properties as the animated icons that Internet Explorer displays in the toolbar, the title that appears in the browser, proxy settings, security settings, home page and other URLs, and several other settings. This branch essentially lets you customize IE without using a tool like the Internet Explorer Administration Kit.

Administrative Templates

As in the Computer Configuration branch, the Administrative Templates branch under User Configuration contains numerous settings that control the way specific applications run and the types of actions users can take with the applications. For example, you can use the policies in the Internet Explorer branch to disable specific tabs in the Internet Explorer properties dialog box to prevent the user from changing certain types of settings.

Many of the policies under the Administrative Templates branch let you apply restrictions on the actions users can take within the operating system as well as in specific applications. I focus on applying restrictions separately in Chapter 36 because this is one of the main uses for modifying local policies when group policies aren't available.

Chapter 36

Reining in Users with Policy Restrictions

Don't you just hate it when someone does something to their computer out of ignorance and you have to fix it? If you could just keep them out of Control Panel and hide all the drives in My Computer—or hide My Computer altogether—wouldn't that be great? Before it happens again and you consider homicide as an option, take a look at what group and local policies can do to prevent the problem.

In Chapter 35, I explained how group and local policies work and how you can use them to control a user's work environment. This includes the Desktop and the location of My Documents and other profile folders.

You can also use policies to restrict the actions a user can take on a computer. For example, if you don't make users a member of the Administrators group, they can't add or remove hardware or make certain other changes. But what if the computer has a FAT file system? There is nothing to prevent someone from opening a folder and deleting a bunch of critical files. Removing My Computer altogether, or at least limiting what it shows, can go a long way toward preventing this type of catastrophe.

In this chapter, I explain how you can use local and group policies to set hardware and software restrictions and to apply restrictions on the Desktop and working environment. For complete control over user settings and data, you should also go a step further, implementing folder redirection and the other suggestions I offer in Chapter 37.

NOTE   Windows XP Home Edition doesn't provide a means to set policies because it doesn't support them. So, most of the restrictions I discuss in this chapter apply only to Windows XP Professional. Where possible, I've noted the manual method for setting these restrictions under Home Edition.

Applying System and Hardware Restrictions

Although nonadministrative users are restricted in what they can do to configure the system, there are still changes that users can make. Some of those changes present security risks, and others increase support calls. You can use group and local policies to restrict the actions that users can take within the system and for configuring hardware. The following sections explain how to implement specific restrictions, but this isn't a complete list; I've included the items most administrators and users want to control. You should take the time to scan through the policies for other possible changes that will benefit your network or the way in which you use Windows XP.

To make the changes I describe in the following sections, you need to edit group policies either at the local level or in Active Directory for domain members. I'll assume you're modifying them at the local level. Click Start ➤ Run and enter **MMC** in the Run dialog box. In the MMC, choose File ➤ Add/Remove Snap-In. Click Add in the dialog box, select the Group Policy snap-in, and click Add. Click Finish in the Select Group Policy Object dialog box. Click Close, and click OK to return to the MMC console.

Disk Quotas

Disk quotas let you restrict the amount of disk space a user can consume on an NTFS volume. Quotas apply on a per-volume basis, so you don't have to worry about limiting a user's space in each folder. Quotas can help reduce wasted space taken up by MP3, AVI, and other nonessential files, and force users to more efficiently manage the space allocated to them.

NOTE FAT volumes don't support quotas. Both Windows XP Professional and Home Edition support quotas on NTFS volumes. However, Home Edition doesn't provide a means to set quotas through policies. Instead, you must configure them through the properties for the NTFS volume.

You can configure quotas manually through the Windows interface, but it's much handier to set them through policy, particularly when you need to apply the quotas to a large number of users. Setting the quota through a policy also ensures that any new users who are added to the computer or who come under the scope of the policy receive the specified quota settings.

To set quotas through a policy, open the \Computer Configuration\Administrative Templates\ System\Disk Quotas branch. Six policies control disk quotas. I covered quotas in Chapter 14, so you can refer there if you need more details.

Remote Assistance

The Remote Assistance branch offers two policies that let you control the actions users can perform for Remote Assistance:

Solicited Remote Assistance Use this policy to specify whether to permit remote control of the computer when the user requests remote assistance. If you enable the policy, you can choose between allowing remote users to control the computer or just to view it. You can also specify the maximum ticket duration, which determines how long a Remote Assistance request can be open.

Offer Remote Assistance This policy determines whether Remote Assistance is allowed when the remote expert attempts to initiate the session without first receiving a request from the user. As with solicited Remote Assistance, you can choose between view-only or remote control if you enable the policy.

NOTE Remote Assistance is covered in detail in Chapter 23.

You can set Remote Assistance options on a Windows XP Home Edition computer with the Remote tab of the System properties (right-click My Computer and choose Properties).

System Restore

System Restore provides a means for Windows XP to automatically restore the system to a particular configuration. Users can create restore points that act as snapshots of the computer's configuration, and later restore the computer to one of those states, if needed. By default, System Restore is turned on. In some situations, however, you might want to prevent users from creating restore points or restoring their systems to a previous state.

Two policies in the \Computer Configuration\Administrative Templates\System\System Restore branch control the System Restore feature:

Turn Off System Restore   Enable this policy if you want to prevent the user from creating snap-shots or performing a system restore operation. If this policy is enabled, the System Restore Wizard and configuration interface are unavailable to the user.

Turn Off Configuration   This option determines whether the user can configure System Restore through its configuration interface (accessed from the System Restore tab of the System properties). Enable this setting if you don't want users to be able to change the System Restore configuration.

NOTE   See Chapter 39 for a complete discussion of System Restore, including how to configure it, create restore points, and restore a system.

Simple Network Management Protocol (SNMP)

A few years ago, security organizations discovered significant bugs in the public-domain code widely used by many companies to integrate Simple Network Management Protocol (SNMP) capabilities into their equipment. Although most vendors—including Microsoft—will move swiftly to address these problems, you might still want to impose some restrictions on SNMP.

The branch \Computer Configuration\Administrative Templates\Network\SNMP provides three policies that control SNMP on the client computer:

Communities   Use this policy to specify the SNMP communities for which the computer can respond to SNMP requests. With this policy enabled and the communities defined, the computer ignores requests from other communities. If the policy isn't defined or is disabled, the computer responds to whatever communities are configured in its local SNMP settings.

Permitted Managers   Use this policy to specify the hosts that can submit SNMP requests to the client computer. With this policy enabled and the managers defined, the client ignores requests from other SNMP managers. If the policy isn't defined or is disabled, the computer responds to the managers defined in its local SNMP settings.

Traps For Public Community   Use this policy to specify the hosts that receive SNMP traps from the local computer. If the policy isn't defined or is disabled, the client sends traps to the hosts specified in its local SNMP settings.

NOTE   See Chapter 26 for a complete discussion of the SNMP service and how to configure communities, managers, and traps without using policies.

Windows Explorer

The \User Configuration\Administrative Templates\Windows Components\Windows Explorer branch contains several policies that control the way the Explorer interface looks and functions. I won't cover all of these in detail; instead, I'll point out some of the policies you'll find most useful.

Several of the policies let you remove certain menus and functions from the Windows Explorer interface. For example, you can remove the Folder Options menu from the Tools menu, remove Map Network Drive and Disconnect Network Drive, hide the Manage item on My Computer's shortcut menu, and remove several other dialog boxes, tabs, and menu items to prevent users from accessing them.

TIP In some cases, you can't completely prevent access to certain features. For example, although you can remove the Map Network Drive command, users can still browse the network by entering the UNC path in the Run dialog box or in an Explorer window. They can also use the net use command to map a drive. Knowledgeable power users can get around many of these restrictions in one way or another.

One other change you might want to make is to restrict the drive icons that show up in My Computer. Use the policy Hide These Specified Drives In My Computer to specify which drives should appear.

The Common Open File Dialog sub-branch lets you specify which items appear in the Places bar, overriding the default set of paths and icons. You can specify local folders, UNC paths, and common shell folders. You can also use the remaining three policies to hide the Places bar or other elements.

Microsoft Management Console (MMC)

Use the \User Configuration\Administrative Templates\Windows Components\Microsoft Management Console branch to control which MMC snap-ins the user can open.

The policy Restrict The User From Entering Author Mode, if enabled, prevents the user from opening the MMC in author mode. This mode allows the user to create console files and add/remove snap-ins. Enabling this policy prevents the user from taking those actions.

The policy Restrict User To Explicitly Permitted List Of Snap-Ins lets you specify which snap-ins a user is allowed to add to a console. After you enable this setting, use the policies in the Restricted/Permitted Snap-Ins sub-branch to specify which snap-ins are allowed and which ones are denied. Enable a policy to allow the snap-in to be used; disable a policy to prevent that snap-in from being used.

If you want to give the user the ability to set some group or local policies but not others, enable the Group Policy Snap-In policy in the Group Policy sub-branch. Then, enable or disable policies in the Group Policy Snap-In Extensions and Resultant Set Of Policy Snap-In Extensions branches to control which ones are allowed or denied, respectively.

Windows Update

The \User Configuration\Administrative Templates\Windows Components\Windows Update branch contains a single policy that you can use to deny access to the Windows Update site. This turns off automatic updates and prevents the user from accessing the Windows Update site through the Windows Update link on the Start menu or from the Tools menu in Internet Explorer. It also prevents Device Manager from automatically installing device drivers from the Windows Update site.

Ctrl+Alt+Delete

The \User Configuration\Administrative Templates\System\Ctrl+Alt+Del Options branch contains four policies that let you control what happens when the user presses Ctrl+Alt+Delete. These policies include the following:

Remove Task Manager Use this policy to prevent the user from running Task Manager. However, keep in mind that Task Manager can be a useful tool for troubleshooting.

Remove Lock Computer Use this policy to remove the Lock Computer option from the Windows Security dialog box that appears when you press Ctrl+Alt+Delete.

Remove Change Password Use this policy to remove the Change Password button from the Windows Security dialog box. The user can still change a password when prompted by the system, such as when the account password expires.

Remove Logoff Use this policy to prevent the user from logging off of the system using any method, including scripts, console commands, or other methods.

Applying Software Restrictions

The previous sections covered policies that controlled system-wide capabilities and tasks, both hardware- and software-related. You can also use policies to control specific applications, allowing or denying the user the ability to perform certain tasks or configuration changes with the application. The following sections explore the policies you will likely find most useful for controlling applications. However, you should review all the available policies for others that might also suit your needs.

NetMeeting

There are two places where you can set policies that control the user's ability to use specific features in NetMeeting. For example, you might want to allow video conferencing and chat but deny application sharing or remote control.

The \Computer Configuration\Administrative Templates\Windows Components\NetMeeting branch contains one policy, Disable Remote Desktop Sharing. If enabled, this policy prevents users on the computer from using Remote Desktop Sharing, which allows a remote user to take control of the computer.

The \User Configuration\Administrative Templates\Windows Components\NetMeeting branch contains many other policies that control NetMeeting in other ways. For example, you can configure NetMeeting, deny automatic acceptance of incoming calls, disable the Whiteboard feature, and control many other settings. You can also hide various menus and options from the user.

Internet Explorer

Use the \Computer Configuration\Administrative Templates\Windows Components\Internet Explorer branch to control machine-wide Internet Explorer settings such as security zones, proxy settings, how Internet Explorer handles updates, and whether IE shows the splash screen on startup.

The \User Configuration\Administrative Templates\Windows Components\Internet Explorer branch contains several settings and sub-branches that control Internet Explorer on a per-user basis. These policies control the items that the user sees in IE's configuration interface and the actions they can take within Internet Explorer. You can also configure a handful of other application settings, including specifying whether Outlook Express should block attachments that could potentially contain a virus or malicious code.

Windows Installer

The \Computer Configuration\Administrative Templates\Windows Components\Windows Installer branch contains several policies that let you control whether the user can run the Windows Installer. Blocking the Windows Installer or limiting the user's access to it restricts the user's ability to install applications.

The \User Configuration\Administrative Templates\Windows Components\Windows Installer branch contains four additional policies that also control the Windows Installer.

Windows Messenger

Use the \Computer Configuration\Administrative Templates\Windows Components\Windows Messenger branch to specify whether users on the computer can run Windows Messenger and, if so, whether it starts automatically. Disable the latter option to require the user to start Windows Messenger manually.

The \User Configuration\Administrative Templates\Windows Components\Windows Messenger branch contains the same settings but applies them at the user level rather than the computer level. This distinction is applicable only when you're imposing the policies at the OU, domain, or site level, where you can define policies so that different groups on the same computer have different policies applied.

Media Player

Use the \User Configuration\Administrative Templates\Windows Components\Windows Media Player branch to configure the appearance and behavior of Media Player. For example, you can specify the skin (appearance) of the player and lock it in that mode, preventing the user from switching views. You can prevent the user from being able to download additional codecs, and configure the ports, proxies, and protocols Media Player uses for streaming media.

Applying Desktop and Environment Restrictions

There are lots of policies you can configure to define the user's Desktop and working environment. For example, you can enable Active Desktop and set it for a particular URL, define what the user sees on the Start menu and Taskbar, and control the working environment in several other ways. The following sections provide a quick overview.

Start Menu and Taskbar

The \User Configuration\Administrative Templates\Start Menu And Taskbar branch is the place to go to control the items you want the user to see on the Start menu and Taskbar. Most of the policies in this branch let you remove from the Start menu specific items such as links to Windows Update, My Documents, Network Connections, Search, and other common items. Removing items not only streamlines the Start menu but also helps keep users out of areas where they don't belong. You can hide the system tray (a.k.a. the notification area), remove the clock from the tray, and make a handful of other tray changes.

If you prefer to give users a classic Start menu rather than use the Windows XP Start menu, enable the policy Force Classic Start Menu. This not only forces the system to use the Windows 2000–style Start menu, but also displays My Computer, My Network Places, My Documents, My Pictures, and My Music icons on the Desktop.

Active Desktop

The \User Configuration\Administrative Templates\Desktop\Active Desktop policy branch lets you enable or disable Active Desktop, which can display dynamic data on the Desktop. In addition to displaying HTML data on the Desktop, you can also display JPEG wallpaper with Active Desktop enabled.

The policies in this branch also let you specify the wallpaper to be used and limit the wallpaper to bitmapped files only, excluding JPEG, GIF, PNG, and HTML documents. You can also add and remove URLs of data to be included or excluded from Active Desktop.

Control Panel

The \User Configuration\Administrative Templates\Control Panel branch is the place to go to restrict the user's ability to perform specific types of actions through Control Panel. For example, you might remove the Add Or Remove Programs icon from Control Panel to restrict the user's ability to modify Windows components or applications. If you're publishing applications from a server with group policies, you might want to use the policy Specify Default Category For Add New Programs to limit the display of application categories to the single specified category.

The other sub-branches in this policy branch specify other restrictions to limit the things users can do through Control Panel. For example, you can use the Display branch and its policies to prevent wallpaper changes, set the screensaver properties, and hide some or all of the tabs in the Display properties.

Use the Printers branch to prevent users from either adding or removing printers, and set the default locations for locating and adding printers. Use the Regional And Language Options branch to restrict the user to a specific language.

Offline Files

The \User Configuration\Administrative Templates\Network\Offline Files branch contains several policies that determine whether the user can use Offline Files and how the feature behaves. For example, you can specify synchronization settings, balloon reminders, and event logging. You can also specify that Windows XP not make redirected folders available offline by default.

Network Connections

The \User Configuration\Administrative Templates\Network\Network Connections branch is the place to go to control the tasks a user can perform in relation to the network. For example, you might use the policies in this branch to prevent the user from making changes to their network configuration, prevent them from enabling or disabling an interface, and prevent access to the New Connection Wizard. You'll also find settings here to control remote access connections and properties.

NOTE   See Chapter 23 for details on configuring and using the remote access features in Windows XP.

Configuring Time

Keeping the time correct on systems is important for a variety of reasons, but in particular for accurate backup, recovery, and event logging. Toward that end, Windows XP includes the Windows Time Service that lets you synchronize the time of a Windows XP computer with a time server. In a domain environment, domain members automatically synchronize their time with a domain controller at logon. In a workgroup, however, time synchronization doesn't happen by default.

You can use the \Computer Configuration\Administrative Templates\System\Windows Time Service policy branch to configure several policies that determine how the computer synchronizes its time. You can also use the Time Providers sub-branch to enable the time client and specify the time server to be used. Several time servers are freely available on the Internet, and the United States government provides its own at `http://time.nist.com`.

In addition, a Windows XP Professional computer can also function as a time server for other computers. Use the Enable Windows NTP Server policy to turn the computer into a time server. However, you also need to use the other policies to ensure that the computer synchronizes its time with a valid time server.

Chapter 37

Managing User Data and Settings

In the preceding chapter, I explained how to use group and local policies to control the changes that users can make to their Desktop and other elements of their working environment. I also explained how to apply change control to prevent users from making changes to their systems, and how to control the elements that appear on the user's Desktop, in My Computer, and in other locations in the interface.

Another aspect of good user management is ensuring that a user's documents and other data are secure and safe from system failures—or, if a failure does occur, that you can recover that data quickly with minimal disruption.

In this chapter, I explain how to use local and group policies to manage user data and settings. You'll see how to redirect user data folders to a server to support roaming users and provide a higher degree of recoverability in the event of a system failure. This chapter also covers user profiles and scripts to help you understand how to create a particular working environment for users when they log on.

Redirecting Folders

System failures are one of an IT manager's worst nightmares. If the failure happens to the CEO, it's even worse! When it happens to your own system, you know the frustration that other users feel when a critical tool suddenly goes away, taking all of their work with it.

Improving and streamlining disaster recovery is extremely important to help minimize downtime and ensure that you can recover a system and its data quickly if the need arises. Equally important, streamlining the process reduces the pressure you'll feel from users to get their systems back up and their data back in their hands, because you can accomplish the recovery more quickly.

Having been a system administrator for a long time, I can tell you that most users are notoriously bad about backing up their data, even if you give them the means to do so. You can implement an agent-based backup mechanism to back up user data from their workstations to a server, but this approach has potential pitfalls. For example, how can you be sure some users won't shut off their computers at the end of the day, preventing the server from backing them up?

A better approach is to place the users' data on a server. There are a couple of ways to achieve that, but one of the best approaches in my opinion is to use group or local policies to redirect user folders such as My Documents to a network server. With the files residing on the server, it's much easier to implement a reliable backup and recovery strategy.

TIP Folder redirection isn't possible on Windows XP Home Edition because Home Edition doesn't support group or local policies. You can redirect folders on a Windows XP Professional system using group policies if the computer is a domain member. You can't redirect folders using local policies, which prevents policy-based redirection for workgroup members.

Redirecting folders also considerably simplifies recovery of a failed workstation. You don't need to restore the documents; just restore the operating system or install a new system, point Windows to the server for the files, and voilà—the user is back to work.

TIP Use RIS or another automated OS deployment method to install the operating system for even better recoverability. See Chapter 3 for a discussion of using RIS for remote deployment.

Redirection Options

You can redirect five user folders: `Application Data`, `Desktop`, `My Documents`, `My Pictures`, and `Start Menu`. Three policy states control redirection of these folders. The first, No Administrative Policy Defined, takes no action on the folder. In the case of nonroaming users, the folder remains on the user's local computer. For roaming users, the folder resides in the roaming profile and is copied across the network to the user's workstation at logon.

The option Basic—Redirect Everyone's Folder To The Same Location lets you redirect folders regardless of the users' security group membership. Generally, you specify a location in the form `\\server\share\%username%` to cause the folder to be redirected to a folder on a network share with a name that matches the username. For example, you might specify `\\srv1\users\%username%\My Documents` to redirect the `My Documents` folder to a network share. For the user jboyce, `My Documents` would be redirected to `\\srv1\users\jboyce\My Documents`.

You can use the Basic option to redirect a particular folder for all users to the same location to provide common content. For example, you might redirect the `Start Menu` folder to a common folder on a network share to ensure that all users see the same Start menu. It's unlikely, however, that you would redirect `My Documents` to a common folder, unless of course you wanted the users to have a common set of documents.

The option Advanced—Specify Locations For Various User Groups lets you specify redirection based on group membership, which provides a lot more flexibility. With this policy setting, you don't specify a single location, but instead specify a location for specific security groups. For example, you might redirect `Start Menu` for the administrators to one folder and `Start Menu` for general users to a different folder. The result is that everyone in the group receives a particular folder. As with the Basic option, you can specify a common folder or use variables such as `%username%` to redirect based on the users' account name.

Setting Up Redirection

You configure folder redirection only at the group policy level, which requires access to the domain controller where you want the policies applied. Follow these steps:

1. Open the Active Directory Users And Computers console on a domain controller for the computer.

2. Open the properties for the container at which you want to apply the policies (such as an organizational unit), and edit or create a group policy object from the Group Policy tab.

3. With the Group Policy editor open, expand the branch \User Configuration\Windows Settings\Folder Redirection.

4. Right-click the folder you want to redirect, and choose Properties.

5. On the Target tab (Figure 37.1), select the redirection method from the drop-down list.

FIGURE 37.1
FIGURE 37.1
Use the Target tab to
specify a redirection
method.

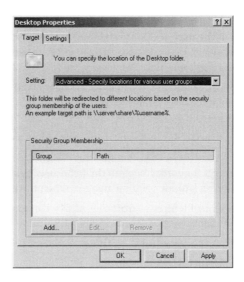

6. If you choose Advanced, the Security Group Membership box appears on the tab. Click Add
to display the Specify Group And Location dialog box (Figure 37.2). Type the group name or
click Browse to browse the Active Directory for it.

FIGURE 37.2
Specify the group and its
folder location.

7. Specify the desired folder location in the Target Folder Location field. Here's where it gets a bit
tricky, regardless of the redirection option you choose. If you specify a local path for the folder,
the effect is that the user is redirected to that local path on their computer, not on the server.
So, the specified folder must exist on each system that comes under the scope of the policy. To
redirect the user to a network share, you must enter the folder path in UNC format, such as
\\srv1\shares\\%*username*%**\My Documents**.

The Settings tab lets you choose other options that control folder redirection:

Grant the user exclusive rights to *folder*   Configure permissions on the folder so the user and local system have full access, but no other users have access (including administrators). If this option isn't selected, no changes are made to the folder's permissions.

Move the contents of *folder* **to the new location**   Redirect the contents of the source folder to the target folder. For example, you would enable this option to have a user's local My Folders contents moved to a server.

Leave the folder in the new location when policy is removed   Files will remain in the redirected location even if the group policy no longer applies.

Redirect the folder back to the local user profile location when policy is removed   Move the folder back to the original location when the group policy no longer applies.

Make My Pictures a subfolder of My Documents   The default location for My Pictures is as a subfolder of My Documents. Select this option to redirect My Pictures along with My Documents.

Do not specify administrative policy for My Pictures   Leave My Pictures in its default location as defined by the user's profile.

Working with User Profiles

In Chapter 34, I explained how to create and manage user accounts, but there were a few user account settings I opted to cover in this chapter because they relate to user profiles.

In Windows XP, each user has a user profile made up of several components, one of which is that user's set of profile folders. These include My Documents, Start Menu, and the others described in the previous section. The file ntuser.dat, a portion of the user's Registry that is stored in the user's profile folder, also becomes part of the user profile. This portion of the Registry defines the user's working environment, such as the Desktop, screensaver, and other elements.

TIP   ntuser.dat is named ntuser.man when a mandatory profile is used.

In Windows NT, the Registry portion of the user's profile was the primary means by which administrators applied restrictions and change control. With the introduction of group policy, the need to control user settings by enforcing the use of a particular ntuser.dat file became largely unnecessary. However, it can still be a useful technique for managing users, particularly those who don't fall under the scope of group policy (such as workgroup members). So, let's look at how you can use a profile to provide change control.

Understanding Profiles

Each user account includes several properties in addition to the username and password. The Profile tab (Figure 37.3) shows some of these additional properties, one of which is the Profile Path setting.

When a user logs on, Windows XP looks in the folder specified by Profile Path for the ntuser.dat file. If it finds one there, it applies that file as the user's portion of the Registry. The settings stored in the Registry file then define the user's work environment. The remaining profile comes from the user's profile store, located by default in C:\Documents and Settings*user*, where *user* is the user's logon name. Or the profile is redirected to a network server by group policy, as I explained in the previous section.

There are three types of profiles: standard, roaming, and mandatory. With a standard profile, the user's `ntuser.dat` file is stored locally. When the user logs on to another computer, it's possible for them to have a different working environment because the profile doesn't follow them to the other computer.

With a roaming profile, however, the profile is stored on a network share and referenced in the user's Profile Path by a UNC path that is accessible from all computers where the user needs to log on. When the user logs on, Windows XP copies the profile across the network from the specified location. This means that a user can have the same Desktop configuration regardless of logon location.

If you rename the `ntuser.dat` file to `ntuser.man`, it becomes a mandatory profile. The user can make changes to the working environment (such as changing Desktop schemes or colors), but those changes are lost when the user logs off; the previous configuration applies when the user logs back on. So, a mandatory profile lets you control the user's initial working environment and prevent permanent changes.

If you can't use group policy to achieve the result you want, you can opt to control user settings through the profile. First decide whether you want to set up a roaming or mandatory profile. Then follow the steps outlined in the following sections to create the profile.

Setting Up a Roaming Profile

To create a roaming profile, follow these steps:

1. Log on as the user to one of the computers where you want the profile to be used.

2. Configure the Desktop and other settings as needed, and then log off.

3. Log on again, this time as Administrator.

4. Open the user's local profile folder, and copy `ntuser.dat` to a network share that will be available to the user from all logon locations.

5. Open the user's account properties, and click the Profile tab.

6. In the Profile Path field, enter the path to the folder where the profile is stored, in UNC format.

> **TIP** Keep in mind that some of the profile settings stored in `ntuser.dat` are hardware-specific, so in many cases the user will have to log on from similar workstations for the roaming profile settings to work properly. This isn't usually a major problem, but it's something for which you should plan.

In cases where the user logs on to a domain, you set the profile path through the domain account properties in the Active Directory Users And Groups console on a domain controller. You can set up a roaming profile for users in a workgroup, although the process becomes more complex. The user must have a logon account at each workstation they use, which means you need to set the Profile Path for each local account to point to the roaming profile path for that user. Use the Local Users And Group branch of the Computer Management console on each computer to set these properties.

Setting Up a Mandatory Profile

To set up a mandatory profile, you use a method similar to the one used to set up a roaming profile:

1. Log on as the user to a target workstation, and configure the work environment.

2. Log off, and log back on as Administrator.

3. Open the profile folder for the account you just modified, and rename `ntuser.dat` to `ntuser.man`.

4. If this is the user's only computer, the job is done. If you're setting up a roaming mandatory profile, however, copy the `ntuser.man` file to a network share accessible to the user at logon. Then open the user's account properties and specify the path to that folder in the Profile Path field.

Applying Logon and Logoff Scripts

Whether you're working in a workgroup or domain, you can use logon and logoff scripts to automatically perform actions when users log on or log off. As you might have guessed, the logon script executes when the user logs on, and the logoff scripts executes when the user logs off. Common tasks for a logon script include mapping network drives and printers and running programs. Common logoff tasks include disconnecting resources, cleaning up local folders, sending notifications, and so on.

> **NOTE** Although it's most common to run batch files as logon scripts, you can run any executable or even launch documents through application association. However, you should use the `Startup` folder or other methods described later in this chapter instead of scripts for those purposes.

Where to Store the Scripts

When you specify a path for a script in a policy, you can enter it as a UNC path, absolute local path, or relative local path. Which method you use depends on how and where you assign the script.

Windows 2000 or Windows Server 2003 maintains a script folder for each policy object. To view the location for the scripts for a particular policy, open the Active Directory Users And Computers console and open the group policy object. Open the appropriate policy, such as \User Configuration\Windows Settings\Scripts\Logon. Click Show Files on the policy's dialog box to open a folder window in the designated folder. If a script resides in this folder, you can specify only the script name in the policy and omit any other path information. Otherwise, you need to specify the path to the script. Enter a UNC path if you want to pull the script from a shared folder that isn't local to the user's logon location. Specify an absolute path to pull the script from the user's local computer. Then make sure you copy the script into the appropriate folder.

TIP If you're dealing with local policy–based scripts, store the scripts in the `%systemroot%`\System32\ GroupPolicy\User\Scripts\Logon folder on the local computer, or a subfolder of that folder.

Account-based scripts are a little different. Store account-based logon scripts in the NETLOGON share on the server, which Windows sets up by default in the \SYSVOL*domain*\SCRIPTS folder. The SYSVOL folder location varies depending on where you specified its location during Active Directory installation.

TIP If you're not sure where NETLOGON is located, open the Shares branch of the Computer Management console. The right pane lists all shares and their physical paths.

If you're specifying logon scripts for users in a workgroup, start by creating a NETLOGON share on the local computer. Place general scripts in that folder, and create user folders under the share for user-specific scripts. When you specify the path to the script in the user's properties, specify only the script name if the script resides in the NETLOGON share, or preface it with the subfolder name if it resides in a subfolder. For example, specify **`special\somescript.bat`** if the `somescript.bat` file resides in \NETLOGON\special.

TIP You can use the `%username%` variable to specify a script located in a folder under NETLOGON that matches the user's logon name.

Now let's get down to business and assign some scripts. You can define logon and logoff scripts in two ways: with policies or through the user account properties.

Policy-Based Scripts

The \User Configuration\Windows Settings\Scripts policy branch contains two policies, Logon and Logoff, which define the scripts that execute for users who fall under the scope of the policy. You can set the scripts either locally or at the site, domain, or OU level, as needed.

To add a script, follow these steps:

1. Open the policy to display the properties sheet, which lists the existing scripts, if any, for the policy.

2. Click Add to display the Add A Script dialog box. Enter the path to the script file. Usually the script is a BAT or CMD file, but you can specify other executables, as well.

3. You can specify optional parameters for the script in the Script Parameters field; they're passed to the script when it executes. This lets you tailor a common script that contains replaceable variables to a specific user by passing those variables to the script at execution time.

4. Make sure you copy the script to the appropriate folder, depending on the default path for the particular policy object.

TIP One advantage of using policy-based scripts is the ability to specify multiple scripts. You can assign only one account-based script (covered in the next section).

Account-Based Scripts

You can also specify logon and logoff scripts through the user's account properties. Doing so gives you a handy means to execute scripts for members of a workgroup who don't receive policy-based scripts. What's more, you can use a combination of policy-based and account-based scripts to execute multiple scripts as needed. For example, you might use a policy-based script to perform general tasks for all users and use the account-based script to perform user-specific tasks.

To specify an account-based script for domain members, open the Active Directory Users And Computers console on the target domain controller, and then open the user's account. Click the Profile tab, and enter the script in the Logon Script field. Then copy the script to the appropriate location in the NETLOGON share.

To specify an account-based script for local users, open the Local Users And Groups branch of the Computer Management console. Open the properties for the account, click the Profile tab, and specify the script in the Logon Script field. Then copy the script to the appropriate location in the NETLOGON share.

Controlling Script Execution

Group and local policy offer a handful of settings that control logon and logoff script execution. The \User Configuration\Administrative Templates\System\Logon\Logoff branch of the group policy offers the following settings that affect logon and logoff scripts:

Run Logon Scripts Synchronously   Enable this policy if you want all scripts to finish processing before Windows XP displays the Explorer interface. If this policy is disabled or not set, the logon scripts need not complete before the Explorer interface appears.

Run Legacy Logon Scripts Hidden   Enable this policy if you want scripts written for Windows NT or earlier to be hidden. When the policy is disabled or not defined, the scripts appear in a console window while they execute.

Run Logon Scripts Visible   Enable this policy if you want Windows XP to display the console window for the script when it executes. When this policy is disabled or not defined, the console is hidden.

Run Logoff Scripts Visible   Enable this policy to display the console window for logoff scripts when they execute. The console is hidden if this policy is disabled or not defined.

You can also set these same policies locally. They're located in \User Configuration\Administrative Templates\System\Scripts.

Alternatives to Logon Scripts

Logon scripts are a handy way to perform tasks during logon, but other methods are available to you as well. The Startup folder, for example, lets you start applications automatically at logon, making it an alternative to logon scripts. You can create a script and place it in your Startup folder to have it execute at startup. This is a useful technique for Home Edition, which doesn't support group or local policies.

You can also consider using the Registry to run applications at startup. To add a program for the *current* user, open the Registry Editor and expand the branch

```
\HKEY_CURRENT_USER\Software\Microsoft\Windows\CurrentVersion\Run
```

Create a new string value in this key and set as its value the program you want to execute at startup. Include the path and enclose the path in quotes. Add any optional parameters for the program outside the quotes, as in the following example, which starts Microsoft Word without the Normal.dot template:

```
"c:\program files\office\winword.exe" /a
```

TIP   If you want the program to run for *all* users at logon, create the entry in the key \HKEY_LOCAL_MACHINE\Software\Microsoft\Windows\CurrentVersion\Run.

Part 8

Backup and Disaster Recovery

In this section:

Chapter 38

Backup

Windows XP includes a powerful set of tools and utilities that can help you recover a failed system. These tools include the Backup Utility program and System Restore. If you use computers long enough, you'll eventually need one of these tools.

Of these, the Backup Utility is the one you should be most familiar with right from the start. You've heard it by now: if it's important, or even if you think it will be, back it up. The hard disk on your system is arguably the most important piece of your computer; without it, your computer would be little more than a calculator or a video game console. People buy computers so that they can work with a set of information day after day, and that data needs to be stored on a hard disk if it is to be available. Yet the hard disk is also one of the more fragile devices of your system, failing on average more times than any other computer component. In the event of a disk crash, your data can be impossible to retrieve without dropping the GNP of New Zealand on a data recovery service.

Along with being at risk because of mechanical failure, your data is also vulnerable, as you may have experienced by now, to the vagaries of human error. People have been known to make typos, and they have also clicked the wrong button a time or two, sending critical data into the ether. In addition, people have been known to "try out" the `format` and `fdisk` utilities for (their own) entertainment. All right, I've made my point: you are, in your lifetime as an experienced user or administrator, going to lose data, and your next paycheck may depend on your ability to get it back. But you'll be able to retrieve data if you're in the habit of following a regular backup strategy and you have a good command of the Windows XP Backup Utility.

Backup Utility Basics

The Windows XP Backup Utility is an updated version of the Backup Utility included in Windows 2000, which in turn was a much more powerful version than was included with NT 4. The job of the Backup Utility is to back up all selected data to a single file that is named with the file extension `.bkf`. The destination of this backup file can be any device that stores files, such as tapes, removable disks, and even network locations.

The first time you access the Backup Utility, you launch the Backup Or Restore Wizard (choose Start ➢ All Programs ➢ Accessories ➢ System Tools ➢ Backup). As Figure 38.1 shows, the Backup Utility always starts with the Welcome screen, unless you clear the Always Start In Wizard Mode check box.

You've used wizards by now, and I won't go through each and every screen of this utility. If you've backed up anything before, you'll find this tool easy to use. You simply tell the wizard which files to back up and where to store the backed-up data. When the backup is done, you can click the Report button to view a log file generated as the files were copied and verify that the backup was a success.

FIGURE 38.1

The Backup Or Restore Wizard opens at the Welcome screen.

Instead of using the wizard, you can back up data manually using Advanced Mode, as shown in Figure 38.2. When you back up manually, you can specify whether to verify the data after the backup, whether to replace the backup files or append them to existing backups, and when to run the backup.

Click the Backup tab, and select the files and folders you want to back up. At the bottom of the Backup tab, choose the location for the backup from the Backup Destination list.

You use the Restore And Manage Media tab to specify what and where you want to restore. Again, it's just a matter of a few clicks. You use the Schedule Jobs tab to schedule backups; I'll show you how to do this later in this chapter.

FIGURE 38.2

You can use Advanced Mode to back up manually.

What About Transferring Backups to a CD?

When you step through the Backup Or Restore Wizard, you're asked where to back up; however, backing up directly to a CD isn't an option. Nevertheless, you can easily copy your backup to a CD using the CD Writing Wizard in Windows XP or your favorite burning software. In fact, this backup strategy is recommended; you can archive your backups on a medium that is effortless to store off-site and that is difficult to damage. Keep in mind that you need enough free space on your target disk to hold the backup file or files and that the backup must be small enough (650–700 MB, depending on the capacity of your CD) to fit onto a single CD-ROM. If the backup job is too big to fit on a single disk, you'll need to break up the backup so that more than one file is created.

What About Backing Up Directly to a CD?

As with all things computer, you have other options if you want to back up straight to the CD, skipping the intermediary step described previously. You can attack this problem two ways:

◆ Back up directly to the CD, using a third-party backup program.

◆ Install software, such as Roxio's Easy CD Creator, to trick the Backup Utility into thinking the CD-R device is just another hard disk on your system.

Here are a couple of great third-party programs that you can use:

Backup to CD-RW (Made Simple)   Distributed by Willow Creek Software, this is an easy-to-use program for backing up to a CD-RW or CD-R. It can also back up to a hard disk or to a network drive.

Nero Burning ROM   This program is distributed by Ahead Software. You can download a trial version at `www.nero.com`.

Where Is the Backup Utility in Windows XP Home Edition?

If you're using Windows XP Professional, the Backup Utility is installed by default and is part of the System Tools. (Many think it better fits under Administrative Tools, because backing up data is usually an administrative task, but we didn't get to write the operating system code, now did we?) If you're using the Home Edition, however, the Backup Utility isn't installed during setup. You must install it from the `\Valueadd\Msft\Ntbackup` folder on the Windows XP CD-ROM.

TIP   Who do you have to be to perform a backup, anyway? Users with Administrator or Backup Operator privileges can back up and restore any files on the system, even files they can't otherwise access. Individual users can back up and restore files that they own.

A Better Backup Method?

Although the Windows Backup tool does a good job of backing up data, I confess I don't use it on a regular basis. I come from an administrative background, and I prefer my backups to take place automatically. What's more, I like to be able to quickly and easily recover data from a backup set when necessary. I fondly remember restoring 20 GB to a server from a tape set a few years back after a worm attack; the restore took more than 24 hours to run. Since then, automated, hard disk–based backup has been my method of choice.

If you need to back up a relatively small number of computers (or one), my favorite solution is an external USB or FireWire hard disk. These backup media offer a handful of advantages:

Backup speed A USB or FireWire hard disk supports much higher transfer rates than a tape backup system, so backups complete in much less time.

Easy access to files If you choose the right backup software solution, the resulting backups are folders and files on the external drive. You can easily recover them en masse or one at a time through a simple click-and-drag operation.

Networked access You can share the backup drive on the network to let multiple users back up their computers to it.

Speedy recovery Just as backups are fast with a speedy hard drive, so is recovery. You can recover data from the drive much more quickly than you can from tape or CD.

Safety You can disconnect an external drive and tuck it away in a fire safe or take it off-site. If a catastrophe befalls your office, your backup will still be safe and easily recovered.

Currently, I'm using an Iomega external USB hard disk as the backup solution for my small network. The Iomega Automatic Backup software that comes with the drive runs in the background and automatically backs up the folders I've specified at a set time without any intervention from me. The software copies the data to the external drive as folders and files, so I don't have to worry about running a special program to recover a folder or file—I can open the drive in My Computer and drag the files where they need to be.

If you're looking for a good backup and recovery solution, consider an external drive and automatic backup/recovery software that stores the data on the drive as individual folders and files rather than as a backup set.

Creating an Automated System Recovery Disk

An automated system recovery (ASR) disk is a backup configuration whose purpose is to get your system partition up and running again quickly. It saves the entire contents of your system drive to a backup medium of your choice. Moreover, it saves information about the current location of system files, detected hardware, and partitions (or volumes) to a floppy disk. It's good administrative practice to create an ASR disk right after a successful installation of Windows XP and then update it any time you significantly change the system—for example, when you change or upgrade any vital device drivers. However, one of the drawbacks of the ASR disk is that it only backs up (and restores) data that exists on the system volume. If you want to be able to restore other disks on your computer, run the Backup Wizard and back up everything on the computer.

To create an ASR disk, click the Automated System Recovery Wizard option in the Welcome To The Backup Utility Advanced Mode dialog box to start the Automated System Recovery Preparation Wizard. Again, I won't walk you though each step of this wizard; it's much more important that you know the purpose of the ASR disk. You'll be asked for the location of the system partition backup; when prompted, insert a floppy disk to save the system recovery information. Keep this ASR floppy disk in a safe place when you're finished.

The ASR disk isn't a complete backup, and for this reason you shouldn't consider your backup strategy comprehensive if all you're using is ASR. Instead, you use the ASR disk to quickly repair and restart Windows XP if your computer won't start or if system files become corrupt. But remember: the ASR floppy disk isn't a bootable disk. To access it, you must first boot the computer using either the Windows XP Professional installation CD-ROM or the setup floppies that can be created from the XP Professional CD. Follow these steps:

1. Set your computer's BIOS to boot from the CD-ROM, and then restart the computer.

2. When prompted to do so, press F2.

3. When prompted to insert the ASR floppy, do so, and follow the on-screen instructions to restore your system files.

TIP ASR is available in Windows XP Professional but not in Home Edition. Although the Backup Utility may appear to make an ASR disk, you can't use this disk to restore because Home Edition doesn't support setups from ASR disks.

Backing Up System State Data

The *system state* of a computer is generally defined as all the files that are critical to the environment. In plain English, the system state includes information about user accounts, hardware and software settings, and files required for startup. However, what exactly is included in the system state differs from operating system to operating system and depends on which services are running on a computer. In this section, I'll expand the discussion to include Windows 2000 and Windows Server 2003 products, to give you a better picture of the importance of backing up the system state. I'll then specify what constitutes the system state on an XP Professional machine, which as you'll see is a subset of system state components.

Backing up the system state is critical when many changes have been made to the computer. For example, if you have a Windows 2000 system that acts as a domain controller on a small network, and the hard disk crashes, you'll most likely immediately reinstall the OS to a new disk. However, this step doesn't restore the contents of the Active Directory (AD) database, which is critical to recovering your network's original environment. You would have to re-create all user accounts and perform other recovery tasks to get the server back to its previous state. When you back up the system state, you ensure that the computer can be easily returned to its original condition.

You can back up and restore the following system state components using the Backup Utility program in Windows XP:

♦ The Registry

♦ The COM+ Class Registration database

♦ Boot files, including the system files

♦ The Certificate Services database

♦ The Active Directory directory service

♦ The SYSVOL directory

♦ Cluster service information

♦ The IIS metadirectory

♦ System files that are under Windows File Protection

When you choose to back up or restore the system state data, all the system state data that is relevant to your computer is backed up or restored; that is, you can't choose to back up or restore individual components because of dependencies among the components. However, you can restore the system state data to an alternate location. If you do so, only the Registry files, the SYSVOL directory, the Cluster service information, and system boot files are restored. The AD service, the Certificate Services database, and the COM+ Class Registration database aren't restored.

As you can see, backing up the system state is critical for most servers on a network: domain controllers, web servers, certificate servers, and the like. It isn't quite as crucial on Windows XP Professional systems.

On XP Professional computers, the system state data comprises only the Registry, the COM+ Class Registration database, files under Windows File Protection, and boot files. In other words, unless you have tons of user accounts on your system or are using it as the network's web server, the system can be (relatively) quickly restored after reinstalling the operating system. However, it can still be useful to back up system state data to make it easy to recover the Registry. The next section explains in more detail.

Backing Up and Recovering the Registry

When you install Windows XP, Setup creates a backup copy of the Registry in the `%systemroot%\Repair` folder. You can use this backup copy of the Registry to recover a system in the event of a Registry problem (such as a corrupted Registry file). Unfortunately, Windows XP doesn't automatically keep the repair copy of the Registry up to date; you have to make sure the files are backed up.

The easiest way to update the repair copy of the Registry is to back up the system state data with the Windows Backup program. When you perform a system state backup, the Backup program automatically updates the Registry files in the `Repair` folder. It also makes a copy of the system state data in the location you specify during backup.

When it comes time to restore the Registry, you could use Backup to restore the system state data. However, that method assumes that your system will boot or, if not, that you've installed a parallel copy of Windows XP on the computer that you can use to restore the system state data. In many cases, the system won't boot if a Registry problem occurs. What's more, you probably want to get the system running right away and not go through the hassle of installing another copy of Windows XP.

Fortunately, you can restore one or more Registry files manually with the Recovery Console (RC). To do so, follow these steps:

1. Boot the computer using the RC. In the RC, change to the `%systemroot%\System32\Config` folder.

2. Rename the existing Registry file(s) you want to restore, giving them an `.OLD` file extension.

3. Copy the Registry file(s) as needed from the `%systemroot%\Repair` folder to `%systemroot%\System32\Config`.

4. Reboot the system to verify that everything is working as it should.

TIP   See Chapter 40 to learn more about the Recovery Console and how to start it.

You may have guessed that you can also back up the Registry from the RC, which is an alternative to using the Backup utility to back up system state data and indirectly create the repair copy of the Registry. To do so, boot to the RC, and then copy the contents of the `%systemroot%\System32\Config` folder to the `%systemroot%\Repair` folder. You'll have to copy the files one at a time, because the RC's COPY command doesn't support wildcards. Or, create a batch file that contains multiple COPY commands to copy all of the Registry files, and then use the BATCH command in the RC to run the batch file.

Automating Backup

Your backup strategy should include scheduling regular backups. You can establish a schedule using the Backup Or Restore Wizard or using the Schedule Jobs tab in the Backup Utility Advanced Mode. To use the wizard, click the Advanced button on the final screen. Then, select the backup type (discussed later in this chapter), how to back up, and what to do with the file. In the When To Backup window, choose to begin the job now or later.

To schedule a backup job from the Backup Wizard, click the Later option, and then click the Set Schedule button to open the Schedule Job dialog box, as shown in Figure 38.3. The contents of this dialog box depend on the frequency option you choose from the drop-down list box. For example, if you select Monthly, you can specify which day of the month the backup will run. You can further fine-tune the schedule by clicking the Advanced button.

You can also open the Schedule Jobs dialog box by clicking the Schedule Jobs tab on the Backup Utility Advanced Mode screen. Click the Add Job button, and you're on your way. In either case, you use the interface just described. To modify an existing job, however, you need to return to the Schedule Jobs tab in Advanced Mode. Click the Schedule Data tab, and then click the Properties button to open the Schedule Job dialog box.

FIGURE 38.3

You can schedule a backup job using the options in the Schedule Job dialog box.

Importing Other Backup Sets

If you've previously saved a backup job, you can use the same settings to perform future backups. The Backup Utility lets you quickly import these settings. Follow these steps:

1. In the Welcome To The Backup Utility Advanced Mode screen, click the Backup tab.

2. Choose Job ➢ Load Selections to open the Open dialog box.

3. Previously used settings are saved with the .bks extension. Select a job, and then click the Open button.

You should see one or more checks next to selections in the Backup tab, as appropriate to the saved settings.

You can now proceed with the backup normally, setting a new schedule if you like or choosing to use a different backup type. This can save you the trouble of making several check box selections each time you back up your data.

Using System Restore

System Restore is an XP service that runs in the background, continually monitoring changes to essential files, folders, and settings. At regular intervals, System Restore takes a snapshot of your system's Registry. If Windows becomes unstable, you can use System Restore in either normal or safe mode to roll back your system files and Registry settings to those that were used at a previous time when your system was working properly.

Using System Restore is especially effective in the following situations:

◆ You install a program that conflicts with other software drivers on your system. If uninstalling the program doesn't fix the situation, you can restore to a point before the program was installed.

◆ You install one or more updated drivers that cause system instability. You can use System Restore to restore all previously installed drivers instead of using the Driver Rollback feature from Device Manager.

♦ Your system develops performance or stability problems for no apparent reason. This situation may not seem plausible at first glance; after all, problems always occur for a reason, right? But consider a situation in which a computer is shared by many people, family members or coworkers who may or may not document changes they make or may install untested or unsupported software or devices without compatible drivers. You can restore to a point where you're reasonably sure that the system was functioning properly (that is, the last time *you* were using it).

TIP Don't count on System Restore to replace a good antivirus program. A system can become infected and not exhibit any symptoms. Thus, files stored in restore points can be infected without your knowledge, even if the computer was functioning properly at the restore point.

System Restore keeps a log of changes to a system in the `%systemroot%\system32\Restore` folder. At regular intervals, System Restore takes snapshots of the system state, looking at the same type of information that is saved when you back up system state data.

By default, System Restore creates restore points without user intervention every 24 hours if you leave your computer on. If you shut down your system, System Restore creates a new restore point when you restart if the most recent restore point was created more than 24 hours ago.

To restore a previous system configuration, you must be logged on as a user who is a member of the Administrators group. Be sure that no other users are logged on to the machine over the network, and shut down all running programs. Then, follow these steps:

1. Choose Start ➢ Help And Support to open the Help And Support Center home page.

2. In the Pick A Task list, click Undo Changes To Your Computer With System Restore, or choose Start ➢ All Programs ➢ Accessories ➢ System Tools ➢ System Restore. Either way, you open System Restore.

3. Click Restore My Computer To An Earlier Time, and then click Next to open the Select A Restore Point screen.

4. Select a date that represents a system restore point, and then click Next to open the Confirm Restore Point Selection screen.

5. Verify the date you selected, and then click Next.

System Restore copies the necessary files and settings from the System Restore archives. Your system then restarts automatically.

TIP You can always run System Restore again and choose Undo My Last Restoration if the results aren't what you expect.

In addition to creating restore points at 24-hour intervals, System Restore creates restore points when you do the following:

◆ Install an unsigned third-party driver. When you install an unsigned driver, Windows displays a warning message. If you continue anyway (who doesn't?), the system creates a restore point before completing the installation.

◆ Install an application using an installer that's compatible with System Restore. Applications that use the Windows Installer and InstallShield Professional 6.1 or later are included in this category.

◆ Install a Windows Update update or a patch. Windows creates a restore point automatically when you download and install an update using Windows Update.

◆ Restore a prior configuration using System Restore. Each time you run System Restore, it creates a new restore point so that you can undo the restore, as mentioned earlier.

◆ Restore data from a backup set created with the Windows XP Backup Utility program. If the restoration of the backed-up files creates problems, you can reverse the effects using System Restore.

Furthermore, you can customize the restore interval. Follow these steps:

1. Open the Registry Editor and locate the key

   `\HKLM\SOFTWARE\Microsoft\WindowsNT\CurrentVersion\SystemRestore`

2. Change the RPGlobalInterval value from its default setting of 86,400 (a value of seconds, which, to save you a trip to your calculator, comes out to 24 hours). Cut it in half (for example, to 43,200) to take a System Restore snapshot twice a day. Double it for snapshots every other day, and so on. Automatic snapshots will still take place.

By default, restore points are deleted every 90 days. You can adjust this interval by changing the RPLifeInterval value, as shown in Figure 38.4, from the default setting of 7,776,000 seconds. RPLifeInterval is also under the Registry key

   `\HKLM\SOFTWARE\Microsoft\WindowsNT\CurrentVersion\SystemRestore`

FIGURE 38.4
The RPLifeInterval value
determines how long re-
store points are kept.

Planning a Disaster Recovery Strategy

Earlier, we stepped through the Backup Or Restore Wizard, telling the utility exactly what to back up.
On the final screen of this wizard, you can click the Advanced Options button to open the Options
dialog box. Click the Backup Type tab, shown in Figure 38.5, to specify the type of backup you want
to make. (You can also open the Options dialog box by choosing Tools ➢ Options in the Backup Utility window.)

FIGURE 38.5
Use the options on
the Backup Type tab to
select the kind of back-
up you want.

Which backup type is best? As is the case with so many computing scenarios, it all depends. The best backup type for your situation depends on how much data you're backing up, how often, how quickly you want the backup to be performed, and how many backups you're willing to apply in the event of a restore. You have the following choices:

Normal   This option backs up all selected files and marks each file as having been backed up; that is, it clears the archive bit. This type of backup is often used as a benchmark that other backup types can use to determine what needs backing up. Because it backs up everything you select, the normal backup takes the longest but is the easiest to restore. Many companies that shut down operation for the night perform a full nightly backup, because time isn't a concern.

Copy   This type of backup backs up all selected files and doesn't mark them as being backed up. A copy is useful as a quick way to archive working data without impacting your overall backup strategy.

Differential   This type of backup backs up only the files that have changed since the last normal or incremental backup and doesn't clear the archive bit, which would mark them as having been backed up. Because it doesn't clear the archive bit, a differential backup always uses as a point of reference the last time the archive bit was cleared. These backups take longer overall than an incremental backup but are quicker to restore. You can restore all data using the last full backup and then apply only the most recent differential backup.

Incremental   This option backs up selected files that haven't been marked as archived and marks the files as having been backed up. These backups are much quicker than a differential backup, but they take longer to restore because more backups must be applied to the last normal backup. To perform a restore, this strategy requires that the last normal backup and all the incremental backups be applied.

Daily   This approach backs up only the selected files that have changed on the current day and doesn't clear the archive bit. Each daily backup and the last normal backup are required for a successful restore. The daily backup is a way to back up a day's work without affecting your overall backup strategy.

TIP   Most of the time, your backup strategies should include the normal, differential, and incremental backup types. Use the other types of backups sparingly, because it can become confusing to keep track of what files are where when it's time to restore data.

How Group Policy Can Provide Easy Recovery

Group policy, which is supported in Windows XP Professional (but not Home Edition), works in concert with other Microsoft server technologies to help automate configuration and other tasks. With group policy and these other technologies, you can

◆ Centralize the management of user data

◆ Distribute and maintain software (that is, install applications and apply service packs, hotfixes, updates, and so on)

◆ Manage user settings (so that programs and computers can easily share settings, such as your Favorites list in Windows Explorer and Internet Explorer)

◆ Automatically install the OS based on group membership in the Active Directory

When you use these features on both the server and the client, a user's data, applications, and settings remain constant throughout their environment. You can mirror data from your computer to the network, which protects your critical work. In addition, you can use any Windows computer on your network and always have access to your data.

These features, when used together, provide for almost completely automated and transparent recovery of the OS, applications, and user data. If a user's system fails, you can give the user a new computer or a blank hard drive and let Remote Installation Services handle the recovery task. After RIS installs the user's OS, group policy then installs the applications and further redirects the user to their data folders, which are tucked away safely on a network server. You save considerable time that would otherwise be required for an administrator or the user to manually recover the system. Plus, redirecting the users' data folders to a network server that is backed up regularly can help prevent lost data.

To implement a truly automatic backup and recovery strategy, perform these tasks:

◆ Deploy Windows 2000 Server or Windows Server 2003 with Active Directory to support group policy assignment across the network.

◆ Deploy a RIS server to handle automatic OS installation.

◆ Use group policy to automatically assign applications for installation.

◆ Use group policy to redirect users' document folders to a server to make them available without disruption even if the user's computer fails.

You'll find more information about RIS and automated OS deployment in Chapter 3. Chapter 37 explains how to redirect user folders with group policy.

Chapter 39

System Recovery Tools

For most users, recovery remains a tedious topic until the solids hit the air-conditioning, whereupon the topic becomes not only interesting but also pressing. But if you've used Windows extensively, chances are that you're aware of the dangers of system damage and data loss, and that you're therefore reading this chapter at leisure without an urgent need to solve a grisly problem immediately.

However you're approaching it, this chapter discusses how to put the backup and disaster recovery plan you created in Chapter 38 into effect recovering your system, and how to use XP's repair and recovery tools and techniques for various categories of problems.

The chapter starts with an overview of those tools and techniques, what they do, and when they're best used. The chapter then discusses the tools and techniques in approximately ascending order of seriousness of problem they're intended for, starting with recovering data from a backup set and rolling back a driver and then moving on to more serious tools such as Automated System Recovery (ASR). It discusses techniques for repairing and recovering remote systems and finishes by discussing manual ways of recovering a system.

Which Recovery or Repair Tool Should You Use When?

Before you start using XP's various recovery and repair tools, make sure you know which tool is suited to which situation. For example, using ASR to solve a driver problem is like using a bulldozer to knock down a sand castle. Sure, it'll do the trick, but it's not the best tool for the job—and you might flatten a couple of other things in the process.

Table 39.1 lists the recovery and repair tools and techniques XP provides, roughly in order of seriousness of problem, with notes on the problems each tool or technique is best used to fix.

TABLE 39.1: Windows XP's Recovery and Repair Tools and Their Purposes

TOOL	PURPOSE	BEST USED FOR
Tools and Techniques Used when XP Starts Successfully		
Backup	Create and restore backups of specified files.	Protecting and restoring data files
Device Driver Roll Back	Replace an updated device driver that seems to be causing problems with the previous driver for the device, and restore any driver settings changed during the update.	Solving problems caused by installing new device drivers

TABLE 39.1:   Windows XP's Recovery and Repair Tools and Their Purposes *(CONTINUED)*

TOOL	PURPOSE	BEST USED FOR
Uninstall a program	Uninstall a program that's causing a problem.	Recovering from problems caused by installing a program
Reinstall a program	Reinstall a program that seems to be causing problems.	Solving problems resulting from a program's files having become corrupt or been deleted
System Restore	Create restore points containing system and application settings. Restore the system and application settings to those specified in the restore point you designate.	Recovering from installing applications or drivers that turn out to have a bad effect
Disable a device	Take a problem device and its drivers out of the equation for solving any system instability.	Recovering from problems apparently caused by, or contributed to by, a device driver
Clean boot	Start XP with fewer services and drivers to avoid problems caused by services that start automatically and drivers that load at startup.	Getting XP to run stably enough that you can repair its configuration manually

Tools and Techniques Used when XP Won't Start Successfully

Last Known Good Configuration	Restore the last control-set configuration with which XP started successfully.	Recovering from control-set problems that prevent XP from starting fully
Automated System Recovery (ASR)	Create a backup set to which XP can be restored when it won't start.	Recovering an XP Professional installation automatically
Recovery Console	Use a character-mode operating environment that provides repair-related commands.	Repairing Windows manually— for example, by replacing individual files
Parallel installation of XP	Install XP in another directory so that you can start it and use its tools to troubleshoot and repair your installation.	Repairing your XP configuration manually when XP won't start
Reinstall XP	Reinstall XP as an upgrade or a fresh installation.	Best *not* used until all else fails

Recovering Data from a Backup Set

If one or more of your data files have become corrupt, run Backup Utility, and restore the appropriate files as follows:

1. Launch Backup Utility from the Start menu (Start ➢ All Programs ➢ Accessories ➢ System Tools ➢ Backup) or by double-clicking the backup file from which you want to restore the files. If Backup Utility launches as a wizard, click the Advanced Mode link.

2. On the Restore And Manage Media tab, select the backup from which you want to restore. To restore from a backup file, expand the File object, and select the appropriate backup file. To restore from a backup on tape, expand the Tape object, and select the media name for the backup set.

3. If you want to restore only some files, select them.

4. If you haven't already done so, choose the appropriate option button on the Restore tab of the Options dialog box to specify what Backup Utility should do when a file it's restoring is already on the computer. Your choices are

   ◆ "Do not replace the file on my computer"

   ◆ "Replace the file on disk only if the file on disk is older"

   ◆ "Always replace the file on my computer"

5. In the Restore Files To drop-down list, choose whether to restore the files to their original location, an alternate location that you specify, or a single folder. If you choose an alternate location or a single folder, specify it.

6. To restore your installation of Windows XP, select the System State check box.

7. Click the Start Restore button. Backup Utility begins restoring the files.

8. If you're restoring System State files to their original locations, Backup Utility displays a Warning dialog box to make sure you intend to do so. Click the OK button to proceed.

9. Backup Utility then displays the Confirm Restore dialog box, in which you can click the Advanced button to set advanced options for the restoration operation:

   "Restore security"   This option controls whether Backup Utility reapplies the security settings (ownership, access permissions, and audit entries) to the restored files and folders. This option is available only for files from NTFS volumes going to NTFS volumes.

   "Restore junction points, and restore file and folder data under junction points to the original location"   This option controls whether Backup Utility restores the junction points on your disk together with the data the junction points reference. If you don't select this check box (which Backup Utility selects by default), Backup Utility restores the junction points, but you may not be able to access the data they point to.

   "When restoring replicated data sets, mark the restored data as the primary data for all replicas"   This option controls whether any File Replication Service (FRS) data you restore is replicated to other servers after the restore operation. (Otherwise, the data you restore may appear to be older than the replicated copies of it, in which case it won't be replicated.)

"Restore the cluster registry to the quorum disk and all other nodes"   This option isn't available for Windows XP Professional or Home Edition because it applies only to server clusters.

"Preserve existing volume mount points"   This option controls whether the restore operation avoids writing over volume mount points. Select this check box when you're restoring an entire drive, partition, or volume to a drive on which you don't want the volume mount points overwritten. By contrast, if you've just formatted the drive, you may want to overwrite the volume mount points with those in the backup.

10. After choosing advanced restore options, close the Advanced Restore Options dialog box. Then click the OK button in the Confirm Restore dialog box to start the restore operation.

WARNING   If you restore files from a backup created before you activated Windows XP on your computer or from a backup created on a computer on which XP hadn't been activated, or if you've made significant hardware changes since creating the backup, XP may prompt you to activate it after the backup, even though you have previously activated it. If this happens, you'll need to reactivate XP. To avoid this happening, make a full or incremental backup after making significant changes to your hardware configuration. (A full or incremental backup includes the Windows Product Activation database files, wpa.dbl, located in \Windows\System32, and wpa.bak, if it exists.)

If a restore operation doesn't give the results you want, you may be able to undo the restoration by using System Restore, which is discussed later in this chapter.

Rolling Back an Installation

If installing a new driver (or updating a driver, either manually or via Windows Update) seems to make your system unstable, use the Roll Back Driver button on the Driver tab of the Properties dialog box for the component to roll back the driver to the previous driver.

If Windows XP becomes unstable after you install a program, use the Add Or Remove Programs feature to uninstall the program. If files for a program become corrupt and it starts crashing, reinstall it.

Using System Restore

System Restore (Start ➤ All Programs ➤ Accessories ➤ System Tools ➤ System Restore) is a powerful tool with a mostly goof-proof interface. You'll have no difficulty creating restore points manually and restoring Windows to them. But System Restore offers plenty of details and complexities—read on.

Who Can Run System Restore

Only members of the Administrators group can run System Restore. Other users receive a message telling them they don't have sufficient security privileges to restore the system if they try to run System Restore.

When Restore Points Are Created

Windows XP creates the first restore point the first time you boot it after installation. Thereafter, by default it creates a restore point every 24 hours of real time, plus restore points at these important events:

◆ When you install Windows Updates

◆ When you perform a restore operation (using System Restore itself or Backup Utility)

◆ When you install unsigned device drivers

◆ When you install or uninstall a program via the Windows Installer or InstallShield

Automatically created restore points are great as a fallback for those times when you fail to notice a disaster heading your way. But you may also want to create restore points manually when you're trying several different drivers for a piece of hardware or when you're installing software that doesn't use the Windows Installer or InstallShield. When you create a restore point manually, you can give it a more descriptive name than Windows manages for restore points created automatically, which should help you identify the restore point later.

There's no harm in creating an extra restore point, other than

◆ It takes a little time.

◆ Sooner or later, you're going to run out of restore space, at which System Restore will discard your oldest restore points.

To create more restore points automatically, use the Registry Editor to change one of the following values in this key:

```
\HKEY_LOCAL_MACHINE\Software\Microsoft\WindowsNT\CurrentVersion\SystemRestore
```

RPGlobalInterval   A DWORD value specifying the number of seconds that System Restore waits before creating an automatic restore point based on calendar date. The default setting is 86,400 seconds (24 hours).

RPSessionInterval   A DWORD value specifying the number of seconds that System Restore waits before creating an automatic restore point based on system uptime. The default setting is 0 seconds, which switches off this function.

When Restore Points Are Deleted

By default, restore points are kept for 90 days and then deleted automatically. If System Restore grows to occupy more than 90 percent of its available storage space before that, it deletes the oldest restore points until about 25 percent of the available space is free so that it can create new restore points. (This process is known as FIFO—first in, first out.)

All restore points are deleted when you turn off System Restore on the system drive. Some restore points are deleted if you reduce the size of the data store manually.

If you run short of disk space, System Restore cedes some of its available space to help out. If necessary, it deletes the oldest restore points so that it has 25 percent or more of the remaining available space free for creating restore points.

If you select the System Restore option in Disk Cleanup, Windows XP purges all restore points but the latest.

To change the length of time that restore points are kept, adjust the RPLifeInterval value entry in the SystemRestore key. The default setting is 7,776,000 seconds (90 days).

TIP   For details of other System Restore Registry keys, see Q295659 in the Knowledge Base at support.microsoft.com.

What's Protected and What's Not

Briefly, System Restore tracks changes to program files. It doesn't protect or restore data files. (For that, you need to use Backup.) Similarly, it doesn't restore trivial user-interface settings such as your wallpaper or Desktop background image.

System Restore also doesn't protect backup files such as those created using Backup Utility. So, you can't use System Restore to restore backup files you've deleted.

System Restore monitors, protects, and restores Start menu shortcuts and HTML links, because these are stored on the system drive. But if a program is installed on a nonsystem drive that isn't using System Restore, the program won't be restored in a restore operation, so these shortcuts or links won't start the program.

For a full list of the files, file types, and folders that System Restore doesn't protect, browse *%systemroot%*\system32\Restore\filelist.xml.

System Restore Quirks

The Select A System Restore screen shows in boldface dates in the current month that contain restore points. Dates in the previous month (at the beginning of the current month) appear grayed out even if they have restore points. To see these restore points, move back a month in the calendar control. This presentation is (to use Microsoft's phrase) "by design," but it's confusing at first, especially given that when System Restore runs out of space, it deletes old restore points to make room for new ones.

In early versions of Windows XP Professional and Home Edition, System Restore failed to update the date if you changed the date on your computer while System Restore was open. (The solution is, of course, to close System Restore before changing the date.)

System Restore is enabled by default. If you disable it temporarily, don't reenable it while installing a program. System Restore creates a restore point when you reenable it, and creating the restore point during the installation of a program can corrupt the restore point.

The only way to tell if a restore point is corrupt is to try to restore the system to it. If the restoration fails, the restore point was corrupt.

TIP   Close all documents before running a System Restore operation. Better, close all programs as well.

For a hard link that you've deleted, System Restore creates a new file *with the same name as the deleted link but with the same contents as the original file.*

System Restore may not fully restore printer drivers that use file extensions that are normally used by data files. If this happens, reinstall the printer drivers manually.

If the system drive has less than 200 MB of free space, or if a nonsystem drive has less than 50 MB of free space, XP suspends System Restore when a file that System Restore is tracking is copied, modified, or deleted. *This suspension applies to all disks, not just the disk that's short of space.* (Microsoft calls this *consistent freeze.*) To get System Restore going again, free at least 200 MB of disk space on the system disk or 50 MB on the nonsystem disk, and either wait 15 minutes for System Restore to notice and restart itself or choose Start ➢ All Programs ➢ Accessories ➢ System Tools ➢ System Restore to start System Restore immediately.

Windows XP doesn't preserve System Restore settings if you reinstall XP or upgrade from Home Edition to Professional.

Taming the Disk Hog

You *can* turn off System Restore for all drives if you want (on the System Restore tab of the System Properties dialog box); however, for most computers, it's a better idea to run System Restore but decrease the amount of space it takes. By default, System Restore lays claim to 12 percent of each hard drive (or 400 MB for drives smaller than 4 GB), giving it the potential to move ahead of notorious disk hogs such as the Recycle Bin, Temporary Internet Files, the paging file, and the hibernation file in the Greed Stakes. That said, System Restore uses disk space only as necessary and up to this maximum setting, so the space isn't gone for good.

Because System Restore doesn't monitor, protect, or restore data files, turn it off for data-only drives. Use System Restore on your system drive (which is listed first on the System Restore tab of the System Restore tab) and on drives that contain programs.

Examining Your Restore Points

To examine your restore points, run SRDIAG.EXE, which you'll find in the *%systemroot%*\system32\ Restore folder. Without any parameters, SRDIAG.EXE creates a CAB file named *ComputerName_ mmddyy_hhmmss*.cab in that same Restore folder. You can use the /CabLoc parameter to specify a folder for the file and the /CabName parameter to specify the filename, as in the following example:

```
srdiag /CabName:Restore1.cab /CabLoc:c:\examples
```

Table 39.2 lists the files contained in the resulting CAB file.

The CAB file also contains, for each restore point, a restorepointsize file (named *driveletter*--RP*n*-restorepointsize—for example, C--RP3-restorepointsize) and a LOG file (named *driveletter*--RP*n*-rp.log—for example, C--RP3-rp.log).

Of the files in the System Restore cabinet, SR-RP.LOG and SR-RSTRLOG.TXT tend to be the most rewarding for human examination.

TABLE 39.2:   Files Contained in a System Restore Cabinet File

FILE	CONTENTS
SR-REG.TXT	Registry settings for System Restore.
MACHINEGUID.TXT	The global universal identification (GUID) of the _restore folder. The system's data store is located in \System Volume Information_restore{*GUID*}.
FILELIST.XML	A list of the files and folders included and excluded in restore operations.

TABLE 39.2: Files Contained in a System Restore Cabinet File *(CONTINUED)*

FILE	CONTENTS
DRIVETABLE.TXT	Details of the status of each drive that System Restore is monitoring. Includes the mount point path, volume GUID, volume status, and maximum size of the data store.
SR-CHGLOG.LOG	The change log containing details of the changes to files on each monitored drive for all available restore points.
SR-EVENTLOGS.TXT	A log of events for the System Restore service (for example, when System Restore is turned on and off, and when restore points are created).
SR-FILELIST.LOG	A list of the System Restore binary files, with their file information.
SR-RP.LOG	A list of the restore points, their type (for example, System Checkpoint), status, and date and time created.
SR-RSTRLOG.TXT	The restore log file for the last restore completed or attempted.
SR-FIFO.LOG	A list of FIFO restore points purged by the datastore. This file isn't created until a restore point is purged.

Locking Down System Restore

To prevent users from changing System Restore settings in Windows XP Professional, use the Group Policy Editor to select the Disabled option button for the Turn Off System Restore item and the Enabled option button for the Turn Off Configuration item in the System Restore object (Computer Configuration ➢ Administrative Templates ➢ System).

Alternatively, run the Registry Editor, and navigate to the following key:

```
\HKEY_LOCAL_MACHINE\SOFTWARE\Policies\Microsoft\Windows NT
```

Create a new subkey named SystemRestore, and create under it a new DWORD value named DisableConfig with the value data 1.

Once you've taken either of these actions, the options on the System Restore tab of the System Properties dialog box appear disabled.

"Restoration Incomplete" Error Message

The message "Restoration incomplete. Your computer cannot be restored to *date restore point*" appears when the computer is shut down improperly during restoration, interrupting the restoration. If this happens, you can try to restore again to the same restore point, restore to another restore point, or undo the incomplete restoration.

How System Restore Handles Passwords

System Restore restores program passwords (such as those for .NET Passport or AOL Instant Messenger, which are stored on web servers), domain passwords, and computer passwords, but it doesn't restore Windows XP passwords, Internet Explorer passwords, or Content Advisor passwords.

Checking that System Restore Is Running

You can check that System Restore is running by viewing the Services tab of System Configuration Utility or by issuing a `net start` command.

When Restoration Fails

If a restoration doesn't produce the effects you want, use the Undo My Last Restoration option to revert to your previous unsatisfactory state, or try restoring to another restore point.

Last Known Good Configuration

System Restore is a powerful tool that can fix many configuration problems by restoring your computer to the state it was in before a problem occurred. But if your computer won't start Windows fully or at all, System Restore can't help you. The next recovery tool to turn to is the Last Known Configuration feature.

Last Known Good Configuration is intended to help you recover from problems caused by installing a driver that turns out to be problematic or by a program (malware or otherwise) trashing Registry data. As its name suggests, Last Known Good Configuration starts the computer using the Registry information and driver settings used the last time Windows started successfully. This information comes from one of the ControlSet00n keys in the Registry. To see which control set key will be used, use the Registry Editor to view the `\HKEY_LOCAL_MACHINE\SYSTEM\Select` key. The LastKnownGood value entry identifies the control set that will be used, the Current and Default value entries are the current and default control sets, and the Failed value entry identifies the last control set with which Windows failed to start correctly. (Using Last Known Good Configuration marks the previous default control set as Failed.)

To start your computer with Last Known Good Configuration, display the Windows Advanced Options menu by pressing the F8 key at the Please Select The Operating System To Start prompt (if you have a multiboot configuration using the NT boot loader) or at the beginning of the Windows startup sequence. Then select the Last Known Good Configuration item from the menu.

Last Known Good Configuration has two disadvantages:

- You lose any configuration changes made since the last successful start. (Given that one of these changes may have caused the problem, this loss may not worry you too much.)

- It doesn't always work. It cures only certain types of problems (such as those described earlier) and can't do anything for problems that don't involve control sets (for example, problems involving passwords or policies). Even for control-set problems, if you made a change and then rebooted and logged in successfully before deciding you want to make a change, Last Known Good Configuration can't help you.

Performing a Clean Boot

If Windows XP is suffering a problem related to a startup program, a driver, or a setting that causes it to crash too soon after starting (successfully) for you to troubleshoot it, performing a *clean boot* may enable you to get XP running stably enough for you to eliminate the problem. A clean boot is one in which you disable startup programs, drivers, and settings so that they can't interfere with XP's starting. Disabling these programs, drivers, and settings of course costs you the functionality they provide until you reenable them, so a clean boot is a troubleshooting tool rather than a way of getting work done around the problem.

To perform a clean boot, follow these steps:

1. Run System Configuration Utility (for example, Start ➤ Run, enter **msconfig**, and click the OK button).

2. On the General tab, select the Selective Startup option button, and clear the check boxes beneath it. (XP includes four check boxes—Process SYSTEM.INI File, Process WIN.INI File, Load System Services, and Load Startup Items—but your computer may include third-party add-ins that place further check boxes here.)

3. Click the OK button to close System Configuration Utility, and accept XP's offer to restart your computer.

When XP comes back up (minus the startup programs, drivers, and settings you've eliminated), it displays a System Configuration Utility message box telling you the computer is in Diagnostic or Selective Startup mode. You'll probably be aware of this, because XP's interface will be missing most of its visual enhancements, such as the rounded upper corners of windows, rounded buttons, and color gradation on the Taskbar and notification area.

By default, XP runs System Configuration Utility automatically in Diagnostic or Selective Startup mode. (You can select the check box in the System Configuration Utility message box to prevent it from doing so.) On the General tab, select the Selective Startup button again. Then make sure that all the check boxes you cleared are still cleared. If one of them is dimmed and unavailable, it typically means that the program's manufacturer has done something subtle to force it to load. In this case, you'll probably need to consult the manufacturer in order to disable it.

If the check boxes are clear, select the first check box, and restart the computer. If XP restarts and doesn't manifest the problem you're troubleshooting, select the second check box, and restart again. Continue the process until you reach the check box that reproduces the problem. Then display the tab of System Configuration Utility that corresponds to the offending check box, and follow the same process of eliminating all items, gradually adding them back in until the problem reappears. For example, if you find that the Load Startup Items check box on the General tab of System Configuration Utility seems to be the offender, display the Startup tab and disable all the items on it. Then reenable them one by one, and see which one's giving XP grief.

Once you've finished using clean boot to troubleshoot your PC, run msconfig, select the Normal Startup option button on the General tab of System Configuration Utility, and reboot.

Recovery with ASR

Automated System Recovery (ASR) is designed to be used after what Microsoft delicately terms a "major failure" or (even more delicately) a "catastrophic system failure"—in other words, a failure so grim that your system isn't recoverable by conventional means such as Safe mode, System Restore, or manual recovery.

ASR is designed to be a set-and-forget process. You create a backup set that consists of a large backup file containing all your system information (your system state, your system services, and all disks that contain OS components) and a floppy disk that contains files that give access to the backup file. After your catastrophic failure, you use the floppy and the backup file to restore XP to the state it was in when you made the backup.

If all goes well and the backup set identified by your ASR disk is up to date or represents a state you're prepared to use again, ASR is viable and far preferable to reinstalling XP from scratch. But if your ASR disk is way out of date, ASR is only marginally more appealing than reinstalling from scratch.

NOTE   ASR saves only your system files. It's designed to be used in conjunction with a full backup of your data, not to supplant the backup.

Creating Your ASR Backup Set

Create your ASR disk by clicking the Automated System Recovery Wizard button on the Welcome tab of the Backup Utility window (or choosing Tools ➢ ASR Wizard) and following the wizard.

WARNING   Don't put your backup file on the boot volume or the system volume, because the ASR restore process partitions the C: drive as a matter of course. When the C: drive is partitioned, any backup file stored on it usually gets corrupted. The restore process then runs fine until approximately its midpoint, when it announces that it can't find the specified backup file and invites you to produce it. You can then navigate to the directory where the backup file was: The directory is there because the restore process has re-created it, but the file is nowhere to be found.

Using ASR

When you've determined that your system has indeed suffered a catastrophic failure and that you can't recover it by using less drastic means, use ASR:

1. Slot the floppy and your XP CD. If your backup is on removable media, make that available.

2. Boot from the CD, and run Windows Setup as if you were going to install XP afresh.

3. When Windows Setup prompts you to press F2 to activate ASR, do so.

4. Sensibly enough, Windows Setup prompts you to confirm the action. When you do, Windows Setup reads the files from the floppy disk and uses that information, the XP CD, and your backup set to restore your system to the state it was in when you created the ASR set.

5. Windows prompts you to press F3 to reboot. Remove the floppy if the computer will try to boot from it, and then press F3.

What the ASR Disk Contains

An ASR disk contains the files `ASR.SIF` and `ASRPNP.SIF`. These SIF files—*state information files*—are just text files, so you can edit them in any text editor (for example, Notepad) if necessary.

You might need to edit them to add information about files and device drivers needed during ASR Setup that the Windows XP CD-ROM doesn't contain and that you need to supply manually. For details, see Q299044 in the Microsoft Knowledge Base at `support.microsoft.com`.

Re-creating an ASR Disk

If you've lost your ASR disk, you can re-create it as follows.

1. Open the backup file for the ASR set on the Restore And Manage Media tab of Backup Utility.

2. Expand the contents of the file.

3. Expand the second item for the drive letter containing the system files so that you can see the `\Windows\Repair` folder.

4. Select the check boxes for `ASR.SIF` and `ASRPNP.SIF`.

5. In the Restore Files To drop-down list, specify Single Folder, and use the Alternate Location text box to specify your floppy drive (for example, A:\). Make sure the files go to the root of the floppy disk—if they're anywhere else, ASR won't work.

6. Click the Start Restore button. Backup Utility displays the Confirm Restore dialog box.

7. Click the OK button. If you're using NTFS on your system drive, Backup Utility displays the Continue dialog box, warning you that "the target file system does not support some [of] the features of the original file system."

8. Click the OK button. Backup Utility copies the files to the floppy disk.

Recovering Systems Remotely

So far in this chapter, we've been assuming that you have direct access to the computer that you need to recover. If it's at the other end of the wire, your options are as follows:

◆ If XP is functional but impaired, you can use the tools discussed in Chapter 23 to perform some of the actions discussed so far in this chapter on a remote computer. For example, if you can log on remotely to a computer that has Remote Desktop Connection (RDC) enabled, you can use RDC to run System Restore across the network. Doing so of course terminates your RDC connection as XP restarts—but you can reestablish the connection once the system comes back up.

◆ Likewise, if you can establish a Remote Assistance connection, you can roll back a driver, uninstall or reinstall a program, disable a device, or take other corrective action.

◆ If the remote system is running the Telnet service, you may be able to log in remotely to perform administration tasks if the GUI tools aren't working.

◆ If XP is running but has a Registry problem, you may be able to recover it by using the Registry Editor to edit the Registry remotely.

◆ You may be able to use MMC snap-ins and extensions to access the computer remotely and to manipulate it into better health.

◆ If the remote computer is sick enough to be inaccessible remotely, you'll need a live body on the ground to get it going again—for example, by inserting a Remote Installation Services (RIS) client disk, restarting the PC, and getting the RIS process going; or by inserting the ASR disk (and removable media, if applicable) and starting the ASR process.

Manual Recovery Methods

This section details some manual recovery steps you may want to try when automated means of recovery don't fit your needs.

Installing a Parallel Copy of Windows XP

Earlier in this chapter, I discussed performing a clean boot to bypass and then isolate a startup problem Windows XP was having. If a clean boot doesn't get you where you want to be, install a parallel copy of XP, boot it, and work from there. The key point is to install the new copy of XP either in a different folder on the same partition or on a different partition so that you keep it separate from the previous copy.

If you're able to get the original copy of XP working again (for example, by editing the Registry from the new copy of XP), you can then revert to the original copy. If not, you'll be able to recover files or back up your data before taking further steps.

Disabling Problem Services

If using Last Known Good Configuration to restore the control set that allowed the previous boot doesn't get XP started again, you may need to disable services that you suspect of preventing XP from starting.

To do so, boot to your parallel copy of XP, fire up the Registry Editor, select the HKEY_LOCAL_MACHINE key, and use the File ➤ Load Hive command to load the \System32\Config\System file from the installation of XP that you're troubleshooting. Use the Current value entry in the \HKEY_LOCAL_MACHINE\SYSTEM\Select key to identify the current control set, and then open the key for that control set and examine the Services key for services that are set to start automatically.

The Start key for each service will have the value 1 (starts during bootup), 2 (starts automatically after bootup), 3 (starts manually), or 4 (is disabled). Don't mess with the 1 values, because these services are critical to boot XP; but try changing any suspect services with the value 2 to either 3 or 4. Change a value for a suspect service (or perhaps two), and then reboot with the installation of XP that you're troubleshooting and see whether things have improved. If not, boot back into your parallel copy of XP, restore the services you changed to their previous setting, and try changing another service or two. Rinse and repeat until you get results.

Reinstalling Windows XP

If worse comes to the worst, you may need to reinstall Windows XP. Try an upgrade installation first, because then you won't need to reinstall and reconfigure all your applications as well as XP itself.

RECOVERING SYSTEM STATE INFORMATION IF YOU DON'T HAVE A SYSTEM STATE BACKUP

If you've never performed a system state backup, the repair folder will contain a backup of your original system state, not of its more recent state. But you can retrieve recent settings from the System Volume Information folder by using Recovery Console, provided the option Recovery Console: Allow Floppy Copy And Access To All Drives And Folders is set to Enabled. This option is in the Security Options folder under Local Policies for whichever security tool you're using (for example, Local Security Policy or Domain Security Policy).

Take these steps:

1. Boot into Recovery Console.

2. Delete the current SAM, SECURITY, SOFTWARE, SYSTEM, and DEFAULT files from the %systemroot%\system32\config folder. (If you're feeling cautious, copy them to a temporary folder, and then delete the originals.)

3. Issue the command **set allowallpaths = true** to enable access to all drives and paths.

4. Change directory to the System Volume Information folder. It should contain one or more folders named _restore{GUID}, where GUID is a globally unique identifier such as 49F88DFF-6A1F-4764-95C7-BE8K701B5C8C.

5. Change directory to the last folder before the one that has the current time. It should contain one or more restore-point folders named RP0, RP1, and so on.

6. Change directory to the latest RP folder and then to the `snapshot` folder it contains.

7. Copy these files to the `%systemroot%\system32\config` folder, and rename them as indicated:

   ◆ _REGISTRY_MACHINE_SAM—Rename to SAM.

   ◆ _REGISTRY_MACHINE_SECURITY—Rename to SECURITY.

   ◆ _REGISTRY_MACHINE_SOFTWARE—Rename to SOFTWARE.

   ◆ _REGISTRY_MACHINE_SYSTEM—Rename to SYSTEM.

   ◆ _REGISTRY_USER_DEFAULT—Rename to DEFAULT.

8. Exit Recovery Console, and restart XP.

If your Windows drive uses FAT32 rather than NTFS, you can retrieve recent settings files from the `System Volume Information` folder using Windows Explorer and copy them to a temporary folder, and then boot into Recovery Console and copy them to the `%systemroot%\system32\config` folder. If you want to do this, make sure XP is displaying protected operating system files. (If it isn't, choose Tools ➢ Folder Options, clear the Hide Protected Operating System Files check box on the View tab of the Folder Options dialog box, click the Yes button in the resulting warning dialog box, and close the Folder Options dialog box.)

Restoring Files with the Recovery Console

Another tool you can use to recover your system when XP won't start is the Recovery Console. The next chapter discusses the Recovery Console in detail. Recovery tasks you can perform with the Recovery Console include restoring your Registry from backup and restoring critical files, as discussed in the following sections.

USING THE RECOVERY CONSOLE TO RESTORE THE REGISTRY FROM A BACKUP COPY

To restore the Registry from a backup copy by using Recovery Console, install the Recovery Console and boot to it (as discussed in Chapter 40). Then use the `copy` command to copy, to the `%systemroot%\system32\config` folder, either XP's default backups of the Registry files from the `%systemroot%\repair` folder or your manual backups of the Registry files from another location. Issue the `exit` command to exit Recovery Console, restart your computer, and then use System Restore to restore your computer to an earlier restore point.

USING THE RECOVERY CONSOLE TO RESTORE CRITICAL FILES

You may also need to restore critical files other than Registry files after a program has damaged a Windows file in such a way that Windows can't recover it. Use the `copy` command to copy files from a local drive or a network drive. (Use the `net use` command to map to a network drive in order to copy backups of files from it.)

Chapter 40

Recovery Console

Sometimes, your Windows get broken, leaving you in great pane. OK, enough bad humor, since this is a serious subject.

If you've been with PCs for more than a few years, you know that repair solutions for the operating system weren't always easy to come by. When you could find them (such as with PC manufacturers who would pack a recovery CD with their systems), these solutions usually weren't too elegant or customizable. Often, such methods resulted in almost as much work to restore a system to operating capacity as it would take to reformat the disk and reinstall the OS and all the applications.

For most of us, the first step in coming back meant having a boot disk handy. But you had to remember to add various commands and utilities (not to mention drivers, scanners, and so on) to the boot disk so that you had everything you needed in the event that Windows or the PC wouldn't boot. Just to assemble what you needed and to reach the point where you could troubleshoot required more than an ounce of skill and perseverance.

Operating system recovery options have changed, and it's time for a somewhat updated approach. To that end, I present you with Recovery Console, the command-line console interface you'll use with Windows XP to try to restore it to operation when lesser methods fail.

Let's get started, because there is a good deal to learn.

Overview of Recovery Console

Recovery Console (RC) is a command-line console troubleshooting tool included with Windows XP.

Do think of Recovery Console as a tool in your arsenal to combat problems encountered in getting Windows XP to load and behave properly.

Don't think of it as a panacea for resolving all that may be wrong.

Later, in "Recovery Console Commands," you'll see many similarities in XP's Recovery Console to what many of us know as a DOS troubleshooting environment. By this, I mean that you execute commands at the command line to try to fix a disk, load or unload a service or driver, or copy/delete a file.

But if you approach RC as just another DOS program, you'll be frustrated, because it's deliberately more limited than DOS. You don't have access to every file and folder, for example, but you do have access to strategic files and to the folders that are most likely to contain the files you need to access, change, or restore from a fresh copy, such as may be found in your root directory or your Windows installation folder. Table 40.1 provides basic information on your capabilities and disabilities when using RC.

By default, you need administrator-level access to use RC. Although other levels of users can be given rights to use RC, that should be done only with care; despite RC's limitations, it can do things that can result in problems such as data destruction and loss of system integrity. For this reason, I advise you take the time to familiarize yourself with the commands and their options so you can use RC most effectively and with reduced chance of mishap.

TABLE 40.1:   Recovery Console System Access Capabilities and Disabilities

CAPABILITY	DISABILITY
Access to root directory for all volumes	Attempts to access anything beyond items in Capability list result in an "Access Denied" message.
Access to Windows installation folder and subfolders (`%systemroot%`)	Can't use any text-editing tools within RC.
Access to Recovery Console folder and subfolders (available only when installed to Startup folder, not from CD execution)	Can't change the local administrator password from RC.
Can read files and folders stored on supported removable media types (CD, floppy, and so on)	Can't write to supported removable media types such as floppy or CD.
	Documents and Settings folder files are unavailable.
	Restrictions apply across both FAT32 and NTFS volumes.

NOTE   For exceptions to the access disabilities, see the section "Administering Recovery Console through Policy Setting" later in this chapter.

Launching Recovery Console

Before we get into details, I strongly recommend that you take time both while reading this chapter and beyond to become hands-on acquainted with RC, its powers, and its limitations. The more experience you have with RC before you hit a problem, the better prepared you'll be to work through the console to fix it. You'll also better understand the types of issues you can't resolve with it. For example, if an operation requires editing several files to restore the system, RC won't let you do this.

Don't overlook the need for a full backup before you do much experimentation. We learn some of our best lessons through making mistakes—sometimes, catastrophic ones. The backup ensures that you can restore your work and operations in the unlikely event this occurs.

Before You Use Recovery Console

Under most circumstances, you should always try to restart your Windows XP system in safe mode or by using the Last Known Good Configuration option from Startup before you use RC.

If you can get into Windows XP at all, there are some additional things you should do, including the following:

◆ Reverse the last operation performed—think about what you did just before the problem developed, and try to reverse it.

◆ Perform a backup of essential data (just in case).

◆ Pare down your Startup menu so you aren't loading unessential services, utilities, and programs, which may be affecting a successful boot.

The Two Ways to Launch Recovery Console

There are two different ways you can make RC available for your use:

◆ Run it from your Windows XP CD.

◆ Install it as a startup option.

Which option you choose to use depends on your preference and, to some degree, the situation at hand. In some situations, one means of launching RC may succeed when the other fails. An example can be seen when the boot disk is damaged or somehow misconfigured, as might happen with a computer virus infection. In this case, the installed version of RC probably won't load, but you can still access it from the CD.

RUNNING RECOVERY CONSOLE FROM CD

When used from the Windows XP compact disk, RC behaves very much like a boot disk or CD, permitting you to try to boot the system enough to get into the command console.

Follow these steps to run RC from the CD:

NOTE You must configure the system's BIOS to make the CD bootable for the following procedure.

1. Restart the PC with the Windows XP CD already inserted into the CD drive.

2. You may be prompted to load certain options to make the system boot from the CD; choose any required.

3. When Setup loads, follow the on-screen prompts until you reach the point where you can select **R** for repair/recovery.

4. Choose the Windows installation you want to recover. (This option is available only on systems running more than one operating system.)

5. When prompted, provide your administrator password.

6. When RC appears, you can begin typing commands, or type **help** for a list of them.

7. Type **exit** to quit RC and restart the PC.

NOTE If you need to load special SCSI or RAID drivers for using RC, press F6 when prompted during the launch process.

NOTE If you choose to run RC from CD, be sure to keep your Windows XP setup CD in a safe location where you can find it when you need it (as you should in any event). This should go without saying, but I talk to a dozen experienced users every day (not to mention the number of novices) who can't find their setup CD when they need it most.

ADDING RECOVERY CONSOLE AS A STARTUP OPTION

For expediency with troubleshooting, you have the option of making RC a Startup option for Windows XP. By doing this, when you subsequently reboot your system, you'll be presented with a list of options, much as you see if you run additional operating systems on separate partitions on your XP system. You can then select RC to try to start the system.

TIP   You must be logged on as an administrator to do this.

To enable this option, perform these steps:

1. With Windows XP loaded, insert your Windows XP CD into your CD-ROM drive.

2. Click Start ➢ Run.

3. In the Run dialog box, type *CD_drive_letter*:\i386\winnt32.exe /cmdcons.

4. Follow the on-screen instructions.

You'll find that, as part of the install and setup process for RC, the module automatically connects to the Internet and downloads and installs dynamic updates before it reports that it has been successfully installed to your system.

To launch the installed RC, do this:

1. Shut down and restart the PC.

2. When prompted by the Startup menu, select Recovery Console.

3. Enter your administrator password, when prompted.

WARNING   After three failed attempted to supply the administrator password, you'll be prompted to press Enter to restart the system.

4. Whether or not you have just one operating system installed, select the Windows installation for which you want to use RC.

5. When RC loads, you're ready to type your commands.

6. When your work is complete, type **exit** to quit RC and restart the PC.

TIP   In some situations, this installed version of RC won't work. In this event, try running RC from the CD; that method may work when the other doesn't.

NOTE   The installed RC takes approximately 7 MB of disk space.

Using Recovery Console

You now know how to launch and exit RC. Next, you need to know the basic tools available to you in this environment and that these tools are entirely command line–driven.

For those of you who haven't worked much with a command line or commands, here are some tips:

◆ Command-line environments demand absolutely correct syntax and are literal in their execution of commands, so double-check them before you press Enter. You may not be able to undo something if you do it improperly.

◆ Anything deleted from a command console will *not* be available for recovery under Windows Recycle Bin.

◆ Don't try to introduce commands from other operating systems; RC works with a fixed, limited list of commands and their options.

In the next section, we'll turn our eye to the major commands available for use in RC, and then I'll provide some examples of how they may be used.

Recovery Console Commands

If you're familiar with standard DOS commands such as `dir`, you'll see that many of these are available under RC. Some updates and new commands reflect that this is a command-line console running in a powerful 32-bit operating environment.

However, if you've done troubleshooting through a DOS environment in the past, you need to realize that RC behaves quite a bit differently, despite the similarity of commands and execution. You don't have the free range of access to virtually everything contained on the disk that you have with DOS. The idea here is to get in, try to recover (a service, a bad boot sector, and so on), get out, and not allow a huge window of opportunity for foul-ups and security breaches, intentional or unintentional.

NOTE   I've heard it asked several times, "Why are we sitting at a command line to fix Windows?" A graphical user environment with massive integration and multiple components and services, as you find with Windows XP, requires a phenomenal amount of power—and variables—to load. A command line doesn't demand that overhead and reduces the variables to make troubleshooting a bit saner.

In Table 40.2, the RC commands are listed along with the function each performs. The switches and parameters for each are too numerous to list here. Please consult Help And Support under Windows XP and search on **Recovery Console**. You can click each command in the Help And Support Center window to expand it to see its options, as shown in Figure 40.1.

TABLE 40.2:   Recovery Console Commands

COMMAND	FUNCTION
`attrib`	Changes the attributes (Hidden, System, and so on) of a file
`batch`	Loads a batch file to run one or more batch commands
`bootcfg`	Launches a utility for boot-file configuration and recovery
`cd` or `chdir`	Changes to a different directory
`chkdsk`	Runs the CHKDSK file-system utility and reports results

TABLE 40.2:   Recovery Console Commands *(CONTINUED)*

COMMAND	FUNCTION
cls	Clears the console screen
copy	Copies a file
del or delete	Erases a file
dir	Lists the contents of a directory
disable	Stops either a specified system service or a device driver
diskpart	Loads the disk partition manager
enable	Starts a system service or loads a device driver
exit	Quits RC and attempts to restart the PC
expand	Extracts a file from a Microsoft-compressed file store, such as a cabinet (.cab) file
fixboot	Overwrites (and repairs) the partition boot sector of a specified partition
fixmbr	Overwrites (and repairs) the specified drive's Master Boot Record (MBR)
format	(Re)formats a drive to prepare it for use or the installation of an operating system
help	Presents a list of available RC commands
listsvc	Presents a list of services and drivers in use
logon	Initiates a logon
map	Shows the drive letters mapped to each drive connected to and recognized by the system
md or mkdir	Creates a directory whose label you specify
more	Pauses between screens when you're reading a text file
net use	Establishes a connection between a particular drive letter and a network share
rd or rmdir	Removes a specified directory
ren or rename	Changes the name of a file from its current name to a different one
set	Displays and/or sets the current environment variables
systemroot	Establishes the current directory (*systemroot*) as that of the root directory of the system you're working from
type	Displays the contents of a text file; often used in conjunction with the |more option

FIGURE 40.1

Help And Support offers details on Recovery Console commands.

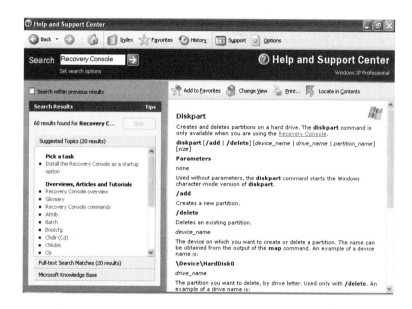

Examples of Recovery Console Command Usage

Table 40.3 presents some examples of RC commands, their switches and parameters, and situations they might be used in.

TABLE 40.3:   Recovery Command Examples

SAMPLE COMMAND	WHAT THE EXAMPLE DOES
attrib -r -h crit.cfg	Removes the Read-Only and Hidden attributes from the file crit.cfg
batch e:\fixit.txt e:\fixed.txt	Runs the commands stored as a text batch file (fixit.txt), and reports the results in another file (fixed.txt)
bootcfg /scan	Checks all Windows installations for boot information, and reports results to the screen
chkdsk /f D:	Checks the D: drive for error, and fixes any that it finds
disable eventlog	Disables the event-logging service in Windows
diskpart /add \device\HardDisk1 100	Adds a 100 MB disk partition to the hard disk designated as 1

TABLE 40.3:   Recovery Command Examples *(CONTINUED)*

SAMPLE COMMAND	WHAT THE EXAMPLE DOES
diskpart /delete *device*\HardDisk0\Partition3	Removes the designated disk partition from the hard disk identified as 0
enable eventlog service_auto_start	Turns on event logging automatically on startup
fixboot E:	Repairs the boot record for the partition of drive E: by overwriting it
fixmbr /*device*/HardDisk0	Rewrites the MBR when corruption or a virus may have caused a problem
format f: /fs:FAT32	Formats the F: drive, and makes it a system drive using FAT32
Logon	Checks the system for all Windows installations, displays options, and prompts you to provide the administrator's password for the Windows installation you want to work with
md c:\logs	Creates a new directory called logs
net use \\pax\\sam /sam /q9e7h F: /d	Connects the system specified as \\pax\sam to the D: drive, using the username sam and a password of q9e7h
set allowwildcards=true	Establishes the ability to use wildcards with supporting RC commands
rd d:\logs	Removes a directory called logs from the D: drive

Administering Recovery Console through Policy Setting

Two settings under \Local Policy\Security Options affect options for RC on Windows XP Professional. Both are disabled by default. These are as follows:

- ◆   "Automatic administrative logon"
- ◆   "Allow access to floppy copy and access to all drives and all folders"

Let's take a moment to understand the functionality and implications for each.

Enabling the automatic administrative logon option allows an administrator to log onto the system without having to provide a password. This is convenient but can be an unwise choice for better security, because anyone with enough knowledge to try to run RC could do so.

TIP Out of the box, no administrator password is required (or assigned) for Home Edition. Users must force an administrator's password onto this edition if they want to use one. I certainly wouldn't feel comfortable running a system where anyone who happens by the keyboard can get instant access, let alone administrator-level access. However, understand that the two policies described in this section don't affect Home Edition.

The second setting ("Allow access to floppy..."), when enabled, permits the use of the `set` command under RC (see the preceding two sections) to show or modify environment variables. Within the `set` command are a limited number of variables you can act on. These can be set to either `=true` or `=false` (example: `AllowWildCards=true`) and include the following:

`AllowAllPaths` Using this opens access to all files and folders on the system on which RC is being used.

`AllowRemovableMedia` Using this grants the administrative user logged onto RC the right to copy files to recognized removable media drives, such as floppies.

`AllowWildCards` Using this turns on support for the use of wildcards (* or !) for commands that support them, such as `dir` and `del`.

Follow these steps to enable one or both of these policy settings:

1. From Control Panel, double-click Administrative Tools, and then click Local Security Policy.

2. Under Security Settings in the left pane, open the Local Policies node, and then click to select Security Options, which opens the options list in the right pane.

3. Locate the two listings that begin with *Recovery Console*.

4. Double-click to select "Allow automatic administrative logon," which produces the Local Security Setting window for that option. Click Enabled, and then click OK.

5. Double-click to select "Allow access to floppy copy and access to all drives and all folders." Click Enabled, and then click OK.

Part 9

Security

In this section:

Chapter 41

Authentication and Data Protection

This chapter discusses what digital certificates are, what they're used for, and how to use them on Windows XP. It shows you how and where to get certificates that meet your needs; how to manage certificates with the Certificates console and with Internet Explorer's Certificates dialog box; and how to update the root certificates to keep XP current.

Understanding Certificates

Before you get a certificate and start using it, you need to understand what certificates are, what they're for, and what problems and weaknesses they have.

What Is a Certificate?

A *certificate* is a relatively small amount of encrypted code intended to identify its holder and to secure communications and documents coming from and going to the holder. To these ends, a certificate contains information about the certificate holder, the purposes for which the certificate has been issued, the keys used, and the certification path from the certification authority (CA) ultimately responsible for the certificate through any intermediate CAs involved in issuing it. Depending on its packaging, the certificate may also contain details of the certificates held by the authorities involved in the certification path.

What Is a Certification Authority?

A *certification authority (CA)* is an organization that issues certificates to individuals or organizations—preferably after verifying their identity thoroughly. CAs can be government organizations, but at this writing, most of the major public CAs are public companies.

A public key infrastructure (PKI) typically consists of a hierarchy of CAs. At the top of the certification hierarchy are the *root certification authorities* (root CAs) or *root authorities*. Root CAs issue themselves their own certificates—in effect, stating that everyone can trust them. (More on this in a moment.) Because root CAs in a PKI trust each other, the intermediate CAs in the different branches of the certification hierarchy trust each other too. This trust cascades down to the holders of the certificates issued by the CAs, who should therefore be able to trust each other as well.

How Do Certificates Work?

Certificates use a *key pair*—a public key and a private key—to secure data. Data encrypted with the public key can be decrypted only with the private key, and data encrypted with the private key can be decrypted only with the public key. The public key and private key are related to each other mathematically, but in such a way that the private key can't be derived from the public key.

Therefore, you (as a key holder) can safely distribute your public key worldwide so that it's available to whomever needs it. When someone wants to send you an encrypted message, they encrypt it using your public key; you decrypt it with your private key. When you want to prove that a message or document comes from you, you sign it with your private key, and the recipient uses the public key to verify that the message or document was signed by you.

How do you distribute your public key? You can of course send it to people, but you'd need to be omnipresent to get the key to everyone who needed it. So, public key cryptography requires a PKI to make the keys available. For protection, the public key isn't distributed on its own: Instead, a CA produces a digital certificate that binds the public key to the key holder's identity. The digital certificate is then distributed.

What Does a Certificate Prove?

Most CAs issue a variety of certificates for different purposes, including the following widely used types of certificates:

Personal certificates   These are for signing and encrypting e-mail and proving your identity to a remote computer.

Developer certificates   These certificates are used for signing macros and software you develop so that other people can be sure that they come from you, that your identity has been verified, and that the software hasn't been tampered with in transit.

SSL server certificates   These certify that a server belongs to the company or organization specified and secure the connection between the browser and the server. (I'll discuss SSL server certificates more later in this chapter.)

As you'd imagine, certificates held by intermediate CAs and root CAs have a wide range of other purposes—for example, verifying Windows system components and recovering keys.

Weaknesses of Digital Certificates

Digital certificates have three main weaknesses:

◆   You need to trust the CA to be trustworthy and to have verified the identity of the individual or organization in question.

◆   You need to trust that the person or organization that has applied the digital certificate to whatever item it's securing was the person or organization they're supposed to be.

◆   Problems with the validity of a certificate aren't necessarily apparent immediately.

Let's look at these problems in detail, because you should understand them if you use digital certificates.

TRUSTING THE CA

The first part of trusting a CA is the old question *sed quis custodiet ipsos custodes*—"but who guards the guards themselves?" In this case, the question is, "but who certifies the CA?"

In a PKI, each intermediate CA is certified by a root CA. So far, so good. But each root CA certifies itself, issuing its own root public key and binding it to its root certificate—a cornerstone of the PKI edifice of trust. In other words, you're required to trust the root CAs in order to use the PKI, and you must trust the root CAs because everybody else in the PKI trusts them and the root CAs trust each other. In *Secrets and Lies*, Bruce Schneier, a leading cryptographer, points out that although CAs may be authorities on making certificates, they're almost never authorities on what the certificates they make contain. For example, most CAs who issue SSL server certificates aren't authorities on the DNS name assignments bound into the server certificates. Schneier comments, "Basically, certificates only protect you from those that the PKI vendor refuses to do business with."

NOTE Trust may be less of an issue for certificates issued within a company. For example, you may feel that you can trust HR and IT between them to ensure that the holder of any certificate is who they claim to be.

Then you need to trust the CA to verify the identity of the certificate holder enough for the purposes of the transaction. For example, if you're using certificates to verify the sender of an e-mail message, you might settle for a modest level of certainty, whereas if you were buying software from them, you'd probably want a high level of certainty.

But most verification takes place at one or more removes, with the CA leveraging an existing means of identification (such as a credit-card or credit-agency listing for an individual or a Dun & Bradstreet listing for a company) instead of performing direct identification. Few, if any, CAs interface directly with national or even state agencies—bodies widely trusted to identify people and companies with a great degree of accuracy. (Consider how many people have problems with inaccurate credit reports and how few have problems with passport mix-ups. Which would you rather have issuing digital certificates that you needed to trust—a credit agency or the passport guys?)

TRUSTING THE CERTIFICATE HOLDER

Even if you feel you can trust the CA or the PKI, you're not out of the woods: You also need to trust the certificate holder to keep their certificate to themselves (or to the appropriate group of people), not lose the private key (certainly not let the private key get stolen), and apply it only voluntarily, consciously, and after due consideration to the appropriate documents or communication sessions.

Depending on the nature of the certificate and the information it contains, you also may not be able to identify the certificate holder conclusively. With most personal digital certificates, the only pieces of information you get about the holder are their name and their e-mail address. Unless you know already that the e-mail address belongs to the person you know by this name, you won't be able to use the e-mail address to distinguish that person from another with the same name or a similar name.

LINKING DIGITAL ID TO PHYSICAL ID

What would it take to make CAs truly trustworthy? Some commentators envision a national (or better, international) identity scheme that would work in both the physical world and the digital world. Each individual would apply to a national (or international) agency for identity documentation that would cover the areas currently covered by passports, driver's licenses, and digital certificates. Digital certificates could be derived from the information supplied by the individual—information that would probably include biometric data such as digital fingerprints, a facial scan, and a DNA profile—and could be verified by using a scanner attached to the computer (for example, a fingerprint scanner built into the keyboard or a facial scanner mounted on the monitor). Then we'd need to create a similar structure for businesses.... Given such technology, you could be pretty sure who was at the other end of the wire.

In any case, many of the personal certificates issued by CAs don't verify the holder's identity. For example, you can get a personal certificate from VeriSign for signing e-mail without proving anything more than that you know a credit card number and its billing details and that the e-mail address works.

Making Sure the Certificate Is Still Valid

Each certificate has its validity period encoded into it, so when a certificate is past its expiration data, applications that use the certificate automatically warn you of the problem and refuse to use the certificate. But if a certificate or its private key is lost or stolen, problems arise. Each user of the public key essentially needs to check that the certificate hasn't been reported lost (or stolen) and isn't on the certificate revocation list (CRL) before each use. There isn't a good mechanism for doing this.

Similarly, a certificate issued by a company's CA might prove that the certificate holder worked for the company in a certain capacity and had authority to take certain actions (for example, making purchases). If the person moves to a different role, they'll need a new certificate. If they're fired, the certificate needs to be removed from them before they can use it when they shouldn't. Any communications encrypted with the certificate's public key (for example, messages sent to the newly unemployed person) will then be unreadable.

What Are Certificates Good For?

As you've seen, at this writing, digital certificates are an unsatisfactory means of proving identity. But once you're clear on their limitations and know why you must keep your wits about you when using certificates, certificates can be very useful.

Certificates are particularly useful in closed systems, such as military or government organizations, in which a competent authority vets each applicant in depth before issuing a certificate limited to their needs and probably with a short validity period.

Where Are Certificates Stored?

Windows XP stores certificates in certificate stores that you can view using the Certificates console, discussed later in this chapter. By using the Certificates console and by using Internet Explorer's Certificates dialog box, you can export a certificate to a file—for example, to back it up or to copy or move it to another computer.

Windows XP can also work with certificates stored on smart cards, provided that you have a smart-card reader installed on or attached to your computer.

To use a smart card or a certificate to secure a network connection, select the Use Extensible Authentication Protocol (EAP) option button in the Logon Security group box in the Advanced Security Settings dialog box for the connection. Then, click the Properties button, and use the Smart Card Or Other Certificate Properties dialog box to specify whether to use a smart card or certificate, whether to validate the server certificate (and if so, how), and whether to use a different username for the connection.

Using the Certificates Console

Windows XP provides two tools for working with certificates: the Certificates console, which is a snap-in for the MMC and which we'll examine in this section, and the Certificates dialog box, which we'll examine in the next section.

To open the Certificates console, open the MMC (choose Start ➤ Run, enter **mmc /a**, and click OK), and add the Certificates snap-in by using the Add/Remove Snap-in dialog box (File ➤ Add/Remove Snap-in; see Chapter 9 for more details).

If you have permission to manage certificates for the services account and the computer account, the Certificates snap-in displays the Certificates Snap-in dialog box. Select the My User Account option button, the Service Account option button, or the Computer Account option button to specify which certificates you want to manage with the Certificates console.

If you want to use this MMC console for managing certificates in the future, save the console. Alternatively, open an existing console and add the Certificates snap-in to it.

Viewing the Certificate Stores

The Certificates console lets you view the certificates listed by their purposes or by the logical stores in which they're kept. Listing certificates by their purposes helps you find certificates for a particular purpose. (Bear in mind that many certificates fulfill multiple purposes and so appear in multiple categories.) Viewing the logical stores lets you see which certificates are in each store.

To change the view, choose View ➤ Options to display the View Options dialog box (see Figure 41.1), and choose the Certificate Purpose option button or the Logical Certificate Stores option button as appropriate.

You can display the physical certificate stores by selecting the Physical Certificate Stores check box in the View Options dialog box. Doing so can be useful for exporting an entire store.

You can also display archived certificates by selecting the Archived Certificates check box. XP archives a certificate when you replace it with a new certificate. Under normal circumstances, you'll seldom need to view archived certificates.

Finding a Certificate

To find a certificate matching certain criteria, choose Action ➤ Find Certificates to display the dialog box shown in Figure 41.2. Specify the certificate store or stores to search, specify the information in the Contains text box, select the appropriate item in the Look In Field list box (Issued By, Issued To, MD5 Hash, Serial Number, or SHA1 Hash), and click Find Now.

Once you've found a certificate, you can take assorted actions with it (such as exporting it, requesting it, or renewing it) by using the commands on the File menu or the shortcut menu for the certificate. The sections after the next section discuss actions you'll commonly take with certificates.

FIGURE 41.1
Use the View Options dialog box to specify how the Certificates console should display the certificates.

Managing Certificates with Internet Explorer

To manage certificates with IE, display the Certificates dialog box by choosing Tools ➢ Internet Options. Then, on the Content page of the resulting dialog, click the Certificates button. Figure 41.3 shows the Certificates dialog box.

As you can see in the figure, the Certificates dialog box breaks the certificates into different categories—Personal, Other People, Intermediate Certification Authorities, Trusted Root Certification Authorities, and Trusted Publishers—each of which appears on a separate tab. You can narrow the display further by selecting a certificate purpose in the Intended Purpose drop-down list.

Once you've selected a certificate, IE makes the View, Export, Remove, and Advanced buttons available. The Import button (which starts the Certificate Import Wizard) is always available. The following sections discuss the tasks you can perform with these buttons: viewing a certificate, changing the properties of a certificate, obtaining a certificate, and exporting and importing a certificate.

FIGURE 41.3
Use the Certificates
dialog box to manage
certificates from Inter-
net Explorer.

Viewing a Certificate

To view a certificate, double-click it in the Certificates dialog box or in the Certificates console. Windows XP displays the Certificate dialog box with its General tab selected (see Figure 41.4). This tab lists the certificate's purpose, the person to whom the certificate was issued, the issuer, and the certificate's validity information. If the Issuer Statement button is available, you can click it to display information about the issuer of the certificate or to connect to the issuer's website.

The Details tab (see Figure 41.5) gives you access to all the fields of data contained in the certificate. You can limit the set of fields displayed by choosing Version 1 Fields Only, Extensions Only, Critical Extensions Only, or Properties Only in the Show drop-down list. To display the full contents of a field in the lower text box, select it in the list box.

FIGURE 41.4

The General tab of the Certificate dialog box includes the certificate's purpose and validity period.

FIGURE 41.5

You can examine all the fields in the certificate on the Details tab of the Certificate dialog box.

The Certification Path tab (see Figure 41.6) shows the certification path for the certificate—the chain of certificates from the current certificate to the CA ultimately responsible for it. Use the View Certificate button to display the certificate for one of the other entities in the certification chain.

Editing a Certificate

From the Details tab of the Certificate dialog box for a certificate, you can click the Edit Properties button to display the Certificate Properties dialog box (see Figure 41.7). Here you can use the controls in the Certificate Purposes group box to enable all purposes for the certificate, disable all purposes, or enable only the purposes you specify. If the certificate and the issuing CA support adding purposes to the certificate, you can do so by clicking the Add button.

FIGURE 41.6
The Certification Path tab of the Certificate dialog box shows the chain of certificates up to the CA.

FIGURE 41.7
You can change the purposes for which the certificate can be used.

In most cases, you won't be able to add purposes to a certificate, and you'll seldom want to disable any of the purposes a certificate has. However, you may well want to edit the Friendly Name (the descriptive name) and Description for the certificate to make it easier to identify.

Obtaining a Certificate

Depending on your circumstances, you can get a digital certificate either from a public CA or from a CA hosted by your company. Public CAs supply certificates that you can use for authentication and security with anyone who trusts the CA through the PKI, whereas CAs run by companies supply certificates mostly for internal use within the company or group. (In some cases, company CAs are part of the PKI, but most aren't.)

TIP If you want to practice importing, exporting, and deleting certificates, look for an applet that lets you create your own certificates for testing. The CDs of most versions of Microsoft Office include an applet named SELFCERT.EXE that creates a sample digital certificate with the name you specify and installs it on your computer. The certificates are limited to signing VBA projects, but you can export, import, and delete them.

Obtaining a Certificate from a Public CA

At this writing, leading public CAs include the following:

VeriSign, Inc. VeriSign provides a wide variety of digital certificates, from individual certificates to SSL server certificates. VeriSign owns Network Solutions, the original Internet registrars, and Thawte (discussed in a moment): www.verisign.com.

GlobalSign NV GlobalSign provides certificates to individual users and companies, including 56-bit SSL server certificates. Headquartered in Brussels, GlobalSign is developing a Europe-based network that extends to 20 countries at this writing: www.globalsign.net.

Thawte Consulting (Pty) Ltd. Thawte provides certificates to individual users, developers, and companies. Its server certificates include SSL server certificates and SuperCerts, SSL server certificates that let browsers with weak encryption (for example, 40-bit encryption) communicate with servers using 128-bit encryption. Based in South Africa and now owned by VeriSign, Thawte has offices in the U.S. and representatives in most First World countries, and claims to have certified 30 percent of the world's servers: www.thawte.com.

TIP For the latest list of CAs that Microsoft recommends, click the Get Digital ID button on the Security tab in the Options dialog box for Outlook Express (Tools ➤ Options).

In most cases, you can get a certificate by filling in an application form on a public CA's website, giving such verifying information as it requires (name, address, phone number, credit card, and so on), paying (by credit card), and supplying via snail mail any supporting documents that the CA requires. For example, for a personal certificate, GlobalSign requires you to send a copy of the identity document you specified in your application, together with a signed membership agreement.

WARNING Usually you need to carry out the whole application from the same computer on which you ultimately install and use the certificate.

GETTING THE RIGHT CERTIFICATE FOR YOUR NEEDS

Before you start filling out an application form for a certificate, assess your needs and make sure the type of certificate you're getting fills them. Some CAs offer free personal certificates that you can use for purposes such as e-mail and proving your identity to a remote computer, but they don't cover heavier-duty uses such as software development or SSL (Secure Sockets Layer—a protocol that enables a web browser and a web server to communicate securely with each other across the Internet).

If you develop software or macros and need to apply a digital signature to them, you'll need a developer certificate. The digital signature assures the people who download your code that it came from you (rather than from anyone else), that your identity has been verified, and that the code hasn't been tampered with since you signed it.

If you need to support SSL on a server, you'll need an SSL server certificate. An SSL server certificate essentially guarantees to the browser connecting to it that the site belongs to the company or organization specified. SSL is vital for any transaction in which the customer needs to trust the company in question.

When you've connected to an Internet server via SSL, IE displays the lock icon in the status bar, indicating that the connection is secured via SSL. This authentication is handled seamlessly by the browser, but users can view the SSL server certificate if they want to verify its details.

For some types of certificates, however, you may need to visit an office or representative of the CA in person to demonstrate that you match your identity documents. For example, the primary way to become a member of Thawte's Web of Trust is to meet enough existing members (and prove your identity to them) to accumulate 50 points. Each member makes an assertion to Thawte confirming the identity of the person they've met. Meeting a member gets you a number of points corresponding to the number of people they've authenticated. Once you meet enough members to get 100 points, you can start making assertions yourself.

Once the CA has verified your identity to the degree required for the type of certificate you're requesting, it provides the certificate. A typical mechanism is for the CA to e-mail you a custom URL at which you can pick up the certificate; you then install it on your computer via an automated process.

Obtaining a Certificate from a Company CA

Companies can get certificates from public CAs, of course, and many do so, particularly SSL certificates for web servers that need to offer secure connections to visitors. But many companies also run their own CA, because doing so gives them far greater flexibility in their use of certificates.

If your company has a stand-alone Windows 2000 Server computer running the Certification Authority service, you can request a certificate from it by using IE. Open `http://servername/certsrv`, where *servername* is the name or IP address of the server. The page displayed provides options for requesting a certificate, retrieving the CA certificate or certificate revocation list, and checking on a pending certificate.

Select the Request A Certificate option button, and click the Next button to access the procedure for requesting a certificate. Once you've submitted the request, it's held in the `Pending Requests` folder in the CA until an administrator reviews it and issues the certificate (or denies the request). So, normally you'd return to the Certification Services page after an interval dictated by the speed of your administrator's reactions and use the Check On A Pending Certificate procedure to see whether the certificate has been issued. If it has, the procedure installs it automatically for you.

If your company's CA is integrated into Active Directory, you can request a certificate by using the Certificate Request Wizard. To run the wizard, right-click the appropriate certificate store in the Certificates console, and choose All Tasks ➤ Request New Certificate from the shortcut menu. (Alternatively, select the store, and choose Action ➤ All Tasks ➤ Request New Certificate.)

Exporting and Importing Certificates

Unless you confine your use of certificates those that are automatically installed on your computer or computers, you'll sometimes need to export a certificate to a file or import a certificate from a file.

Reasons for exporting a certificate include backing up the certificate (with or without its private key) and copying or moving the certificate to another computer so that you can use it on that computer as well as or instead of the computer it's currently installed on.

Reasons for importing a certificate include installing the certificate on the computer in the first place (if it wasn't installed automatically) and restoring from backup a certificate that's been damaged or deleted.

Certificate File Formats

XP supports the following standard file formats for certificates:

Personal Information Exchange (PFX or PKCS #12)   You can use this format to transfer a certificate with its corresponding private key from one computer to another or to copy the certificate and its private key to removable media. Public Key Cryptography Standard number 12 (PKCS #12) is an industry standard for backing up, restoring, and transferring certificates. PKCS #12 files use the .pfx extension.

Cryptographic Message Syntax Standard (PKCS #7)   Use this format to transfer a certificate, together with all the certificates in its certificate path, from one computer to another or to copy the certificate to removable media. PKCS #7 files use the .p7b extension. If you don't need to transfer the private key with the certificate, PKCS #7 is usually the best format to use.

DER-encoded binary X.509   Use this binary encoding format to transfer certificates to other Windows applications (for example, other browsers) that don't support PKCS #12. DER-encoded files use the .cer extension.

Base64-encoded X.509   Use this ASCII-based format to transfer certificates to and from operating systems other than Windows. For example, if your CA is running on Linux, you may receive a certificate in a Base64-encoded X.509 file. These files use the .cer extension.

NOTE   Depending on the type of certificate you're exporting and on whether the certificate's issuer marked its private key as exportable, the Certificate Export Wizard may not offer you all these formats.

Exporting a Certificate

To export a certificate, start the Certificate Export Wizard by taking either of these actions:

◆   In the Certificates console, right-click the certificate, and choose All Tasks ➤ Export from the shortcut menu. Alternatively, select the certificate, and choose Action ➤ All Tasks ➤ Export.

◆   In the Certificates dialog box, select the certificate, and click the Export button.

The Certificate Export Wizard makes the export process easy, but you have two key decisions to make. The first is whether to export the private key with the certificate. This choice applies only if you hold the private key to the certificate *and* the private key is marked as exportable. If you don't hold the private key, the wizard doesn't display the Export Private Key page. If you hold the private key but it's not marked as exportable, the wizard displays the page but makes the Yes, Export The Private Key option button unavailable.

The second choice is which file format to use for the certificate. This choice comes on the Export File Format page of the Certificate Export Wizard (see Figure 41.8).

If you chose to export the private key with the certificate, you can use only the Personal Information Exchange – PKCS #12 format. You can then choose the following options:

"Include all certificates in the certification path if possible"   Select this check box if you want to include in the exported certificate file all the certificates in the certification path. Doing so is usually a good idea.

"Enable strong protection"   Select this check box if you want to use strong encryption on the exported certificate file. Using strong encryption is usually a good idea, and the wizard checks this box by default.

"Delete the private key if the export is successful"   Select this check box only if you're moving the certificate from one computer to another.

If you chose not to export the private key (or if you didn't have the choice), you can choose among DER Encoded Binary X.509 format, Base-64 Encoded X.509 format, and Cryptographic Message Syntax Standard – PKCS #7 format.

If you choose the PKCS #7 format, you can select the "Include all certificates in the certification path if possible" check box to include all the certificates in the certificate's certification path.

If you chose to export the private key, you then get to enter a password for it. If not, or after you do so, you specify the name for the certificate file, check the details on the Completing The Certificate Export Wizard page, and click the Finish button. The wizard then exports the certificate file and notifies you when it has done so.

FIGURE 41.8
Choose the file format to use for the certificate—if you have any choice.

Importing a Certificate

To import a certificate, start the Certificate Import Wizard by taking any of these steps:

- Double-click a certificate file.

- In the Certificates console, right-click the certificate store into which you want to import the certificate, and choose All Tasks ➢ Import from the context menu. Alternatively, select the store, and choose Action ➢ All Tasks ➢ Import.

- Click the Import button in the Certificates dialog box.

The wizard then walks you through the steps of importing the file:

1. Identify the certificate file to import.

2. Enter the password for the private key (if it's included in the certificate).

3. Choose whether to enable strong private key protection. Use this option if you want Windows XP to prompt you to enter the password every time an application needs to use the private key. This is good security, but it can get old fast.

4. Choose whether to mark the private key as exportable, so that you can back up or export the private key with the certificate. (For security, you may choose to mark the private key as not being exportable.)

Updating the Root Certificates

As you'll recall from earlier in the chapter, root certificates are the certificates that are held by the highest-level CAs and that underpin the PKI. To make sure that your root certificates are current, you need to update them periodically. Given that different certificates last for different periods, and that they're issued at different times, updating them manually would be a miserable job. So it'll be no surprise that Windows XP can update the certificates for you. In fact, XP is configured to update the root certificates automatically by using its Update Root Certificates component, which is installed by default.

To prevent XP from updating its root certificates, you need to remove the Update Root Certificates component. To do so, launch the Windows Components Wizard by choosing Start ➢ Control Panel ➢ Add Or Remove Programs and clicking the Add/Remove Windows Components button. Clear the Update Root Certificates check box, and click the Next button.

To reenable updating of root certificates, reinstall the Update Root Certificates component by selecting the Update Root Certificates check box in the Windows Components Wizard and clicking the Next button.

Chapter 42

Encrypting File System

If your files contain sensitive or confidential information, consider encrypting them with Encrypting File System (EFS) to prevent other people from being able to read the files if they're able to access them or steal them.

The chapter begins by providing an overview of EFS: what it is, why you might use it, and things you should consider before you start using it. I then discuss how to implement EFS and encrypt and decrypt files and folders using both the GUI and the `cipher` command. I'll show you how to share encrypted data and end by discussing how to plan and implement a recovery policy for EFS.

Overview of EFS

EFS is a security feature of Windows XP Professional (Home Edition doesn't include EFS) that lets you encrypt specified files or folders on your computer to protect them from intrusion.

Windows XP handles encryption transparently as it does compression on NTFS volumes, so you perform file operations (creating, saving, deleting, copying, and so on) as usual—you don't have to decrypt a file before you can work with it.

WARNING   EFS is a powerful feature with strong appeal to many users, but you need to approach it with caution: If you get things wrong, you can end up with encrypted files that you'll never be able to decrypt. This danger is eminently avoidable, but you need to understand how EFS works before you start using it. So, please read the whole of this chapter before experimenting with EFS.

How Does EFS Work?

EFS encrypts data using a key linked to the public key based on the security identifier (SID) for your user account. The data can be decrypted only by using the key for that SID; someone using another user account can't decrypt it, because other accounts have different SIDs. If you designate another user as a recovery agent, that user can also recover files.

As you'd imagine, encrypting and decrypting files takes more processor cycles than does handling unencrypted files. Generally speaking, a computer that can run Windows XP Professional comfortably should be able to handle EFS without breaking a sweat; if the computer is struggling to run Professional, EFS will diminish the computer's performance further.

What You Can and Can't Encrypt

EFS can encrypt files and folders stored on NTFS volumes. (You can't use EFS on FAT or FAT32 volumes.) You can encrypt either folders or individual files. In most cases, it's much better to encrypt folders. (More on this in a moment.)

TIP   If you need to encrypt folders or files currently on a FAT/FAT32 volume, convert the volume to NTFS. Then, encrypt the folders or files on the converted volume.

You can't encrypt files in the `%systemroot%` folder, nor can you encrypt any files marked with the System attribute.

You also can't encrypt compressed files or folders. If you mark a compressed file or folder for encryption, XP decompresses it before applying the encryption.

Similarly, if you tell XP to compress an encrypted file or folder, XP needs to decrypt it first. Before doing so, it warns you in the Confirm Attribute Change dialog box that it will decrypt the file, so you have a chance to cancel the action.

How Encrypted Files and Folders Behave

You can apply encryption to files and folders (with the constraints discussed in the previous section). When you encrypt a folder, you can choose whether to encrypt all its contents (all files and subfolders) or just the folder itself.

Once you've encrypted a file or folder, only you or a designated recovery agent can decrypt it, unless you explicitly choose to share an encrypted file (not a folder) with other specified users.

Once you've encrypted a file or folder, you can access it transparently from your user account. Other users can't access the file or folder. If they try to do so, XP stops them with an "Access denied" message. (The wording of the message depends on the application from which the user is trying to access the file or folder.)

Here's how XP handles encryption for files you move or copy:

♦ When you move or copy unencrypted files into an encrypted folder, XP encrypts them without comment.

♦ When you move encrypted files from an encrypted folder to an unencrypted folder on an NTFS volume, they stay encrypted: If you want them decrypted, you need to decrypt them manually.

♦ If you copy or move encrypted files from an encrypted folder to a volume that doesn't use NTFS (for example, a FAT volume), XP decrypts them. Before doing so, it displays the Encrypted File dialog box to let you decide whether to carry out the operation for this file (click the Ignore button) or for all files you're copying or moving (the Ignore All button), or whether to cancel it.

♦ XP's Backup Utility supports EFS, so files and folders that you back up using Backup Utility remain encrypted.

(Why) Should You Use EFS?

The usual reason for using EFS is to protect your files from being read by unauthorized persons. (A less usual reason is curiosity.) Although you can use Windows XP Professional's user accounts and NTFS permissions to keep other users out of your files, these features don't protect your computer against direct physical attacks (such as theft of a laptop, CPU, or hard disk) or against someone accessing your files by booting with a different operating system or from a utility that lets them mount NTFS volumes from a floppy disk.

EFS isn't a substitute for using XP's user accounts and permissions to keep people out of your files, because anyone with permission to read a folder can view the list of its contents (even though they can't read the contents of files). Worse, anyone with permission to delete files or folders can delete encrypted files or folders.

Why Must You Be Careful with EFS?

You need to be careful with EFS because if you lose your private key for decrypting data and haven't designated a recovery agent, you'll never be able to decrypt the data. Thus, in effect, you lose access to the contents of the encrypted files or folders forever.

Even if you don't lose your private key, system problems can effectively lose it for you. In particular, be aware that reinstalling Windows prevents you from accessing encrypted files. Because reinstalling Windows creates accounts with different SIDs, you won't be able to access encrypted files directly, even if the account names are the same. Instead, you'll need to import your EFS certificate in order to be able to access encrypted files.

Tips for Implementing EFS for Maximum Protection

This section provides tips on implementing EFS for maximum protection of your files.

ENCRYPT FOLDERS RATHER THAN INDIVIDUAL FILES

Microsoft recommends encrypting folders rather than individual files, but you can encrypt individual files if necessary. The reason for encrypting folders is that doing so makes sure the temporary files that many programs create while working are encrypted as well as the files themselves. Because many programs (particularly older programs) place their temporary files in folders other than the folder containing the file they're working with, you may need to encrypt your temporary folders as well.

CREATE FILES IN ALREADY-ENCRYPTED FOLDERS

To keep a file as secure as possible, create it in an already encrypted folder so that it's never saved to disk in an unencrypted file.

If you use the My Documents folder for your personal documents, encrypt it.

ENCRYPT YOUR TEMPORARY FOLDERS

Encrypt your temporary folders (the %temp% and %tmp% folders) so that temporary files created by programs that don't use the current folder are encrypted as well.

TURN OFF PRINT SPOOLING, OR ENCRYPT YOUR PRINT SPOOL FOLDER

If possible, turn off print spooling—writing print files to disk before printing them. If this isn't possible, encrypt the folder in which print spool files are stored.

EXPORT YOUR EFS CERTIFICATE, AND KEEP IT SAFE

To implement its encryption, EFS uses a key bound to a certificate. Because you won't be able to decrypt your encrypted files without this key, it's vital to back up the certificate and keep the backup in a safe place.

SET UP A RECOVERY AGENT

If you use your computer in a stand-alone configuration or in a workgroup (in other words, it's not part of a domain), create a recovery agent as described in "Planning and Implementing an EFS Recovery Policy" later in this chapter. Then back up the recovery agent's certificate.

KEEP YOUR OLD RECOVERY AGENT CERTIFICATES

If you update your recovery agent certificates, keep your old certificates so that you can recover previously encrypted files if necessary.

SECURE ENCRYPTED DATA IN TRANSIT ACROSS YOUR NETWORK

If you're connecting to a computer on which remote encryption has been enabled, you can encrypt or decrypt files and folders from across the network. But be aware that when you open an encrypted file over the network, the data that's transmitted back and forth isn't encrypted. To encrypt the data in transit, you need to use another protocol, such as IPSec or PPTP.

Before you can encrypt on a remote computer in a domain, the administrator has to designate the remote computer as trusted for delegation in Active Directory Users And Computers. However, if the remote computer is running WebDAV, it doesn't need to be designated as trusted for delegation. WebDAV can encrypt the file at the local computer and transmit encrypted data.

NOTE　In order to use EFS on remote folders, your computer and the remote computer need to be in the same domain. If the remote computer is in another domain, XP displays the error message "Key not valid for use in specified state" when you try to encrypt a file on the remote computer.

CLEAR YOUR PAGING FILE AT SHUTDOWN

Because your paging file may contain sensitive information that was temporarily stored in virtual memory by a program, you may want to clear it when you shut down your computer so that nobody can glean data from it.

To clear the paging file at shutdown, run Registry Editor, navigate to the key

```
\HKEY_LOCAL_MACHINE\SYSTEM\CurrentControlSet\Control\Session Manager\Memory
Management
```

and change the value of the value entry ClearPageFileAtShutdown to 1. Restart XP to make the change take effect.

BEWARE OF SYSTEM RESTORE

If you encrypt only file types that aren't monitored by System Restore, you don't need to worry about someone being able to use System Restore to restore the files to their unencrypted state. For example, if you encrypt only data files, System Restore won't pose a threat to the encryption.

But if you need to encrypt files of types that are being monitored by System Restore, you have two choices. Either store the encrypted files on a drive on which you're not using System Restore (for example, a data-only drive); or turn off System Restore (as discussed in Chapter 38) before encrypting the files, and then turn it back on once they're encrypted.

Encrypting Files and Folders

To encrypt a folder, you set its Encryption property. The easiest way to do so is as follows:

1. Display the Properties dialog box for the file or folder by right-clicking the item in an Explorer window and choosing Properties from the context menu.

2. Display the Advanced Attributes dialog box by clicking the Advanced button on the General tab.

3. Select the Encrypt Contents To Secure Data check box in the Compress Or Encrypt Attributes group box.

4. Click the OK button to close the Advanced Attributes dialog box.

5. Click the OK button or the Apply button in the Properties dialog box for the file or folder.

6. If you're encrypting a folder, XP displays the Confirm Attribute Changes dialog box. Select the Apply Changes To This Folder Only option or the Apply Changes To This Folder, Subfolders And Files option, as appropriate, and click the OK button.

7. XP applies encryption to the file or folder. Depending on the size of the file or the folder's contents, applying the encryption may take a while.

To decrypt a file or folder, repeat this process, but clear the Encrypt Contents To Secure Data check box. If you're decrypting a folder, XP displays the Confirm Attribute Change dialog box so that you can indicate whether to decrypt only the folder or the folder and all its contents.

NOTE By default, encrypted files and folders appear in a green font in Explorer windows. To display them in the same color as unencrypted files and folders, clear the Show Encrypted Or Compressed NTFS Files In Color check box on the View tab of the Folder Options dialog box (Tools ➤ Folder Options).

Encrypting and Decrypting with the *cipher* Command

XP provides GUI tools for performing most encryption and decryption operations, but it also provides the `cipher` command for working from the command prompt. As you'll see in a moment, there are a couple of operations for which you *must* use `cipher`; the rest of the time, it's there as an option.

If you're prepared to put in a little work with the switches shown in Table 42.1, `cipher` gives you greater flexibility than the GUI tools for encrypting and decrypting files and folders.

TABLE 42.1: Switches for the *cipher* Command

SWITCH	EXPLANATION
[no switch]	Displays the encryption state (E for encrypted, U for unencrypted) for the current folder and the files and subfolders it contains.
/D	Decrypts the specified folders.
/E	Encrypts the specified folders.
/A	Encrypts or decrypts both files and folders.
/F	Forces the encryption on all the objects specified, even if they're already encrypted. (By default, `cipher` skips objects that are already encrypted.)
/H	Includes files with the Hidden attribute or System attribute in the listing. (By default, `cipher` doesn't list files that have these attributes.)
/I	Ignores any errors encountered and continue encrypting or decrypting files. (By default, `cipher` stops when it encounters an error.)
/K	Creates a new encryption key for the current user.
/U	Examines all the encrypted files on local drives, updating the user's file encryption key or the recovery agent's key.
/U /N	Examines all the encrypted files on local drives, but without updating keys.
/Q	Reports a minimal set of information.
/R	Creates an EFS recovery agent key and certificate. (More on this switch in a moment.)
/S	Performs the specified operation on the specified folder and its subfolders, but not on files in that folder and those subfolders.
/W	Removes data from available unused disk space on the volume.

A word of explanation about the `cipher /K` command, which you'll see from the table creates a new encryption key for the user currently logged on. This encryption key isn't a replacement for a lost key, and you can't use it to decrypt data encrypted with the original key—you can use it only to encrypt new data.

Sharing Encrypted Data

Once you've encrypted a file, you can't blithely share it with other people the way you can an unencrypted file, because they won't be able to decrypt it. Instead, you need to take the actions discussed in this section.

Sharing an Encrypted File with Other Users

Windows XP lets you share an encrypted file (but not a folder) with specified other users who each have an EFS certificate. Other users of your computer can create EFS certificates by encrypting one or more files under their accounts. Remote users will need to export their EFS certificates and supply them to you so that you can import them on your computer.

To share an encrypted file, display the Advanced Attributes dialog box for the file. Then click the Details button to display the Encryption Details For dialog box (Figure 42.1). Click the Add button to display the Select User dialog box, and use it to add the appropriate people to the Users Who Can Transparently Access This File list.

Using Your Encrypted Files from Another Computer

To use your encrypted files from another computer, you need to have your encryption certificate on that computer. If your network administrator has set you up with a roaming profile, Windows XP automatically makes the encryption certificate available to any computer at which you log on successfully. If you don't have a roaming profile, import your certificate manually on the computer by using the techniques described in Chapter 41.

Disabling and Enabling EFS

You can disable EFS on a computer attached to a domain by creating a domain policy that denies the use of EFS and applying that policy to the computer (or, more likely, to the appropriate group of computers).

If the computer isn't part of a domain, run the Registry Editor and create a new DWORD value entry named EfsConfiguration in the key

```
\HKEY_LOCAL_MACHINE\SOFTWARE\Microsoft\Windows NT\CurrentVersion\EFS
```

Assign the value 1 to the value entry, and then restart the computer.

To reenable EFS, assign the EfsConfiguration value entry the value 0.

FIGURE 42.1

To share an encrypted file with another user, add them to the list in the Encryption Details For dialog box for the file.

WARNING If you're going to disable EFS, do so before any user of the computer has had the chance to encrypt any of their files. Otherwise, any user who has encrypted files or folders will no longer be able to access them. Use efsinfo on the system to identify encrypted files (and decrypt them) prior to disabling EFS.

Planning and Implementing an EFS Recovery Policy

As discussed earlier in this chapter, EFS provides strong encryption. However, that encryption necessarily comes with some major gotchas against which you need to protect yourself so that you can recover encrypted files if anything goes wrong.

If your computer is part of a domain, Windows XP automatically sets up the domain administrator as the recovery agent. The administrator can set up other recovery agents as necessary by using the domain's enterprise certification authority (CA) to create recovery agent certificates and then adding them to the domain security policy—but even if the administrator doesn't add any recovery agents, the domain's users are automatically covered for data recovery.

If your computer stands alone or is part of a workgroup, however, XP doesn't automatically create a recovery agent, leaving you with the potential of losing all access to your encrypted files. If you're not part of a domain, you need to designate one or more recovery agents who can recover encrypted files if your certificate goes AWOL.

Creating a Recovery Agent Certificate

Before you designate a recovery agent, you need to create a recovery agent certificate by using the cipher command. Take these steps:

1. Log on to your computer as administrator, and open a Command Prompt window.

2. Enter **cipher /r:*filename***, where *filename* is the name (and, if necessary, path) of the files in which you want the certificate files stored. (Files? Yes—the cipher command creates certificate files in both the CER format and the PFX format.)

3. When cipher prompts you for a password, enter an unguessable password, and press the Enter key. cipher creates the certificate files.

4. Copy the certificate files to a safe location *away from your computer* (for example, on a floppy disk, another removable medium, or a secure online drive), and delete the original files.

Designating a Recovery Agent

Once you've created the recovery agent certificate, you can designate your recovery agent. You can use any account to which you have access, other than the account with which you're creating the encrypted files. In most cases, the Administrator account provides the best solution.

To designate your recovery agent, log on to the account you'll use as the data recovery agent. Then, use the Certificates console (or an MMC console with the Certificates snap-in) to import the recovery certificate's PFX file to the Personal branch under Certificates – Current User. On the Password page of the Certificate Import Wizard, select the Mark This Key As Exportable check box. On the Certificate Store page, select the "Automatically select the certificate store based on the type of certificate" option.

Run the Local Security Settings console (for example, choose Start ➤ Run, enter **secpol.msc**, and click OK), and perform the following actions:

1. Under Security Settings, expand the Public Key Policies item.

2. Right-click the Encrypting File System item, and choose Add Data Recovery Agent from the context menu to start the Add Recovery Agent Wizard.

3. On the Select Recovery Agents page of the wizard, click the Browse Folders button.

4. Use the resulting Open dialog box to select and open the recovery certificate's CER file. The wizard adds the contents of the certificate to the Recovery Agents list, listing the user as USER_ UNKNOWN.

5. Finish the wizard.

You've now set up the current user as a recovery agent. Any files encrypted from now on will be encrypted with both the user's public key and the recovery agent's public key, so they can be recovered by either the user or the recovery agent. It's a good idea to add another level of protection by removing the recovery agent's key from the account you just designated as recovery agent so that nobody can log on under that account and easily decrypt the encrypted files.

To remove the recovery agent's key, log on to the recovery agent account (if you're not still logged on), and use Certificates console to export the certificate. On the Export Private Key screen of the wizard, select the Yes, Export The Private Key option button. On the Export File Format screen, select the Enable Strong Protection and Delete The Private Key If The Export Is Successful check boxes.

Keeping Your Encryption and Recovery Certificates Safe

When the wizard has finished the export, store the certificate in a secure location away from your computer. In order to use the recovery agent to decrypt files, you'll need to import the certificate again to the recovery agent account—but that's the price of security.

If you lose your encryption certificate and the recovery agent certificate, there's not much you can do to recover your encrypted files. As I mentioned earlier, you can create a new encryption certificate by using the cipher command (cipher /K), but this certificate will work only for new files you encrypt—you won't be able to use it to decrypt the files you encrypted using the previous certificate. It's vital to keep a backup of your encryption certificate and the recovery agent certificate.

Recovering Encrypted Data

Once you've designated your recovery agent, you can recover encrypted data by logging onto the recovery agent account and importing the recovery agent certificate (if you removed it for security).

FINDING AND EXAMINING ENCRYPTED FILES AND FOLDERS

Of course, recovering the encrypted files and folders presupposes that you can find them in the first place and decrypt only those for the user who has lost his private key. Even if you've designated a central location for all your encrypted files, working out which belong to whom can be a daunting task.

As you saw earlier in the chapter, you can use the cipher /u /n command to produce a list of the encrypted files on your system (without updating the encryption key). But this list doesn't tell you who encrypted the files. You can use the Encryption Details dialog box for a file to see who encrypted it, but doing so means plugging through file by file, which could take you halfway till eternity for a system with many encrypted files.

Before you ask—yes, Microsoft is aware of the problem. Load your Windows XP Professional CD, and install EFSINFO.EXE from the \SUPPORT\TOOLS folder, either by extracting it from the SUPPORT.CAB cabinet file or by running SUPTOOLS.MSI from the \SUPPORT\TOOLS folder and using the Windows Support Tools Setup Wizard to install either the Typical set of tools or the Complete set of tools.

EXAMINING ENCRYPTED FILES WITH *EFSINFO*

Once you've installed EFSINFO.EXE, open a Command Prompt window, and run the program from the location to which you installed it (XP doesn't add it to your path). Table 42.2 lists the switches for efsinfo.

TABLE 42.2:   Switches for the *efsinfo* Command

SWITCH	EXPLANATION
[no switch]	Displays the encryption state (Encrypted or Not Encrypted) for the current folder and the files and subfolders it contains.
/U	Displays the user information for the file. (This is the default option.)
/R	Displays the recovery agent information for the file.
/C	Displays the thumbnail information for the certificate.
/I	Ignores any errors encountered and continue listing. (By default, efsinfo stops when it encounters an error.)
/Y	Displays the thumbnail information for the current EFS certificate on the local PC.
/S	Performs the specified operation on the directories and subdirectories in the current directory.

For example, you could use the efsinfo /r /u command to return user information and recovery agent information for all the files in the current folder.

TIP   Another tool for examining encrypted files is EFSDump (for *information dumper*), a free utility that you can download from the Sysinternals website (www.sysinternals.com/ntw2k/source/misc.shtml).

Group Policy Settings for EFS

As you might expect, a couple of group policy settings are related to EFS, and you should consider these policies if you're developing an EFS strategy for your company. The following sections explain these policies.

Do Not Automatically Encrypt Files Moved to Encrypted Folders

This policy, located in Computer Configuration\Administrative Templates\System, controls whether files that are moved to an existing encrypted folder are encrypted. If this policy is enabled, Windows XP doesn't encrypt the files. If this policy is disabled or isn't configured and isn't overridden by a policy at a higher level, Windows XP automatically encrypts any file that is moved to an encrypted folder.

The setting applies only to files that you move on the same volume. If you move a file to an encrypted folder on another volume, Windows XP encrypts the file by default.

This group policy setting corresponds to the Registry value `HKEY_LOCAL_MACHINE\Software\Microsoft\Windows\CurrentVersion\Policies\Explorer!NoEncryptOnMove`.

Encrypt the Offline Files Cache

This policy is located in Computer Configuration\Administrative Templates\Network\Offline Files and determines whether the files in the Offline Files cache are encrypted. The Offline Files cache contains the local copy of files that the user has made available offline. If this setting is enabled, Windows XP automatically encrypts all files in the cache and encrypts new files as they're added to the cache. However, understand that Windows XP encrypts the local copy in the cache but does nothing to the original file on the network server—its encryption status remains as it was.

If this setting is not configured or is disabled, Windows XP doesn't encrypt files in the Offline Files cache, potentially creating a security risk. After all, the Offline Files cache is simply a hidden folder managed by Windows, so anyone with a little know-how can steal a computer and read all the files in the Offline Folders cache.

This policy corresponds to the Registry value `HKEY_LOCAL_MACHINE\Software\Policies\Microsoft\Windows\NetCache\AssignedOfflineFolders!EncryptCache`.

Chapter 43

IPSec

As you'll know only too well if you surf the Web and read the news, Internet Protocol (IP) is a truly wonderful invention, but it suffers from having been designed with flexibility and robustness rather than security in mind. The result is that networks running on IP (such as the Internet) are vulnerable to a wide range of attacks, from the undetectable sniffing of unencrypted data to distributed denial-of-service (DoS) attacks launched by "zombie" computers commandeered by malicious hackers.

Chances are that you don't want any attacks happening to your IP traffic. To secure your IP traffic on computers running Windows XP Professional, you can use IP Security (IPSec), as discussed in this chapter. (Windows XP Home Edition doesn't include IPSec.)

You can also apply TCP/IP filtering to your network connections on either Professional or Home Edition to limit the traffic that passes across them. I discuss this topic briefly at the end of the chapter.

Understanding IPSec

IPSec is a suite of protocols and services for securing IP traffic across a network connection. By establishing trust from a source IP address to a destination IP address, IPSec aims to provide end-to-end security combined with ease of use. IPSec includes mechanisms for encrypting data, authenticating the computers connected, securing the transmission and receipt of data, and filtering IP traffic.

Windows XP Professional implements IPSec through policies. IPSec policies can be stored either in Active Directory or in a local computer's Registry. Usually, global IPSec policies are stored in Active Directory and apply to computers that connect to the domain. If a computer gets disconnected from the domain, the domain's IPSec policy information is cached in the computer's Registry. For computers that don't connect to a domain, local IPSec policies are stored in the computer's Registry.

This chapter discusses how to configure local IPSec policies on computers running Windows XP Professional.

How to Use IPSec

You can use IPSec when establishing VPN connections using Layer 2 Tunneling Protocol (L2TP), as discussed in the next chapter, for either remote-access connections or for ultra-secure communications on an internal network. You can also use IPSec by itself (which is referred to as *IPSec tunnel mode* or *IPSec pure tunnel*) to secure communications on an internal network or intranet.

As I mentioned a moment ago, Windows XP Professional can use global or local IPSec policies. Global IPSec policies (which are set on the domain using Domain Security Policy) override local IPSec policies (which are set on the local computer by using Local Security Policy).

When to Use IPSec

Use IPSec when you need to secure communications between two computers. But don't use it unthinkingly on all network connections just because you can. Evaluate your need for IPSec by assessing the following considerations:

◆ How vulnerable is your network to attacks from outside? If your network isn't connected to the Internet or other external networks, its vulnerability will be low.

◆ How vulnerable is your network to attacks from inside? In most cases, this consideration boils down to whether your network carries sensitive data that you need to protect from the rest of the company. For example, you might need to protect financial data or patent information from the regular users of the network. But if such data is already cordoned off in secure systems, you shouldn't need to use IPSec to secure it.

◆ Do you need to secure traffic on the LAN or just data on remote-access connections?

◆ Will your IPSec policies work for all the computers that need to access the data in question? You may need to upgrade some of the computers in order to use IPSec effectively.

If you decide you need IPSec, bear the following in mind:

◆ If your network uses a domain, you'll almost always do best to manage your IPSec policies at the domain level. In other cases, you may want to let server administrators apply IPSec policies on an as-needed basis. Only rarely will you do well to apply IPSec policies at the local computer level in a domain.

◆ IPSec encryption—like any other strong encryption—involves considerable processor overhead. Now that gigahertz-plus chips are so widely used as to be hard to avoid, this is less of an issue than it used to be; but even so, don't run IPSec unless you need it, because it will slow down your computer. If you're using a legacy computer that's struggling to run XP Professional, adding IPSec to its burden may hamstring it entirely. Check to see whether your network adapter can handle encryption duties, and, if so, offload them onto it.

◆ Because misconfigured IPSec policies can cripple communications between vital computers rather than secure communications, test your IPSec policies thoroughly in the lab or on test workstations and servers before deploying them for real.

Requirements for Using IPSec

In order to use IPSec, your computers need a means of authentication and the capability for encryption. Your firewall or other filtering devices need to apply filters that allow IPSec traffic to pass. The following sections contain details about these requirements.

KERBEROS V5 OR CERTIFICATES FOR AUTHENTICATION

Windows XP Professional systems that are part of a domain can use Kerberos V5 for authentication, so they don't need certificates for authentication on an intranet. Windows XP Home Edition systems (which can't connect to a domain) and Windows XP Professional systems that don't connect to a domain need certificates for authentication.

DES OR 3DES ENCRYPTION

To use IPSec, your systems need to be capable of at least Data Encryption Standard (DES) encryption, and preferably Triple DES (3DES) strong encryption. DES uses a 56-bit key, and Triple DES uses two 56-bit keys.

For Windows XP Professional systems, this isn't an issue. But if you want to apply 3DES to your IPSec-secured connections, make sure you've applied Service Pack 2 (or later) or the High Encryption Pack to your Windows 2000 computers. Otherwise, the Windows 2000 machines will knock the encryption back to DES.

PACKET FILTERING

In order for IPSec to be implemented, the source computer and the destination computer need to know about the traffic that's being secured. The computers through which the traffic is routed don't need to know about the traffic—unless they're filtering IP traffic.

If you use a device that filters packets between your Internet connection and computers in a DMZ or perimeter network, you need to apply filtering to make sure IPSec-secured packets can pass through the device. Table 43.1 lists a basic set of filters that the device should permit to pass.

TABLE 43.1: Basic Filters for a Firewall Device to Allow IPSec Traffic to Pass

PURPOSE	ITEM	VALUE (DECIMAL)	VALUE (HEX)
IPSec Encapsulating Security Protocol (ESP) traffic	IP protocol ID	50	0x32
IPSec Authentication Header (AH) traffic	IP protocol ID	51	0x33
Internet Key Exchange (IKE) traffic	UDP port	500	0x1F4

Depending on the packet-filtering software you're using, you may be able to improve on the basic set of filters shown in Table 43.1 by defining separate input filters and output filters for each network interface involved and by specifying IP addresses for the computers in the DMZ. Table 43.2 lists restrictive filters for IPSec traffic based on a computer secured with IPSec communicating through a dedicated interface with a firewall device in a DMZ.

TABLE 43.2: Restrictive Filters for a Firewall Device to Allow IPSec Traffic to Pass

PURPOSE	SOURCE/DESTINATION IP ADDRESS	PORT/PROTOCOL	VALUE (DECIMAL)	VALUE (HEX)
Input Packet Filters for Computer's DMZ Interface				
Incoming IKE traffic	Destination	UDP destination port	500	0x1F4
Incoming IPSec ESP traffic	Destination	IP protocol	50	0x32

TABLE 43.2: Restrictive Filters for a Firewall Device to Allow IPSec Traffic to Pass *(CONTINUED)*

PURPOSE	SOURCE/DESTINATION IP ADDRESS	PORT/PROTOCOL	VALUE (DECIMAL)	VALUE (HEX)
Incoming IPSec AH traffic	Destination	IP protocol	51	0x33

Output Packet Filters for Computer's DMZ Interface

Outgoing IKE traffic	Source	UDP source port	500	0x1F4
Incoming IPSec ESP traffic	Source	IP protocol	50	0x32
Outgoing IPSec AH traffic	Source	IP protocol	51	0x33

Input Packet Filters on DMZ Interface of Firewall

Outgoing IKE traffic	Source	UDP source port	500	0x1F4
Outgoing IPSec ESP traffic	Source	IP protocol	50	0x32
Outgoing IPSec AH traffic	Source	IP protocol	51	0x33

Output Packet Filters on DMZ Interface of Firewall

Incoming IKE traffic	Destination	UDP port	500	0x1F4
Incoming IPSec ESP traffic	Destination	IP protocol	50	0x32
Incoming IPSec AH traffic	Destination	IP protocol	51	0x33

Overview of Preconfigured Policies

Windows XP Professional provides three standard IPSec policies that you can use as they are or edit to suit your needs:

Client (Respond Only)   Usually used on a client, this policy uses unsecured communication unless a server requests security. When one does, the client uses security only for the protocol and the port requested by the server. Other traffic remains unsecured.

Secure Server (Require Security)   Usually used on a secure server, this policy requires security using Kerberos trust for all IP traffic. This policy doesn't allow any unsecured communication.

Server (Request Security) Usually used on a server, this policy requests security using Kerberos trust for IP traffic but allows unsecured IP traffic from clients that don't respond to the request for secured traffic.

To use one of these policies as it stands, assign it as described in "Assigning IPSec Policies," later in this chapter. To modify a policy before assigning it, follow the steps in the next section.

Modifying Existing IPSec Policies

In many cases, the best way to start working with IPSec policies is to modify one of the existing policies, because they're already fully enough formed to need little further configuration. To work with IPSec policies using Local Security Policy, take the following steps:

1. Open Local Security Policy (choose Start ➤ Control Panel ➤ Performance and Maintenance ➤ Administrative Tools ➤ Local Security Policy).

2. Click the IP Security Policies branch to display its contents.

3. To view the description of a policy, double-click it to display its Properties dialog box with the Rules tab foremost, and then click the General tab.

4. On the General tab, you can change the following items:

    ◆ The name of the rule. (This appears in the IP Security Policy snap-in.)

    ◆ The description of the rule. For example, clarify the changes you're making and their intended effects.

    ◆ The interval at which Windows XP Professional should poll Active Directory for policy changes. This setting applies only if the computer is part of a domain.

5. Also on the General tab, you can click the Advanced button to display the Key Exchange Settings dialog box (shown on the left in Figure 43.1), in which you can choose the following settings:

    ◆ Select the Master Key Perfect Forward Secrecy check box if you want to force Windows XP Professional to reauthenticate and negotiate a new master key each time it needs a new session key.

    ◆ Reduce the Authenticate And Generate A New Key After Every *nn* Minutes setting to tighten security by changing keys more frequently.

    ◆ To force Windows XP Professional to get a new key after a specific number of sessions, enter the number in the Authenticate And Generate A New Key After Every *nn* Settings box. The default setting, 0, doesn't force a change. If you select the Master Key Perfect Forward Secrecy check box, Windows XP Professional applies a value of 1 to this option and doesn't let you change it.

    ◆ To specify your preferred security methods, click the Methods button and work in the resulting Key Exchange Security Methods dialog box (shown on the right in Figure 43.1).

FIGURE 43.1

Use the Key Exchange Settings dialog box (left) to tighten IPSec authentication and key security. If necessary, click the Methods button and use the Key Exchange Security Methods dialog box (right) to specify these methods.

6. On the Rules tab, you can select or clear the check boxes for the existing rules in the IP Security Rules list box to apply them to the policy or turn them off. You can edit a rule by double-clicking it and working with the options on the tabs of the resulting Edit Rule Properties dialog box; Figure 43.2 shows an example of this dialog box. (Note that the selection of tabs in the Edit Rule Properties dialog box varies depending on the rule you're editing.)

FIGURE 43.2

Use the Edit Rule Properties dialog box to edit an existing IPSec policy to meet your needs.

7. On the Security Methods tab of the Edit Rule Properties dialog box, you can make changes such as the following:

◆ Use the Move Up and Move Down buttons to change the preference order of the security methods.

◆ Add a new security method by clicking the Add button and choosing the appropriate option in the New Security Method dialog box: Encryption And Integrity (which uses ESP), Integrity Only (which uses AH), or Custom. If you select the Custom option button, click the Settings button and use the resulting dialog box to define the custom settings.

◆ Edit an existing security method by selecting it, clicking the Edit button, and working in the Modify Security Method dialog box and the Custom Security Method Settings dialog box as necessary.

◆ Remove a security method by selecting it, clicking the Remove button, and then clicking the Yes button in the IP Security Policy Management confirmation dialog box.

◆ Tighten security by selecting the Session Key Perfect Forward Secrecy check box. This option forces Windows XP Professional to renegotiate a new master key each time it needs a new session key.

8. On the Authentication Methods tab of the Edit Rule Properties dialog box, you can change the types of authentication used by the rule and the order in which to apply them. The default for Windows XP Professional in a domain is Kerberos V5. The alternatives are to use a specified certificate or a preshared key.

Creating New IPSec Policies

If the preconfigured IPSec policies don't suit you, and you don't want to change them, you can create new IPSec policies from scratch from the Local Security Settings snap-in.

To create a new IPSec policy, you can either use the IP Security Policy Wizard to create the basic details of your new policy and then edit some settings manually, or you can create the whole policy manually. For your first policies, you may prefer to use the wizard. Subsequently, you'll probably want to graduate to creating your policies manually.

To run the wizard, right-click the IP Security Policies item, and choose Create IP Security Policy from the shortcut menu.

To create an IP security policy manually, you need to turn off the IP Security Policy Wizard. To do so, right-click an existing IPSec policy, and choose Properties to display the Properties dialog box for the policy. On the Rules tab, clear the Use Add Wizard check box, and then click the Add button to display the New Rule Properties dialog box. This dialog box contains most of the same tabs and controls as the Edit Rule Properties dialog box, shown earlier in Figure 43.2. (Like that dialog box, the New Rule Properties dialog box contains different sets of tabs depending on the type of rule you're working with.)

SHOULD YOU USE ESP OR AH?

As you've seen, Windows XP Professional lets you choose between using Encapsulating Security Protocol (ESP) or Authentication Header (AH) to protect your IP traffic. What's the difference, and which should you use?

Briefly, AH computes a keyed hash for each IP packet and header being transferred. It then includes this hash with the packet, thus providing data authentication and integrity. Each packet includes a sequence number for packet replay services.

ESP also computes a keyed hash for each IP packet and includes it with the packet. But with ESP, the hash doesn't protect the IP header—the hash calculation includes the ESP header, trailer, and payload, but not the IP header. ESP encrypts the payload using DES or (better) 3DES and includes a sequence number with each packet for packet replay services.

AH offers better performance than ESP, whereas ESP offers better protection than AH. Consider using AH to secure LAN traffic and ESP for more vulnerable traffic, such as traffic that crosses the Internet. If you have network adapters on which you can offload IPSec encryption, you may want to use ESP for internal traffic as well.

Assigning IPSec Policies

Once you've chosen or modified an IPSec policy, you need to assign it in order to put it into effect. To assign a policy in Windows XP Professional, run the IP Security Policy snap-in, right-click the policy, and choose Assign from the shortcut menu.

Only one IPSec policy can be assigned at a time, so assigning a policy unassigns any currently assigned policy. You can also unassign the currently assigned policy without assigning another by right-clicking the policy and choosing Un-assign.

Managing Global Filters

Instead of creating IP filters as necessary when you need them while creating a policy, you can define global filters ahead of time so that you can apply them to policies easily.

To manage global IPSec filters, right-click the IP Security Policies item in Local Security Settings, and choose Manage IP Filter Lists And Filter Actions from the context menu to display that option's dialog box; its two tabs are shown in Figure 43.3.

To add an IPSec filter, click the Add button on the Manage IP Filter Lists tab. In the resulting IP Filter List dialog box, enter the name and description for the new filter list. Then, click the Add button, and follow the steps of the IP Filter Wizard as it walks you through specifying the source address of the IP traffic, the traffic's destination, the protocol, and other details. To edit the resulting filter, select the Edit Properties check box on the final page of the wizard before clicking the Finish button.

To edit an IPSec filter, double-click it on the Manage IP Filter Lists tab. In the resulting dialog box, change the name or description as appropriate; use the Edit button to edit an existing filter, the Remove button to remove an existing filter, or the Add button to add a new filter.

To create a new filter action, click the Add button on the Manage Filter Actions tab, and follow the steps of the Filter Action Wizard. These steps involve supplying the name and description for the filter; choosing whether to permit, block, or negotiate security; (if you chose to negotiate) specifying whether to refuse to communicate with computers that don't support IPSec or to fall back to unsecured communication; and specifying which methods of IP traffic security to use.

To edit an existing filter action, double-click it on the Manage Filter Actions tab, and work in the resulting Properties dialog box. For example, you might choose to apply Session Key Perfect Forward Secrecy to a filter action.

FIGURE 43.3

Use the Manage IP Filter Lists And Filter Actions dialog box to manage global IP filters.

Using TCP/IP Filtering

Another tool for restricting the IP traffic that your Windows XP computer receives is TCP/IP filtering. You can filter TCP ports, UDP ports, and IP protocols on a port-by-port basis. Filtering applies to *all* the network adapters that your computer is using: You can't apply filtering to one adapter but not to the others.

By default, XP doesn't apply filtering. This means that it allows all the IP traffic to pass across the network adapters. You can tighten up your security considerably by filtering ports and protocols, but it's a ticklish business, because filtering the wrong ports can cripple your network. So before you start applying filters, you need to know which ports are used for which purpose. Visit `www.iana.org/assignments/port-numbers` for the latest list of TCP/IP port assignments.

To configure and apply TCP/IP filtering, follow these steps:

1. Choose Start ➢ Connect To, right-click any network interface, and choose Properties.

2. Double-click the Internet Protocol (TCP/IP) item on the General tab to display the Internet Protocol (TCP/IP) Properties dialog box.

3. Click the Advanced button to display the Advanced TCP/IP Settings dialog box.

4. On the Options tab, double-click the TCP/IP Filtering item in the Optional Settings list box to display the TCP/IP Filtering dialog box.

5. Select the Enable TCP/IP Filtering (All Adapters) check box.

6. For each type of filter (TCP Ports, UDP Ports, and IP Protocols) that you need to apply, select the Permit Only option instead of Permit All, and then use the Add button and the resulting dialog box to add your port or protocol number. Use the Remove buttons to remove a selected filter that has outlived its usefulness.

7. Click the OK buttons to close the TCP/IP Filtering dialog box, the Advanced TCP/IP Settings dialog box, the Internet Protocol (TCP/IP) Properties dialog box, and the network interface's Properties dialog box.

8. Make sure your network is functioning as it ought to. If it isn't, chances are that you need to tweak the filters you applied.

Once you apply TCP/IP filtering, Windows XP accepts only TCP packets destined for the TCP ports you've added, UDP packets for the UDP ports you've added, IP protocols matching the list of protocols you've specified, and all ICMP packets. TCP/IP filtering doesn't filter ICMP traffic—for ICMP filtering, use RRAS to configure IP packet filters.

Chapter 44

VPN Connections

This chapter discusses how to create and manage virtual private network (VPN) connections for connecting securely to remote networks via a shared or public network, such as the Internet.

VPNs are popular with corporations for allowing secure remote connectivity at low cost, but individual users can also use them to good effect. Windows XP provides both VPN client and VPN server capabilities.

Understanding Virtual Private Network Connections

Virtual private network (VPN) connections let you establish a secure connection across an unsecured network (such as the Internet) so that your computer becomes a node on the remote network. The computer connecting to the network is the VPN client, and the computer to which it connects is the VPN server.

You're most likely to need to use XP (Professional or Home Edition) as a VPN client, but both versions of XP also include a minimal VPN server that can accept a single incoming connection. This chapter shows you how to use both the VPN client and the VPN server components, starting with the client.

How VPN Connections Work

A VPN connection establishes a secure connection by *tunneling* under the protocols of the unsecured network (for example, TCP/IP in the case of an Internet connection) to create a virtual direct connection between the VPN client and the VPN server. This connection operates as a dedicated WAN link on a logical level and is secured by encrypting each packet or frame to be transmitted and enveloping it in another packet or frame with a new header for transmission. This process is called *encapsulation*. When the packet or frame reaches its destination, the header is removed, the envelope (as it were) is opened, and the packet or frame inside it is decrypted *(unencapsulation)*.

As a VPN client, Windows XP can use the Point-to-Point Tunneling Protocol (PPTP) or the Layer 2 Tunneling Protocol (L2TP). As a VPN server, XP can use only PPTP, whereas Windows 2000 Server and Windows Server 2003 can use either PPTP or L2TP. Both PPTP and L2TP are based on the Point-to-Point Protocol (PPP), the suite of standard protocols commonly used for connecting to an ISP.

If your configuration allows you the choice, use L2TP rather than PPTP for your VPN connection, because it offers greater security. (I'll discuss VPN security in detail later in this chapter.) To use L2TP VPN connections, you need to install a certificate on the VPN client or use a smart card.

NOTE   See Chapter 41 for a discussion of certificates.

NOTE Another option for creating VPN connections is to use IPSec tunnel mode (also known as *IPSec pure tunnel*). You may need to do this when working with routers or gateways that don't support PPTP tunneling or L2TP tunneling. If you're using a Windows XP/2000/2003 solution for your VPN, use L2TP or PPTP rather than IPSec tunnel mode. (See the previous chapter for details on IPSec.)

What VPN Connections Are Used For

VPN connections are typically used to enable remote users to access a corporate network securely across the Internet. In this scenario, the remote user connects to her ISP for Internet access as usual and then establishes an encrypted connection across the Internet to a VPN server attached to the corporate network. By connecting to the ISP using her usual Internet connection rather than establishing a dial-up connection to the corporate server, a user with a broadband Internet connection can connect at broadband speeds rather than being limited to modem speeds. If the user has a dial-up Internet connection, there's no speed advantage to a VPN connection, but the Internet connection should at least be a local call rather than a long-distance call.

VPN connections benefit the company as well by reducing costs in two ways. First, the company can offload the burden of supporting dial-up connections to the remote users' ISPs, so its remote access servers don't need to be stuffed with modems and connected to a large number of phone lines. Second, instead of users dialing long-distance (presumably at company expense) to connect, they can connect with a local call to their ISP, greatly reducing the cost of remote access.

VPN connections can also be used within secure networks to cordon off ultra-sensitive data from areas where users who are authorized to use the network but not to see that data could otherwise access it. Authorized users can establish VPN connections across the network to the VPN server containing the protected data, whereas unauthorized users can't even see the VPN server.

Creating Outgoing VPN Connections

To create an outgoing VPN connection, follow these steps, clicking the Next button to drive each screen of the wizard:

1. Start the New Connection Wizard (for example, choose Start ➢ All Programs ➢ Accessories ➢ Communications ➢ New Connection Wizard).

2. Select the Connect To The Network At My Workplace option on the Network Connection Type page of the wizard.

3. Select the Virtual Private Network Connection option on the Network Connection page.

4. Enter the name for the connection on the Connection Name page. The wizard names the text box Company Name, but you can call the connection anything you want.

5. If the wizard displays the Public Network page offering to dial an initial connection to the Internet before establishing the VPN connection, select the Do Not Dial The Initial Connection button or the Automatically Dial This Initial Connection button, as appropriate. If you choose the latter, select the appropriate preconfigured connection in the drop-down list.

6. Enter the VPN server's host name or IP address on the VPN Server Selection page of the wizard. (If your VPN server has a dynamic IP address rather than a static IP address, leave this page blank. You'll need to fill in the information when you use the connection.)

7. Click the Finish button on the completion page. The wizard creates the connection, assigns it the name you specified, and closes.

If necessary, display the Properties dialog box for the connection, and choose further options, such as the following:

General tab options   In the Host Name Or IP Address Of Destination text box, enter the IP address or host name of the VPN server. You shouldn't need to change this entry unless the VPN server has a dynamic IP address that you need to update each time you connect. If you need to change your setting for dialing an Internet connection before connecting to the VPN server, select the Dial Another Connection First check box and choose the connection in the drop-down list.

Security tab options   Use the Typical option button or the Advanced option button to specify how to authenticate your identity. If you choose Typical and your VPN requires encryption, select the Require Data Encryption (Disconnect If None) check box.

Networking tab options   By default, Windows XP automatically negotiates the VPN type— L2TP with IPSec (which XP tries first, because it's more secure) or PPTP. To override this behavior, choose the PPTP VPN item or the L2TP IPSec VPN item instead of Automatic in the Type Of VPN drop-down list. To specify an IP address for the VPN instead of having the VPN server assign an IP address automatically, double-click the Internet Protocol (TCP/IP) item to display the Internet Protocol (TCP/IP) dialog box, select the Use The Following IP Address option button, and enter the address.

Advanced tab options   You can share a VPN connection with other computers on your network by selecting the Allow Other Network Users To Connect Through This Computer's Connection check box. You can use ICF on the connection by selecting the Protect My Computer And Network By Limiting Or Preventing Access To This Computer From The Internet check box.

Connecting to a VPN Connection

To connect to a VPN connection, choose Start ➢ Connect To, and select the connection's name from the submenu to display the Connect dialog box for the VPN.

TIP   If your computer doesn't show a Connect To menu, you can open the Network Connections folder to access the VPN connection. You can also customize the Start menu to show the Connect To menu. To do so, right-click the Start button, and choose Properties. Click Customize, click Advanced, and scroll through the Start Menu Items list to find Network Connections. Choose the Display As Connect To Menu, and click OK twice.

If you need to tweak any of the parameters for the connection, click the Properties button to display the connection's Properties dialog box, and make the changes as discussed in the previous section.

Enter your username and password, choose whether to save them and for whose use (if applicable), and then click the Connect button.

Once XP has established the connection, you'll be able to connect to resources on the VPN server or its LAN (if you're permitted to do so) as if you were connected directly to the network. The big difference is that the connection happens at the speed of your Internet connection rather than at LAN speeds, and the overhead of encrypting the packets or frames slows down the connection a little further. If you have a slow connection, running programs across the wire takes a long time.

To disconnect the VPN connection, right-click its icon in the notification area and choose Disconnect from the context menu.

Configuring Incoming VPN Connections

As I mentioned earlier in this chapter, Windows XP includes a minimal VPN server that can accept one incoming connection. You might want to implement a VPN server so that other people can connect to it across the Internet to access files you're sharing or upload files—for example, to work together on a project.

This section describes how to configure an incoming connection on an XP computer that connects directly to the Internet, on an XP computer that connects to the Internet through ICS, and on a Windows 2000 Server or Windows Server 2003 computer.

Incoming Connection on an XP Computer with an Internet Connection

To configure Windows XP to accept incoming VPN connections, log on as an administrator and take the following steps:

1. Start the New Connection Wizard (for example, click the Create A New Connection link in the Network Tasks list on the Network Connections screen).

NOTE If you haven't set up a modem and specified your location, XP displays the Location Information dialog box. Enter your country, area code, and any other information needed for a modem connection. (Even if you don't have a modem, enter your area code.) When you dismiss the Location Information dialog box, XP displays the Phone And Modem Options dialog box, in which you can rename your default location and create new locations and dialing rules as necessary.

2. Select the Set Up An Advanced Connection option on the Network Connection Type page of the wizard.

3. Select the Accept Incoming Connections option on the Advanced Connection Options page.

4. If your computer has a modem, parallel port, or IrDA port, the wizard displays the Devices For Incoming Connections page, which lists those devices installed on your computer and invites you to select the check box for each device you want to use for incoming connections. You *can* select one or more check boxes (for example, select the check box for your modem), but you don't have to.

5. Select the Allow Virtual Private Connections option on the Incoming Virtual Private Network (VPN) Connection page.

6. Select the check boxes for the users you want to be able to use the VPN connection on the User Permissions page. Use the Add button and the resulting New User dialog box to add a user *to the computer* (not just to the connection). Use the Remove button to remove a user account *from the computer*. Use the Properties button and the resulting Properties dialog box to change the full name for a user, to specify a password for them, or to set callback options if necessary.

7. Select the networking software to use for the connection on the Networking Software page. If necessary, use the Install button to install an additional protocol, service, or client.

8. In most cases, it's a good idea to check the TCP/IP settings for the incoming VPN connection. Double-click the Internet Protocol (TCP/IP) item on the Networking Software page to display the Incoming TCP/IP Properties dialog box (shown in Figure 44.1), and choose settings as appropriate:

FIGURE 44.1
Use the Incoming TCP/IP
Properties dialog box to
specify whether to allow
callers access to your LAN
and whether to assign
TCP/IP addresses auto-
matically or manually.

◆ Select or clear the Allow Callers To Access My Local Area Network check box to allow or
deny access to your LAN. (Callers will be able to access shared folders and other resources
on your computer either way.)

◆ Designate how to assign TCP/IP addresses—automatically or manually—in the TCP/IP
Address Assignment group box. If you select the Specify TCP/IP Addresses option button,
use the From and To text boxes to specify the range of addresses, and check the readout
shown in the Total text box. Note that selecting the Allow Calling Computer To Specify Its
Own IP Address check box could cause an address conflict with a computer already connected to the network.

9. Click the Finish button on the completion page. The wizard creates the connection, names it
Incoming Connections, and closes.

You can turn off the VPN connection by clearing the Allow Others To Make Private Connections
To My Computer By Tunneling Through The Internet Or Another Network check box on the General
tab of the Incoming Connections Properties dialog box.

If your computer's Internet connection has a dynamic IP address rather than a static IP address,
you'll need to communicate the current IP address to anyone who wants to connect. (To get the IP
address, run an `ipconfig` command and look at the appropriate line of the readout—for example, the
PPP Adapter line for a dial-up connection.)

Incoming PPTP Connection via ICS

If your VPN server connects to the Internet via Internet Connection Sharing (ICS), configure the ICS
host to pass PPTP traffic on TCP port 1723 to the VPN server as follows:

1. On the ICS host, display the Properties dialog box for the shared Internet connection.

2. Click the Settings button on the Advanced tab to display the Advanced Settings dialog box.

3. On the Services tab, select the Incoming Connection VPN (PPTP) item, and click the Edit button to display the Service Settings dialog box for the service.

> **NOTE**   If you want to change the name of the incoming connection to make clear that it's being redirected to the internal VPN server, use the Delete button to delete the Incoming Connection VPN (PPTP) connection and the Add button to create a new entry. Use 1723 for the external port number and the internal port number, and select the TCP option button.

4. Change the contents of the Name Or IP Address Of The Computer Hosting This Service On The Network text box to the IP address (for example, 192.168.0.145) or qualified name (for example, VPNServer.MSHOME.NET) of the VPN server.

5. Click the OK buttons to close the Service Settings dialog box, the Advanced Settings dialog box, and the Properties dialog box.

Incoming Connection on Windows 2000 Server or Windows Server 2003

To configure an incoming VPN connection on a Windows 2000 Server, enable Routing and Remote Access Service as follows:

1. Choose Start ➢ Programs ➢ Administrative Tools ➢ Routing And Remote Access to display the RRAS console.

2. Right-click the server, and choose Configure And Enable Routing And Remote Access from the shortcut menu to run the RRAS setup wizard. The wizard walks you through the setup process; steps 3–7 describe the key decisions.

3. On the Common Configurations page, select the Virtual Private Network (VPN) Server option.

4. On the Remote Client Protocols page, make sure the appropriate protocols are listed. If they aren't, select the No, I Need To Add Protocols option, and add them on the next page.

5. On the Internet Connection page, select the Internet connection through which the VPN clients will access the server.

6. On the IP Address Assignment page, choose whether to assign IP addresses to VPN clients automatically or use a range of addresses that you specify.

7. On the Managing Multiple Remote Access Servers page, choose whether you want to use RADIUS to manage your remote access servers. If you use RADIUS, provide the necessary information.

The process is slightly different on Windows Server 2003, but the steps are generally the same; you should have no problems setting up a Windows Server 2003 VPN server.

Implementing Optimum Security on Your VPN Connections

To implement optimum security on your VPN connections, follow the suggestions in the following sections.

Restrict VPN Users to a Minimum

Allow VPN use only to those users who need it. Deny access by default to each user on the Dial-In tab of the user's Properties dialog box or through your remote access policy.

Prefer L2TP to PPTP

Use L2TP rather than PPTP if possible, because L2TP is more secure. If your VPN clients are running Windows XP or 2000, the only reason to use PPTP is if your VPN *server* is running XP—which it shouldn't be, because XP limits the server to a single incoming connection at a time—or if you haven't installed a certificate on the clients.

Close All Unnecessary VPN Ports

By default, Windows 2000 Server sets up five ports for PPTP connections and five ports for L2TP connections when you enable RRAS. Reduce these numbers of ports to the minimum practicable for the degree of connectivity you want to provide. For example, if your server will never need to support more than three simultaneous VPN connections, and all the clients will be using Windows 2000 or XP, disable the PPTP ports and reduce the number of L2TP ports to three.

To change the open ports, right-click the Ports item for the server in the Routing And Remote Access Console, and choose Properties from the shortcut menu to display the Ports Properties dialog box; then, double-click the relevant WAN Miniport entry, and work in the Configure Device dialog box:

◆ To disable ports, clear the Remote Access Connections (Inbound Only) check box.

◆ To reduce the number of ports, change the setting in the Maximum Ports box.

As I mentioned earlier, XP provides only a single port for VPN connections. When you don't need the VPN, turn off access to it by clearing the Allow Others To Make Private Connections To My Computer By Tunneling Through The Internet Or Other Network check box on the General tab of the Incoming Connections Properties dialog box.

Require Encryption on Passwords and Data

Require encryption on passwords and data for all clients that connect. For example:

◆ In Windows 2000 Server or Windows Server 2003, define a group profile that requires users who connect via the VPN to authenticate using EAP and use 128-bit encryption to encrypt their data.

◆ On a Windows XP VPN server, select the Require All Users To Secure Their Passwords And Data check box on the Users tab of the Incoming Connections Properties dialog box.

The VPN clients will then need to select the Require Data Encryption (Disconnect If None) check box on the Security tab of the Properties dialog box for the VPN connection in order to connect.

Use Strong Authentication—Preferably EAP

Make sure your VPN server requires authentication for each user who connects. If possible, use Extensible Authentication Protocol (EAP) with a certificate or a smart card.

If you can't use EAP, use encrypted authentication such as Microsoft Challenge Handshake Authentication Protocol version 2 (MS-CHAP v2). Using MS-CHAP v2 rather than MS-CHAP may require you to update NT4, Windows 95, and Windows 98 clients with MS-CHAP v2, but v2 provides stronger authentication. (You can download the MS-CHAP v2 updates from the Microsoft website.)

Use DHCP, or Configure a Static IP Address Pool

Configure your VPN server to use Dynamic Host Configuration Protocol (DHCP) to assign IP addresses to VPN clients, rather than let VPN clients specify their own addresses. If you can't use DHCP:

◆ If your network has a single subnet, configure a static IP address pool consisting of a subset of the IP addresses for the subnet that contains the VPN server.

◆ If your network has multiple subnets and a routed infrastructure, configure a static IP address pool with a range of addresses in a different subnet from the subnet that contains the VPN server. Enable the routing protocol for your infrastructure on the VPN server, or add static routes for the address ranges to the routing tables of your routers.

Create Input and Output Filters

Create input filters and output filters for your VPN connections to restrict the packets that can pass through the connections.

In the Routing And Remote Access console, expand the IP Routing branch, and select the General item. Display the Properties dialog box for the interface on which you want to edit the IPSec filters.

To create an input filter, click the Input Filters button on the General tab of the Properties dialog box to display the Input Filters dialog box. To create an output filter, click the Output Filters button on the General tab to display the Output Filters dialog box. From either dialog box (as appropriate), click the Add button to display the Add IP Filter dialog box.

L2TP/IPSEC INPUT AND OUTPUT FILTERS

For an L2TP VPN connection, set the following filters:

◆ An input filter with the Destination Network check box selected, the IP address of the network interface, the subnet mask 255.255.255.255, the protocol UDP, the source port 500, and the destination port 500.

◆ An input filter with the Destination Network check box selected, the IP address of the network interface, the subnet mask 255.255.255.255, the protocol UDP, the source port 1701, and the destination port 1701.

In the Input Filters dialog box, select the Drop All Packets Except Those That Meet The Criteria Below option.

Then, set the following output filters from the Output Filters dialog box:

◆ An output filter with the Source Network check box selected, the IP address of the network interface, the subnet mask 255.255.255.255, the protocol UDP, the source port 500, and the destination port 500.

◆ An output filter with the Source Network check box selected, the IP address of the network interface, the subnet mask 255.255.255.255, the protocol UDP, the source port 1701, and the destination port 1701.

In the Output Filters dialog box, select the Drop All Packets Except Those That Meet The Criteria Below option button.

PPTP INPUT AND OUTPUT FILTERS

For a PPTP VPN connection, set the following input filters:

◆ An input filter with the Destination Network check box selected, the IP address of the network interface, the subnet mask 255.255.255.255, the protocol Other, and the value 47 in the Protocol Number box. (This box appears when you choose Other in the Protocol drop-down list.)

◆ An input filter with the Destination Network check box selected, the IP address of the network interface, the subnet mask 255.255.255.255, the protocol TCP, the source port 0, and the destination port 1723.

◆ If your PPTP VPN server also acts as a PPTP VPN client, a third input filter with the Destination Network check box selected, the IP address of the network interface, the subnet mask 255.255.255.255, the protocol TCP (Established), the source port 1723, and the destination port 0.

In the Input Filters dialog box, select the Drop All Packets Except Those That Meet The Criteria Below option button.

Then, set the following output filters from the Output Filters dialog box:

◆ An output filter with the Source Network check box selected, the IP address of the network interface, the subnet mask 255.255.255.255, the protocol Other, and the value 47 in the Protocol Number box

◆ An output filter with the Source Network check box selected, the IP address of the network interface, the subnet mask 255.255.255.255, the protocol TCP, the source port 1723, and the destination port 0.

◆ If your PPTP VPN server also acts as a PPTP VPN client, add a third output filter with the Source Network check box selected, the IP address of the network interface, the subnet mask 255.255.255.255, the protocol TCP (Established), the source port 0, and the destination port 1723.

In the Output Filters dialog box, select the Drop All Packets Except Those That Meet The Criteria Below option button.

USING INTERNAL VPN CONNECTIONS FOR SENSITIVE DATA

As I mentioned earlier in the chapter, although VPN connections are typically used for remote access, they can be used on an internal network as well—for example, to cordon off servers that contain ultra-sensitive data from the casual depredations of regular users. Issue the appropriate permissions to the authorized users so that they can establish VPN connections to the hidden servers across the LAN. You then get the full security that VPN connections offer together with full LAN speeds (minus the overhead of encryption).

Chapter 45

Security Configuration Tools

In today's world, you can't assume that your system or network is free from unwanted and/or harmful visitors. Nor can you ignore the potential for abuse caused by the normal user with access to a single workstation or a network.

Unfortunately, however, security is all too often overlooked for two basic reasons. First, we have a tendency not to resolve a problem until disaster has struck (sometimes multiple times); and second, security configuration tends to involve a lot of pesky detail work, as you struggle to be sure only the right people have access, of the appropriate level of ability, with the proper features turned on or off.

Windows XP—in a slight evolution from previous versions—strives to provide, under the umbrella of its Security Configuration And Analysis feature, the tools and templates necessary to let you tweak settings to fit the problems and particular needs of your setup without requiring a graduate degree in user access and security. This package also provides a decent administrative interface to control some of the security/usage components, such as establishing types of users and groups, setting policy, and others you've already read about in the chapters leading up to this.

In this chapter, I'll walk you through the tools and the options, and how they may best apply to the way you're most likely to use them. Remember as you go, however, that you as both a user and an administrator represent one of the most powerful tools available for protecting a system or network. Thus, you need to understand these tools, actually review the logs and other information they provide, and make the changes necessary to institute that security.

NOTE Most of the features discussed in this chapter are specific to Windows XP Professional. Although Home Edition employs some security (including Windows Firewall), only Professional is designed for stronger, corporate-style security configuration and implementation.

Overview of XP Security Tools

I just mentioned some of the tools you've already discovered in earlier reading or work. Now it's time to review the specific security tools in XP and how/why to use them. Among these tools are the following:

Security Configuration And Analysis This tool is used for configuring and reviewing the security established.

Auditing Although it isn't security specific, this feature's ability to monitor the successes and failures of selected objects and events can offer invaluable information about how a system is being used and abused as well as what changes in security may be necessary.

Resultant Set of Policy Wizard (RSoP) This wizard-driven utility aids in the successful implementation of group policy, even where different policy settings conflict with one another.

Security templates This is a set of predefined security policy measures.

Where appropriate, you'll find tips indicating how you can access or use the same tool process from the command line (there are still more than a few of us command-line commandos).

Determining Your Level of Security

Before you begin working with the tools discussed here, it makes sense to understand what policies are already in effect on the system on which you're working.

You can check local security settings one of two ways: from the command line or Run dialog box, by typing **secpol.msc**, or by following this procedure:

1. From Control Panel, click Administrative Tools.

2. Choose Local System Policy.

3. Click to expand and review policies and settings in place under each object listed in the console.

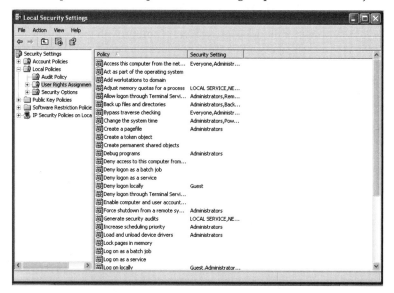

To modify entries listed here, click the device as it's listed in the right pane, and choose to Enable or Disable, and so on. When you're finished, right-click the Security Settings listing on the left and choose Reload, which reloads the security settings, including the changes you just made.

Here's an example of something you might want to do for security. Let's say your company has always allowed—even encouraged—individuals to perform their own backups, but now you want to have them performed regularly (so they get done) only by trusted people with Administrator or Backup Operator access. You'll follow the steps just described, locating the Users Rights Assignment entry under Local Policies. Then you'll right-click the Back Up Files And Directories listing in the right pane, click Add/Remove, and remove everyone but Administrators (or Administrators and Backup Operators). Once this policy has been applied, only someone belonging to one of those sacred groups may perform backups.

NOTE   Be aware that many security authorities and reporting agencies say that most of the damage and information theft encountered on computer networks and systems is done internally, by employees or others who have been granted access to the services as part of their normal work.

Using These Tools to Configure Security

Starting with Security Configuration And Analysis, I'll take you through a swift power tour of the installation, configuration, and use of these security tools.

WARNING   As we work through these points, understand that you'll need to be logged in on your administrator account to have full access to some (if not most) of these features.

Using Security Configuration And Analysis

The Security Configuration And Analysis tool features two main components: a basic interface for performing adjustments to system security setup and a utility to review that setup to identify where security may be lacking or where precautions may be missing altogether. A log is created as part of the process, which you can then eyeball in search of nasty surprises.

INSTALLING SECURITY CONFIGURATION AND ANALYSIS

If you're like many (based on those I've spoken with) who looked around for this tool before discovering where it's hidden, you already know that it's available as a snap-in you add and manage through the MMC.

Follow these steps to add it:

1. Open the MMC.

2. Choose File ➢ Add/Remove Snap-in.

3. In the Add/Remove Snap-in window, click Add.

4. Locate Security Configuration And Analysis in the list, and then click Add. Click OK and click Close.

A new console opens, and you'll find Security Configuration And Analysis listed. Click to open it.

USING THE SECURITY CONFIGURATION AND ANALYSIS TOOL

Once you have the tool installed, you need to create a database that is used for storing the information collected as part of the analysis. To do this, perform the following steps from the Security Configuration And Analysis tool:

1. Right-click Security Configuration and Analysis under Console Root.

2. Choose Open Database.

3. Provide a name for the database. Click Open.

4. When prompted, select a security template to import (see "Using Security Templates," later in this chapter). Click Open.

Once this is done, you see a screen that reports the location of your newly created security configuration and analysis database and tells you that you may now review the information collected. The type of information depends on which of the security templates you selected; I'll take you through those soon.

TIP   Security database files are stored with the file extension .sdb.

CONFIGURING THE COMPUTER WITH THIS TOOL

Once you've established the database you need, you have an additional step to perform before you can reap the benefits of the analysis. This step involves configuring the computer based on XP standards for security, performing an analysis, and viewing the results:

1. Right-click Security Configuration And Analysis under Console Root.

2. Choose Configure Computer Now.

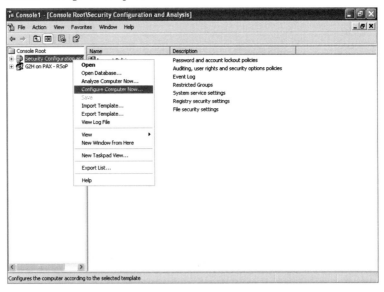

3. The location of your error log for this procedure appears in a Configure System dialog box. To change it, click Browse, and provide the alternate location. By default, this is under the My Documents security section—for example:

```
D:\Documents and Settings\user\My Documents\Security\Logs\011102A.log
```

The screen will report that it's processing the configuration, and then return you to the MMC Security screen.

Next, let's finally look at the analysis.

TIP You can't access Configure Computer Now? You must create a database (as detailed in the previous section) first or the option will be unavailable.

ANALYZING THE CONFIGURATION

Now it's time for the final results of this effort. To finish, perform these steps:

1. From MMC, right-click Security Configuration And Analysis, and choose Analyze Computer Now.

2. The Perform Analysis window reports the location of the log file. Change the location, if needed, and click OK.

A status screen should report that the analysis is being performed. When it's finished, you'll be returned to the MMC Security console. Please note that the Security Configuration And Analysis entry automatically expands to show the various areas checked in the survey, as shown in Figure 45.1.

Click any of the options to open the report for each. When you find an item that reports that it was Not Analyzed, this may be because the information collected under this particular template doesn't apply for the situation (as one example).

FIGURE 45.1

After analysis, the MMC Security console displays each area that was analyzed.

VIEWING THE ANALYSIS LOG

To view the log created during the analysis process, from the MMC Security console, right-click Security Configuration And Analysis, and choose View Log File (if it's already on, clicking it will turn it off). The log file appears in the right pane, available for your review.

TIP Be sure to note any settings that surprise you or that may leave obvious security holes that could be exploited or unintentionally abused.

AUDITING SERVICES

You may have noticed the term *auditing* in relation to security in Windows XP. Auditing refers to another method used by XP to monitor many of the events that occur on a system, and it can be used not just for security, but for performance, troubleshooting, and more.

When it's used in the realm of security, *auditing* often means to keep an eye on the policies established for the system and the people who access it. For example, you could use it to see how many times (and when) users log on, how frequently passwords are changed (for better security), which users are accessing which resources or making what modifications, what programs are being run, and other issues of this nature. Some audit policies, such as auditing directory service access, can work only on domain setups, whereas others apply only to servers and workstations.

NOTE For a complete description of Windows XP auditing, see Chapter 13.

NOTE Like the monitoring for performance you learned about in Chapter 12, using auditing services can affect the overall operation of the system (the act of documenting an event requires more effort than just performing the event).

Using the Resultant Set of Policy Wizard

Although you learned about group policy in Chapter 35, understand that Resultant Set of Policy (RSoP) is an extension of it, specifically added to try to increase the success rate with which group policy is implemented and problems can be resolved. The latter is an attempt to make it easier to identify and troubleshoot difficulties encountered when policies established at different levels cause conflicts. Such conflicts may include one policy's natural precedence overriding the work of another policy's settings.

RSoP is intimately tied to the Windows Management Interface (WMI); its primary job is to scan the policies and analyze them based on various sets of criteria, including domain and domain controller, site, and defined organizational unit. RSoP then reports the results in a relatively easy-to-comprehend interface for your perusal. By presenting it in wizard form, Microsoft hopes to help facilitate the configuration process even further.

To run the Resultant Set of Policy Wizard, try this:

1. Open the Microsoft Management Console.

2. Choose File ➢ Add/Remove Snap-in.

3. In the Add/Remove Snap-in window, click Add.

4. Highlight Resultant Set of Policy Wizard in the list, and then click Add to open the wizard.

5. In the wizard, click Next, and then select Logging mode (if you work with Active Directory, Planning mode is also available). Click Next.

6. Choose the computer whose policy settings you want to display.

7. In the User Selection window, choose the user whose policy settings you wish to review. Click Next to see a summary of your selections, and then click Next again to start the analysis.

8. When prompted, click Finish, and note that the results for the user are added as an MMC snap-in addition.

To review those policy settings, open and look at the appropriate console, as shown in Figure 45.2.

FIGURE 45.2
Review the policy settings.

Using Security Templates

Templates, as you already know, are preconfigured or designed entities that serve as the foundation for creating new documents and files based on the standards provided within the prototype. Specifically, security templates offer a basic—and in some cases, quite advanced—security configuration, which you can customize to fit the particular needs of your situation.

In Windows XP, you can use these security templates to help configure and tweak a host of essentials, including Account and Local Policies, Restricted Groups, Event Log specifics, System and File System Services, and Registry settings.

By default with Windows XP Professional, security templates aren't installed. However, you can quickly add them by performing these steps:

1. Open the Microsoft Management Console.

2. Choose File ➤ Add/Remove Snap-in.

3. In the Add/Remove Snap-in window, click Add.

4. Select Security Templates from the list, and then click Add. Click OK.

TIP   You can also run `secedit.exe` from the command line to apply a security template.

Available Security Templates

The following security templates are available for use by default with Windows XP Professional:

Compatws   The Compatibility template is charged with trying to employ security policies that are consistent with application operation compatibility for all users regardless of the operating circumstances.

Hisecdc   The High Secure template for domain controllers is responsible for employing the highest security measures through a much stronger implementation of authentication and encryption practices. All domain controllers must be running Windows 2000 or later to allow its use.

Hisecws   The High Secure template for workstations is the same as the previous template but tailored to workstations. Notably, High Secure removes the Power Users group on networks for better security.

Rootsec   The Root Directory Permissions template is new to this version. It provides specific new permissions available for securing the boot or system drive's root directory to limit the potential for damage among key files residing in the root, necessary for trying to maintain system integrity. One big bonus: if something fouls up your root directory permissions, you can use this template to reapply the default configuration.

Securedc   The Secure template for domain controllers is used to create improved (but not aggressive in a way that may negatively affect operating compatibility) security settings over default domain controller security. Specifically, it works with features such as more stringent password usage, audit settings, and the ability to lock out accounts.

Securews   The Secure template for workstations is the same as the previous template but is specifically for workstation setups.

Setup security   This is the one PC-specific template that basically lays out the security setup established by XP when the operating system was first installed. For this reason, it's a good choice when you want to restore the default security configuration for troubleshooting or when you're restoring a compromised system to operation.

TIP Templates are saved with the .inf file extension.

NOTE If you're not administering a domain-based setup, you probably won't use Securedc or His-ecdc; and Hisecws presents several obstacles to normal user and advanced connections. For example, users who try to connect to a High Secure–enabled server using clients that don't support NTLMv2 and client-side packet signing won't be able to do so.

IMPORTING AND EXPORTING SECURITY TEMPLATES

To import a security template for use, do this:

1. In MMC, right-click Security Configuration And Analysis.

2. Choose Import Template.

3. Select the template you wish to import, and click Open.

To export a security template, follow these steps, but choose Export Template in step 2, and then provide a name for the exported template.

APPLYING A SECURITY TEMPLATE

To apply a security template, try this:

1. In the MMC Security Configuration console, locate the Local Computer Policy console, and click to expand it.

2. Double-click \Computer Configuration\Windows Settings.

3. Right-click Security Settings, and then select Import Policy.

4. Choose your template, and click OK.

CREATING YOUR OWN SECURITY TEMPLATE

Want to create your own security template? You can do so by performing these steps:

1. From the MMC Console Root *after* you've added the Security Templates snap-in, locate and click to expand the Security Templates listing.

2. Right-click the default templates directory listed.

3. Choose New Template.

4. Create your original template.

5. To save, right-click a template name in the list, and choose Save As.

6. Provide a unique name for your new template, and click Save.

Implementing Tight Security

Unless you're the only one using your system or network and it's located behind locked doors, unconnected to the Internet or other outside communications, you run the risk of having someone try to gain access to your information. But most of us don't live and work with our computers walled off from the rest of the world, nor can we afford to turn our attention away from work to indulge our paranoia. So we need protection against tampering and data theft, and we need to implement it *before* a situation arises to bite us. Once protection is employed, we need to keep a watchful eye to make sure that it stays viable. After all, the greatest office alarm system in the world won't save you if it's not turned on or if one of the locks on your door is broken.

Scattered throughout this book (because security and privacy are addressed throughout the Windows XP operating system, particularly in Professional) are many references to the tools you can use—from the newly included Firewall and beefed-up encryption to the configuration and analysis features discussed here—to secure your system or network from intrusions. I encourage you to review them all as you begin to formulate a security plan that works best for you, as well as follow these basic common-sense practices:

◆ Understand your system(s) and network configuration—this information is critical in knowing where holes may exist.

◆ Employ good password security (see the following subsection).

◆ Regularly check security alerts and virus warnings issued by governing bodies, manufacturers, and others, to keep abreast of matters that may compromise security and possibly system integrity.

◆ Don't give everyone Administrator status. This is done too often; and, like having too many cooks, it frequently leads to intentional or unintentional mayhem and disasters.

◆ Frequently review policies, users and their access (remove users who should no longer have access, and monitor the level of access for everyone else), and other security issues (including the analysis tools discussed here), and identify problems to correct immediately as well as those to watch in the future.

◆ After you make adjustments to security and access, remember to reanalyze the configuration and check relevant logs to determine whether the modifications cause any problems.

◆ Beware of the trade-off between convenience and security, and make policies (system and office administration) that don't compromise good security principles.

WARNING   Simple but unsecured: The use of the Welcome screen to let users click their names and automatically access the system makes it easy for anyone happening by the keyboard to use it. Disable the Welcome screen, and have users log on using their ID and password.

Smart Password Control

Through user education and by getting tough—employing security policy settings such as the set expiration of passwords and locking out accounts that fail to provide the correct password after a limited number of tries—you may be able to seriously reduce the number of users who either intentionally or unintentionally make a password (and thus an account) available to others.

Smart password implementation should include the following:

◆ Promote and/or enforce the use of passwords that are between 7 and 12 characters in length and that include a combination of both letters and numbers.

◆ If a user loses or compromises his password, force the change of the password rather than reissuing the same one.

◆ Be absolutely certain you supply the password to the correct person and do so using a secure means.

◆ If one password needs serious consideration, it's the one linked to Administrator accounts. Exercise particular caution in its choice (no pet names or birthdates), and change it regularly.

◆ Be aware that programs exist that can successfully remove passwords in a variety of operating systems, including Windows NT/2000/XP/2003.

Index

TELL US WHAT YOU THINK!

Your feedback is critical to our efforts to provide you with the best books and software on the market. Tell us what you think about the products you've purchased. It's simple:

1. Go to the Sybex website.
2. Find your book by typing the ISBN or title into the Search field.
3. Click on the book title when it appears.
4. Click **Submit a Review.**
5. Fill out the questionnaire and comments.
6. Click **Submit.**

With your feedback, we can continue to publish the highest quality computer books and software products that today's busy IT professionals deserve.

www.sybex.com

SYBEX Inc. • 1151 Marina Village Parkway, Alameda, CA 94501 • 510-523-8233